# HITCHCOCK'S
## *notebooks*

Alfred Hitchcock and Jack Cox photographing
the British Museum for *Blackmail*

# HITCHCOCK'S

*An Authorized and Illustrated Look
Inside the Creative Mind of
Alfred Hitchcock*

# *notebooks*

## DAN AUILER

SPIKE

AN AVON BOOK

Grateful acknowledgment is given to the following:

*The Estate of Alfred Hitchcock and The Margaret Herrick Library of the Academy of Motion Picture Arts and Sciences* for access and permission to reprint letters, memos, screenplay excerpts, production notes, floor plans, telegrams, blueprints, storyboards for *Lifeboat, The Wrong Man, North by Northwest, Psycho, The Birds,* and *Family Plot,* and other documents.

*BFI Stills, Posters, and Designs* for photographs or stills from *Number 13, The Mountain Eagle, The 39 Steps, Young and Innocent, Rebecca, The Ring, Champagne, The Farmer's Wife, Number 17, Rich and Strange, Secret Agent, Sabotage, Foreign Correspondent, Shadow of a Doubt, I Confess, The Man Who Knew Too Much,* and *Flamingo Feather,* and the photograph of Alfred Hitchcock with the lion.

*Warner Brothers Archives / USC* for photographs from *Rope, Under Capricorn, Strangers on a Train, Dial M for Murder, Rear Window,* and *The Wrong Man.*

AVON BOOKS, INC.
1350 Avenue of the Americas
New York, New York 10019

Copyright © 1999 by Dan Auiler
Interior design by Stanley S. Drate/Folio Graphics Co. Inc.
ISBN: 0-380-97783-4

Library of Congress Cataloging in Publication Data:
Auiler, Dan.
    Hitchcock's notebooks : an authorized and illustrated look inside
the creative mind of Alfred Hitchcock / Dan Auiler.
        p.   cm.
    1. Hitchcock, Alfred, 1899–   —Criticism and interpretation.
I. Title.
PN1998.3.H58A84   1999                                    98-31904
791.43′0233′092—dc21                                          CIP

First Spike Printing: April 1999

SPIKE TRADEMARK REG. U.S. PAT. OFF. AND IN OTHER COUNTRIES, MARCA REGISTRADA, HECHO EN U.S.A.

Printed in the U.S.A.

FIRST EDITION

QPM   10  9  8  7  6  5  4  3  2  1

www.spikebooks.com

*To my parents*
*Wilk and Faris Auiler*

# Acknowledgments

This book could not have been written without the gracious support of Leland Faust and Patricia Hitchcock O'Connell. In addition to the Hitchcock trust, I must thank the dedicated Faye Thompson and film archivist Michael Friend, as well as their staffs at the Margaret Herrick Library of the Academy of Motion Picture Arts and Sciences. At the British Film Institute, I am indebted to Janet Moat and Kathleen Dickson and Mandy Rowson. I also owe an enormous debt to Hitchcock's creative team: the late Peggy Robertson, C.O. "Doc" Erikson, Henry Bumstead, Herbert Coleman, Herb Steinberg, Leonard South, Samuel Taylor, Evan Hunter, Jack Cardiff, Hume Cronyn, Manny Yospa, Alan Lawson, Bob Allen, "Minty" Huebner, Constance Cummings (Mrs. Benn Levy), and Arthur Schatz.

The book would not have been possible without my agents Christy Fletcher and Laura Morris and my editors Stephen S. Power of Avon Books and Matthew Hamilton of Bloomsbury. Thanks also to Kevin Brownlow for information on Jack Cox, Martina Hall at the BBC for help in tracking down *Kaleidoscope* participants, and J. Lary Kuhns for sharing his research on *The Mountain Eagle*.

My gracious friends in Denmark, Povl and Annelise Bronsted, provided a place to stay and a tour of some of *Torn Curtain*'s locations in Copenhagen. Ken Mogg provided much needed editorial assistance, and Sid Gottlieb helped at an important moment.

And, as always, my family remained dedicated during long absences.

# *contents*

# *chapter one*
# BEGINNINGS

*Well, little boys are always asked what they want to be when
they grow up, and it must be said to my credit that I never
wanted to be a policeman.*

—HITCHCOCK TO TRUFFAUT

t he world owes a debt of thanks to Hitchcock's able secretaries. For while
he himself kept no diaries, journals, or meditations on his art, they
helped create a lasting record of the building plans for more than fifty
years of filmmaking. And as I began to sift through the enormous collection of
personal papers that his daughter Patricia graciously donated to the Academy
of Motion Picture Arts and Sciences (gracious, because the Academy's members only acknowledged Hitchcock's genius in his twilight), I found that if the
material were placed into some kind of context, some kind of shape, profound
lessons could be learned.

There is no doubt that many, if not most, of the important filmmakers of
the second half of this century learned from looking carefully at his art. Virtually every member of the French new wave was an apt pupil of Hitchcock. In
America his students are everywhere. The most powerful and significant were
the seventies wunderkinds Spielberg and Lucas. Indeed, it would be difficult to
find a filmmaker who was not shaped by Hitchcock and his work—even among
the few out there who often react against the kind of tension Hitchcock created
in his films.

There was a second element to this collection that I found personally moving: the uncompleted Hitchcock ouevre, from the fortunately short list of films
that didn't come to fruition from the pipe dream, the Cary Grant *Hamlet* (just
a well-publicized afterthought that ended in court), to the projects that fell
apart because of star anxieties. Others fell apart for the usual reasons. But there
were two deeply personal films that, despite his enormous power, despite his
being one of the largest stockholders in MCA, he could not convince his friend
and boss Lew Wasserman to let him make.

One project reached romantically back into his youth. The other, the one that perhaps caused Hitchcock the most pain, was a daring, provocative film that would have certainly been considered one of the great ones. This story of the unproduced *Frenzy* is the bittersweet connective tissue of this working "biography" of Hitchcock.

To begin to understand Hitchcock, you have to stand on the streets of Leytonstone, London, where he came from. The home that he was born into in August 1899 no longer exists. A blue oval plaque on a gas station marks the spot today. The town, though, is still the working-class community that it was at the turn of the century. His father was a grocer who died when his son was fifteen years old. His illness had forced the young Hitchcock out of school and into work.

The police station that his father allegedly took him to to be incarcerated for five minutes is also torn down. This well-known story was told so often by Hitchcock that even he wasn't sure if it had actually happened. It certainly reveals a certain ambivalence toward his father.

He may have been close to his mother and sister, but he said little about his family to journalists. His mother would die during World War II, and perhaps it is no coincidence that immediately after this he makes the only film with such a warm portrait of a mother: *Shadow of a Doubt.*

We know that Hitchcock was intrigued by the theater and film from an early age. He was an avid playgoer and his early films are certainly testament to that. So many of the films revolved around theaters and so many of his first actors were from the stage he had grown to love. The early British films are the most indebted to his middle-class upbringing: the films are almost documentary in their depiction of middle-class London life, and occasionally the biographical element creeps in—like the greengrocer next to the cinema in *Sabotage.*

His interest includes the technical as well. An engineering student when his father died, he interestingly continued to drift toward the arts. His ability to draw stood him well at Henley Telegraph and Cable, where he worked for a time in their art department, creating advertisements. He used these same skills to convince the American company of Famous Players-Lasky (which would later merge with Paramount) that he could design their title cards. They were impressed, and the rest conveniently for us is a history that has been fairly well documented. If we only knew as much about Shakespeare's early years.

At Famous Players-Lasky, Hitchcock would encounter the first of his teachers, and even though the company would collapse in a few years, he would have time enough to see just how motion pictures were put together. The early editor and scenarist who had the greatest impact on his career and his life was Alma Reville.

She was born in Islington and began her career in the new motion picture industry much earlier than Hitchcock. As early as 1916, she worked as a young actress for the London Film Company (according to Kevin Brownlow, a 1918 film has recently been discovered that features the young Alma). Beyond small parts, she was an editor and evidently one of the best in the nascent industry. Hitchcock would have learned from Alma. And as the photographs and interviews show, Alma was with the young Hitchcock from his first film to his last. During this run, she would also play the part of his wife. They married on December 2, 1926.

Their closeness in temperament and Alma's evident humility have obscured her contribution to what we know as the Hitchcock film. The record indicates Alma helped shape each film's fundamental story from his first film to well after World War II. The fact that she was continuing a position that she had before she married Hitchcock indicates that this was not just padding the Hitchcock family income. (Charles Bennett, who wrote with Hitchcock some of his finest British and American films from the twenties to the forties, often claimed Alma was hired and given credit to add to Hitchcock's income. Unfortunately, this claim has no basis in fact but, instead, seems to come from the anger Bennett felt over not working with Hitchcock after the war.)

Little is known about Hitchcock's first directorial effort. Some sources say that the incomplete *Number 13* was partially financed by Hitchcock's family. The project ended, evidently, when the family and the company ran out of money. Famous Players-Lasky closed shop and all that remains for *Number 13* is a production still.

Hitchcock's second film has also disappeared. *The Mountain Eagle* is considered one of the 100 most wanted films in the world. No copy currently exists in any known film library and until recently it was assumed that only half a dozen stills existed.

This is until the work of J. Lary Kuhns. Kuhns looked in the most obvious place: Hitchcock's own collection. He discovered what must be a complete set of stills from the film and an additional set of production stills that features Hitchcock in every shot (Alma, his recent fiancée, also appears in a number of the stills). The publication of the stills here and in *The Hitchcock Annual* will hopefully stir enough memories so that a print of this important Hitchcock film may be found. This is not altogether impossible, as a rare, tinted print of *The Pleasure Garden,* Hitchcock's first complete film, was found in 1992 in Waco, Texas, and restored by G. William Jones Film and Video Collection based at Southern Methodist University.

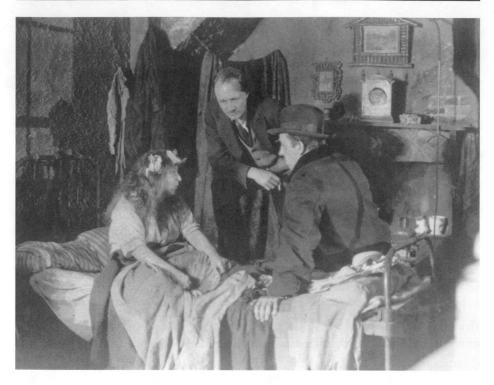

The young director on the set of his first film

What we know reliably about the film comes from a few contemporary sources. The best of which is the trade review of the film in *The Kinematograph* in October 1926:

OCTOBER 7, 1926

## The Mountain Eagle

*W. and F. Anglo-German. Featuring Nita Naldi, Malcolm Keen and Bernhard Goetzke. 7,503 feet. Released May 25, 1927.*

**Story.**—Pettigrew, J.P. of a small mountain village, hates John Fulton, a lonely dweller in the mountains, known as Fearogod to the inhabitants, as much as he loves his son Edward, who was born a cripple as his mother, whom Fulton has also loved, died. Pettigrew sees his son apparently making love to Beatrice Talbot, the village schoolmistress, and, going to reprove her, he tries to take her in his arms. The son sees this, and leaves the village. Pettigrew determines to have Beatrice thrown out, but Fearogod intervenes, and takes her to his cabin. Pettigrew here sees the chance to arrest Fearogod for abduction and Beatrice as a wanton, but Fearogod forestalls him by coming and demanding that Pettigrew marry them. The pair then fall in love, but Pettigrew has Fearogod arrested and thrown into prison on a charge of murdering his son, who has not returned. Fearogod breaks out of prison after a year, and attempts to fly with his wife and child, but the latter falls sick, and Fearogod returns to the village for a doctor. There he finds Edward has returned, and his affairs cleared up. Pettigrew is accidentally shot.

Rather wandering and not too convincing story, which is redeemed by good, if somewhat slow, direction and excellent acting.

**Acting.**—Bernhard Goetzke is very fine indeed as Pettigrew, and one can almost feel the train of his thoughts by his expressions. Malcolm Keen, too, gives a fine performance as John Fulton, while Nita Naldi is quite good, but not very sympathetic, as Beatrice. John Hamilton is fair in the small part of the crippled Edward Pettigrew.

**Production.**—Alfred Hitchcock's direction is, as usual, thoroughly imaginative, but in this case he has rather over-stressed the slow *tempo,* and has had a story which is too full of unconvincing twists. For instance, there appears to be no reason why Beatrice could not have communicated earlier with Edward, who had written her a letter before her husband's arrest.

The continuity is jerky, which is due rather to the lack of story motive than to the director's handling.

Characterisation, on the other hand, is very good, and many individual scenes are very cleverly handled to the extent of the dramatic force.

**Settings and Photography.**—Settings suffer from being unplaced geographically, and the English-named characters appear incongruous with their surroundings. The mountain scenery is very good, and the small village interiors and exteriors are also sound. Baron Ventimiglia's photography is excellent.

**Box-office Angle.**—Fair character drama, with the main appeal in the acting.

While Hitchcock always discounted the quality of this film, Kuhns points out that another contemporary writer called *The Mountain Eagle* far superior to *The Lodger* (the film Hitchcock describes as the first true "Hitchcock" picture).

The available stills are provocative and show a number of what became Hitchcock touches: the dark, "Germanic" lighting (compare the stills in the cabin to the scene in the hardware store in *Psycho*); the jeering laugh (the unidentified laughing man still is framed nearly identically to the jeering jester painting in *Blackmail*); and the fascination with strangulation—in particular the image of the hands throttling the victim's throat.

*The Mountain Eagle stills.* These production stills are presented in an order that may match the story's progression, but it is pure guesswork on my part. The synopsis provided in Chapter One is all that remains of the storyline.

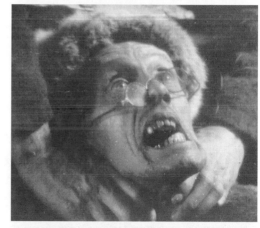

The production stills show a much trimmer Hitchcock—clearly in his element despite the bitter cold of the Tyrolean Mountains where *The Mountain Eagle* was filmed. And the production stills reconfirm the close professional relationship Hitchcock had with Alma Reville. She is constantly at his side (she was the film's editor).

More than a decade later, Hitchcock wrote about filming *The Mountain Eagle* with Nita Naldi, who was a big American star at that time:

I was still in Munich, working for a joint control: half an English company, half a German one. I was given a script. I was told to go on location and get some pretty shots. I was told my star would be coming out for the studio stuff later.

When I read the script, I found it was set in the Kentucky hills. My heroine was a pleasant, simple, homely schoolmarm. My star was glamorous, dark, Latin, Junoesque, statuesque, slinky, with slanting eyes, four-inch heels, nails like a mandarin's, and a black dog to match her black swathed dress.

But the worry was for later. First of all, I had to get my mountain scenes. I had no time to go looking for them. I had to ask. I asked everybody in sight: "Where can I get a nice thatched village with snowy mountains in the background and nice tree stuff in the foreground, and no modern stuff that would be out of the picture?"

I was recommended to this place, to that place, to the other place. But this place's only claim to fame was a new glazed-tile town hall; and that place had

Hitchcock and Alma in the Tyrolean Mountains (1926)

been recommended because it had just had lampposts installed; and the other place because the beer was good.

But as I walked along, I glanced into a picture shop. I saw a postcard of the perfect location. I went in and asked where it was. "Obergurgel," said they. Yes. You do remember it. It's where Professor Piccard came down from the first stratosphere flight.

I took the German assistant director I had just been given and went out to see the place. To get there we took a train to Innsbruck. We then drove for seven and a half hours in an open Victoria. We then walked for two and a half hours on our feet—no transport could reach it.

With every step we swore conditions would be so primitive, the place so out of the way, that to film anything there would be out of the question. But it had cast a spell upon me, that postcard. That was the ideal place to shoot the Kentucky hills (in Germany). Snow on the high ground, woods on the village level, thatch, a forgotten, almost a vanished, civilization. Grand.

I reached the place. For once it was up to the pictures of it. It was perfect. I went back to Munich as happy as a sandboy. But on the way I wanted to speak English. I was tired to death of German gutturals. I was sick of flogging my brain to think in another language. I was as mad to hear the sound of an English voice, as mad to speak and be understood in my own tongue as a claustrophobe is anxious to get into the open air. I know that feeling too: I had it in an Italian seaplane.

However, I got back to Munich. There I picked up my company: Malcolm Keen was one of them. He was the most important to me: he brought out my en-

*The Mountain Eagle* cast and crew on the track into "Obergurgel"

gagement ring. Nita had not yet arrived, so we went out to do the out-of-doors shots.

We got to Obergurgel. We settled in a cottage. We went out in the evening and plotted out the work for the next day. A few long shots of the snow and the close-ups and medium shots amid the woods. Content as a dog promised a nice bone, we went to bed.

When we woke up next day, the village was a foot under snow.

That washed us out. The snow meant that we should have to wait six months at least to make the picture at Obergurgel. We took our snow scenes and made our way down the valley, hoping just to beat the falls as they too made their way steadily to the lower ground.

We got to a place called Umhaus. It seemed only a fraction less perfect than Obergurgel. We made all our arrangements. We went to bed.

And the next morning the village was under snow.

What made it even better was that we were snowed up. It was still snowing. We couldn't shoot a foot of film. We couldn't stick our noses outside the door.

We spent four days sitting round a German stove. I had bought a few delicacies to take: 100 lemons, for I love lemonade and all soft drinks; a bottle of Cointreau; a couple of bottles of whiskey; and some biscuits. One of the actors was head-over-heels in love with a girl in England. He wrote to her every day. That was grand for the rest of us. It was grand for him. It wasn't so good for the girl: the post only went once a week!

When the snow stopped snowing, we seemed sunker than ever. It had traveled farther and farther down the valley. The long shots we had taken committed us to this valley and the whole place was under feet of snow.

There was only one thing to do: produce a thaw.

I got hold of four men who formed the local fire brigade. I convinced them that they must get out the fire engine and wash the snow away. They argued, finally they agreed. They pulled out the great manual pump with its leaky hose and they turned it on the village.

We washed the snow from the houses, from the roofs, from the trees, from the ground. But one of the houses had a leaky roof, and the old peasant woman who lived there complained she was being really washed away.

I saw the mayor. I told him my troubles. He said that a rich film company could probably get what it wanted—at a price. I asked him how much I should give her. He said, "A schilling"—the Austrian coin then worth 7d. I gave her two. If I had given her ten, I think I could have flooded the whole countryside, she was so pleased.

And on that small area of land, washed clean of snow with a fire engine, our exteriors were made.

I went back to Munich to meet my star. As she stepped off the train, Munich quite audibly gasped. They had never seen anything like her before. She traveled with her father, who looked like Earl Haig. Her Louix XIV heels clicked down the platform. The dog on its leash was long and gleaming with brushing. Her maid followed her. It was like the royalty Germany hadn't seen for five years.

But I was thinking of a simple Kentucky miss in a gingham gown and a cotton apron. I had to produce a strong

talked to everybody in her heavy New York drawl. The Germans, accustomed to the starchiness of the Hohenzollerns, fell hard for this American royalty, with her father and her dog, and her maid, who was more democratic than the stage-hands.

I shall never forget one afternoon. We had been working hard all the day, and

Alma and Bernhard Goetzke

woman of the midwestern mountains who handled a gun instead of a lipstick.

First, we quarreled about her nails. They came down from half an inch beyond the finger to a quarter. We had another discussion. They came down to an eighth. Another discussion and they were all right.

The heels came down layer by layer. The makeup was altered shade by shade. The hair was changed curl by curl.

Nita put up a magnificent fight for the appearance that had made her, but it was nothing to the fight that she put up for the clothes she wanted to wear. Fortunately, I was not concerned with that: it was Alma's job.

But Alma, who took her round and made her buy cotton aprons instead of silk and compelled her to choose cloth instead of satin frocks, nearly fainted when she saw her lingerie.

Munich is a cold city, and it was winter. But Nita under her frock wore just one garment: such scanties as even today would be considered—well, scanty.

However, Nita turned out to be a grand person. For all her entourage, there was nothing high-hat about her. She

Nita was nearly all in. She had to play one more scene, where she was cleaning Malcolm Keen's rifle when a face appeared at the window and she pointed the gun at him.

The scene was going well when, just as she turned the gun to the window, I saw it waver. It veered from side to side. It moved up and down. It went round in circles.

Then, without a word, Nita tilted to one side and fell headlong.

Nita just before fainting from exhaustion

The floor was very hard. The set was built on a foundation of stones set in cement. Before the camera had even stopped turning, she had recovered. And all she said was: "Why don't they build these lousy sets right over here? This floor's too gol-darned hard for comfort!"

She got to her feet and wanted to go on playing, but we called it a day.

Owing to that delay, and the delay caused by the snow, we got a little late with the production. Nita had one bit scene still to play. It was half-past four in the afternoon and her train—for Paris—left at half-past six.

Nita was playing a scene where she had been run out of town (unjustly, of course) by the Kentucky farmers. She had to turn on them and tell them just what she thought of them.

In silent days, we never wrote dialogue, except for close-ups where anyone could lip-read. In a big emotional scene, we let people say just whatever came into their heads. It helped them to get over the atmosphere.

When Nita finally turned on these "farmers," I called, "Give them all you've got."

She did. She gave them, in English, Italian, American, Bowery, Park Avenue, and, maybe, double Dutch. She called them anything and everything she could lay her tongue to. She told them where they got off, where they came from, where they were going to. She used words we had never before heard.

When, shuddering and shaking with emotion, she stopped and I called out "Cut," the whole studio—none of whom understood a word she had said—burst into spontaneous applause.

She caught up her dress, her dog, her maid, her father. She piled into a taxi. She rushed to the station. She caught her train still in her gingham gown, with the makeup still on her face.

She went to Paris. When Alma and I were married, we went to Paris for our honeymoon and spent the first day of it with Nita . . . but that is another story—and one I'm not going to tell.

*The Mountain Eagle,* in a quirk of fate and distribution, was actually released after *The Lodger,* the film that firmly established Hitchcock as England's brightest directorial star. His next films were at times unevenly received, but never indifferently and it was as the premier British director that Hitchcock made one of the first British "talkies": *Blackmail.*

After a few stumbles leading into the thirties, this next decade was a remarkable period of success for Hitchcock—beginning with *The Man Who Knew Too Much* and continuing on through *The 39 Steps, Sabotage, Secret Agent, Young and Innocent, The Lady Vanishes,* and *Jamaica Inn.*

This last film was to predict the future. Like *Rebecca, Jamaica Inn* was based on a Daphne du Maurier novel, introduced a new actress (a young Maureen O'Hara) teamed with an established screen and stage star (Charles Laughton), and was set on the dramatic Cornish coast (a locale not too different in temperament from the setting for the Manderley mansion).

In America, with the world's finest film production tools available, Hitchcock moved from being a gifted amateur to the rank of a master whose solid professionalism marks all of his American work. His tenure with David O. Selznick was mostly successful, with each giving the other a limited amount of space to work in (unusual for the typically dominating American producer). After Selznick, there were the occasional stumbles (*Under Capricorn, Stage Fright, I Confess*), but for the most part, one financial and critical success followed another: *Strangers on a Train, Dial M for Murder, Rear Window, The Trouble with Harry, To Catch a Thief, The Man Who Knew Too Much, The Wrong Man, Vertigo, North by Northwest, Psycho,* and *The Birds.* This extraordinary list is unparalleled in film history—except perhaps by Hitchcock's earlier run of hits in the thirties—from the first *The Man Who Knew Too Much* to *The Lady Vanishes.*

The golden decade of Hitchcock's work—from 1954 until 1962 (*Rear Window* through *Psycho*)—was dominated by his years at Paramount. The Paramount team was made up by professionals largely collected by Hitchcock while at Warner Bros.: Robert Burks, Leonard South, George Tomasini. The essential staff would move with Hitchcock to his final studio, Universal, but the period beginning with *Marnie* is one marked by a steady decline. He seemed to be finding his footing once more in the seventies (once he solidified his financial control at MCA), but his output had slowed to retirement speed. He completed only two films in that final decade—compared to a dozen in his golden decade (and indeed, he seemed to average that many in each decade—not including the twenty television productions he directed. Hitchcock completed fifty-seven films from 1925 to 1975).

Over his career, Hitchcock's modus operandi for constructing a film was refined, but it remained fairly consistent. So the material that follows is organized according to the progressive stages of his creative process, rather than chronologically. The first step in a film's production is the creation of the script—the process Hitchcock seemed the most enamored with. Once the script is completed (or near completion), preproduction begins. During this phase, plans and storyboards are drawn up, actors are cast, and production teams are put together.

The actual physical production of the film follows. Naturally, very little paperwork exists at this stage. I've gathered a number of stills of Hitchcock at work from various periods of his career, as well as comments from those who worked with Hitchcock on the set. Despite his penchant for showmanship, Hitchcock was only filmed at work twice (or, rather, there exist only two examples of Hitchcock at work on film). The first is from the early period—silent footage of Hitchcock directing Anny Ondra and Cyril Ritchard in a kiss from *Blackmail.* The last is home movie footage from a Catholic priest taken at San Juan Bautista during the filming of *Vertigo.*

The final phase of production is called postproduction. During this step the film is pieced together: edited, scored and tested before audiences.

Throughout the chapters on these stages, I've included material on the work Hitchcock completed for *Kaleidoscope,* the first unfinished version of *Frenzy* that the director attempted in 1967. In Chapter Six, "*Kaleidoscope* and other Dreams Deferred," I've related the full story of the unmaking of this film. Here I've also cataloged the other projects Hitchcock did not complete.

Finally, the book examines the genesis of Hitchcock the pitchman for his films. Hitchcock was wisest when he dealt with the media. He had proclaimed early in his career that a successful director had to learn to sell his films to the critics—and the audiences. His trademark appearances in his films and his witty trailers from the late fifties and sixties were important in selling the Hitchcock package.

# chapter two

# BUILDING THE SCREENPLAY

*To insist that a storyteller stick to the facts is just as ridiculous as to demand a representative painter that he show objects accurately.*

—HITCHCOCK TO TRUFFAUT

ew people realize that besides being the Master of Suspense, Hitchcock was truly the master of cinema. He even wrote the Encyclopaedia Britannica's entry on "Film Production" in 1965. It is instructive to read part of Hitchcock's entry on the screenplay:

The screenplay, which is sometimes known, also, as the scenario or film script, resembles the blueprint of the architect. It is the verbal design of the finished film. In studios where films are made in great numbers, and under industrial conditions, the writer prepares the screenplay under the supervision of a producer, who represents the budgetary and box office concerns of the front office . . .

In its progress toward completion, the screenplay normally passes through certain stages; these stages have been established over the years and depend on the working habits of those engaged in writing it. The practice of these years has come to establish three main stages: (1) the outline; (2) the treatment; (3) the screenplay.

The outline, as the term implies, gives the essence of the action or story and may present either an original idea or, more usually, one derived from a successful stage play or novel.

The outline is then built up into the treatment. This is a prose narrative, written in the present tense, in greater or less detail, that reads like a description of what will finally appear on the screen.

This treatment is broken down into screenplay form, which like its stage counterpart, sets out the dialogue, describes the movements and reactions of the actors, and at the same time gives the breakdown of the individual scenes, with some indication of the role, in each scene, of the camera and the sound. It likewise serves as a guide to the various technical departments: to the art department for the sets, to the casting department for the actors, to the costume department, to makeup, to the music department, and so on.

The writer, who should be as skilled

in the dialogue of images as of words, must have the capacity to anticipate, visually and in detail, the finished film. The detailed screenplay . . . enables the director to hold securely to the unity of form and to the cinematic structure of the action, while leaving him free to work intimately and concentratedly with the actors.

This chapter then follows this collaborative process from idea to finished screenplay. Hitchcock was intimately involved in the writing of most of his films. There were the occasional variations, but for the most part throughout his career, he would develop the film's core story first with his wife Alma.

"Father would bring home the story or the novel and if Mother didn't like it, then he wouldn't do it. It was that simple," Patricia Hitchcock O'Connell, Hitchcock's daughter, remembered.

Even if he was adapting a novel or short story, the process began with a treatment, often developed by the Hitchcocks in their home. Each film history is its own variation, but Hitchcock worked with a remarkable consistency in his fifty-four feature films.

After this core was developed (which almost always included at least two or three of those Hitchcock moments for which he was famous—like the Albert Hall scene in both versions of *The Man Who Knew Too Much* or the crop dusting scene in *North by Northwest*), he would assign a writer to help him construct the film story. For most of his career, the first writer was an expert in "construction." Charles Bennett was Hitchcock's first "constructionist."

Bennett enjoyed a career that lasted into his nineties. As a young man, he was a success on the British stage, then he turned to playwriting. His first play, *Blackmail,* was an enormous success. The production that the equally successful Hitchcock saw and enjoyed starred Tallulah Bankhead as the duplicitous young woman who kills her attacker.

The rest is well-known film history. Hitchcock began the film version as a silent film but reworked it as sound technology and the market developed, making it one of the first "talkies" in England. The British press hailed it nearly unanimously.

Ironically, according to Bennett, he never wrote anything for *Blackmail,* the movie, but it was easy to see why Hitchcock became attached to the charming, elfin character who was comfortable on and off the stage, telling stories.

"Hitchcock and I used to go to a local pub—not far from the studio—and we would spend most of the afternoon just talking. Sometimes we talked very little about the film we were writing," Bennett remembered during a series of meetings that would turn out to be his final interviews. Bennett preferred to meet in the late afternoons, in time for that first glass of white wine.

"Hitch referred to me as his constructionist and felt I was the best. For dialogue he would bring in someone else—but no one else could build a story like I could," Bennett would say.

The first film that Bennett actually wrote for Hitchcock was *The Man Who Knew Too Much*. Bennett and Hitchcock began working on the screenplay in 1933.

"It originally had nothing to do with an assassination and Albert Hall. We were supposed to adapt the popular Bull Dog Drummond series [specifically, the novel *Bulldog Drummond Baby*] for the screen. But during our long lunches, we abandoned Drummond and began *The Man Who Knew Too Much*. Abandoned is not right, really. The story grew out of our conversations about Drummond. Eventually, Hitch said, "Why don't we just drop the Drummond business?"

Together they built the new plot: a parent is told vital information about an assassination by a dying spy; the conspirators kidnap their child to keep their silence. The genius in the construction is the dynamic it creates for the third act: the race against time to save their child and the assassination victim. This can be hack work in the wrong director's hands. But in Hitchcock's hands, the story works incredibly, both in the 1934 film and the 1955 remake.

Another writer from Hitchcock's British period (1921 to 1939) was Sidney Gilliat. Gilliat cowrote *The Lady Vanishes* and *Jamaica Inn*. He recalled Hitchcock's working style:

"Hitch, by the way, never wrote dialogue first. Hitch is a complex story in himself. He always had a very curious relationship with writers. He seldom or never took writing credit officially. He might be responsible for all sorts of things in the script, but he'd never taken screen credit—to his credit."

So much has been lost from Hitchcock's early period. What does exist indicates that the younger Hitchcock was the model for the older: the screenplay is where the director dreamed his films. Hitchcock was frequently quoted saying that he almost didn't want to go on to make the film because filmmaking is constant compromise. On paper, there in the study with another writer, no compromise was demanded.

The film director was fortunate on four different occasions to work with writers who were nimble constructionists and witty dialogue writers. The first writer to master both tasks effectively was the former Chicago journalist Ben Hecht. Hecht worked with Hitchcock during the war years; their undisputedly best work was *Notorious*. The next was John Michael Hayes in the fifties. Their collaboration led to Hitchcock's finest run of films: *Rear Window, The Trouble with Harry, To Catch a Thief,* and the remake of *The Man Who Knew Too Much* (the latter of which also benefited from substantial contributions by Hitchcock's longtime friend Angus MacPhail).

Hayes has bitter memories of the end of their relationship, but he also drew a picture of the typically engaged Hitchcock in his interviews with Patrick MacGilligan:

"As for Hitchcock, he let me write on my own, and then we conferred afterward. We had some conferences, but he didn't go over pages. We'd sit and discuss the thing in general. I'd do a first draft and a second draft; then we would do a shooting script, and that's when he would break the story in shots, specific camera angles. He'd draw sketches. If I had a film with two hundred shots in it on my first or second draft, we'd end up with six hundred, because he broke it down into every single camera angle. Hitch did not like to make changes. When we finished setting up the shots before the picture was started, he'd say, 'The picture is made now. All we have to do is sit on the set and make sure they follow what we've worked out here.'"

Hayes added: "Hitch would never change the script unless the writer agreed to it. Too many directors think just because they're a director they know how to write, and they don't.

"I like to write dialogue. It's one of my skills, character and dialogue. Hitchcock taught me how to tell a story with the camera and tell it silently."

After Hayes, Hitchcock worked with a series of writers. Samuel Taylor was another gifted dialoguist. He also remembers the long lunches and lively conversation, but from his home in Maine he also recalled the important quiet moments:

"We would get to a point where we just sit quietly and Hitchcock would say, 'The wheels are turning,' meaning that we were at work on the screenplay even though not a word was being said.

"Those were great times. We really had a marvelous time together. I can't really say where Hitch's input began or ended. When you worked with him on a film, you wrote a Hitchcock picture."

The Taylors and the Hitchcocks became close friends. After *Vertigo,* which Taylor saved from oblivion, he worked for a long time on the aborted *No Bail for the Judge* and then returned to Hitchcock's side for *Topaz*—but to much less spectacular results.

"*Topaz* was not at all a typical Hitchcock production. We were writing scenes the night before filming, which Hitchcock didn't like at all. The studio really put him in an awkward position," Taylor concluded.

Despite Hitchcock's legendary status as the director who prepared, one of his finest films also saw last-minute revisions. Hitchcock's calendar shows a daily meeting with Ernest Lehman for nearly a year while they prepared and then filmed the now classic *North by Northwest.*

Lehman wrote thousands of pages in the various drafts of this film whose genesis was in an idea pitched to Hitchcock nearly a decade earlier by a journalist (as you will see in the papers that follow). Judging from the resulting friendship and film, Lehman and Hitchcock were a very amiable team. To read the 500-plus pages of the recorded transcript of their work on Hitchcock's final film, *Family Plot,* is a lesson in scriptwriting. There is a constant give-and-take—with Hitchcock tossing inventive filmic ideas into the mix and Lehman either incorporating the plan or explaining why it wouldn't work.

For *North by Northwest,* Lehman wrote in his notes that after the second draft of *The Man on Lincoln's Nose* (the film's original title), he sat with Hitchcock and a typist at the St. Regis Hotel in New York, going through the screenplay page by page. Hitchcock would argue changes and then Lehman would write out the new scene, which the secretary would then type up. Even Cary Grant got into the rewriting act, going over the script with Lehman in his trailer at the famed crop-dusting location, again with a typist formalizing the last-minute changes.

Hitchcock worked with many of the world's finest writers: Robert E. Sherwood (*Rebecca*), John Steinbeck (*Lifeboat*), Raymond Chandler (*Strangers on a Train*), Thornton Wilder (*Shadow of a Doubt*), Dorothy Parker (*Saboteur*), Maxwell Anderson (*The Wrong Man, Vertigo*), Brian Moore (*Torn Curtain*), and Anthony Shaffer (*Frenzy,* 1970). He gave all of them the freedom to write Hitchcock films. That was his "trick." By the time he moved to America, he had codified the Hitchcock film—a thriller of a certain type and style—and these writers weaved stories with this idea in mind. If the writer was unfamiliar with the genre or needed to be refreshed, Hitchcock gladly screened his core films. During the summer of 1957, for instance, Ernest Lehman screened nearly every great Hitchcock film in his preparation for *North by Northwest.*

## THE EARLY FILMS

There are few personal papers left from Hitchcock's silent period and only the finished scripts from the sound period of 1928 to 1939. Those scripts do reveal the occasional trivia. For example, in the original *The Man Who Knew Too Much,* the screenplay ends with Peter Lorre's character escaping, his chiming watch hanging from his empty coat behind the door, whereas in the film Lorre is shot and, dying, stumbles from his hiding place behind the door—with his watch chiming.

The first treatment of *Sabotage* was apparently written by Hitchcock, and the scenes that this interesting film is memorable for are strangely muted:

- The original bus explosion is not nearly as dramatic. Missing are the puppy and the older woman that add tension to the scene, which is incredible in the film.

- The killing of Verloc is much different. The version originally scripted is more like a stabbing from *Psycho*, "Verloc is riveted to his chair—a flash of knife midair—he slumps forward." The filmed scene is classic montage (in fact, the scene is often used in cinema classes): subtle and emotionally riveting as Sylvia Sidney decides to kill her husband with a knife, then approaches him—their eyes meet, he realizes what she's decided— then the knife pierces Verloc (below camera framing).

Regrettably, there is nothing left to indicate how the film evolved between Charles Bennett and Hitchcock, and Bennett, then in his nineties, could no longer recall the specific details of the film's writing.

One film that was problematic was *Secret Agent*.[1] Like his later spy thriller *Topaz*, Hitchcock had a hard time bringing the picture to an end. In addition to the ending present in the film, two other endings were written (just as *Topaz* had three different endings):

**ALTERNATE ENDING 1**

An oblique shot showing that while the American drinks, the revolver is being slowly pointed at his heart.

CU
Ashenden and Elsa. Suddenly they realize what the Mexican intends to do. They are about to speak when the revolver shot is heard. They clutch each other in horror.

CU
The flask drops from Martin's lips. He slumps forward, dead.

SCU
The Mexican is alarmed at the possible loss of his brandy. He grabs it from the floor as it is running out. He wipes the mouthpiece, then as the camera PANS he offers the flask to Ashenden and Elsa. They both turn away, shudderingly. The Mexican, with a show of nonchalance, proceeds to drink the brandy himself as the picture. FADES OUT.

**ALTERNATE ENDING 2**

SCU
The American is drinking from the flask. The flask suddenly drops from his lips, and with an almost inaudible sigh of thanks, his head slumps forward.

SCU
Ashenden and Elsa, still clutching each other, see what has happened.

[1] *Secret Agent* was made after *Sabotage*, which was based on Conrad's novel *The Secret Agent*. Hitchcock's film *Secret Agent* was based on W. Somerset Maugham's *Ashenden, or The British Agent* and subsequent stories.

SCU

The Mexican withdraws his revolver and, throwing it aside, picks up the fallen flask; he shrugs his shoulder.

CU

Almost in ecstasy, Ashenden shouts out:

"He's beaten you—thank Christ, he's beaten you!"

Elsa breaks down, sobbing, into Ashenden's arms.

The second alternate ending, which is in producer Michael Balcon's script, has Peter Lorre's character say, after shooting the American, "This job take much long time, my friends. Maybe I am getting old." Ashenden and the girl support each other, their heads intimately together. Music rises as we FADE OUT.

This incredible period of creativity and professional growth is unfortunately very poorly documented. Much of the paperwork from the studios of that era was destroyed in World War II or thrown away in later years. The great bulk of what is left in the way of Hitchcock's script development is from the American period.

## THE AMERICAN PERIOD

Hitchcock's work with the American studios is well documented in his personal files, which are held at the Margaret Herrick Library of the Academy of Motion Picture Arts and Sciences. Each film is represented by multiple scripts and sometimes ample notes and transcripts from meetings with writers. By far the most complete period is Hitchcock's final work at Universal Studios.

Obviously, all of the material cannot be reproduced here. Indeed, the vast majority of it is script after script with subtle changes. These are only interesting in the full context of the screenplay and the film. So I've limited what's present to those samples that can indicate in some way the full arc of development—from original story to a complete script. Nor can representations from all the films be present here. In selecting which films to include, I tried to choose material from those most significant and popular or the material, if from a lesser film, that is in some way exceptional.

I've also tried to avoid repetition. Fine work has been done on a number of films already, in a variety of mediums. For example, the story development of *Rebecca*, *Notorious*, and *North by Northwest* are available respectively on the excellent Criterion laserdisc editions, while the screenplay development of perhaps Hitchcock's most important films, *Vertigo* and *Psycho*, are well documented in my book on the former and Stephen Rebello's excellent book on the latter.

# *Rebecca*

A draft comparison is a tool frequently used during the development of a screenplay, comparing the various versions of the story against each other. This helps clarify where each scene came from and also helps the screenwriter now working out the project to sort the story threads. For a historian, it is a bird's-eye picture of the screenplay development.

The following draft comparison of the variations on *Rebecca* gives an extraordinary account (in shorthand) of what each filmmaker brought to the project.

## Rebecca Comparison

BETWEEN:
ONE-LINE CONTINUITY OF NOVEL
AND
ONE-LINE CONTINUITY OF STORY OUTLINE
      OF JUNE 3, 1939, BY
          MACDONALD & HARRISON
AND
ONE-LINE CONTINUITY OF TREATMENT
      OF JUNE 24, 1939, BY
          HITCHCOCK, HARRISON, & MACDONALD
AND
PLAY IN THREE ACTS BY DAPHNE DU MAURIER

                MARY BOWIE
                JULY 19, 1939.

| ONE-LINE CONTINUITY OF NOVEL | ONE-LINE CONTINUITY OF STORY OUTLINE JUNE 3, 1939 | ONE-LINE CONTINUITY OF TREATMENT JUNE 24, 1939 | PLAY IN THREE ACTS BY DAPHNE DU MAURIER |
| --- | --- | --- | --- |
| DESCRIPTION OF MANDERLEY: DAPHNE DREAMS SHE GOES BACK, DESCRIBES OLD BEAUTY AND NEW RUIN. | DESCRIPTION OF MANDERLEY: AFTER OPENING TITLES, GIRL'S VOICE DESCRIBES BEAUTIES OF PLACE WHILE SCREEN SHOWS DESOLATE RUINS. "I SUPPOSE IT FIRST REALLY STARTED ON THAT JOURNEY TO THE SOUTH OF FRANCE . . ." | DESCRIPTION OF MANDERLEY: SCREEN SHOWS RUINS. GIRL'S VOICE DESCRIBES BEAUTIES, THEN: " . . . I WONDER WHAT MY LIFE WOULD HAVE BEEN IF I HADN'T GONE TO MONTE CARLO WITH MRS. VAN HOPPER . . ." | ALL OF THE STORY POINTS, CHARACTERIZATIONS, BACKGROUND, ETC., CONTAINED ON THIS AND THE FOLLOWING PAGE (MONTE CARLO SEQUENCE), ARE COVERED IN THE FIRST SCENE, IS ACT OF THE PLAY WHICH BEGINS WITH THE ARRIVAL OF MAXIM AND HIS BRIDE AT MANDERLEY. |
| INTRODUCTION OF MRS. VAN HOPPER & MAXIM: AT HOTEL IN MONTE CARLO | INTRODUCTION OF MRS. VAN HOPPER & MAXIM: AT STATION IN DOVER, ON CHANNEL STEAMER. DAPHNE CHATS WITH STRANGER, MAXIM DE WINTER, ON DECK. BOTH BECOME SLIGHTLY ILL. | INTRODUCTION OF MRS. VAN HOPPER & MAXIM: AT HOTEL IN MONTE CARLO. | DUE TO THE OBVIOUS LIMITATIONS OF THE STAGE, AND THE NECESSITY FOR COMPRESSION OF ACTION, ETC., THERE WILL BE MANY PLACES WHERE IT WILL BE IMPOSSIBLE TO MATCH DETAILS IN ANY SORT OF INTELLIGIBLE ORDER IN THIS COMPARISON. WHERE THERE IS MUCH OF THIS TRANSPOSITION, I HAVE MADE A NOTE OF IT, GIVING ITS PLACE IN THE PLAY AND THE PAGE NUMBER IN THIS COMPARISON. |
| NEW ARRIVAL SEATED AT NEXT TABLE IN DINING ROOM: "IT'S MAX DE WINTER . . . WHO OWNS MANDERLEY . . . THEY SAY HE CAN'T GET OVER HIS WIFE'S DEATH . . ." | ON BLUE TRAIN, MRS. VAN HOPPER GLIMPSES MAXIM IN CORRIDOR: "THAT'S MAX DE WINTER . . . WHO OWNS MANDERLEY." | MRS. VAN HOPPER ENTERING DINING ROOM WITH GIRL, "I," SPIES MAXIM. SENDS GIRL FOR HER NEPHEW'S LETTER, WAITS IN LOUNGE TO WAYLAY MAXIM. "IT'S MAXIM DE WINTER, ETC.," SAME AS NOVEL. | FOR EASE IN READING AND COMPARISON, I HAVE BEGUN THE PLAY ON PAGE THREE OPPOSITE CORRESPONDING ARRIVAL IN NOVEL AND TREATMENTS. |
| MRS. VAN HOPPER INSISTS MAXIM JOIN THEM FOR COFFEE AFTER LUNCHEON. HER ATTEMPTS TO INCLUDE DAPHNE, HIS KINDNESS TO GIRL—REFUSING TO LET HER RUN ERRAND (EXTRA CUP—RUDENESS TO MRS. VAN HOPPER. | DINING CAR. MRS. VAN HOPPER INSISTS MAXIM DINE WITH THEM. HER ATTEMPTS TO INCLUDE DAPHNE, HIS KINDNESS TO GIRL—REFUSING TO LET HER RUN ERRAND (CIGARETTES). | SAME AS NOVEL | |
| LATER, MRS. VAN HOPPER SCOLDS DAPHNE FOR MONOPOLIZING CONVERSATION. | MRS. VAN HOPPER SCOLDS DAPHNE FOR MONOPOLIZING CONVERSATION—CAN'T INTEREST A MAN WHO HAS A FAMOUS ENGLISH BEAUTY FOR A WIFE. WHEN HE RETURNS WITH CIGARETTES, MAX ANSWERS MRS. VAN HOPPER'S QUESTION QUIETLY: HIS WIFE DIED SOME TIME AGO. | SAME AS NOVEL | |

| ONE-LINE CONTINUITY OF NOVEL | ONE-LINE CONTINUITY OF STORY OUTLINE JUNE 3, 1939 | ONE-LINE CONTINUITY OF TREATMENT JUNE 24, 1939 | PLAY IN THREE ACTS BY DAPHNE DU MAURIER |
|---|---|---|---|
| NOTE COMES TO DAPHNE FROM MAXIM APOLOGIZING FOR HIS RUDENESS TO MRS. VAN HOPPER. | | SAME AS NOVEL. | |
| DAPHNE AND MAXIM BECOME AC-QUAINTED: MRS. VAN HOPPER ILL NEXT DAY. THEY LUNCH TOGETHER, DRIVE; DAPHNE TALKS ABOUT HERSELF, POETRY; HE WITHDRAWS INTO HIMSELF AT MENTION OF HOME. AT HOTEL, MRS. VAN HOPPER SAYS: "THEY SAY HE NEVER TALKS ABOUT IT. SHE WAS DROWNED IN A BAY NEAR MANDERLEY ..." | DAPHNE AND MAXIM BECOME AC-QUAINTED: BREAKFAST ALONE TOGETHER ON BLUE TRAIN NEXT MORNING. DAPHNE TALKS ABOUT HERSELF—HE BECOMES QUIET AT MENTION OF BOATS OR SAILING. DAPHNE HELPS MRS. VAN HOPPER PREPARE FOR ARRIVAL AT MONTE CARLO, LEARNS FROM HER THAT MAXIM'S WIFE WAS DROWNED IN PARTICULARLY SAD CIRCUM-STANCES. | GIRL AND MAXIM BECOME ACQUAINTED: SAME AS NOVEL. <br><br> NOTE FROM TREATMENT: "WE NOW GET A SERIES OF IMPRESSIONS OF 'Y' COMING AND GOING FROM MRS. VAN HOPPER'S ROOMS ON VARIOUS DAYS AT VARIOUS TIMES. PROBABLY WE SHALL HAVE THREE OR FOUR EXTREMELY SHORT SCENES ... CREATING A GENERAL EFFECT OF "Y'S" DE-CEPTION OF MRS. VAN HOPPER CONCERN-ING HER VARIOUS EXCURSIONS ..." | THIS LINE OF DIALOGUE SPOKEN BY MAXIM AT MANDERLEY, NIGHT OF ARRIVAL. SCENE 1, ACT 1. PAGE 5 OF COMPARISON. |
| DAPHNE FALLS IN LOVE WITH MAXIM—SECRET DRIVES, MEETINGS, WITHDRAWAL AT MENTION OF MANDERLEY OR WIFE: "SOMETHING HAPPENED A YEAR AGO THAT ALTERED MY WHOLE LIFE ..." | DAPHNE FALLING IN LOVE WITH MAXIM—HE HELPS HER WIND WOOL, "WALK THE DOG," GET AWAY FROM READ-ING ALOUD SESSION, ETC. | THIS SCENE AND FOLLOWING ARE SAME AS IN NOVEL BUT TRANSPOSED. "BLACK SATIN AND PEARLS, ETC." PRECEDED "SOME-THING HAPPENED A YEAR AGO, ETC." | |
| | RIDING IN SPEEDBOAT, THEY ARE HAILED BY HIS FRIENDS ON YACHT, INVITED ABOARD. DAPHNE SELF-CONSCIOUS, SEA-SICK; THEY LEAVE. | | |
| RETURNING FROM A DRIVE, HER DESIRE TO BE MORE WORLDLY AND SOPHISTICATED INFURIATES HIM. | IN SPEEDBOAT AGAIN, DAPHNE'S DISSATIS-FACTION WITH HERSELF—ENDING IN OBLIQUE COMPARISONS TO REBECCA, EN-RAGE HIM. | SAME AS IN NOVEL—BUT HER DISSATISFAC-TIONS DO NOT ANGER HIM. | THIS MAXIM—"I" SCENE OCCURS DURING FIRST EVENING AT MANDERLEY, AFTER GIRL'S FIRST INTERVIEW WITH MRS. DAN-VERS HAS DEPRESSED HER. SCENE 1, ACT 1. PAGE 5 OF COMPARISON. |

| | | |
|---|---|---|
| RECONCILIATION. HE KISSES HER, ASKS HER TO CALL HIM MAXIM. | RECONCILIATION. HE PROMISES TO TAKE HER TO THE SPORTING CLUB AS A PEACE OFFERING. | |
| LATER, MRS. VAN HOPPER SPEAKS FURTHER OF BRILLIANCE OF REBECCA AND HOW HE ADORED HER. DAPHNE SECRETLY JEALOUS. | | OMITTED. |
| | AT CLUB THAT NIGHT, MAXIM—SEEMINGLY ALONE—IS INVITED TO JOIN MRS. VAN HOPPER'S PARTY. CONSTERNATION WHEN DAPHNE APPEARS SUDDENLY BESIDE HIM. YACHTING HOST OF AFTERNOON (DUKE OF WESTMINSTER) SPIES DAPHNE, FRIENDLY GREETINGS, ETC., ENRAGE MRS. VAN HOPPER. | |
| ONE MORNING, A CABLE FROM HER DAUGHTER DECIDES MRS. VAN HOPPER TO LEAVE NEXT DAY FOR NEW YORK. | FOLLOWING MORNING MRS. VAN HOPPER UNPLEASANT TO DAPHNE ABOUT MAXIM. SAYS SHE HAS DECIDED TO LEAVE MONTE CARLO AT ONCE. | CABLE, ETC., SAME AS NOVEL. |
| DAPHNE TRIES TO CONTACT MAXIM TO SAY GOOD-BY. HE HAS LEFT HOTEL FOR DAY AND EVENING. | DAPHNE TRIES TO RING MAXIM BUT HE HAS LEFT EARLY TO RIDE. TRIES TO TELEPHONE BEFORE IMMINENT DEPARTURE, CALLS DINING ROOM, BARBER SHOP, ETC. HE IS BATHING ROOM AND DOES NOT HEAR TELEPHONE WHEN IT RINGS. | GIRL GOES AT ONCE TO MAXIM'S ROOM— THERE IS NO TIME LAPSE HERE. |
| EARLY NEXT MORNING, SHE GOES TO HIS ROOMS. HE IS SHAVING; HE DRESSES, INSISTING THEY BREAKFAST TOGETHER. | LUGGAGE AND TAXI WAITING AT DOOR WHEN DAPHNE FINALLY FINDS HIM IN HIS ROOM SHAVING. | SCENE IS THE SAME. |

| ONE-LINE CONTINUITY OF NOVEL | ONE-LINE CONTINUITY OF STORY OUTLINE JUNE 3, 1939 | ONE-LINE CONTINUITY OF TREATMENT JUNE 24, 1939 | PLAY IN THREE ACTS BY DAPHNE DU MAURIER |
|---|---|---|---|
| MAXIM PROPOSES, MATTER-OF-FACTLY, AT TABLE IN DINING ROOM. DAPHNE INCREDULOUS. | MAXIM PROPOSES, IN HIS ROOM, WITH LATHER ON HIS FACE, ETC. | MAXIM PROPOSES, AT BREAKFAST ON TERRACE. 'IT'S A PITY YOU HAVE TO SHOW UP ...' MAXIM'S DOUBTS ABOUT HIS BEING TOO OLD FOR HER (IN NOVEL THEY OCCUR LATER, AT MANDERLEY) | MRS. DANVERS SUGGESTS THAT LONELINESS AT MANDERLEY HAS INDUCED MAXIM TO MARRY, DURING FIRST INTERVIEW WITH GIRL. SCENE 1, ACT 1. PAGE OF COMPARISON #4 |
| HE GOES TO TELL MRS. VAN HOPPER. | MRS. VAN HOPPER GONE LOOKING FOR DAPHNE, WHO TURNS FROM MAXIM'S ARMS TO TELL HER THE NEWS. | SAME. (AS IN NOVEL, GIRL BURNS DEDICATION PAGE OF BOOK OF POETRY MAXIM HAD LENT HER.) | |
| MRS. VAN HOPPER WARNS DAPHNE AFTERWARD THAT IT IS A BIG MISTAKE—SHE IS NOT HIS KIND, HE IS ONLY MARRYING HER TO ESCAPE LONELINESS AT MANDERLEY. | | MRS. VAN HOPPER'S REACTION SAME AS IN NOVEL. | ACT 1, SCENE 1. GREAT HALL AT MANDERLEY MAY 7, 6:15 P.M. MRS. DANVERS ALONE ON STAGE AT RISE, LEAVE AT ONCE. BEATRICE, GILES, CRAWLEY ARRIVE TO WELCOME BRIDE AND MAXIM. DIALOGUE ESTABLISHES BACKGROUND, ETC. |
| ARRIVAL AT MANDERLEY: (AFTER HONEYMOON IN VENICE) THEY GET HOME ABOUT TEA TIME. RAIN STOPS. DAPHNE IMPRESSED BY BEAUTY OF HOUSE, ETC. | ARRIVAL AT MANDERLEY: | ARRIVAL AT MANDERLEY: SAME. ON STEPS, GIRL ALMOST SHAKES BUTLER'S HAND. | ARRIVAL OF MAXIM AND "I": MOOD, INCIDENT, DIALOGUE SAME AS THE LUNCHEON SCENE IN NOVEL WHEN GIRL MEETS LACYS AND CRAWLEY. "IS BATHING SAFE IN BAY? ... ETC." |

BEATRICE—"I" SCENE: DISCUSS GIRL'S HAIR, CLOTHES, SAILING, ETC., WHILE MEN GO TO SEE GILES' NEW CAR. BEA AND GILES LEAVE. FRANK EXPLAINS LOCAL INTEREST IN BRIDE—ALSO NEIGHBORS DEMANDING REVIVAL OF FANCY DRESS BALL. MAXIM GOES OUT WITH FRANK WHEN HE LEAVES.

SAME.
DRIVING UP TO HOUSE, MAXIM MENTIONS AGED GRANDMOTHER WHO IS ALMOST ALWAYS CONFINED TO HER ROOM, AND EFFICIENCY OF HOUSEKEEPER MRS. DANVERS WHO IS THE ONLY ONE WHO CAN HANDLE THE OLD LADY.
(NOTE: IN NOVEL, GRANDMOTHER HAS HER OWN HOME. BEATRICE TAKES DAPHNE TO VISIT HER MUCH LATER.)

OUTSIDE HOUSE, FRITH (BUTLER) SAYS ENTIRE STAFF ASSEMBLED FOR WELCOME AT MRS. DANVERS' ORDERS  MAXIM ANNOYED.

FADE OUT ON GIRL MEETING TALL, GAUNT WOMAN: "THIS IS MRS. DANVERS . . ."

SAME.

MAXIM IS ANNOYED THAT STAFF HAS BEEN ASSEMBLED FOR WELCOME; SUSPECTS MRS. DANVERS OF DOING THIS.

DAPHNE, TERROR-STRICKEN, STARTS TO SHAKE HANDS WITH FRITH, THE BUTLER FLUSTERED, SHE NOTICES MRS. DANVERS' INIMICAL PRESENCE.

DAPHNE'S EMBARRASSMENT INTENSIFIED WHEN SHE MEETS MRS. DANVERS—CONFUSED, SHE DROPS HER GLOVES. HOUSEKEEPER, CONTEMPTUOUS, PICKS THEM UP. FRITH, THE BUTLER, ROBERT, YOUNG POSTMAN, MAIDS, ETC.

| ONE-LINE CONTINUITY OF NOVEL | ONE-LINE CONTINUITY OF STORY OUTLINE<br>JUNE 3, 1939 | ONE-LINE CONTINUITY OF TREATMENT<br>JUNE 24, 1939 | PLAY IN THREE ACTS BY DAPHNE DU MAURIER |
|---|---|---|---|
| MAXIM BUSY WITH LETTERS. MRS. DANVERS TAKES DAPHNE TO INSPECT NEWLY DECORATED EAST WING. | MAXIM BUSY WITH ESTATE BUSINESS—MRS. DANVERS TAKES DAPHNE ON TOUR OF HOUSE. | SAME AS NOVEL. | MRS. DANVERS' SCENE WITH "I": APPEARS SILENTLY—STARTLES GIRL WHO DROPS HAND BAG. MRS. DANVERS' ATTITUDE SAME AS IN NOVEL, CONSTANT REFERENCES TO MRS. DE WINTER, ETC. EXPLANATION OF MAXIM'S CHANGE FROM WEST WING TO EAST WING. |
| MRS. DANVERS' CONTEMPT AND DISLIKE, OBVIOUS. SAYS THESE ROOMS HAVE NEVER BEEN USED BY MAXIM BEFORE—WEST WING, CLOSER TO SEA, HAD BEEN LOCATION OF HIS SUITE. | MRS. DANVERS' ATTITUDE MAKES TOUR AGONY FOR DAPHNE. (NOTE FROM OUTLINE: "AFTER THE LOCATION OF WEST WING SUITE OF REBECCA HAS BEEN ESTABLISHED EXTERNALLY—") DAPHNE IS PREVENTED FROM OPENING CERTAIN DOOR, TOLD BY MRS. DANVERS SHE CANNOT GO IN THERE: DOOR LEADS TO ROOMS WHICH WERE PRIVATE DOMAIN OF MRS. DE WINTER. | SAME AS NOVEL.—CONTEMPT AND DISLIKE UNDER-EMPHASIZED. | |
| MRS. DANVERS SHOCKED DAPHNE HAS NO PERSONAL MAID. SHE SUGGESTS USING PARLOR-MAID, ALICE, TEMPORARILY. (NOTE: ALICE IS LATER REPLACED BY CLARICE.) | NOTE FROM OUTLINE, P. 23: "IT IS NECESSARY TO STATE THAT IN TREATMENT TWO MATTERS NOT YET DEALT WITH IN THIS OUTLINE WILL HAVE TO BE INSERTED—NAMELY, THE EARLY MENTION OF DAPHNE'S MAID, CLARICE . . ." | SAME AS IN NOVEL. | SHOCKED GIRL HAS NO PERSONAL MAID. |
| MRS. DANVERS: "I CAME HERE WHEN THE FIRST MRS. DE WINTER WAS A BRIDE . . ." | | SAME | "I CAME HERE WHEN FIRST MRS. DE WINTER WAS A BRIDE . . ." ETC. GIRL ASKS FOR HELP—MRS. DANVERS COLDLY SPEAKS OF STAFF'S DEVOTION TO MRS. DE WINTER—HINTS MAXIM MARRIED TO ESCAPE LONELINESS. |

GIRL APOLOGIZES FOR TROUBLE OF REDECORATING SUITE. MRS. DANVERS DESCRIBED SUPERIORITIES OF WEST WING, HINTS IT IS KEPT INVIOLATE BECAUSE "THAT WAS MRS. DE WINTER'S BEDROOM . . ."

MAXIM—"I" SCENE 1 (SIMILAR TO SCENE IN NOVEL, RETURNING FROM DRIVE IN MONTE CARLO.) HER DISSATISFACTIONS WITH HERSELF, ETC. MAXIM COMFORTING. "SOMETHING HAPPENED A YEAR AGO THAT ALTERED MY WHOLE LIFE . . ."

LATER, DAPHNE CONFESSES REACTIONS TO MRS. DANVERS' ATTITUDE. MAXIM HALF-ANGRY: "DON'T MIND HER. . . . IF SHE REALLY MAKES HERSELF A NUISANCE WE'LL GET RID OF HER."

OMITTED.

GIRL CONFESSES REACTIONS TO MRS. DANVERS. MAXIM: "DON'T MIND HER, ETC. . ." AS IN NOVEL.

FIRST EVENING AT MANDERLEY MAXIM AND DAPHNE SPEND QUIET EVENING ALONE TOGETHER.

FIRST EVENING AT MANDERLEY:

AFTER TOUR DAPHNE JOINS MAXIM IN OFFICE—MEETS FRANK CRAWLEY, ESTATE AGENT. SHE OFFERS TO TYPE REPLY TO BUSINESS LETTER—MEN LEAVE HER TO IT. DEEP IN WORK, DAPHNE IS INTERRUPTED BY MAXIM'S SISTER BEATRICE WHO MISTAKES HER FOR A SECRETARY.

OMITTED.

| ONE-LINE CONTINUITY OF NOVEL | ONE-LINE CONTINUITY OF STORY OUTLINE JUNE 3, 1939 | ONE-LINE CONTINUITY OF TREATMENT JUNE 24, 1939 | PLAY IN THREE ACTS BY DAPHNE DU MAURIER |
|---|---|---|---|
| NOTE: IN NOVEL, DAPHNE MEETS BEATRICE AND GILES, AND FRANK CRAWLEY THE NEXT DAY AT LUNCHEON. | MAXIM, CRAWLEY, BEATRICE AND HER HUSBAND GILES, IN LIBRARY BEFORE DINNER. DAPHNE, DISHEVELLED, APPEARS, WORK IN HAND, MAXIM SEES OPPORTUNITY FOR JOKE—HE KEEPS UP MASQUERADE, CALLING HER "MISS SNODGRASS," TREATING HER LIKE SECRETARY. JOKE GETS OUT OF HAND—HE FINALLY RESCUES DAPHNE AND INTRODUCES HER AS HIS WIFE. AT DINNER, BEATRICE'S CONSTANT TACTLESS REFERENCES TO REBECCA EMBARRASS DAPHNE, MAKE HER FEEL INADEQUATE AND AN INTRUDER. | | |
| | MAXIM SUDDENLY CALLS FOR JASPER, (DOG). SCENE OF JASPER LYING DISCONSOLATE OUTSIDE DOOR OF REBECCA'S SUITE. HE COMES TO DINING ROOM BUT DROOPS WITH DISAPPOINTMENT WHEN DAPHNE STOOPS TO PAT HIM. | | |
| JASPER COMES TO DAPHNE IN THE LIBRARY AFTER DINNER AND LAYS HIS HEAD ACROSS HER KNEES. THEY ARE FRIENDS AT ONCE. | HE REFUSES HER CARESS—WILL NOT ACCEPT HER. | | |
| FOLLOWING CONTINUITY CHANGED IN OUTLINE. | | | |
| NEXT MORNING: MAXIM ALREADY DOWN WHEN DAPHNE APPEARS FOR BREAKFAST—HE LEAVES THE HOUSE ALMOST AT ONCE. HIS SISTER BEATRICE HAS INVITED HERSELF FOR LUNCH. | NEXT MORNING:DAPHNE FROM WINDOW IN HER ROOM SEES MAXIM START OUT ON HORSEBACK WITH FRANK. (BREAKFAST IN ROOM.) | NEXT MORNING: SAME AS NOVEL. | |

LEAVING BEDROOM, SHE LOSES HER WAY, AND FINDS HERSELF BEFORE FORBIDDEN DOOR IN WEST WING.

DAPHNE FINDS UNLIGHTED FIRE IN LIBRARY—GOES TO LOOK FOR MATCHES—CAUGHT BY FRITH WHO SUGGESTS GOING TO MORNING ROOM: "MRS. DE WINTER ALWAYS USED THE MORNING ROOM." AND,

"MRS. DE WINTER ALWAYS ... DID HER CORRESPONDENCE ... THERE ... IN THE MORNINGS ..."

DAPHNE FLEES—FOLLOWS SOUND OF GIGGLING—COMES UPON TWO MAIDS, WHO GET BACK TO THEIR WORK QUICKLY.

DAPHNE FINDS UNLIGHTED FIRE IN LIBRARY—LOOKS ABOUT FOR MATCHES—CAUGHT BY FRITH, WHO SAYS THERE'S FIRE IN MORNING ROOM, STOPS HIMSELF SAYING:—"BY MRS. DE WINTER'S ORDERS ..." DAPHNE TOO EMBARRASSED TO ASK WHERE ROOM IS. SHE LOSES HER WAY AGAIN—FINDS HERSELF IN SERVANTS' HALL—SENIOR MEMBERS OF STAFF BREAKFASTING—

FOLLOWING CONTINUITY CHANGED IN OUTLINE.

MEMBER OF STAFF LEADS HER TO MORNING ROOM. JASPER, LYING ON THE HEARTH, LEAVES ROOM WHEN DAPHNE ENTERS.

SAME AS NOVEL.

THESE SUGGESTIONS COME FROM MRS. DANVERS DURING HER FIRST INTERVIEW WITH "I."

SCENE I, ACT I, PAGE 4

| ONE-LINE CONTINUITY OF NOVEL | ONE-LINE CONTINUITY OF STORY OUTLINE JUNE 3, 1939 | ONE-LINE CONTINUITY OF TREATMENT JUNE 24, 1939 | PLAY IN THREE THREE ACTS BY DAPHNE DU MAURIER |
| --- | --- | --- | --- |
| SCENE AT DESK IN MORNING ROOM: AT REBECCA'S DESK, DAPHNE FEELS INCOMPETENT AND AN INTRUDER. REBECCA'S MONOGRAMMED PAPER—ENGAGEMENT PADS AND BOOKS—NOTES, ETC. | SCENE AT DESK IN MORNING ROOM: SAME | SAME AS NOVEL. | |
| DISCONSOLATELY, DAPHNE TRIES TO WRITE TO MRS. VAN HOPPER. | OMITTED. | TRANSPOSED: NOTE IS BEGUN TO MRS. VAN HOPPER FOLLOWING INTERVIEW WITH MRS. DANVERS. | |
| TELEPHONE RINGS. DAPHNE ANSWERS WOMAN'S VOICE ASKING FOR MRS. DE WINTER: "I AM AFRAID YOU HAVE MADE A MISTAKE. MRS. DE WINTER HAS BEEN DEAD FOR OVER A YEAR . . ." | TELEPHONE RINGS. DAPHNE ANSWERS—MAN'S VOICE ASKING FOR MRS. DE WINTER: "I AM AFRAID YOU HAVE MADE A MISTAKE, ETC." | TELEPHONE RINGS. GIRL ANSWERS FOR MRS. DE WINTER. A MAN'S VOICE ASKING FOR MRS. DE WINTER. "I'M AFRAID YOU HAVE MADE A MISTAKE . . ." | GIRL SPEAKS THIS LINE, SIX WEEKS LATER, WHEN SHE IS ACCOSTED BY JACK FAVELL, DAY OF BALL. SCENE II, ACT I, PAGE 10 OF COMPARISON |
| SHE IS DOUBLY APPALLED AT THIS HORRIBLE MISTAKE WHEN SHE LEARNS IT IS MRS. DANVERS CALLING ON HOUSE PHONE TO DISCUSS MENUS | | | |
| SOUND MAKES HER TURN, HORRIFIED, TO DISCOVER MRS. DANVERS IN ROOM. HOUSEKEEPER SAYS IT WAS HEAD GARDENER CALLING FOR INSTRUCTIONS. | | SOUND MAKES HER TURN, HORRIFIED, TO FIND MRS. DANVERS HAS BEEN A WITNESS. HOUSEKEEPER SAYS IT WAS PROBABLY HEAD GARDENER CALLING FOR INSTRUCTIONS. | |
| DISCUSSION IS SHEER AGONY, DUE TO MRS. DANVERS' ATTITUDE AND CONSTANT REFERENCES TO REBECCA'S PREFERENCES. | SAME | SAME | MRS. DANVERS INFORMS GIRL OF REBECCA'S PREFERENCES DURING FIRST INTERVIEW, FIRST EVENING AT MANDERLEY. SCENE I, ACT I, PAGE 4 |

| | | |
|---|---|---|
| FOLLOWING CONTINUITY CHANGED—OR OMITTED—IN OUTLINE | MRS. DANVERS SUGGESTS DAPHNE VISIT GRANDMOTHER AS SOON AS OLD LADY IS WELL ENOUGH TO RECEIVE HER. | NOTE TO MRS. VAN HOPPER HERE. |
| DAPHNE FLEES AT SOUND OF ARRIVING CAR—LOSES HER WAY—MEETS SCULLERY MAID. | SAME AS NOVEL. | |
| FINDS HERSELF IN WEST WING—TRIES ONE DOOR, ROOM WITHIN IS DARK SHROUDED IN DUSTSHEETS—SOUND OF THE SEA. ACCOSTED BY MRS. DANVERS, WHO DISAPPROVES HER PRESENCE THERE, SAYS LACYS HAVE ARRIVED FOR LUNCH. | SAME AS NOVEL. | |
| DAPHNE MEETS BEATRICE AND GILES LACY, AND FRANK CRAWLEY THE ESTATE AGENT. THEY ARE KIND. MAXIM DISTRESSED BY REFERENCES TO 'A YEAR AGO.' CONSTERNATION WHEN DAPHNE SAYS, "IS BATHING SAFE IN THE BAY? . . ." | SAME AS NOVEL: BEATRICE, GILES, FRANK INTRODUCED, ETC. | "I" MEETS LACYS, CRAWLEY AS PREVIOUSLY NOTES DIALOGUE, ETC., SAME AS NOVEL. SCENE I, ACT I PAGE 3 OF COMPARISON. |
| BEATRICE'S KINDLY COUNSEL ABOUT MRS. DANVERS: SHE CRITICIZED DAPHNE'S APPEARANCE—SUGGESTS THEY GO TO CALL ON GRANDMOTHER SOON—ASKS IF DAPHNE SAILS—ANSWER IS NO—BEATRICE RELIEVED. | CONVERSATION BETWEEN WOMEN IS SAME AS NOVEL EXCEPT THAT IT TAKES PLACE BEFORE LUNCHEON (MEN HAVE GONE TO WASH UP) INSTEAD OF AFTER. NOTE: CHARACTER OF GRANDMOTHER OMITTED. | NOTE: CHARACTER OF GRANDMOTHER IS OMITTED IN PLAY. |

| ONE-LINE CONTINUITY OF NOVEL | ONE-LINE CONTINUITY OF STORY OUTLINE JUNE 3, 1939 | ONE-LINE CONTINUITY OF TREATMENT JUNE 24, 1939 | PLAY IN THREE ACTS BY DAPHNE DU MAURIER |
|---|---|---|---|
| "YOU ARE NOT A BIT WHAT I EXPECTED . . . YOU ARE SO DIFFERENT FROM REBECCA . . ." | (NOTE: APPROXIMATELY THIS SAME LINE APPEARS IN OUTLINE DURING DINNER WHEN DAPHNE MEETS BEATRICE). | THIS LINE SPOKEN DURING INTRODUCTION. NOTE: BEATRICE APPARENTLY DID NOT KNOW BEFORE THAT THEY ARE NOT NOW USING WEST WING SUITE. | |
| (NOTE: IN NOVEL, BEATRICE TAKES DAPHNE TO CALL ON THE GRANDMOTHER. A NURSE AND A PARLOUR MAID ARE PRESENT. ATMOSPHERE AND INCIDENT OF SCENE IS USED IN OUTLINE) | DAPHNE MEETS GRANDMOTHER "AFTER AN INDEFINITE TIME-LAPSE." IT IS AFTERNOON. BEATRICE AND A MAID ARE WITH OLD LADY AND KEEPS ASKING FOR MRS. DANVERS. MRS. DANVERS INTRODUCES DAPHNE—OLD LADY CANNOT GRASP DAPHNE'S POSITION—ASKS WHY "DEAR REBECCA" HASN'T BEEN TO SEE HER. | | |
| DISCOVERY OF COTTAGE ON BEACH: DAPHNE BORROWS MACINTOSH FROM CLOSET TO GO FOR WALK WITH MAXIM AND JASPER, AFTER THEIR GUESTS HAVE LEFT. HAPPY VALLEY—JASPER WANTING TO TAKE A DIFFERENT PATH THROUGH WOODS. THEY PLAY WITH HIM ON THE BEACH—HE RUNS AWAY—DAPHNE INSISTS ON GOING AFTER HIM—MAXIM STAYING BEHIND. | DISCOVERY OF COTTAGE ON BEACH: MAXIM AND DAPHNE IN A HAPPY MOOD ARE PLAYING GOLF—HE IS COACHING HER. SHE DRIVES—IT GOES WILD—LOOKING FOR HER BALL, SHE COMES TO THE BEACH. | DISCOVERY OF COTTAGE ON BEACH: SAME AS IN NOVEL BUT HAPPY VALLEY OMITTED, AND JASPER DISAPPEARS BEFORE THEY REACH THE BEACH. SHE GOES TO LOOK FOR DOG, LEAVES MAXIM, ETC. | DISCOVERY OF COTTAGE ON BEACH: COVERED IN DIALOGUE, "Y" AND FRANK CRAWLEY, IN SCENE II, ACT I, PAGE 11 |
| INTRODUCTION: IDIOT BOY, BEN. SHE ASKS FOR STRING—HE MAKES SENSELESS ANSWERS— | | INTRODUCTION OF IDIOT BOY BEN: SAME AS NOVEL. | NOTE: CHARACTER OF IDIOT BOY BEN, OMITTED FROM PLAY. |

| | | | |
|---|---|---|---|
| SEES A COTTAGE (CONVERTED BOAT HOUSE), GOES INSIDE FOR STRING—SURPRISED TO FIND IT FURNISHED BUT IN A STATE OF DISREPAIR. | SHE SEES A SMALL (STONE) COTTAGE AND GOES TO EXPLORE IT—CAN SEE IT HAS ONCE BEEN LIVED IN. | SAME AS NOVEL—COTTAGE BUILT OF SAME STONE AS BREAKWATER. WINDOWS BOARDED UP BUT INTERIOR FURNISHED. | |
| OUTSIDE AGAIN, BEN SPEAKS TO HER: "SHE DON'T GO IN THERE, NOW. SHE'S GONE IN THE SEA, AIN'T SHE?" | INTRODUCTION, BEN: HE PULLS HER AWAY FROM DOOR, EXCITEDLY TELLING HER SHE CANNOT GO IN THERE, IT BELONGS TO THE OTHER ONE . . . | SAME AS NOVEL. | |
| DAPHNE REJOINS MAXIM, WHO IS CROSS. THEY ALMOST QUARREL ON WAY BACK TO HOUSE. | MAXIM COMES TO COTTAGE FOR HER, DISMISSES BEN. THEY RETURN TO THEIR GAME—MAXIM IS KIND BUT CONSTRAINED AND NERVOUS. | SAME. | |
| ". . . I NEVER GO NEAR THE BLOODY PLACE, OR THAT GOD-DAMNED COTTAGE. AND IF YOU HAD MY MEMORIES YOU WOULD NOT WANT TO GO THERE EITHER . . ." | | SAME. | THESE LINES SPOKEN BY MAXIM DURING NEAR-QUARREL AFTER INTERVIEW WITH MRS. DANVERS OVER BREAKAGE OF CHINA ORNAMENT. SCENE II, ACT I, PAGE 11 OF COMPARISON. |
| ". . . WE OUGHT NEVER TO HAVE COME BACK TO MANDERLEY. OH, GOD, WHAT A FOOL I WAS TO COME BACK." | | SAME. | SAME AS ABOVE. |
| RECONCILIATION. AT TEA, DAPHNE DISCOVERS SHE HAS UNCONSCIOUSLY REMOVED A HANDKERCHIEF FROM MACINTOSH POCKET—REBECCA'S MONOGRAM. | | CHANGE: DISCOVERY OF REBECCA'S HANDKERCHIEF IN POCKET OF MACINTOSH DURING WALK HOME WHEN "I" BEGINS TO CRY DURING QUARREL. | |

| ONE-LINE CONTINUITY OF NOVEL | ONE-LINE CONTINUITY OF STORY OUTLINE JUNE 3, 1939 | ONE-LINE CONTINUITY OF TREATMENT JUNE 24, 1939 | PLAY IN THREE ACTS BY DAPHNE DU MAURIER |
| --- | --- | --- | --- |
| FIRST MENTION OF FANCY DRESS BALL: NEIGHBORS CALL, DAPHNE RETURNS CALLS SENDING UNSPOKEN CRITICISMS, ETC. CALLING ON A BISHOP'S WIFE AND ASKS IF MANDERLEY FANCY DRESS BALL WILL BE GIVEN THIS YEAR, MENTIONS REBECCA. DAPHNE PRETENDS SHE HAS HEARD OF BALL—DEFIANT AND BRAZEN SHE SPEAKS OF REBECCA TOO. | NOTE FROM OUTLINE, P. 23: "BEFORE GOING FURTHER, IT IS NECESSARY TO STATE THAT, IN TREATMENT, THE MATTERS NOT YET DEALT WITH IN THIS OUTLINE WILL HAVE TO BE INSERTED: . . . AND THE EARLY MENTION AND CONSTANT REFERENCE TO THE ANNUAL FANCY DRESS BALL AT MANDERLEY WHICH IS A TRADITIONAL AND INESCAPABLE FUNCTION." | FIRST MENTION OF FANCY DRESS BALL: CALLS AND VISITS OMITTED IN ACTION, COVERED IN CONVERSATION WITH FRANK CRAWLEY DURING FOLLOWING SCENE: "I" IN GREAT HALL PEERING PENSIVELY OUT AT COVE. SEES MRS. DANVERS AT WINDOW IN WEST WING. IMPULSIVELY "I" SEEKS OUT THE ESTATE AGENT. | FIRST MENTION OF FANCY DRESS BALL: OFTEN CALLED MIDSUMMER EVE BALL, IN PLAY. SCENE I, ACT I, PAGE 4. |
| NOTE: THERE IS A CHANGE OF CONTINUITY HERE: IN THE NOVEL, DAPHNE GOES TO REBECCA'S SUITE MUCH LATER ON, FROM DIFFERENT MOTIVES AND WITH A DIFFERENT RESULT. | DAPHNE GOES TO REBECCA'S SUITE IN WEST WING: (INDETERMINATE TIME-LAPSE) DAPHNE AT WINDOW OF HER ROOM, LOOKING DOWN AT COVE—ACROSS AT FORBIDDEN WEST WING. RESTLESS, SHE DECIDES TO EXPLORE REBECCA'S ROOMS. SHE IS ASTONISHED AT FRESH, CARED-FOR, LIVED-IN LOOKING ROOM. JASPER IS THERE, GROWLS AT HER. ENTERING ANOTHER ROOM, IN THE SUITE, DAPHNE SEES MAXIM AT WRITING TABLE, HIS HEAD IN HIS ARMS. DAPHNE LEAVES WITHOUT DISTURBING HIM. | | |
| SCENE WITH FRANK CRAWLEY: RETURNING FROM VISIT WITH BISHOP'S WIFE, DAPHNE MEETS HIM IN DRIVE OF MANDERLEY. | SCENE WITH FRANK CRAWLEY: FROM REBECCA'S ROOMS, DAPHNE GOES AT ONCE TO FRANK IN THE OFFICE. | SCENE WITH FRANK CRAWLEY: HE IS IN HIS OFFICE BEYOND LIBRARY. SHE TELLS HIM THAT SHE CALLED ON BISHOP'S WIFE YESTERDAY WHO MENTIONED FANCY DRESS BALL. | SCENE WITH FRANK CRAWLEY: OCCURS IN GREAT HALL, AFTER "I" HAS MET FAVELL. OTHERWISE SCENE IS SAME AS IN NOVEL. SCENE II, ACT I, PAGE 11 |
| HE EXPLAINS FANCY DRESS BALL, HOW REBECCA USED COTTAGE (PICNICS, PARTIES, ETC.) | OMITTED. | SAME AS NOVEL. | SEE ABOVE. |

SAME AS NOVEL

SAME BUT THAT THERE IS NO HINT HERE THAT SHE FEARS MAXIM STILL LOVES REBECCA.

FRANK IS SYMPATHETIC.

"I CAN'T TELL YOU HOW DELIGHTED I AM THAT YOU MARRIED MAXIM . . ."

BUT HE HAS TO ADMIT TO HER THAT REBECCA WAS THE MOST BEAUTIFUL CREATURE HE EVER SAW.

NOTE: THERE IS NO SPECIAL POINT IN THIS TREATMENT AT WHICH ALICE IS REPLACED BY MAID CLARICE.

SCENE WITH FRANK CRAWLEY, CONTD.: OCCURS GREAT HALL, AFTER "I" HAS MET FAVELL, DIALOGUE, ETC., SAME AS NOVEL. SEE BELOW
ACT I, SCENE II. PAGE 11

CURTAIN.

NOTE: ALICE (PARLOR MAID) REMAINS PERSONAL MAID THROUGHOUT PLAY.

ACT I, SCENE II. GREAT HALL. SIX WEEKS
LATER.
FOGGY
MORNING.

---

BARE DETAILS OF HER DEATH, AND MAXIM'S LATER IDENTIFICATION OF BODY.

SAME.

DAPHNE UNBURDENS HER HEART TO HIM: CONFESSES HER FEAR AND JEALOUSY OF REBECCA—BECAUSE MAXIM STILL LOVES HER.

SAME.

FRANK IS SYMPATHETIC:

OMITTED

"NONE OF US WANTS TO BRING BACK THE PAST—" HE SAYS.

SAME.

BUT WHEN DAPHNE ASKS HIM HE ADMITS REBECCA WAS THE MOST BEAUTIFUL CREATURE HE EVER SAW IN HIS LIFE.

CLARICE, A COUNTRY GIRL, REPLACES ALICE AS DAPHNE'S PERSONAL MAID. THEY BECOME GOOD FRIENDS.

SHADOW OF REBECCA CONTINUES TO HANG OVER DAPHNE'S LIFE.

| ONE-LINE CONTINUITY OF NOVEL | ONE-LINE CONTINUITY OF STORY OUTLINE JUNE 3, 1939 | ONE-LINE CONTINUITY OF TREATMENT JUNE 24, 1939 | PLAY IN THREE ACTS BY DAPHNE DU MAURIER |
| --- | --- | --- | --- |
| DAPHNE BREAKS CHINA ORNAMENT IN MORNING ROOM: | DAPHNE BREAKS CHINA ORNAMENT IN MORNING ROOM: | INCIDENT OF CHINA ORNAMENT IN MORNING ROOM: | CHINA ORNAMENT BROKEN: "I" KNOCKS ORNAMENT OFF MANTLE WHILE ARRANGING FLOWERS. WRAPS IT IN NEWSPAPER—GIVES IT TO ROBERT TO DISPOSE OF. CONTINUITY CHANGED HERE: |
| WEDDING PRESENT FROM BEATRICE, SIX VOLUMES OF HISTORY OF ART. KNOCKS CHINA CUPID OFF DESK IN MORNING ROOM, WHILE DAPHNE IS PLACING THEM. IT BREAKS ON FLOOR. | DAPHNE RUSHES BLINDLY FROM FRANK'S OFFICE TO MORNING ROOM. SLAMS DOOR VIOLENTLY, CHINA FIGURINE CRASHES TO FLOOR. | (THE MANNER IN WHICH THE CHINA CUPID WAS BROKEN IS NOT DISCLOSED.) | |
| TERRIFIED, SHE HIDES PIECES IN DRAWER. | SAME. | THE ACTUAL BREAKING OF THE ORNAMENT DOES NOT OCCUR AS ACTION, BUT IS COVERED BY DIALOGUE IN THE FOLLOWING SCENE: | INTRODUCTION OF JACK FAVELL: CALLS TO HER FROM WINDOW—ANSWER: "YOU'VE MADE A MISTAKE. MRS. DE WINTER HAS BEEN DEAD A YEAR." OTHERWISE, SIMILAR TO INTRODUCTION OF FAVELL. |
| | SHE DOES NOT KNOW THAT MRS. DANVERS HAS BEEN A WITNESS TO ENTIRE INCIDENT. (CAMERA SHOWS THE HOUSEKEEPER.) | | SCENE WITH FRANK CRAWLEY: "I" ASKS ABOUT COTTAGE DISCOVERED ON ONE OF HER WALKS—OTHERWISE, SAME AS SCENE IN NOVEL. |
| NEXT DAY, FRITH TELLS MAXIM THAT MRS. DANVERS ACCUSES ROBERT OF STEALING, OR BREAKING AND HIDING, ORNAMENT. | MRS. DANVERS TELLS MAXIM THAT ORNAMENT HAS BEEN STOLEN BY CLARICE—DEMANDS GIRL'S DISMISSAL. | IN THE MORNING, FRITH COMES TO MAXIM IN MORNING ROOM: MRS. DANVERS ACCUSES ROBERT OF STEALING CHINA ORNAMENT OFF WRITING TABLE. | SAME AS NOVEL: FRITH BRINGS NEWS OF TROUBLE BETWEEN ROBERT AND MRS. DANVERS OVER CHINA ORNAMENT, ETC. |
| DAPHNE IS FORCED TO CONFESS. | SAME. | GIRL CONFESSES BEFORE MRS. DANVERS APPEARS—WANTS TO ESCAPE WHILE MRS. DANVERS IS TOLD. MAXIM SURPRISED BUT NOT IMPATIENT OR ANGRY. MRS. DANVERS RECEIVES NEWS COLDLY. | SAME. |
| MAXIM'S SHOCK, MRS. DANVERS' CONTEMPT—HE SCOLDS DAPHNE BEFORE HOUSEKEEPER FOR MAKING A FOOL OF HERSELF. | SAME—BUT HE DISMISSES MRS. DANVERS BEFORE CRITICIZING DAPHNE. | | |

| | | |
|---|---|---|
| THEY QUARREL—MAXIM'S DOUBTS ABOUT THEIR MARRIED HAPPINESS, DAPHNE REASSURING, MAXIM'S STRANGE REACTION WHEN SHE SAYS: "I SUPPOSE THAT'S WHY YOU MARRIED ME . . . THERE'LL NEVER BE ANY GOSSIP ABOUT ME." | SAME AS NOVEL. | SAME AS NOVEL. (ACT I, SCENE II, CONTD.) ADDED TO SCENE: "I" SUGGESTS PUTTING REBECCA'S PRECIOUS THINGS ALL TOGETHER IN COTTAGE—MAXIM'S OUTBURST— "I NEVER GO NEAR THE BLOODY PLACE . . ." ETC. "WHAT A FOOL I WAS TO COME BACK," FROM SCENE IN NOVEL AFTER DISCOVERY OF COTTAGE ON BEACH. |
| MAXIM'S FIRST SAYING OF REBECCA'S NAME—ORNAMENT WAS WEDDING PRESENT TO HER. | SAME AS NOVEL. | |
| MAXIM GOES TO LONDON FOR A FEW DAYS. DAPHNE GOES TO COTTAGE AGAIN—MEETS IDIOT BOY BEN—HE TELLS HER ABOUT REBECCA AT COTTAGE, HER THREATS TO SEND HIM TO ASYLUM. | NOTE: MAXIM'S ABSENCE IS EXPLAINED BY "I" IN FOLLOWING SCENE: HE HAS GONE TO LONDON. | |
| NOTE FROM OUTLINE: "——IN TREATMENT, FAVELL SHALL BE INJECTED INTO STORY IN ONE OR TWO SEQUENCES—BUT WITHOUT IN ANY WAY IDENTIFYING HIM: HE WILL BE MERELY A PERSON—PRESUMABLY UNPLEASANT AND OF SINISTER IMPORT—WHOM WE SEE MAKING UNEXPLAINED VISITS TO MRS. DANVERS." | INTRODUCTION OF FAVELL: SCENE OPENS WITH GIRL LEAVING COVE, BACK AT HOUSE FINDS STRANGE CAR IN DRIVE, ETC. AS IN NOVEL. | (INTRODUCTION OF FAVELL HAS TAKEN PLACE EARLIER AS NOTED ABOVE.) |
| INTRODUCTION OF FAVELL: DAPHNE FINDS FAVELL WITH MRS. DANVERS—HIS PRESENCE AND IDENTITY UNEXPLAINED—JASPER GLAD TO SEE HIM. FAVELL ASKS DAPHNE NOT TO MENTION HIS VISIT TO MAXIM. DAPHNE, SUSPICIOUS OF HIM AND MRS. DANVERS, DECIDES TO GO INSPECT WEST WING. | AFTER FAVELL'S DEPARTURE, "I" GOES DETERMINEDLY UP TO REBECCA'S SUITE. | |

| ONE-LINE CONTINUITY OF NOVEL | ONE-LINE CONTINUITY OF STORY OUTLINE JUNE 3, 1939 | ONE-LINE CONTINUITY OF TREATMENT JUNE 24, 1939 | PLAY IN THREE ACTS BY DAPHNE DU MAURIER |
|---|---|---|---|
| DAPHNE SEES REBECCA'S ROOMS: SHE IS ASTONISHED AT BEAUTY AND LIVED-IN ATMOSPHERE. MRS. DANVERS DISCOVERS HER, TORTURES HER WITH INTIMATE DETAILS OF REBECCA—HER MARRIAGE TO MAXIM—FURTHER DETAILS OF NIGHT OF HER DEATH—"DO YOU THINK THE DEAD COME BACK? . . . SOMETIMES I WONDER IF SHE WATCHES YOU AND MR. DE WINTER TOGETHER . . ." | VISIT TO REBECCA'S SUITE USED PREVIOUSLY AND TREATED DIFFERENTLY IN OUTLINE. | DAPHNE SEES REBECCA'S ROOMS: SHE IS ASTONISHED AT BEAUTY AND LIVED-IN ATMOSPHERE. ACCOSTED BY MRS. DANVERS, "I" MAKES FEEBLE EXCUSE FOR PRESENCE THERE.<br>SAME AS NOVEL.<br>FOLLOWING IS ADDED: MRS. DANVERS SAYS WEST WING SUITE IS NOT USED BY MAXIM BECAUSE OF UNBEARABLE SOUND OF SEA. SHE LEAVES "I" REPEATING "LISTEN TO THE SEA . . ." "I" BURSTS INTO UNCONTROLLABLE SOBBING. | MRS. DANVERS—"I" SCENES: SHE RETURNS TO HALL TO RUB-IN BREAKING OF ORNAMENT—<br>COSTUME: SHE BRINGS GOWN OF MAXIM'S GREAT-GRANDMOTHER'S—SUGGESTS "I" WEAR IT, "I" AGREES.<br>SAME AS NOVEL, TELLS INTIMATE DETAILS OF REBECCA, ETC.,—BUT LESS PASSIONATELY.<br>CONTINUITY CHANGED:<br>SCENE IS INTERRUPTED BY ROCKETS, ETC., "IT MUST BE A SHIP GONE ASHORE IN THE BAY—"<br>CURTAIN. |
| DAPHNE MEETS GRANDMOTHER: BEATRICE INVITES HER TO GO VISIT OLD LADY. GRANDMOTHER CANNOT REALIZE WHO DAPHNE IS—ASKS FOR "DEAR REBECCA." | USED PREVIOUSLY. | | |
| RETURNING TO MANDERLEY, DAPHNE FINDS MAXIM HAS GONE HOME—SHE OVERHEARS HIM WARNING MRS. DANVERS ABOUT HAVING FAVELL AT THE HOUSE. | | LATER, IN HER OWN ROOM, "I" COMPOSES HERSELF. SEES MAXIM'S CAR DRIVE IN—GOES TO GREET HIM—HEARS HIM WARN MRS. DANVERS ABOUT FAVELL. | "I" OVERHEARS WARNING LATER ON, IN ACT II, SCENE I, PAGE 13. |

| | | | |
|---|---|---|---|
| FANCY DRESS BALL SEQUENCE<br><br>ONE SUNDAY, A LADY GUEST SUGGESTS FANCY DRESS BALL BE GIVEN—MAXIM RELUCTANT—FINALLY AGREES. | GILES, IN FANCY DRESS COSTUME, INTERRUPTS SCENE BETWEEN MAXIM AND DAPHNE (THE QUARREL FOLLOWING HER CONFESSION THAT SHE BROKE ORNAMENT). | FANCY DRESS BALL SEQUENCE<br><br>IMMEDIATELY AFTER MAXIM'S ARRIVAL, FRANK CRAWLEY SAYS LADY COWAN IS A NUISANCE, CALLING ABOUT FANCY DRESS BALL. MAXIM IS RELUCTANT, CONSULTS "I"—"I" THINKS IT MIGHT BE FUN. | FANCY DRESS BALL SEQUENCE: ACT I, SCENE I, FRANK CRAWLEY SAYS NEIGHBORS ARE ALREADY DEMANDING BALL BE REVIVED. SCENE II OF ACT I (IMMEDIATELY ABOVE) TAKES PLACE ON DAY OF BALL. |
| MAXIM'S SUGGESTION: "PUT A RIBBON AROUND YOUR HAIR AND BE ALICE-IN-WONDERLAND ..." | | SUGGESTS "I" GO AS ALICE-IN-WONDERLAND. | (LINE USED PREVIOUSLY, ACT I, SCENE I, PG. 11) |
| HE SAYS HE NEVER DRESSES UP. | MAXIM SHOWS HIS DISTASTE FOR BALL AND THE COSTUME GILES BRINGS FOR HIM TO TRY ON. | SAYS HE WEARS ORDINARY CLOTHES. | ACT II, SCENE I, GREAT HALL, THAT EVENING. SERVANTS PREPARING FOR BALL. FRITH AND CRAWLEY DISCUSS GROUNDED SHIP—WHAT DID DIVER FIND? ... CRAWLEY, WORRIED, CALLS HARBOUR MASTER FOR NEWS—NO RESULT. |
| DAPHNE, HURT, DECIDES TO KEEP COSTUME SECRET. | MAXIM AND DAPHNE APPEAR TO BE ESTRANGED. | "I" PROMISES TO GIVE FRANK AND MAXIM SURPRISE OF THEIR LIVES WITH HER COSTUME. | |
| UNDECIDED ABOUT COSTUME UNTIL MRS. DANVERS COMES TO HER ROOM AND SUGGESTS COPYING PORTRAIT IN GALLERY. | MRS. DANVERS AND DAPHNE IN GALLERY LOOKING AT PORTRAIT—HOUSEKEEPER SUGGESTS COPYING IT. | "I" SKETCHING POSSIBLE COSTUMES—MRS. DANVERS FINDS DISCARDED DRAWINGS, SUGGESTS SHE COPY PICTURE IN GALLERY. AT FIRST RELUCTANT, GIRL GOES ALONE TO INSPECT PICTURE: "CAROLINE DE WINTER 1760–1808." | (COSTUME SUGGESTION USED PREVIOUSLY, ACT I, SCENE II, PAGE 11) |
| SHE IS DREADING THE BALL. | SHE IS LOOKING FORWARD TO THE BALL—HOPING TO IMPRESS MAXIM—EFFECT RECONCILIATION—WITH BEAUTY OF HER COSTUME. | | MAXIM WARNING MRS. DANVERS: ABOUT FAVELL, OVERHEARD BY "I" ON STAIRS—SHE HAS COME DOWN FOR ROSE FOR HER COSTUME WHICH IS STILL A SECRET. MAXIM NOTICES NEW EXPRESSION ON HER FACE. |

| ONE-LINE CONTINUITY OF NOVEL | ONE-LINE CONTINUITY OF STORY OUTLINE JUNE 3, 1939 | ONE-LINE CONTINUITY OF TREATMENT JUNE 24, 1939 | PLAY IN THREE ACTS BY DAPHNE DU MAURIER |
|---|---|---|---|
| PREPARATIONS FOR BALL. | MONTAGE. | MONTAGE OF PREPARATIONS FOR BALL | |
| BEATRICE AND GILES ARRIVE EARLY, DISCUSS COSTUMES—DAPHNE SECRETIVE. | | | BEATRICE AND GILES ARRIVE IN COSTUMES, ALSO CRAWLEY. BAND ARRIVES. |
| CLARICE HELPS DAPHNE CHANGE. | CLARICE AND MRS. DANVERS HELP DAPHNE DRESS. MAXIM FORGETS TO CHANGE UNTIL REMINDED BY SERVANTS. | "I" DRESSING, CLARICE ASSISTING. SHE REFUSES TO ADMIT BEATRICE: COSTUME STILL SECRET. | |
| MAXIM, BEATRICE, GILES, CRAWLEY WAITING IN LOWER HALL FOR DAPHNE—NO GUESTS HAVE YET ARRIVED FOR DINNER PARTY. | STORM COMING. GUESTS ARRIVING BEFORE DAPHNE APPEARS. HALL CROWDED—GRANDMOTHER IN WHEELCHAIR. | BALL HAS ALREADY STARTED—MUSIC, FEW COUPLES DANCING. MAXIM, BEATRICE, GILES, FRANK, A FEW OTHERS NEAR FOOT OF STAIRS. | SAME AS NOVEL. |
| DRESSED, DAPHNE GIVES DIRECTIONS TO BAND LEADER— "MISS CAROLINE DE WINTER!" | MRS. DANVERS GIVES DIRECTIONS TO BAND LEADER. SAME. | "I" APPEARS IN COSTUME, ANNOUNCES HERSELF: "MAY I PRESENT MISS CAROLINE DE WINTER." | SAME BUT BAND LEADER ANNOUNCES: "MRS. MAXIMILIAN DE WINTER!" |
| DAPHNE MAKES GRAND ENTRANCE DOWN STAIRS. | SAME. | SAME AS NOVEL: PLAYS OUT HER FANTASTIC LITTLE SCENE— | SAME. |
| HORROR-STRICKEN SILENCE. | GRANDMOTHER: "REBECCA!" MURMURINGS OF GUESTS—SHOCKED. | | SAME. |
| MAXIM: "WHAT THE HELL DO YOU THINK YOU ARE DOING? ... GO AND CHANGE NOW ... BEFORE ANYBODY COMES ..." | PUSHING HIS WAY THROUGH GUESTS— WHAT THE HELL DOES SHE THINK SHE'S DOING IN THAT DRESS?—TELLS HER TO GO AND CHANGE ... | MAXIM: "WHAT THE HELL DO YOU THINK YOU'RE DOING?" ... TELLS HER TO GO AND CHANGE. | SAME. |
| MRS. DANVERS EVILLY TRIUMPHANT IN UPPER HALL. | | IN THE GALLERY, MRS. DANVERS EVILLY TRIUMPHANT—"I" RUSHES BLINDLY PAST HER. | CHANGE: AS "I" EXITS, FRITH ANNOUNCES FIRST GUESTS. |
| | | | CURTAIN. |

| CONTINUITY CHANGED OR OMITTED IN OUTLINE. | | ACT II, SCENE II, GREAT HALL, 4:30 A.M. |
|---|---|---|
| | "I" HAS IMMEDIATELY TAKEN OFF COSTUME—CLARICE UNABLE TO FIND MRS. DANVERS FOR HER— | BALL IS JUST ENDING—BEA, GILES, CRAWLEY DISCUSSING GIRL'S FAUX PAS WHICH MAXIM BELIEVES TO BE DELIBERATE, BALL, SHIP, ETC., MAXIM HAS BEEN ABSENT FROM BALL FOR SOME TIME. |
| BEATRICE COMES TO HELP DAPHNE CHANGE—EXPLAINS IT WAS COSTUME REBECCA WORE—MAXIM THINKS IT WAS DELIBERATE JOKE. | NOTE: INTERMEDIATE SCENES IN NOVEL ARE OMITTED. FOLLOWING SCENES TAKE PLACE IMMEDIATELY AFTER GIRL'S FAUX PAS, WHILE BALL IS STILL GOING ON. | |
| DAPHNE REFUSES TO GO DOWN—BEATRICE AND GILES TRY TO PERSUADE HER. AT LAST DAPHNE GOES DOWNSTAIRS. BALL IS SHEER AGONY. | | BEATRICE AND GILES LEAVE. |
| MAXIM DOES NOT SPEAK TO HER, NOR COME TO BED THAT NIGHT IN THEIR ROOM. | DAPHNE, MISERABLE, SITS IN HER ROOM HEARING VOICES CLAMORING IN HER MIND—ACCUSING, CRITICIZING, ETC.—THEN MRS. DANVERS' VOICE IN REALITY— | FRANK—"I" SCENE: AS IN NOVEL OVER TELEPHONE. |
| | | SHE IS BROKEN-HEARTED: |
| NO SIGN OF MAXIM NEXT MORNING—BEATRICE AND GILES HAVE LEFT. | | "HE DOESN'T LOVE ME—HE LOVES REBECCA—WILL NOT LISTEN WHEN HE TRIES TO EXPLAIN. |
| DAPHNE TELEPHONED FRANK CRAWLEY—"HE DOESN'T LOVE ME, HE LOVES REBECCA"—BUT SHE REFUSES TO SEE FRANK WHO SAYS HE HAS SOMETHING IMPORTANT TO TELL HER. | | |
| DAPHNE SEEKS OUT MRS. DANVERS FOR EXPLANATION. | "I" GOES RESOLUTELY TO WEST WING TO FIND MRS. DANVERS. | |
| IN REBECCA'S ROOM, MRS. DANVERS EXPLAINS HER HATRED AND CONTEMPT: "WHAT DO YOU KNOW ABOUT . . . MEN? YOU THINK YOU CAN TAKE MRS. DE WINTER'S PLACE—WHY, EVEN THE SERVANTS LAUGHED AT YOU . . ." | SCENE IN REBECCA'S ROOM SAME AS IN NOVEL—"I" ACCUSES MRS. DANVERS OF MAKING HER WEAR REBECCA'S COSTUME:—"MRS. LACY TOLD ME—" | MRS. DANVERS APPEARS. "I" HYSTERICALLY DEMANDS EXPLANATION—"YOU MADE ME WEAR THAT DRESS!" MRS. DANVERS, AS IN NOVEL: "NOBODY WANTED YOU AT MANDERLEY—WHAT DO YOU KNOW ABOUT MEN—EVEN THE SERVANTS LAUGHED AT YOU . . ." |
| | MRS. DANVERS' TIRADE: | |
| | SAME—BUT SHE ADDS THAT HER CAREFUL TENDING OF REBECCA'S ROOMS IS DONE WITH MAXIM'S KNOWLEDGE AND APPROVAL. | |

| ONE-LINE CONTINUITY OF NOVEL | ONE-LINE CONTINUITY OF STORY OUTLINE JUNE 3, 1939 | ONE-LINE CONTINUITY OF TREATMENT JUNE 24, 1939 | PLAY IN THREE ACTS BY DAPHNE DU MAURIER |
| --- | --- | --- | --- |
| DAPHNE IS AT THE WINDOW. | DAPHNE MOVES TO WINDOW, THROWS IT OPEN—STORMING OUTSIDE—SOUNDS OF MUSIC FROM BALL. | SCENE AT WINDOW SAME AS IN NOVEL BUT MRS. DANVERS' ATTEMPTS TO MAKE "I" JUMP ARE MORE SUBTLE AND SUGGESTIVE— | "I" IS NEAR RAILING OF GALLERY—<br><br>MRS. DANVERS PRESSING "I" CLOSER TO RAILING. |
| MRS. DANVERS TRIES TO MAKE DAPHNE JUMP OUT OF WINDOW: "...THERE'S NOT MUCH FOR YOU TO LIVE FOR—WHY DON'T YOU ... ETC. EASY DEATH—NOT LIKE DROWNING ..." | SAME. | LINE OMITTED: "EASY DEATH—NOT LIKE DROWNING——" | "WHY DON'T YOU ... ETC.," AS IN NOVEL. |
| INTERRUPTED BY SOUNDS OF RUNNING FEET. | ROCKET BURSTS IN SKY ABOVE THE SEA.<br><br>MEN RUN FROM HOUSE (FROM THE BALL) TOWARD THE SEA—SIRENS SCREAMING—MORE ROCKETS. | INTERRUPTED BY SIRENS AND ROCKETS. MRS. DANVERS: "... THERE MUST BE A SHIP ASHORE IN THE BAY." | INTERRUPTED BY TELEPHONE BELL...<br><br>SCENE CONTINUED ON FOLLOWING PAGE |
| SHIP GROUNDED IN BAY: | SHIP SINKING IN COVE: | SHIP GROUNDED IN BAY: | (USED PREVIOUSLY, ACT I, SCENE II, PG. 12) |
| IT IS MAXIM RUNNING ON TERRACE—DAPHNE JOINS CROWD ON BEACH—LOOKS FOR MAXIM— | | "I" AND MRS. DANVERS HEAR SHOUTS, ETC., FROM BELOW—MUSIC STOPS—THEY SEE GUESTS, MAXIM, FRANK, ETC., RUNNING OUT OF THE HOUSE TOWARD SHORE. | |
| DIVER IS BEING SENT DOWN TO INSPECT BOTTOM OF SHIP. | NEXT MORNING: DAPHNE IS PACKED, DRESSED FOR TRAVELING—SHE IS READY TO LEAVE MANDERLEY. | NEXT MORNING: | (ACT II, SCENE II, CONTD.) |
| MAXIM, CRAWLEY SAYS, HAS TAKEN INJURED SEAMAN TO DOCTOR. | MAXIM, FRITH TELLS HER, HAS TAKEN INJURED SEAMAN TO DOCTOR. | "I" AT WINDOW IN CORRIDOR OF WEST WING, WATCHING SCENE DOWN IN BAY. ROBERT SAYS MAXIM HAS NOT RETURNED; HE HAS TAKEN INJURED SAILOR TO KERRITH. | |
| | DAPHNE READY TO LEAVE WITHOUT FAREWELLS— | | |

| | | | |
|---|---|---|---|
| CAPTAIN SEARLE COMES TO HOUSE TO SEE MAXIM. IN HIS ABSENCE DAPHNE RECEIVES THE MAN. | CAPTAIN SEARLE IS ANNOUNCED. | ROBERT ANNOUNCES ARRIVAL OF CAPTAIN SEARLE. | INSPECTOR WELCH IS CALLING CRAWLEY—CRAWLEY MIRACULOUSLY APPEARS. AFTER 'PHONE CONVERSATION, HE SAYS MAXIM HAS BEEN WITH POLICE ALL EVENING—DIVER FOUND REBECCA'S BOAT AND A BODY—"THEN THERE MUST HAVE BEEN SOMEONE ELSE WITH HER, ETC." |
| HE TELLS HER DIVER FOUND REBECCA'S SAILING BOAT—INVESTIGATION MUST BEGIN AT ONCE BECAUSE THERE IS A BODY IN THE BOAT—"THEN THERE MUST HAVE BEEN SOMEONE ELSE WITH HER . . ." | SAME. | SAME AS NOVEL. | |
| MAXIM RETURNS. SEARLE TELLS HIM NEWS ALONE. | MAXIM RETURNS—ASKS WHERE DAPHNE IS GOING—SEARLE TELLS HIM NEWS ALONE. | MAXIM RETURNS—GIRL GOES INTO HALL, GAZES REFLECTIVELY AT PORTRAIT OF CAROLINE DE WINTER. SHE GOES BACK TO MAXIM WHEN SEARLE LEAVES. | MAXIM ENTERS—HE WILL JOIN OFFICIALS TOMORROW WHEN THEY RAISE THE BOAT— |
| | DAPHNE TELLS CLARICE TO UNPACK. | | |
| MAXIM'S CONFESSION: TELLS DAPHNE. | MAXIM'S CONFESSION: TELLS DAPHNE SHE'D BE BETTER OFF TO LEAVE: REBECCA HAS WON. | MAXIM'S CONFESSION: SAME AS NOVEL. "I" ASKS LAST NIGHT BE FORGOTTEN. HE TELLS HER IT'S TOO LATE. "WE'VE LOST OUR LITTLE CHANCE AT HAPPINESS . . ." ETC. "THE WOMAN'S BODY IN THE CRYPT IS NOT REBECCA'S . . ." ETC. LINE OMITTED: "WILL YOU LOOK IN MY EYES AND TELL ME YOU LOVE ME NOW?" ADDED LINE: "YOU'RE NOT TO BE DRAGGED INTO THIS, ETC. . . ." | MAXIM'S CONFESSION: "I" SAYS SHE'S SORRY, CAN'T THEY BEGIN AGAIN— "IT'S TOO LATE . . . REBECCA HAS WON . . ." WOMAN BURIED IN CRYPT IS NOT REBECCA—ETC. AS IN NOVEL. |
| "WE'VE LOST OUR LITTLE CHANCE AT HAPPINESS . . . REBECCA HAS WON . . . REBECCA WAS NOT DROWNED AT ALL. I KILLED HER. I SHOT REBECCA, ETC. . . . IT'S REBECCA WHO'S LYING DEAD THERE ON THE CABIN FLOOR. WILL YOU LOOK IN MY EYES AND TELL ME YOU LOVE ME NOW?" DISCUSS DETAILS OF REBECCA'S DEATH. | DAPHNE, MISUNDERSTANDING, SAYS SHE'LL STAND BY—KNOWS HOW HE LOVED REBECCA. | | |
| "YOU THOUGHT I LOVED REBECCA? I HATED HER . . ." | SAME. | SAME. | "YOU THOUGHT I LOVED REBECCA? . . . I HATED HER . . ." ETC. |
| | SAYS IN A FEW HOURS EVERYONE WILL KNOW IT'S REBECCA'S BODY IN BOAT—THAT HE KILLED HER. | | |

| ONE-LINE CONTINUITY OF NOVEL | ONE-LINE CONTINUITY OF STORY OUTLINE JUNE 3, 1939 | ONE-LINE CONTINUITY OF TREATMENT JUNE 24, 1939 | PLAY IN THREE ACTS BY DAPHNE DU MAURIER |
|---|---|---|---|
| DAPHNE'S JOY IN DISCOVERING THAT HE LOVES HER. | DAPHNE'S JOY THAT HIS LOVE FOR HER HAS NOT LESSENED. | | |
| MAXIM DESCRIBES HORRORS OF MARRIED LIFE WITH REBECCA—EARLY DISCOVERY OF HER TRUE NATURE— | SAME. | SAME AS NOVEL. | MAXIM DESCRIBES HORRORS OF MARRIED LIFE WITH REBECCA—DISCOVERY OF TRUE NATURE. |
| —"SHABBY, SORDID FARCE" THEY PLAYED—INFIDELITIES, JACK FAVELL, ETC. | | SAME AS NOVEL. | SAME. "SHABBY, SORDID FARCE" THEY PLAYED—INFIDELITIES, JACK FAVELL, ETC. |
| THAT NIGHT AT COTTAGE WHEN REBECCA RETURNED FROM DAY IN LONDON, SHE TOLD HIM OF PREGNANCY—NOT HIS CHILD THAT WOULD INHERIT MANDERLEY. | SAME—BUT THAT REBECCA NAMED FAVELL OU'RIGHT AS FATHER OF CHILD. | SAME AS NOVEL. CHANGED LINE: "IF I HAD A CHILD NEITHER YOU NOR ANYONE IN THE WORLD COULD EVER PROVE IT WASN'T YOURS . . ." | THAT NIGHT AT COTTAGE, WHEN REBECCA RETURNED FROM LONDON: "JACK AND I ARE GOING TO HAVE A CHILD AND NEITHER YOU NOR ANYONE WILL BE ABLE TO PROVE IT ISN'T YOURS . . ." "I'LL BE THE PERFECT MOTHER . . . ETC." |
| DESCRIBES SHOOTING REBECCA, TAKING BODY TO BOAT, ETC. | DESCRIBES HITTING REBECCA, SO THAT IN FALLING SHE WAS KILLED, ETC. | METHOD OF KILLING UNDISCLOSED. | DESCRIBES DISPOSING OF BODY (NO MENTION OF METHOD OF KILLING UNTIL LATER IN PLAY) |
| DESCRIBES IDENTIFYING NAMELESS WOMAN'S BODY AS REBECCA'S. | SAME. | USED PREVIOUSLY IN THIS SCENE. | |
| | HE ASKS IF DAPHNE CAN STILL LOVE HIM NOW. | | |
| "I KNEW REBECCA WOULD WIN IN THE END . . ." | SAME AS NOVEL. | | "I KNEW REBECCA WOULD WIN IN THE END . . ." "I" TRIES TO MAKE UP CONVINCING STORY. |

PHONE RINGS—IT IS COLONEL JULYAN, MAGISTRATE.—HE IS GOING OUT TOMORROW TO SEE BODY WITH DOCTOR AND INSPECTOR WELCH AND MAXIM.

SAME—BUT THAT IT IS GILES WHO IS COMING OVER TO SEE MAXIM OFFICIALLY. NOTE FROM OUTLINE: —IN TREATMENT, ANOTHER VERY IMPORTANT ESTABLISHMENT WILL BE MADE EARLY IN THE STORY—THAT COLONEL GILES LACY, BEATRICE'S HUSBAND IS CHIEF CONSTABLE OF COUNTY.

PHONE RINGS—IT IS COLONEL JULYAN, CHIEF CONSTABLE FOR THE COUNTY—

PHONE RINGS—DUMBFOUNDED, NEITHER ANSWERS.

CURTAIN.

ACT III, SCENE I. GREAT HALL. TWO O'CLOCK ON THE AFTERNOON OF 25TH.

PHONE AGAIN—NEWSPAPER REPORTER.

PHONE AGAIN—NEWSPAPER REPORTER.

AT RISE, FRITH ON PHONE TO REPORTER.

CHANGE IN CONTINUITY IN OUTLINE:

MAXIM, DAPHNE, FRANK, THE LACYS HAVING PRE-DINNER DRINKS IN LIBRARY—DETERMINEDLY GAY—

DAPHNE HAS MATURED SOMEHOW—SHE AND MAXIM CLOSER TOGETHER. EVERYONE SYMPATHETIC TO THEM.

(MAXIM HAS GONE TO EXHUMATION.)

NEXT DAY, MAXIM OFF TO INSPECT BODY—

DAPHNE ASSUMES MANNER OF MISTRESS OF MANDERLEY—DISCIPLINES SERVANTS—EVEN MRS. DANVERS. MRS. DANVERS SUSPICIOUS ABOUT BODY—

DAPHNE GOES TO CONSULT MRS. DANVERS—FINALLY PUTS WOMAN IN HER PLACE.

NEXT MORNING, IN MORNING ROOM, "I" CALMLY ASSERTS HERSELF WITH MRS. DANVERS. MRS. DANVERS DOES NOT MENTION BODY OR BOAT. MAXIM TELEPHONES: JULYAN AND FRANK COMING BACK WITH HIM TO LUNCH. HE RINGS OFF IN MIDDLE OF HER QUESTIONS.

FRITH TELLS "I" OF LOCAL SUSPICIONS THAT BODY IS REBECCA'S . . . MRS. DANVERS IS ILL.

FRITH SAYS INQUEST TO BE HELD IN KERRITH FOUR O'CLOCK THAT AFTERNOON (OCCURS LATER IN NOVEL).

| ONE-LINE CONTINUITY OF NOVEL | ONE-LINE CONTINUITY OF STORY OUTLINE JUNE 3, 1939 | ONE-LINE CONTINUITY OF TREATMENT JUNE 24, 1939 | PLAY IN THREE ACTS BY DAPHNE DU MAURIER |
|---|---|---|---|
| JULYAN, FRANK, MAXIM, COME TO LUNCH AFTER EXAMINATION OF BODY—IT HAD BEEN IDENTIFIED AT ONCE AS REBECCA'S. | MEANWHILE, GILES TELLS MAXIM INQUEST SET FOR MONDAY MORNING. | AT LUNCHEON: CONVERSATION DESULTORY—JULYAN SORRY ABOUT NECESSITY FOR INQUEST BUT LATTER IS JUST A CASE OF GETTING BOAT BUILDER TO CONFIRM BOAT'S SEAWORTHINESS. | MAXIM, PRECEDING ENTRANCE OF JULYAN AND CRAWLEY, TELLS "I" BODY WAS IDENTIFIED AT ONCE: BULLET DID NOT TOUCH BONE (OCCURS LATER IN NOVEL). |
| EVERYONE SYMPATHETIC TO MAXIM AND DAPHNE. | SAME. | COL. JULYAN EXTREMELY REASSURING. | COL. JULYAN'S FACILE EXPLANATION OF REBECCA'S DEATH, SAME AS IN NOVEL. |
| JULYAN SUGGESTS EASY SOLUTIONS OF REBECCA'S ACCIDENT. | AT DINNER, GILES DISCUSSES ANOTHER MURDER—SO OFTEN MURDER JUSTIFIED BUT CANNOT FORGIVE IT—MUST BE PUNISHED. | | |
| INQUEST ARRANGED FOR TUESDAY MORNING. | | OMITTED. | (INQUEST MENTIONED PREVIOUSLY—ARRANGED FOR AFTERNOON OF 25TH.) |
| MAXIM TELLS DAPHNE NO SIGN OF HAVING SHOT REBECCA—BULLET DID NOT TOUCH BONE. | | OMITTED. | (USED PREVIOUSLY AS NOTED) |
| "I'M GLAD I KILLED REBECCA . . . BUT . . . I CAN'T FORGIVE WHAT IT HAS DONE TO YOU . . . YOU ARE SO MUCH OLDER . . ." | | OMITTED. | (THESE LINES APPEAR LATER IN SCENE——) |
| INQUEST | INQUEST | INQUEST | INQUEST |
| DAPHNE HIDES NEWSPAPERS NEXT DAY—MRS. DANVERS ILL, DOES NOT APPEAR—FRANK WORRIED ABOUT INQUEST—DAPHNE THINKS HE SUSPECTS THE TRUTH—MAXIM SHORT WITH HIM. | | | FOR THIS SEQUENCE IN NOVEL, THERE IS SUBSTITUTED THE FOLLOWING SCENE WHICH TAKES PLACE IN GREAT HALL AT MANDERLEY. ACTION AND DIALOGUE AND INCIDENT FOLLOWS NOVEL EXACTLY, EXCEPT FOR TIME AND PLACE. |
| | | | ACT III, SCENE I, CONTD. |

| | | | |
|---|---|---|---|
| DAPHNE INSISTS UPON DRIVING WITH THEM TO INQUEST—STAYS OUTSIDE AT FIRST— | INQUEST BEING HELD IN MAIN SCHOOL ROOM OF COUNCIL SCHOOL. MAXIM AND DAPHNE SIDE BY SIDE—FAVELL IN INCONSPICUOUS CORNER—MRS. DANVERS ALONE—BEATRICE AND FRANK CERTAIN IT WILL END SATISFACTORILY—GILES, DISTRESSED. | | "I" STAYS OUTSIDE AT FIRST, THEN GOES INTO SMALL ANTEROOM, THEN INTO COURT— |
| WHEN SHE GOES IN FRANK AND MAXIM HAVE ALREADY TESTIFIED— SHE SEES MRS. DANVERS BESIDE FAVELL— | EVIDENCE IS CONCLUDED WHEN NOTE IS BROUGHT TO CORONER— | SAME AS NOVEL. | SAME AS NOVEL. |
| TABB, SHIPBUILDER, IS ON THE STAND, TELLS ABOUT EXAMINING REBECCA'S BOAT: | HE CALLS JAMES TABB, SHIPBUILDER, TO STAND AND TABB TELLS THE SUSPICIOUS FACTS HE FOUND ON EXAMINING REBECCA'S BOAT. | SAME AS NOVEL. | TABB ENTERS—JULYAN HAS ASKED HIM TO CALL FOR PRELIMINARY EXAMINATION—HE TELLS ABOUT BOAT: |
| "WHO DROVE HOLES IN HER PLANKING? . . . AND TURNED THE SEA COCKS ON? . . . THAT BOAT NEVER CAPSIZED AT ALL. SHE WAS DELIBERATELY SCUTTLED. | FAVELL SHOWS SURPRISE AND INTEREST.<br><br>TABB DESCRIBES HOLES IN PLANKING—SEA COCKS TURNED FULL ON. | TABB'S TESTIMONY, SAME AS IN NOVEL. | "WHO DROVE HOLES IN HER PLANKING? . . ." ETC. AS IN NOVEL. |
| MAX RECALLED TO STAND—QUESTIONED. | | SAME AS IN NOVEL. | COLONEL JULYAN RESUMES QUESTIONING MAXIM: |
| "WERE RELATIONS BETWEEN YOU AND THE LATE MRS. DE WINTER PERFECTLY HAPPY? | | SAME. | "WERE RELATIONS BETWEEN YOU AND LATE MRS. DE WINTER ETC. . . ." |

| ONE-LINE CONTINUITY OF NOVEL | ONE-LINE CONTINUITY OF STORY OUTLINE JUNE 3, 1939 | ONE-LINE CONTINUITY OF TREATMENT JUNE 24, 1939 | PLAY IN THREE ACTS BY DAPHNE DU MAURIER |
|---|---|---|---|
| DAPHNE FAINTS. | | SAME. | "I" FAINTS.—JULYAN AND CRAWLEY LEAVE MAXIM ALONE WITH WIFE WHO IS RECOVERING. |
| | CONSTERNATION. CORONER ADJOURNS COURT FOR LUNCHEON. | | |
| CONTINUITY CHANGED IN OUTLINE | IN COFFEE ROOM OF INN, DAPHNE TRIES TO CHEER MAXIM. | | LINES HERE: "I DON'T REGRET ANYTHING BUT I CAN'T FORGET WHAT IT'S DONE TO YOU," AS IN NOVEL PRECEDING INQUEST. |
| | | | CURTAIN. |
| FRANK TAKES DAPHNE BACK TO MANDERLEY. | | "I" AT MANDERLEY, WAITING IN LIBRARY FOR RESULTS OF INQUEST. | |
| VERDICT: MAXIM RETURNS WITH NEWS OF VERDICT: SUICIDE WITHOUT SUFFICIENT EVIDENCE TO SHOW STATE OF MIND OF DECEASED. | | VERDICT: MAXIM TELEPHONES, VERDICT IS: SUICIDE WITHOUT SUFFICIENT EVIDENCE TO SHOW STATE OF MIND OF DECEASED. SHOT OF MAXIM AT PHONE—BREAKS OFF WHEN FRANK APPEARS BESIDE HIM. | ACT III. SCENE II. FRANK CRAWLEY'S OFFICE VERDICT: "I" WAITING—FAVELL ENTERS, TELLS VERDICT SAVAGELY: "SUICIDE, WITHOUT SUFFICIENT EVIDENCE . . . ETC." "YOU AND I KNOW IT WASN'T SUICIDE. . . ." |
| MAXIM GOES WITH FRANK, JULYAN, TO SERVICES FOR REBECCA'S BODY. | | | |
| REBECCA'S NOTE: FAVELL COMES DURING ABSENCE—WHEN MAXIM RETURNS, HE TURNS NASTY—ACCUSING MAXIM OF PART IN REBECCA'S DEATH. HE READS NOTE FROM REBECCA—ATTEMPTS TO BLACKMAIL MAXIM. | REBECCA'S NOTE: FAVELL COMES TO THEIR TABLE, INTRODUCTION TO DAPHNE—HE IS OFFENSIVELY HEARTY—DISBELIEVES SUICIDE THEORY—SAYS HE HAS NOTE TO DISPROVE IT. DOES NOT SHOW REBECCA'S NOTE,—VEILED BLACKMAIL. | REBECCA'S NOTE: FAVELL COMES TO HOUSE BEFORE MAXIM RETURNS—OFFENSIVELY FAMILIAR, WANTS DRINKS—"YOU AND I KNOW IT WASN'T SUICIDE . . . THAT DODDERING OLD FOOL OF A CORONER MUST HAVE BEEN SQUARED! . . ." MAXIM AND CRAWLEY RETURN. FAVELL CONTINUES NASTY INNUENDOES—MENTIONS NOTE—SUGGESTS HE AND MAXIM COME TO AGREEMENT TO KEEP NOTE QUIET.— | REBECCA'S NOTE: MAXIM AND CRAWLEY RETURN. FAVELL TURNS NASTY—READS NOTE, ETC., AS IN NOVEL. |
| | INQUEST RESUMED—RE-EXAMINATION OF WITNESS DUE TO TABB'S EVIDENCE. FAVELL SILENT. | | |

ACCUSATION OF MURDER:
MAXIM DEFIANTLY CALLS JULYAN TO COME TO HEAR FAVELL'S ACCUSATIONS. JULYAN UNIMPRESSED BY FAVELL'S DRUNKEN MANNER AND STORY OF REBECCA'S LAST DAY.

FAVELL'S ADMISSION THAT HE AND REBECCA WERE LOVERS—

VERDICT: JURY OUT A LONG TIME—
VERDICT: SUICIDE WHILE OF TEMPORARILY UNSOUND MIND.

SCENE IN STREET OUTSIDE GILES' AND MAXIM'S CARS—GILES ADVISING MAXIM AND DAPHNE TO TAKE A TRIP WHILE GOSSIP DIES DOWN.
SCENE IN COTTAGE ON BEACH THAT NIGHT: FAVELL ENLISTING MRS. DANVERS' AID— SHE IS MERELY VINDICTIVE, HE KEEPS HER IGNORANT OF HIS PLAN TO BLACKMAIL MAXIM.

FAVELL ASKING FOR NAME AND ADDRESS OF CERTAIN DOCTOR—MRS. DANVERS PROMISES TO FIND IT BEFORE MAXIM AND DAPHNE LEAVE FOR TRIP.

ACCUSATION OF MURDER:
MAXIM AND DAPHNE READY TO LEAVE ON TRIP. FAVELL APPEARS, MAKES ACCUSATION OF MURDER AND COMES OUT IN THE OPEN WITH BLACKMAIL—MAXIM LEAVES, RETURNS WITH GILES AND FRANK—FAVELL GROWS INSULTING TO DAPHNE, AND MAXIM STRIKES HIM.

FAVELL SAYS HE AND REBECCA WERE LOVERS AND THAT REBECCA WAS TO BEAR HIS CHILD—REASON FOR MURDER BY MAXIM.

SLIGHT CHANGE IN ABOVE: IN NOVEL, FAVELL READS NOTE TO MAXIM, CRAWLEY AND GIRL.

ACCUSATION OF MURDER:
MAXIM TELEPHONES JULYAN—CRAWLEY TRIES TO PREVENT THIS. FAVELL: "ALL RIGHT, MAX, IF YOU REALLY WANT TO HANG YOURSELF ..." JULYAN ARRIVES—FAVELL INSISTS REBECCA WAS MURDERED.

GIVES NOTE TO JULYAN TO READ.
FAVELL ADMITS HE WAS REBECCA'S LOVER.

ACCUSATION OF MURDER:
MAXIM CALLS JULYAN IN—HE IS WAITING OUTSIDE IN CAR—

SAME.

| ONE-LINE CONTINUITY OF NOVEL | ONE-LINE CONTINUITY OF STORY OUTLINE JUNE 3, 1939 | ONE-LINE CONTINUITY OF TREATMENT JUNE 24, 1939 | PLAY IN THREE ACTS BY DAPHNE DU MAURIER |
|---|---|---|---|
| —"I HAVE A RIGHT TO SPEAK, NOT ONLY AS REBECCA'S COUSIN, BUT AS HER PROSPECTIVE HUSBAND . . ." | | | SAME. |
| —"THERE'S YOUR MURDERER FOR YOU, MR. MAXIMILIAN DE WINTER . . ." | | "—SHE WAS MURDERED—AND THE MURDERER IS OVER—THERE, MR. MAXIMILIAN DE WINTER!" | SAME. |
| THEY SEND FOR BEN TO SUBSTANTIATE FAVELL'S STORY—NEGATIVE RESULTS. | | THEY SEND FOR BEN BECAUSE FAVELL SAYS BOY WOULD HAVE SEEN MAXIM AT COTTAGE NIGHT OF MURDER. NEGATIVE RESULTS OF INTERVIEW. | |
| THEY SEND FOR MRS. DANVERS FOR SAME REASON; SHE DENIES REBECCA LOVED FAVELL OR ANY MAN. | | THEY SEND FOR MRS. DANVERS. NO MENTION HERE OF REBECCA LOVING OR NOT LOVING MEN. MRS. DANVERS KNOWS OF NO REASON FOR SUICIDE. | THEY SEND FOR MRS. DANVERS TO SUBSTANTIATE FAVELL'S STORY—NO ANSWER ON PHONE TO MANDERLEY. CRAWLEY GOES TO GET HER—BRINGS HER IN: SHE WAS PACKED, READY TO LEAVE MANDERLEY FOREVER. MRS. DANVERS DENIES REBECCA LOVED FAVELL OR ANY MAN. |
| MRS. DANVERS PRODUCES REBECCA'S ENGAGEMENT BOOK FOR HINTS OF HOW REBECCA SPENT LAST DAY——DISCOVER BAKER'S NAME AND A NUMBER—TRY TELEPHONING—DISCOVER BAKER IS A DOCTOR—— JULYAN DECIDES THEY MUST ALL GO SEE HIM NEXT DAY. | FAVELL OFFERS TO TAKE GILES, ETC., TO DOCTOR WHO CAN CORROBORATE HIS STORY. GILES DECIDES TO INVESTIGATE. MAXIM, FRANK, FAVELL TO GO TO LONDON WITH HIM—THEY PUT DAPHNE IN A CAR FOR MANDERLEY. | CONSULT REBECCA'S ENGAGEMENT BOOK. FIND BAKER'S NAME AND NUMBER— LONDON TELEPHONE DIRECTORY PROVES BAKER A DOCTOR AT 127 ARONRIGHT ROAD, BARNET. | MRS. DANVERS PRODUCES REBECCA'S ENGAGEMENT DIARY—DISCOVERY OF BAKER'S NAME, ETC., SAME AS NOVEL. |
| AT FAVELL'S SUGGESTION, MRS. DANVERS LOCKS MAXIM AND DAPHNE IN THEIR ROOM THAT NIGHT. | | OMITTED. | |

| VISIT TO DOCTOR BAKER'S | VISIT TO DOCTOR BAKER'S | VISIT TO DOCTOR BAKER'S | VISIT TO DOCTOR BAKER'S |
|---|---|---|---|
| JULYAN AND DAPHNE IN MAXIM'S CAR—FAVELL FOLLOWING IN HIS—DRIVE THROUGH LONDON TO BARNET (SUBURB). | DEPRESSING PART OF LONDON: SHEPHERD'S BUSH—MAXIM'S, GILES' AND FAVELL'S CARS. | | OMITTED. |
| BAKER'S HOUSE PLAIN, DECENT, SEMI-DETACHED SUBURBAN VILLA TYPE. DOCTOR HIMSELF IS DECENT, EFFICIENT; HE HAS BEEN A WELL-KNOWN WOMAN'S SPECIALIST. | HOUSE NEXT TO ROW OF SHOPS—SQUALOR OF SURROUNDINGS—TWO WOMEN OF OBTRUSIVELY EASY VIRTUE DESCENDING FROM DOCTOR'S OFFICE. | TYPICAL SUBURBAN HOUSE—MAXIM'S AND FAVELL'S CARS, COLONEL JULYAN AND GIRL ALSO PRESENT. DOCTOR IS BRISK, BUSINESS-LIKE. | |
| | CONSULTING ROOM, DINGY BUT EFFICIENT—SOUR NURSE. DOCTOR IS GRIM UNPLEASANT, INHUMAN. | CHANGE OF TIME: ASKING FOR INFORMATION CONCERNING REBECCA'S VISIT: "—IT WAS THE 12TH OF JULY EXACTLY TWO YEARS AGO—" | |
| DOCTOR INFORMS THEM HE HAS NEVER ATTENDED A MRS. DE WINTER—CONSULTING RECORDS AND FILES, THEY FIND REBECCA CAME AS MRS. DANVERS. | SAME. | CONSULTING FILES, ETC., SAME AS NOVEL. DISCOVER REBECCA CAME AS MRS. DANVERS. | FINALLY GET DR. BAKER ON PHONE, HE INFORMS JULYAN HE NEVER ATTENDED A MRS. DE WINTER—ETC., AS IN NOVEL, DURING PERSONAL VISIT TO DOCTOR. |
| SUSPICIOUS OF PAINS, ETC., REBECCA CAME FOR CONFIRMATION OF HER FEARS. SHE WAS SUFFERING FROM INCURABLE MALIGNANT DISEASE WHICH WOULD SOON CAUSE HER DEATH. | REBECCA HAD COME UNDER IMPRESSION SHE WAS TO HAVE A CHILD—DIAGNOSIS DISPROVED THIS. SHE WAS SUFFERING FROM CANCER, ETC. | SAME AS NOVEL. | INFORMATION DISCLOSED DURING PHONE CALL. SAME AS NOVEL. |
| AFTER THIS, ALL REGARD EVIDENCE SUFFICIENT TO PROVE REBECCA'S DEATH SUICIDE—CASE CLOSED. | SAME. | SAME. | SAME AS NOVEL. |
| OUTSIDE BY THE CARS—JULYAN WARNS FAVELL TO LEAVE MAXIM AND MANDERLEY ALONE. | SAME. | SAME—FAVELL VENTS FURY BY BURSTING OUT AGAINST ORGAN GRINDER. | BEFORE FAVELL EXITS: "DOES ANYONE KNOW IF CANCER IS CONTAGIOUS—" AS IN NOVEL. |

| ONE-LINE CONTINUITY OF NOVEL | ONE-LINE CONTINUITY OF STORY OUTLINE JUNE 3, 1939 | ONE-LINE CONTINUITY OF TREATMENT JUNE 24, 1939 | PLAY IN THREE ACTS BY DAPHNE DU MAURIER |
| --- | --- | --- | --- |
| FAVELL'S THREAT: "—IT'S BEEN A STROKE OF LUCK FOR YOU, MAX, HASN'T IT? BUT THE LAW CAN GET YOU YET, AND SO CAN I, IN A DIFFERENT WAY ..." | FAVELL, DEFEATED, SILENTLY LURCHES OFF TOWARD BAR. | OMITTED.—FAVELL LURCHES OFF: "ALL RIGHT, MAX ..." | MRS. DANVERS MAKES THREAT BEFORE SHE LEAVES WITH FAVELL: "... AN EYE FOR AN EYE ..." |
| MAXIM AND DAPHNE DROP JULYAN AT HIS SISTER'S. HE ADVISES THEM TO GET AWAY UNTIL GOSSIP DIES DOWN. | | JULYAN REFUSES OFFER OF LIFT—ADVISES THEM TO GET AWAY UNTIL GOSSIP DIES DOWN. | JULYAN AND FRANK LEAVE. |
| DURING QUIET DINNER ALONE TOGETHER, MAXIM TELEPHONES NEWS TO FRANK AT MANDERLEY—LEARNS THAT, AFTER RECEIVING TELEPHONE CALL FROM LONDON, MRS. DANVERS HAS LEFT. NEWS MAKES MAXIM RESTLESS, WORRIED—THEY DECIDE TO HURRY BACK TO MANDERLEY. | | OMITTED. | MAXIM AND "I" ALONE TOGETHER AT LAST, WONDER IF JULYAN AND CRAWLEY KNEW TRUTH. MAXIM BELIEVES SO. |
| DESTRUCTION OF MANDERLEY<br><br>DAPHNE DOZES RESTLESSLY AS MAXIM DRIVES RAPIDLY THROUGH THE NIGHT. ALMOST HOME, FROM TOP OF HILL, THEY SEE GLOW IN SKY.<br><br>IT IS MANDERLEY, BURNING. | DESTRUCTION OF MANDERLEY<br><br>FRANK DOZES AS MAXIM DRIVES RAPIDLY THROUGH THE NIGHT. ALMOST HOME, FROM TOP OF HILL, THEY SEE GLOW IN SKY. IT IS MANDERLEY, BURNING. THEY HURRY ON.<br><br>AT MANDERLEY, HOUSE IS IN FLAMES; MAXIM'S CAR COMES TO SCREECHING STOP—HE DASHES TOWARD AN ELM TREE UNDER WHICH IS A GROUP LOOKING AT SOMETHING ON THE GROUND ... "DAPHNE!" BUT DAPHNE RISES FROM BESIDE MRS. DANVERS' BURNED, TWISTED, LIFELESS BODY—MAXIM TAKES HER IN HIS ARMS. DAPHNE SAYS MRS. DANVERS HAD RATHER SEE MANDERLEY DESTROYED THAN BELONGING TO ANOTHER WOMAN. | DESTRUCTION OF MANDERLEY<br><br>NIGHT IN CORNISH COUNTRYSIDE—MAXIM DRIVING WITH ONE ARM, HOLDING GIRL WITH THE OTHER. "WHAT TIME IS IT?" ... "TWENTY PAST TWO ..." SAME AS NOVEL: LIGHTS IN WESTERN SKY, DIALOGUE, ETC., "THAT'S NOT DAWN, THAT'S MANDERLEY!" | DESTRUCTION OF MANDERLEY<br><br>MAXIM BELIEVED REBECCA PERPETUATED LAST CRUEL JOKE DELIBERATELY—"I'M NOT SURE SHE HASN'T WON EVEN NOW ..." THEY TRY TO PHONE MANDERLEY TO TELL FRITH THEY ARE COMING HOME. LINE IS DEAD ...<br><br>"I" AT WINDOW SEES GLOW IN SKY—THINKS IT MAY BE SUN SETTING—OR "NORTHERN LIGHTS" ...<br><br>MAXIM: "THAT'S NOT THE NORTHERN LIGHTS—THAT'S MANDERLEY!"<br><br>STAND AT WINDOW WATCHING FLAMES— |

RETURN TO OPENING SCENE: DAPHNE AND
MAXIM AGAIN ON CHANNEL STEAMER—
CIGAR SMOKE BLOWING ACROSS HER FACE.
GIRL'S VOICE FINISHING DESCRIPTION OF
MANDERLEY—"—AND SO I SHALL NEVER
SEE MANDERLEY AGAIN . . ."

RETURN TO OPENING SCENE: CAMERA
DRAWS BACK FROM RUINED HOUSE—"I'S"
VOICE: "WE CAN NEVER GO BACK TO MAND-
ERLEY AGAIN . . . BUT SOMETIMES IN MY
DREAMS I DO GO BACK . . ."

CURTAIN.

## Suspicion

Hitchcock's fourth American film was adapted from the novel *Before the Fact* by Anthony Berkeley (writing under the pseudonym Francis Iles). Alma Hitchcock did the first adaptation. Joan Harrison, perhaps the family's closest friend, worked on this adaptation, which eventually was developed into a screenplay by Samson Raphaelson. The evidence suggests that Hitchcock was involved in the day-to-day construction of the screenplay.

The screenplay developed rather easily, but had problems with its ending from the very first treatment. Lina McLaidlaw (Joan Fontaine) has fallen in

---

MEMORANDUM

Dear Hitch:

Just a reminder of the few minor things we talked about—

1. In the car scene let Johnny use "monkey face" sparingly—I suggest not at all.

2. In the car scene I think it would enrich it if we put back Johnny's line about counting the number of women he has kissed like sheep over a fence, etc.

3. When Lina overhears her father and mother calling her a spinster—if, before Johnny is discovered, we could see him walking toward her, we would not have the feeling that he has overheard, which I think we may have at present. I don't think that feeling is good. If she thinks he has heard her parents calling her a spinster, she wouldn't be likely to kiss him.

4. In the scene between Isobel and Lina, I think we should cut Isobel's mention of Beaky's death, because if Isobel is aware of that and its parallel with the footbridge murder she's an idiot if she doesn't instantly suspect Johnny. Also, I think it's pretty obvious writing there to slam the parallel into the audience's face, the parallel being already so clear.

5. I also suggest that in the big final scene, she doesn't send Johnnie out, and then he comes back. We expect something to happen while Johnnie is out, and nothing happens. Besides, it makes all the longer our wait for the poison to work on her.

Rapho

love with and married the dashing playboy Johnny Aysgarth (Cary Grant). Over time, Lina discovers that Johnny has lied to her on numerous occasions and she begins to suspect that Johnny plans to kill her for her insurance money. The audience is never sure either. Neither was Hitchcock. The debate over the ending continued into the shooting, with even the president of RKO (which produced the film) weighing in with an ending.

A memo (page 62, bottom) from Raphaelson to Hitchcock listed various points in the script that he suggested should be changed. Point five concerns the ending of the screenplay, which is the one that Hitchcock told François Truffaut he preferred.

Filming began in April 1941, yet the screenplay was still in turmoil. The next pages are from the working script. Notice that even during production, the film was referred to as *Before the Fact*. During a film's production, as new scenes are written or rewritten, the color of the pages is changed to keep track of the latest version. The first set of pages (dated 5/26/41) was the most recent. There are also in these pages three different endings, none of which is the ending that was finally shot in July 1941.

Reading a screenplay in development can be a challenge. The reader's best guide is the page number. For example, the first page to follow is the new draft of page 217—followed by the old page. This pattern continues throughout the script.

Above the page number is the date of the revision. In the left margin of the new pages are indications of the status of each shot—note that these revisions were being made during the film's production.

Changes                5/26/41

"BEFORE THE FACT"          217

| | | |
|---|---|---|
| (ALREADY SHOT) | 437 | SEMI-LONG SHOT—from Lina's eyeline   Johnnie stands framed in the doorway, holding the glass of milk. |

**JOHNNIE**
**I—I brought you something, Monkey-face.**

| | | |
|---|---|---|
| (ALREADY SHOT) | 438 | CLOSEUP—a BIG HEAD of Lina. She almost instinctively braces herself. |

**LINA**
**Bring it to me.**

| | | |
|---|---|---|
| (ALREADY SHOT) | 439 | SEMI-LONG SHOT—Johnnie watching her, starts to move forward. His eyes drop to the glass of milk in his hands. |

| | | |
|---|---|---|
| (ALREADY SHOT) | 440 | CLOSEUP—Lina's eyes follow the glass as it travels towards her, round the end of the bed, getting nearer and nearer. As it comes right up to her. |

CAMERA PULLS BACK and shows Johnnie putting it down on the table by her.

|  |  |  |
|---|---|---|
| (ALREADY SHOT) | 441 | CLOSEUP—Johnnie looks down at her with a slightly compassionate look. |
| (ALREADY SHOT) | 442 | CLOSEUP—Lina looks up from the glass to Johnnie's face. |

> **LINA**
> Give it to me.

Johnnie hands her the glass of milk—she starts to drink it.

|  |  |  |
|---|---|---|
| (TENTATIVE) | 442a | A CUT of the dog lying in the room—looks up. |
| (ALREADY SHOT) | 442b | CLOSEUP—Lina in profile, Johnnie standing just beyond her—as she drinks the glass of milk. Then lowers glass. |

ff

437    SEMI-LONG SHOT—from LINA's EYELINE—Johnnie stands framed in the doorway, holding the glass of milk.

> **JOHNNIE**
> I—here's something for you to drink, darling.

438    CLOSEUP—a BIG HEAD of Lina. She almost instinctively braces herself.

> **LINA**
> Bring it to me.

439    SEMI-CLOSEUP—Johnnie watching her, starts to move forward. His eyes drop to the glass of milk in his hands.

440    CLOSEUP—Lina's eyes follow the glass as it travels towards her, round the end of the bed, getting nearer and nearer. As it comes right up to her, the

CAMERA PULLS BACK and shows Johnnie putting it down on the table by her.

441    CLOSEUP—Johnnie looks down at her with a slightly compassionate look.

442    CLOSEUP—Lina looks up from the glass to Johnnie's face.

> **LINA**
> Give it to me.

443    SEMI-CLOSEUP—Johnnie stretches out his hand, picks up the glass and hands it to her. Lina takes it simply and drinks it right down. As she sets the glass down, she looks up at Johnnie, who is half smiling and watching her. She takes her tiny handkerchief from under her pillow and wipes her lips. She rises, slides her feet from the bed, and stands.

CAMERA PULLS BACK. She holds her arms out to him.

> **LINA**
>
> **Kiss me, Johnnie.**

gh                                    (CONTINUED)

5/26/41

218

443    SEMI-CLOSE SHOT—Lina and Johnnie—as he takes the glass from
her. A little milk remains in the glass. He puts the glass on the tray.

> **JOHNNIE**
>
> **Feeling all right?**

> **LINA**
>
> **I feel very strange—as if we're not going to be together much
> longer.**

> **JOHNNIE**
>
> *(sharply)*
>
> **Don't say that, darling. That's a terrible thing to say.**

> **LINA**
>
> **But it's how I feel.**

> **JOHNNIE**
>
> **I don't want to hear you talk like that.**

> **LINA**
>
> **But people do die sooner or later—and if I were dying now, I'd
> feel—oh, as if I hadn't really known you. I look at you, and I love
> you. I was made to live for you, to die for you—and yet I don't really
> know you.**

> **JOIINNIE**
>
> *(uncomfortably)*
>
> **Now, relax, darling. Shut your eyes and go to sleep.**

> **LINA**
>
> **My Johnnie. My own. All those lives you lived that I don't know
> anything about. What were you like when you were a boy—when
> you were a child?**

> **JOHNNIE**
>
> **Darling, please—not now.**

ff                                    (CONTINUED)

443 (CONTINUED)

He takes her in his arms and kisses her lightly. She draws away from
him.

LINA (cont'd)
**Not let me be alone, Johnnie.**

JOHNNIE
**Monkey-face, I—**

LINA
**Please go, darling.**

He looks at her a little nervously then turns towards the dressing room.

444    SEMI-CLOSEUP—Lina watches him.

445    SEMI-LONG SHOT—At the door Johnnie glances back at her for a moment, then goes through. Lina subsides onto the bed once more and leans her head against the padded bed back.

446    SEMI-CLOSEUP—A tear trickles slowly down her cheek—she closes her eyes.

447    SEMI-CLOSEUP—The door of the dressing room opens slowly. Johnnie looks through into the bedroom, watching her.

448    SEMI-LONG SHOT—from HIS EYELINE. We see Lina's head bow, while still leaning against the bed back.

449    SEMI-LONG SHOT—Johnnie starts to tiptoe across towards the bed. He comes around the side, close to her. He goes down on one knee and peers into her face.

450    SEMI-CLOSEUP—Lina opens her eyes. She sees Johnnie kneeling there. He makes a move forward—comes and sits beside her and takes her in his arms—

CAMERA MOVES IN to the two heads—

gh                                                                          (CONTINUED)

5/26/41

443 (CONTINUED)                                                                219

LINA
**Oh, Johnnie—I want to know these things more than anything in the world. Tell me about that boy.**

JOHNNIE
**Oh, he wasn't bad. How can I describe him? I guess he was pretty bad. As a matter of fact, he was a spoiled, dishonest little brat.**

He sees the dog.

JOHNNIE (cont'd)
**Hello, boy.**

444    CLOSE SHOT—of the dog.

445–   Johnnie takes the milk—puts the tray on the floor and pours the
457    remainder of the milk into the tray.

> **LINA**
> *(almost a cry that escapes her)*
> Johnnie—

> **JOHNNIE**
> It's all right, dear. He won't make a mess.

We see the dog lap up the milk. At the same time, Johnnie moves to
the other side of the bed—saying as he goes:

> **JOHNNIE (cont'd)**
> Yes—I was a dreadful child—and a dreadful boy—gambling and
> cheating at school. Summing it up, Monkey-face, at the age of
> twenty-one I was what you might call a cad . . . Sleepy?

ff                                                        (CONTINUED)

450 (CONTINUED)

As he holds her tightly, her head rests against his shoulder. She
knows she is dying, and she is in a mood of quiet exaltation. All her
love for Johnnie shines from her face.

> **LINA**
> It's all right, dearest. I know I'm dying. But it's all right

A frightened look comes into Johnnie's face which he
masters—uneasily.

> **JOHNNIE**
> Why do you say that?

Lina hushes him by putting her fingers on his lips.

> **LINA**
> Sshh . . . Don't look at me like that, dear. I didn't mean to tell you
> I knew. I was going to die quietly, peacefully. But when you came
> back—oh, Johnnie, . . . I wanted you to know I forgive you.

> **JOHNNIE**
> *(staring at her)*
> What are you talking about?

> **LINA**
> *(wandering—in a tiny voice)*
> But poor Beaky—he was so good, and kind, and trusting—I wish it
> hadn't had to be Beaky—

451    CLOSEUP—Johnnie staring at her, alarmed.

JOHNNIE
*(in a strange voice)*
Beaky! . . .

445–(CONTINUED)                                                5/26/41
457                                                                   220

LINA
Sleepy? Oh, no, I've never been more wide awake in my life.
Oh, darling, darling, darling!

She controls herself from an overwhelming impulse to embrace him.

JOHNNIE
*(prosaically puzzled, as he turns on the other light beside the bed)*
What's the matter?

LINA
Nothing—tell me more—I'm hungry for every word—

JOHNNIE
*(sitting on the side of the bed)*
You know, I've never talked about myself before—I've never even
thought about myself.
*(slowly)*
I sound pretty bad.

LINA
Oh, no you don't. You have no idea how harmless, how wonderful
you sound.

JOHNNIE
Lina—I've got to tell you this—it's not very nice.

LINA
Yes—

JOHNNIE
Darling, I'm in a devil of a mess. I may have to go to jail.

LINA
*(after a pause)*
Go on, Johnnie.

ff                                                          (CONTINUED)

452        CLOSEUP—Lina looks into his eyes.

LINA
Oh, Johnnie, I know you were with him in Paris—

Suddenly she breaks off, bewildered.

LINA (cont'd)
Johnnie! I'm still talking to you!

453      CLOSEUP—the two.

**JOHNNIE**
**Of course you are.**

**LINA**
**I'm still here! I'm lying here talking to you! I'm still alive!**

Lina turns her head towards the empty milk glass. Johnnie follows her eyes.

454      CLOSEUP—Johnnie stares at the glass then his eyes turn to Lina again—he begins to understand her meaning.

**LINA'S VOICE**
**Isobel said it would happen quickly.**

**JOHNNIE**
**Isobel!**
*(then getting the full shock)*
**What did you think was in that glass?**

455      SEMI-CLOSEUP—The two. Lina stares at him wide-eyed.

**JOHNNIE**
**There was nothing in that glass but milk.**

(CONTINUED)

445– (CONTINUED)                                    5/14/41
45 /                                                   221

**JOHNNIE**
**Are you sure you're well enough?**

**LINA**
*Very* **well.**

**JOHNNIE**
**I stole money from Melbeck.**

**LINA**
**Stole?**

**JOHNNIE**
**That's the word for it—I never used it before. I had other words for it . . . Oh, darling, I don't know why I'm telling you this now. I was going to wait a few days—until you were well.**

**LINA**
*(radiant)*
**But you—you had made up your mind to tell me.**

**JOHNNIE**
**What else could I do?**

LINA

Oh, so many things—you're very clever—you might have done many things.

JOHNNIE

I *am* clever—and I *have* tried to do other things—but I've been getting tired—awfully tired of—well, of cheating.

LINA
*(adoring him)*
Have you?

(CONTINUED)

445–(CONTINUED)                                                    5/26/41
457

JOHNNIE

Are you sure you're well enough?

LINA
*Very* well.

JOHNNIE

I stole money from Melbeck.

LINA
Stole?

JOHNNIE

That's the word for it—I never used it before. I had other words for it . . . I fooled nobody but myself.
*(turning to her)*
Melbeck threatened to prosecute. That's why I got Beaky into that silly real estate thing, intending to—well, to cheat him. It didn't work, thank God. But when I went to London to see Beaky off, I borrowed from him—and I didn't stay at my club—

LINA
*(apprehensively excited)*
You didn't?

JOHNNIE

I had to win a lot of money somehow—so I went to the Goodwood Races.

LINA
*(with a great sob of relief)*
You went to the races!

JOHNNIE

I lost Beaky's money—lost my best friend's money, while he was dying . . .

> LINA
> *(leaning towards him)*
> **Oh, darling!**

ff                                                                (CONTINUED)

455–457 (CONTINUED)

> As he speaks the realization of what it all means grows. He rises—

> JOHNNIE (cont'd)
> **Lina!—Lina!—Lina—Lina, what have I said. How could I—you thought—you believed that I—**

> LINA
> **I was loving you all the time—I forgave you—**

> JOHNNIE
> **Yes—but you thought I murdered Beaky. You thought I was in Paris—I wasn't. I was at the races. And then my curiosity about the poison—and my interest in Isobel's books—**
> *(pause)*
> **You saw me as Beaky's murderer and as yours!**

> LINA
> **Yes, I did. But now I don't know why I did—Johnnie, I'm so confused—help me to understand. Why only yesterday I saw a picture of you as a boy—that young eager boy couldn't have—**

> JOHNNIE
> **Perhaps you're right. That boy couldn't have—but I'm beginning to understand how you came to think that I could. You see, that boy wanted everything—every luxury in the whole world.**

> LINA
> **Yes of course he did, Johnnie.**

> JOHNNIE
> **But that took money, and I was broke. I didn't know how to earn my living—my family were too well-connected to think of equipping me for that! So I made up my mind to do something about it—I discovered the art of gambling. You could win enough—if you were lucky—to live like a lord, or at least so I thought. But then I started losing—I learned that you just *had* to be lucky; and that there were ways of making oneself lucky. (cont'd)**

(CONTINUED)

455 (CONTINUED)

> As he speaks the realization of what it all means grows.

> JOHNNIE (cont'd)
> **Lina!**

Overwhelmed, he drops his head in his hands.

> **JOHNNIE (cont'd)**
> Oh, Lina . . . Lina, Lina . . .

Lina sits up straight—just beginning to realize how distorted her
fantasy has been.

> **LINA**
> Oh, darling—what have I said! How could I—

> **JOHNNIE**
> *(to himself)*
> You believed—you thought I was your murderer . . .

> **LINA**
> I didn't—I was loving you all the time—I forgave you—

> **JOHNNIE**
> And you thought I murdered Beaky. You thought I was in Paris . . .
> I wasn't. I was at the races losing some more money that I didn't
> have . . .
> *(turning to her)*
> But you saw me as his murderer, and as yours! . . .
> *(turning away from her)*
> That makes me as guilty as if I had done it!

He suddenly gets up, leaving Lina staring after him.

gh

455-(CONTINUED)
457                                                          6/14/41

                                                                                  222

> **JOHNNIE**
> You know, Melbeck threatened to prosecute. Oh, I may as well tell
> you the rest. That's why I got Beaky into that silly real estate thing,
> intending to—well, to cheat him. It didn't work, thank God. But
> when I went to London to see Beaky off, I borrowed from him—and
> I didn't stay at my club—

> **LINA**
> *(apprehensively excited)*
> You didn't?

> **JOHNNIE**
> I had to win a lot of money somehow—so I went to the Goodwood
> Races.

> **LINA**
> *(with a great sob of relief)*
> You went to the races!

JOHNNIE

I lost Beaky's money—lost my best friend's money, while he was dying . . .

LINA

*(leaning towards him)*
Oh, darling.

JOHNNIE

*(backing away from her embrace)*
And then I even tried to steal ideas from Isobel—I thought I might make something by writing a thriller. I *was* desperate . . .

LINA

Oh, Johnnie.

She embraces him and now he holds her close.

v                                                                                (CONTINUED)

455-(CONTINUED)                                                        5/26/41
457

JOHNNIE

*(backing away from her embrace)*
And then I even tried to steal ideas from Isobel—I thought I might make something by writing a thriller. I *was* desperate . . .

LINA

Oh, Johnnie.

She embraces him and now he holds her close.

LINA (cont'd)

I love you so.

JOHNNIE

I wish I knew why.

LINA

You'll never know—not really.

JOHNNIE

I'll never make you happy—you know that, don't you?

LINA

You're making me happy right now.

JOHNNIE

You don't know what you're talking about. We can't live in this house any longer. We can't keep a car. And what if I have to go to jail?

> LINA
> *(breaking out of the embrace)*
> Never! I'll never let that happen—I'll get the money for
> Melbeck—Mother has money—we'll get it somehow—

> JOHNNIE
> No—I could never live with myself if you did one more thing for
> me.

ff                                                      (CONTINUED)

455–457 (CONTINUED)

> JOHNNIE (cont'd)
> So I invented tricks . . . little lies . . . little cheatings—and, after a
> while, big ones—until I got myself in so deep I couldn't stop. But
> people liked me—women liked me—I saw to that. And Johnnie
> Aysgarth was a terrific social success. He lived off his friends—even
> exploited their wives—then suddenly . . . he fell in love.

He moves toward bed.

> JOHNNIE (cont'd)
> Oh, he had an honest minute or two—he knew what the girl was in
> for—He tried to tell her when he first fell in love—but he didn't try
> hard enough—he did a pretty feeble job.

> LINA
> I loved you so much you didn't have a chance.

> JOHNNIE
> No—wait a minute. It was true about Melbeck. I stole that money.
> And I never once stopped gambling at the races—I've been doing it
> all the time—sneaking away—borrowing right and left. And I *did*
> try to cheat Beaky. You were right about that, too, when you
> warned him against me. I didn't give a rap whether that land was
> any good or not. As long as I could draw a salary and write checks,
> what did I care about Beaky? Oh I loved him in my own way, I
> suppose. I loved him and I loved you.

> LINA
> Oh, Johnnie, I must have been insane to—

                                                         (CONTINUED)

                    Changes                            4/23/41
                *"BEFORE THE FACT"*

456    SEMI-LONG SHOT. Johnnie stands in the middle of the room, his
       back to the bed. Lina cries after him.

> LINA

Johnnie! I don't know what to say—I—I'll never forgive myself. *How* could I? Why, I was looking at a picture of you yesterday—when you were a small boy—that boy could *never* . . . That lovely little boy, with his bright, eager face—a boy who should have had everything . . . everything . . .

> JOHNNIE

*(harshly, as to himself)*

Yes—and that boy *wanted* everything. Every *luxury* in the whole world.

> LINA

Why shouldn't you want them? I love you for wanting them.

457    SEMI-CLOSEUP. Johnnie swings 'round on her. He starts talking in a low bitter voice.

> JOHNNIE

But getting that took money, and I was broke. I couldn't earn my living—my family were too well-connected to think of equipping me for that!

In the b.g. Lina has come from the bed and approaches him as he continues:

> JOHNNIE (cont'd)

So I made up my mind to do something about it . . . I discovered the art of gambling. You could win enough—if you were lucky—to live like a lord. Then I started losing—and I learned that you just *had* to be lucky; and that there were ways of making yourself lucky. That is, if you were clever. (cont'd)

kl                                                          (CONTINUED)

456    SEMI-LONG SHOT—Johnnie stands in the middle of the room—his back to the bed—Lina cries after him.

> LINA

Johnnie,—I don't know what to say—I—I'll never forgive myself. *How* could I—Why, I was looking at a picture of you yesterday—when you were a small boy—that boy could *never*—. . . . That lovely little boy, with his bright, eager face—a boy who should have had everything . . . everything . . .

> JOHNNIE

*(harshly—as to himself)*

Yes—and that boy *wanted* everything! Everything in the whole world! Wealth, and luxury, and fame, and excitement, and power, and love!

LINA
Why shouldn't you want it? I love you for wanting it.

457    SEMI-CLOSEUP—Johnnie swings 'round on her—he starts talking in a low bitter voice:

JOHNNIE
He asked himself the same question. Why shouldn't he want it? His father's name was Sir William Aysgarth—*Sir* . . . That meant something. His uncle's name was Lord Middleham. Oho, *Lord*!—that's a beautiful word—there's magic in it! Magic, indeed! That Lord had thousands of acres, houses like a dream, with rooms in them like pictures in a picture book. The Sir and his Lady—they lived in a shabby flat, and occasionally they visited the Lord. And oh, they wanted to be like the Lord—they couldn't hide that from the little boy. Oh, no—they managed to be at the right places for the right seasons. Their clothes were always correct and fine, and there was always a butler—and the boy went to Eton, the school where the sons of the Lords go. (cont'd)

(CONTINUED)

445-(CONTINUED)                                          5/14/41
457                                                          223

LINA (cont'd)
I love you so.

JOHNNIE
I wish I knew why.

LINA
You'll never know—not really.

JOHNNIE
I'll never make you happy—you know that, don't you?

LINA
You're making me happy now.

JOHNNIE
You don't know what you're talking about. We can't live in this house any longer. We can't keep a car. And what if I have to go to jail?

LINA
*(breaking out of the embrace)*
Never! I'll never let that happen—I'll get the money for Melbeck—Mother has money—we'll get it somehow—

JOHNNIE
Would you do that?

**LINA**

Of course I would—I will! Why, if I set my mind to it—Johnnie, I could never live without you. I *won't* live without you, although I'd die for you—

**JOHNNIE**
*(slowly)*

There's something strange about you tonight—I don't think I've ever loved you as much as I do right now . . . Do you know that?

v

(CONTINUED)

445-(CONTINUED)                                          5/26/41
457

**LINA**

Johnnie—you *are* changing, aren't you?

**JOHNNIE**

Maybe I am.

**LINA**

Well, I'll tell you one thing—I could never live without *you.* I'd die for you, but I won't *live* without you. And you can't live without me. I know that now.

**JOHNNIE**

I know it, too.

He holds her very close.

**JOHNNIE** (cont'd)

Darling, I'll find a way somehow.

**LINA**

I know you will.

**JOHNNIE**

And it won't be by cheating, borrowing, or lying. You believe that, don't you, dear?

**LINA**

Of course I do, my dearest, of course I do.

**JOHNNIE**
*(slowly)*

Do you know—I'm beginning to believe it myself!

They both laugh.

458-      OMITTED.
474

FADE OUT

ff                              THE END

455–457 (CONTINUED)

> **JOHNNIE**
> No, dear, you weren't insane. You were writing my story more accurately than I've lived it . . . In your mind, what was to prevent me from pouring that brandy down Beaky's throat? And, after that, you knew I was still desperate. I even tried to raise money on your insurance.

> **LINA**
> I know.

> **JOHNNIE**
> If you knew that, why shouldn't you think I meant to kill you? You believed it—and why shouldn't you?

> **LINA**
> Oh—please don't go on.

> **JOHNNIE**
> You saw me standing there, watching you drink—looking at you sadly as you drank. One part of me horrified, and the other part counting the insurance money.

> **LINA**
> Oh, my darling—

> **JOHNNIE**
> Why—you were willing to—you loved me enough to die for me.

> **LINA**
> Yes, I would have died for you if you wished it. But see it was really all my fault. Beaky once told me I didn't know you—the real you. But now I do, and I love you more than ever—if that's possible. I don't care what you do. You can lie—you can gamble—you can steal. I love you and I shall always love you.

(CONTINUED)

457 (CONTINUED)                                        4/23/41

> **JOHNNIE (cont'd)**
> So I invented tricks . . . little lies . . . little cheatings—and, after a while, big ones—till I got myself in so deep I couldn't stop. And people liked me—women liked me—I saw to that. So Johnnie Aysgarth was a terrific social success. He lived off his friends—even exploited their wives—then suddenly . . . he fell in love.

During this, the CAMERA HAS FOLLOWED him as he paces up and down. Now he stands still for a moment, facing Lina.

JOHNNIE (cont'd)

Oh, he had an honest minute or two—he knew what the girl was in for—He tried to tell her when he first realized he was in love—but he didn't try hard enough—he did a pretty feeble job.

LINA

It didn't matter. I was also in love with you. You didn't have a chance.

JOHNNIE

(raising his voice again)

It was true about Melbeck—that was true. I stole that money. And I never once stopped gambling at the races—I've been doing it all the time—sneaking away—borrowing right and left. And I *did* try to cheat Beaky. You were right about that, too, when you warned him against me. I didn't give a rap whether that land was any good or not. So long as I could draw a salary and write checks, what did I care about Beaky? I loved him in my own way, I suppose. I loved him and I loved you.

Lina comes closer to him and breaks in.

kl

(CONTINUED)

457 (CONTINUED)

JOHNNIE (cont'd)

Then his father died—and the boy had to take a shabbier room at Eton. The boy didn't like the shabby room—he didn't like it *one bit.* He couldn't rest until he did something about that—

In the b.g. Lina has come from the bed and approaches him.

LINA

Of course he couldn't! How I wish I had known that boy!

Johnnie continues:

JOHNNIE

Do you know what he did about it? He discovered the art of gambling. You could win enough—if you were lucky—to live like a Lord for the rest of the year. Then he lost—and he learned that you just *had* to be lucky; and there were ways of making yourself lucky. That is, if you were clever. He invented more tricks, little lies, little cheatings—and after a while big ones—so that he almost never lost. And people liked him—he saw to that. He could stand by the side of a beautiful woman and make such delicious fun of her hard-working, successful husband, that the husband would suddenly dwindle, become a dull, plodding little fellow—and Johnnie Aysgarth, at twenty and twenty-one, was sought after by the most sought-after ladies. He laughed and loved his way through the pocketbooks of his friends and the reputations of their wives—and suddenly . . . he fell in love.

During this the CAMERA has followed him as he paces up and down—now he stands still for a moment facing Lina.

gh                                                        (CONTINUED)

445-(CONTINUED)                                          6/14/41
457                                                      224

          LINA
*(deeply)*
Yes, I know it.

          JOHNNIE
I couldn't live without *you,* either.

          LINA
*(holding him close)*
We've *got* to be together.

          JOHNNIE
But I can't take anything from you . . . Somehow, the way things are now, I—I've got to do this myself.

          LINA
*(yearning over him)*
Oh, Johnnie!

          JOHNNIE
And I'll find a way.

          LINA
I know you will.

          JOHNNIE
And it won't be by cheating—I love the way you're looking at me—I want you to look at me like that always—

          LINA
I always will—

          JOHNNIE
And it won't be by borrowing, or lying, or—I don't know what's got into me—I've never felt like this before. Maybe it's something you've done to me, the way you're looking at me, the way I can feel your heart beating for me. Somehow I'm not the same as I was. I feel myself changing . . .

v                                                        (CONTINUED)

455–457 (CONTINUED)

>           JOHNNIE
> Oh my darling, there won't be any more of it—I promise you that. I
> won't give you any cause for further unhappiness. There'll be no
> more betting—no more lying—no more cheating. Never, never
> again! You believe that, don't you, dear?

>           LINA
> Yes, darling—of course, I do.

FADE OUT

457 (CONTINUED)                                                    4/23/41

>           LINA
> Oh, Johnnie, I must have been insane—to—to . . .

>           JOHNNIE
> You weren't insane. You were writing my story more accurately
> than I've lived it . . . In your mind, what was to stop me from
> pouring that brandy down Beaky's throat? And, after that, you
> knew I was still desperate. I even tried to raise money on your
> insurance.

>           LINA
> *(quietly)*
> I know.

>           JOHNNIE
> If you knew that, why shouldn't you think I meant to kill you for
> your insurance? You believed it—and why shouldn't you?

>           LINA
> Darling, darling, don't say any more . . . I can't bear it.

>           JOHNNIE
> *(continuing ruthlessly)*
> You saw me standing there, watching you drink that glass—looking
> at you sadly as you drank it—one part of me horrified, and the other
> part counting the insurance money.

>           LINA
> No, no—never—!

She buries her head in his shoulder.

kl                                                         (CONTINUED)

Changes                                          3/15/41
"BEFORE THE FACT"

457 (CONTINUED)

> **JOHNNIE** (cont'd)
>
> He had an honest minute or two—he knew what that girl was in for. He tried to tell her—but he didn't try hard enough—he did a pretty feeble job.

> **LINA**
>
> It didn't matter. I was so in love with you. You didn't have a chance.

> **JOHNNIE**
>
> *(raising his voice again)*
>
> It was true about Melbeck—that was true, do you understand? I stole that money. And I never once stopped gambling at the races—I've been doing it all the time—sneaking away—borrowing right and left. And I *did* try to cheat Beaky. You were right about that, too! I didn't give a rap whether that land was any good or not. So long as I could draw a salary and write cheques—what did I care about Beaky! I loved him, I'll grant myself that much. I loved him, and I loved you.

Lina comes closer to him and breaks in:

> **LINA**
>
> Oh, Johnnie,—I must have been insane—to—to . . .

> **JOHNNIE**
>
> You weren't insane. You were writing my story more accurately than I've lived it. . . . In your mind what was to keep me from pouring that brandy down Beaky's throat? And, after that, you knew I was still desperate. There was no more to be borrowed—I had no luck at the races. . . . What was to keep you from thinking I meant to kill you for your insurance? You believed it—and why

(CONTINUED)

457 (CONTINUED)

> **JOHNNIE** (cont'd)
>
> He had an honest minute or two—he knew what that girl was in for. He tried to tell her—but he didn't try hard enough—he did a pretty feeble job.

> **LINA**
>
> It didn't matter. I was so in love with you. You didn't have a chance.

> **JOHNNIE**
>
> *(raising his voice again)*
>
> It was true about Melneck—that was true, do you understand? I stole that money. And I never once stopped gambling at the

races—I've been doing it all the time—sneaking away—borrowing right and left. And I *did* try to cheat Beaky. You were right about that, too! I didn't give a rap whether that land was any good or not. So long as I could draw a salary and write cheques—what did I care about Beaky! I loved him, I'll grant myself that much. I loved him, and I loved you.

Lina comes closer to him and breaks in:

### LINA

Oh, Johnnie,—I must have been insane—to—to . . .

### JOHNNIE

You weren't insane. You were writing my story more accurately than I've lived it. *You* thought of it—so why wouldn't I? . . . What was to keep me from pouring that brandy down Beaky's throat if I had been in Paris with him? I might have done it. I was desperate. There was no more to be borrowed, and I had no luck at the races. What was to keep me from killing you for your insurance? Only just that I didn't think of it . . . But as the days went by, I might have thought of that.

(CONTINUED)

445– (CONTINUED)                                                 6/14/41
457                                                             225–232

### LINA
*(brimming over with happiness)*
Do you?

### JOHNNIE
Oh, Lina, I'm going to be good enough for you one of these days!

### LINA
*(thrilling)*
Are you?

### JOHNNIE
You've no idea how much I want to. You believe me, don't you, dear?

### LINA
Of course I do, my own—of course I do.

### JOHNNIE
*(slowly)*
Do you know—I'm beginning to believe it myself!

He looks at her wide-eyed. She begins to smile, and so does he. Then gradually she begins to laugh, and so does he—the laughter of great relief.

FADE OUT

458— OMITTED.
474

                         THE END

457 (CONTINUED)                                    3/15/41

    Lina throws her arms around him—

### LINA

**Darling, darling! Don't say any more! I can't bear it!**

### JOHNNIE

*(continuing ruthlessly)*

**You saw me standing there, watching you drink that glass, looking at you sadly as you drank it—one part of me horrified and the other part counting the insurance money.**

### LINA

**No, no.—never—!**

    She buries her head in his shouders.

### JOHNNIE

*(savagely)*

**Why not? Why shouldn't you think of me like that?—You—you loved me enough to—why, you were willing to die for me—but you never in all those days and weeks and months we lived together,—you never knew the one thing about me that was true and *never* changed from the second I laid eyes on you—that at any moment *I* would have died for *you*—**

### LINA

*(tears streaming down her face)*

**God help me, Johnnie, I didn't—but I do now—I do now—**

    Johnnie looks out ahead—staring, Lina's face pressed against his shoulder, sobbing. He remains staring out into the room as we

                                         DISSOLVE OUT

457 (CONTINUED)                                    4/23/41

    Johnnie doesn't hear her—he is struck with wonder at what he is realizing.

### JOHNNIE

**Why—you—you loved me enough—you were willing to die for me.**

### LINA

*(raises her head—looks at him steadily
and sweetly)*

**Yes, Johnnie, I would have been willing to die, if that's the way you wanted it. But you see, it was really all my fault. Beaky once told**

me I didn't know you—the real you. But now I do, and I love you
more than ever—if that's possible. I don't care what you do. You
can lie—you can gamble—you can steal. I love you and I shall
always love you.

                    JOHNNIE
(eagerly)
But, darling, there's not going to be any more of it. I promise you
that. I'm not going to cause you any further unhappiness. There
won't be any more betting—any more lying—any more cheating.
Never, never again! And this time I really mean it.

As there is no immediate response from Lina, he bends down and
looks anxiously into her face.

                    JOHNNIE (cont'd)
You believe that, don't you, dear?

Lina clasps him to her. He lays his head on her shoulder.

                    LINA
Yes, darling—of course, I do.

As she says this, she looks out over his shoulder at the audience—she
smiles very, very maternally and very understandingly, while she
strokes his hair. But we know that she cannot believe him. . . .

kl        458–     OMITTED                                FADE OUT
          474

                         THE END

457 (CONTINUED)                                       4/23/41

                    JOHNNIE
(savagely)
Why not? Why shouldn't you think of me like that—you—you loved
me enough to—Why, you were willing to die for me—but you never
in all those days and weeks and months we lived together—you
never knew the one thing about me that *never* changed from the
second I laid eyes on you—that at any moment *I* would've died for
*you*—

In a surge of emotion, Lina flings her arms around him and kisses
him with the utmost passion. For a moment Johnnie stands rigid, his
arms by his side—but her love brings its response. As he responds
to the kiss with equal passion, the scene

                                        FADES OUT

          458–     OMITTED
          474

                         THE END

kl

457 (CONTINUED)

Lina throws her arms around him—

**LINA**

**Darling, darling! Don't say any more! I can't bear it!**

**JOHNNIE**

*(continuing ruthlessly)*

**I can see myself standing there, watching you drink that glass—I look at you sadly as you drink it—one part of me horrified, and the other part counting the insurance money.**

**LINA**

**No, no—never—!**

She buries her head in his shoulder.

**JOHNNIE**

*(savagely going on)*

**Why not? *You* could think of me like that—you—who loved me enough to—why, you were willing to die for me—but you never in all those days and weeks and months we lived together, you never knew the one thing about me that was true and *never* changed from the second I laid eyes on you—that at any moment *I* would have died for *you*—**

**LINA**

*(tears streaming down her face)*

**God help me, Johnnie, I didn't—but I do now—I do now—**

Johnnie looks out ahead—staring, Lina's face pressed against his shoulder, sobbing.

**JOHNNIE**

**You thought of me as your murderer—**

gh                                                                                 (CONTINUED)

457 (CONTINUED)

**LINA**

*(sobbing—almost inaudible)*

**Don't, don't! Oh, please, darling, don't! . . .**

Johnnie remains staring out into the room as we

DISSOLVE OUT

DISSOLVE IN

INSERT  CLOSEUP A NOTE—in Johnnie's handwriting, it reads:

"Lina—

Please tell Melbeck I'll pay him back his money. It may take some time. As for you—I owe you a greater debt. I'll try to find some way to pay that debt, and if I do, we'll see each other again.

Johnnie."

DISSOLVE

INT. AYSGARTH BEDROOM—DAY

458    SEMI-CLOSEUP. Lina, in her dressing robe, is reading the note. She takes off her glasses and slowly looks about the room. She dashes over to the window—looks down—then back to the dressing room. She throws the door open—then over to the bedroom door, where we hear her calling:

**LINA**
**Ethel! Ethel!**

DISSOLVE

MONTAGE

459    A MONTAGE OF SHOTS of Lina searching for Johnnie. On the race
465    track—night clubs—etc. During this we get an impression of the outbreak of War—but always the searching Lina is prominent—An insert in the Personal columns and then finally—

DISSOLVE

INT. RAILWAY CARRIAGE—DAY

466    SEMI-CLOSEUP. Lina seated as she was at the opening of the picture, glancing at her "Illustrated London News." Suddenly her eyes widen with excitement as she sees:

INSERT  A PHOTOGRAPH of a group of R.A.F. men, lounging and laughing, perhaps half a dozen in all. Among them, in the uniform of a pilot, turned three quarters away from the camera, is a young man who might be Johnnie. (cont'd)

eg

(CONTINUED)

466 (CONTINUED)

INSERT (cont'd)

The CAMERA MOVES IN to the caption underneath:

"A typical group of our R.A.F. flyers enjoying a respite between flights over enemy territory. Reading from left to right: Gunner G. Policzki, Albert Levy, James Allen, Viscount Allerdyce, Herbert Matthews. These men are all from Unit 3, Corps 89.''

BACK TO SCENE Lina is studying the picture with great excitement—then lowering the magazine for a moment, as she did in the first scene, she stares across at the empty seat opposite her, remembering with sudden nostalgia her first meeting with Johnnie. She looks quickly back at the picture again.

INSERT   Lina's finger comes into the photograph and follows from the names beneath to the men from left to right—counting as she does so—when she comes to the third—JAMES ALLEN—CAMERA MOVES IN STILL CLOSER until we just have the man who is three quarters turned away—it is unmistakably Johnnie. CAMERA PANS DOWN AGAIN to the Caption until it rests on the words: ''Unit 3, Corps 89''

DISSOLVE

EXT. AIRFIELD—EVENING

467      CLOSEUP—a painted sign on a shed or railing—''Corps 89''

DISSOLVE

INT. AIR COMMODORE'S OFFICE—EVENING

468      SEMI-LONG SHOT. The Air Commodore is stepping out from behind his desk and comes around to Lina.

CAMERA MOVES IN with them as he leads her across to another door—he pauses before opening it, hand on doorknob.

> **AIR COMMODORE**
> **Perhaps I'd better tell you this—I doubt if your husband will—but he's one of our finest pilots.**

eg                                                            (CONTINUED)

468 (CONTINUED)

> **LINA**
> *(her eyes shining—murmurs)*
> **Is he?**

> **AIR COMMODORE**
> **Only yesterday his flight fought off ten enemy fighters—downed three himself, disabled one, and chased the rest of them halfway across the Channel.**

> **LINA**
> *(quietly and deeply)*
> **Thank you.**

The Commodore opens the door and they pass through.

INT. PASSAGE—EVENING

469    SEMI-LONG SHOT. They pass across the passage and the
Commodore throws open another door.

INT. RECREATION ROOM—EVENING

470    SEMI-LONG SHOT. Over the shoulders of Lina and the Commodore
we see about half a dozen pilots, who are resting before their next
take-off. Four of them are sleeping, while two are playing cards—one
of these is Johnnie. He smacks down a card just as the Commodore
speaks:

        **COMMODORE**
**Time for a visitor, Allen?**

Johnnie turns quickly, and seeing Lina, rises suddenly. He comes
slowly towards her with a growing grin on his face. The Commodore
steps back into the passage, Lina and Johnnie with him.

        INT. PASSAGE—EVENING

471    SEMI-CLOSEUP. Johnnie half closes the door to behind him. The
Commodore looks tactfully at Lina—

        **COMMODORE**
**See you later.**

Johnnie and Lina stand looking at each other, neither speaking, while
the Commodore goes. Then Johnnie takes both her hands in his and
grips them tightly—

        **JOHNNIE**
**Hello.**

Lina lays her head against his shoulder—he puts an arm around her
shoulder.

        **LINA**
**Johnnie! . . .**

        **JOHNNIE**
**James Allen is the name.**

        **LINA**
**Johnnie . . .**

        **JOHNNIE**
**No. James Allen. I like him better. He may seem like a stuffed shirt,
but I'm getting very fond of him.**

Lina looks at him, tears starting down her cheeks.

        **LINA**
**Oh, darling, when can we be together again?**

JOHNNIE

My leave starts next Tuesday—I was planning to drop in on you.

LINA

*(searching his face)*
Were you?

(CONTINUED)

471 (CONTINUED)

JOHNNIE

*(very tenderly—his feeling being too deep to be expressed)*
Yes—I miss home cooking. How's Ethel?

The grip of his hand around her shows all the emotion he is restraining. Lina looks at him with adoration.

LINA

Oh, Johnnie . . .

JOHNNIE

Better tell me quickly how Ethel is—or I'll start crying myself.

LINA

*(smiling through her tears)*
Ethel is fine!

JOHNNIE

I'm glad to hear that.

During all this, the corridor has resounded with the tramping of feet as various pilots and mechanics are passing. We hear an occasional name called in the middle distance, like: "Lieutenant Harrison—wanted at K-3. Sergeant Whitford—report at G-1. Sergeant Whitford!" Now suddenly Johnnie hears:

VOICE

Lieutenant (?) Allen—

Johnnie glances down at his wristwatch—

VOICE (cont'd)

—Report at J-9.

JOHNNIE

I have to be off now.

LINA

*(anxiously)*
Where are you going?

(CONTINUED)

471 (CONTINUED)

> JOHNNIE
>
> Well, darling, it's a military secret—promise you won't tell anybody—it's Berlin.

> VOICE
>
> Lieutenant Allen!

> JOHNNIE
>
> Got to go.

Suddenly he takes her in his arms and kisses her fervently. As they break apart:

> JOHNNIE (cont'd)
>
> See you Tuesday—

Lina, as he starts to hurry away—takes a step after him saying:

> LINA
>
> What would you like for dinner?

> JOHNNIE
>
> *(over his shoulder)*
>
> Leg of lamb!

He is gone. Lina stands a moment in the passage [as] other airmen hurry by. Then she crosses to the door of the Commodore's office, and knocks.

INT. AIR COMMODORE'S OFFICE—EVENING

472    SEMI-LONG SHOT. The Commodore is busy with orders, etc. He looks across as Lina enters, and smiles. Lina indicates the window through which we can see an impression of the Airfield beyond.

> LINA
>
> May I stay here a moment?

> COMMODORE
>
> Certainly.

eg                                                                                    (CONTINUED)

472 (CONTINUED)

He watches her for a moment as she looks out of the window, and then picks up from his desk a pair of field glasses.

> COMMODORE
>
> Will these be any good to you?

CAMERA MOVES IN as he hands them to her. We can see through the windows pilots running towards their machines—and through a half open window can hear the roar of the running engines. Lina raises the glasses to her eyes.

EXT. AIRFIELD—EVENING

473    LONG SHOT. Through the glasses she can see Johnnie climbing into a machine. As he closes the glass top with a wave in her direction, she pans her glasses slightly along the plane, until we see painted on the side of the machine—"Monkey-face." The engine roars louder as his plane starts to taxi off, still held in the circle of the field glasses. The plane gets smaller and smaller. She sees it rise from the field. Other planes rise in succession as Johnnie's plane gets smaller. The whole scene blurs as though an irregular film were coming over it.

474    CLOSEUP—Lina lowers the glasses. We see that her eyes are filled with tears, but her face bears a look of tremendous pride.

FADE OUT

THE END

Most would agree that few of these endings are very satisfying. In June, George Schaefer, the head of RKO production, submitted to Hitchcock his own idea as to how the film should end:

---

Nothing in the picture is to be changed until the final scene, where he brings her a glass of milk.

He brings the glass of milk just as shown now, puts it on the table, and says to her "I have brought you something. Go ahead and drink it." She looks at him with an earnest knowing expression and in a most solemn but devoted tone of voice says "Do you want me to drink this? If so, hand it to me yourself. Give it to me out of your own hands, because if you want me to drink it I will gladly drink it and forgive you." He looks startled and replies "So you know?" She answers "Yes, I Know."

He says at first incredulously and then later in self-abasement "You would drink this, knowing what is in it? You love me so much you would die for me, that I might accomplish my purpose? Without much qualm I was about to give you this drink. But low as I have sunk, to realize you would die for me in this way makes me know that I am not fit to live - that I should not live." With which he puts the glass to his lips and empties it, falling on the bed unconscious.

She in panic takes up the telephone, phones the woman detective writer and exclaims excitedly: "Johnny took what you told him about in a glass of milk a minute ago. He is unconscious. Is there anything I can do?" The writer replies: "Don't worry. I did not tell Johnny, and of course I would not, the real poison , but I wanted to see what he would do and I gave him a prescription that is a potion from which he will awake unharmed within a few hours. I did not even share with you the fact that I had not told him the real prescription, because knowing all of you, I wanted to bring this thing to a climix."

Lena hangs up the phone, notices beads of perspiration on Johnny's head takes his head in her lap, wipes off the perspiration and with a beatific expression of hope, looks into the camera.

---

A week later, Raphaelson, the original screenwriter, gives his final two cents:

June 28, 1941.

Dear Hitch:

In case I don't see you before I go, I want to leave these impressions of the last scene:

I think it is very good up to where Lina gets the first inkling that Johnnie didn't kill Beaky. From then on, I think it is out of focus. What is wrong with it contains the clue, I believe, of what can make it a fine scene.

Johnny fails to rise to the "lift" of the "happy ending" finale. This would be all right if it weren't the intent that he should rise. I think it is impossible for Johnnie, in that situation, to do anything but sternly regard the realities of the present, the past, and the future.

So I suggest that Johnnie makes no contact with Lina -- hardly looks at her, never once touches her hand, doesn't stand up. In other words, he plays practically all of that scene talking to himself, so to speak.

But as for Lina ... When she gets the first inkling that Johnnie didn't kill Beaky, I don't think she begins to get enough "lift". I think she must carry the whole finish. I think she should rise to an ecstasy unprecedented in the acting career of Miss Fontaine at the second beat when she fully realizes Johnnie didn't kill Beaky. I could conceive of the camera on Lina as she does what amounts to a lyric dance of solemn happiness, while Johnnie, on the sound track, continues his succeeding speeches. I could see her by the window, looking with exaltation into the brightly moonlit night, while the sound track continues with Johnnie. I could even see her say speeches like the one about her mother helping out with money -- while she stands by the window.

Then, for the finish -- and by the finish, I mean actually her last line -- I could see her sweep back to Johnnie, who is still sitting with his elbows on his knees, and over his shoulder tell him the last speech. Then, as he slowly looks up at her with the first glimmering of realization, we fade out.

In other words, I think it is impossible, under these story conditions, to have Johnnie meet Lina even one-tenth of the way in these few minutes. Lina must do all, and rightly so. The less Johnnie meets her, the more we believe in his sincerity.

Mr. Hitchcock                                    Page Two

        And I wish to protest most strenuously against
what has happened to my last line.  She says now:  "Those are
the most beautiful words any woman ever heard!"  I regard that
speech as inane, pointless, silly, and affected.  I regard my
original speech -- "Those are the most beautiful words you
ever said to a woman in your life" -- as rich with meaning,
and unchangeably right.  I consider that speech vital to the
picture.

        In case I don't see you -- my love and blessings
on you and Alma.

                                        Sincerely,

                                        *[signature]*

*Address all summer:*

*%o Marion Inn*
*Marion, Mass.*

*P.S.  Also I don't think she should
say the line about "is it
a painful death." That comes
from a supine, licked woman.
Just heard you're not coming until
Tuesday — awfully sorry to
have missed you both —*

Hitch was away in New York doing a radio show, "Information Please,"
June 26 through July 2—although he talked extensively on the phone to the
writers and cutters about shooting and cutting in the new ending.

The ending that survives in the finished film was finally accepted on July
18, 1941, thus completing the film's screenplay and film on the same day. Lina
pulls away from Johnny as their car races along the cliffs, thinking that he's

trying to push her out. In reality, he's trying to keep her from falling out. They confront each other and, although the dialogue is far from hopeful, the car turns around to head back to their home rather than continuing on to Lina's mother.

In addition to problems with the ending (problems, by the way, that Hitchcock asked not be publicized by the studio—he had Joseph Breen, the owner of RKO, quash a magazine story that listed the problems), the studio was unhappy with the film's title. They suggested *Suspicion,* to which Hitchcock strongly objected by telegram:

To George Schaefer from Alfred Hitchcock, August 18, 1941:

> MY DEAR GEORGE PLEASE DO NOT CALL BEFORE THE FACT SUSPICION IT IS SUCH A CHEAP AND DULL TITLE AND MAKES IT SOUND LIKE A B PICTURE WHAT ABOUT CALLING IT JOHNNIE LOVE AH

Schaefer's August 20 reply:

> DEAR ALFRED WE HAVE CHECKED WITH EVERY IMPORTANT CIRCUIT TO SECURE THEIR REACTION ON PROPOSED TITLE BEFORE THE FACT IT IS THUMBS DOWN WITH EVERYONE THEY ARE ALL UNANIMOUS IN THEIR OPINION THAT THEY LIKE TITLE SUSPICION AND AS YOU KNOW THE GALLUP POLL GAVE US A THREE TO ONE VOTE ON TITLE SUSPICION IN PREFERENCE TO THE ORIGINAL TITLE. PERSONALLY I LIKE TITLE JOHNNIE BUT HAVE BEEN UNABLE TO CONVINCE OTHERS THANK YOU SO MUCH FOR YOUR INTEREST KIND REGARDS

*Suspicion* had a longer gestation than normal. The film didn't open until November 1941, but when it did, all the tinkering paid off. Evidence, this memo from Schaefer:

November 24, 1941:

> DEAR ALFRED ORCHIDS TO YOU AGAIN REVIEWS EXCELLENT AND PICTURE DOING OUTSTANDING BUSINESS WE ARE ALL VERY HAPPY AND KNOW YOU MUST BE TOO REGARDS

## *Shadow of a Doubt*

Hitchcock made three "nonwar" movies between 1940 and the end of the war, starting with *Suspicion*. The next was Hitchcock's dark look at small-town America and his personal favorite: *Shadow of a Doubt*. *Spellbound* would round out the trio.

The genesis of the story for *Shadow of a Doubt* is quite interesting. To understand the screenplay's development fully, one needs to go to the end. Gordon McDonell, who authored the original story, sent this revealing congratulatory letter to Hitchcock when the movie was released in January 1943:

Apartment 702
1314 North Hayworth
Hollywood

January 10, 1943

Dear Hitch:

    I saw it on Friday. . . I shook like a jelly for a full two hours afterwards. . .
    Frankly, I have never seen a murder picture to touch it. It is so very, very real. . . One just lived with them. I don't know how to tell you what a wonderful job I think you have done. I predict here and now that it will do terrific business and make a whole lot of money for you. I imagine you must be very pleased it with it, although I realise you are probably still a bit close to it to be so sure as I feel about it. You obviously put so much into it. I want to see it again and again. (An that's nothing to do with the fact that it was anything to do with me. As a rule I do not care for my stuff in books or on the screen).
    Everything about it was so utterly right. Script, dialogue, actin casting -- and as for the music and the way you handled the camera:-- that was everything. That close up of him, getting closer and closer until he looks straight into it. And when he remembers, that on the staircase, that now she is the only one who knows, and looks back, down at her there in the doorway. . . And the tremendous, shattering impact of the music in conjunction with the newspaper headline, in the library. . . And that wonderful shot, downwards, macabre, of her leaving the library. You got so much into that shot. . .
    But there is so much to talk about. I keep thinking of this bit and that bit. Herb -- he was wonderful, you were so clever with him. And of course the two stars were perfect: Teresa is so very sweet (I've thought that since Pride of the Yankees that she is the best actress in town) and Jo Cotten, well he just *was* Uncle Charlie. . . But it was you all the way through. You certainly did put the whole of yourself into that picture. . .
    The whole thing too, to me personally, is a satisfaction very particular: you know how first I thought of it when we were staying dow. in Hanford when our car had broken down in the high Sierra and we had gone down to get it repaired. It was in 1938, just while I was beginning to mull over the vague stirrings of my present book that I am still working on. There we were, stuck in that little place and it was so hot and dry and dusty and small town. And then I thought of it and later when we were up in the mountains again I told Margaret and she said I must write it as a book. I said I never would, because I wanted to write what I am writing and nothing else. Ever since then 'Uncle Charlie' has been in our family and we have often spoken of him as though he existed. Then, so long afterwards, M said to me one day she was searching and searching for a story for you. By then we had forgotten about Uncle Charlie and then that evening he came into my head, I did not know why nor then he

did just then: I wasn't consciously thinking of a story for you because
I never think of anything except my book.  Suddenly I connected up you and
Uncle Charlie and I jumped up and said: "Margaret, what about Uncle Charli
for Hitch."  And she said, "Why, of course - what fools we were not to
think of him sooner.". . . You know the rest.  When, then, you asked me
through Margaret if I would add to it I said no because, as always, my
mind was taken up so fully with my book that I had none to spare for
anything else.  And also I felt this: that you had there a story which
you, being an artist, would see in your own way and in nobody else's way.
And I, if I did go on with it, would see any further parts in my own
particular way which would inevitably have been a different one from
yours,  I knew that that would have destroyed your keenness because I
have had so much experience of just that process happening to me.  If
I have an idea for a story and I tell it to someone too early and they
then seize upon it eagerly and start adding to it, immediately I get a
feeling: 'Oh dear, oh dear, that's not at all what I was wanting to do
and because of this fellow crashing in with his own darned ideas he has
now stopped my own libido from rushing on with it.  Now I have gone cold
on the whole thing.  He has spoilt it.  Okay, then to hell with it.  It's
dead.'  Hasn't that often happened to you?  I feel sure it must have done.
I am putting all this partly to explain why I didn't add anything, to
show you that it was not rudeness on my part or lack of enthusiasm but
because I knew well how vital it was for an artist, any artist, not to
have one particle of his intitial keenness taken away.  And also it was
that, because I knew you had adopted Uncle Charlie into your own system,
then that was where Uncle Charlie lay and no longer in mine.
     And, oh boy, look what you did with him. . .
     Very rarely have I seen a picture where it ceases to be a picture
and you are sitting there in the theatre not realising you are, transporte
completely into the life which is there upon the screen.  Never before has
such an experience happened to me in a murder picture.  I do think it is
a masterpiece which you have created.
               Please give my regards to your wife,
               Yours,
                        Gordon McDonell
          Gordon McDonell.

It is interesting that, like McDonell thinking that Uncle Charlie was made
for Hitchcock, the other sin qua non Hitchcock, *Vertigo*, was also rumored to
be written with Hitchcock in mind (this is unfortunately not the case, as my
book on *Vertigo* reveals).

The story that McDonell gave to Hitchcock (by way of his wife, who
worked for Selznick) on May 5, 1942, follows. This copy has been edited by
Hitchcock:

May 5, 1942

~~UNCLE CHARLIE~~
by
Gordon McDonell

*Hitchcock #2
UNTITLED
BY
GORDON McDONELL*

The story is set in the little town of Hanford in the San
Joaquin Valley, a typical American small town almost lost between the
desert and mountains.  In Hanford lives an unimportant little family
of four -- father, mother, daughter and son.  They are little
people, leading unimportant little lives.  The father is a small and
rather timid employee in the local bank.  The son, about 19, has a
job but not a very good one, and there are very few prospects for
him in the small town.  The daughter ~~(Fontaine type)~~ is a girl of
about 18 with great potentialities of charm.  Given the right chances
one feels she could develop her real, natural intelligence and make somethin
out of her quite considerable beauty.  But in Hanford there is nothing
for her.  She takes on much of the burden of housekeeping in the
little household, trying all the time to spare her semi-invalid mother
the work which seriously affects her health.  She has become engaged,
half against her own better sense, to the town's ne'er-do-well
~~(John Garfield type)~~.  He is always half in trouble, footloose, dis-
contented, often railing in speech against the humdrum respectability
of the smug little town.  As a result, whenever anything goes wrong
in town, when a small local holdup finally attributed to tramps
empties the cash register of the local drug store, town gossip at
first ascribed the holdup to the ne'er-do-well.  The instinct throughout town is to fasten blame on him whenever possible.  The girl, herself, is often swayed by public disapproval and yet she clings half-

heartedly to their engagement just because the future is so empty.

The little family are always struggling to come up in the
world socially.  It is very important to them, and they count their
small social successes very tenderly, for instance, the evening
when the mother has to deputize as chairman of the local meeting of
the Women's Club, is a red letter day.  It is almost THE BEGINNING
OF BETTER THINGS.  The struggle to "climb to reach the Jonses" is
just as hard a one in the little town of Hanford as it would be in
London or New York and just as important to the climbers, but when the
story opens and the hot weather has descended once again to burn
up the smug little streets and fill the air with biting desert dust,
it looks like just another year when nothing will ever happen.  Life
passes Hanford by; there are no high spots, there are never even
any crimes.

A letter addressed to the mother arrives which is the whole
key note of life for the little family.  It comes from Uncle Charlie,
the gay, handsome, successful, debonair brother whom the mother has
not seen for ten years.  To the girl and her brother, Uncle Charlie
in anecdote has become quite a legendary figure, the hero of so many
exploits of the mother's girlhood.  Always it has been their hope
that one day they would see and know Uncle Charlie for themselves,
and now a letter comes from a fashionable New York hotel telling
them that Uncle Charlie is on his way west and is coming to visit
them.  At once the summer becomes exciting and lively and the little
house is alive with plans.  The girl sees the flush of vitality
again in her mother's cheeks as her mother hurries from house to house
to tell everybody proudly the news of Uncle Charlie's visit.  Little
teas are arranged in advance, and a whirl of small town gaiety is

planned.  The President of the Women's Club approaches the mother
hoping that Uncle Charlie will favor them with a talk on some of his
travels.

Then Uncle Charlie arrives and he is all and more than
any of them expected.  Distinguished, entirely charming, very polished, and a man of the world, he captivates them all, and the household takes on an entirely new lease of life.  Uncle Charlie has the
gift of unique sympathy and is able to deal with every member of the
family in just the way needed to galvanize them into making better
use of themselves.  Under his influence, the father loses much of
his feeling of inferiority and gets a better position in the bank,
the young son is spurred by Uncle Charlie's vigorous encouragement
to go out and look for a job in a bigger city with a future to it.
The mother becomes an entirely different person.  She once again
takes an interest in her appearance and her faded prettiness blooms
again.  On that account alone Uncle Charlie wins the gratitude of the
girl.  To her it is the greatest gift he could have brought that he
has given so much of health back to her fading mother.  Between Uncle
Charlie and the girl there springs up a very close relationship.
He is wonderful to her in a way that no man has ever been before,
bringing to her a breath of that wide outside world she has longed to
visit.  Evidently well supplied with money Uncle Charlie showers her
with pretty things, brushing away her protests by saying that this is
the least an uncle can do for his pretty niece.  He is unalterably
set against her fiance.  The two men start off on the wrong foot and
are antagonistic from the start.  The worst side of the fiance always
seems to be brought out in ugly contrast to Uncle Charlie's polished
manner so that many an evening ends in the young man making a surly

fool of himself.  Uncle Charlie is quite outspoken in urging the
girl to have done with this misalliance, saying that she is throwing herself away on such an oaf and that he himself will take her
along with him and show her some of the world.

Then gradually, although her head is almost turned by the
attentions of this good-looking man of the world, little things
begin to bother the girl about him.  She begins to wonder about his
life, about his past, and one day while tidying up his room in his
absence, she is impelled by curiosity to go through his trunk.  In
it she finds some clippings dealing with two or three isolated
murder cases.  A terrible instinct hits her.  Then she is furious
with herself for having such thoughts about the man who has become
their benefactor.  She tries not to think about it again, but again
and again she returns to search his room and each time she finds
something that makes her suspicion grow.  Finally tucked away in a
corner of his trunk she finds a pretty dainty chiffon scarf.  A
memory strikes her and she ruffles through the clippings to find the
description of the most recent murder, that of a young girl which took
place a couple of months earlier.  The murder weapon had been a
flowered chiffon scarf.

She slams the trunk shut and turns to run, but as she
rushes out of the door Uncle Charlie comes in.  Her eyes are unguarded
and as she faces him for that brief instant he sees in her eyes that
she knows he is the murderer.

She is utterly torn between whether to hand him over to the
police or whether to let things slide.  If she hands him over to the
police, the whole life of the little family, above all her mother's
life, will be ruined for good and all.  In a small town like Hanford
such a scandal could never be lived down.  The town would have been

made a fool of, having opened its hospitable doors to a murderer.
The revelation of the truth might even kill her mother. Feeling unable to bear this choice alone she tells her fiance about it and he
turns out in this, her greatest crisis, to be a strong and solid
prop. He does not try to force her to go to the police, understanding that she has to work that out alone, but he does stand by her in
a way which welds them very closely.

    The girl's one object while making her decision is to
avoid Uncle Charlie, and Uncle Charlie's one object is to get her
alone. Terrified, she realizes that his only means of silencing her
is to kill her. Several times he almost succeeds in getting her
alone, once when he sends the whole family out to a movie and returns
to the house, but she escapes out of her bedroom window, although
she knows that this cannot go on for long.

    Then Uncle Charlie arranges a large picnic in the foothills.
They all drive out in cars across the desert floor and park below
the towering, crumbling sandstone cliffs which are the beginning of
the mountains. It is the gayest of picnics, but to the girl it is
a haunted evening for she has decided that even if it kills her mother,
she cannot let the murderer go free. Then by clever planning, when
they start home Uncle Charlie manages so that the whole of the cavalcade
of cars leave and start off into the sunset across the desert floor,
no one realizing that the girl has been left behind a little way up
one of the cliffs they have been climbing. When the last car has
driven off into the dusk and the evening silence has settled down over
the desert, he begins to climb to meet her. Coming down she sees
him approaching and knows that this is the end, that soon she will be
found entirely crushed and broken at the foot of the crumbling rocks,
the victim of a tragic "accident". She turns and, panic-stricken,

struggles wildly up the crumbling hillside, but the man gains on her.
She reaches the crest and turns as he comes toward her. They are on
the edge of the cliff, and neither sees that a crack is slowly widening
in the ground at their feet where the loose sand has been shaken
by their hurried footsteps. Uncle Charlie's hands go out but the
girl jumps aside, behind the crack in the ground. From a little below
comes the sound of a sudden shout. The fiance has realized that the
girl has been left behind and is racing up the hillside, Uncle
Charlie makes a lunge but the shout startles him and he misses his
hold just as the piece of cliff on which he is standing breaks away
and falls carrying Uncle Charlie down with the mass of rocks and loose
earth to crash to the desert floor below.

    The broken body of the well-liked Uncle Charlie is brought
reverently and tragically home to Hanford by a score of willing
volunteers who rush out to the scene of the "accident". Condolences
and glorious floral tributes pore into the grief-stricken little
household and the whole of Hanford turns out to do honor to the
guest in a funeral the like of which has seldom been seen in the
small town. As they drive along in the funeral procession, the girl
and her fiance are the only people who know what Uncle Charlie
really was and what his death has spared the mother.

---o---

Less than a week after receiving McDonell's story, Hitchcock outlined his ideas for a screenplay to be developed from it:

Alfred Hitchcock
May 11, 1942

NOTES ON POSSIBLE DEVELOPMENT
OF UNCLE CHARLIE STORY FOR
SCREEN PLAY

At present the story indicates a shape consisting of four phases:

1. The family and their lives existing at the time the story opens.

2. The arrival of the Uncle; the effect of his influence on their social status. The beginning of the attraction of the daughter to her Uncle, culminating in her first suspicions about him being not quite everything he appears to be.

3. The growth of her suspicions, culminating in final proof that her Uncle is a murderer.

4. The girl's problem -- the Uncle's problem -- and finally his attempts to extricate himself by attempting to murder her.

The main treatment of the story at the outset should not give any indication of the ultimate development which takes place. It should start out as a comedy of small town manners with the implication that after the arrival of the Uncle and his subsequent happy effect on them all that something dramatic is going to develop between him and the daughter; that is to say, that her being attracted to him is going to possibly upset the harmonious state of affairs between the Uncle and the family. If this situation is developed at all and is seen by the mother who becomes apprehensive, it can be used as a pointer to the girl as to how really distressed the mother might become if she knew the real truth about her younger

2.

brother, Uncle Charlie. From this point on, if the girl becomes less cordial towards the Uncle and this is apparent to her mother,

the latter might construe this with some measure of relief that
the situation between her daughter and the Uncle has not developed
according to her fears.   I put it this way because, while I am
suggesting some situation between daughter and Uncle might develop,
it should never really reach a stage which would call for some showdown between mother and daughter -- or should it?  Looking at the
shape again in the light of the above remarks, several things stand
out fairly clearly:

1.    That the beginning of the story should be pure comedy.

2.    That it should continue right through the scenes concerned
      with the Uncle's arrival and his subsequent effect on the
      family.

3.    From the point where the girl first suspects her Uncle, the
      comedy should continue as overtones right up to the end of
      the story and should be got from the characters 'not in the
      know'.

                    ------------------

                                        Alfred Hitchcock
                                        May 11, 1942


                    SOME NOTES ABOUT THE SMALL
                         TOWN ATMOSPHERE
                    ---------------------------

      If possible I am extremely anxious to avoid the conventional
small town American scene.  By conventional I mean the stock
figures which have been seen in so many films of this type.   I
would like them to be very modern; in fact, one could almost lay
the story in the present day so that the social ambitions could
concern themselves possibly with war work and such like.  The
only drawback to this is that it might date the film because
things change so rapidly nowadays.  But by modern I mean that
the small town should be influenced by movies, radio, juke boxes,
etc.; in other words, as it were, life in a small town lit by
neon signs.

Concerning the last section, Hitchcock had felt that *Saboteur* was not as successful in re-creating the real America he had been discovering on weekends.

To paint this portrait of small-town America, Hitchcock turned to the small-town American playwright Thornton Wilder. The resulting handwritten script, a few pages of which follow, is an extraordinary accomplishment, a striking testament to Wilder and Hitchcock's ability. Hitchcock was so touched by Wilder's abilities, in fact, that he gave him special credit in the titles, in addition to his screenplay credit.

SHADOW OF A DOUBT

(Temporary title)

*Thornton Wilder's original material*

Screen Play

by

Thornton Wilder

1

SHADOW OF A DOUBT
PART ONE

The New Jersey marshes near Jersey City. Soot and waste heaps. Then some streets at the edges of the Towns in early evening.

Working-men's rooming-houses.

An abandoned station on a siding with the sign: "Passaic New Jersey."

More rooming-houses.

Uncle Charlie's back as he goes up the steps of one of them. The hall. He climbs up the stairs to his room, and enters.

In the room. Considerable light comes in the windows from the street-lights outside.

Before he closes the door he listens a moment, then closes it and locks it in one rapid accustomed gesture. He stands lost in thought. Then savagely unlocks it again. He goes to the window and looks down into the street, obliquely from the left and the right sides of the window frame. Without pulling down the blind, he comes back into the room and turns on the light.

Uncle Charlie is bulky; about forty-seven; well, but a shade ostentatiously, dressed; red carnation in his button-hole. His fleshy, slightly florid face is set in fatigue and bitterness. His movements alternate between tense stillness and rapid nervous precision.

Ia

## SHADOW OF A DOUBT
### PART ONE

Views of the Jersey marshes near Jersey City. Soot and waste heaps. Then some street of workingmen's boarding houses. A view of ~~Part~~ an ~~Hudson~~ station on a siding with a sign "Passaic ~~½ mi y~~" ~~More ~~ ~~? yes.~~ Uncle Charlie's back as he enters one of them.

Room in a working-men's boarding-house, ~~~~ New Jersey. Night. Considerable light enters through the windows from the street-lights outside.

Enter Uncle Charlie... He is Bulky; about forty-seven; well but a shade ostentatiously, dressed; carnation in his Buttonhole. His fleshy, slightly florid face is set by fatigue and Bitterness. His movements alternate between tense stillness and rapid nervous precision.

Before he closes the door he listens a moment. Then closes and locks the door in one accustomed gesture.

He stands lost in motionless thought. Then savagely ~~un~~ unlocks the door.

He goes to the window and looks down into the street, obliquely, from the left and right of the window-frame.

Without pulling down the Blind, he comes back into the room and turns on the light.

He empties his pockets on upon the Top of the bureau, papers, purse, cigars, glasses. Some of the objects fall on the floor.

Without taking off his hat or shoes he ~~~~ lies down on the Bed, hands clasped behind his head, and stares up at the ceiling.

Knock on the door. He makes no response. Second Knock.

The landlady, Mrs Martin, puts her head in, and hems apologetically.

## MRS MARTIN

Two men were here and asked for you while you was out, Mr. Spencer. Young man and a kinda older man. I think they was sorry you wasn't in.

(pause.)

I guess they'll be Back, though. I saw them up at the corner about an hour ago, when I went to the A. and P. for a minute. I just wanted to change your Towels Mr. Spencer, I hope I'm not disturbing you.

(she goes to the washstand.)

You look kinda tired to me and that's a fact. Have you got a headache or something? I think maybe you need a real rest, that's what I think. — Why, Mr. Spencer, you oughtn't to leave all that money lying around that way. Always makes me nervous to see money lying around. Everybody in the world ain't honest, you know. — Though I must say I haven't had much trouble that way. Some people say New Jersey has a bad reputation for things like that, but I haven't had much trouble, I'll say that.

(She goes to the door.)

Well, wouldn't you want I should turn out the light and you can get a good rest? You'd better lock the door when I'm gone.

(He nods slightly)

I think those two men'll be back. Looked to me like they were really sorry you was out.

### UNCLE CHARLIE

(without change of expression)

Well, if they come back, Mrs Martin, you show them right up.

### MRS MARTIN

I'll do that, Mr. Spencer, I'll do that.

### UNCLE CHARLIE

Up to now I've always been out when they came. Yes, sir, they've never found me in yet. (Pause.) Funny thing, — they've never seen my face once. No, Mrs Martin, your friends have never clapped eyes on me in all their born days. But I'm in this time. Everything's got to end some time or other. You can show them right up when they come.

### MRS MARTIN

(bewildered; softly)

Yes, Mr. Spencer.

(She turns out the light and shuts the door. In the streaked shadows we see his eyes staring at the ceiling. Suddenly he turns over with a choking noise and we see the bulk of his back and his fists pounding into the pillow in impotent rage. He springs from the bed and gulps down two glasses of water at the washstand. He turns on the light, then stands motionless staring at the floor. Breathingly heavily he can be heard whispering:)

### UNCLE CHARLIE

What do they know? They're bluffing. They don't know anything.

(Sudden fever of activity. Crams money, papers, etc into his pockets and goes out.
Foot of the stairs. He calls "Mrs Martin".
She appears.
Same concentrated pause, eyes on the ground.)

### UNCLE CHARLIE

I'm going away on a business trip. Just collect the things I've left upstairs and put them aside somewhere. 'Be back some day.

(He gives her a ~~Twenty dollar bill~~ Ten dollar bill.)

### MRS MARTIN

Why, Mr. Spencer, you don't owe me a penny. No, no, Mr. Spencer, I couldn't take it. I really couldn't.

### UNCLE CHARLIE

(eyes on the distance)

Why..... find something to do with it. Find something or other. It's only money, — that's all it is. Throw it away.

(He goes out the front door.
On the top step he takes a deep breath and straightens his shoulders.
In the street, not far from the house, two men are waiting under the trees, one on each side of the side walk, though several yards apart. He walks straight down the walk between them. They make no move until he's passed. One turns to follow him; the other quickly crosses the street.

A Telephone-Booth.
Uncle Charlie holds the receiver to his ear. In his other hand is a heap of silver change.

### UNCLE CHARLIE

Yes, it's under fifty words. How much money do I have to have ready? All right, I have it...... Wait a minute: what Town am I in now?.... All right, I'm ready. It's going to Mrs Joseph Newton, Santa Rosa, California...... "Dear Emma, am coming to pay you a visit at last arriving about next Thursday. I will wire train."

(Same dead pause)

"Give my love to everybody, especially our little Charlie." No. Cross out that 'last, — from "especially our little Charlie" ...... euh..... "Much anticipation. Your affectionate Brother, Mouser."...... M.... O.... U.... No, say "Your affectionate brother, Charles". There's no return address. All right, all right, say, Charles Otis, Waldorf-Astoria, New York. No, don't read it to me. Here's the money. A quarter. A quarter. A quarter.

(Sound of the Bell registering the coins changes to The telephone bell in the Newton home.

~~SEQUENCE II~~

(Ann Newton, 10, bespectacled, competent and solemn is lying on her stomach on the floor of the sitting-room, reading. Book in hand, her eyes glued to the page, she goes to the ~~~~ wall Telephone Pulling before her a foot stool that will enable her to reach the height of the mouthpiece. During the following she continues reading.

### ANN

Hello...... This is Ann Newton. Mr. Slocum. No, my mama isn't home yet. Yes, Mr. Slocum, I'll tell her to Telephone you at the depot about a ~~~~ telegram.... before Ten o'clock. Thank you very much, Mr. Slocum.

(Not Taking her eyes from the page she returns to her former place on the rug. Her father appears in the dining room beyond her. Mr. Newton is 45, lanky, absent-minded. A wing of pepper-and-salt hair falling over one eye. He carries two cheap magazines with lurid covers, of the pulp mystery story type. He stores them in the wood box, ~~~~ furtively.)

~~~~~ ~~~~~~ ~~~~~~~~~~~~~~~~~~~~~~~~    change. (first page)

**5**

"Give my love to everybody, especially our little Charlie". No. Cross out that last;— from "especially our little Charlie"...... euh.....  "Much anticipation. Your affectionate brother, Mousie".... M....O....U— No, say "Yo affectionate brother, Charles." There's no return address. ~~address~~, no, don't read it to me. Here's the money. A quarter, a quarter, a quarter.....

(sound of Bell registering the coins. DISSOLVE to long view of the valley in which Santa Rosa lies. sound of distant church Bells. spirits sound of city. shots closer into village. The Newton home. The window of YOUNG CHARLIE'S room. Enter room. YOUNG CHARLIE is lying on her bed, staring at the ceiling. Both the disposition of her room and her mood are reminiscent of UNCLE CHARLIE'S in the earlier sequence.
    YOUNG CHARLIE is between 17 and 18. Very pretty. Capable of high spirits, but with a strong sense of responsibility. Her present mood is without self-pity or tearful exaggeration. The sound of the telephone ringing downstairs is heard. She turns her head slightly, then returns to her fixed gaze at the ceiling.
CUT to sitting-room of the NEWTON home, downstairs.

     (Ann Newton, 10, bespectacled,
     competent and solemn, is
     lying on her stomach on the
     floor of the sitting room,
     reading. Book in hand, her
     eyes glued to the page, she
     goes to the wall telephone,
     kicking before her a foot-
     stool that will enable her
     to reach the height of the
     mouthpiece. During the
     following she continues
     reading.)

       **ANN**

Hello. This is Ann Newton, Mrs Henderson. No, my mama isn't home yet. Yes, Mrs Henderson, I'll tell her to telephone you at the telegraph office..... Before nine o'clock. Thank you very much, Mrs Henderson.

Second Sequence: Childhood Memories

47

UNCLE CHARLIE

Good morning. What do you know about this?

MRS NEWTON

Charlie wasn't here. But, Charles, the way he put it,—it was a useful thing to do.... it was like a... our duty as citizens. It's something the government wants.

UNCLE CHARLIE

Oh, the government's in it, is it?

MRS NEWTON

Maybe, not exactly.... I don't know; but it's for the public good. And, Charles, of course. I told him you were here, and he seemed very interested.

UNCLE CHARLIE

I won't have anything to do with it. I'm just a visitor here. ~~I won't be photographed, they wouldn't have been photographed in my life... and I won't be photographed now.~~ And my advice to you is to slam the door in his face.

MRS NEWTON

You don't have to meet him, if you don't wish to, Charles. I know he'll be disappointed.

YOUNG CHARLIE

I wish you'd consent, if only for the reason that we could have a photograph of you. He'd give us one free.

UNCLE CHARLIE

No, ma'am. No, thank you. I've never been photographed in my life, and I won't be photographed now.

MRS NEWTON

Why, Charles, I have a photograph of you.

UNCLE CHARLES
(astonished)

I tell you there are none.

MRS NEWTON

(Taking a small snapshot out of an envelope)

I guess you've forgotten all about it.

(YOUNG CHARLIE moves around by her uncle's shoulder to look at it. It is the photograph of a boy of nine; high forehead; singularly idealistic expression.)

UNCLE CHARLIE

(taken aback)

39 Burnham Street.

YOUNG CHARLIE

(in awe)

Uncle, how beautiful!

UNCLE CHARLIE

(after looking at it a moment under his breath)

The whole world's crooked, that's what's the matter. The whole world's gone down hill. Oh, Emmy, if we could only turn back the clock.

(The photograph fills the screen. Over it we hear MRS NEWTON'S voice:)

MRS NEWTON

I can remember the day it was taken just as though it were yesterday. You'd thrown a snowball, and hit the policeman, — what was his name?

UNCLE CHARLIE

(sharply)

No!

MRS NEWTON

You certainly did. And mama wouldn't speak to you the whole rest of the day, except when we had that appointment at the photographer's. Don't you remember, — mama cried all the way home!

4.7 — ch

(Camera returns to take in the room. UNCLE CHARLIE pushes the photograph back at her almost roughly)

## UNCLE CHARLIE

Doesn't do to look backward or forward, —that's my philosophy. Keep your eyes on the present moment, —that's all we can manage. Now you girls run away. I've got to dress and go downtown to the bank. Charlie's going to have lunch with me downtown, special treat.

## MRS NEWTON

Well, Charlie! Don't be late for the questionnaire-man. He's coming at four o'clock.

## The Dinner Table

~~Roger~~ remember that: don't ~~hum~~ that tune. And, mama,  74

don't you ~~at~~ ~~p~~ ~~on~~ the t~~ick~~. ~~You~~ ~~I~~ ~~it~~ ~~sit~~ ~~true~~  I se
a ~~way~~ ~~without~~ a single care on your mind.

### MRS NEWTON

If you say so, but I *like* to help.

      (She opens the door to the ~~dining~~ dining-room

Roger, dinner's almost ready. Have you washed your
hands? Charles! — Joe! — you can sit down at the
table, if you like.

      (~~Ann~~ Ann enters the kitchen)

### UNCLE CHARLIE'S VOICE

Where's our Charlie? Where's our Charlie, I've missed
her all day.

### MRS NEWTON

She'll be in ~~at~~ in a minute, Charles.

      (Ann has been pulling her skirt, trying
    to whisper something. Mrs Newton closes
    the kitchen door all ~~said~~)

### ANN

Mama.

### MRS NEWTON

What is it?

### ANN

Mama, I want to ask you something.

### MRS NEWTON

What ~~@~~ is it you want? I can't hear you. Don't whisper
what is it you want?

### ANN

I want to sit by you.

### MRS NEWTON

... What? Don't you like sitting by your Uncle

75

ANN

I want to sit by you.

YOUNG CHARLIE

Let her change with Roger, if she wants to

MRS NEWTON

Certainly not. Uncle Charles might think that......, certainly not.

YOUNG CHARLIE

Oh, mother, — let her change if she wants to.

MRS NEWTON

All right; but I don't like it

YOUNG CHARLIE

Go on in. Go on in.

(She practically pushes them through the
door. Then she stands listening at it, her
face concentrated in loathing.

Dissolve to the dinner-table.
They are finishing their soup.

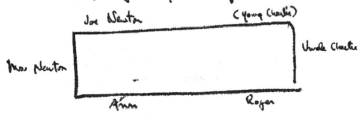

(Mrs. Newton is catching a quick view of the
first page of the newspaper.
UNCLE CHARLIE becomes aware of
the change of seating at his left.)

UNCLE CHARLIE

Hel — lo! What's this? Have I lost my little girl?

76

MRS NEWTON
(hastily)

I want them both to have a chance to sit by you, Charles

UNCLE CHARLES
(but with his eyes on Ann.)

Roger: Wait till you see your new present; sent for it yesterday. You'll open your eyes.

MRS NEWTON

Now, Charles, promise me, — not another thing.

🖐 MR NEWTON                                          7¹
(handing Uncle Charlie the paper)

Nothing special in the paper as far as I can see. Want a look, Charles?

MRS ANN ?

You can start taking up the plates, Ann, if you want to.

(The Kitchen. YOUNG CHARLIE prepares herself to enter the dining-room. She faces the door — almost nose to it — and takes a deep breath. Suddenly she turns, goes back to the other end of the kitchen, gropes in her handbag, and takes out a lipstick. She goes to a cracked hanging mirror and applies the stick, with a concentrated look on her face.)

(The Dining Room. Uncle Charlie has been glancing through the inner sides of the newspaper with increasing satisfaction. ~~Suddenly~~ he feels ~~YOUNG CHARLIE enter from kitchen~~ ~~following continues she~~ about ~~Taking up the empty soup plates.~~ ~~On the~~ fine.)

UNCLE CHARLIE

~~No, no, no. nothing special tonight. Nothing special.~~

77

(But he continues to glance through the back
pages.
YOUNG CHARLIE enters. During the
following speeches she moves about, taking
up the empty soup-plates. On her
entrance she receives an ovation)

UNCLE CHARLIE

There you are! Here's Charlie at last, folks.

ROGER

Hey!!

MR NEWTON

~~Yes poor poor fielded~~ Yes, here's our girl.

YOUNG CHARLIE
(drily
~~unsympathetically~~ deprecating the welcome.)

I live here.

MR NEWTON

Where you been, Charlie?

MRS NEWTON

She was asleep. She slept like a log all afternoon.

UNCLE CHARLIE
(with a wink)

Are you sure?                                    72

YOUNG CHARLIE
(boldly)

I've been dreaming about you, Uncle Charlie. Perfect
nightmares. — Mama, as the play to be in and out
all the time, you come up here and sit in my
place by Uncle Charlie.

MRS NEWTON

Charlie!

10

### YOUNG CHARLIE

We may not have him with us forever, so you get a good visit with him now.

(She stands holding out her chair for her mother. MRS NEWTON rises and comes to it).

### MRS NEWTON

(choked)

Why, Charlie, what a thing to say! I hope he stays with us a good long time.

### YOUNG CHARLIE

(smiling brightly at Uncle Charlie)

Well, we have to face the fact that we'll lose him some day or other, don't we?

(UNCLE CHARLIE, over his newspaper gets Tids and has been watching her musingly)

### UNCLE CHARLES

Yes, that's what I like, — people that look facts in the face.

### MRS NEWTON

(patting his hand, though he's still holding the newspaper)

Charlie didn't mean a thing by that, not a thing.

~~AnN~~

(~~announces the plate~~)

~~Should be read aloud table~~

### ~~UNCLE CHARLIE~~

~~Aunt, you're right. I'm forgetting all my manners. Thank you for the lesson, little lady.~~

78 – a

(ANN is standing beside him about to
take his soup-plate from under the folds
of his paper.)

UNCLE CHARLIE

Want to see the funnies, Ann? They're right here.

ANN

(removing his plate; lowered eyes)

We don't read at the Table.

UNCLE CHARLIE

Ann, you're right. I'm forgetting all my manners.
Thanks just for the lesson little Lady. Roger,
will you go and look at the back of the icebox and
bring me a big red bottle you see there?

(ROGER goes out.)

(73) 79

YOUNG CHARLIE

Anyway, now that father's finished with the paper, you can
do anything you like with it. We throw them
away, — or we just line bureau drawers with them.

(She goes out into the kitchen. Now
UNCLE CHARLIE is uneasy.

MRS NEWTON

Ann, go out and help Charlie bring in the vegetables.

UNCLE CHARLIE

How late was Charlie out last night, — gallivanting
about with that young journalist or whatever you
call 'em.

MRS NEWTON

She got back quite early. I was surprised. I went to
take a look at Ann and there was Charlie already
asleep by quarter of ten. She must have gone
up the back way.

UNCLE CHARLES

Did she see him today?

MRS NEWTON

No. He called twice, but I wouldn't disturb her.

UNCLE CHARLES

What do you think of him, Emma?

MRS NEWTON

Why I ? .... why-ah..... he seems to be a very
nice young man.

(UNCLE CHARLIE raises his eyes
suspiciously and clutches his
napkin in his fist.

74-A

(ROGER returns with a bottle of burgundy he places beside Uncle Charles.)

MRS NEWTON

Goodness! What's that Charles? Wine ?!!

UNCLE CHARLIE

St. Paul said: Take a little wine for thy stomach's sake.

MRS NEWTON

But, Charles, we never, never, — in fact, we've all taken the pledge. Ann took it just last week.

UNCLE CHARLES

(74)

This is sparkling what's called Sparkling Red Burgundy. It's weaker than the Worcester sauce you put on your steak, Emma. In hospitals they give it to invalids.

MR NEWTON

That's a fact, Emma, — its a tonic for anybody that's run down.

MRS NEWTON

But you can do what you think best, won't touch it.

UNCLE CHARLIE

Roger!

(He whispers a direction to him. Roger returns in a moment with four glasses.)
YOUNG CHARLIE enters with the roast, which she places before her father. She sits down in her place with lowered eyes.)

80

**MRS NEWTON**

Charles, the bank president's wife, Mrs ____, is president of our women's club. She called up this afternoon again. She wants to know the title of the speech you're going to make for us. She has to give it to the newspapers.

**UNCLE CHARLIE**

It's got to have a title, does it? Let's see. Shall we give 'em current events or a travel talk? —

**MRS NEWTON**

Oh, travel, Charles! We get current events every week.

**MR NEWTON**

(serving)

Fact is, Charles, Rotary and Kiwanis are fighting over you now. Mr. Green's Rotary, and he wants you for them; and the Kiwanis, and it looks like I've got to produce you for them.

**MRS NEWTON**

Do you make many speeches, Charles?

**UNCLE CHARLIE**

Oh, it's one of those things you can't get out of when you're in public life. Easier to do 'em than refuse 'em.

**MRS NEWTON**

Mrs Green says I'll have to introduce you at the lecture. I know I'll die of fright before I ever get on the platform.

(75)

**UNCLE CHARLIE**

Now, ____, listen to what I'm saying to you: when you've got some kind of text or ordeal ahead of you, — see? —

**MRS NEWTON**

Yes, Charles.

81

(UNCLE CHARLIE starts unwinding the
wire from the neck of the bottle.)

## UNCLE CHARLIE

First, prepare your speech or make your plan, — whatever it is,
thoroughly. Then don't think about it again. Nothing in the
world is difficult, if you just fix your will on it.
Do it!! — But don't let your imagination fool with it
beforehand, or afterwards.

(He now is rubbing the neck of the bottle
with a rotary motion and pulling at
cork.)

... No. Just take it for what it's worth. Realize that
it'll all be over in a few moments. Don't keep
turning it over in your mind. Soon it'll be
in the past, — and you'll be thinking of other
things. There! Like that!

(He pulls the cork. YOUNG CHARLIE has
been watching his hands with fascinated
horror. She shuts her eyes, but recovers
herself.)

## MRS NEWTON

Oh, Charles, you always did do things easily.

## UNCLE CHARLES

(pouring out the glasses.)

What kind of audience will it be?

## MRS NEWTON

Oh, we're middle-aged women, mostly. Pretty busy
with our homes, most of us.

## UNCLE CHARLIE

That's right. You're doing something.

(YOUNG CHARLIE abruptly drains half her
glass. UNCLE CHARLIE falls into brooding
thought for a moment, then continues from some
deep resentment)

In the cities it's a different matter. Thousands of middle-aged women
— their husbands spent forty and fifty years building up a fortune
... work, work, work. They die and leave their money to their wives

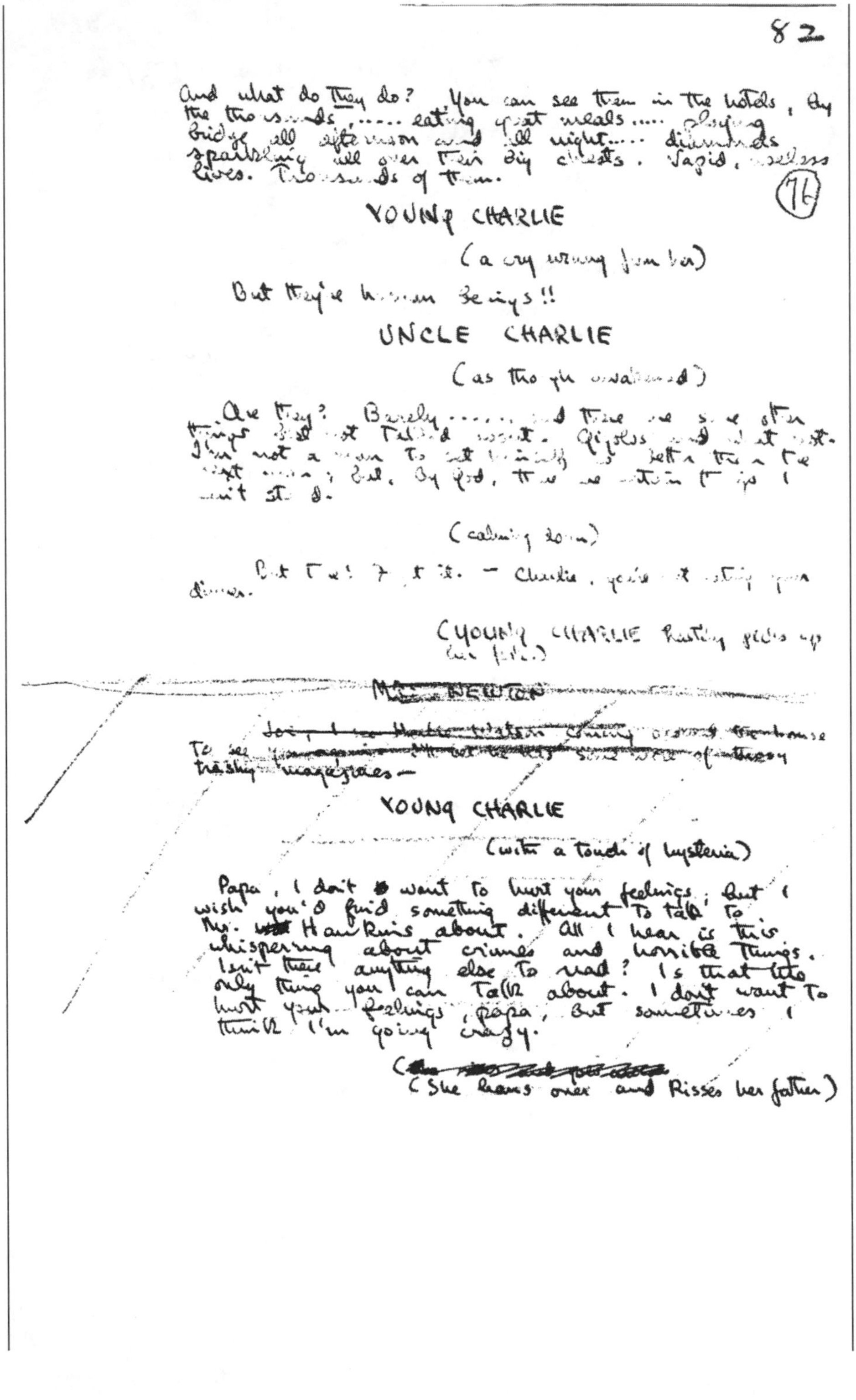

82

And what do They do? You can see them in the hotels, by the thousands,..... eating great meals..... playing bridge all afternoon and all night..... diamonds sparkling all over their big chests. Vapid, useless lives. Thousands of them. (76)

YOUNG CHARLIE

(a cry wrung from her)

But they're human beings!!

UNCLE CHARLIE

(as though he awakened)

Are they? Barely...... and there are some other things that not talked about. Gigolos and what not. I'm not a man to set himself up better than the next man, but, by God, there are certain things I can't stand.

(calming down)

But that's [illegible] it. — Charlie, you're not eating your dinner.

(YOUNG CHARLIE hastily picks up her fork.)

~~MR. NEWTON~~

~~Joe, I [illegible] Hattie Watson [illegible] around the house~~ To see ~~[illegible]~~ some one of ~~those~~ trashy magazines—

YOUNG CHARLIE

(with a touch of hysteria)

Papa, I don't ~~[illegible]~~ want to hurt your feelings, but I wish you'd find something different to talk to Mr. ~~[illegible]~~ Hawkins about. All I hear is this whispering about crimes and horrible things. Isn't there anything else to read? Is that the only thing you can talk about. I don't want to hurt your feelings, papa, but sometimes I think I'm going crazy.

(~~[illegible]~~

(She leans over and kisses her father)

**Family on a Train**

136

UNCLE CHARLIE *(on the platform by the list to e)*

MRS NEWTON

Be sure and write to us, Charles.

UNCLE CHARLIE

I certainly will. I'll send you my address and you write me.

MR NEWTON

Yes, don't forget to write.

UNCLE CHARLIE

Yes, write you often. And you write me, Joe. Goodbye.

EVERYBODY

Goodbye. Goodbye.

*(The compartment. The children dash in and out examining things. At the door, UNCLE CHARLIE is talking to the porter.)*

UNCLE CHARLIE.

Porter .... a large black brief case .... very important to me.... I swear I thought I saw it being carried into that next car. Go and look for it.

PORTER

Yes, sir.

*(He hurries off. The train whistle sounds.)*

ANN

Charlie, the train's starting. We gotta go.

ROGER

The train's starting.

UNCLE CHARLIE

Plenty of time. Run along; ~~Annie~~. ~~Street~~ we'll follow you.

(The children dash along the corridor and off. UNCLE CHARLIE at the door detains YOUNG CHARLIE)

Just a minute, Charlie. Plenty of time. Perhaps that brief case is here. Look under the couch.

YOUNG CHARLIE

Goodbye, I have to run.

UNCLE CHARLIE

(pointing to the upper ~~so~~ niches)

Isn't that it up there?

YOUNG CHARLIE

The train's going! Goodbye. Let me pass. Uncle. I'll have to jump over you.

(He is on his hands and feet blocking the way. He straightens himself.)

UNCLE CHARLIE

I'll come out to the platform with you.

YOUNG CHARLIE

Why, the train's going!!

(They reach the platform. The door has been closed. He opens it quickly. She stands on the steps, shrinking from the jump. UNCLE CHARLIE grasps her upper arm in a grip of iron. He murmurs soothingly:)

15

UNCLE CHARLIE

Wait...... just a little faster, just a little faster.

(YOUNG CHARLIE turns blazingly on him.)

~~YOUNG CHARLIE~~ YOUNG CHARLIE

You won't! You won't!

(They start to struggle.)

(CUT TO JACK and SAUNDERS passing without hurry along the compartments of a car.)

JACK

Still in the Town.

(Cut to UNCLE CHARLIE ~~and~~ and YOUNG CHARLIE in a furious struggle.) YOUNG CHARLIE, with a powerful hold on the iron rail, twists her body and by crouching pulls herself up to the platform.

AS JACK appears on the platform he is in time to see YOUNG CHARLIE give her uncle a tremendous push.

YOUNG CHARLIE

You won't!

(UNCLE CHARLIE weakens. She gives him a second push, just as the oncoming train is about to pass the open door. UNCLE CHARLIE's hold is broken and he falls.) DISSOLVE in a crash of noise and lights.

DISSOLVE To an impressive funeral procession passing through the square of the town. The hearse; a score of automobiles. Solemnized crowds line the streets.

# HITCHCOCK'S NOTEBOOKS

126

139

(Quick glimpses into the automobiles moving the mourners. In the first limousine MR NEWTON mutely presses his wife's hand, as she weeps into a black-edged handkerchief. Beyond her, YOUNG CHARLIE looks resolutely out of the window. The two children are sitting sideways on the adjustable seats, darting their heads out of the window to count the automobiles in the procession.)

**ANN**

Twelve.

**ROGER**

Eleven.

**ANN**

There's twelve.

**ROGER**

That last one don't belong to us. It's just somebody driving in the street.

**ANN**

Yes, it does too belong to us. It's ~~HERBIE~~ Herbie Hawkins; and he _likes_ funerals, too.

**MR NEWTON**

Children, if you can't sit quiet you can go home.

(Glimpse of JACK with the GREENES)

**MR GREENE**

No, we don't grow much alfalfa around here. That's grown farther south.

**MRS GREEN**

(fumbling a ~~black-edged~~ handkerchief)

Oh, my father grew miles of alfalfa.

**JACK**

You don't say.

140

(Cut to the last car. HERBIE driving his own. With a sedate lift of an eyebrow he acknowledges the greetings of an acquaintance on the sidewalks.)

121

The church door. People going in. MR and MRS NEWTON with ANN and ROGER close behind them. YOUNG CHARLIE pauses with one foot on the stair. JACK catches up with her. Without exchange of signals she turns from the door and starts toward the street at the side of the church.

The side-walk under the church windows. Both sides of the street are lined with cars. Organ music is coming from the church.

YOUNG CHARLIE and JACK are moving very slowly. They come to a stop.

YOUNG CHARLIE

I did know more than I could tell you.... will you ever forgive me?

JACK

Yes. oh. yes.

(He kicks some gravel in the path, thoughtfully. The minister's voice comes through the windows.)

DR MacCurdy.

Santa Rosa has gained and lost a son, — a son that she can be proud of. brave, generous, —

(His voice fades out)

141

YOUNG CHARLIE

Jack, he said that the whole world was just one big heap
of lies and evil; and that people like us —

(a movement of the head indicates the
congregation in the church)

have no idea what the world's really like. "You'd know. Is it as bad as that."

JACK

(turning and looking in her face)

No, of course not.

(taking her hand)

But it takes a lot of watching. It's not necessary that
they know about whatever bad there is. We'll watch it.

(They move on, slowly, hands clasped
(The organ in the church swells)

END OF THE PLAY

The film has only the slightest variations on what's excerpted here. The ending is in essence the same, although the children's dialogue has been eliminated. Hitchcock's pleasure with *Shadow of a Doubt* may spring from how close the final film matched his and Wilder's original realization.

## Lifeboat

From the felicitous to the nightmarish. Hitchcock's last full-fledged war movie (*Notorious* takes place after the war) was *Lifeboat*, made for 20th Century-Fox in 1944. Hitchcock tried turning to another American original for the story, but lightning did not strike twice. John Steinbeck wrote the first treatment of the film in the form of a novella, one which has never been published, but Hitchcock considered it unusable. Steinbeck then wrote a scenario with Harry Sylvester that was published in the November 13, 1943, issue of *Collier's*. Jo Swerling wrote the screenplay based on this short story. The initial draft of the screenplay was finished in August 1943.

The film has dated perhaps more than any other Hitchcock film. The performances are stylized and the rather overt themes weigh down what there is of a plot. Of interest in the development of the screenplay is the interaction between Hitchcock and Darryl F. Zanuck (head of 20th Century-Fox). Zanuck's initial response on the screenplay:

Twentieth Century-Fox Film Corporation

STUDIOS
BEVERLY HILLS, CALIFORNIA

INTER-OFFICE CORRESPONDENCE ONLY

DATE___AUGUST 19,_____ 19 43

TO  MR. KENNETH MACGOWAN                FROM_____DARRYL ZANUCK_____
MR. ALFRED HITCHCOCK
MR. JO SWERLING    SUBJECT _____LIFEBOAT_____
CC:  Molly Mandaville

When I read the script through again last night, and tried to analyze its length, I became very worried. I have had the script read today and timed with a stopwatch. We did not make any allowances for business and we put the storm sequence in for three minutes.

The result confirmed my convictions about the length of the script. We have 13,000 feet of dialogue. It is my opinion that the finished picture will be 15,000 feet.

There is no question but what this would be fatal for this type of a picture. In my opinion, the story can hold for no more than a total of 10,000 feet at the very outside.

This means that drastic eliminations are necessary, and you are not going to get your eliminations by cutting out a few lines here and there in each sequence. You are going to have to be prepared to drop some element in its entirety.

I am going to try to make some suggestions in the latter half of the story. The long, drawn-out card game which goes on for pages; the talk about the baseball game, and all of these things can help the length, but I still feel that we have got to be prepared to drop an entire episode.

I now regret that we have Mrs. Higgins and the baby in the picture at all.

The quicker you get to the discovery of the compass and the ensuing storm, the better off we are, purely from the standpoint of audience interest. I got impatient from listening to long, drawn-out arguments in German. When they find the compass watch, they are idiots if they don't pounce upon him, instead of talking. This is concrete evidence that even a child could understand.

There is a long, rather monotonous stretch, previous to the point where the German kills Gus. It seems to me that he is the strong man over too long a period of time.

I have not yet studied in detail the last third of the script.

I still think we are making an error in retaining the sequence where they tie up Mrs. Higgins, and I'll be willing to bet $1000, to go to any charity, that it is not in the picture after the first preview.

D. F. Z.

He fired off another, longer memo the next day:

Twentieth Century-Fox Film Corporation

BEVERLY HILLS, CALIFORNIA

INTER-OFFICE CORRESPONDENCE ONLY

DATE_____ AUGUST 20, ____19 43

TO MR. ALFRED HITCHCOCK          FROM_____ DARRYL ZANUCK
CC: MR. KENNETH MACGOWAN
                    SUBJECT _____ LIFEBOAT _____

My dear Hitchcock:

The timing of the script was not done by an expert, nor by anyone who was deliberately attempting to mislead us. One person merely read the dialogue aloud,
while the other person took down the timing with a stop-watch. Now, of course,
they did not overlap any dialogue, and they might have read slowly, or they
might have paused too long between speeches, and, of course, they are not aware
of any of the cuts in dialogue or script pages that we have recently eliminated.

According to your calculation, the script will run to 7,500 feet. I will bet
you $1,000, the winner to donate the amount to charity, that you are wrong by
2,000 feet. I am now speaking about the script as it stands, and I believe I
am allowing myself plenty of footage for protection.

A picture of this scope, in my opinion, should hold up very well at 9,000 feet,
and perhaps even longer, but if we actually are over 10,000 feet, then I know
that you agree the matter is serious, not only from the standpoint of economy.

You are making excellent progress, and certainly no one could complain about
the amount of film you have exposed in the last few days.

It still remains my opinion, however, that our story is repetitious in places,
and monotonous. I am certain that the cuts we have made in the last few days
have not harmed the quality of the production one iota. As a matter of fact,
I feel that they have been helpful. If we can continue to do this throughout
the balance of the story, and not kid ourselves, I believe we can improve the
piece generally, and save you a great deal of extra work on the set, as well as
money. Under ordinary circumstances, I would be perfectly willing to go right
ahead and shoot the entire script, and then worry about the editing in the cutting
room, but you are up against such a terrible mechanical handicap, that I feel
that we should make every effort to keep everything in the picture that we are
going to shoot.

I do not make a habit of interfering with productions placed in such capable
hands as yours. Any interference in this case comes from an emergency problem,
which I inherited. On all sides, I have been advised to call off the production.
The picture was devised originally, so I understand, to be a million dollar cost
project. Suddenly its cost has doubled, and no one could possibly dislike the
idea of butting in any more than I do. I have plenty of worries on my own personal productions, and nothing would give me greater joy than to forget all
about LIFEBOAT until the night I go to the preview.

You felt you could make the picture in eight or nine weeks. You told me so.
Lefty Hough thought that you could. He told me so, and so did Macgowan. We took
into consideration this fact, and arrived at a fair budget. We were all wrong.
It would be folly now, in my opinion, to butcher the story in an effort to save
a penny here and there, but it is also folly to fail to study each scene, each
line and each episode, and see if we cannot find ways and means to eliminate non-
essentials.

                              Darryl

Hitchcock seemed to be running out of patience with Zanuck. He deflected criticism at "some menial," but this was very thinly veiled.

[8-20-43]

**Twentieth Century-Fox Film Corporation**

STUDIOS
BEVERLY HILLS, CALIFORNIA

August 30, 1943

INTER-OFFICE CORRESPONDENCE ONLY

TO   COL. DARRYL F. ZANUCK                         DATE _____ 19 ___

FROM   ALFRED HITCHCOCK

SUBJECT   LIFEBOAT

Dear Mr. Zanuck:

I have just received your note regarding the length of LIFEBOAT. I don't know who you employ to time your scripts, but whoever ~~had done~~ it is misleading you horribly. I will even go so far as to say disgracefully. In all my experience in this business, I have never encountered such stupid information as has been given you by some menial who apparently has no knowledge of the timing of a script or the playing of dialogue.

According to the note, in paragraph two you express your opinion, based upon this ridiculous information, that the picture will be 15,000 feet in length. I can only think that the person who did this for you is trying to sabotage the picture. Maybe it is a spy belonging to some disgruntled ex-employe.

Now let us get down to facts, and let us base our calculations on facts that come from persons of long experience and also the fact of actual shooting time. Through Page 28 of the script, which includes a fair amount of silent action, the shot footage is actually timed at 15 minutes. This, on the basis of a 147-page script, works out to actually 79 minutes. Add to this a maximum of 5 minutes, (which is generous for the storm sequence), we arrive at an extremely generous estimate of 84 minutes. Films run through at 90 feet a minute. Therefore, we arrive at a length of 7560 feet, which, in my opinion, is considerably inadequate for a picture of this calibre and importance.

I am gravely concerned at the suggestion of cutting the story for fear that after the shooting is completed we will find that the picture is so short that we will have to commence writing added sequences to make the picture sufficiently long for an important release.

In view of our previous discussions regarding the shooting time, I would like to repeat that we are all considerably misled by the cumbersome methods of shooting on an exterior stage which could never be repeated under normal conditions in the studio. As I pointed out to you in our previous conversation, I am at present shooting a sequence of 9 pages which will take approximately 2 days - which is exactly one day under the allotted time in the production schedule.

Dear Mr. Zanuck, please take good note of these above facts before we commit ourselves to any acts which in the ultimate may make us all look extremely ridiculous by giving insufficient care and notice to these considerations.

Your obedient servant,

ALFRED HITCHCOCK

In the quicksilver world of Hollywood, hard feelings evaporate with good work. It is customary to cut together a rough of the film during production. *Lifeboat* was unique in that it was filmed in sequence, so that a good sense of how the film was being shaped could be determined early in the process. Zanuck's first look brought this response:

---

### Twentieth Century-Fox Film Corporation

STUDIOS
BEVERLY HILLS, CALIFORNIA

INTER-OFFICE CORRESPONDENCE ONLY            DATE____September 4,_____19 43

TO _MR. ALFRED HITCHCOCK_____    FROM____DARRYL ZANUCK_____

SUBJECT _____

DEAR HITCH:

I saw the first reel of the picture and I am enthusiastic about it. It has tempo, interest, and a feeling of being very much on the level. The characterizations are perfect.

My criticisms are minor. The cutting of the camera business looks clumsy. I think it would be much smoother without using the insert of the camera falling in the water. It now looks as if we couldn't get it to fall, and we had to result to an insert.

I think we need one line for Mary Anderson where she says, "It's a baby." This can be cut in when her back is to the camera as they reach to get the baby out of the water. I strongly felt the need of it.

I have always wondered about the line, "Dankeschoen." It is a wonderful kick for me, but I wish he would have said it twice so that there could be no doubt in the mind of the audience that they have pulled a Nazi aboard. If this punch is lost on half of the audience it will be regrettable because it is a wonderful curtain for the first act.

D.F.Z.

---

At this point, it should be apparent the writing of a screenplay is often far from linear and seldom ends when filming begins.

I consider *Notorious* and *Shadow of a Doubt* Hitchcock's finest films from the forties. The development of Ben Hecht's screenplay for *Notorious* is available in an extensive laserdisc set available from Criterion. Developed from a magazine story, *Notorious* followed much the same process. Hecht wrote Hitchcock's *Spellbound* prior to this and the two seemed to work well together.

After the war, Hitchcock began to move out on his own. His next project would conclude his obligations to Selznick.

## The Paradine Case

*The Paradine Case* is an often underrated Hitchcock film. It is a courtroom drama where the lawyer fails on such a spectacular level that he is destroyed professionally and personally. The film is similar in effect to *Vertigo,* which also received a rather mixed reception. *The Paradine Case* is daring for its time and may perhaps find an audience. The gist of the film's plot can be gathered from the following draft comparison. I include this rather lengthy comparison as evidence of Hitchcock's own writing ability (one he never took credit for) and his ability to set ego aside and chart a course on what was best for the film's narrative. In that single sense, Hitchcock was perhaps the only auteur willing to not do it only his way. I can recall numerous times in the recorded meetings between Ernest Lehman and Hitchcock where he gladly threw away an idea that he loved in service of the film. Finally, I include this draft comparison as a full demonstration of the constant interaction between the director, his wife, and the assigned writer during the creation of the screenplay.

THE PARADINE CASE

   Comparison of

Book by Robert Hichens
Hitchcock draft -  No.1. Script.
Bridie treatment- No.2. Script.
Reville adaptation-No.3. Script.

 

Compiled by
Muriel Elwood
September 5m 1946.

| HICHENS BOOK | NO.1. Script (Hitchcock) | No. 2. Script (Bridie) | No.3. Script (Reville) |
|---|---|---|---|
| | | G.Is looking over Law Courts. | omitted |
| | Paradine Home - Mrs. Paradine arrested. | Same Portrait added | same Portrait added. |
| | Mrs. P. charged at Bow Street - asks Flaquer, solicitor to engage Keane for defense | Same | Same |
| Keane virile, dignified, emotional. | Same as book | Keane - selfmade, inferior to wife, not sure of self, highly emotional Irishman | Same as 2. |
| Theatre Flaquer, Keane, and wife, Gay. | Theatre Flaquer, Keane, Gay and Judy, Flaquer daughter | Theatre Same | Theatre Same |
| Lord and Lady Horfield in box Horfield talks Gay interval | omitted | omitted | omitted |
| Flaquer & Keane interval asks Keane to take Paradine case. | same | same | same |
| Keane does not know Mrs. P. | same as book | Keane knew Col. Paradine. Mrs. P. reminds Flaquer of Gay Mrs. P. unsavory past | omitted same as 2 same as 2 |

2.

| Book | No.1 Script | No.2.Script | No.3. Script. |
|------|-------------|-------------|---------------|
| | Keanes home after theatre: | Keanes home after theatre: | Keanes home after theatre: |
| | Their devotion shown. Dog, Sausage | same | same |
| | Gay has never seen Mrs. P. | Gay knew Col. P. Seen but not met Mrs. P. | Same as 2. |
| Theme of No.1 script comes in later - no mention of case on way home | Keane never discusses cases with Gay. She has never been in court. | Keane does discuss cases with Gay. She has never been in court. | Same as 2. |
| | | Keanes son at Eton. | Same as 2. |
| Ethics of defending guilty party (later p.30) | Same as book | Same content | Same content |
| Strindberg mentioned by Horfield (p26-27) Also discussed with Gay.(p31) | Mrs. P. compared to Strindberg type of woman. | omitted | omitted |
| Flaquer-Keane discuss case: | Flaquer-Keane discuss case: | Flaquer-Keane discuss case: | Flaquer-Keane discuss case: |
| Mrs. P. mother Swedish; Mrs.P worked barber shop Copenhagen; mixed up with gang; servant to American diplomat who brought her to America. | Same as book. | Mrs. P. father Swedish; mother cabaret dancer; worked barber shop; mixed gang; adopted by Chicago businessman who took her America and sent her to college | Same as 2. |
| Col.P. blinded war hero; Mrs.P accused poisoning him. | Same | Same | Same |
| Gays's dislike p.5 & 7 - "lot of vinegar in his blood." | Horfield mentioned as Judge. Gay thinks him "nasty old man" | Same Gay -"he gives her the creeps; thinks him bit mad". | Same<br>Same |

3.

| Book | No.1.Script | No. 2.Script. | No.3. Script. |
|---|---|---|---|
| Keane buys photo-graph of Mrs. P. | omitted | omitted | omitted |
| Holloway Prison | Holloway Prison | Holloway Prison | Holloway Prison. |
| Keane meets Mrs. P. - impressed | same | same | same |
| Mrs. P. mentions past being against her - once a ser-vant - "came from mud, must be muddy" | same | same - but "came from gutter" | same as 2. |
| Coached re state-ment "had to be his eyes". | same | same | same |
| | | Assizes Court Sequence added here. | |
| | Horfield criti-cism of Keane's emotionalism comes next seq-uence. | Horfield-Keane. Horfield criti-cizes Keane's emotionalism. | Same as 2. |
| Horfields dine at Keanes: | Same as book. | Reversed- Keanes dine at Horfields | Same as 2. |
| Guests- Lady Flaquer, Judy, Mrs. Geo.Blason Martin Latrobe, Arthur Lieber-stein,- and Horfields. | Guests -Flaquer, Judy and Horfields. | Keanes only guests. | Same as 2. |
| Lady H. pitiable, highly nervous, devoted but afraid of hus-band. | Same | Same | Same |
| Lady H. discusses husband with Keane - her dread when he condemns intimates sadism. | Same as book. | Lord Horfield changed to "Sir Thomas" - Lady H. intimates husband's sadism to Gay | same as 2. same as 2. |

4.

| Book | No.1 Script | No.2 Script | No.3. Script. |
|------|-------------|-------------|---------------|
| | Gay uncomfortable under Horfields lecherous glances. | Horfield lechery shown - Gay gets angry with him. | Same as 2. |
| Keane studies photograph of Mrs. P. before going to bed. | omitted | Keane and Gay study picture of Mrs. P. in "Tatler" | Same as 2. |
| | **Holloway Prison.** | **Holloway Prison** | **Holloway Prison** |
| Mentioned different place - (p.45;also p.92) | Keane mentions Mrs. P. likeness to wife. | Same | Same |
| Mentioned in first interview Keane and Mrs.P. p.37 and p.92 | Mrs. P. emphasizes feeling as servant | Mrs. P. mentions English caste system and her lack in this respect. | Same as 2. |
| same p.93 | Keane emotional - says will save her. | Same | Same |
| **Bow St. Hearing.** | **Bow St. Hearing.** | **Bow St. Hearing** | **Bow St. Hearing.** |
| Hatred of Col's valet, Wm.Marsh for Mrs. P. | Flaquer and Keane discuss Marsh's hatred for Mrs.P. | Same | Same |
| Keane wonders whether Marsh murderer and first thinks of /assisted suicide defense." | Keane mentions these two points to Flaquer. | Same | Same |
| **Flaquer Apt.** | **Flaquer Apt.** | **Swimming Club.** | |
| Gay-Judy; Gay nervous and upset over Paradine case. Discusses her feelings with Judy. Begins to smoke cigarettes. | Same as book. | Same content - different setting and dialogue | omitted. |

5.

| Book | No.1. Script | No.2. Script | No.3. Script. |
| --- | --- | --- | --- |
| Baron Sedelsward, Swedish painter introduced at tea party at Flaquers. Invites Keanes to his art show. Keane accepts when learns Baron had known Mrs. P. in Copenhagen. Invites Baron to dine at Club. Baron defends Mrs.P. character. | | omitted in all scripts. | |
| Flaquer and Judy discuss difficultoes of case is causing between Keane and Gay. Flaquer wishes he hadnt briefed Keane. Flaquer mentions Keane's "assisted suicide" defense; collusion between Mrs. P. and Marsh. Realize Keane in love with Mrs. B. | Same as book. | Same content. | Same content. |
| Gay goes alone to church - she very unhappy. | Same as book. | Same - but no indication yet of rift. | Same as 2. |
| This incident comes later at Flaquers party. | Lady H. calls on Keane; begs him to get Mrs.P. off. so that husband cannot indulge his sadism. | Same content | Same content. |
| Holloway Prison | Holloway Prison | Holloway Prison | Holloway Prison |
| Keane says he believes Marsh murdered Paradine. Mrs. P. defends Marsh. Flare up between Keane and Mrs.P. Keane tries to find out what was between Marsh and Mrs. P. -unsuccessful. | Same wording as book. | Same content dialogue differs. | Same as 2. |

6.

| Book | No.1. Script | No.2 Script | No.3. Script. |
|------|--------------|-------------|---------------|
| Keane reports his interview with Mrs. P. to Flaquer and tells him she has practically agreed to line of "assisted suicide" defense. | Same as book. | Dialogue differs. | Same as 2. |
| Keane joins reception at Flaquers; guests include Horfields; at this time Lady Horfield pleads with Keane to get Mrs. P. off. (in scripts comes in when Lady H. visits Keane at home) | omitted | omitted | omitted |
| Keane and Flaquer continue discussion same evening; Keane flares up when Flaquer calls Mrs. P. "Infernally clever". Flaquer disapproves Keanes "assisted suicide" defense They nearly quarrel. Keane refuses to retire from case. | Taken from book. but continues on without interruption of reception. | Content same - dialogue different. | same as 2. |
| Flaquer sends Keane letter placating him and agreeing to line of defense but not to direct attack on Marsh. | omitted from all scripts. | | |
| Holloway Prison | Holloway Prison | Holloway Prison | Holloway Prison. |
| Mrs.P. alarmed over suggestion Keane will give up case. | Taken from book dialogue same. | Same content different dialogue | Same as 2. |

7

| Book | No.1. Script | No.2. Script | No.3. Script. |
|---|---|---|---|
| Keane suggests not putting her on stand at trial. She does not agree. She states that after herself she relies on Keane. He is hurt; gets angry and emotional. | Taken from book - dialogue same. | Same content - dialggue different. | Same as 2. |
| She agrees to "assisted suicide" defense as long as Marsh not made to appear murderer. | | | |
| Keane tells Gay he is going to visit Hindley Hall - Mrs. P's home. | same as book. | Content same - locale changed to Scotland. dialogue different - Keane and Gay more friendly. | Same as 2 - except changed back to original locale. |
| Here Keane meets Lady H. at art gallery and she tells him more of husband's sadism. Lord H. appears and she is in panic. | omitted from all scripts. | | |
| Keane takes Gay to theatre - rift widens. | omitted from all scripts. | | |
| Gay has talk with Keane. Asks to go north with him; says his work becoming "separating monster" between them; he refuses to take her on trip. | Taken from book - dialogue same. | Content similar - dialgue different- more understanding between Keanes less rift. | Same as 2. |
| Keane gets angry over Judy putting ideas into Gay's head. | Same | Similar | Same as 2. |

8.

| Book | No.1.Script | No.2.Script. | No.3. Script. |
|---|---|---|---|
| Keane visits Mrs. P. home. Gossips with landlady at inn. Goes to see Hindley Hall. Marsh admits him and then disappears. Keane sees Marsh from window; asks him to show garden; Marsh agrees, then disappears. | Taken from book; dialogue same. | Content approx. same - dialogue differs - locale changed. | Same as 2 - locale same as book. |
| Marsh calls to see Keane at Inn; sure Keanes visit to see him; calls Mrs. P. "woman of Babylon". Keane worried over interview. | Taken from book - dialogue same. | Content same - dialogue different. Keane more uncontrolled and less dignified. Marsh says Mrs.P. "bad to the bone" Leaving he remarks "I know what's the matter with you and God help you." | Same as 2. |
| Return to London | Return to London. | Return to London | Return to London |
| Keane talks with man in dining car about Paradine case, now common gossip. Man refers to Marsh as "woman hater". | | omitted from scripts. | |
| This scene comes later in book: | From train Keane goes direct to Holloway Prison. | From train Keane goes direct to Holloway Prison | From train Keane goes direct to Holloway Prison |
| Keane tells Mrs. P. has seen house because "you drew me there." Very emotional. | Taken from book; dialogue same. | Scene omitted | Scene omitted. |
| Tries to find out why Marsh hates her so. Suggests she and Marsh have been lovers. | Taken from book dialogue same. | Content same, differently worded | Same as 2. |

9.

| Book | No.1. Script. | No.2. Script. | No.3. Script. |
| --- | --- | --- | --- |
| Keane receives letter from Flaquer about Horfield warning him "not to get his back up" as Horfield in rather extraordinary mood lately. He finds out Horfield's mood due Gay having gone to theatre with him (Lady Ho. ill) and Horfield having made unpleasant advances to her. Keane does not wait to hear why she was annoyed with Horfield. | Letter omitted in all scripts. Scene with Gay follows after Keane's return from Holloway Prison.  Gay having gone to theatre with Horfield same as book. | Gay tells Keane about Horfield but with less restraint and he is more sympathetic; rift widens but less so. | Same as 2. |
| Keane goes to see Flaquer who confirms that Horfields mood is due to woman but does not mention Gay. | omitted from all scripts. | | |
| Keane meets Horfield at Club and speaks lightly of incident at theatre with Gay; makes up to Horfield because of Mrs. P. Invites him to theatre. | omitted from all scripts. | | |
| Gay is hurt over husband's attitude re Horfield. Tells Keane never wants Horfield in house again and that she has good reasons. Keane will not listen. Gay hates Mrs. P. | This scene is omitted from scripts but indicated at beginning with scene between Gay and Horfield at dinner party. | | |
| Keane insists upon theatre party. He drives Lady H. and leaves Gay with Lord H. He is extremely obnoxious and she tells him "I shall keep dirty people out of my life." | omitted from all scripts. | | |

| Book | No.1. Script | No.2. Script | No.3. Script. |
|------|--------------|--------------|---------------|
| After theatre Gay tells husband what happened in car and says she will never see H. again and will go to country to avoid complications with H. until trial is over. | omitted from all scripts. | | |
| Gay goes to country house. Judy comes to see her. Says she should not leave Keane alone during trial. Gay eager to see trial but afraid. Judy arranges so they can go secretly. | omitted from all scripts. | | |

### FIRST DAY OF TRIAL

### No.1. Court Old Bailey.

Camera pans to show different views of Court.

| Book | No.1. Script | No.2. Script | No.3. Script. |
|------|--------------|--------------|---------------|
| Gay goes with Judy to trial and sits in gallery. | Same | Same | Same |
| Sir Joseph Farrell, Counsel for Crown summing up case. | Same | Same | Same |
| Keane examines Lakin butler re glass of burgundy in which poison placed and as to habits of Colonel. | Same | Same | Same |
| Keane returns home to find Gay there. She does not reveal has been to trial. Tenseness between them. | Same | Same | Same |

Flashes to homes of Flaquers, Horfields and Mrs. Paradine in cell.

| Book | No.1. Script | No.2. Script | No.3. Script. |
|------|-------------|--------------|---------------|

SECOND DAY OF TRIAL.

| Book | No.1. Script | No.2. Script | No.3. Script. |
|------|-------------|--------------|---------------|
| Farrell examines Marsh re cause of quarrel on night of murder. Marsh insists cause was that Mrs. P. had told Col. he was leaving his service. | Same | Same | Same |
| | | Farrell introduces plan of London house and has Marsh mark it for positions on night of murder. Plan shown to jury. | Plan introduced but more briefly. |
| The fact is brought in here - but omitted in all scripts - that after quarrel Mrs. P. played "Blue Danube". This ties up with earlier statement of Arthur Lieberstein (p.63) that the "Blue Danube" always upset Colonel. Introduced to show Mrs. P. callousness in playing this when husband upset over quarrel. | | | |
| Keane examines Marsh. Brings in his having been jilted by woman. | Taken from book - dialogue same. | Same content | Same content. |
| Frequent altercations between Keane and Morfield. | same | Same | Same |
| | | Keane reviews Marsh's war record to bring out that Marsh "holds lives pretty cheaply" | Omitted. |

12

| Book | No.1. Script | No.2. Script | No.3. Script. |
|------|--------------|--------------|---------------|
| Keane badgers Marsh as to whether Col. did not frequently say he wished he were dead. | | | |
| Accuses Marsh of having lied about quarrel. Indicates familiarity between Marsh and Mrs. P. Marsh much shaken. | | | |
| Outlines events of night of murder. Col. dining alone; asks for glass of brandy to be left in his room; Marsh's going up to Col. room for reconciliation; Col sends him away. Sees Mrs. P. on landing. Marsh insists he did not go into Col. bedroom while Col. in bathroom. | All Taken from books Dialogue same. | Same content. | Same content. |
| Keane produces plan of landing and has Marsh mark it for positions. | | | |
| Keane allows jealousy of Marsh to get better of him and throws out "assisted suicide" defense and indicates Marsh murdered Colonel. | | | |
| | | Introduction of incident where Marsh procured poison to put away Col's spaniel. | Same as 2. |

| Book | No.1. Script | No.2. SCript. | No.3. Script. |
|---|---|---|---|
| Flaquer much disturbed over Keane changed line of defense. | Taken from book. Dialogue same | Content same Different wording | Same as 2. |
| Keane suggests scrapping all witnesses except Mrs. P. so that he can have last word with jury. | Taken from book. Dialogue same. | omitted | omitted. |
| Keane sees Mrs.P. before she leaves. He is pleased with way things are going; she stony-faced. | Taken from book. Dialogue same. | Content same. | Content same. |
| Keane leaves note for Gay not dining home - has to go to Holloway. | Omitted | Omitted | Omitted. |
| Holloway Prison | Holloway Prison | Holloway Prison | Holloway Prison |
| Mrs. P. angry with Keane because he has incriminated Marsh. | Taken from book. Dialogue same. | Content same. Dialogue diff. | Content same. Dialogue diff. |
| She refers to Marsh as Will - this angers Keane. | ditto | ditto | ditto |
| He declares his love for her. She ignores it. | ditto | ditto | ditto. |
|  |  | Mrs. P. accuses Keane of wanting Marsh out of way so that he can have her for himself. | Same as 2. |
| Mrs. P. admits love for Marsh and that they were lovers. | Same | Same | Same |

| Book | No.1. Script | No.2. Script. | No.3. Script. |
|---|---|---|---|
| Omitted | omitted. | Mrs. P. denies having killed husband. | Same as 2. |
| Keane tells her intends to scrap all witnesses. | same | same | same |
| Mrs. P. insists that Keane must not save her at Marsh's expense. Says"If you do I shall hate you as I have never hated a man". | Taken from book. Dialogue same | Same - but says: "Shall hate you from depths of my soul". | Same as 2. |
| | | <u>New scene.</u><br><br>Farrell and his Junior crossing street. Farrell nearly run over. Argue advisability bringing in Keane visit to Mrs. P's home up north. | Same as 2. |

THIRD DAY OF TRIAL

| | | | |
|---|---|---|---|
| <u>Keane examines Mrs. Paradine.</u> | <u>Keane examines Mrs. Paradine</u> | <u>Keane examines Mrs. Paradine</u> | <u>Keane examines Mrs. Paradine.</u> |
| | | New note: Mrs. P. had met husband while nurse during war. | Same as 2. |
| She never saw husband before blinded in war. | Same | Same | Same |
| She testifies husband being very miserable over blindness and sometimes unkind to her. | Taken from book Dialogue same | Same | Same |

15

| Book | No.1. Script | No.2. Script | NO.3. Script. |
|---|---|---|---|
| Keane forces Mrs. P. to admit that Marsh attempted to make love to her. | Taken from book. Dialogue same. | Same but with addition she says Marsh "one night climbed roof of porch and tried to get into window." | Same as 2. |
| States Marsh denied to Col. he had been familiar with her and defended himself. | ditto. | States that Marsh admitted he had been familiar and asked forgiveness. | Same as 2. |
| Keane appears to be cross-examining own witness. | ditto | Same | Same |
| Repeated altercations between Horfiled and Keane. | ditto. | Same | Same |
| Marsh shouts that Mrs. P. is lying. Removed from Court. | ditto. | Same | Same. |
| Keane continues examination after interruption - checks details of Col.'s death; her behavior on night of murder; her playing of "Blue Danube" | In this script Keane ceases examination after interruption and Farrell take it up. | Keane continues examination  Approx. same as Script No.1. variations in dialogue.  Mention of Mrs.P. having own annuity apart from husband's will. | Keane continues examination.  Same - but details of night of murder omitted.  Same as 2. |
| Farrell follows Keane: | Farrell follows Marsh interraption: | Farrell follows Keane: | Same as 2. |
| Farrell request Judge to allow Marsh to be brought back for question. Left to Horfield to decide. | This comes in script after Farrell's examination. | Omitted | Omitted. |

15

| Book | No.1.Script | No.2.Script | No.3.Script. |
|---|---|---|---|
| Farrell asks Mrs.P. if Marsh was a woman-hater. | | Omitted from scripts. | |
| Ask Mrs. P. if she thinks Marsh good-looking. She says never has noticed. | Taken from book - dialogue same. | Omitted | Omitted |
| Keane objects frequently - re-buffed by Hor-field. | Same | Same | Same |
| Farrell refers to Mrs. P. having been servant. | Same as book | Omitted | Omitted |
| Accuses her of being "madly in love" with Marsh and having set herself to make him love her. | Taken from book | Same content different wording. | Same as 2. |
| She becomes hysterical | ditto | Same | Same |
| Farrell reviews events of fatal night - refers to her playing waltz. | Omitted | Omitted | Omitted |
| Farrell's exam-ination ends. | Same as book | Brings in her past and refers to her as "gansters moll" | Same as 2. |
| | | Mrs. P. causes sen-sation by stating she does not agree with her own lawyer who "has been trying to make people think William Marsh killed my husband." | Same as 2 |
| | | She now states she washed wine glass - having previously denied this in exam-ination by Keane. States did so because thought Marsh might have put something in glass (cont) | Same as 2 |

| Book | No.1. Script | No.2. Script | No.3. Script. |
|------|-------------|--------------|---------------|
| | | Mrs. P. admits to Judge that her statement to Keane re wineglass was untrue. | Same as 2. |
| **Luncheon adjournment** | **Luncheon adjournment** | **Luncheon adjournment** | **Luncheon adjournment** |
| Keane very disturbed. Hurries out after few hasty words with Flaquer who says if Marsh recalled they have lost case. | Taken from book dialogue same. | Keane goes to nearby restaurant Very disturbed. Given secluded table. Gay and Judy come in, see him and sit at table. Gay admits being at trial. Keane gets very angry when Judy says obvious to all that Keane in love with Mrs. P. and that he wants Marsh out of the way. Leaves angrily. | Same as 2. |

<u>Court reassembles.</u>

| Book | No.1. Script | No.2. Script | No.3. Script. |
|------|-------------|--------------|---------------|
| Marsh recalled. Admits perjury. Now tells truth that Mrs. P. had pestered him until he gave hm. Very ashamed. Loudly denies having anything to do with poisoning. | Taken from book. Dialogue same. | Marsh <u>not</u> permitted to return to stand. This does not come in until beginning of next day's trial. Judge says Marsh will be charged with perjury. He is dismissed. | Same as 2. |
| Keane opens <u>next</u> day of trial with summing up. | Omitted | After luncheon interval Keane sums up to jury emphasising that have no proof of who administered poison. Points to Mrs. P.'s noble effort to shield Marsh by washing glass. Pleads for complete exoneration for her. | Same as 2 |

|  | | | 18 |
| Book | No.1.Script | No.2. script. | No.3. Script. |
| --- | --- | --- | --- |

### End of Third day of Trial

| Book | No.1.Script | No.2. script. | No.3. Script. |
| --- | --- | --- | --- |
| Horfields - he calm and happy - she extremely nervous. | Taken from book. Dialogue same. | Same | Same |
| Lady H. enraged over Farrell's "abominable cruelty" and asks husband never to invite him to house again. He sneers at her. | ditto. | Omitted | Omitted |
| Please with husband not to condemn Mrs. P. He sneers again. | ditto. | Same | Same as 2. |
| Admits telling Keane of husband's sadism. He is angry. | ditto. | Omitted | Omitted |
| Tells her Keane in love with Mrs. P. | ditto. | Omitted | Omitted |
| Calls her "silly old woman". Sends her to bed. | ditto. | Love of cruelty shown as he threatens to send her to asylum. | Same as 2. |
| Gay undecided whether to go to trial last day. Keane silent night before and abrupt departure for bed. Decides will go to trial. | Taken from book. Dialogue same. | Omitted | Omitted. |
|  | | Keane drinking that night. Fla-quer phones concerned over Keane. Gay come in. Keane kind but does not want to talk. | Omitted |

| Book | No.1. Script. | No.2. Script. | No.3. Script. |
|------|---------------|---------------|---------------|
| | | Last Day of Trial. | |
| Keane sums up here | (see page 17 for scripts) | | |
| Horfield sums up against Mrs. P. | Same | Same | Same |
| | | **New scene** | |
| | | Marsh looking at area ruined by recent bombings. Caretaker from Hall comes up to him. He relieves his feelings by telling her that Mrs. P is a "vampire" and that she taunted him until he could no longer resist her. | Same as 2. |
| | | Return to Courtroom Horfield finishes summing up. | Same as 2. |
| Jury files out. | Jury files out. | Jury files out. | Same as 2. |
| Foreman of jury returns to ask judge about Marsh. Judge tells him to ignore Marsh's first testimony and consider evidence given when he returned. | | Omitted from all scripts. | |
| Jury brings in verdict of Guilty. Horfield sentences Mrs. P. to be hanged. As she leaves she turns and looks at Keane and says "It is his fault". | Taken from book. Dialogue same. ditto. | Changed. | Changed. |

| Book | No.1. Script | No.2. Script. | No.3. Script. |
|------|--------------|---------------|---------------|

## 20

**Different ending in No.2 and No.3.**

**Prisoner's Room.**

Mrs. P. calm. Asks for her bag so can make up before being sentenced. Admits to wardress "Will Marsh was my lover." Sensing that Judge will condemn her she talks glibly of having killed "the blind man". As she makes up lips, swallows ampule and dies.

**Not included in scripts**

Newspapers announce Horfield shot by person unknown as leaving Court. It is thought revolver was fired through a pocket.

Throughout book dog Sausage is frequently pointed as tearing cushions, etc. After first day of trial Keane deliberately gives his coat to dog and directs his attention to tearing pocket Night after verdict given Gay opens door to husband's dressing room and sees dog ripping coat Keane had worn that day. Then connects Horfield's shooting with husband but says nothing. It is not discovered who shot Horfield.

Keane gives up Bar and goes abroad with Gay.

Omitted from all scripts.

Keane broken, walks home in rain. He and Gay reconciled.        Content same        Content same

Horfield recovers from bullet. He also retires from Bench.

## THE TRANSATLANTIC/WARNER YEARS

After *The Paradine Case,* Hitchcock formed a production company with Sidney Bernstein. They produced two films: Hitchcock's first color film, *Rope,* and the box office disappointment *Under Capricorn.*

Two projects that started as Transatlantic Pictures were completed for Warner Bros.: *Stage Fright* and *I Confess.* The latter, in particular, took a number of years and drafts to reach the screen.

*I Confess* is the story of a priest who is wrongfully accused of a murder. This is complicated by the fact that the real murderer has confessed to him and that the victim was in fact blackmailing the priest over a past relationship.

In the original treatments, the priest is convicted and condemned, and only after he is hanged does the real murderer confess. Hitchcock worked on this screenplay with Alma and a number of writers for several years. More than a year into the process, during the filming of *Stage Fright,* Victor Peers wrote this letter to Sidney Bernstein describing the project and Hitchcock's state of mind at the time:

Dear Sidney,

We met last night—Hitch, Lesley Storm, Peggy Singer, and myself. Before Lesley Storm's arrival, I sensed that Hitch wasn't too happy with the story line, which is enclosed here.

He did not care for the first scene at the Grandfort home and the scene of the priest going to Malotte's home is apparently out of the question from the Catholic point of view.

Lesley Storm, however, argued her point so well that Hitch was obviously most interested and suddenly turned to me and said that he would like her to return with him to CA and to work with him on the actual scenario.

I promised him I would telephone to you and I hope I have been able to speak to you before you get this letter.

From my angle, Storm appears to be getting hold of the story and thinking constructively and, in clarifying the characterization, for example, she thinks that in their youth it is Ruth who is much more in love with Michel than he with her. He leans toward priesthood and it is because she is afraid that she may lose him that she gives herself to him in an effort to keep him.

It is the parents, of course, who destroy this plan.

This idea of characterization impressed Hitch very much indeed. The position then is that Storm will wait until the end of this week for word from you as to whether 1) she continues and 2) she goes to America.

Hitch is certainly very low in spirit. I gather that yesterday morning's rushes were all to be retaken and the editing dept. was causing quite some concern. Moreover, he has been working continuously and late hours and undoubtedly needs a rest.

Yours,

Victor Peers

They courted a number of writers at the time. Graham Greene flat-out refused, saying he was interested in adapting only his own stories for the screen. In the end, *I Confess* would not be made until 1952, under Hitchcock's contract with Warner Bros. George Tabori and William Archibald wrote the screenplay based on Hitchcock's original treatments and the play *Nos Deux Consciences* by Paul Antheme.

This was a challenging period for Hitchcock and marked by some disappointment. But it was the failure of his production company that may have created a dynamic that led to the great films of the fifties, starting with *Strangers on a Train.*

Indeed, the period was difficult for all filmmakers, as the following revealing letters (written in 1953—a few years after *Strangers on a Train* and just prior to his departure to Paramount) from Hitchcock to his friend and former partner Bernstein reveal. Hollywood was beginning to feel the impact of television and struggled with different formats to keep audiences in the theaters.

Dear Sidney,

At this moment of writing everything here seems to be in what the "Paycock" calls 'a state of chassis.' Warners as you have read by now are concentrating on 3D with Polaroid glasses, while 20th announce that they are making everything in Cinemascope. Warners appear to be the more smart of the two, because their system, using two films can be also used as a regular 'flat' film by just using one of the negatives for small houses not equipped for 3D. 20th on the other hand, using Cinemascope must have a very wide screen and this is so large (64 feet wide) that only about 1500 houses are capable of taking it. They have not made any public announcement but secretly they are having to make a regular 35 mm version at the same time with a consequent slowing up of production. I understand for example that in the case of "The Robe" so much time is lost while waiting for the 35 mm to be shot requiring more set

②

ups than is necessary in Cinemascope.
I have seen a demonstration of the latter.
It is quite effective in big panoramic scenes
but questionable for intimate scenes. This
same problem arises with 'Cinerama'
which I saw in New York. Cinerama
is strictly for Road Show. (Brochure enclosed).
Metro have announced some productions
for Cinemascope but nothing definite.
Paramount are making some 3D's and
have also announced a big screen for
'backlog' flats.
       Warners are also experimenting with
one 35mm film to take both negatives.—

This means two negatives in shooting but
one print for the two. Also, to save putting
a polaroid lens over the projector lens
the polaroid screen would be laminated
into the print as well.
There is also a big problem with light
both in the studio and in the projector as
well - this especially with Cinemascope

③

with such a big area to cover.
Another problem with Cinemascope is
whether the 'rake' of the throw in a
theater will cause distortion on a
curved screen. In the demonstration
I saw at Fox Western Av. Studio, the
projector was practically on the same
level as the screen, but I imagine
that 20th must be working on the
problem of the projection from a high
balcony.

Take the "y" off the last word
and he is here at present 'casing
the joint' — I haven't seen him.

The Hollywood Reporter, no doubt
subsidized by Zanuck is carrying
on a campaign for Cinemascope with
slogans like "Throw away your glasses"
J. L. Warner naturally insensed.

Skouras announced this morning
800 old films for TV as soon as
the successful Cinemascope is launched!

Now comes Magnascope. This
is sponsored by Mike Todd who was
cased out of Cinerama. Magnascope
is a 65mm film somewhat like t

④

old Fox "Grandeur." ~~⋈~~ but modernized
by the Amer. Optical Co who are helping
to finance. This again is strictly
road show. 'Oklahoma' has been
announced for this system.

And so it goes.
I think the switch to Dial M will
enable me to be in London when
the script of Thief is started. I have
talked to Cary and he is still very
interested. He also wants to play
the lead in Dial M. but Warner
does not see it. So far no leading
man set, but we have talked
to Olivia de Havilland who wants
to play the woman but her price
$175,000 may preclude using her unless
she comes down. She is in Europe
at present & wants to stay a while
— this may be an incentive to come
down in price.

The Rear Window situation would
necessitate a script being started
in the next couple of months so that
it could be shot around November
or December. The shooting time on

⑤

this could not amount to more than four weeks.

I would have to make special arrangements with Warners to do this extra outside picture, but I have a strong point, in view of the fact that I lost an outside picture owing to the I Confess switch.

In any case Dial M would be my last "official" picture for Warners, so I could make my own terms for the extra picture that I am giving them.

The Warner lot is the deadest that anyone can remember. They have just paid off Michael Curtiz after 26 years in addition to many actors. I think they only have about six or seven contract players left.

I am leaving for New York in the next day or so to see Dial M again. Will be there about three days.

No baby yet.

Love  Hitch.

_..... 4. 1953_
1.

Dear Sidney,

Am now preparing

Dial M.

Warner gives reason for not doing the picture in England is that he does not want to send one of the only new 3D cameras away to run risk of going wrong and thus holding up production. I personally think the real reason is that he will create a bad impression by making a picture abroad when the studio is virtually at a standstill.

Cary Grant is very, very keen to play the lead but Warner is against him — does not think it is possible to overcome public being used to Cary as a light comedy type. Again I think there is another reason. You see, with "Wax" such a smash Warner (at present) thinks any 3D will do a big gross and he obviously thinks that Cary's 10% of the gross is too much to pay & also that Hitchcock also gets 10% of the

2.

and Dial M need not
much over $1,000,000.
This thinking is of course
inspired by the fact that Gunzberg —
the man who supplied the camera
for "Wax" gets 3% up to negative
cost + 5% after. That is why
Warners have built their own
cameras — they will have two by
the end of this year.

Dial M script is not a great
problem. It will have to follow the
play very closely because if any
attempt is made to open it up the
"holes" will show so I am treating
it on a modified "Rope" style. After
all its great success as a play has
been its speed and 'tightness'.

Mary Elsom sent me the London
notices of I Confess — not too bad on
the whole. By God I am tipped,
though, what with the label 'thriller'
and 'the search for 'Suspense'.

Have you seen any book reviews
on 'Catch a Thief' yet?

3.

Cinerama opened here the other day and looks like repeating its other successes in N.Y and Detroit.

Would you ask Chris to throw a tiny red carpet at the "Express" for Irv Kupcinet when he comes over. "Kup" as he is known in Chicago is the leading journalist there. He runs the most important column in the City. He is on the Chicago Sun Times — NOT the Tribune. He also has his own Television show.

Yours truly

HW

P.S. Ray Milland is latest suggestion for Dial M lead. Cost. $125,000.

V.P. to note 28.7.53.

Ⓨ

ALFRED HITCHCOCK

July 22.

Dear Sidney,

Just received your letter this morning.

Dial M for Murder goes on Aug 4ᵗʰ 30 days schedule with Ray Milland, Grace Kelly, Robert Cummings as the American Radio writer, John Williams as the detective (he won the N.Y. Critics award for the best supporting performance in Dial M.) We haven't cast the heavy yet because we are waiting for a test of the man who played it in London.

The script is in polish stage (I have the original author on it). It follows the stage play very closely because opening it up would show up all the holes and lose tautness. I will send you a copy when completed.

Rear Window script is well on the way. Have a young man on it called John Michael Hayes. Picture goes around October at Paramount.

Dial M does not call for any 3D gimmicks. No spears or chairs to throw at the audience.

Screen size for Dial M. 1.75 to 1.00.

Budget $805,000 without overhead. The present overhead figure is 50% but with two or three pictures going, it may come down, so they haven't given any overhead yet.

Exteriors for Dial M are only three seen through a window into the street, so I am having normal flat plates made in London to be re-shot here with foreground window in 3D. The head of the lab told me yesterday that there is no known way to use 3D background plates.

What about John Dighton for Catch a Thief to stress comedy.

Freddie Knott who wrote Dial M. is quite a bright boy.

While waiting between bouts on Rear Window script, am starting to lay out "Trouble with Harry".

(2)

ALFRED HITCHCOCK

Confidentially I think there is
a slight resistance to Cary's
terms of 10% of the gross. Warner
turned him down for Dial M even
though Cary was terribly keen to do
it. Then there was the Judy Garland
picture "A star is born" musical version.
They are desperate for a leading man
but Cary's terms are a stumbling
block again.
Dial M cast cost.

| | |
|---|---|
| Milland | 125 |
| Cummings | 25 |
| Kelly | 14 |
| Williams | 9 |
| Heavy | 8 (allowed) |

Louis Hayward wants 10 for last part
(the heavy), but Warner balking.
Remember the appalling difference
in dressing the Rope set? Well,
I'm going through the same thing
again — the shocking taste of the
set dresser (a contract man, so he's
a must).

Why has Korda publicized that he received £26,000 for Dial M. When he actually got $150,000 as a down payment plus a little more later?

Ask Joan Harrison to show you the picture I took of her.

More later.

Love

Hitch

V.P. to note  28.7.53.
*[initials]*

ALFRED HITCHCOCK

July 23

Dear Sidney,

More. It is quite obvious to me why Victor Peers' experiment didn't come off. His 'guinea pigs' were used to the big screen, having always sat in the front row of the movies.

Apropos of the 'Queen is Crowned' I suppose the english papers carried the story of the woman who was watching the coronation on TV and called to ask "who was the star playing the part of the Queen?"

It's not being mentioned anywhere but FOX are making an ordinary 35mm version of the Robe in addition to Cinemascope.

It is called 'The Trouble with Harry', not 'What Happened to Harry'.

Can Alan Moorehead write a film script?

Hw

Have you considered Rogers
MacDougall for Dark Duty.
I feel it essential not to
play _into_ the heaviness of the
subject matter but rather
_against_ it.

Harold Hecht (of Norma Prods.
— Hecht & Lancaster) asked me
to consider directing 'Operation
Heartbreak' by Duff Cooper — I
turned it down on account
to free a schedule.

Have to think about Catch a
Thief date in order to advise
Warners that I want to do
_two_ outside pictures in a row.

Yours truly
Alfred.

Oct 1953

ALFRED HITCHCOCK

My dear Sidney

I imagine you are back from Margate by now, was it chosen because they have a 'Dreamland' there?

I had a long phone chat with Cecil. I phoned him at The Alvac on Sunday morning and found him quite bewildered and quite in a dreamland of "screens and systems". I was able to enlighten him on one or two points however.

Firstly, Warner has no more 3d pictures on schedule. In fact, I understand that it is quite possible that Dial M, for murder may even go out as a 'flattie'.

The studio has an 'ant horror' picture ready to go, and they have just changed it back to flat and black + white.

Warner also talks about only making big pictures and cutting out the programmer altogether. This will certainly add to the product shortage which is being looked to with apprehension by the small exhibitor here.

②

### ALFRED HITCHCOCK

Dial M for Murder is at present being assembled for a first cut. I followed the play pretty closely and did so for two reasons. One – I felt that to open up a taut shape would dissipate the very element that made the play a success. It's bound to be a bit talky and I've tried to reduce this but unfortunately all the lines mean so much plotwise. The other reason is more potent — one cannot show modern London exteriors on the back lot, although the front office could see no difference between the Brownstone N.Y. street and Randolph Crescent, Maida Vale! Anyway I've got to cut at least 500 feet out to bring it down to the maximum 4600 feet per reel to allow for only one 3D intermission making a total of 9200 feet. If there are no 3D then the question of length is academic.

ALFRED HITCHCOCK

Had a note from Alex Korda
the other day thanking me for
some cigars I sent him. They were
in honour of his engagement.
They were "King Edward $\overline{VII}$" Six cents
each! Box of 50 $2.75. I told
him to offer them to those whom he
liked the least.

Cecil told me that his last
picture didn't go over too well.

Paramount had great hopes for
Roman Holiday, but Hartman told
me they were somewhat disappointed
because it was extremely "spotty".

Cecil told me that was his
opinion also.

The Robe is momentarily keeping
the wolf from the Zanuck and
Skouras doors.

Hottest day of year 100°. Today.

Rear Window script well on way
Dialog will be finished this week
then I will start on final shooting

(4)

ALFRED HITCHCOCK

script next Monday oct 12th. I
will just about finish it before
shooting time Nov. 15. The set
starts being built this week,
to be completed by Nov 1st. Then
I will have the cameraman light
it completely except foreground
room before the shooting date.
In other words he will have
two weeks to light all the
apartments and the backyards
for Day, Evening and Night,
so that when one is shooting
the action in the room, all that
has to be done is to just switch-
on the background. I hope it
works. The whole thing is a bit
of a rush but Jimmy Stewart
is only available for four weeks
before Xmas. He is committed for
a big air force picture in January.

ALFRED HITCHCOCK

So it doesn't look as though my free days will start until after xmas, although once I start shooting my evenings will be free then. Or would you think it better if you put off coming over until Jan?

I have seen a lot of Cary and he still talks about doing 'catch a thief' next summer. His last picture at M.G.M. 'Dream Wife' was N.G at the box office.

Warners have asked me to make a play they have bought called "Anastasia" I read it and thought the writing by our mutual friend atrocious. Alma said the same. Yet I understand it is a success and has the

ALFRED HITCHCOCK

discerning sponsorship of the leaders of the London Stage!

What about the Beggars Opera — not much business here in L.A.

Am phoning Cecil again at the end of the week. I tried to persuade them to fly to Santa Cruz for next week end but Cecil said his doctor would not agree to it. Pity.

Lost $25,000 on the Canadian stocks recommended by O'Connell senior — the hell with new in-laws Can I have balance Rope salary Jan 6th 1954 because tax deadline Jan 15th. Do not want before because there may be a tax reduction next year

Alma & I both miss you    LOVE    Hitch.

## The Man Who Knew Too Much

Hitchcock certainly dealt in familiar thematic territory for most of his career, but he remade only one of his films: *The Man Who Knew Too Much*. He toyed with remaking *The 39 Steps* and *The Lodger* (both of which were remade by other directors), but only *The Man Who Knew Too Much* captured his full attention.

The plot for each film is in essence the same. As recounted earlier, a couple's only child is kidnapped during a family vacation in order to keep the parents from revealing a secret assassination plot about which one of the parents was given the vaguest facts from a dying spy.

There are a number of classic scenes in the first film:

- The spy is killed while dancing in a St. Moritz hotel ballroom—he's shot through the large windows that look out on the Swiss Alps. In his dying moments, he tells his dance partner (the original film's mother was a sharpshooter) that there is something important hidden in his shaving brush that the enemy must not find.
- Back in London, the husband takes what few clues he has to try and find their daughter. With "Uncle" Clive—although it's unclear whether he's related to the couple or just a close family friend—their investigation first takes them to a dentist, then to a church (Ambrose Chapel) where they encounter the assassins and learn that the assassination is to take place that evening at Albert Hall. Clive escapes and informs the mother.
- The assassination attempt at Albert Hall.
- The climax where the child is rescued.

In early 1955, Hitchcock began work on updating this film by making the British couple an American couple. The script would eventually be penned by John Michael Hayes, but the principal construction took place during February with Angus MacPhail.

The notes that follow, arranged in sequence, offer an insight into the day-to-day evolution of a story. You'll notice certain ideas come and go, some thankfully: the business about the supersonic jet, for example. By the end of the notes, however, a very recognizable shape forms. Hayes would often denigrate MacPhail's contribution to the film (indeed, he claimed that one of the reasons he broke with Hitchcock was over MacPhail receiving credit on the film). This snapshot of the screenplay's construction clearly shows a substantial contribution by MacPhail. The following notes developed by Angus presuppose knowledge of the first version and some knowledge of the later.

MAN WHO KNEW TOO MUCH. Notes: January 31st, 1955.

1. If we substitute Jill for Clive, it is she who is hypnotised in the chapel scene.

In the existing construction, Lawrence spots the ticket for the Albert Hall in Levine's pocket: this causes him to shout to Clive to tell Jill to proceed to the Albert Hall. Now, Lawrence will simply instruct Jill herself to proceed to the Albert Hall.

If we argue that she would not desert her husband at such a juncture, we can emphasise that she is still under the hypnotic influence: and she will unhesitatingly obey the command of the man she loves.

2. We have to reconsider this. Perhaps the yells and screams of Jill having her teeth wrenched out would not be highly funny. Suggest you consider that we reverse the roles of Lawrence and of Jill: she does the snooping, while he has his teeth wrenched out.

3. A new Cover Story for them also requires consideration. This raises the tiresome point that an American couple would scarcely journey to Wapping, lion's-denwards, unless they had some effective form of disguise. Their mere presence in Wapping would be anomalous; even in normal circumstances.

I think the set-up was weak in the original: it would be much weaker today; and with the husband-wife set-up I fear their conduct would seem more than rash.

Illogically, in terms of the potential Miss Day, it might be fun to play the pub scene, referred to in the original but not shown. Miss Day, whooping it up at the Prospect of Whitby, has undeniable charms for me. (The pub was where they discovered the address of the dentist).

4. This raises the slightly pedantic question of the locale. Do you feel strongly about Wapping and the East End in general? In a district such as Notting Hill, the presence of Americans would scarcely be remarked . . . and Bayswater is spotted with odd religions. Jehovah's Witnesses have their headquarters just behind Lancaster Gate.

I won't now go into the question of the National Health Service and t he casual pulling of teeth. Might be worth an alternative take for the British market . . .

5. The temporary capture of Lawrence, as discussed. I suggest the following general line. Abbott lets Lawrence meet the boy; but tells Lawrence that they are moving out. He has made this locale too hot. They are taking the boy with them: just in case. Lawrence will be left alone, bound and gagged, to meditate on his sins.

But: the boy contrives to pass to Lawrence some object with which he can free himself from his bonds. Some object which we will have planted in the opening sequences.

6. The crooks depart. Lawrence manages to release himself. This is intercut with the Albert Hall. A routine set-up, of course: but it might be redeemed if the object passed to Lawrence by the boy is some absurdly ingenious kid's toy.

7. Presumably this is also intercut with the arrival of Abbott and co at the Embassy. Extreme irritation of Ambassador. They listen to the broadcast of the concert. They

learn that the murder attempt has failed. This is followed by a phone call to say that the gallant intended-victim is going to keep his date as the guest of honour at the Embassy party when the concert is over.

The Russian Ambassador, Peter Ustinov, no doubt, is really livid at this.

8.  You didn't react to my suggestion that Levine commits suicide at the Albert Hall, rather than face capture . . . ? I find it too silly that he should turn up, whimpering, at the Embassy. He must know that he himself is now for the high jump at the hands of Abbott.

8.  Lawrence joins Jill and others backstage at the Albert Hall. Discussion of ways and means. They have guessed, now, what was in the wind . . . But you can't make a casus belli out of a chap whose right ear has been slightly grazed by a bullet.

Scotland Yard can't budge. Question of extraterritoriality. But a police cordon will be thrown round the Embassy. And if Mr. and Mrs. Lawrence care to intervene, a blind eye will be turned.

9.  Jill contrives her invitation to the party, via the grateful would-be victim.

10.  Very unnatural, to me, that the kid should not be gagged. How inefficient can these Commies be? If you want real hokum, the kid has given his word of honour that he won't speak a word. He doesn't speak a word. He sings: the end of his mother's song. This is valid psychology for the kid, I think; but leaves the Commies teribly soft and silly.

11.  General carping point. The c rooks cannot, at any moment, tell whether Lawrence has in fact Told All to Scotland Yard. As Vile Cynical Eurasians, they would naturally assume he has double crossed them. It will be small satisfaction to them to chop his son into small pieces, if the assassination has failed . . . Afraid I can't think of any answer to this one, so far. But perhaps it is only remote ice-box?

12.  If the crooks had any sense, they would dope the kid for his transfer from the chapel to the Embassy. But do I understand that there is a heavy U.S. tabu on the suggested use of drugs?

13.  Would like to emphasise that the crooks threaten torture of the kid. This is far more horrible to me than the straight threat of death. Besides, they know, and Lawrence knows, that they cant afford to play this ace of trumps.

MAN WHO KNEW TOO MUCH. Notes: February 1st, 1955.

1.  Attempted summary of previous discussions about opening sequences:

2.  Bob and Jill Lawrence are in the local bus on their way to Marakesh. With them is their young son, Philip, aged eight. Bus jolts and Philip grabs at yashmak. Hell breaks loose. Local types are pacified by a Frenchman, Louis. The grateful Lawrences ask him to dinner at the hotel in Marakesh.

3.  Seven o'clock in the Lawrences' suite in the hotel. Louis arrives for cocktails. Philip has finished his evening meal a nd is due in bed. But it's his birthday. He begs to stay up

for a bit, so his mother will sing him his favourite song. Listening to t he song, Louis moves out casually on to t he balcony, leans against a supporting pillar.

There is the sound of a gunshot. Louis moves back in; you couldn't actually swear he hurries. Bob comments that it sounded like a revolver shot. Louis is quite positive it was a back-fire from a car. "They dope the gasoline around here with coconut oil."

Down the street a figure moves swiftly and furtively away xxxxxxxxxxxxxx from camera.

4. Next morning. (Note: I don't think that Abbott and Costello, I mean Levine, would in any public circumstances allow themselves to be seen together. Such conduct, I need hardly remind you, is contrary to all undercover practise. Therefore, I suggest, we must use either Abbott or Levine for the sightseeing sequence; but not both.

5. We have not yet discussed characterisations for these two men. Are you at all devoted to Abbottt as the fake invalid?

6. Well, until we have had this important discussion, I sugggest it would be nice, in theory, to start the next morning sequence with a scene in which Abbott xx (or Levine, according to characterisation) has made fast friends with Philip. They are indulging in a wild game of something or other. This is broken by the arrival from inside the hotel of Bob, xxxxxx xxxxxxxxxxxxxxxxxxxxxxxxxxxxxxxxxxxx and Jill, all set for sightseeing.

xxxxxxxxxxxxxxxxxxxxxxxxxxxxxxxxxxxxxxxxxxxxxxxxxxxxxxxxxxxxxxxxxxxxxxxx
xxxxxxxxxxxxx

8. Anyway, Phil introduces his newfound friend, and off the party sets. An equivocal line, I suppose, to account for the absence of Louis?

9. The above analysis is interesting. It shows that we haven't yet allowed for any material to substitute for the original chi-chi flirtation between Jill and Louis. Whatever is decided on, I think the key element should be a mysterioso quality about Louis: quite the opposite of his character in the original. I doNt mean cloak-and-dagger. Something enigmatic. A question mark. Charm itself, but his story about being in the French wine business, being the great-great grandson of the original Veuve Cliquot, somehow doesnt ring true; and maybe he doesnt mean it to ring true. (Ah, shades of Uncle Pendragon).

The sort of man who, ifthe sequence went on longer to the bedtime of the Lawrences, would have Bob and Jill indulging in all sorts of fantastic speculations about Louis.

10. Suggest this is v. important matter: has to be balanced perfectly against the surprise when he falls, dying, into Bob's arms.

11. Small point: but we have to have enough Lawrence-Louis material to justify Louis's dying confidence in Bob.

12. Sorry: I recollect, now, we said there should be a separate scene between Abbott and Levine the evening before. Can we mnage this without it being too much on the nos e about the attempt on Louis and his subsequent murder? Or, conversely, should we have it stark, brutally to the point.

MAN WHO KNEW TOO MUCH. Notes: February 2nd, 1955.

1. Recap. of this morning's conversation:

2. London. Bob wants to go off on his own to Notting Hill. But Jill will have none of this. She insists on accompanying him. How c an he refuse?

3. Perhaps short scene at the Mitre; which puts them onto the address of George Barber?

4. Dentist's. Jill is left in the waiting room, to snoop as much as is practical. Bob submits himself as the patient. Jill sees Abbott and Levine arrive by taxi below. Jill tries, without success, to warn Bob of the impending danger.

   Abbott and Levine arrive in waiting room. Jill is able to avoid recognition.

   Abbott puts his head round the door of the consulting room. Angle such that he doesn't identify Bob. Discreet line from Abbott to dentist about keeping on the alert?

   Abbott and Levine exit through back door; which is observed by Jill.

   Meantime, dentist scrtinises Bob more carefully, asks him awkward questions. Attempt to apply gas to Bob. Jill enters and helps Bob to get the dentist under.

5. Bob and Jill exit through back door, find themselves in an alley. Sound of singing. This takes them to the Chapel.

6. Here, the script seems to make an important point of the fact that Bob recognises Abbott's "Nurse" from St. Moritz. . . . What are your views about this?

7. The hypnotism. Of course, I agree, the present set-up is inadmissible; in which Bob gives Clive the high-sign to submit to the fluence. But would it really be too much if Jill volunteers? As for Bob, perhaps we might here use Clare Greet and her gun, she is his neighbour . . . He is compelled to watch, helplessly, as Jill is put under the influence.

8. The manner in which Bob gets the clue about the Albert Hall is montrous. Besides, it can now be regarded as Pat Hamilton's copyright. Will t ry and think up something a little less corny.


### "THE MAN WHO KNEW TOO MUCH"

#### SKELETON

February 7th, 1955


1. Bus bound for Marakesh. Establish characters of Bob, Jill and young Philip Lawrence.

   Bob is a professional man, an architect. Under a slow manner, he is quick tempered, impulsive, emotional. He has never traveled outside the United States before. He regards the details of this holiday trip with sardonic amusement.

He is deeply in love with Jill. She too is a professional: a professional singer. She has rubbed shoulders in a cosmopolitan way. Circumstances don't find her at a loss. Unlike Bob, she is no intellectual. She trusts her hunches and her impulses.

They both have a sense of humour. They are both devoted to young Philip. They are determined that he shan't be spoiled. So, of course, he is spoiled. But, at the age of eight, he is doing pretty well, just the same.

The family atmosphere is affectionate. Bob and Jill are so secure that they can afford to quarrel. They are quarreling, mildly. Bob wanted to go and see the foundations of the ancient city of Carthage: Jill, the romantic, has opted forthe snake-charmers of Marakesh.

2.  Yashmak incident. Louis Bernard comes to the rescue. Louis, it would seem, is also a professional: a professional Frenchman. Give him a boater, it would seem, and he would be the young Maurice Chevalier.

With friendly amusement, he warns Bob and Jill to watch their step in Morocco. The assassination statistics are racing neck a nd neck with the road casualties. Bob and Jill invite Louis to dine with them in their suite in the hotel in Marakesh.

3.  Arrival at hotel in Marakesh. Philip's supersonic interplanetary jet-bomber gets out of control. It is prevented from large-scale wrecking by the Reverend Hugh Abbott and his wife, Agnes, a delightful English couple.

4.  Hotel suite. Philip is due for bed as Louis arrives for cocktails. Bob has taken to Louis, who has taken to Jill. One of those quick holiday friendships seems to be forming.

Jill and Louis have a mutual interest in music. The talk gets around to the work of Take Jonescu, the Roumanian composer, whose cente[n]ary is being celebrated this year.

Phil and Bob are at one in thinking this to be deplorable highbrow stuff. Phil begs that his mother sing his favourite song. It happens so Louis says, to be his favourite too. So Jill sings it.

5.  Louis goes out on the balcony. Shot is aimed at Louis. But Louis passes this off as a backfire of a car.

Louis had promised to show them the sights, such as they are, of Marakesh tomorrow. But now, he excuses himself. He is vague. It seems a little odd . . .

6.  ? Perhaps guarded encounter between Louis and the Abbotts as Louis departs?

7.  Next morning. Philip is trying out his jet bomber with the Abbotts in the grounds of the hotel. Jill and Bxob arrive to collect him for a sightseeing expedition, into which the Abbotts get included.

8.  Sightseeing expedition; which climaxes in the bizarre death of Louis. Abbott, as a priest, is solicitously helpful.

9.  Fresh set-up at xxxxx police headquarters, to involve the Abbotts, in an innocent and helpful capacity. Climaxing in phone call to Bob. He xxxxxx refuses to tell the French detective what the call was about.

9.  Bob and Jill make xxxxx their way back to their hotel. Jill, relieved after all the tension, is xxxxxxxxxxxxx talking freely. Bob is trying, desperately, to brace himself to tell Jill the content of the phone call. At last, he tells her . . .

10.  Phil is stowed into aircraft.

11.  Car on the way to the airport. Bitterly unhappy dialogue between Jill and Bob. Establish that Louis's dying words have provided the clue of "London".

12.  Where, at the Connaught Hotel, the formidable Gibson, from the Foreign Office, is waiting patiently to interview Bob and Jill.

We learn, from Gibson, something of the F.O. conjecture about the criminal plan. We satisfy our curiosity about Louis: he was an agent of the Deuxieme Bureau.

Bob is inclined to throw Gibson unceremoniously out. But Jill, with a woman's practical sense, realises they must be prepared to come to terms if necessary.

Gibson goes. If Bob changes his mind, he conveys tactfully, a phone call will put the whole state machine into action.

Siting of phone call xx with Philip not yet exactly determined.

14.  Adventure which culminates in arrival at Chapel.

13.  Bob and Jill, in a taxi, are on their way to Notting Hill. Hot dispute about what Louis's dying words really meant

15.  Chapel. Routine of Jill singing, trying to draw Bob's attention to Mrs. Abbott at the organ.

Abbott mounts the pulpit. He announces the text of his sermon, The Wicked Shallbe Turned Into Hell, then falls a prey to asthma, closes the proceedings.

16.  Battle. Bob gets his clue to the Albert Hall, shouts same to Jill, before they are separated. (Note: I suggest there is no place for Jill's return with policeman. She must be despatched directly to the Albert Hall.)

17.  Bob is captured. Scene with Phil. Levine is musically instructed.

Bob is left to rot; and the criminals move out.

17.  Albert Hall. Cross-cut with Bob making his escape?

18.  Also cross cut: the arrival of Abbott at the Russian Embassy with his embarrassing supercargo?

19.  Albert Hall. Assassination attempt fails. Suicide of Levine?

20.  Backstage, Albert Hall. Bob arrives. Scene with Gibson. Extraterratoriality problem Polite inquiries from Rumanian Prime Minister. Jill leaps at chance to attend reception at Russian Embassy.

21.  Russian Embassy. Jill sings her number, which is faintly segued by Phil, upstairs.

22.  Climax to, as they say, be devised.

MAN WHO KNEW TOO MUCH. Notes: February 8th, 1955.

1. There is a Protestant hymn which runs:

> Welcome Festival Day,
> Thrice Hallowed for ever and ever.

Subsequent wording, I seem to recall. makes it clear that the reference is to the Birth of Jesus Christ. But this reference could be avoided.

It is a good reusing tune. I will sing it to you, if not forcibly prevented.

2. It is this reference to "Festival" which makes all the pieces of the jig-saw puzzle suddenly fit together in Bob's mind.

3. The first of Louis's dying words is "London", repeated with emphasis. He goes on to say: "Contact Champion Barman Urgent."

4. This, after some dispute, leads Bob and Jill to a swift tour of pubs called "The Champion". I dare say a more esoteric name will be necessary, to reduce the potential number of pubs.

5. Louis's dying words continue: "Service. xxxxxxxxxxxxxxxxxxxxxxx Choral. Sunday. xxxxxx Premier. . . ."

6. Bob and Jill, spent but determined, reach the Champion, Notting Hill, at lunch time on Sunday. It is bizarre: a funeral procession is leaving the pub. Bob and Jill learn that the barman met with a sudden accident, a couple of days ago.

7. Bob and Jill manage to get into xxxxxxxx one of the mourning cars, along with the guvnor and other mourners. The guvnor is inconsolable. Best barman he ever had. Pious, too. Why, if he'd survived, he'd have been reading the lessons in the little chapel in Portobello Road this very afternoon.

Remembering "Service. Choral" Bob and Jill exchange a glance. They ask politely to be dropped off by the chapel. The guvnor amiably humours this whim. Mad Americans. Nice, but mad.

8. Final clewing, as Jill and Bob make to enter chapel. "Choral"? Premier? Well, after all, today is the first of June; and premier is the French for First. But who's going to do an internationally significant assassination in this one horse little chapel?

9. Bob, eventually, conveys his thought about the Festival Hall to Jill. Contrive the combat in such a manner that Jill doesn't realise Bob is hopelessly outnumbered. She does not return with a cop, but goes straight to the Festival Hall.

10. Bob is captured. The gang make off, carrying small Philip with them. Bob is left in charge of one captor. Bob, Iw ill now reveal to you, is a psychiatrist in good standing. He hypnotises his captor and makes his getaway.

MAN WHO KNEW TOO MUCH. Notes: February 9th, 1955.

1.  In the last sequence, does it, do you feel, boil up to single combat between Bob and Abbott? If so:

2.  After the death of Louis, in Marakesh, Bob, professionally, comments that the knife blow was incompetently struck. The victim should never have lived to speak.

3.  In last sequence, work the two men into a holding stance with a knife. Abbott is at Bob's mercy. Those powerful surgeon's wrists can do what they wish with him. People are battering at the doors.

Abbott, who is not a coward, says: "Go ahead. Finish me off. But you'll hang for murder."

Bob says: "Even the greatest surgeons sometimes slip up, on a difficult operation. And I'm a very average surgeon."

He strikes the blow. Death is instantaneous.

4.  Bob's captor in the post-Chapel sequence. Might he not be a punch-drunk ex-pug? He fancies himself as Joe Louis. It is with no great difficulty that Bob persuades him he is indeed Joe Louis, about to win the world heavyweight championship.

Bob rigs up an opponent from pillows and things; a small mountain of inanimate objects. He persuades his captor that the right technique with this formidable opponent is to box clever, rest for a round, etc, etc. He leaves his captor engaged in this agile activity.

5.  Before this: Abbott discovers Mrs. Abbott in the act of knotting sheets so that young Phil xxxxx may slide to the ground and safety. He knifes her: but the boy has gone.

Afterwards, Jill finds Mrs. Abbott, dying. The latter indicates the knotted sheets at the window, says: "I told him . . . to run as fast as he could . . . across the Park . . . to the American Embassy . . ."

6.  If we are using the first introduction of the Abbotts on the morning after the arrival in Marakesh, it might be nice to make this between Mr. and Mrs. Abbott in the swimming pool; and Phil.

After they are all clothed, Abbott is wearing his dog-collar. (This was effective with Tracy in "San Francisco").


"THE MAN WHO KNEW TOO MUCH"

Revised Skeleton

February 12th, 1955


1.  Bus is on its way to Marakesh. Plant the Lawrence family. Young Philip has trouble with his balance and with yashmak. Louis Bernard springs to the rescue.

Louis ingratiates himself with the Lawrences. He is amiably curious about the backgrounds of Bob and Jill. This, Jill does not care for; as her eyes betray. Bob, on the contrary, is flattered by Louis's interest.

By means of Louis's questions, we learn that Bob is a surgeon in a sound, though not famous, way of business. We learn also that Jill used to be a top-line singer. She gave up show business when she married.

Louis offers to show them round Marakesh next day. Bob asks him to dinner in their suite at the hotel that evening.

2. The Lawrences' suite at the hotel. Bob and Jill are having an affectionate marital difference of opinion about Louis. Jill's feminine intuition tells her that Louis is not the simple charming boy he seems. Bob ridicules this.

Louis arrives. They go out on to the balcony to drink cocktails. They gaze idly down as fresh guests arrive. Jill, now, is trying delicately to pump Louis about himself: but the results are unrewarding.

A handsome couple arrive below. English, from their voices. Suddenly, rather surprisingly, Louis tells Bob and Jill that he will not, after all, be able to show them the sights of Marakesh next day. He invents some graceful reason for this defection. Jill gives Bob a look.

Jill sings her lullaby, at the [insistence] of young Philip, who is wrapt; and joins in.

Louis has remained on the balcony. A bullet is fired. It misses Louis and buries itself in the plaster of the outside wall, above his head. Jill is sure that it was a gunshot. But Louis easily passes the incident off as the backfire of a car; as he gracefully re-enters the room.

Young Phil, being tucked up in bed, seems to share his mother's romantic notions about Louis.

(Note: Is Louis invited for cocktails only: or do we make a point of the fact that he excuses himself from the meal?)

3. Next morning. Phil at the swimming pool. He has made friends with the handsome English couple who arrived the evening before. We learn that they are called Mr. and Mrs. Abbott.

Bob and Jill arrive to collect their offspring for breakfast. Phil

3. cont. introduces his new friends. It seems that the Abbotts plan a sightseeing tour of Marakesh that morning. The Abbotts and the Lawrences agree to join forces.

4. The party sets off from the hotel. We find that Mr. Abbott is wearing a dog-collar. He is a parson. He and his wife have been on a tour of the Holy Land.

Young Phil is fascinated by the snake-charmers and other side-shows of Marakesh. He keeps on darting off. Jill anxious. Abbott re-assures her. The Arabs are devoted to children. He will come to no harm.

So, Phil is not present when a macabre incident occurs. An Arab is running, pursued by the police. The Arab puts the police off his trail. He leans, panting, against a white-painted wall. The shadow of a knife looms. It strikes. The Arab runs, the knife in his back.

He impinges on the Abbott-Lawrence group. He falls. Lawrence takes him in his arms. He speaks, as Locals gather round. The words we hear loudly are: "London . . . London . . ."

The remainder of his dying words are heard only by Bob. The Arab's dark hue streaks with sweat and blood. Bob wipes the dying man's face. It is Louis.

5.  Police Station. Bob is grilled. He won't talk. A telephone call comes through for Bob. He gives a non-committal reply to the caller. He refuses to communicate the content of the call to the police. But we have heard the voice on the telephone. We do not identify this voice. It says that Phil has been kidnaped. He will be held as hostage: to ensure Bob's silence about Louis's dying words.

6.  Bob and Jill are on their way home to the hotel. Jill is mystified, shocked; yet, in an odd way, relieved. She talks excitedly. Bob is trying to nerve himself to tell her the content of the telephone call. He is in a state of violent emotion, rigorously repressed.

7.  Hotel suite. Bob breaks the news to Jill . . .

8.  Small airstrip. Phil is bundled into an aircraft. Through a porthole, we see his brave protest. But a hand comes over his face: which disappears from sight.

9.  Hotel bedroom. Bob and Jill are in their beds. Moonlight. Neither can sleep. Pitiful argument about ways and means. Jill is positive. They must go to London, follow the clew of Louis's dying words. She silences Bob's objections. They must act on their own. What else can they do? It is their only chance that they will ever set eyes on Phil again.

Bob takes her into his arms; what consolation can he offer her?

10.  The Connaught Hotel, London. Gibson, of M.1.5., sits moodily at a writing desk.

Bob and Jill enter, with porters bearing their luggage. The porters depart. Gibson explains himself. He is as frank as an M1.5. man can be. He tells them that The Enemy plans an aggressive act, next Sunday, here, in London. This act may well touch off World War Three. It is essential that Bob tell him the content of Louis Bernard's dying words.

His argument is specious, plausible. The Enemy cannot ever know whether Bob has or has not conveyed Louis's dying words. So what have Bob and Jill to lose?

The scene is broken by a telephone call. Philip is put through to his father and to his mother. The warning voice at the other end tells Bob to hold his tongue with Gibson.

All the same, Bob weakens, seduced by Gibson's arguments. But Jill intervenes. She is a trifle brutal with Gibson about Scotland Yard's security system. She says it's just as bad as it would be, back home.

Gibson recognises present defeat. He asks Bob and Jill to ponder the matter. The Enemy daren't kill young Phil. He is their trump card. Gibson will await a call from the Lawrences.

Gibson departs. Jill seizes on the most likely clew in Louis's dying words. Tomorrow, at dawn.

11. Hiatus. Adventure for Bob and Jill, which puts them on the track of the Chapel.

12. The Chapel. Bob spots Mrs. Abbott at the organ. Under cover of the hymn, he sings this to Jill. She, professional singer that she is, unfortunately responds in a clarion soprano. Which causes all eyes to be turned upon them.

13. Abbott, in full canonicals, ascends the pulpit steps. He has not been inattentive to the disturbance. Melodiously he announces the text for his sermon. Then, is overcome by an apparent fit of coughing. He calls the service off, begging the congregation to go home.

The innocent members of the congregation disperse; leaving only enemy agents.

Battle. But Bob has picked up the final clew from the mention of Festival in the hymn. He shouts this to Jill, ordering her to proceed to the Festival Hall. She doesn't realise how hard pressed Bob is; obediently departs.

14. Back premises of Chapel. The captive Bob is brought in. The sharpshooter is briefed by ABBOTT.

14. cont. Mrs. Abbott, sickened, protests when Abbott says they are going to shift to the Embassy and take the kid with them. But Abbott over-rules her.

Bob is left in the, seemingly, secure charge of a plug-ugly. The Abbotts and their entourage scamper: with Phil.

15. Start of Festival Hall sequence.

16. Back premises of Chapel. Bob hypnotises plug-ugly, who is a thwarted heavyweight boxer. Bob makes his escape, leaving plg-ugly to plug-ugly.

17. Festival Hall. Unsuccessful attempt to assassinate Pomanian Premier. Up to, and including, suicide of sharpshooter.

18. Abbotts arrive at Embassy with Phil in tow. The Ambassador is coldly furious. We get the impression that Phil's neck will be wrung without scruple, if the Dialectic demands this.

19. Gibson, Jill, Bob and others assembled. Plant that H.M. Government can take no steps about the Embassy: it possesses extraterritorial rights.

Grateful inquiries to Jill from the Pomanian premier. Bob and Jill decide to attend the reception at the Embassy.

20. Embassy. Smashing reception in progress. Jill and Bob arrive, are cordially received.

Jill is asked to sing: and sings the Lullaby. Faintly, from upstairs, a small voice, realised only by Bob and Jill, chips in.

Jill continues to play and sing; to cover Bob as he makes his way upstairs.

21. Events upstairs at Embassy still to be sorted out.

"THE MAN WHO KNEW TOO MUCH"

First London Episode

February 15th, 1955

1.  One of the words that the dying Louis lets fall is Sorter. Or, it might be, Sorta. Sorta what? Bob and Jill do not consider this to be a valuable clew.

2.  The Lawrences arrive in London. Gibson wants to persuade Bob to reveal Louis's dying words. He decides to "show willing". He says there is some evidence that Louis had a private English contact at Mount Pleasant, a refugee from the Communist terror.

Does this ring a bell with Bob? It does not ring a bell with Bob. Gibson departs. The floor waiter serves breakfast to Bob and Jill.

On an impulse, Jill asks the floor waiter what is this Mount Pleasant? The waiter explains that Mount Pleasant is the central London clearing house for all mail: the place where all the letters get sorted.

He departs. Bob and Jill gaze at one another. So the word Sorter does mean something, after all.

3.  Jill is taking the initiative, when the two of them arrive at Mount Pleasant. Glibly, she passes herself off as a foreign correspondent of the Washington Post: a name that comes aptly to her lips.

The P.R.O. is all smiles. He will show them how Mount Pleasant ticks over. The pride and joy is the miniature railway which connects Mount Pleasant, underground, with the principal railroad termini.

The convoys of miniature railroad trucks emerge in seemly fashion from the tunnel, carrying their cargoes of mail. But the last truck carries no mail: instead it contains a corpse.

4.  A checkup reveals the identity of the corpse: a man named Lajos Vassily. Jill and Bob would like to investigate this further. But the P.R.O. is adamant. It is now a matter for the police and for the Coroner's Court. However, Jill has gleaned the address at which the dead man lodged: 21, Delamere Terrace, Notting Hill.

5.  Delamere Terrace, romantically sordid, gives on to the basin of the Regent's Canal. The landlady, an eccentric character, specialises in Siamese cats. Bob and Jill are not accustomed to cats leaping athletically on to their shoulders.

The landlady is not sentimental about Vassily. She always thought he would come to a sticky end. "Queer sex," she says darkly. "That was the trouble with him.

Bob and Jill are baffled by this. But further questioning reveals that Vassily belonged to one of those queer religious sects. He regularly attended services at a fusty chapel in the Portobello Road.

Bob disentangles a Siamese which evinces a desire to nest round his neck. They start off for the chapel.

MAN WHO KNEW TOO MUCH. February 17th, 1955.

1. First shot at analysing the plot.

2. The Russians, pursuing their usual tactics, have decided to put the Western Allies in the wrong. It so happens that the Hungarian Prime Minister is paying an official visit to London. He will be the guest of honour at a special programme of Hungarian music, to be given at the Festival Hall. Subsequently, he will be the guest of honour at a reception given by the Russian Ambassador at the Russian Embassy in London.

The Russians intend to arrange that this Prime Minister, their own stooge, shall be assassinated at the Festival Hall.

3. The job has to be an expert one. Amongst the best of the Russian agents in Britain are Mr. and Mrs. Abbott. They are instructed to go and vet a Killer in Morocco: some character who will not be instantly picked up by Scotland Yard.

4. The Deuxieme Bureau, in France, has got wind of this project, though only in the slenderest way. They send one of their best men, Louis Bernard, to Morocco, to try and identify the enemy agents; who are known to be passing as a married couple.

5. Louis meets the Lawrences. Momentarily, he fancies they may be the persons he is after; and questions them accordingly. He revises his opinion, when the Abbotts arrive.

6. The Abbotss are well aware that Louis is a dangerous man. They instruct the Killer xxx to murder Louis; to prove that he can cope with the much more difficult problem of the Hungarian Prime Minister.

The Killer does the job. The Abbotts put the Killer on to tail Bob.

7. The Chapel is an entirely practical Front for the dissemination of code instructions to enemy agents in Britain.

8. After the fracas in the Chapel, Jill escapes. The place is now hot. Abbott decides they must seek refuge in the Russian Embassy.

9. The Russian Ambassador is, not unnaturally, a trifle annoyed at his current cargo of wanted agents and kidnaped kid. But he carries it off with the Russian chic and grace that only Peter Ustinov can command.

MAN WHO KNEW TOO MUCH. Notes: February 17th, 1955.

1. Louis's dying words are as follows:

London . . . London . . . Barmaid Collins . . . Chapel Front . . . Rhapsody . . . Sunday deadline . . . deadline . . .

2. Suggest you consider that we do glimpse Louis's killer, however fleetingly.

3. Bob and Jill decide that Louis's dying words justify their journey to London. But the

interview with Gibson, followed by the telephonic ultimatum from Abbott, brings them to a temporary halt.

Jill is on the edge of a breakdown. Bob insists that she come and visit Harley Street specialist, already known to Bob.

4. Harley Street. The wise old doctor breaks down their resistance to telling him all about it.

5. Nearby, the Killer keeps the doctor's house under view.

6. Doctor elucidates "Barmaid Collins". Of course, it doesn't mean a barmaid whose name is Collins. It means a barmaid who works behind the bar at Collins Music-Hall, Islington Green. This is a place where they give weekly touring revues, of a xxxxxxxxxx sexy type.

Bob sets off for Collins. It is agreed that the Doctor will deliver Jill, in better shape, back at the hotel, in three hours' time. Mood: that Jill is to have a respite, however brief, from her ordeal. She even manages a pathetic little joke to Bob about the barmaid.

7. Bob sets off for Islington; and the Killer follows.

8. At Collins, "We Couldn't Wear Less" seems to be enticing the customers.

The bar is packed. Several coachloads of workers from factories at Luton are present to celebrate.

The barmaid in charge is in the majestic forties: she is a French tart, retired with honours from the Piccadilly run.

It seems to Bob that there is almost no hope of a word, quiet or otherwise, with Marie. His politest attempts to penetrate the crowd are illregarded.

Suddenly the word goes round that Hazel Dawn, the Fruity Cutie with the Big Blue Eyes, is about to do her strip tease act on stage. Magically, the bar empties.

9. Bob advances to the bar. He orders a drink and engages Marie in conversation.

The Killer has entered. He sits down unobtrusively in a corner.

Bob broaches the matter of "Chapel Front"; Marie fences, one eye on the killer.

She writes something, privily, under the bar counter.

The killer moves, leisurely, to Bob's side. The conversation becomes ominous.

Marie holds out her hand to Bob: "Here's your change, sir."

The Killer doesn't care for this. At this moment the Luton boys flood back into the bar: the Fruity Cutie has finished her act . . .

10. Perhaps Bob runs for it, with brief chase backstage? He finally eludes pursuit.

11. Hotel. Bob shows Doctor and Jill the slip of paper that Marie handed to him. It gives the address of the Chapel.

MAN WHO KNEW TOO MUCH. Notes: February 20th, 1955.

1. Some queries and details about Louis's murder:

Bob is holdingthe dying man in his arms. Amongst the first enclosing "ring" of spectators are Mr. and Mrs. Abbott.

After his first words, "London—go to London . . ." Louis pauses, his eyes straying to the spectators: though there is no direct visual emphasis on the Abbotts.

Louis then deliberately drops his already weakeneing voice, addresses Bob in such a way that Bob has to put his ear right close up to Louis's lips.

Meantime, young Phil, amusing himself in another section of the market has been attracted, like the rest of the c rowd, by the drama round Louis. He moves with the crowd, but is prevented xxxx by Jill from forcing his way to t he front.

2. A pompous French sergent-de-ville appears and takes command, just after Louis has died. The native crowd tactfully melts away, but the Europeans stay put. The French cop says that the Europeans will have to go to police headquarters and be questioned.

3. Police headquarters are fetid and hot. Bob is with the Abbotts. Bob is totally mystified by the murder of the blacked-up Louis. Abbott sees no mystery: the Reds are trying to stir up big trouble in Morocco: Louis Bernard, obviously, was an agent of the French Deuxieme Bureau: the Reds got him.

Jill enters. She had received police permission to go and settle Phil down in bed at the hotel. He has faitfully promised to stay put until the return ofhis parents.

An Arab policeman announces that the Prefet is now ready to talk to Mr. and Mrs. Abbott. The latter tells Jill she hopes they may see more of each other the following day.

The Abbotts go off down the corridor, in converse which we do not hear.

Jill tells Bob she would like to cut short their trip in Morocco. She fears the effect of the incident on Phil. She would like to erase it from his mind.

The policeman says that the Prefet is ready to talk to Bob and Jill.

4. Prefet's Office. Bob and Jill are closely questioned about Louis Bernard. Bob is asked: what were Louis's dying words?

Bob is on the defensive. He doesn't care for the bullying manner of the Prefet. How does the Prefet know that Louis spoke any dying words?

Two.

The Prefet replies non-committally that there were many witnesses. There is, perhaps, a grotesque misunderstanding, because the Prefet suspects that Bob may be an agent of the F.B.I.?

A phone call. It is for Bob. An unknown voice tells him that Phil has been kidnaped. If he opens his big mouth, his son's life will be forfeit.

Bob conceals his emotion, manages to ring off on some calming phrase. To the Prefet, he explains the call as having been concerned with some trifling technicality at the hotel.

The Prefet says, dismissively, that he may wish t o talk to Bob and Jill further. Bob becomes a little tough. The Lawrences propose to leave next morning by charter plane.

The Prefet replies that there is only one charter plane available. But he cant stand up to Bob's aggressive attitude. He asks that they leave their future addresses.

5.  Bob and Jill hire a Victoria horse-cab outside the Prefecture, to drive back to their hotel. Bob is in torment. How can he bring himself to tell Jill the content of the telephone call?

Jill is talking away about their future itinerary. The Eiffel Tower will certainly take Phil's mind off that ghastly episode in the market place.

6.  Query. They reach Phil's room in the hotel. Empty. Jill spots at once that Phil's pajamas are on the bed, his day clothes gone.

Bob tells her the content of the telephone call.

7.  Charter Plane. Through a porthole we glimpse Phil's face: a hand is clapped over his mouth. He is drawn back, out of sight.

8.  Bob and Jill are packing. We find that Jill, xxxxxxxxxxx psychologically, has risen to he occasion. No tears. A plan of action. She has a powerful hunch about the Abbotts. Why have they suddenly left the hotel, after the invitation to get together next day?

A phone call. Bob has asked the hotel to check about the charter plane. It was booked by Mr. and Mrs. Abbott, for a routine flight to Brussels.

Bob continues sceptical. But this is enough for Jill. What did Louis say? "London—go to London." And xxxxxx Abbott overheard these words. Abbott has taken their son to London. That is her feminine intuition. She was right in her feminine intuition about Louis, w asn't she? Brussels is only a blind. To London they must go.

MAN WHO KNEW TOO MUCH. Feb. 21st., 1955.

1.  Bob's solo adventure in London. I think it is agreed that this should be a solo adventure, not involving Jill?

2.  You laid it down that this sequence must involve an immediate, continuous, physical menace to Bob. Hence, the suggestion that he is tailed by the Killer.

3.  But, I suggest, your requirement is not fulfilled, unless we known that the man tailing Bob is a Killer.

4.  Hence the suggestion that we glimpse the murderer of Louis: and that it is the same man, who is tailing Bob.

5.  I can't see any other practical means of achieving what you want, here.

6.  You will have noticed that I suggested pinning Bob's actions on the fact that the Enemy warns against: "Any OFFICIAL interference with their plans." This is chi-chi.

But how justify any action on Bob's part? Perhaps J.M.H. will be able to think up a way of capitalising this weakness.

And yet, I think Bob's actions after the interview with Craig are psychologically correct.

7.  Time lapses. I don't know whether you would like to suggest that, after the murder of Louis, our principals have been kept hanging around for hours: so that the drive back in the Victoria to the hotel is Night?

8.  Time lapses in London. These must, in a measure, be governed by Bob's solo adventure.

I xxxxx mean, I have an old Presbyterian feeling that the Chapel scene should be on a Sunday. Conducting religious services on a weekday seems so jolly odd, specially choral ones.

So, if Bob's adventure involves something secular, such as a musichall performance, a full night must elapse.

9.  However, the timing could be thus:

Sunday morning. Lawrences arrive at Connaught Hotel. Interview with Gibson.

Lawrences proceed to Harley Street.

Bob goes (e.g.) to Madame Tussaud's. (Open all day Sunday.)

zzzzzzzzzzzzzzzzzzzzzz
Afternoon service at Chapel.

Festival Concert about six-thirty.

Reception at Embassy, about eight-thirty.

10.  In any case, I would register a personal vote in favour of the overnight time-lapse. The Quatre-Arts Ball feeling is rather strong: if Bob comes back from his solo adventure and hoicks his wife off at once to the Chapel.

I would have thought that your own stylistic postulate would demand a small quiet scene here, between husband and wife. A let-up on the meldramatic fallals: and a poignant reminder of the deep human values at stake

MAN WHO KNEW TOO MUCH. February 21st, 1955.

1.  Bob and Jill arrive at the Connaught Hotel, London. They are amazed to learn from the desk clerk that there is somebody waiting to see them. They know nobody in London.

"It's a Mr. Gibson," says the clerk with a discreet cough. "We took the liberty of letting him wait in your suite. In t he - er - circumstances."

The dumbfounded Lawrences are conducted to their suite, where the suave but formidably intel ligent Gibson introduces himself. (Note: we must decide whether he is to be F.O. or M.1.5.) It is a matter of urgent national and international importance.

Though the man is obviously no faker, Bob resents the Mysterioso and the highhanded reception. A glance between Bob and Jill determines that they are not going to be helpful. On the contrary.

As in the original, Bob and Jill put over their story that they left the kid behind in charge of r elatives. Gibson has little difficulty in breaking t he story down.

Suddenly he threatens. If Bob denies that yuong Phil was kidnaped, xxxxxxxx he will either instantly produce verifiable details of the boy's whereabouts; or else he will be liable to a criminal charge of deserting a minor a nd a dependant.

Bob and Jill realise that they have got to tread carefully with this formidable man Gibson. They cautiously admit the possibility of kidnaping.

"Very well," says Gibson. "And now I am asking you t he same question that the Prefect of Police at Marakesh asked you: what were the dying words of Louis Bernard?"

But Bob dries up again at t his. Gibson advances two excellent arguments why Bob should reveal what he knows. First, it cannot endanger Phil, because the Enemy cannot know that, if anything, Bob has revealed to Gibson. Second, the kidnapers are in the usual stalemate condition: they dare not harm their hostage; or their bargaining weapon would at once disappear.

"Only till Sunday," says Bob, without thinking.

Gibson picks him up sharply. "Sunday? What do you know about Sunday? What is going to happen on Sunday? Tell me, man!"

At this moment there is a phone call. (For Bob? For Jill?) They take the call in the adjoining room.

2.  A big black Rolls is gliding through the streets, it's side curtains drawn. Inside is Phil, in the charge of two men: not the Abbotts. (Perhaps the Killer; and the man who will later drive Abbott's car from the chapel?)

Phil, who appears, submissing, is put through to his parents on the radio-telephone. In the middle of calm reassurances

Two.

about his state of health, etc, he segues quietly and swiftly into a description of the Rolls, registration number, etc. His captors at once disconnect the radio-telephone remlve him from the radio telephone.

(Note, it might be a small touch that Phil is a boy scout. What he does here and later are very fair examples of the virtues of self reliance and presence of mind which the Scouts advocate.)

At the hotel, Bob gets a Final Warning over the radio-telephone. They know that Gibson is with him. They even know, they tell Bob, the kind of arguments that Gibson has been using. Well, to cut out the debating points, it comes down to this: if there is any kind of official attempt to obstruct the plans of the Enemy, Bob and Jill will never see Philip again.

3. The latter end of this conversation has taken place in the bedroom of the Lawrences' suite; with both Jill and Bob present. The call is cut off; and t hey rejoin Gibson who has been left alone. He is just replacing his telephone receiver; a separate line fromthe one in the bedroom.

"Radio-telephone from a car," he says matter-of-factly. "Operating under a fake registration number, of course. Still, your small boy did a good job. Seven-seater black Rolls-Royce, 1955 model. Maybe they wont have the sense to dump it."

Bob is angry at this wiretapping. Gibson is unmoved. "You have chosen to act like a good father—instead of like a good citizen of the Western Alliance. What do you care—if World War Three is sparked off on Sunday? Must say I should behave just the same as you, if I were in your shoes. Not that that's any excuse . . ."

He says that Bob knows where to find him, any time, day or night, if Bob changes his mind. He exits.

Jill's control so far has been miraculous. Now, she has reached breaking point. The doctor and the considerate husband in Bob come uppermost. He persuades her that she must come and see Dr. Craig, in Harley Street. Craig was his onetime teacher, whom he had rencountered at the Medical Conference in Paris.

4. Note: we discussed the idea that Gibson, in the course of conversation, confirmed Jill's intuitive hunch about the Abbotts. They did indeed charter the charter plane; on a course set for Brussels. But, as Gibson, explains, the plane could sneak in across the English coast, touch down for a minute, then resume its course to Brussels. Technical details would have to be checked about this.

5. We also discussed that Jill challenges Gibson to round up

xxx

Three.

the Abbotts. Gibson points out that this would be a needle in a haystack. The Abotts, if guilty, would surely possess alternative passports in other names.

In this context, I suggest the overriding consideration must be how much total footage the whole of the Gibson sequence will stand.

5. Harley Street. Craig is a wise and sympathetic old boy. He takes a serious view of Jill's state of mind. Bob and Jill didn't mean to tell Craig all about everything: but they realise they must.

6. The Killer moves, leisurely, up Harley Street, as the Rolls vanishes round a corner. He locates the house in which he is interested. He settles down to watch it.

7. Bob and Jill have t old Craig everything. He pounces on one of the phrases from Louis's dying words. As a Londoner himself, he realises at once that the words possess a specific meaning, which was incomprehensible to Bob and Jill.

Bob fires up at this.He is determined, instantly, to follow up the clew. Jill protests. But Craig approves. It will do Jill a world of good to stop worrying about her son for a while, and start worrying about her husband.

Meantime, Craig will give Jill a spot of hynopedic therapy. (We take this opportunity of reminding the audience that hypnopedia is, nowadays, a commonplace of medical treatment.) Craig will escort Jill back to the hotel in two hours' time.

8.  Bob leaves the Harley Street house and is duly tailed by the Killer.

9.  There follows an adventure for Bob in which he secures the clew to the Chapel; and also throws the Killer off his trail. (Barmaid at Collins Musichall yet to be discussed).

10.  Bob rejoins Craig and Jill at the hotel. Jill is now in much better shape.

11.  Note: Gibson would undoubtedly have had both Bob and Jill efficiently tailed. I suppose we must either ignore this, or make a virtue of it.

MAN WHO KNEW TOO MUCH. Notes: February 24th, 1955.

1.  The dying Louis says "London—London". Then, he drops his voice. What he says sounds to Bob as follows:

> Ambrose Chappell . . . Contact him . . .

What he really means, poor fellow, as we discover later, is:

> The chapel in Ambrose St. xxxx used by enemy to communicate with subsidiary agents by means of a hymn which contains a code of instructions.

The misunderstanding is thus, both on the word Chapel and on the word Hymn.

2.  Harley Street. While old Craig is dealing with Jill, Bob checks the name Ambrose xxxxxx Chappell in the telephone book. There is only one Ambrose Chappell listed.

(We would have to check with the London Telephone Directory and find a first name for Mr. Chappell which gives us only one directory entry. Or, rather, no actual entry, because of libel.)

3.  Now: for size. There is, I believe, in Camden Town, an establishment which is the last stronghold in Britain of Taxidermy. They will stuff you anything, from an elephant to a gnat. (It was given a splash in Picture Post or Illustrated, a couple of years ago.)

All sorts of obscene eviscerations are in progress as Bob arrives: though nothing which blatantly reveals the innocent taxidermist reason for same.

The employees are laconic. Bob has some difficulty in entering the presence of Ambrose Chappell, who is Ernest Thesiger. (Or Sim, of Course, if he would do it).

Bob tries to box clever. He realises that he must proceed with caution. But he, a straightforward American, is not accustomed to devious talk.

Ambrose, unhappily, gets the impression that Bob has murdered a Frenchman in Marakesh and wants him stuffed. The honour of Ambrose's firm is at stake. He proposes to call Scotland Yard and give Bob in charge.

2.

The intervention of Scotland Yard, as we realise, is the last thing Bob desires. He is compelled to reveal everything to Ambrose.

4. Perhaps, back to Craig and Jill. She is better. This would be the last scene in the picture to be played on a purely emotional note, with no melodramatic content. Craig will take her back to the hotel.

5. Back to Ambrose and Bob. Ambrose believes Bob's story. ("Ah, the Secret Service. On some moresuitable occasion, I must tell you about the ostrich I stuffed for General Pershing in World War One.")

He ventures an interpretation of

Ambrose Chappell . . . Contact him . . .

"There is," he says, "a non-comformist—an extremely noncomformist—chapel in Ambrose Street, in Somers Town, behind St. Pancras Station. But who is the Him, or He, whom you have to contact, I really cannot surmise."

6. Bob rejoins Craig and Jill at the hotel. Bob and Jill set off for the chapel in Ambrose Street.

These pages are indicative of the kind of work Hitchcock did throughout the period. *Vertigo,* Hitchcock's next Paramount film, would develop in much the same way.[2]

---

[2]For an extensive examination of this script's development, see my book *Vertigo: The Making of a Hitchcock Classic.*

The script work with his friend MacPhail was not progressing to Hitchcock's satisfaction, so Hitchcock sat down and began outlining the picture. The following are his own notes on how two key sequences should be shaped:

1. Ben arrives
2. Ben confronts AC Jr.
3. "My name is Mackenzie and I arrived from Marakesh a few hours ago.
4. AC dead pan.
5 Ben says "you probably know why I've come here."
6 AC "My dear sir I haven't the faintest idea."
7. Ben I was given your name by someone I happened to meet in Marakesh.
   AC oh yes?
8. Ben I expect you've heard of him — Louis Bernard — a french
9. AC Uh Uh.
9a  Ben says a deal could be done — involuntary
    Ben goes on to suggest that a deal might be made if he kept his mouth shut about the killing that is to take place in London.
10 AC reacts. (?)
11 Ben is prepared to put down $20,000.
12 "Father phone for the police

13 Ben says you're bluffing
you wouldn't dare.

14 AC I don't know what you're
talking about etc but the
police had better be told etc

15 Ben desperate starts to go.

16 Bar the door - Ben
pulled off - Hullaballoo.

17 Lions - Swordfish. Montage
fight - Ben gets to go.

---

1. Ben arrives outside. To explain
about Addison's collar in the
photo that gave her the idea of
the chapel being a place

2 They enter the chapel and stand
at the back. No Addison's in
evidence

3. They sing in the Hymn tune that
there is no one is identifiable ?
are they barking up a wrong tree.

4. Suddenly they are startled by the
appearance of Mrs Addison coming
down the aisle with a collecting bag.

They try to hide. She comes nearer and nearer and finally is startled to see them. Ben puts a £1 note in. She turns to go back.

5  Addison appears in the pulpit he sees his wife's startled face.

6  Addison starts sermon.

7  Ben instincts Jo — Jo goes.

8  Addison changes sermon.

9  Congregation goes.

10  Addison descends from pulpit and instincts wife and Reissar

11  Ben goes up the aisle — The two men meet.
~~Dialogue scale~~ (M) ⚡

~~Addison is suave and quite dead pan as he compliments Ben on his discovery of the cho~~

9  Congregation goes.

10  Addison comes down from Pulpit and gives intructions to wife + Reissar.

11 Ben goes up aisle

12 They meet. Dialog.

~~13 Two horses appear.~~

13 Main door bangs.

14 Ben sees two men.

15 Ben manoeuvers to pulpit

16 He grabs mike & yells Hank

17 Faint reply from Hank.

18 Ben leaps from pulpit to door

19 Men grab.

These notes were given to John Michael Hayes—who, rather quickly, wrote his draft. Hitchcock, in turn, wrote numerous notes on the Hayes version. Here is a sample of the careful detail that Hitchcock loved:

Page 7 (notes 4-27-55)
I have eliminated the intervention of the other Arabs in the bus because this may affect the French reception of the film. There is some political trouble between France and Morocco and I don't think we should point up an overall antagonism between the Arabs and the white man. It should be left entirely to the one Arab who is angry. As Ben is an educated man, and not just a brash American tourist abroad, I don't feel he would expect any Arab to be able to speak English. If he were some stage Texan type, this might be all right, but I feel the character Jimmy is playing is a little more understanding of his surroundings. Just in the same way, turning around to the rest of the bus and calling "English!" seems unnecessary, so that Ben's first speech when he says, "Now wait a minute, etc.," it should [come] more or less spontaneously from him without him realizing what he is saying. This makes the intervention of Louis Bernard not obnoxious and makes Louis an understanding bilingual Frenchman.

Page 8
Sc. 30 Again I am disturbed in the final speech on this page where Louis mentions Basheesh from the foreigner. Again I feel that think we might get in trouble from the French, and in any case, I feel that this attitude toward dark-skinned people is out-of-date. Perhaps this speech could be readjusted without this reference. To go a little further, I am not sure that this giving of money to the Arab shouldn't be altogether eliminated and just rely upon the calm and pleasant diplomacy of Louis to save the situation, so that the Arab retreats grumblingly. The reason I feel fairly strongly about this is because tearing the veil is a delicate matter anyway. It is a religious thing and the idea of offense being settled with a pittance may again get us into trouble.

Hitchcock loved to work out the fine detail. When Hayes wrote later that there were no trains into Marrakech, Hitchcock, ever the train buff, corrected him: "No, there are three trains that come into Marrakech."

## North by Northwest

*North by Northwest* deserves a book-length treatment. The writing of the script was a fascinating and extensive process and the space available here could never do it justice, so I'll limit myself to the very brief but interesting genesis of the original story. Hitchcock had an amazing ability to file away ideas that decades later would see fruition. The first letter from journalist Otis Guernsey is unfortunately not dated, but appears to have been sent to Hitchcock in the early fifties.

**New York Herald Tribune**

*A European Edition is Published Daily in Paris*

PEnnsylvania 6-4000

230 West 41st Street, New York 18

Dear Hitch:

This note has been long in coming, and I hope
that the delay has not caused you any embarassment. I
wanted to make sure of my ground before I got in touch
with you again about the script idea we talked over in
"21".

Kay Brown got in touch with me, and she has been
very patient and helpful about the whole thing. She has
stressed the need for speed in this matter, and that is
why I am writing you although nothing constructive has
been accomplished.

As you remember, the idea was originally this:
that a diplomatic controvery exists in a Near Eastern
country, involving, possibly, something active like the
smuggling-in of American arms collected in Europe where
they were sold on abandoned and brought in to create
a sub rosa rebellion; that the "Good Guys", in order
to decoy the "Bad Guys'" espionage, create a fictitious
character of a masterspy; that a young, ingenuous American salesman, entering the country for respectable purposes is saddled by accident with this identity; that,
subject to this unexpected melodrama he turns like the
American worm always does and tries to clear himself;
that, in the course of his searches he meets a girl who
is part of the "Good Guys'" plan to establish the fictional masterspy, and, finally, that he contributes to
the downfall of the bad guys in a flurry of denouement
and romance.

The idea of an innocent man suddenly saddled
with a highly romantic and dangerous identity still
sounds to me like a good one for a picture. But it does
not seem to stand up under development. I have worked
for a considerable time on it, covering some 65 pages
with notes and detail in four different approaches.

It still does not seem to work, instead developing faults of a) logic b) corn or c) overcomplicated
devices in order to establish situations.

**NEW YORK**
**Herald Tribune**
*A European Edition is Published Daily in Paris*

PEnnsylvania 6-4000                                    230 West 41st Street, New York 18

I admit the possibility that the flaws may
exist only in the eye of the beholder; that it does not
suffer development simply because I personally am unable
to develop it. After many frustrations I can only say that
I'm not sure, but I am not yet convinced that it is I
who am at fault.

There's no point in going into detail about
the plot avenues I have explored, except to say that
I can think of yet one more possibility that has not at
this writing shown the signs of cracking apart under
the strain of development. I haven't given up, and I
intend to continue working on it until I run out of
ideas.

At the same time, I don't want to hold you up
by pretending that I have the perfect outline just
waiting to go to the typist's. Do whatever you wish
with the idea--abandon it, or cause it to be worked on.
In the meantime, I will keep my nose to the grindstone
and if I come up with anything I'll forward it to you
via Kay Brown.

In the meantime, best of luck to you and yours
and don't fail to let me know when you pass through
this metropolis.

Yours,

The importance of the idea in the development of what became *North by Northwest* is revealed in this letter from 1957 to Hitchcock and MGM, giving the story to Hitchcock.

NEW YORK
## Herald Tribune
*A European Edition is Published Daily in Paris*

PEnnsylvania 6-4000                                    230 West 41st Street, New York 36

October 14, 1957

Mr. Alfred Hitchcock
% M-G-M
1540 Broadway
New York, New York

Dear Hitch,

    A few years ago I suggested to you an idea for a movie, vaguely based on something which actually happened in the Middle East during World War II. At that time, a couple of secretaries in a British embassy invented--for the fun of it and to relieve the boredom of an inactive post--a fake masterspy. They gave him a name, and a record and planted information around to lure the Nazis onto his trail.

    To their delight and astonishment, the enemy gobbled the bait and spent some valuable time and energy trying to hunt down the non-existent operative.

    I suggested to you that this escapade might be built into a good movie melodrama in any one of a number of ways. The actual treatment we discussed at the time involved an ingenuous young American--probably a traveling salesman--who has the fake identity pinned on him by accident and finds that he cannot get rid of it. He is on the spot: the enemy is trying to capture and kill him, and his friends cannot help him because they cannot afford to have their ruse exposed.

    However you plan to use the idea at this time, I hereby hand it over to you, blithely and with best wishes, with all rights and privileges, etc., etc., with no purpose of evasion or mental reservations, etc., etc., for such consideration as may have been discussed between my agent and yours, for all the good it may do you which I hope will be plenty.

Cordially yours,

Otis L. Guernsey Jr.

OLG:rec

## The Birds

The development of *The Birds* has also been extensively discussed in screenwriter (and noted author of crime fiction) Evan Hunter's book *Hitch and Me*. The idea for the film came from a terrific short story by Daphne du Maurier (Hitchcock's third film based on a du Maurier text; the first two were *Jamaica Inn* and *Rebecca*).

Hunter described the day-to-day process in his book:

"Tell me the story so far."

These are the words Hitch would say to me every working weekday morning.

"Tell me the story so far." And every morning, after we'd had our coffee, he would sit back in his big black leather chair with his hands folded over his belly, and I would tell him the story to date, ending with wherever we had left off the afternoon before.

In the beginning, there was no story to tell. Day after day, we grappled with vague ideas and ephemeral notions, doing what the cartoonists call "snowballing," but the only recurring approach was the kernel of the Stranger-in-Town idea I'd brought from New York. The schoolteacher was gone, of course, an early casualty. What remained was the concept of a woman coming to a strange town, which is attacked by birds shortly after her arrival. Do the townspeople have something to hide? Is there a guilty secret here? Do they see this stranger as a messenger of revenge? Are the birds an instrument of punishment for their guilt? All very heavy stuff.

We toyed with this approach for days on end, stopping only for lunch taken in Hitch's office.

Of interest from Hitchcock's files is this letter from Hitchcock to Hunter after reading the first full draft of the screenplay:

November 30, 1961

Mr. Evan Hunter
R.D. #1 Horseshoe Hill
Pound Ridge
Westchester, New York

Dear Evan:

I have had the opportunity of going over the script a couple of times and, in consequence, would like to make some further observations.

The script has also been read by a number of other people, mostly the technicians who are working on the picture, such as Art director, production personnel, etc. probably not more than 8 or 9 people in all.

With the comments I have, I'm also going to include their observations. Naturally, of course, where someone might have made some comment which I didn't agree with I am, as Sam Goldwyn would say, "including them out".

The first general impression is that the script is way too long. This, of course, I know you are already aware of. However the concensus seems to indicate that it is the front part of the script that needs some drastic pruning. I will suggest some ideas to you later on in this letter.

Now the next prevalent comment I have heard is that both the girl and the young man seem insufficiently charaterized. In endeavoring to analyze this critisism I have gathered the impression 'there doesn't seem to be any particular feature about the young man himself to warrant the girl going to all the trouble she does in delivering a couple of love birds'. Another comment about him was obviously misconstrued from the wording in the script—some people looked upon him as a shy, awkward young man. Now I think this was caused because the reader failed to appreciate the fact that his manner was awkward only because in our script he behaves self-consciously about wanting to purchase such things as "love birds". When I reflected upon this it looked to me as though the joke about buying love birds and the young man's self-consciousness about it wouldn't come off. In other words, people would say, "What's difficult about buying a pair of love birds?" After all they are not contraceptives!

Now, maybe this scene in the bird shop hasn't come off. It certainly has inspired the comment that there is nothing particular about the young man at present to warrant the girl chasing out to get his car number, etc. It could be that the whole scene is too mild for the young man to make any sharp impression on the girl at all.

Evan, would you please permit me to interpose here with an observation that I think we should look out for in this script and this scene in the bird shop is a fair example of what I mean. We run the risk of having in a picture what I call 'no scene' scenes. By this I mean that the little sequence might have narrative value but in itself is undramatic. It very obviously lacks shape and it doesn't within itself have a climax as a scene on the stage might. I remember many years ago when I made the movie LIFEBOAT I got John Steinbeck to do a story outline for me and the script was done by Jo Swerling. Now Jo Swerling was a very prominent and successful screenplay writer and had worked on a lot of Frank Capra's early pictures. Now, of course, as you probably remember if you ever saw the picture, LIFEBOAT was a group story lasting several days and within the narrative a number of sequences. These were very well written but I found that they were 'no scene' scenes—in other words, they lacked dramatic shape and I remember having to have sessions all during the shooting of the picture in order to correct these particular dramatic lapses.

Now we have a number of these in our present script. For example, in the newspaper office in the scene between Melanie and her father I feel the audience will get nothing much out of this scene. In fact, one of the comments made was that the father was just a stock figure whose relationship with his daughter seems fairly conventional.

Now at Bodega Bay I can clearly see that we do have one or two scenes with no particular shape. These are the scenes of Melanie buying temporary garments and going to the hotel for a room. They really accomplish very little and account for some of the excessive length in the front part of the picture. I feel sure these could be eliminated so that the scene when she presents herself at the school teacher's house with only a paper bag can be dramatically capitalized. This is to say that she explains her purchases and wish for a room—after the fact.

But here again her relationship with the young man must have a very solid premise for her going to the trouble of taking a room for the night. Now perhaps this may have already been taken care of in the bird shop. But if that isn't sufficient then we need a further propellent in the dockside scene on page 46 of the present script.

Now, Evan, there is, I am sorry to say, an almost unanimous comment that the interior of the church scene should go because, apparently to the script reader, the story does not progress as all. The scene outside the church, of course, serves a very good purpose for us. It brings our couple together again and sets up the children's party.

Incidentally, at the children's party I think Bob Boyle, our production man, had quite an interesting thought that it would be more interesting and, I am inclined to agree with him, that the bird attack might take place during the blindman's buff sequence so that we get a little blindfolded girl attacked. Of course, we could have the entrance of the cake about the same time.

Generally speaking, Evan, the rest of it seems to be in pretty good shape except perhaps for some pruning here and there.

Now for some other thoughts. In order to keep the suspense alive from the very beginning I do think we ought to punctuate the sequences with some more positive ideas that will keep the audience a little on edge in the matter of "birds". And, I think we could start this right from the very beginning.

I know you had an idea of this when you had Melanie walking down the street and a flock of pigeons fluttered away. Now an audience might get some significance in this or they may not but somehow I think if we are going to put in ideas of this nature they should be a little less blurred. For example: How would it be to open the picture on a San Francisco street with a series of cuts of upturned faces, some stationary, others moving slowly along, and what they are looking at is an unusual number of sea gulls flying above the buildings of the city. We could continue the upturned faces until at last we came to Melanie also looking up and pan her right into the bird shop where she could make some comment to the woman inside who dismisses it with a remark to the effect that when the weather is bad at sea they often get driven inland. Another spot that occurs to me where we could have a sharp moment—at the end of the night scene between Annie and Melanie there could be the sound of a thump on the front door. They open it to find a dead bird lying there and the scene could fade out on this. This will also tie in with Annie's last line in this scene. There are probably some other spots which might lend themselves to this kind of treatment in the earlier part of the script. Incidentally, I still think that at some moment Annie should see the cut on Melanie's head.

You know I've often wondered what the Audubon Society's attitude might be to this picture. And if we have any fears that they might be a little "frowning" we might find a spot towards the end where Kathy theorizes about "It's all because we put them in cages, we shoot them down, we eat them, etc." This, of course, leaves only one other question as to whether the Audubon Society will frown at birds having a revengeful nature!

Well, Evan, there you are. Until we have further conversations these are all the things that I can think of to put down. Naturally there may be a few more things to be done. I'm still wondering whether anything of a thematic nature should go into the script. I'm sure we are going to be asked again and again, especially by the morons, "Why are they doing it?"

I have had some conversations with your agent, Hal Landers, about the timing for these adjustments. As you know, we originally talked of your coming out just prior to shooting time to make any corrections in the script that may be needed. I fear, however, that this is going to be too late for the production department to make their preparations without a final script. And it would seem, consequently, that these adjustments will have to be made almost immediately. Now I don't know what your present arrangements are and whether it would be convenient for you to do these changes but I would be grateful if you would discuss this with Mr. Landers.

My best wishes to Anita and yourself.

Sincerely,

AJH:sg

cc: Mr. Hal Landers

---

This letter is particularly rich for not only its adept story analysis but also for its interesting recollection concerning the development of other screenplays.

Hitchcock was concerned enough about the screenplay for *The Birds* that he enlisted two other writers to analyze the screenplay. The first was his old friend Hume Cronyn, who recalled his experiences with Hitchcock in his memoirs:

Early on in our working relationship, I discovered a curious trick of his. We would be discussing some story point with great intensity, trembling on the edge of a solution to the problem at hand, when Hitch would suddenly lean back in his chair and say, "Hume, have you heard the story of the traveling salesman and the farmer's daughter?" I would look at him blankly and he would proceed to tell it with great relish, frequently commenting on the story's characters, the nature of the humor involved, and the philosophical demonstration implied. That makes it sound as though the stories might be profound or at least witty. They were neither. They were generally seventh-grade jokes of the sniggery school, and frequently infantile.

After several days' work together, punctuated by such stories, I challenged him—politely. "Why do you do that?"

"Do what?"

"Stop to tell jokes at a critical juncture."

"It's not so critical—it's only a film."

"But we were just about to find a solution to the problem. I can't even remember what it was now."

"Good. We were pressing. . . . You never get it when you press."

And while I may have failed to appreciate Hitch's jokes, I've never forgotten that little piece of philosophy, either as an actor or as a sometime writer.

On another occasion, we were arguing about some story point or other when he seized my pad and pencil and drew a large circle.

"This is the pie. We keep trying to cut into it here." And he drew a savage wedge into the circle's perimeter. "What we must try to do is this—" and the pencil raced around the opposite side of his pie and dug a wedge in there. I blinked. "What does that mean? . . . Turn day into night? Color into black and white? Change our antagonist into our hero? . . ." "Maybe. What we're doing is all so . . . expected. I want to be surprised." It was a very old lesson demonstrated in graphic form. Logic is so frequently boring. It's the contradictions that are fascinating. In the year following *Rope,* Hitch asked me to do another treatment, this one based on Helen Simpson's novel *Under Capricorn.* It was to star Ingrid Bergman and Joe Cotten, a sprawling panoramic story of Australia in the days of penal transportation. Hitch wanted to shoot *Capricorn* in the same style he'd used so successfully in *Rope*—a series of long takes. That was a mistake, and I knew it, but even I, as friend and collaborator, was not about to tell him so. You simply did not tell Alfred Hitchcock how to shoot—or how not to shoot—a film.

I went to London with Hitch to work on *Capricorn.* We would meet for our story conferences at Sidney Bernstein's offices in Golden Square. From the beginning, the work was fraught with problems. On one particular morning, with Hitch at the end of the table and Sidney and I on either side of him, Hitch suddenly reared back in his chair, scowling like an angry baby, and announced, "This film is going to be a flop. I'm going to lunch." And he stalked out of the room, pouting. I was appalled; Sidney was immediately solicitous. "Now, Hume, don't be upset. You know Hitch: he'll have a good lunch, come back, and everything will be serene." It was true; I'd seen Hitch suffer these tantrums before. He never had them on the set; by the time we got there, the whole film was already shot in his head, down to every cut and camera angle. (He used to say that the actual shooting of a film bored him; he'd already made it.) But during a film's preparation, he could become very mercurial; his emotional thermometer would soar to over a hundred degrees in enthusiasm, only to plunge below freezing in despair. We were alike in that, and I should have been more philosophical about the morning's upset. The trouble was that in this particular instance I had the awful, nagging suspicion that Hitch's premonition was accurate. During the afternoon's work, we found a way round the morning's gridlock, and while I found the detour less than satisfying, Hitch was restored to a benign humor. He asked me to have dinner with him at the Savoy. When I arrived, he was positively purring. There were two long-necked bottles of wine sitting in the cooler. I remember that they had mauve caps. "The last two bottles of this in the Savoy cellar . . . and we're going to drink them both." The wine was Schloss Johannisberger, Furst von Metternich, of a rare vintage which I've forgotten. We had dinner, we drank the two bottles, and I staggered out of the hotel in need of fresh air and a long walk. I weaved down the Strand, across Trafalgar Square and along Piccadilly to my hotel, and fell into bed. I remember that walk because of my anxiety over the treatment—but to Hitch, at least on that one evening, it was "only a film."

It was with some sense of this history that Hitchcock turned to Cronyn on this occasion to examine *The Birds* (which is a little ironic, since he would tell Truffaut a few months later that he felt Cronyn was rather weak as a writer).

---

Piazza Margana 19
Rome.

January 13th 1962.

Alfred Hitchcock, Esq.,
10957 Bellagio Road
Los Angeles 24,
California.

Dear Hitch,

I think it's a marvellous story. I told you that—and we don't need to be reminded of "The cinematic as well as oral values". They're wonderfully obvious. I'm delighted by the counterpoint of the pastoral, almost lyric quality of the settings. . . . sunlight on the bay, the coast-road, the flights of birds (at least in the beginning) the flowers, the singing children etc. And against all that the mounting tension and horror.

I could go on and enumerate the many scenes I like but that's not what this letter is about. You were kind enough to encourage my writing to you, so I will plunge into my reservations. If they're unhelpful you can quickly file this in the round file under your desk.

First, I agree that there's room for improvement in the development and relationship of the principal characters, and these seem particularly important in view of the extreme and macabre nature of the events. However, I don't think the deficiencies are alarming and the construction seems sound. At any rate I was continually held by the story, never bothered by a sense of manipulation or unreality, and delighted that no attempt was made to explain the phenomena. (Ice-box trade)?

MITCH: Is it possible to give him even more humor? I like his cockiness, but he sounds a trifle smug, even priggish on page 10, Sc. 22. Does he have to explain why he does what he does here? Suppose he just did it without talking about it? Isn't the mystery of his behavior intriguing? Might it not lend an even stronger motivation to Melanie's trip to Bodega Bay? I realise you want to establish the "practical joker" aspect of Melanie's character, but isn't that already implied in her behaviour with Mitch, with Mrs. MacGruder, on the telephone, and in Mitch's apartment house.

I suspect that these scenes (13 through 22) can be even more amusing and every bit as infuriating to Melanie, without the immediate, on the nose revelation of motive. And that the motive can become explicit and will seem more graceful if it appears later—perhaps on Page 40, Sc. 160. The action here (First Aid) will counterpoint such straight talk and the motivation for Mitch is stronger now, less gratuitous.

More about Mitch later in relation to Lydia.

MELANIE: The best moment in her development seems to come in that "Maybe I ought to join the other children" speech (Page 79, Sc. 237). I am a little vague as to the other sign-posts in her growth. I have a sense that they're announced in description and may not be fully dramatized.

The implied arrogance, silliness and selfishness of the early Melanie may need heightening, so that the change to consideration, responsibility and maturity are more marked—and more endearing.

ANNIE: I recognise her plot function. I'm not sure I understand her catalytic effect on the other characters. She's not really a threat or a spur to Melanie is she? The "capucino" speeches are good ones, they give her a background (they might almost come from an older Melanie). However, are they, or rather, is Annie really serving the function you intended?

Either I'm obtuse here or the script is wooly. Perhaps you need more of Annie, or do you need less?

LYDIA: At first reading I had the impression of a basic contradiction in Lydia's character. She seemed to be one sort of person up until Sc. 412 and then another emerged. Nothing wrong with that if you buy it. However, I smelled a herring. I was not only unprepared for this scene—as well as the last Lydia-Melanie scene in the film—I was prepared for something else. I imagine that's exactly what Mr. Hunter intended but I don't think it quite comes off. I'm confused about Lydia and I feel Annie has set up a straw threat which is really a cheat.

On rereading the script and rechecking all the references to Lydia, I agreed that her development could be logically justified. She would be apprehensive about losing Mitch, she might seem possessive and Annie could consider this as bad ("she's not a bad person really") So why the confusion? Why am I prepared to dislike Lydia, then like and sympathise with her (in 412—the tea scene with Melanie) then dislike her again (in 555 when she attacks Mitch) and end up feeling a sense of contrivance in her final scene when she comforts Melanie.

I think the trouble may lie in the strength of the cliche of possessive mommism. We've had a lot of that, and consequently Annie's remarks followed by Lydia's guarded and anxious attitude provoke a conditioned reaction. "Uh huh, here's the heavy".

I don't like black and white characters and I don't see why Lydia shouldn't be possessive, but I sense a better way of doing it than as it stands. I also think a basic decision has to be made as to whether Lydia is fundamentally "good" or "bad". It would seem to me both more original and more interesting if the choice was "good".

Following that premise, I think Lydia is most effective when she's consistent with what she says about herself in Sc. 412. She seems to be telling the truth here.

"I wish I were a stronger person"—"I'd love to relax sometime"—"I don't fuss and fret over my children"—"I feel safer with him here"—"I don't think I could bear being left alone"—"I want to like any girl Mitch chooses".

This all adds up to a picture of someone extremely vulnerable: apprehensive, lonely, and insecure. I think that vulnerability is becoming, and should be emphasized. It serves the story. Of all the characters, Lydia seems the most likely to be affected by the birds. Because of that I hope the audience will like her, identify with her and tremble for her. The preparation in her character will be important, and if achieved I think her hysterics can be hair-raising because they are understandable, even predictable— predictable in precisely the same fashion that Michele's situation is when her glasses fall off. (444) The same thrill of horrid anticipation based on vulnerability.

I feel sure you won't want to steal this business for Lydia. I suggested it really as "for instance". It's the sort of thing—being lost without her glasses—which dramatizes the peculiarly defenceless nature of the character. There are others, but offhand I can't think of one as vivid, (My brother went through a terrible period once when he couldn't talk—a form of shell-shock. When he got upset he couldn't tell you what was wrong. It was horrifying. He just stood there gibbering.)

You might also consider having Lydia admire birds, really care about them to begin with. It's already suggested in her concern over the chickens.

Conversely, I think the effectiveness of Lydia's character may be damaged by any suggestion that she is consciously bitchy. I felt that occasionally before I got to Sc. 412. I think she should be possessive in her loneliness, but perhaps Mitch should carry some part of that element. If he feels a reasonable sympathy and responsibility for his mother's aloneness, I think it recommends him to us more than does the strained patience with which he presently treats her. If he's aware of her insecurity and can handle her anxieties with humor rather than controlled exasperation, it can only add to his sense of conflict over Melanie. It won't lessen it.

So much of all this is a matter of playing attitude rather than rewrite. If my premise has validity the only spots that I think might need reconsideration are the following: Sc. 202, Pages 64–65. Sc. 555, Page 157. Sc. 188, Page 58.

MISCELLANEOUS: I wonder if the sleeping business (Sc. 574, Page 161) is not unreal and the dialogue in Sc. 579 in danger of seeming ludicrous? Could they possibly sleep in the face of the noise and circumstance described? Also might it not be better to keep the sleeping business for Sc. 589 alone—in the Hiatus. Silence, exhausted sleep, and the gradual emergence of a new sound.

Jess is very good at the terrifying business of hysteria. The danger, of course, is hysterics for hysteria's sake, which is why I harp on establishing vulnerability and preparation. It is just possible that somewhat greater preparation maybe needed for Lydia's hysterics in 555, but I'm not at all certain about this. We haven't seen her since 413. I'm not suggesting another scene or cuts to Lydia where they don't belong, I just wonder what has happened to <u>her</u> in this interim. I wonder, if unseen by Mitch and Melanie, she should come out of the house to tell them she has got something on the radio, and overhear Mitch's line "It may not be last week again for a long, long time" as well as see the birds coming.

I don't know what your plans are for the script. A number of times in the past you've asked me about writers. If you are looking for someone to polish, I will risk a suggestion. Millard Lampell—my collaborator on MAN RUNNING. It was for that reason that I cabled New York to have our script air-mailed to you, although I would have much preferred to have held it back until we cut twenty pages of it and done our own polishing job—which is now in the works.

Millard dramatized Hersey's THE WALL which ran for 5 months in New York last season and is an enormous current hit in Germany. He is very good with character and with comedy. He has also had problems—black list—but I think that's behind him now. Paramount can fill you in. They bought and released a film of his called CHANCE MEETING. I didn't like it, but it got wonderful reviews.

Millard's address is 789, West End Avenue, New York City. Telephone University 5 6790. You've probably got ideas of your own and won't be interested in this one. However, I would never recommend anyone to you for whom I didn't have considerable regard—and if you are on the hunt for someone who is available and prepared to do this sort of job, I think he might be.

Of course, he doesn't know anything about this suggestion.

Sorry I can't make this shorter. I had hoped to get it off days ago but I haven't been well. Now I must rush it to the post office.

Love to Alma.

Yours,

HUME CRONYN

P.S. When agents have nothing to do with getting one a job, I think they feel they have to prove something. This always makes me nervous. Joe had to cable me in the Bahamas to ask me if it was true that I demanded a $1000 a week for expenses on this film. It wasn't. If GAC makes unreasonble difficulties, please let Jess know—not of course that I won't be delighted to see her take every penny from you that she possibly can.

Cronyn was not the only writer Hitchcock tapped for ideas on *The Birds*. He asked the venerable V. S. Pritchett to give his opinion of the screenplay:

1489 Summit Road,
Berkeley 8.
Thornwall 9-0556.

16th March, 1962

Dear Mr. Hitchcock,

I have now read the script of <u>THE BIRDS</u> and enclose my criticism of it, as we arranged. Let me say at once, it is obviously going to be a superb picture. I am not at all worried about the terror scenes—they will be magnificent. But I am, as you will see, rather dubious about the characterisation of the protagonists in the early part. I do understand that the early meetings of Mitch and Melanie are a skilful means of misleading us and of increasing the surprise when it does come, but it did seem to me to take a long time. I have, of course, been thinking of it purely in the terms of story and without perhaps giving full consideration to the brilliant visual effects of scene and atmosphere that you always get in your films. But I do think that the link between the characters' love story and the terror is not very strong.

Anyway, you'll see from the enclose what I think in detail.

Thank you for letting me see it. It was exciting.

Good wishes for your wife and yourself,

Yours ever,

V.S. Pritchett

V.S. Pritchett,
1489 Summit Road,
<u>Berkeley 8. Calif.</u>

The Birds.

This story has two phases. There is a love story of some piquancy, with an ex-girl friend and a jealous mother making complications for the lovers. This part occupies just under half the script—reckoning by pages; I dont know about running time. This is done in the sense of light comedy: a city girl arriving in a rural place. The second phase is enormously more important—the inexplicable terror of the birds who attack not only the main characters, but the whole community, with the suggestion that this is a revolt of the birds against the human race. This drama takes 100 pages and is brilliantly managed. The arrival of the swift in the fireplace at Brenner's house is a splendid moment. The school scene with the crows is admirable. In order to tie in the first phase of the story with the second, the effect of the terror is shown to settle the problem of the lovers: to teach the socialite that the "gags" of Nature are grim, to reconcile the mother to the love affair. They blindly escape from the village, like panic stricken refugees on the road or soldiers that have thrown away their guns and are left, as we are, in a state of pure terror, asking, Why? There are theories but there is no answer. The crime is one of Nature's wanton efforts. The unresolved doubt is whether the birds "know" or can "organise". So although this may be a science fiction story without the science, there is a suggestion of allegory or fable underneath.

How to link such a fantastic story with ordinary people? Somewhere here is the weakness of the script. It tends to split dangerously into two. The main reason for this is that the chief people, as at present characterised are only mildly interesting. Their private imbroglio is tame. Mitch might just as well be a stockbroker as a criminal lawyer. The girl is said to have once been a wild young socialite, but from the beginning she is merely mischievous and is even being cured of that. Her rival (Annie) is obligingly good-natured and has already left the field; Lydia, the mother, although said to be possessive, is well on the way to being simply the normal watchful mother. Their common problem is not shown to be very serious, let alone desperate, bitter, passionate or emotionally intractable. I know it is a convention that the characters in a thriller must not be so strongly characterised that they divert the audience from the thrills of fear and suspense that are the overwhelming interesting of the story and that the very mildness of the people accentuates the effect of the horror they will undergo: what have ordinary, harmless people done to deserve it is a highly dramatic question. But if the people are under-characterised the story will fall apart when the terror strikes; one will get the impression that they are in two different stories—in this case a light comedy and a terror tale—that do not weld together.

There are other reasons for the failure to knit the two satisfactorily. The opening is slow. The gull does indeed strike on page 36, but the shock is—quite correctly, no doubt—used to precipitate the love affair, not to make us uneasy. The chicken business (52) makes us curious but does not alarm; only on page 72 do we suddenly sit up and feel that here may be a frightening omen. These events are well-timed but it has taken us a long time to get to that point.

This raises another question: ought we to have been so thoroughly deceived from the beginning? Oughtn't some small hint of disturbance to be introduced into our minds either through one of the characters or in the scene itself. The flight of birds in formation across San Francisco is of course significant and could strike this note—but someone would have to say "Bombers" or something like that. If this is too crude, isn't the pet shop the ideal place for someone to show or say that birds _are_ pretty, but. . . . "Have you seen doves kill off their young, and birds beat one of a group to death—chickens to everyone's knowledge—but also beautiful, terrifying creatures like swans?" in short the kind of remark that the salesman makes much later (473). What is the sinister side of the life of love birds—apart from their self-conceit in the total bliss of domesticity? The object of such hints is not to "explain" because the film must avoid explanation—but to create an atmosphere of possible disturbance. Reading the script I notice that the one really effective character, although minor, is Mrs. Bundy; she is the only character who knows anything about birds and she is comically vain of her knowledge, but her very oddity and her knowledge imply that she has a sense that she almost knows. The other characters are too frightened before the inexplicable to have any deep sense that they face a real mystery. Incidentally, Mrs. Bundy's suggestion of "rabies" is very dramatic, just because it is a conjecture that heightens the terror. It is a more frightening idea than the idea of a [ILLEGIBLE] of the bird [ILLEGIBLE].

But to turn back to the characters as they establish themselves at the beginning. In their different ways they are all insipidly good. There is a suggestion—in the scene at the Tides during the terror—that man in the vague general sense is warlike and destructive—but there is no specific instance of a destructive man. Perhaps there should not be. But one looks for a character who, at any rate, conveys some wildness. Mitchy as a criminal lawyer must know about human monsters—he must know about the jail birds in their cages—but his few words on this are lightly uttered. In any case, he is a prig. But what about Melanie? We gather from him that Melanie has had real wild potentialities. It is true that she is mischievous and that her love affair amuses because it is an affair between a mischievous girl and a prig; but I think a lot might have been gained within the story, as it is conceived, by making her wildness more [ILLEGIBLE] evident. If she is a mere nuisance as a practical joker, Mitch is making very heavy weather of it. But how much more suggestive the situation becomes if her jokes were really dangerous—for example, when she was pushed into the fountain or broke a window, was not somebody injured or even killed? Couldn't she be a person who attracts real disasters? Wouldn't that kind of wildness at once give more dramatic force to all the people she is close to? Obviously her relationship with Lydia—now very mild—would become more dramatic. The terror would give a special meaning to being at "the wrong end of a gag". The moment Melanie becomes stronger the other characters take shape, too. Annie, who is at present so passive. She has stayed on at Bodega Bay out of a sort of protective friendship for Mitchy and—as the script stands—performs no striking act of protecting him; but, if Melanie is strong, Annie is bound to react more interestingly. At present she is goody-goody; and I dont like her moralistic talk about it being "better" to teach in a public school. Obviously Annie was weak vis-à-vis Lydia in the old days and even with Mitch; one would like to see the terror bringing out one touch of original sin in her. In general, strengthen Melanie and the others take on more life. If you leave Melanie as she is in the script, there is very little that she has done wrong and therefore very little to be reformed of. Anyway she is full of good works in a socialite way already so that if the terror has changed her, the change had begun *before* the terror.

As for the terror, it goes fantastically well. Mrs. Bundy might be shown as, ultimately, seriously or comically conveying inside knowledge of the mystery. Could there not be a tame bird—a parrot—in the inn which reacts against its own kind, is frightened by them and which she protects or stares at in horror or event [ILLEGIBLE]? The drunk's words are good but in the end couldn't he rise in drunken defiance? I am uncertain about the effect of the President's speech on the radio but as irony it succeeds, and I wonder if it is right to preserve the love birds in the end. Suppose at the climax of the attack, the attacking birds have knocked the cage over, made it fly open and the love birds have gone—to join the enemy! Cathy could even be attacked while going to look for them—by the owl.

At the very end it is surprising that only Mitch, Melanie etc. are seen driving away in flight. Does no one else fly from the town? Why haven't they jumped into their cars too?

I have noted weaknesses of dialogue on the following pages. Some are minor matters of phraseology, others where sharpening or cutting is required. They occur on pages: 6–10; 27–29; 37; 40; 48; 49; 50; 53; 54; 65; 74; 132; 188; 194.

Incidentally when Mrs. Bundy says "Rabies" this ought to horrify and I, for one, reacted with the idea of germ warefare. "Who infected them?" The horrified reply is: "If the human race has fallen as low as that it ought to be exterminated."

Of course, the consistent complaint here is the weakness in the character development, something that never was fully worked out.

## Marnie

Hitchcock seems to have lost his bearings in the early sixties. He struggled with character development. Indeed, it was the weakest aspect of his films from this point on, although he seemed to recover some with *Frenzy* and *Family Plot,* which are weak films but stronger in effective character development than the previous films of the sixties.

*Marnie* is a special film, as it occupies the turning point in Hitchcock's career. *Marnie, Torn Curtain,* and *Topaz* were failures critically and financially, putting him in an awkward position at Universal, with a lessening degree of control over the films he directed. *Marnie* was the scene of many battles. The development of the screenplay was a two-year process, beginning with Evan Hunter and ending with Jay Presson Allen. Hunter's work was eventually abandoned in preference of Allen's work.

Allen, who came to Hitchcock's attention from her play *The Prime of Miss Jean Brodie,* recalled writing her first screenplay with Hitchcock:

He was a great teacher. He did it naturally, easily, and unself-consciously. In that little bit of time that I worked for him, he taught me more about screenwriting than I learned in all the rest of my career. There was one scene in *Marnie,* for example, where this girl is forced into marriage with this guy. I only knew how to write absolutely linear scenes. So I wrote the wedding and the reception and leaving the reception and going to the boat and getting on the boat and the boat leaving. . . . I mean, you know, I kept plodding, plodding, plodding. Hitch said, "Why don't we cut some of that out, Jay? Why don't we shoot the church and hear the bells ring and see them begin to leave the church. Then why don't we cut to a large vase of flowers, and there is a note pinned to the flowers that says, 'Congratulations.' And the water in the vase is sloshing, sloshing, sloshing."

Lovely shorthand. I often think of that. When I get verbose, I suddenly stop and say to myself, "The vase of water."

The story of *Marnie* begins with a treatment of the Winston Graham novel by Hitchcock. He had intended the role of *Marnie* for Grace Kelly, who had read the novel and agreed to make her return to the screen with the director. Unfortunately, the citizens of Monaco strongly disagreed with her plan. A referendum was held, which gave the thumbs-down to the idea, and Princess Grace regretfully declined the role. Tippi Hedren would inherit it.

"MARNIE"
As Revised by Alfred Hitchcock
Treatment, November, 1961

We don't see her face, this girl in a plaid coat who carries a worn, inexpensive suitcase to the ticket counter of the New Haven Railroad Station, pays for a ticket, and then loses herself in the crowd. We do notice her hair—long and black, almost too black; and her handbag whose contents she took plains to conceal when she extracted her fare. It's her handbag that would give a thief pause. Full and fat, that handbag. Unnaturally so. . . .

George Pringle, owner and manager of the Pringle New Haven Department Store, closes the empty cash drawer of the safe in his office. Thirty-two hundred dollars is missing, he tells investigating detectives, and so is "Peggy Holland," the girl he hired some months ago to work in the Cashiers Department. No, he hadn't insisted on references when she told him she was a recent widow who had never worked before. Pringle's chief cashier, Miss Summers, gives him and the detectives a look, as if to say that she would have insisted on references, but then she wasn't the one who was beguiled by a pretty face. But from the description they supply, it would seem that Peggy Holland was plain rather than pretty, a soft-spoken girl with long black hair, trim ankles, and a good figure. She usually favored a plaid coat and . . . Her personality? Here Pringle and Miss Summers must rely on Peggy's two co-workers whose eager accounts of what she was like conflict one with the other; in short, neither girl knew her. Having already checked Peggy's rooming house with negative results, the detectives doubt that either Peggy or the money will ever be found. Her description fits that of thousands of young women; the money can't be traced . . .

Grimly, and with a vengeful look in his eyes, big behind heavy, rimless glasses, Pringle hopes the detectives are wrong. "She really ought to be found," he says, adding somewhat hopelessly, "wherever she is. . . ."

She is in a hotel room in New York City, unrecognizable as the "Peggy Holland" that Miss Summers and Pringle described. A delectable redhead now, she is the girl we shall call "Marnie." A new suitcase full of new clothes stands next to the old suitcase filled with the cast-offs of "Peggy Holland," all tell-tale labels removed. Taking up her handbag, Marnie gives the room and her appearance a final check, then calls the desk. . . .

At Pennsylvania Station, Marnie leaves her old suitcase with the baggage clerk, tears up the stub when his back is turned, picks up her new suitcase and boards a southbound train which takes her to Maryland and—Garrods' Inn.

The Woman behind the desk of the cozy, parlor-like lobby welcomes "Miss Elmer" as a dear and familiar customer. And what a becoming new hairdo! Well, now, will Marnie be staying longer than usual this time? No, just three days, Marnie says, smiling through these pleasantries, a certain eagerness in her eyes. And now she would like to change into her riding habit. She's come, as always, you know, to see "Forio." The Woman understands and motions for the Inn's Young Man to take Marnie's suitcase to her "regular room" right away. . . .

At the stables in back of Garrods', Marnie waves a friendly hello to the groom, then moves on to a stall where she stops, looks in, and softly calls, "Forio." The horse comes forward, noisily and happily. Marnie reaches out to him, a look of sweetness and warmth suddenly flooding her face. . . .

In the following days Marnie is seldom away from Forio. The wind blows her hair loose and free as she rides him about the countryside. There is a sensed happiness and understanding between this horse and this girl. And Marnie rides as if she were born to it; rides as if she would cheat the time that is soon over. . . .

The Marnie who leaves the bus depot in Pittsburgh is not the Marnie of the New York hotel or of Garrods' Inn. This is the sober, business-like Marnie, her red hair plainly fixed, her eyes framed in glasses. Consulting the Want-Ads, she finds a room and a job—as an usherette ("Experience Unnecessary") in a movie theatre. The ticket money, she is careful to note, goes from the box office to the safe in the manager's office. As a trusted cashier she would have it made. Well, time enough to work on that. With a free weekend ahead of her, Marnie (now using the name of "Molly Jeffrey") decides on a quick trip to her real home in Norfolk, Virginia. . . .

As Marnie pauses on the steps of the old, shabby-genteel house she knew as a child and young girl, the door is opened by Lucy Nye, a small, superstitious old woman, who squeals her welcome, then rushes Marnie into the kitchen where her mother, Mrs. Elmer, is waiting. A semi-invalid in her late forties, Mrs. Elmer greets Marnie with a strange mixture of reserve and warmth. There is, in fact, something odd about Mrs. Elmer, as though she combined a feminine sensuality and an old-time, fire-and-brimstone fear of God. She disapproves of Marnie's red hair ("Looks like you're trying to attract the men!"); yet considers her position (fictitious, of course,) as secretary and traveling companion to a generous millionaire employer as evidence that Marnie has grown up "good and straight," in spite of "losing her Pa," and "that nasty stealing business" when she was just a kid. Mrs. Elmer briefly mentions Marnie's Uncle Stephen who is, as usual, "on the road" and of little comfort to her. During their conversation, Lucy, a former neighbor who moved in to care for Mrs. Elmer years ago, suddenly stops her food preparations and listens in fear to the thunder of approaching storm. Mumbling prayers, she goes about the house covering mirrors, for to her a reflection of lightning will strike one cold. The years haven't changed Lucy, Marnie sees, herself frightened by the storm—and something else—something there in the kitchen; something she doesn't understand. Rising to go, she hands her mother a stack of bills, which should, she says, tide her over until she can visit again. Mrs. Elmer takes the money and smiles: "Nothing like a lot of God and a little hard-earned money to take care of an old woman!"

Within two months Marnie is in the Box Office cashier's spot that she wanted. The last late customer has gone inside, the theatre lobby stands empty. As the manager leaves his office and comes to the lobby, Marnie waits until she has his eye, then lowers her head and presses her temples. When he crosses to her, she makes a great show of straightening up. Just one of her bad headaches, she says, grateful for his concern. Well, if he doesn't mind taking over, she'll just accept his kind offer and go home. . . .

Gathering her handbag, she would seem to be leaving, but is instead on her circuitous way to the manager's office. Slipping in, she closes the door, unlocks the safe and empties every bill and coin from the cashbox into her handbag. Suddenly she stands quite still. The door is opening. She waits—No one is there. A draft from the corridor, probably. After making sure the latch is secure, she closes the safe, returns the key to its hiding place, and leaves. . . .

A bus out of Pittsburgh takes Marnie to Washington, D.C. and to a hotel room where, again, new clothes and a new suitcase replace the old. She arrives in Philadelphia, a blonde who definitely doesn't wear glasses; a blonde named "Mrs. Mary Taylor" who applies for a job at John Rutland and Company, one of Philadelphia's oldest printing firms. . . .

Marnie's interview concludes favorably, not because the office manager, Sam Ward, approves of her, but because Terry Holbrook, one of the firm's junior partners, does. Terry, a good-looking, rather too charming man in his mid-thirties, matches Marnie wistful smile for wistful smile as she tells her sad, brave widow's story. And he nods as she hastens to tell her interviewers that in spite of her inexperience, she is "good at figures," seemingly blessed by nature with one of those orderly and statistical minds that make for excellent bookkeeping. Marnie knows that Terry, behind his smiles, has been studying her in a one-track male way, and she resents it, as if, in some curious, moral way she does not approve of being hired for other than business reasons. But she does want the job, so she smiles sweetly at him, knowing full well that he will be the yea-sayer, and not Sam Ward, whom she instinctively recognizes as her enemy. . . .

Old Christopher Holbrook himself welcomes Marnie to the firm on her first day of work. It is, he explains in his friendly, expansive way, a "family firm," run by him and his son Terry, in association with Mark Rutland, the son of Holbrook's late partner. And now, calling Terry in, Holbrook instructs him to show "Mrs. Taylor" around and to introduce her to "other members of the family"; most particularly to her immediate supervisor, Miss Clabon, under whom she will work as a cashier. Until that moment, Marnie didn't know just how much she had to thank Terry for. And as they tour the printing plant, she expresses her gratitude. "I'll always forgo a girl with experience in favor of one with potential," he says, neglecting only to wink.

After introducing Marnie to Miss Clabon, a young, middle-aged woman, and to Dawn Witherbee, with whom Marnie will be sharing a cubicle, Terry takes her to meet Mark Rutland, a good-looking, quiet-faced man in his early forties. Mark stares at her, hardly smiling. No one can hear the thundering thing happening to him; Marnie least of all. As she turns to go to her desk, he continues gazing at her, and finally has to make himself look away. It is obvious that she has hit him, as they say, where he lives.

Marnie's job, as Dawn explains it, is payroll bookkeeping of the simplest sort and couldn't be duller; but to Marnie, the view through the glass partition to Miss Clabon's desk is anything but dull. She watches Miss Clabon extract cash from a great box, count it out, place it in a pay envelope, seal the envelope, and write the receiver's name on it. And though Marnie keeps her attention there where she feels it belongs, she listens well enough to Dawn, who, bored by the elementary job instructions, eagerly supplies information about "the family."

It seems that Old Holbrook, Terry's father, and Old Rutland, Mark's father, didn't get on too well; and when Rutland died, no one expected Mark to come into the firm. But he stepped right in, and for two years now has kept things humming, introducing new ideas which old Holbrook finds downright disturbing. And it's no secret that Terry and Mark don't get on at all.

Mark's a widower whose wife died less than a year ago, Dawn tells Marnie, and he lives alone in an "awfully grand house" somewhere along the Main Line. He was in the Navy, an officer, and his mother is alive, but never comes to the Company. Mark's the nice one; quiet, even moody. And Terry's the "tomcat," the kind a girl has to watch out for. Marnie agrees off-handedly, adding that "any kind has to be watched out for." Dawn cuts off her giggle as Miss Clabon enters the cubicle and hands Marnie a ledger to take into Mr. Rutland's office. . . .

As Marnie delivers the ledger and turns to go, Mark calls out, "Mrs. Taylor?" He seems to be searching for an excuse to talk to her, to keep her there. The company, he says, is holding its annual dinner-dance tomorrow evening; and while it's customary for all employees to attend, he suspects that she, as a recent widow, may not wish to. He'll gladly explain to. . . .

Bue she's going, Marnie says. She's already told Mr. Terry Holbrook she'd be there. . . .

The wind-up of the company affair is as dull as its beginning. Mark has left, annoyed that Terry has monopolized Marnie as a dancing partner. And now Terry invites Marnie to join "a few of the fast ones" at his house for a night of poker. Even if she doesn't know how to play, there'll be drinks and dance records—the sort of things to make up for the dullness of these family affairs. Marnie hesitates, knowing she shouldn't allow herself to be tempted. But she is, and she accepts. . . .

At Terry's tastefully appointed bachelor house, only the die-hards are left at the poker table. Marnie, playing with feverish concentration, has given them all a lesson in beginner's luck. She rakes in her winnings; the game breaks up. Left alone with Terry, Marnie knows she should get out, but she is hungry, and his suggestion of breakfast before driving her home appeals to her. Busying herself in the kitchen, Marnie wonders why Terry didn't invite Mark to the party. "Business reasons," Terry says. Besides, Mark's a widower and wouldn't go partying anyway. Marnie's sharp look doesn't faze Terry. Is she really a widow? he says. There's something about her that tells him she hasn't—"been touched." He goes to her at the stove, pulls her around to him, and kisses her. Fighting back like a cornered animal, she tears away. The frying pan clatters to the floor. The moment has all the aspects of rape. Half appalled, half amused, Terry says he only tried to kiss her. Why the jungle fight? She doesn't like being handled, Marnie says, still shaken. She turns away and goes out, without saying goodbye. . . .

At Terry's suggestion, Marnie fills in for his father's secretary while the latter is on vacation; but proximity to Terry, who shares his father's office, does nothing to thaw Marnie's iciness toward him. Trusted with opening and sorting the ordinary mail, Marnie unthinkingly opens an envelope marked "personal" and bearing the letterhead of Hobson and Hobson, a stockbroker's firm. She scans the letter, puts it on top of the others and takes them to Mr. Holbrook, whose "thank you" turns to a bellow of anger when he discovers she has read the Hobson letter. Personal means personal! he says, ignoring her apologies and waving her out. Fuming, Marnie tells Dawn she has a mind to quit. She doesn't like these "family type firms," she . . . Marnie's complaints fade away at the sight of the great box of beautiful cash on Miss Clabon's desk. She almost smiles as she opens her ledger and starts to work, a girl who let off a little steam and feels better for it. . . .

Marnie looks up from her desk to see Sam Ward standing over her, a cold smile on his face. Mark Rutland is at his home with a "faint cold," he says, and has asked that Marnie deliver some proofs to him there. Ward hands her a large envelope, adding, and it hurts, that the company will furnish her cab fare. . . .

Welcoming Marnie to his large, quietly impressive house, Mark sends his housekeeper, Mrs. Leonard, for tea. The cab—and the proofs—can wait, he says, showing Marnie into the living room where he has been watching a horse race on television. Seeing her eyes light up, Mark asks if she's interested in racing. Racing and horses—especially horses, Marnie says, her voice suddenly vibrant. Mark notes the change and is about to say something when there is a crash of thunder, a sizzle of lightning, and an abrupt downpour of rain. Marnie backs into a corner, sees a mirror, and almost cries out as another flash illumines the room. Grateful for Mark's compassion, Marnie tells him it was her "old Aunt Lucy" who put the fear of lightning and thunder in her when she was a child—fear she can't shake. Children learn things so permanently, Mark says. That's ninety percent of a psychoanalyst's job—unlearning the child and reteaching the adult. Marnie smiles weakly, knowing he is trying to distract her.

Mrs. Leonard brings in the tea and leaves, sensing Marnie's fear and sympathizing with it. Marnie refuses the tea. Perhaps later when . . . A crash, like a bomb, hits the house and sends Marnie into Mark's arms. When she realizes where she is, she pulls away, knowing that for a moment there she had felt safe. Mrs. Leonard comes in to see if they're all right. A tree was hit, she says, and fell against the house. Mark looks at the two women, goes to a sideboard and pours them each a brandy. Neither needs urging. . . .

When the rain eases and Marnie leaves in the taxi, Mark stands looking after her, confident that there can now be a relationship between them. . . .

With Miss Clabon about to go on vacation, Marnie has been selected to fill in for her while she is gone. After a brief instruction period, Marnie tells Miss Clabon that she "understands the system." On Thursdays the envelopes are filled, and any not completed are taken care of Friday morning. And on Friday they're handed out. Miss Clabon adds that the filled envelopes are kept in the safe over Thursday night, and that Mr. Ward will open and close it as required. Any questions? Well, then, Marnie can go to lunch.

Marnie returns to her cubicle and is about to go out when Mark appears and asks if she would like to join him at the races Saturday. He has called her "Mary," his tone has implied an intimacy she is far from feeling, but she can't refuse a chance to see a race—to see horses. . . .

At the paddock before the race, Mark singles out a horse called Telepathy, telling Marnie he has a good feeling about this one and would like to place a bet for her. She doesn't bet, Marnie says, but he should follow his hunch about Telepathy. She'd seen the horse trained as a one-year-old at Garrods' Stable in Maryland and had thought then he had promise. (Unwittingly, Marnie has named the stable where she keeps Forio.)

After placing his bet, Mark returns to the stands in time to see Marnie curtly dismissing a man who claimed to have known her as "Peggy Nicholson" from Boston. He was wrong, she tells Mark, turning to the race as the starting gun goes off. In Mark's eyes, Marnie is much more interesting than the race. He doesn't know her either, he says. One minute she seems about to catch fire, and the next she's withdrawn, mysterious. . . . Marnie stands suddenly. The race is over—and Telepathy has won! She's brought them both luck, Mark says. He placed a bet for her, and she's won at least a hundred dollars. For the next race he's picked a horse named Hobson's Choice.

The name causes Marnie to frown. She asks Mark if he knows of a firm called "Hobson and Hobson." Mark does; it's a firm specializing in buy-outs and transfers. They haven't offered Marnie a better job, have they? No, nothing like that, Marnie says. She just wondered. And now if Mark wants to make that bet, he'd better hurry. . . .

That night as Mark pulls up in front of her rooming house, Marnie deftly counters his attempts to discover her "secret" with questions of her own. Why did he go into the firm when he doesn't seem to like printing? To look after his father's interests, to protect the things he had loved, Mark says. Old Holbrook and Terry were plotting for control of the firm when Mark's father died, and Mark stepped in to prevent it then, and he intends to prevent it now. But that's enough about him, Mark says. Gently, he draws Marnie to him and kisses her. She lies cold and still in his arms. Letting her go then, he brings his hand to her hair and strokes it. She pulls away, shivering, and turns to go. Mark looks at her wonderingly. Did she enjoy herself today, as he did? Marnie nods, thanking him. Then she'll go to the races with him again—next Saturday? Marnie withdraws into her private thoughts, then suddenly agrees, a bit too willingly. But then she has the advantage of knowing she won't be around on Saturday. . . .

On Thursday, Marnie works through the quiet of the lunch hour in Miss Clabon's cubicle, the pay envelopes spread out on the desk. An employee from the printing room has supplied her with stacks of plain paper cut to the size of "a dollar bill," to be used, Marnie explained, as props in a game she's planning for a church social. She selects the next name from the ledger, writes it on a pay envelope, and counts out the prescribed amount of cash. Then comes the switch: a stack of paper "dollars" goes into the envelope, the cash into her handbag. She seals the envelope and places it on a growing pile. . . .

By the end of the day Marnie has all the envelopes stacked neatly in a large box. As Sam Ward enters the cubicle, she picks up her fat handbag and stands. He nods to her, opens the safe, and then steps aside, allowing her to place the box inside. With the safe closed and locked, Marnie feels elated, set free. She even tries to bait Ward for disliking her, certain that when she leaves tonight she will never return. But Ward remains coldly impersonal. As long as she does her work, why should he have anything against her? Ward says. Marnie shrugs, bids him goodnight, and leaves. Ward stands a moment, watching her, a faint, sardonic smile on his face. . . .

Marnie heads straight for Maryland and—Forio. Everything else seems far away as she rides him about the countryside, the wind blowing her hair, her face carefree and smiling. She is bringing Forio back to the stable when suddenly she stops, her smile dying. Mark is there. She'd better get her things from the Inn, he says, and come with him. Still too stunned to speak, Marnie sadly relinquishes Forio to the groom, then turns to Mark as to her executioner. . . .

Mark won't tell Marnie how he found her or where he is taking her in his car. He has found most of the money intact and is now satisfied that he is at last getting the truth out of her. She admits that her real name is Margaret (Marnie) Elmer and that she has never been married. She was orphaned when she was a little girl, she tells him, and raised by her "Aunt Lucy," in Norfolk, Virginia. Until she worked for a living, she was always poor and stole occasionally, but only in the way children will steal. Keeping Forio at the stable is not a sign of "sudden" wealth, she says. She'd always loved riding and used to go to Garrods' once in a while when she'd saved up a little money. Forio was for sale—cheap—she had the money, and, well, she bought him. Riding Forio is the only time she feels free, but she doesn't expect Mark to understand that. It was, she says, the thought of being able to live at Garrods' and to be with Forio all the time that made her steal. She hated to do it, but . . . "I always seem to have two drives at the same time. One belongs to me, the girl I'm trying to be, and the other to the little lost girl—the 'child of the streets.' I mean I'm not hungry any more, and I'm not teased and treated like dirt, but it's as if I still want to react as if I were. I can't explain it, Mark." Whether she realizes it or not, Marnie has hit the truth here, and Mark instinctively knows it.

Mark takes her to his house then, and it is here that Marnie really goes to work. There is, she says shyly, another reason she stole—perhaps the real reason. She was afraid she was taking their friendship—too seriously. He's "Main Line"; she's nothing. She could only wind up hurting him, so she decided to hurt him once and for all: steal from him and then go where he could never find her. Well, if he's smart now, he'll turn her over to the police and get rid of her. She doesn't care what happens.

She's to come back to the office as though nothing had happened, Mark says. And as far as Holbrook or any of the others knows, nothing has. Mark alone discovered the theft and made it good out of his own pocket. Why? Because . . . "Ward always said you were too good to be true, and Terry once said you were too true to be good. I hated giving either of them the satisfaction of being right."

She can't go back to the office, Marnie says. And now that he's covered for her, he can't very well go to the police. Why doesn't he simply let her go?

He won't let her get away again, Mark says. It's no good her running away from him—or herself—any longer. She's going to stay at a hotel for the night, and in the morning he's going to take her to visit his mother. "I want her to meet the girl I'm going to marry." Marnie stares at him, dumbstruck. . . .

That night Marnie lies in the hotel bed, her face troubled in sleep. In her dream she sees her mother sitting in bed, reading a romance magazine, and Marnie as a little girl asleep in the bed with her. A tapping comes at the window, insistent and loud. Marnie's mother raises the shade to Mark Rutland, handsome in his Navy officer's uniform. She smiles warmly, and after letting him in, shuts Marnie in a cold room. Hearing their laughter from the bedroom, the child Marnie throws herself down on a cot and tries to shut out the sound. But there is something there—under the cot. She looks down, screams, and wakes up screaming. . . .

With Mark's mother, a charming, handsome woman of middle years, in attendance, Mark and Marnie are married by a judge in his courtroom chambers. Included at the wedding breakfast in a fashionable restaurant's private dining room are old Holbrook and Terry, Dawn Witherbee, and, of course, Mark's mother. Throughout, Terry keeps glancing at Marnie, as if to say, "What's behind all this?" He cynically joins the toast to their "good fortune" and then salutes their choice of Jamaica as a honeymoon spot, where, he says suggestively, the climate is sultry. . . .

The Jamaican setting is a dream place for a honeymoon, provided, of course, one dreams of a honeymoon. After a week, Marnie still refuses to sleep with Mark. She had indicated she would if only he would tell her (as he has refused to do) how he traced her; but when he reminds her that she spoke of Garrods' Stable at the races that day, and then tries to make love to her, she pulls away violently. The thought of sex makes her sick, she says. And he might as well know the truth now. She doesn't love him and never has. She only married him because she was afraid he'd turn her over to the police if she didn't.

Mark doesn't see how she can believe that. She might try recalling it was she who pointed out that once he had covered for her, calling the police was out of the question. Well, his love for her isn't as blind as she thought. He's suspected her true feelings toward him for the past few days. He had thought he could use reason to overcome her fear of love. But love, Mark says, is not always patient, not always gentle. He pulls her to him, and as she draws away, he grabs her and forces her to the bed. She fights like a wildcat, but he subdues her. He turns off the light, shutting out her tears, her look of anguish. . . .

The next morning Mark is, perhaps, overly solicitous about Marnie's comfort, but he makes no attempt to apologize. She won't suffer his company on the beach and leaves him to go for a swim. Turning in disgust from the bruise on her shoulder, she looks at Mark staring moodily into space; then she looks out to sea. Coming to a swift, and calming, decision, she starts to swim toward the horizon. She is an almost indiscernible dot in the distance when Mark looks up, senses her purpose, swims after her, and reaches her just as she is going under. She tries to fight him, but he hauls off and socks her, then pulls her to shore. After making certain Marnie is safe, Mark starts back to their cottage. She follows a short distance behind, looking like an obedient prisoner on the heels of her jailer.

Returning to Philadelphia, Marnie and Mark reach a truce of sorts. Mark has respected her wish for separate bedrooms, but in an effort to help her overcome her revulsion of sex, he makes a deal with her: if she will promise to see a psychiatrist of his acquaintance, he will have the old garage converted into a stable and have Forio brought there. If she'll oblige him, he'll oblige her. And he won't tell the psychiatrist about her stealing; in fact he won't tell him anything. Besides, Mark is sure that her stealing is a symptom of some far deeper disturbance. She has mentioned an infant brother who died because money and food were denied her mother by an indifferent welfare worker. Surely this wasn't the cause, Mark suggests.

Well, if he won't believe her, what's the use of talking? Marnie says. No more use than in her seeing a nosy psychiatrist. But if that's the price she'll have to pay to have Forio near her, all right. It's worth it. She'll see this Dr. Roman on Monday. But he won't get anything out of <u>her</u>!

On the Saturday before her appointment, Marnie gets a call from Terry. He's sorry she can't make his poker blast. She did so well the last time that it's a pity Mark refused Terry's invitation to them both. Said they were busy . . . Then he spoke for himself, Marnie says. She'll be there. Telling Mark she has accepted an invitation from Dawn Witherbee for a night out "with the girls," Marnie goes to Terry's where she again wins, playing even more avidly than before. Amused, Terry stands behind her, his hands on her shoulders. But Marnie's concentration is so intense that she is unaware of his touch. . . .

Returning home in the middle of the night, Marnie gets to her room without waking Mark, and includes the cash she has won in the envelope of a letter to her mother, who remains ignorant of her marriage. Poker money will come in handy, Marnie figures. And neither Mark nor her mother need know where it came from. . . .

At her first meeting with Dr. Charles Roman, Marnie tells the psychiatrist substantially the same story she told Mark. Both her parents died when she was six, she says, and she barely remembers either of them. Her father was a seaman, that's all she knows. Yes, she had a brother, but he died at birth. No, she remembers nothing about him, not a damned thing. She does remember that her mother was God-fearing and strict. Lucy Nye, a sort of aunt, raised her, and Marnie's Uncle Stephen helped them out occasionally. She was a widow at twenty-three when she met Mark—and married him. There's nothing more to tell, really.

Dr. Roman seems pleased their first meeting has gone so well. In psychiatric treatment, he says, intelligence such as hers can be a springboard—or a stumbling block. She must decide which her intelligence is to be. . . . He'll see her Wednesday, then? The same hour?

Marnie leaves, her confidence somewhat shaken. Clearly, Dr. Roman is not the fool she had supposed. . . .

Leaning on a fence on his grounds, Mark watches with pleasure as Marnie rides Forio. The wind splashes her hair; she laughs; and for a moment she is the Marnie we saw at Garrods'. Finally, she pulls Forio to a halt, hops off, and pats him gently. In her happiness she gives Mark a heart-shattering smile. And it is her friendly suggestion that they have breakfast together followed by her genuine thanks for Forio that gives Mark hope. He thanks her for seeing Dr. Roman. She's happier now, he can see, and . . . Marnie looks away, surprised at the guilt she feels. As if in compensation, she tells him about the Hobson and Hobson letter meant for Christopher Holbrook that she had read by accident. She had put it out of her mind; but now, remembering it, she thinks Mark ought to know that the letter concerned an inquiry old Holbrook had made as to the purchase of all available stock in the John Rutland Printing Company.

Interesting, says Mark. If Holbrook is out to get control of the company, Terry must be in on it, too. Well, if there's to be a fight, Mark can take steps to bring it into the open, thanks to Marnie.

At her next session with Dr. Roman, Marnie's contempt for his little game of "free association" slowly changes to anger and fear as she loses control of her responses to words such as Man, Woman, and Marriage. Her fear of sex evident in her answers, Dr. Roman calmly tells Marnie that the desire for sex is not only natural but essential in a balanced, liberated human being. Fear of sex leads to its sublimation, to a substitute of some kind; and that substitute is usually unhealthy, if not anti-social. He doesn't yet know what she's afraid of revealing, but he can only help her when she stops being frightened of what she might say. Well, they'll continue next time. . . .

Marnie returns to Mark's house and to Forio. Refreshed and happy from her ride, she enters through the kitchen, scoops up a pile of shirts Mrs. Leonard has just ironed, and takes them to Mark in his bedroom. He is stripped to the waist, standing before a mirror and trying to remove something from his eye. Her gaze lingers on his smooth, muscular torso. She goes to him, takes the towel he offers, and, standing very close, removes the particle. Aware of a sensual stirring within her, she immediately withdraws, angering Mark. These poker parties at Terry's get later and later, he says. Isn't she ever going to tire of them? Once he learned Dawn was spending her weekends out of town, it wasn't hard to find out where Marnie has been spending her Saturday nights. And Mark won't have it! Except for her sessions with Dr. Roman, he's tried to let her live her own life. But at Terry's, she's in the enemy camp. It would seem that she's opposing Mark's interest in the firm by going there . . . playing fast and loose with Terry.

She can't bear for Terry to touch her, Marnie says, genuinely surprised at Mark's jealousy. But she'll respect Mark's wishes and not play poker at Terry's tonight. Or any other night. That's a promise. She's going to Norfolk on Sunday, however. Aunt Lucy called to say she's selling the house (Marnie's house, really, since Uncle Stephen put it in her name) and needs Marnie's signature on some papers. (At least that's Marnie's story.) So she'll run down there Sunday morning and be back Sunday night. . . .

The money that Marnie hands her mother the next day is her poker winnings from the night before. She came, Marnie says, to find out how her father died. And she won't be put off. As Lucy watches fearfully, Mrs. Elmer takes from her handbag a faded clipping and hands it to Marnie—a clipping telling of Mr. Elmer's death at sea during the war. Why should the manner of his death have been kept from her? Marnie wonders. Why wasn't she told about this, about her brother's death? Where is this Welfare Woman, by the way? The one her mother blamed for the baby's death . . .

She's forgotten her name! Mrs. Elmer cries. What's got into Marnie? All these questions . . .

"Was I all right, I mean when I was born?" Marnie says.

"Of course you were!" Why, Mrs. Elmer couldn't have asked for a better daughter. Only that once—when she stole—was she any trouble. And God and Mrs. Elmer can be thanked for putting her straight after that. No one could ever call her daughter a trollop! "You're worth a dozen ordinary girls, Marnie, and don't ever think different! You're a good girl and you're so clever and . . ."

"I'm not sure it's wise to be too clever," Marnie says and gets up to go. . . .

Again with Dr. Roman, Marnie fights his suggestion that having children might answer some need in her. What does it matter that she loves—or loved—her own mother? "Don't you think it right that someone should come into the world who feels for you what you feel for her?" Getting no response, Dr. Roman continues. "If a child could be got by injection, without having any intercourse with a man at all, would you object then?"

"What the hell does it matter what I object to?" Marnie yells.

Seeing that the idea of childbirth frightens her, Dr. Roman asks her to give him her free association of thought on the word childbirth.

Reluctantly, Marnie settles back on the couch. "Kettle on stove. Boiling water. Lucy Nye. Cold. More blankets. Maybe newspapers will do . . ." Suddenly, she gives a strangled cry. "I was always warm . . . till that tapping at the window . . . why do those men tap at the window . . . Why do I have to be put in the spare room . . ." She begins to cry. "She looked like a witch . . . coming in that room, carrying something wrapped in newspapers . . . I thought she was going to give it to me . . . I couldn't <u>bear</u> to have it . . ."

In terror and agony, Marnie bolts up and starts across the room. Gently, Dr. Roman leads her back to the couch. Her mother couldn't ever have looked like a witch, she says, her cries subsiding. "And when that man was trying to get her to sign me away . . . she refused, she'd never part with me, she said . . . she loved me . . . even when I stole that handbag . . . and got caught . . . She brought down her wrath, but she said she knew I'd never steal again . . . I'm not a trollop flying after men . . . Men just make my nerves shatter . . . They're usually calm, my nerves, when I stole . . ."

She stops abruptly, realizing she has admitted more than she'd ever dreamed it would be possible for her to admit, much less remember. Immediately she adopts a flippant tone. She can't imagine what made her cry. She's been feeling quite happy the past week or so. . . .

"You were doing very well, Mrs. Rutland. Have you any idea what it was you said that upset you, put up your defenses again?"

"I didn't say a damned thing." She goes to the door and waits for him to open it.

"I thought it might have been your mentioning having stolen," Dr. Roman says, reminding her that by opposing him she is only hurting herself. Well, perhaps next time they'll be able to get back in the swing of it. . . .

There'll be no next time, Marnie tells Mark. She's sorry and she tried, but she's through with her analysis. And Mark, having conferred with Dr. Roman, agrees that further treatment against her will would be useless. They are on their way to a dinner party at the home of Rex Newton, a major stockholder in the John Rutland Company, who hopes, Mark tells Marnie, that getting him there with the Holbrooks will put an end to the still undercover battle for control of the firm. Rex Newton favors him, Mark says, but hopes the whole thing can be dropped and life can go on as always.

"That's more or less the feeling I had about my analysis," Marnie says.

At the Newtons, Marnie is the center of attraction as Mark's bride. She is acknowledging introductions when, suddenly, she goes pale. Too late, she recognizes George Pringle, the New Haven department store owner from whom she stole thirty-two hundred dollars. And Pringle recognizes her as "Peggy Holland" within everyone's hearing. His persistence over her denials brings Mark to her aide. He tells Pringle that Marnie's maiden name was Elmer and that he knew her two years before they were married. Begging Marnie's pardon, Pringle turns away, his mind plainly unchanged. Terry, already convinced that Marnie has plenty to hide, has watched the confrontation with amusement. And as Mark and Marnie are leaving—the hoped-for peace talks with the Holbrooks forgotten—Terry gets in his private dig, remarking that deceit seems to be everywhere. . . .

Marnie tenses as Mark enters her bedroom without knocking. He'll have the truth now, he says quietly. All of it. He talked to Pringle and knows why he was so worked up at the thought of meeting "Peggy Holland" again. One lie this time, Mark says, and he will tell Pringle there was no mistake. Marnie admits she's wanted by the police in three cities, admits her aliases; admits everything, in fact, except that her mother is living. She doesn't know why she stole, she says. Perhaps it was a—substitute for something.

The situation can't stay as it is, Mark says. Every time they meet new people, there's the danger she'll be recognized. Leaving him, disappearing, as she suggests, would solve nothing for either of them. They're in this together. No, he'll just have to think of something—and do it. . . .

A few nights later Marnie is in the kitchen with Mrs. Leonard, having left Mark in the drawing room to discuss "business" with their dinner guest, Humphrey Westerman, an elderly gentleman who was a friend of Mark's father. Pleased with Marnie's praise of her dinner, Mrs. Leonard admits she outdid herself for a guest like Mr. Westerman. Philadelphia's Chief of Police, no less! Retired, that is, but still a power in the city. Been like a second father to Mark. . . . Marnie stares at the housekeeper, then goes out on the pretence of tending Forio.

Crouching by the drawing room window, she hears Westerman advising Mark to get her to Headquarters to make a full confession. She'll still have to stand trial, Westerman says, but if Mark makes it clear he intends to repay all the money, the chances are better than fifty-fifty she'd be released and put on probation. Mark could, of course, go to the three firms in question and offer to make up the stolen amounts; but the police would still have to be notified in order to have the warrants against Marnie withdrawn. But a voluntary confession is the better way in Westerman's view. And the quicker Mark gets her to do this, the better. Otherwise, Westerman will have to reveal what Mark has told him.

The next morning Marnie furiously charges Mark with betrayal. If his liberty were at stake, he wouldn't go sneaking to the police. But he'll rat on her and see that she lands in prison!

His liberty and happiness are at stake, Mark says. He had to talk to someone, and Westerman was the only one he could turn to. Mark's on her side as he's always been. If she'll trust him to make private calls on the people concerned . . .

Trust him! Why should she trust him now? Marnie says. And as he tries to comfort her, caress her, she scorns him. Looking at her in grief and pity, Mark leaves her room and, later, the house. . . .

Her decision made, Marnie wastes no time. She packs a suitcase, bids a gentle goodbye to Forio, and drives her car to the back entrance of the Rutland Printing Company. To Mark's secretary she plays the dutiful wife who has come to drive her husband home and pretends surprise to hear he has gone to New Haven. She starts out—and runs into Terry, who tells her he wants her to be at his house Friday night. It's business, he says, and concerns Mark and herself, as well as him and his father. Marnie agrees, knowing she'll be nowhere near Terry's place come Friday, then goes to the hallway, glances about, and quickly enters the Ladies Room. . . .

It is night, the Rutland offices are quiet. Marnie comes out of the Ladies Room, opens the door to the main office and looks in. Terry and Sam Ward are at a desk in the far corner of the room. Only their area is lit. Going to Miss Clabon's booth, she crouches below the partition, reaches the wall safe, works the combination. She edges the safe door open and empties all the cash into her handbag. As footsteps approach the booth, she almost drops her bag. The footsteps stop. She chances a look and sees Terry just as he turns to start on again. He walks to the door and goes out. Marnie closes her bag, half rises, and sees Sam Ward reaching for the light switch. In the darkness she makes it through the door, down the stairs, and out to her car at the back exit. . . .

It is past midnight when Marnie reaches her mother's house in Norfolk. The window shade of the living room window is drawn, and behind it a light burns. As she starts up the front steps, the door is opened—by Lucy, who throws herself on Marnie, sobbing. Mrs. Elmer is dead. She died two days ago, Lucy says, leading Marnie to her mother's coffin while tearfully explaining how she "couldn't contact" Marnie. She "just knew," though, that Marnie would somehow "just know" and come home. Marnie stares at her mother's body, her sense of loss sweeping and terrible. . . .

There's some insurance money, Lucy tells Marnie after they have spent their grief and settled in the kitchen. Uncle Stephen is expected in the morning and will know how to handle everything. Insisting she can manage alone, Marnie goes through her mother's handbag, sorting out policies and deeds from the clutter of newspaper clippings and pills. She comes across the bag's "mystery pocket," opens it, and pulls out an old, much-folded newspaper clipping. As Lucy putters about, paying no attention, Marnie reads the heading, "Norfolk Woman Held On Child-Murder Charge." Reading further, Marnie learns that the "Norfolk Woman" was Mrs. Edith Elmer and that she'd been charged with the murder of her newborn male child. The article further explains that Mrs. Elmer was considered a woman of "loose morals." Marnie lets the clipping fall. Lucy sees it and is horror-struck. Mrs. Elmer never meant for Marnie to know, she gasps. But now it's as if her hand guided Marnie to that clipping! And Lucy begins to talk, almost joyous with the thought of relieving herself of the heavy, horrible secret she has kept for years. . . .

Mrs. Elmer was a "strong one," all right, but weak when it came to being "lonely and poor." With her husband at sea most of the time, she had started "getting friendly with sailors." There were always so many around Norfolk, and they always had a little money to share . . . Well, Mrs. Elmer got pregnant, refused to admit it, and wouldn't have a doctor. The night it happened, she'd called Lucy and made her help. Lucy didn't want to lock Marnie in the cold back room, but she had xx to. When the baby was born, Mrs. Elmer had ordered Lucy to leave her alone for a while and not to tell anyone about the baby. . . .

But when Lucy came back, she'd found Mrs. Elmer hemorrhaging and had called a doctor. The doctor came with a nurse and they'd found the baby, wrapped in newspapers, under the cot in the room Marnie had been locked in. . . .

Marnie remembers now—too well—the "thing" stashed under the bed. . . .

It was the doctor's testimony that Mrs. Elmer was insane at the time of the murder that got her off, Lucy continues. Then when Mr. Elmer divorced her, she'd gone after sailors with a vengeance. Losing her guilt in them, you might say. They'd come by at night, tap on the window, and she'd let them in . . .

And Marnie remembers the tapping on the window, the strange, smiling men, the being locked in the cold back room.

But Mrs. Elmer always "looked respectable," Lucy says. She taught the Good Word to Marnie and always kept her clean and dressed pretty. She won a court fight to keep Marnie, and then when Mr. Elmer's death in action came on top of that, she gave up the sailors, swallowed her loneliness, and began to raise Marnie as a God-fearing child

Why didn't she just keep her mouth shut? Marnie says, remembering her mother's constant warnings against love, sex, anything natural and normal. Marnie remembers, and bitter, burning anger rises in her throat, and tears of silent fury run down her face. . . .

Uncle Stephen, a rather handsome, middle-aged man, accompanies Marnie to the cemetery in the funeral's lone limousine. He understands her reaction against her mother, but begs her not to judge too harshly. Until her marriage, Mrs. Elmer was xrepressed by her father, a fire-and-brimstone preacher. Uncle Stephen went to sea and got away, but his sister had to stay and bear the brunt of their father's narrow, tortured mind. And his sister, Marnie's mother, was what you might call a highly sexed woman.

She might have found a substitute like—others do, Marnie says.

Self-deception was her substitute, Uncle Stephen says. She was trying to be a respectable wife and mother . . . and grasping at love wherever she could, even though it was physical. "She was leading a double life, Marnie. When the baby came, it knocked the lid off that make-believe world of hers."

Well, <u>she</u> remembers too much now, Marnie says, and she doesn't want to understand her mother. It's enough to know she was either a murderess or a lunatic. And, Marnie fears, the heritage passes on.

Marnie and Uncle Stephen are approaching the open grave now. "There's no reason on God's earth why your mother should have passed on to you a character that couldn't hold under pressure, Marnie. You may have suffered from shocks, from seeing her hide the dead baby, but . . . it isn't 'inheritance.' "

"Can you beat it! All her life she poisoned me against sex and love . . ."

"She was suppressing it . . . and when you have to suppress something, you wind up hating it!"

They are at the graveside. Marnie stares down at the coffin, hysteria mounting within her. "Liar!" she cries. "Thief! Murderer!" Neither Lucy nor Stephen can stop her or help her. She opens her handbag, takes out the envelope of money she took from the Rutland safe, and flings it into the grave. "Here, take it!" she screams. "I took it for you . . . now take it!" She then turns on the startled gravediggers. "Cover her! Shovel it in! Go ahead, work, you lazy bastards!" She is weeping now as the earth strikes the coffin. Blindly, she goes to Uncle Stephen. "You have a child . . . and you murder it . . . and live with that all the rest of your life . . . you want sex and tell yourself you hate it . . . it's dirty . . . you lie and steal and hurt . . . is that . . . what I'll come to . . ."

Uncle Stephen tries to hold her close, but she breaks away and runs—right into Terry Holbrook.

He thought she might need some friendly help, Terry says, so he followed her. He has his car there and will take her home—to Mark. Oh, she needn't be afraid to go back. Terry's sure Mark will make good the money she just threw into the grave . . . Terry smiles at her astonishment. He saw her at the safe, he says, but Sam Ward was there and Terry didn't want to make a scene or to hear Ward's I-told-you-so's. Terry was waiting in the parking lot for her, but she got away so fast that the only thing he could do was to follow . . . Seeing there was a "death in the family," he had decided not to intrude until—well—until after the funeral. . . . Terry satisfies Uncle Stephen that Marnie is in good hands, and then drives off with her.

Why does he want to help her? Terry continues. Well, for one thing, she's his sort—one of the misfits of the world; for another, he likes her, in spite of the fact she helped Mark pull the company out from under him and his father. He doesn't understand why she stole (and Marnie can't bring herself to explanations now), but it had occurred to him that she was taking the money in order to run off with another man. Now he knows there never was any man—except Mark. And Mark's loving her so much has suddenly become very important to Terry, for "if he doesn't, he may not cover up for you, and then it'll look as if I did, and that'll make me an accomplice and . . ."

At his intimation that he might make up the loss, if necessary, Marnie thanks Terry for his kindness. And she's glad he's taking her back to Mark. Maybe—someday—Mark will be glad, too. She's sorry about the trouble between Mark and Terry; sorry they can't all be friends.

Oh, in twenty years, Terry says, they'll have forgiven and forgotten the dirty tricks they played on each other. He laughs softly. But now Marnie should try and get some rest. . . .

At a filling station stop, Terry sees Marnie is alseep. He goes to a phone booth and puts in a call to—Mark. . . .

It is night when Terry pulls to a stop in front of a house. Marnie, though awake, is lost in her thoughts and has paid no attention to her surroundings. She thanks Terry again. "I'll try somehow to make it up between you and Mark."

"It'll be impossible," Terry says, blowing the car horn.

Marnie looks out, puzzled, and sees they are at Terry's house, not Mark's. Terry reminds her she had promised to be at his place this evening, so he arranged to have a few people . . .

Dazed, Marnie gets out of the car. At that moment the front door of Terry's house opens. Marnie sees George Pringle standing in the foyer and behind him, a Plainclothesman and an officer in uniform. Terry's almost sorry he has to do this to her, but through her, he can get back at Mark. Terry was certain that Mr. Pringle wasn't mistaken about her, so he talked to him . . . The rest was easy.

Marnie starts toward the house, ready now to face the inevitable. Terry stops her, pointing to a car that has just come up. Mark gets out and hurries to her. It's all over, she tells him. Terry took care of everything . . .

"We'll do everything we can," Mark says. "Westerman will help. We're in this together. I've waited . . . I can wait a bit longer."

"That's something to hold on to," Marnie says. And as Mark kisses her, she responds warmly, fully. Then she starts away. He catches her hand, whispers for her to wait, that he will go in with her.

"No. I'll be back, Mark. I'll come back to you."

Turning abruptly, she walks up the path, climbs the steps, and enters the house. Terry closes the door. . . .

—End—

Since the film is a testament to Allen's screenplay, it is interesting to see how Hunter interpreted Hitchcock's treatment. The following are notes on a draft that he was preparing in February 1963.

"MARNIE"
STORY NOTES
By
Evan Hunter
February 1, 1963

SCENES YET TO BE WORKED OUT IN DETAIL

1) OFFICE #1
2) THE RUTLAND ROBBERY
3) THE LANTERN SLIDE
4) PRE-PARTY
5) REX'S PARTY
6) THE TRAUMA
   a) The details of it.
   b) The sprinkling throughout.
7) THE SYNDROME MONTAGES

SUSTAINED SCENES

| | |
|---|---|
| 1) Strutt | 16) The First Night |
| 2) Mother # 1 | 17) Poolside |
| 3) Norfolk Theater | 18) The Rape and Suicide Attempt |
| 4) Sam Ward Interview | 19) The Lantern Slide and Dinner Bargain |
| 5) Office # 1 | 20) Analyst # 1 |
| 6) Factory-Mark | 21) Analyst # 2 |
| 7) Poker Party # 1 | 22) Poker Party # 2 |
| 8) Pre-Lightning | 23) Analyst # 3 |
| 9) Lightning | 24) Pre-Party |
| 10) Racetrack | 25) Rex's Party |
| 11) Tuesday Night Date | 26) The Showdown |
| 12) Mother # 2 | 27) Mark-Westerman |
| 13) The Rutland Robbery | 28) Mother # 3 |
| 14) Caught | 29) The Journey Back |
| 15) The Reception | 30) The Final Scene |

-I-
## MARNIE IS A THIEF

1) HARTFORD RAILROAD STATION
   A short scene showing Marnie as a brunette, and from the rear, as she approaches the ticket counter. She is carrying a suitcase and a large bulging handbag. She buys her ticket, heads for New York-bound trains. CAMERA comes in close on her big bulging bag.

2) BIG HEAD OF MR. STRUTT—in office where safe was robbed.
   a) Establish Strutt solidly.
   b) Establish that Strutt hired Marnie without references, and was indeed rather taken with her.
   c) Establish modus operandi for Marnie (as tie-in for later Rutland robbery.)
   d) Describe some of the clothing Marnie wore to work.

3) A HOTEL ROOM IN NEW YORK
   a) Marnie is cutting labels out of clothes, some of which were described in previous scene.
   b) She discards these, and replaces them with new clothing.
   bc) She tears up old social security card, chooses new one from pile.
   c) She washes the brunette rinse out of her hair.

4) NEW YORK BUS TERMINAL
   Marnie checks her old suitcase, disposes of the key to pay locker, buys ticket to Laurel, Maryland, and boards the bus.
5) THE BUS TERMINAL IN LAUREL—A station wagon from the Old Colonial is waiting for her. The driver greets her as an old guest.
6) THE OLD COLONIAL—Mrs. Putnam, the manager, elaborates on "familiar guest" theme, and brings in first mention of Forio. It is clear from Mrs. Putnam's talk that Marnie <u>owns</u> the horse, but more than this we do not learn. It is also clear that she will stay here for a week or so before leaving again.
7) BIG HEAD OF MARNIE—ecstatic as she rides Forio.
8) SERIES OF LONG SHOTS—as Marnie rides the countryside.

9) MOTHER # 1
   a) Establish Mr. Pemberton fiction.
   b) Establish Edith as hoyden.
   c) Establish forthcoming trip to Norfolk.
   d) Establish and maintain a mysterioso in this house.
   e) Drop first trauma hint. Marnie, asleep, hears rattling at the window. She half-wakes, searches for sound, but the tapping stops. She drifts off into sleep again, but the tapping begins once more, and her sleep is disturbed and troubled.

10) DISSOLVE into Marnie arriving in Norfolk with new color hair and hairdo, a new bag. She looks around tentatively.

11) <u>THE NORFOLK THEATER</u>

   a) Open with big black and white screen on which is our parody of Italian movie. Marnie is coming up the aisle with a flashlight. As she moves into the CAMERA, we see she is wearing an usher's uniform. She comes out into the lobby. Crowds of people are coming in for the last showing. She glances at the cashier's booth, and we come in for a close shot of the money being taken in.

   b) The manager comes down and chats with Marnie in a friendly, jovial way. She is well-liked, rather amusing, popular with everyone. The cashier is putting receipts into sacks as Marnie and the manager joke. He asked her to help him with them, and she carries one of the bags up to his office. She leaves as he is going to the filing cabinet to get key for safe.

   c) In the lobby again, she sees the manager returning. She goes into the theater, watches screen for a moment—our second parody—and then tells the other usher she is going to the ladies room, will be right back. She goes directly upstairs, passing the manager in the lobby, going directly past the ladies room, and into his office. In an unbroken shot, she moves swiftly to the filing cabinet, takes key from finger of glove, goes to safe, inserts key, and opens safe door.

   d) We cut to the manager who is chatting with the cashier, who then peeks in at the movie (our third and final parody) and goes upstairs to his office. He is about to turn the knob, his hand is in fact on the knob, when one of the projectionists stops him and they get into a highly technical discussion about one of the projectors. The projectionist asks him to come take a look, and he leaves the office door to follow him—when the phone inside the office begins ringing. He goes into the office. It seems empty. He answers the phone, has a discussion about what a good take this has been for a foreign film, says he's not sure exactly how much, but will check it now. He hangs up, takes key from glove in cabinet, opens safe. His BIG PROFILE fills the screen as he discovers it is empty. We CUT to: (Red hair being washed out over bowl? Or:)

12) BIG HEAD OF BLONDE MARNIE—riding the horse. And then dissolve into the long shots of the countryside. Dissolve to the exterior of railroad station in Philadelphia. Marnie emerges with soft brown hair in new style, carrying new luggage. Dissolve to a pencil going down a list of jobs in the local newspaper. It stops at one marked ASSISTANT CASHIER, circles it. Dissolve to exterior establishing shot of Rutland's.


-II-

LIFE AT RUTLAND'S


13) <u>THE SAM WARD INTERVIEW</u>

   Mark is talking with Ward when Marnie enters. He goes to table, sits on edge of it, leafs through trade journal, but puts it down when girl and interview capture his attention. Marnie tells the lies about her new fictitious personality. When it comes to references, she can supply only a scanty background. Ward is about to dismiss her when he gets a nod from Mark to hire her. Marnie leaves without once glancing at Mark. When she is gone, Ward voices his doubts about hiring a girl without the proper references. But Mark is sure she will work out.

14) OFFICE # 1—This is our key office scene and should establish:
   a) The nature of Marnie's job (to be worked out)
   b) The background office routine and characters (to be worked out)
   c) DAWN—who as Greek chorus explains comings and goings and also histories of principals.
   d) TERRY
   He comes in to get something from the safe and, through casual conversation with Dawn, lets us know of their past relationship, and also invites her to a poker party this Friday night. Throughout this (after giving Marnie only the faintest onceover) he unlocks petty cash drawer with a key on his keychain, looks in at safe combination scotch-taped to inside, and then goes to safe and opens it. After he leaves, DAWN elaborates on the Terry-Is-A-Wolf theme, and then suggests that Marnie take a look around the factory before they get down to work. Marnie leaves.

15) FACTORY-MARK
On her tour of the factory, Marnie stops to watch a man engraving glass. Mark comes up, introduces himself, and explains the process. We also learn a little about him and his family, and the craftsman nature of the business. His attitude is one of personal contact. Marnie's is one of arm's length strict business. His attempt at establishing contact fails. She leaves him to "get back to work," and he stares after her in puzzlement. When Marnie gets back to the office, Dawn tells her Terry has called to ask if she wouldn't like to come along to the poker party this Friday. Marnie hesitates a moment. Sam Ward is at the petty cash drawer, going through the identical routine Terry had earlier. Marnie, observing this, says Yes, she'll be delighted to come. Dawn wryly observes that she seems to be off to a flying start.

16) POKER PARTY # 1
   a) Establish the poker players (to be worked out)
   b) Make it clear that Marnie remains after others leave only in an attempt to make an impression of Terry's key.
   c) Terry makes his pass.
   d) Marnie runs off, revulsed.

17) THE CASHIER'S OFFICE
Dawn tells Marnie that Mark Rutland would like her to bring some material over to his house. She is surprised by his sudden interest because—and here she goes into Mark's bg, dead wife, etc. She tells Marnie to take a cab, goes to petty cash drawer, and opens it with a key identical to the one on Terry's key chain. Marnie leaves.

18) THE LIGHTNING SCENE
Almost as now written, but strengthen red herring that Marnie is responding to Mark's approach, and have her accept invitation to racetrack.

19)  THE RACETRACK SCENE
Almost as now written, but indicate that Marnie is frightened by "Haven't I seen you before?" because she is falling for Mark and does not want him to know of her past. Mark asks her to dinner with his mother on Tuesday night, and she accepts.

20)  THE TUESDAY NIGHT DATE
Where we meet Mark's mother, gracious, dignified, gentle, and warm, for the first time. It is apparent that she takes to Marnie at once. In a scene with the two women alone, she talks warmly of her son, and it seems now as though Marnie will really not go through with the planned robbery.

21)  MOTHER # 2—at Marnie's childhood home.
Almost as now written, with talk of father and what happened to him, establishing black box under bed, and with much talk of marriage, slanted to lead us into thinking Marnie is seriously considering Mark now.

22)  THE RUTLAND ROBBERY

23)  REPRISE MONTAGE—rinsing out hair, station wagon, big head of Marnie riding, then into long shots, and down to camera and MARK!

24)  CAUGHT
This will be done with continuous dialogue over cutting changes of scene, the stables, the car ride, the hotel room, the car again, or however many changes we need to cover the dialogue. The dialogue should tell us:
a)  What happened when the robbery was discovered (with attitudes of principals revealed in Mark's silent flashback)
b)  The explanation of how Marnie got the key.
c)  The lies Marnie tells about past history.
d)  The explanation of how she got her horse, and Mark's apparent dismissal of the animal.
e)  The explanation of how Mark found her.
f)  The relating of how he alibied her, and . . .
g)  His marriage proposal.

-III-
THE WEDDING AND HONEYMOON

25)  THE RECEPTION
This is essentially a scene between Dawn and Marnie, in an upstairs bedroom of Mark's house, where Marnie is changing for her forthcoming trip. Dawn tells Marnie how no one believed for a minute she could have been the thief, comments on change of hair, etc. But Marnie doesn't believe this for a moment. When she comes downstairs to the wedding party, the excessive geniality of Holbrook, Ward, etc. indicate she was right. They do think she robbed the safe. Terry offers a wryly sardonic farewell toast, and they depart on their honeymoon.

26) <u>THE LEONARDO DA VINCI—FIRST NIGHT</u>
Marnie is at dressing table in peignoir. Mark comes up behind her, kisses her hair. She rises and goes into sitting room. He comes to the door. With the room between them, he asks her what is wrong. She tells him. Her anxiety makes this scene somewhat comic, though we will play it straight. Mark, patiently angry at the end of the scene, goes back into the bedroom alone.

27) <u>POOLSIDE—THE NEXT DAY</u>
Wherein Marnie elaborates on her sex theories, with Graham's dialogue tuned up and minus the sex lecture, and ending with the tagline from Mark: <u>Love isn't always gentle. Nor is it always patient.</u>

28) <u>THE RAPE AND SUICIDE ATTEMPT</u>
To be worked out in minute detail, to express Marnie's fear, revulsion, pain, and dismal resignation. Pan from her face to open porthole and heaving sea. Dawn lightens the sky. Pan back to the bed with Mark in it alone. He awakens. The bedside clock tells us it is 5:00 A.M. Alarmed, he leaves the suite, searches the empty witching-hour ship for Marnie, glancing over the side at the ocean, rushing past rows of deck chairs, empty decks, a grey sky and a grey sea. He finally comes upon the pool. Marnie is floating in it face downward. He drags her out, administers artificial respiration, and carries her back to the cabin.

MARK

With all that ocean, why'd you pick the swimming pool?

MARNIE

I'm afraid of sharks.

MARK

I wouldn't try that again, darling.

MARNIE

Go to hell.


-IV-

LIFE WITH MARK


29) <u>THE LANTERN SLIDE AND DINNER BARGAIN SCENE</u>
   a) Exact nature of slides to be worked out, but they should reflect the entire Italian trip and Marnie's state of mind on honeymoon. They interrupt the showing of the slides when dinner is announced and her attitude throughout the meal is a continuation of what we saw in the slides: she is a prisoner here; she hates the house, she hates her new clothes, she hates the food (it is Mark who moves his plate closer to hers and asks a servant to set it there from now on) she hates the paintings on the wall, she especially hates Mark, her keeper. The dialogue leads to his suggestion that she see Dr. Roman. She flatly refuses until he offers to bring Forio up from Maryland in return. She accepts the deal.

30) <u>ANALYST # 1</u>
An introduction. Three-quarters comic, one-quarter serious toward very end. Hardly anything emerges about Marnie's past.

31) <u>THE ARRIVAL OF FORIO</u>
Simply shots of Marnie riding ecstatically, with Mark watching.

32) <u>ANALYST # 2</u>
Half comic, half serious. A bit of Marnie's past begins to emerge.

33) <u>PHONE CALL TO LUCY</u>
Wherein it is established that Mother is ill and more money is needed. This is immediately followed by a call from Terry inviting Marnie to a poker game. She accepts because she needs more money.

34) <u>POKER PARTY # 2</u>
But this time she loses. The "loser" concept is the springboard for an intimate scene with Terry. In the entrance foyer, with the voices of the poker players in the bg, he describes himself as a loser, and we foreshadow here the terrible wrath of which he is capable at the picture's end.

35) <u>ANALYST # 3</u>
One-quarter comic, three-quarters serious. It is here that Marnie comes very close to remembering the trauma. She is greatly shaken at the end of the scene.

36) <u>PRE-PARTY</u>
Wherein Mark explains the nature of the business deal and the party they are going to, and again foreshadows what Terry can be expected to do when he finds out. Marnie tries to beg off, but he tells her they needn't stay for more than a little while, and wearily she goes along with him.

37) <u>REX'S PARTY</u>
To be worked out in detail, concerning the nature of the discovery of Strutt and his wife at the party. But Mark and Strutt are in conversation at one point, observed by Marnie, who believes Strutt is telling Mark all about her. When they are finally introduced, however, Strutt doesn't seem to recognize her at all. She tells Mark she has a headache and would like to go home, and then goes upstairs for her coat. Only the faintest backward turn from Strutt indicates the memory-wheels are beginning to grind in his head. But it seems, for the moment, that Marnie has escaped undetected. In the upstairs bedroom, she is confronted by Mrs. Strutt, who accuses Marnie of having known her husband. Marnie assures her this is fantasy and leaves the bedroom, anxious to get away now. Mark, Terry and Strutt are in conversation near the front door. As she approaches, it seems apparent that they were discussing her—and yet nothing is said directly to her when she presents herself to the group. They say their goodnights. Terry and Strutt go back to their conversation as Marnie and Mark leave.

38) <u>THE SHOWDOWN</u>
Following our jump-cut pattern (as in Maryland CAUGHT sequence) Mark gets the full story of Marnie's past robberies from her. He decides to call his friend Judge Westerman at once, and does so without Marnie's knowledge.

39)  <u>MARK-WESTERMAN</u>
Marnie, coming downstairs, learns from Mrs. Leonard that Westerman is in the
study with Mark. She sneaks outside, eavesdrops, hears Mark telling Westerman
all, hears Westerman saying he will have to report this to the authorities unless
they can work it out themselves within the next few days. She goes upstairs, packs
some jewelry and flees.

40)  <u>MOTHER # 3</u>
She arrives at her mother's house and is told by Lucy that Edith is dead. The
undertakers are waiting to claim the body but Marnie asks them to wait. In
searching for mementoes of her mother in the black box under the bed, she comes
upon the single item that triggers memory of the trauma. The trauma flashback
must still be worked out in detail in terms of <u>continuous</u> and <u>smooth-flowing</u>
present-and-past action <u>interwoven</u> and of a <u>single piece</u>. At the end of the
flashback, Mark and Dr. Roman are discovered. They heard the whole thing. He
wants to take her home now. They will come back tomorrow for the funeral.

41)  <u>THE JOURNEY BACK</u>
Wherein Dr. Roman explains the psychological meaning of all this, and wherein
Marnie and Mark plan on a way out of her legal entanglements. They will contact
the people she robbed from, offer to repay the stolen money if all charges are
dropped. But they must do this before she is discovered.

42)  <u>THE FINAL SCENE</u>
When they reach the house, Strutt, Terry, and a Uniformed Cop are waiting in the
doorway. Marnie and Mark play a love scene in the driveway, where she offers
herself freely and willingly for the first time, and where we know he will wait for
her. Then she walks toward the front door.

END

The following letter outlines the battle to come between Hitchcock and
Hunter over one scene in particular:

April 2, 1963

Mr. Alfred J. Hitchcock
Alfred J. Hitchcock Productions, Inc.
Universal City, California

Dear Hitch:

Here is MARNIE, which I believe has shaped up very well. There are a few things I would
like to call to your attention, however, since they are deviations from the story as we
discussed it. I found that some of our story line simply would not work in the writing,
and I adjusted the screenplay accordingly.

The major change I have made concerns the honeymoon night. You will notice that there are two versions of this sequence in the script, one in white, one in yellow. The yellow version is the sequence as we discussed it, complete with the poolside scene, and the rape. I wrote and rewrote and polished and repolished this sequence, but something about it continued to disturb me. I finally wrote the white version—which is the version I would like to see in the film.

I know you are fond of the entire honeymoon sequence as we discussed it, Hitch, but let me tell you what I felt was wrong with it, and how I attempted to bring it into a truer perspective.

To begin with, Marnie's attitude was misleading. We were asking an audience to believe that putting off Mark was on her mind from the top of the scene. This makes her frigidity a cold-blooded thing (no pun intended) rather than something she cannot help. She can respond to warmth and gentleness, she can accept love-making—until it gets serious. Which brings us to a further examination. WHY DOES MARNIE MARRY HIM? The answer is simple: she loves him. She may think she is marrying him to avoid the police, but she really does love him (as we bring out at the picture's end.) It is only her deep emotional disturbance that makes it impossible for her to accept or enjoy this love.

I have, therefore, written a rather playful honeymoon night scene, showing Marnie in a gay and likable mood, a bit giggly (we have never seen her this way in the picture before), playing our entire Garrod's exposition as a warm love scene, which I think works. It is only when Mark's intentions get serious, only when his love-making reminds her of that night long ago, that she panics and pulls away. Her retreat is a curious thing, and the audience—for the first time—realizes that something is seriously wrong with this girl. The scene is frightening, and it also provides a springboard for the later scene in which Mark suggests psychiatric help. To me, it is believable and sound. The way we discussed it was implausibility bordering on burlesque.

Which brings us to the second major change.

In the yellow version, I have gone through the rape sequence as we discussed it. In the white version, I have eliminated it entirely. I firmly believe it is out of place in this story. Mark is not that kind of a person. Marnie is obviously troubled, and he realizes it. Stanley Kowalski might rape her, but not Mark Rutland. Mark would do exactly what we see him do later on—he would seek the help of a psychiatrist. And, without an out-of-character rape, there was no need for a poolside discussion. The entire honeymoon sequence now takes place on a single night. Marnie's panic is followed immediately by her suicide attempt. There is no long stage wait. I am convinced that the rape has no place in this sequence, Hitch, and I hope you will agree and throw away the yellow pages.

Along these lines, I know we both liked the flippant business about being afraid of sharks, etc. as the tag line to the suicide scene. I wrote it that way, and kept it that way almost until I completed my final version—but I did not believe it for a minute. Marnie has tried to drown herself. Mark has brought her back with artificial respiration. This is damn serious business. He would never be glib or flippant in this scene—so I've thrown away the lines, keeping only the "Go to hell" tag.

One last deviation. I know we discussed what we called the post-Westerman scene—which I wrote and finally discarded. To me, it seemed like a no-scene scene, especially in the light of what I learned from my attorney. I don't know what the law is in England, but in America, an attorney would be under no obligation to reveal information gained through privileged communication. Besides, it is not important that Mark and Marnie <u>discuss</u> her reaction. It is only important that we <u>see</u> her reaction and then <u>exaggerate</u> it via use of the fox hunt the following day. I think you'll agree this works, and that it cuts a dead spot from the scenario.

I think that's it. I will be waiting to hear from you, and expecting to come West whenever you say.

My very best wishes.

Sincerely,

Evan Hunter

EH:sb
Enclosure

P. S.  I have three additional copies of the script and if you want them, please let me know, and I'll send them to you immediately.

---

The rape scene was a hotly contested sequence in the film. The scene is in the finished film. The following pages show that the options at that point in the story are limited. Hitchcock had built a trap for himself that required some action on the part of Mark. The tension of the honeymoon sequence is in this unresolved sexual question. The "rape" balances the scales—Mark now has something to be guilty over in the relationship or, rather, it gives Marnie some power over Mark. Regardless, the relationship's dynamic changes from this point in the film.

This first sequence is how Hunter preferred the scene.

pg 7 - research
pg 16   "

141

III D                                    1

EXTERIOR-NIGHT...LONG SHOT OF AN OCEAN LINE AT
SEA.   GAILY LIGHTED.

INTERIOR...CABIN SITTING ROOM  a luxuriously appointed cabin
This is the sitting room of
           MARK, in evening dress, his tie loose, is
fixing himself a drink.  He talks, addressing his remarks
through the partially open bedroom door.

                    MARK
          We're really a couple of tourists, old
          girl...first night out, and dressed up like
          Miss America and Bert Parks.
                   (there is no answer from
                    the bedroom)
          Shall I fix you a drink?
                   (still no answer.  He
                    goes to the door, and
                    although it is half-
                    open, taps)
          Booze?
                   (looks in.  MARNIE is
                    not there.  He moves
                    in and taps on bathroom
                    door)
          I said would you like some bourbon
          to brush your teeth?

                    MARNIE
                   (her voice scarcely audible
                    behind the door)
          No, thank you.

                    MARK

                   (moves back from door, sits
                    on bed.  Continues to speak.
                    Not altogether as a means of
                    quieting a nervous bride...
                    we must feel that he, too,
                    is not completely at ease in
                    this situation.)
          You've never been married, of course, so
          you've no way of knowing...but  marriage
   is not  exactly the way The Ladies' Home Journal
          tells it.  It is definitely not the bed-
          room that is the battleground.  The
          real field of battle is the bath.  That's
          where the lines are drawn and no quarter
          given.  Now it seems to me that we are
          getting off to a rather poor start,  darling.
          You have been in the bathroom...

> MARK
> (consults his watch)
> ...for the better part of forty-five minutes.
> Time for me to finish two drinks and start
> a third.  Have you hopes of my passing out?
> Is that your rotten plot?  It won't work.
> I can drink any bride on this boat under
> the bed...
> (the bathroom door opens and
> MARNIE steps out.  She is in
> gown and robe...not noticeably
> bridal.  Her face is scrubbed and
> very pale.  She makes no pretense
> of smiling)

> MARNIE
> You can have the bath now.

> MARK
> (smiles at her)
> Thank you.
> (continues to sit where
> he is.  SHE cannot decide
> where to move...in which
> direction safety might lie.)

> You're very sexy with your face clean.
> (she neither moves nor answers.
> She doesn't even look at him.
> After a moment of this, he puts
> down his glass, speaks gently)
> Marnie? Come here.
> (Like a prisoner responding to
> a warden's order, she obeys,
> walks directly to him, stands,
> hands at her side.  He doesn't
> touch her, but sits, looking
> up at her)
> It's going to be all right, Marnie.
> Believe me.  I make every-
> thing all right for you.
> (he reaches out and, gently,
> takes her wrist and pulls her
> down beside him.  She is holding
> her breath, and tiny beads of
> perspiration begin to pop out
> on her drawn face as she allows
> this to be done to her.  Then,
> when he moves to kiss her...
> it all breaks.  Violently, she
> pushes him from her, fighting
> to free herself from even the
> air around him...)

CONTINUED                III D                              143 ³

                        MARNIE
           (hoarsely          as she
           breaks for the other room)
     I can't! I can!tI can't!
                        (even MARK    is not expecting a
                        reaction like this..
                        bewildered
                        he        to follow her)

SITTING ROOM

MARNIE is huddled in a corner...as far as she can get from
the bedroom, the bed, MARK.  As MARK stands in the doorway
looking at her in utter bewilderment, she tries to withdraw
even further...she is panting...

                        MARK
           For God's sake, Marnie...

                        MARNIE
           If you touch me again...I'll kill you!
           I'll kill you!
                        (MARK stares at her, dumbfounded,
                        and she, like a cornered animal
                        glares back at him.  For a long
                        moment they are face to face...
                        utterly estranged...without any
                        possibility of communication.
                        Finally, MARK moves, slowly,
                        cautiously, not toward her,
                        but parallel, until he finds a
                        place to sit.  A place from
                        which he can watch her and talk
                        without frightening her any
                        further.

                        MARK
           Marnie,..you don't have to try to push your
           way through the wall.  I won't touch you.
           I promise.
                        (she doesn't move)
           What's all this about?

                        MARNIE
           I don't want you to touch me!

                        MARK
           I won't touch you.  I promise I won't touch
           you.  Just get out of that goddam corner and
           sit down someplace.  Please.
                        (after a moment, she moves,
                        cautiously into a chair as
                        far removed from MARK'S as
                        possible.  There she sits,
                        straight, tense, poised for
                        instant flight)

CONTINUED                    III D

MARK

Now suppose you just tell me what this is
all about?  Is it your little way of saying
you don't find me particularly attractive?

MARNIE

I told you not to marry me! I told you!

MARK
(watching her every gesture...
looking for some clue as he
talks, trying to keep his tone
light...)
Well, yes...you suggested that certain
criminal tendencies...

MARNIE

I don't mean that...
(a small agonized sound caught
in her throat)
Oh, God...why couldn't you just let me go?

MARK
(moves impulsively forward in
a gesture of sympathy)
Marnie...

MARNIE
(immediate withdrawal)
Don't! Please...please don't!

MARK

Look! I said I wouldn't touch you, and won't...
but I'm going to talk to you and you're going
to talk to me.  You owe me that much.

MARNIE

I don't owe you anything! It was you or the police,
that's what you said! And I wish to God
that it had been the police!

MARK

Let me fix you a drink.

MARNIE
(dully)
I don't want a drink.

MARK
I think a brandy...

MARNIE

I don't want it! Just leave me alone!

46    CONTINUED            III D                    145

              MARK
          (patiently, but firmly)
    No, I can't leave you alone...not til I find
    out what's the matter with you and find some
    way to help you...

              MARNIE
    The only way you can help me is to let me
    alone. Can't you understand? Isn't it plain
    enough? I cannot stand to be...handled.

              MARK
    By anybody, or just me?

              MARNIE
    You. Men. ████████

              MARK
          (A beat of silence, then...
           composed, casual)
    Really? You didn't seem to mind that
    day in my office...at the races. All
    this last week...I've..'handled' you...
    I've kissed you...
          (cannot help ████████ smiling slightly - at himself
    ...eight times this last week. I
    counted. Why didn't you break out
    in a cold sweat and back into a corner
    then?

              MARNIE
    I...I thought I could stand it...I had to...

              MARK
    I see.
          (contemplates her for a
           moment)
    Have you always felt like this?

              MARNIE
          (passionately)
    Always! Yes!

              MARK
    Why? What happened to you?

              MARNIE
    Happened? Nothing. Nothing ever happened
    to me. I just never wanted anybody to
    touch me. ████████████████

              MARK
    Have you ever tried to talk about it? To
    a doctor,..somebody who could help you?

              MARNIE
    No. Why should I? I didn't want to get
    married! I was doing all right the way I was...

*96* CONTINUED                    III D                        *146.*

> **MARK**
> (mildly)
> Oh, I wouldn't say that.  If I
> hadn't caught you, Marnie, you
> would have kept on stealing...

> **MARNIE**
> No...no, I wouldn't...

> **MARK**
> Yes, you would...again and again.
> Eventually you'd have got caught...
> by somebody.  You're such a pretty,
> tempting little thing...
> (a faint smile)
> some other...sexual blackmailer...
> would have got his hands on you...
> the chances of it's being someone
> as...let's just say, as 'permissive'
> as me, are pretty remote.  Sooner or
> later you'd have gone to jail or onto
> your back across an office desk with
> some angry old bull of a business man
> taking what he figured was coming to
> him...you'd probably have got him <u>and</u>
> jail.  So I wouldn't say you were
> doing all right, Marnie.  I'd say you
> needed all the help you could get.

> **MARNIE**
> (sullenly)
> I don't need <u>your</u> help.

> **MARK**
> I don't think you are capable of judging
> what you need or from whom you need it.
> What you <u>do</u> need, I expect, is a psychiatrist.

> **MARNIE**
> (laughs angrily)
> Men!  All ▬ you have to do is
> say 'no thanks' to one of them and
> wham!  You're a candidate for the
> funny farm!  It's really laughable.

> **MARK**
> (trying to answer her
> calmly, rationally)
> Marnie...it's not that you see fit to
> say 'no thanks' to me...maybe you have
> some right to feel the way you do...

> **MARNIE**
> That's big of you!

CONTINUED

CONTINUED                    III D

MARK
(ignores this)
...but you're saying 'no thanks' to
everything and everybody, to life in
general.  Can't you understand that's *all wrong?*

MARNIE
I'll tell you what I understand!
I understand that I took some of
the precious Rutland money and that
I'm paying for it with my life!
What do I have to do?  Serve a
life sentence for stealing seven
thousand dollars!

MARK
(sees that she is in a
totally irrational state.
He sighs, leans back)
Look, Marnie...I don't think either one
os us is in any condition to hash this
out tonight.  Let's try to get some
rest...we'll talk it all out tomorrow.

MARNIE
There's nothing to talk out! You know
how I feel.  I'll feel the same tomorrow
and the day after and the day after that!
(in a violent impulse to escape
even the sight of him, she turns...
it is a wall she faces...she makes
a small, hopeless gesture...her
fist against its solid, unyielding
expanse)

MARK
(moved to pity)
Marnie...listen, Marnie...We won't talk
about it until you want to. Look, we're
going to be on this damn boat for
(     ) days and nights...let's just drop
the whole thing for the present and try
to get through this bloody honeymoon
cruise with as much grace as possible...
let's try at least to be kind to one
another...

MARNIE
(bitterly)
Kind!

MARK
All right.  If that's too much...I'll be
kind to you and you be polite to me.

                    MARNIE
You won't...bother me?

                    MARK
No.  I won't 'bother' you, Marnie.
          (at the doubting look
          on her face, he essays
          a grin)
I give you my word.
          (holds up both palms)
Look, Ma!  No hands.

                    MARNIE
          does not smile, but
          draws a deep, shuddery
          breath

Now why don't you go to bed and try
to get some rest?

                    MARNIE
Thank you.
          (              'politely')
I think I'd like to stay in here for
a while.  But, thank you.
          (MARK assesses her          un-
          yielding, defensive posture, *nods agreeably,*
                    and turns toward the
          bedroom.  He grabs up a pair of
          pajamas and a shaving kit, goes
          into the bathroom.  At the sound
          of the closing bathroom door,
          MARNIE slumps, drained, exhausted.
          She closes her eyes and rubs her
          damp face and hairline with the
          sleeve of her robe.  The bathroom
          door opens, and MARK returns to
          the doorway seperating the bed
          and sitting rooms.  He is still
          dressed.  He holds up an electric
          tooth-brush of the cordless
          variety)

                    MARK
*Hey marnie!* Look at this,     .
          (with a TV-like exposure of
          toothy delight, he demonstrates
          the brush)

*66*  CONTINUED                 III D                      *149*

                        MARK
            There.  You must see that you have
            nothing to fear from a man who takes
            his electric toothbrush on his honey-
            moon!
                        (his efforts are rewarded.
                        The faintest, most fleeting
                        ghost of a smile has been
                        forced from her.  He coaxes)
            How about it?  You way over here in your
            bed, and me miles away over there in mine?

                        MARNIE
            In a little while...I'll...come in in a
            little while.

                        MARK
            That's better.
                        (from the distance of
                        the doorway...it might
                        as well be a thousand
                        miles, he looks at her)
            Well...
                        (turns, toothbrush in hand,
                        back to the bath...then
                        stops and looks at her once
                        again...she seems infinitely
                        further away)
            ...if you hear me knashing my teeth in my
            sleep...at least I'll be...
                        (holds up the toothbrush)
            ...knashing them hygienically.

*67*  INTERIOR BEDROOM.    DARK

      MARK, in his bed.  He is on his side, facing the sitting
      room door through which light shows.  He looks at his
      watch.  It is after four.  He gets out of bed and walks
      softly to the door, looks through into the sitting room.
      MARNIE, still in the chair where we saw her last, is
      sleeping, huddled miserably, her arm shielding her eyes from
      the brightly lighted room.  MARK, in his pajamas which by
      this time look thoroughly creased--tossed in--stands in the
      doorway and stares at his bride.  No longer trying, for
      MARNIE'S sake, to make light of the situation, his face is
      weary, saddened.  Immobile, he stands half in the dark,
      watching her troubled sleep.

*68*  EXTERIOR  DECK OF SHIP.   DAYLIGHT.

      MARK is showing MARNIE around the ship.  They are on the
      topmost deck.  His manner is light, urbane.  Her's is quiet,
      subdued.

*150*

CONTINUED                    · III D                                ~~10~~

                         MARK
        ~~You are~~ The Captain has to be a heavy-weight.
        He shouldn't be under five foot nine
        nor weight less than one-eighty.
                    (bows gracefully and
                     smiles at the officer
                     whom they now pass)
        ...Captain.  Fine day, isn't it?
                    (The Captain returns the
                     greeting.  MARK continues,
                     sotto voce, his lecture to
                     MARNIE)
        Five-eleven, one-eighty-five.  Splendid
        specimen.  The other officers are generally
        middle-weights.  Their duties require rather
        speedier foot-work... There are a great many
        single women...married and otherwise on these
        ships.  And what they're all looking for is
        a little action. First and second officers,
        pursers...they've got to be battlers, and
        they hold up only as long as their legs do.
                    (he points out a young ship's
                     officer gallantly dancing
                     attendance on a lady whom only
                     the most generous spirit would
                     describe as middle-aged)
        The ladies do not pay (3000?) dollars round
        trip for the ocean air and a couple of bingo
        games.
                    (they stop at the rail and
                     look down at the water)

                         MARNIE
                    (turns and walks forward
                     toward the section of the
                     rail that overlooks the
                     lower deck.  MARK follows
                     her.  They stand, side by
                     side and gaze down at the
                     empty swimming pool.)
        How long before it will be warm enough
        to swim?

                         MARK
        They'll fill the pool about the third
        day out.
                    (they stand, side by side,
                     and miles apart, looking
                     out to sea)

III D

*however, as* ~~11~~  *151*

*669*

INTERIOR CABIN BEDROOM     DARK

In the darkened room we see MARK in bed.  His head is
propped up as he stares into the dark, silently smoking.
MARNIE, in the other bed, is turned toward the wall.  She
appears to be soundly sleeping.  THE CAMERA closes in on
her, ~~and~~ we see that she is awake.  Her eyes,
pacing the wall, ~~are open as dark as~~ the night.

*101*

EXTERIOR SUNDECK

MARK and MARNIE in deckchairs.  They watch a gull circle the
boat.

                    MARNIE
          Has it come out too far?  What if
          it can't get back?

                    MARK
          It'll get back.

                    MARNIE
                (concerned)
          But what if it can't?

                    MARK
          Gulls know how to get around...if that
          one's in trouble it will hitch a ride... *CATCH A BOAT*

                    MARNIE
          Maybe it wants to catch this boat.

                    MARK            *mediterranean*
          Then it will be in trouble.  This boat
          is headed for the ▓▓▓▓▓.  That's an
          American gull.  It won't be able to speak
          ~~mediterranean~~.

                    MARNIE
          What are you talking about?

                    MARK
          The same specie of birds speak different
          languages if they live in different areas.
          Crows who have never had the initiative to
          get out of Pennsylvania cannot understand
          the cries of crows who have stayed down on
          the farm in Maine.  But you take a crow who
          gets around, ~~He~~'ll be multilingual... Able
          to speak to both the Pennsylvania crow and
          the Down Easter crow.

                    MARNIE
          You're kidding.

III D

CONTINUED

                              MARK
          Not at all.  It's been proven.  They've
          taken tape recordings of the alarm
          calls of the American herring gulls...
          all American herring gulls respond to
          the alarm call...and then they've taken
          the recordings to France and played the
          American alarm calls to the French
          herring gulls, who either ignore the
          calls or else gather around to listen
          and make fun of the barbaric American
          accents.  French gulls despise gulls who
          don't speak French.

MARNIE continues to watch the circling gull.  Her face
is withdrawn and lonely.

                         MARK (cont'd)
          What are you thinking, Marnie?

                              MARNIE
          That it's the same even with animals.
          When a thing is different, it is
          despised.

MARK regards her enigmatically.

INTERIOR SHIP'S LOUNGE

It is rather late.  MARK and MARNIE, in evening dress,
are at the bar.

                              MARNIE
          I'm tired.  If you don't mind, I'll
          go on to the cabin.

                              MARK
                         (avoids her eye)
          All right.  Go along.  I think
          I'll stay and have another drink.
          It's getting so much warmer...I
          may even sit outside for a while.

                              MARNIE
          All right.  Goodnight.

                              MARK
          Good night.

She leaves.  MARK does not watch her out.  He quickly
swallows his drink, pushes out glass to bartender for a
refill.

9?) (Show Mark coming to cabin looking at her?)

182     INTERIOR, CABIN, SITTING ROOM       153
                                                                                 13

MARK in pajamas and robe sits, ostensibly reading.
Actually, attuned only to the sounds from the other room,
sounds made by MARNIE as she moves about the bedroom.  At
last she appears in the doorway.  She too is wearing night
apparel.

                     MARNIE
    Mark?

He appears to respond slowly, reluctantly
looking up from his book.

                     MARK
    Yes?

                     MARNIE
    How long do we have to stay?  In Greece?

                     MARK
              (a moment of
                silence)
    We don't have to stay in Greece at all.
    If you don't like it, we can go on to any place you
like.

                     MARNIE
    That's not what I mean.  I mean how
    long...how long will it be before I...
    before we go back?

                     MARK
              (narrows his eyes)
    Why, Mrs. Rutland...can you be suggesting
    that these halcyon, honeymoon days and
    nights...of just the two of us alone
    together...should ever end?

MARNIE gives him a short, piercingly hostile look, turns
back into the bedroom, smartly shutting the door between
them.  At the insulting sound of the slammed door, MARK
is immediately on his feet.  In a few fast strides, he
crosses the room and enters the bedroom.  His precipitous
entrance instantly alarms MARNIE who has removed her robe
and is about to get into bed.  She whirls around to face
him.  For a brief moment they face each other...on the
ready.

                     MARNIE
              (the more defensive of
                the two)
    If you don't mind...I want to go to bed
    ...the light from the sitting room
    bothers me.

CONTINUED                    III D

                    MARK
        Well, we certainly can't have anything
        'bothering' you, can we?
                    (steps back enough to
                    reach through doorway
                    and flip off the principal
                    sitting-room light.  This
                    leaves them in almost total
                    gloom)
        There.  Heaven forbid that any ray of *penetrate*
        light should be permitted to ███████ the
        night of your soul, Mrs. Rutland.

                    MARNIE
                    (who has not moved so
                    much as a muscle)
        If you don't want to go to bed...
        please get out.

                    MARK
        I have at no point suggested that I
        did not want to go to bed.  I want to
        go to bed...
                    (moves slowly toward
                    her)
        Marnie...I very much want to go to bed...

                    MARNIE
                    (her reflex is immediate...
                    her hands go up to ward
                    him off...to push him
                    away)
        No!
        ████████

        The violence of her rejection triggers an equal, long
        controlled violence in MARK.  In one cruel and brutal
        movement, his hand streaks out and tears the gown from
        her body...there is no outcry from her...only silence as
        THE CAMERA focuses on her bare feet and legs, and the
        violated gown that lies around them.  When THE CAMERA
        cuts away, it comes up to include...close-up...both their
        faces...MARNIE, her eyes closed, her face rigid and white...
        MARK, shocked, sorry...but terribly moved at the sight of
        her, naked and helpless before him.  Slowly he takes off
        his own robe and covers her with it.

                    MARK
        Marnie...I'm sorry...

        His hands, placing the robe around her bare shoulders, seem
        unable to leave her.  Still she does not move from her icy
        stance.  Gently, but compulsively, he pulls her to him,
        softly, coaxingly covers her face with kisses...it is not
        just his desire that has finally overflowed, but his very

CONTINUED            III D

real love for her. And it is love that dictates the
manner in which he takes her...not simply using her, but
courting, caressing, desperately urging her ~~response~~ *response*
MARNIE, her fear and revulsion manifest in her frozen
face and body, yields only to his superior weight and
strength and will. As she is pressed back onto the bed,
THE CAMERA closes in on their heads. MARK'S face
pressed first against her cheek and neck, then against
her breast, ~~~~ is hidden from our view, but
MARNIE'S face, stark, staring blindly at the ceiling
above her, is completely exposed to us, and on it is
written...nothing. There is no flicker of expression,
of emotion. It simply...endures.

Slowly, THE CAMERA moves from this waxen, lifeless face
upwards to the porthole, through which we see the night,
the calm sea. As THE CAMERA holds this view, we slowly
become conscious of a time lapse as the sky gradually
fades into the murky gray of pre-dawn. Now THE CAMERA
returns to the bed. What we see: the sleeping form of
MARK alone on the bed. THE CAMERA draws back, enlarging
our view enough to include MARNIE'S torn gown on the
floor and her discarded robe on the chair where she first
laid it. The other bed is empty, untouched. MARK'S robe
lies in a heap on the floor near it. We hear a faint
sound, a surreptitious rustle...MARK stirs...there is a
hushed moment of quiet, and then the sound of a door... *furtive*
not the bedroom door, but another...being ~~~~ opened
and closed. Instantly, MARK is awake. Wide awake. With
one guilty look he takes in the empty room; then he is on
his feet, swiftly exploring the bath and the sitting room.
*Now* ~~~~ moving rapidly, he grabs up his robe from the floor,
secures it around him and makes his way into the deserted
ship's corridor.

103   EXTERIOR - SHIP'S CORRIDOR

He listens. There is no sound to guide him. His in-
stinctive urgency drives him to a quick decision. He
turns left, runs silently down the hall's length.

104   EXTERIOR - GLASSED-IN PROMONADE, SECOND DECK

The place is deserted, bathed in the foggy half-gloom of
pre-morning. MARK paces swiftly to the end of the protected
section, emerges onto the sports deck...deserted shuffle-
board courts, folded deck-chairs, swimming pool. There is
no one. He turns and bounds up the stairs to the upper deck.

III D                                                                156

105    EXTERIOR - UPPER DECK    on an empty, abandoned ship,

Stacks...he moves swiftly around them.  They hide nothing...
he races toward the back of the deck...deserted...he seems to
be absolutely alone.  There is no sound but his own, the
muffled, muted underscoreing of the ship's engines and the
yielding waters.  He runs foreward again, toward the
rail across which he and MARNIE gazed in Sc. 5.  He grips
the rail and scans from this new angle the empty spaces
below...the shuffle board courts, the empty sundeck, the
pool...but the pool is not empty.  It has been filled, and
at the bottom of it's tropical blue waters there is a
figure.  It is MARNIE.  XMMXXIMMXXMMXXMMMX  She is
dressed in slacks and shirt and shoes...she lies face down
...her hair floating free in the water.

106    EXTERIOR - PLAY DECK

In seconds MARK is down the stairs and into the pool's
depths, desperately working the limp body toward the
surface.  In the dreadful silence        he gets her
out of the pool and lays her face down on the tiles,
immediately starting to give her respiration...and it is
only moments before she stirs, coughs...MARK redoubles his
efforts    she    , frowns, and shakes her head crossly
like a sick child, and at last spits up the swallowed water.
Still holding his own breath, MARK turns her over.  Her
eyes open focusing first on the gray dawn.  Slowly they
lower to take in MARK'S face drawn into lines of anxiety,
shame, love, anger.  Their eyes lock in combat...they each,
at last, understand to whom and what they are joined.
Neither gaze gives way.

The next sequence is how the finished screenplay reads:

*MARNIE* RAPE SCENE, FINAL SCREENPLAY VERSION

242    CONTINUED

**MARNIE**

Yes.

**CHRISTOPHER**

What time do you sail?

**MARNIE**

I think it's six. Mark knows.

**TERRY**

We shouldn't let you get away without a farewell toast. Father? You're the
speechmaker.

**CHRISTOPHER**

*(Raising his glass)*

To Mark and Mary . . .

*(Correcting himself)*

*Marnie* . . . may you have a long and happy life together.

      TERRY
*(Like a curse)*
Good luck . . . *Marnie.*

DISSOLVE

243    LONG SHOT—THE LEONARDO DA VINCI—EXTERIOR—NIGHT

on the open seas, her lights ablaze.

244    FULL SHOT—THE LUXURY SUITE—INTERIOR—NIGHT

As Mark and Marnie enter the darkened cabin. He is in black tie, she in a gown. They have been dancing and drinking, and are in a gay and giggling mood as they enter. Marnie is especially relaxed, vivacious and alive.

      MARK
Let there be light!
*(He turns on the switch)*
And there was light!

      MARNIE
*(Giggling)*
Don't joke at sacred words.

      MARK
Forgive me, madam, I beg your pardon.
*(He holds out his hands to her; she goes to him, and they kiss)*
Mmmmm. I love you.

      MARNIE
*(In his arms)*
You said you'd tell me when we got back to the cabin.

      MARK
I just told you. I love you.

      MARNIE
*(Laughing)*
Not that. How you found me.
*(She goes into the bedroom)*

      MARK
*(Following her)*
I find you *ra*vishing.
*(He kisses her again)*

      MARNIE
I meant in Maryland.

      MARK
Let's forget Maryland. That's all behind us.

He sits on the edge of the bed, gently pulls her down beside him.

245    TWO SHOT—MARNIE AND MARK

> MARNIE
> Please, Mark. I'm curious.

> MARK
> (Kissing her)
> Nope. Never tell you. Never, never, never.

> MARNIE
> (Smiling)
> Never?

245    CONTINUED

> MARK
> Never. Torture me, flay me, kill me, but I'll never . . .

> MARNIE
> (She kisses him, stopping the words)
> How'd you know where to look?

> MARK
> I didn't.
> (He kisses her hand)
> You're beautiful, do you know that?

> MARNIE
> Go ahead, I'm listening.

> MARK
> I said you're beautiful.

> MARNIE
> Thank you.

> MARK
> And you like horses. Which was the one real thing I knew about you. So I figured you
> were going to take that money and splurge it on the races.

> MARNIE
> I'd never have done that.

> MARK
> I know, you never bet.
> (He kisses the tip of her nose)
> But I had to get you back to Philadelphia by Monday, you see, and I had nothing else
> to go on. So on Saturday morning, I drove down to Monmouth Park. No luck.
> (He kisses her ear)
> While I was there, though, I remembered a tip you'd given me.

                    MARNIE
What tip?

                    MARK
Guess.
*(He kisses her cheek)*

245     CONTINUED

                    MARNIE
Mark, I can't guess.

                    MARK
Guess who loves you?

                    MARNIE
Tell me what tip.

                    MARK
On a grey filly in the fourth race. A horse named Telepathy. You said you'd seen her training as a one-year old.

                    MARNIE
Oh!
*(Pause)*
Yes!

The following dialogue is punctuated with kisses as Mark becomes more and more amorous. The words, as he delivers them, are almost a seduction, with the CAMERA moving in closer and closer on their faces and their lips. Marnie is succumbing to the seduction, enjoying the warmth of his arms, his gentleness, his lulling voice. A lassitude seems to spread through her.

                    MARK
So I looked up Telepathy in the *Racing Guide,* and found she belonged to a Major Marsten of Tampa, Florida. I love your mouth, do you know that?
*(He kisses her)*
I called the major long distance that afternoon.
*(He kisses her)*
He told me he'd bought the horse from a man named Fitzgibbon and had no idea where she'd been trained. But he said he'd originally met Fitzgibbon at the Laurel track, and he suggested I contact them. I did. They gave me Fitzgibbon's phone number.

                    MARNIE
*(Lazily succumbing)*
Did you call Fitzgibbon?

245     CONTINUED

                    MARK
*(Kissing her)*

Three times. He was out, and I didn't get to talk to him until Sunday. He told me the horse had been trained by a man named Charles Davis at Garrod's Farm. It was a chance. I drove right down.

*(Pause)*

I should throw a party for them when we get back.

      MARNIE

Who?

      MARK

*(Kissing her)*

The major . . .

*(Another kiss)*

. . . and the people at Laurel . . .

*(Another kiss)*

. . . and Fitzgibbon, too. For bringing you back to me.

He is suddenly serious. His arms tighten around her, and he kisses her in earnest, a long passionate kiss. Slowly, they fall back onto the pillow. His mouth closes on hers. And now a panic starts on Marnie's face. Behind his back, her hands suddenly clench, something unconscious is rising within her, something she cannot control, something which warns of danger. Suddenly, she twists her mouth away from his.

      MARNIE

Mark . . . don't. Please.

*(As he persists)*

Mark, please!

      MARK

*(Puzzled)*

Darling, what . . . ?

She pulls away from him and sits on the edge of the bed. She is suddenly trembling. She hugs herself.

      MARK

What is it? Marnie, you're trembling. What's the matter?

245    CONTINUED

      MARNIE

Please . . . please keep away from me. Please, Mark.

      MARK

*(More alarmed now)*

Darling, darling . . .

*(And tries to take her in his arms to comfort her)*

      MARNIE

*(Recoiling, screaming)*

No! I don't want this! I'm not an animal! Stay away from me!

МARK

Marnie!

MARNIE

It's filthy and disgusting, I don't *want* it!

MARK

Marnie, I love you.

MARNIE

*(Trembling, wild-eyed)*

I don't care what you . . . look . . . keep away from me. Do you hear me? Don't . . . just don't . . . something terrible's going to happen, do you hear me?

Mark is staring at her in complete confusion now. Marnie sits on the edge of the bed, trembling.

MARNIE

Something terrible.

MARK

*(Gently, alarmed)*

All right, Marnie, try to . . . try to calm down now.

MARNIE

I don't want you to come near me, Mark, do you understand? I don't love you! I never did! That's the truth. That's the honest truth. Never. So . . . just . . . just stay away from me. Because I'm . . . I'm . . . warning you.

245    CONTINUED

MARK

*(Hurt, gently)*

Why'd you marry me, Marnie?

MARNIE

*(On the edge of hysteria)*

Marry you? You *have* a wife!

MARK

What are you . . .

MARNIE

I heard, I saw!

MARK

Marnie, my . . . my wife is dead.

*(He moves toward her)*

MARNIE

Keep *away*!

And suddenly she begins sobbing, and throws herself onto the bed, her head buried in the pillow.

246     CLOSE SHOT—MARK

Looking down at her compassionately, troubled, concerned.

DISSOLVE

247     MEDIUM SHOT—MARK

Asleep in a chair in the other cabin. The first dim rays of the sun awaken him. He gets out of the chair, goes to the door between the cabins.

248     FULL SHOT—THE BEDROOM

The bed is empty.

>           **MARK**
> **Marnie?**

249     CLOSE SHOT—MARK

Turning to look at the clock.

250     INSERT—THE TIME

5:10 A.M.

251     FULL SHOT—MARK

As he enters the bedroom and goes quickly to the bathroom door, throwing it open.

>           **MARK**
> **Marnie?**

She is not there. He comes out of the bedroom and goes swiftly to the door of the suite, opening it.

252–   OMIT
259

260     FULL SHOT   THE PROMENADE DECK   EXTERIOR   DAY

As Mark comes out of the cabin. The ship is empty. The deck chairs are lined row upon row. The morning is grey, the sea is grey. He looks quickly over the side.

261     FULL SHOT—THE OCEAN

Rushing past the side of the ship.

262     FULL SHOT—THE PROMENADE DECK

As Mark makes his way down it. He glances over the side every now and then, his panic mounting. Marnie is nowhere in sight. He begins climbing a ladder glancing back over his shoulder as he climbs, and then reaching the deck above, and turning, and looking down. He is looking into the pool.

263     CRANE SHOT—THE POOL

Marnie, in a nightgown, is floating face downward in the water.

264   FULL SHOT—MARK

As he rushes to the pool's edge and dives in after her. He swims to the side, pulls her out.

265   MEDIUM SHOT—MARK

As he bends over her, begins to administer artificial respiration.

266   CLOSE SHOT—MARNIE'S FACE

The head sideways, lying on the deck lifelessly as Mark works over her.

267   TWO SHOT—MARNIE AND MARK

As he works. It seems she is dead. His face gets more and more frantic. The time seems to stretch interminably.

268   CLOSE SHOT—MARNIE'S FACE

As she coughs.

269   CLOSE SHOT—MARK'S FACE

Relieved.

270   TWO SHOT—MARK AND MARNIE

As he continues working over her.

271   TWO SHOT—MARK AND MARNIE

As he carries her in his arms back to the cabin. She is trembling against him.

> **MARNIE**
> **Why didn't you let me die?**

> **MARK**
> **Because I love you.**

> **MARNIE**
> **Go to hell.**

*FADE OUT*

*MARNIE* rape scene as it appeared in the final film.

*FADE IN:*

272   FULL SHOT—THE BOW OF THE LEONARDO DA VINCI AND THE BAY OF NAPLES BEYOND

242    CONTINUED

>           MARNIE
> Yes.

>           CHRISTOPHER
> What time do you sail?

>           MARNIE
> I think it's six. Mark knows.

>           TERRY
> We shouldn't let you get away without a farewell toast. Father? You're the
> speechmaker.

>           CHRISTOPHER
> *(Raising his glass)*
> To Mark and Mary . . .
> *(Correcting himself)*
> *Marnie*. . . may you have a long and happy life together.

>           TERRY
> *(Like a curse)*
> Good luck . . . *Marnie*.

DISSOLVE


243    LONG SHOT—THE LEONARDO DA VINCI—EXTERIOR—NIGHT

on the open seas, her lights ablaze.


244    FULL SHOT—THE LUXURY SUITE—INTERIOR—NIGHT

Marnie is at the dressing table in a robe, brushing out her hair. There is a nervousness
about her. Mark comes into the room behind her, wearing trousers and an unbuttoned
white shirt. He puts his hands on her shoulders, kisses the side of her neck. He smiles
at her in the mirror. She smiles back, but does not respond to his kiss.

>           MARNIE
> *(Brushing again)*
> Mark?

>           MARK
> Mmm?


244    CONTINUED

>           MARNIE
> *(A delaying tactic)*
> You said you'd tell me how you found me.

MARK

I find you beautiful and radiant.

MARNIE

I meant in Maryland.

MARK

I know what you meant. I'd like to forget that, Marnie. It's behind us now.
*(He kisses her neck again)*

MARNIE

*(Rising)*
Please, I'm curious.

She goes to the other side of the room, away from him, finds busy work there. He notices this with a faintly curious glance.

MARK

Well . . . actually, I didn't know where to begin looking.

MARNIE

You seemed to find me soon enough.

MARK

It was mostly luck. I asked myself what you seemed most interested in and the answer, of course, was horses. I figured you were going to take that stolen money and splurge it on the races.

MARNIE

I'd never have done that.

MARK

I realize that now. But all I knew *then* was that I had to get you back to Philadelphia by Monday morning. So I drove to Monmouth Park on Saturday. We'd been there, you know, and I thought maybe, just maybe . . .
*(He shrugs)*
It was hopeless, of course. But while I was there, I remembered a tip you'd given me.

MARNIE

A tip?

MARK

Yes. On a grey filly in the fourth race. A horse named Telepathy. You said you'd seen her training as a one-year old.

MARNIE

Oh!
*(Pause)*
Yes.

MARK

So I looked up Telepathy in the *Racing Guide,* and found she belonged to a Major Marsten of Tampa, Florida. I called the major long distance that afternoon. He told me he'd bought the horse from a man named Fitzgibbon and had no idea where she'd been trained. But he said he'd originally met Fitzgibbon at the Laurel track, and he suggested I contact them. I did. They gave me his phone number.

          MARNIE
So you called him.

          MARK
Three times. He was out, and I didn't get to talk to him until Sunday morning. He told me the horse had been trained by a man named Charles Davis, at Garrod's Farm. It was a chance. I drove right down.
(Pause, smile)
I should throw a party for them when we get back.

          MARNIE
Who do you mean?

          MARK
The major, and the people at Laurel, and Fitzgibbon, too.
(Pause)
For bringing you back to me.

He comes across the cabin to her. Tenderly, he takes her in his arms and kisses her. She endures the kiss for a moment, until Mark really begins to kiss her, and then a panic begins on her face. Behind his back, her hands suddenly clench, something unconscious is rising within her, something she cannot control, something which warns of danger. Suddenly, she twists her mouth away from his and leaves the bedroom, going into the other cabin where she sits in a chair facing the bulkhead. Mark comes to the door between the cabins. Marnie is sitting with her back to him.

          MARK
What's the matter?

          MARNIE
Nothing.

          MARK
Then why'd you . . .

          MARNIE
I said nothing's the matter!

          MARK
(More puzzled now)
What is it, Marnie? You're trembling.

          MARNIE
I'm cold, that's all.

          MARK
Shall I get you something to . . .

        **MARNIE**
*(Sharply)*
**No!**

Silence. Mark continues to watch her. The following speeches overlap.

| **MARK** | **MARNIE** |
|---|---|
| **Maybe you're overtired . . .** | **No, I feel . . .** |

244     CONTINUED

| **MARK** | **MARNIE** |
|---|---|
| **. . . the wedding, the long drive to . . .** | **I'm *not* tired!** |

Silence. Mark is troubled and concerned now. He watches her in gentle bewilderment.

        **MARK**
**I love you, Marnie. You know that, don't you?**

        **MARNIE**
**What has that got to do with anything?**

The following speeches overlap.

| **MARK** | **MARNIE** |
|---|---|
| **Darling, it has *everything* to . . .** | **I'm not an animal!** |

| **MARK** | **MARNIE** |
|---|---|
| **What?** | **I don't want this!** |

| **MARK** | **MARNIE** |
|---|---|
| **What do you mean?** | **I hate even the *thought* of it!** |

| **MARK** | **MARNIE** |
|---|---|
| **The thought of what?** | **This!** |

| **MARK** | **MARNIE** |
|---|---|
| **You keep saying 'This,' but I don't . . .** | **You know what I mean!** |

| **MARK** | **MARNIE** |
|---|---|
| **. . . know what you . . .** | **You do!** |

        **MARK**
**No, Marnie, I don't. I'm sorry.**

Silence. Marnie sits rigid and still in her chair.

        **MARNIE**
*(Almost inaudibly, a mumble)*
**The idea of it makes me ill.**

        **MARK**
**What?**

244       CONTINUED

Marnie whirls for the first time, her eyes blazing.

> **MARNIE**
> I said the idea makes me *ill*!

Silence.

> **MARK**
> *(Gently)*
> Marnie, you're my *wife*!

> **MARNIE**
> I don't care *what* I am! You knew what you were marrying.

> **MARK**
> And what was that?

> **MARNIE**
> A liar, a thief . . .

> **MARK**
> *(Moving toward her)*
> A *woman*.

> **MARNIE**
> No! Not if it means this! It's *disgusting* to me! It's degrading and cheap and *filthy*!
> *(Trembling, wild-eyed)*
> Keep away from me, Mark! If you touch me, I'll . . .

> **MARK**
> *(Stopping)*
> What?

> **MARNIE**
> *(A throaty whisper)*
> I'll *kill* myself!

Mark stares at her for a moment, and then wearily turns and walks toward the door between the cabins. In the doorway, he turns, faces her, seems about to say something more and then, instead, goes into the other cabin, quietly closing the door behind him.

DISSOLVE

245       TWO SHOT—MARNIE AND MARK—POOL DECK EXT—DAY

The sound of people splashing and laughing in the water is behind them as they lean on the rail. Marnie is staring broodingly out to sea. Mark is watching her face.

> **MARK**
> Marnie?
> *(She does not turn)*
> Marnie, look at me.

*(Wearily, she turns)*
Why'd you marry me?

MARNIE
Because I knew if I didn't, you'd turn me over to the police.

MARK
Is *that* what you thought?

MARNIE
It's the truth, isn't it?

MARK
No. Marnie, look, we're . . .
*(He covers her hand with his)*

MARNIE
*(Pulling her hand away, her voice dropping to a whisper)*
Listen to me, Mark. I haven't any feelings for you at all, do you understand that, none at all. I don't love you, I *never* loved you. I didn't want to marry you, but you left me no choice.

MARK
That's putting it pretty plainly.

MARNIE
As plainly as I know how.

MARK
Fine. I'll speak just as plainly. I don't give a damn *why* you married me, Marnie. But we *are* married, and we're going to stay married, and I think you'd better start getting used to the idea.

DISSOLVE

246    FULL SHOT—MARNIE—IN BED

The cabin is dark, except for the light coming through the open porthole. We can hear the sound of the wind and the sea outside. Her eyes widen as she hears the sound of her cabin door opening. A shaft of light falls across the bed. The door closes. The cabin is in shadow again. We hear footsteps aproaching the bed.

247    CLOSE SHOT—MARNIE'S FACE

Looking directly up into the CAMERA as a shadow falls across it. She makes a motion to rise from the pillow. MARK'S HAND enters the shot, forcing her back.

248–    A SUCCESSION OF SHOTS
252
As Mark forces her to submit. The CAMERA stays on Marnie with Mark out of the frame, the struggle on her face, her clawing hands, her twisting head, her terrified eyes.

253    CLOSE SHOT—MARNIE'S FACE IN PROFILE

Trapped. There is pain on her face now, and she suddenly turns it directly into the

CAMERA and closes her eyes. Teeth clenched, her entire body straining, sweat standing out on her brow, eyes closed—tears begin to stream down her cheeks.

254    PAN SHOT

From MARNIE'S FACE to the OPEN PORTHOLE and the turbulent sea outside. There is only the sound of the wind and the ocean.

DISSOLVE

255    CLOSE SHOT—THE PORTHOLE

The sea grows more placid, the wind dies. Dawn is breaking sunlessly on the horizon.

256    PAN SHOT

From the OPEN PORTHOLE back to the BED. Marnie's pillow is empty. The CAMERA keeps panning to where MARK is asleep on the pillow beside it.

257    FULL SHOT—THE BED

As Mark stirs and awakens. He turns to the pillow beside him. Marnie is gone. He sits up.

>           MARK
> Marnie?

No answer. He reaches for the bedside clock.

258    INSERT—THE CLOCK FACE

The time: 5:10 A.M.

259    FULL SHOT—MARK

Getting out of bed.

>           MARK
> Marnie?

He crosses the cabin quickly, pulls open the door to the bathroom, looks in, crosses again to the bed and pulls on a robe.

260    FULL SHOT—THE DECK—EXTERIOR—DAY

As Mark comes out of the cabin, tying the belt on his robe. The ship is empty. The deck chairs are lined row upon row. The morning is grey, the sea is grey. He looks quickly over the side.

261    FULL SHOT—THE OCEAN

Rushing past the side of the ship.

262    FULL SHOT—THE PROMENADE DECK

As Mark makes his way down it. He glances over the side every now and then, his panic mounting. Marnie is nowhere in sight. He begins climbing a ladder glancing back over his shoulder as he climbs, and then reaching the deck above, and turning, and looking down. He is looking into the pool.

263    CRANE SHOT—THE POOL

Marnie, in a nightgown, is floating face downward in the water.

264    FULL SHOT—MARK

As he rushes to the pool's edge and dives in after her. He swims to the side, pulls her out.

265    MEDIUM SHOT—MARK

As he bends over her, begins to administer artificial respiration.

266    CLOSE SHOT—MARNIE'S FACE

The head sideways, lying on the deck lifelessly as Mark works over her.

267    TWO SHOT—MARNIE AND MARK

As he works. It seems she is dead. His face gets more and more frantic. The time seems to stretch interminably.

268    CLOSE SHOT—MARNIE'S FACE

As she coughs.

269    CLOSE SHOT—MARK'S FACE

Relieved.

270    TWO SHOT—MARK AND MARNIE

As he continues working over her.

271    TWO SHOT—MARNIE AND MARK

As he carries her in his arms back to the cabin. She is trembling against him.

> **MARNIE**
> Why didn't you let me die?

> **MARK**
> Because I love you.

> **MARNIE**
> Got to hell.

*FADE OUT*

*FADE IN:*

272    FULL SHOT—THE BOW OF THE LEONARDO DA VINCI AND THE BAY OF NAPLES BEYOND

## Torn Curtain

Alma Hitchcock's presence was felt on Hitchcock's fiftieth film in the form of these handwritten notes on the script. There may have been hundreds of pages like these over the years; however, these are all that survive.

Page 2.  I assume you will shoot this entire scene without underwear on floor, in case of censorship or foreign countries.

" 9    Sarah might ask Manfred does he know where sheet on slip of paper is.

" 10   Wouldn't Sarah say it was she Freddy spoke to on phone?.
"      ? Enigmatic look. isn't it risky to associate them
" 11   Isn't it a little familiar for Sarah to call him 'Karl'?

" 12.  Shouldn't the message be more cryptic — I don't feel he would have took at it in a hotel lobby.

" 14-15  The whole scene seems underwritten — Surely at one point she would say he never wanted her to come on this trip in the first place etc. This is covered in her character delineation but I don't think in script, and would build up now.

" 19   Is it that easy to board plane for East Germany (or anywhere else behind curtain) without showing passport and visa?

**Page 21** — I feel Michael would give a fuller excuse, telling of quarrel, which would lead into Sarah saying 'he thought he was going to be rid of her'.

**Page 23** — We seem a long time away from Sarah — I question whether she shouldn't hear the first DEFECTOR line —

**24-25.** Sarah should definitely hear the line 'Anyone at home know of your intention to defect.'

**" 30** — Couldn't reporter hear Gromek say 'Miss Sherman' — which would give reporter clue to who she is

**" 33.** I don't understand the 'murderer' lines — the whole scene seems underwritten. I feel she would bring up their intended marriage — (it seems confusing, does he want her to stay — surely he does not want her??)

**" 40** — The line 'I can't run out on him now' doesn't seem right.

**46.** Would it be clearer if he said Senator Sherman? or girl's father

Page 58. | might not Sarah talk a little more professionally - instead of 'fascinating'?

" 60 | I would think Sarah's face would be set and hard as now with the strain and, only at the end show the tears in her eyes.

" 70 | ?. the line 'the man who has the thing' you came for.

The script was written by Brian Moore, based on a story by Alfred Hitchcock. They appeared to work well together, but they did not part amicably. In fact, Moore was barred from screenings of the film at the studio because of some unflattering interviews about his work with Hitchcock that had been published.

Peggy Robertson responded to Bernard Herrmann's positive response to the screenplay (the film had already been completed—the screenplay was sent to London, where Herrmann was working at the time):

Dear Benny:
Was so glad to get your letter and reactions to the Torn Curtain screenplay. Am really looking forward to the time when you screen the film which is really and truly marvelous—I think it will be Hitch's greatest. I read your letter to him and he was most pleased, as you can imagine.

## Frenzy/Kaleidoscope

This most intriguing of Hitchcock's unproduced films began with this rough outline of the story by Hitchcock's old ally Benn Levy.[3]

[3]Levy wrote some of the first dialogue heard in British cinemas—that for Alfred Hitchcock's *Blackmail*. Hitchcock produced Benn Levy's first film, *Elstree Calling* (and it was allegedly their work together on this musical revue film that created a rift between the two men). The only record of such a disagreement is Taylor's biography, which is curious, since his source on this rift was undoubtedly Hitchcock, as Levy died in 1972. The actress Constance Cummings, Levy's wife, had only fond memories of the Hitchcocks.

It is really only a catalog of ideas for the film. Levy worked with Hitchcock for the next few months on the project, but Hitchcock felt his draft wasn't working. He subsequently wrote his own draft. Drafts were also written by Hugh Wheeler and Howard Fast.

Hitchcock's inspiration was the British killer Neville Heath, the sweet-faced seducer-murderer. Stephen Rebello alleges that Hitchcock abandoned the project because it was too much like *Psycho*. In reality, the project was rejected by Universal, a rejection that led to the desperate assignment of *Topaz,* which ended in disaster for Hitchcock.

There is even more to this singular project, further proof that Hitchcock was serious about doing this film.

## Original Story Outline by Benn W. Levy

January 18, 1967

The Neville Heath story is a gift from heaven. You'd start with a "straight" romantic meeting, handsome young man, pretty girl. Maybe he rescues her from the wild molestations of a drunken escort. "I can't stand men who paw every girl they meet". Get us rooting for them both. He perhaps unhappily married and therefore a model of screen-hero restraint. She begins to find him irresistibly "just a little boy who can't cope with life"—least of all with domestic problems such as he has described. She's sexually maternal with him, she'd give him anything—and we're delighted. Presently a few of us get tiny stirrings of disquiet at the physical love-scenes but don't quite know why. By the time we see the climax of his love in action and her murder, then even the slowest of us get it: But we shouldn't know till then.

Next, the disposal of the body sequence. And next—which should be the most bloodcurdling scene ever seen on the screen—the mere encounter, preferably not in too dissimilar circumstances, with a second girl. And drag it out forever. Will she? Won't she? At first she seems increasingly drawn to him, then she seems to be backing out, maybe because a former boy friend appears on the scene. But then they have a row (yes, about the recent murder story in the newspapers!!) "I bet she asked for it". He disagrees, they fight.) So she phones Heath, who meets her, dries her tears, is infinitely understanding and comforting, takes her off to the scene of the crime (as near as maybe), makes love to her and does her in.

The mechanism of discovery and catpure is to be devized but it should still be "told forwards", i.e. more from the angle of the pursued than the pursuers. And, at one point, I don't doubt but that Heath, with his maximum of charms, will accost a policewoman!

The ultimate irony of his psychoses, of course, is that he truly *is* "just a little boy who can't cope with life."

Levy and Hitchcock worked hard on the story. Their research included a number of primary texts on Neville Heath and an extensive location scout during April 1967. In May, Levy returned to London. Hitchcock found Levy's finished script dissatisfying and immediately began his own draft of the story.

Hitchcock had not penned his own screenplay since *The Paradine Case*. At the beginning of his career, he actually wrote quite a bit on his own, but all of his films from *The Pleasure Garden* to *Family Plot* were all cowritten efforts. To take up the gauntlet again just before he turned sixty-eight is remarkable. Even more remarkable is the quality of his brave, disturbing screenplay.

The entire screenplay cannot be printed here. I've excerpted one sequence, though, which I think is one of the most incredible sequences in any screenplay. It is as shocking and perhaps more disturbing than the famed shower sequence or the rape scene in *Frenzy* (1970). Willie, the Neville Heath character, is on a date with Caroline. His approach is gentle, almost weak. The trick is in getting Caroline to feel protective, almost motherly toward him. In Hitchcock's draft of the screenplay, Willie takes Caroline to a fairly secluded waterfall not far outside New York City.

A Scene from *Kaleidoscope*

**WILLIE**
They're the mothball fleet. Freighters left over from the war.

**CAROLINE**
They're sad-looking, aren't they?

**WILLIE**
They're dead. Shall we see if we can gate-crash them?

Caroline shivers a little and shakes her head.

**CAROLINE**
No.

Willie looks at her inquiringly.

**CAROLINE**
They're spooky.

**WILLIE**
Okay, we'll stick to our original plan.

He starts the car up and they move on OUT OF PICTURE.

EXT. WOODED COUNTRY—LONG SHOT—DAY

WE SEE Willie's car about a hundred feet away. It is tilted down as though they had turned off the roadway. There is no one in it. The CAMERA PANS and in the distance, through the trees, WE SEE Willie and Caroline. They are hand in hand. Willie carries a large paper sack in the crook of his arm.

ANOTHER ANGLE—LONG SHOT—DAY

WE SEE them crossing and coming NEARER TO CAMERA which is PANNING with them, with trees crossing the f.g. from time to time. We LOSE them behind one large tree in the f.g. so the CAMERA MOVES and has a PEEK. WE FIND them in an embrace.

CLOSEUP—THE TWO

still in an embrace. As Willie shifts his position slightly to envelope her more closely, first an orange then a tomato, then another falls out of the sack. He releases her.

> **CAROLINE**
> **What is it?**

Willie looks down.

> **WILLIE**
> **Tomato.**

He stoops to retrieve it, the CAMERA PANNING DOWN as he does so without mishap. Still bent down he reaches for the orange.

CLOSEUP—WILLIE'S FOOT

stepping on the second tomato.

> **WILLIE**
> **There we go again!**

> **CAROLINE**
> *(grinning at him)*
> **Romantic, aren't you?**

> **WILLIE**
> **Well, you can't have everything. Come on.**

ANOTHER ANGLE

Willie stretches out his hand to her and starts to move but, as he is looking over his shoulder, he bumps into a small tree.

> **CAROLINE**
> **Round the tree, Willie, not through it.**

> **WILLIE**
> **Oh, I see.**

WE LOSE them behind some bushes or ferns for a moment. They emerge from the bushes and as they both FILL THE SCREEN they stop and look.

LONG SHOT—WATERFALL—DAY

From their viewpoint is a waterfall. During the previous scenes, the sound of this waterfall has been growing and at this moment it is at the loudest we have heard it.

CAROLINE
(shouting)
Where are we going to eat?

WILLIE
(shouting)
There's a place over there. Let's get across.

CAROLINE
(shouting)
Do you think we can?

WILLIE
(shouting)
Easy.

LONG SHOT

WE SEE the two tiny figures starting to cross the stepping stones at the foot of the first part of the waterfall. We can just about hear their voices above the roar of the water as they shout to each other.

CAROLINE
Willie, I know I can't make it!

WILLIE
Of course you can.

WE SEE Willie stretch out a hand and help her across.

WILLIE
There you are . . . That's a girl . . . That's it . . . Easy does it. . . .

They have nearly reached the other side when his foot slips.

CAROLINE
(in alarm)
Willie!

WILLIE
(grinning)
You nearly lost *me* that time! On we go . . . Just a pair of mountain goats . . . Careful with that one. . . .

Willie loses his balance again. His arms wave upwards in an effort to regain equilibrium.

CLOSE SHOT—CAROLINE

reaches out for him but her hand succeeds in grabbing only the paper bag. He flops down into a swirling pool.

CAROLINE
(screams)
Willie!

ANOTHER ANGLE

The water is deep where he falls. When he surfaces he splutters. . . .

**WILLIE**
By God, you *have* lost me!

He scrambles his way up the nearest rock to the shore. Caroline leaps competently until she lands on the top of this same rock, helpless with laughter.

CLOSER SHOT—WILLIE

now seated looks up. Caroline drops INTO PICTURE beside him. The waterfall is seen OUT OF FOCUS behind them.

**CAROLINE**
Oh, Willie!
*(she puts her head on his wet shoulder)*
Darling, you're not fit to be let out alone.

**WILLIE**
*(grinning)*
That's right; you notice everything.

**CAROLINE**
*(she rises to her knees)*
Let's get you out of those wet clothes.

**WILLIE**
Oh? And into what?

**CAROLINE**
Into anything. Do you want double pneumonia? We'll hang your things on the bushes; they'll soon dry in this sun.

**WILLIE**
Well, what am I going to wear?

**CAROLINE**
You're going to wear this.

Caroline removes her sloppy-joe revealing a plain white, open-neck shirt underneath.

**WILLIE**
How can I get into that? It's a woman's.

**CAROLINE**
It's not. It was my brother's, he gave it to me. He's just as big as you.

**WILLIE**
But for God's sake, Caroline, it'll only come down to here!

The CAMERA PULLS BACK as he rises to indicate a position barely below his waist.

> **CAROLINE**
> You won't wear it as a sweater, stupid. Just wrap it round your middle.

> **WILLIE**
> Oh!

> **CAROLINE**
> Go round the back there and I'll get out the food. Be seeing you.

Willie holds the sweater in front of him held high to the shoulders. It does not quite reach——!

> **WILLIE**
> You've said it sister.

He goes off and wanders away to the bushes taking off his clothes as he does so.

> **WILLIE'S VOICE (o.s.)**
> Hey, my cigarettes are all wet.

CLOSE SHOT—CAROLINE

She now squats on the ground and starts to unload the brown paper sack.

> **CAROLINE**
> *I've* got some.

She takes out a couple of bottles of beer and cokes, a package of sandwiches, some paper cups, etc . . .

> **CAROLINE**
> Hurry up. How does it look?
> *(she glances up)*

MED. SHOT—CAROLINE'S VIEWPOINT

Willie appears. The arms of the sweater are tied round his waist and the body of it hangs down in front of him like an apron. He carries the rest of his clothes in his arms.

> **WILLIE**
> Well, it's not exactly my color.

He turns round to spread his wet clothes over a nearby bush.

CLOSE SHOT—CAROLINE

breaks into laughter at the sight of his bare behind.

MED. SHOT—WILLIE

He turns good-naturedly.

> **WILLIE**
> Alright, alright!

He advances toward her.

CLOSE SHOT—CAROLINE

rises and crossing, goes into his arms. She is still laughing.

**CAROLINE**
**I'm sorry, darling. You look so sweet. You just look like a little boy, I don't know why. Here, come and sit down; let's eat.**

The CAMERA PANS THEM DOWN ONTO the grass, side by side. Willie freezes for a moment.

**CAROLINE**
**What's the matter?**

Willie puts his hand under his behind.

CLOSEUP—WILLIE'S HAND AND HIS BARE BEHIND

He leans his body over to permit his extracting a pine cone.

CLOSE SHOT—THE TWO

**CAROLINE**
**Oh no! You would!**

Caroline turns and starts to busy herself with the lunch. She takes out a bottle opener; turning to Willie she asks him. . . .

**CAROLINE**
**Coke?**

Willie shakes his head, a different mood seems to envelope him.

**CAROLINE**
**Sandwich? Ham or tuna?**

**WILLIE**
**What? No, I'm not hungry yet.**

**CAROLINE**
**Anything the matter?**

**WILLIE**
**No.**

Caroline glances at him watchfully and then bites into her sandwich. Willie leans out and slightly behind him, he breaks off a dried branch from the bush. He starts to play with it, stripping the leaves off as he does so. There is silence for a moment then Willie turns to Caroline.

**WILLIE**
**Why do I like being with you?**

**CAROLINE**
**I like being with you.**

WILLIE
*(he barely smiles; pursuing his own mood)*
**Why do you never ask me questions?**

CAROLINE
**About yourself! But I do, don't I?**

Willie shakes his head.

CAROLINE
**I suppose because you tell me all you want me to know.**

WILLIE
**What I want you to know is everything.**

CAROLINE
**I know. There isn't much that you hold back, is there?**

WILLIE
**Not from you.**

There is a slight pause.

WILLIE
**But there *has* been one thing.**

Caroline waits.

WILLIE
**It's—it's kind of difficult.**

CAROLINE
**I've got a shrewd idea.**

Willie looks at her.

WILLIE
**Have you? What?**

CLOSEUP—CAROLINE

CAROLINE
**You're married. Right?**

CLOSEUP—WILLIE

looks straight ahead.

WILLIE
**Right.**

CLOSEUP—CAROLINE

looks away.

LONG SHOT—CAROLINE'S VIEWPOINT—THE WATERFALL

CLOSEUP—CAROLINE

without turning she quietly says. . . .

> **CAROLINE**
> I think—I think you should have told me earlier.

CLOSEUP—WILLIE

> **WILLIE**
> I'm sure I should . . . But when it comes to self-destruction, I always play my trump card at the right moment! If you want to know, I ducked it. I was afraid you might—might lose interest.

CLOSEUP—CAROLINE

still looking away.

> **CAROLINE**
> Are you—happy?

CLOSEUP—WILLIE

> **WILLIE**
> That's a silly question, I wouldn't be here, would I? . . . She's older than I, quite a bit older. We came together because—I don't know. . . .

CLOSEUP—CAROLINE

turns back and says to him. . . .

> **CAROLINE**
> Because *you* thought you needed somebody to look after you . . . and she needed somebody to look after.

The CAMERA EASES BACK to INCLUDE Willie as he continues.

> **WILLIE**
> Smart, aren't you? Well, I don't need it now. At least I probably *need* it but don't *want* it! I suppose nobody wants . . . a warden . . . I shouldn't say that. She's very nice really. I'm probably more to blame than she is. God knows I make her as unhappy as she makes me . . . a tough life, you know. She doesn't get much work; not as much as she deserves. And it makes her nervous and unhappy . . . she's rather fond of the bottle.

> **CAROLINE**
> Oh, no.

> **WILLIE**
> That's one reason why I've never left . . . Maybe I haven't had the guts, anyway . . . Maybe I haven't had the incentive—before.

> **CAROLINE**
> Would she mind?

> **WILLIE**
> **Would she mind.**

Willie thinks for a moment. He continues with genuine bitterness.

> **WILLIE**
> **I think she'd be glad to get shot of me. I'm her cross!**

CLOSEUP—CAROLINE

startled by the tone of his voice, looks directly at him.

> **CAROLINE**
> **Is—is there another man?**

She waits and then we hear Willie's voice off. . . .

> **WILLIE (v.o.)**
> **Could be.**

There is a pause.

> **CAROLINE**
> **Is he—around?**

CLOSEUP—WILLIE

shakes his head.

> **WILLIE**
> **Someone . . . she knew before me. I guess he's still in her system.**

He turns his head away from her.

CLOSEUP—CAROLINE

as she watches him.

BIG HEAD OF WILLIE—CAROLINE'S VIEWPOINT

He covers his eyes with one hand. We hear Caroline's voice off. . . .

> **CAROLINE (v.o.)**
> **Oh, Willie, don't.**

WE SEE her hand on his shoulder. It strokes his back tenderly.

BIG HEAD OF CAROLINE

She murmurs softly. . . .

> **CAROLINE**
> **Willie!**

The CAMERA PANS her over as she presses her cheek against his bare shoulder.

> **CAROLINE**
> **Oh, please!**

BIG HEAD OF WILLIE

He turns his face back towards her, the CAMERA PANS SLIGHTLY as Caroline's face comes up INTO PICTURE. They look at each other. The CAMERA EASES BACK SLIGHTLY as he takes her in his arms and kisses her. WE SEE her arms go about him. The CAMERA GOES WITH THEM as he presses her back gently onto the grass.

CLOSEUP—BIG PROFILES

FILLING THE SCREEN. They kiss at great length.

CLOSEUP—WILLIE'S HAND

travelling over her back. It moves on past her waist and WE SEE his arm pressing her to him.

BIG CLOSEUP—THE ZIPPER

coming undone. It FILLS THE SCREEN. WE SEE Willie's hand come between their bodies as he starts to unbutton Caroline's shirt.

Back to their NOSES AND MOUTHS still kissing. The CAMERA GRADUALLY PULLS AWAY until the back of Willie's head FILLS THE SCREEN. We see nothing but his hair. The CAMERA CONTINUES TO RECEDE, passing a bush which obscures the lower part of their bodies until their two reclining figures FILL THE SCREEN. The CAMERA PULLS AWAY CONTINUALLY until the figures are so tiny and the scenic waterfall FILLS THE PICTURE. The CAMERA is so far away now that we have LOST SIGHT of them altogether. The only sound is the loud roar of the waterfall, which somehow seems to increase with the size of the picture.

LOW CAMERA SHOT—WILLIE

His feet FILL THE SCREEN in the f.g. WE SEE that he has his pants on. The CAMERA MOVES IN until his head FILLS THE SCREEN. A cigarette dangles from his lips. He is staring ahead. A puff of smoke emerges from his mouth.

The CAMERA MOVES OFF him and down to the head and shoulders of Caroline. She is lying on her back, the sweater by her head. Her eyes are open and glazed. There is a trickle of blood from one nostril. His hand ENTERS SHOT and strokes her hair for a moment. There are scratches on the back of his hand.

CLOSEUP—WILLIE

He turns and eyes the body.

CLOSEUP

The CAMERA PANS FROM the dead face down onto the body.

CLOSEUP—WILLIE

His eyes are travelling down.

CLOSEUP

The CAMERA ARRIVES on the girl's abdomen where WE SEE rivulets of blood.

LONG SHOT—THE WATERFALL

WE SEE Willie rise. He stoops to pick up some clothes including his coat and shirt from the bush. He glances down at the reclining figure which WE can FAINTLY SEE and then he moves away. He crosses the rocks and goes back in the direction of his car.

LONG SHOT—WILLIE

in the distance making his way towards his car. He gets in it and drives off. The CAMERA PANS into a different direction up the road. Round the bend WE SEE a GROUP OF CHILDREN, perhaps a dozen or so, accompanied by an adult WOMAN. They are obviously out on a picnic and are singing together in unison.

INT. MIRIAM'S BEDROOM—LONG SHOT—NIGHT

Miriam is reclining on her bed and looking at a portable television.

The scene is the first of several brutal moments. The screenplay anticipated Jodie Foster's role in *The Silence of the Lambs* by making the lead detective a woman who is put in harm's way at the film finale. And while there are problems with the screenplay's structure (problems Hitchcock was very much aware of and evidently could not beat), the screenplay would make a remarkable film even today.

As he did with *The Birds,* Hitchcock sent *Kaleidoscope* to a respected artist for evaluation. François Truffaut, whose book on Hitchcock is still the primary text for scholars, had by this time directed a number of what are now considered classic films. His evaluation of the screenplay follows:

Dear Mr Hitchcock,

I really am very sorry not to have written to you sooner about *Frenzy,* but I was determined to give you a detailed account of my impressions of the script, scene by scene; unfortunately, we started shooting my latest film, *Stolen Kisses,* rather earlier than expected.

Then there was the whole business of the Cinémathèque Française,[1] about which I am sure Odette Ferry has told you and which has taken up most of my time when I am not shooting.

Here then is my report on *Frenzy,* and I must ask you to forgive me if, at times, I sound like someone who has made 50 films preaching to a young underground film-maker!

You know how much I respect, admire and esteem you; you know, also, how intimately familiar I am with your films, but I consider that, as a script represents simply one stage of the completed work, one should be able to criticize it sincerely and frankly, even if none of my criticisms strikes you as justified.

*Frenzy* certainly contains the germ of a great film, a film of the stamp of *Shadow of a Doubt, Strangers on a Train* and *Pyscho,* which is why I am in no doubt whatsoever as to the final result.

Report on the script

1. I very much like the beginning of the film on the _New Jersey Flats_ as well as the presentation of the President and his family.

2. The presentation of Willie is excellent. Many people will probably tell you that he reminds them of Perkins in _Psycho,_ but I think he could just as easily be a relation of Bruno in _Strangers on a Train_ or Uncle Charlie.

3. The scene in New York's Shea Stadium also seems to me perfect.

4. The following scene with Willie Cooper and his mother does not seem quite satisfactory at this stage of the script, but it would be hard for me to explain why. Perhaps it will work better when it has been given some dialogue.

5. The scene with Willie and Caroline in front of the United Nations building sounds extremely promising and I know it will work very well, as always when you depict a high-minded criminal explaining his ideals.

6. The other scene which complements the one in the graveyard strikes me as equally promising.

7. Then there comes the murder in Central Park and there we know we'll have a brilliant scene with the _Hitch touch_[5] working a hundred per cent.

8. Now, I can't help wondering whether Willie's relationship with his mother is quite right, since we so quickly have the impression she suspects her son that I am afraid it subsequently becomes very hard for us to believe in the idea that she might wish to help the police in their inquiries—even in the hope of proving her son's innocence. This is the only important reservation I would make about the script, but I must say that it has persisted through several detailed readings. Given the business about the roses whose thorns have been removed by the florist, the injury on the hand and the newspaper article, the public will be left in no doubt whatsoever about what Miriam really believes.

9. I think the scene of the rehearsal in the theatre will be first-rate.

10. The episode in the artists' studio also strikes me as first-rate except for the single point that Patti falls for Willie a little too easily and too arbitrarily; naturally, the notion of her obsession with him can be established by the acting and the dialogue.

11. The next scene, in which Patti takes Willie home and we unexpectedly discover that she has a boyfriend there, seems to me very good.

12. I also like the scene at Miriam's with all the people from the theatre.

13. Patti's murder on the boat strikes me as excellent. Of course, there does rather seem to be an insistence on sex and nudity, but it does not worry me too much because I know that you shoot such scenes with real dramatic power, and you never dwell on unnecessary detail.

14. The following scene with Willie and Miriam is perfect.

I begin to wonder if, from this point on, the script is perhaps just slightly too predictable.

15. For instance, I think the audience will expect to find the police at the studio and I wonder if it might not be an idea to show Willie also expecting to find the police and being a little hesitant about going there. You might show the contradictions in his behaviour. I do see that you have adopted another solution, with the imaginary voice-over in the stairwell, but I am not sure that I completely understood what you were trying to do.

16. The next scene between Willie and Miriam bothers me a little because it is simply too explicit. The spectator might feel the action has ground to a halt. Also, it reinforces Miriam's suspicions even further, which might pose a problem later.

17. The scene with Miriam at Willie's father's house does not seem to me to be right yet. It seems to be there for the sole purpose of conveying information to the audience and what makes it disappointing is the passive attitude adopted by Willie's father. I can't quite see the point of the scene anyway; it has neither a beginning, a middle nor an end and I do think that, if we are to see the President at this juncture, we will expect to see him again for a third time.

18. Similarly, I am not sure about the scene between Miriam and Lieutenant Hinckel. It raises a question which we discussed in the book (Simon and Schuster, pages 76 and 77) about showing a collusion (or even a love affair) between a character from the police and a character who is intimate with the murderer. I am afraid the audience will find this scene very hard to take.

a) because Miriam's doubts as to her son's guilt are not, at this stage, believable;

b) it is not plausible that she should agree to help the police, even if it is a matter of preventing further murders. I do know, of course, that all scripts contain scenes which are not really comprehensible until the dialogue is written, or even until they are shot, edited and inserted into the film, but I have difficulty imagining how this scene might work. I know that there have been other, similar scenes in your work (and this is what we discussed on pages 76 and 77), but, in your previous films, the unease which they might have provoked was compensated for either by a romantic element or by the fact that the degree of kinship was a lesser one (uncle and niece) or, then again, by references to Nazism; in *Frenzy*, the plot is more simplistic: a mother agrees to help the police set a trap for her son.

I would not be so insistent on this point if I felt it to be an essential element in the narrative. But, in fact, I don't. I know you want to make the mother's part a very real and active one, but I am sure there is another way of going about it, even if you are afraid it might make the plot a bit more complicated.

In fact, I cannot help wondering if the second half of *Frenzy* may not be a little too simple.

I think the reason for this lies in the fact that this is an original screenplay. When you adapt a novel, even if it is distilled to its bare essentials, subsidiary scenes always survive which, even if they might appear odd or unexpected, do enrich the finished film. In this case, we have only the main, essential plotline and I worry that such directness, which is so effective in the first half, might make the second half a trifle banal.

19. Of course, I do admit that the film picks up again as soon as Julie Cook arrives on the scene, but wouldn't it work just as well if Miriam too thought that Julie was a reporter?

20. I do like the way you develop the romantic relationship between Julie and Willie and I feel that these will be very good scenes. The character of Willie becomes genuinely moving as he gradually falls in love with Julie. (My negative feelings, however, about the Miriam-Lieutenant Hinckel scenes remain unchanged.)

21. Now comes the scene in the car when the cop checks Willie's driving licence and, as it stands at the moment, the cop's reactions seem very exaggerated, but I am sure that this can be rectified during shooting.

22.  Willie has gone to so much trouble to shake off the police who are chasing him, that the arrival of the inspectors is a bit of a disappointment.

23.  In the last scene, the idea of breaking the news to Miriam when she's on stage is intriguing but I don't think it's quite right yet. I assume you want the plot to go very quickly at this point, but that is a pity because the ending would be crueller and more ironic if, for example, the policeman were to decide not to tell Miriam the news until she had calmly finished her performance or part of her performance, in other words, there could be a relation set up between her work as an actress and the news which she is about to receive, which she is expecting to hear and is afraid to hear (on the same principle as in the wonderful scene no. 9).

### A note on characterization

I know that the quality of the characterization will depend on the final script, but I will nevertheless give you my first impressions.

a)  I don't really like the character of the father (there's either too much or not enough of him), the character of Milton Korfe (who does not yet come across clearly) or Patti (insufficiently detailed) or Hinckel (unless he turns out to be as interesting as Arbogast).[6] (Do you call him Hinckel because it was Chaplin's name for Hitler in *The Great Dictator*?)

b)  I very much like Willie, Miriam (despite my one reservation), Caroline and Julie.

Naturally, if you are not too upset by these criticisms, I should be delighted to read the next version of *Frenzy,* and I am sure that, even as I write, you have already solved most of the problems which I have mentioned.

I trust also that you have got a good cast in mind. Willie will be a great break for somebody.

And those, Mr Hitchcock, are my thoughts on reading *Frenzy.*

*The Bride Wore Black* won't be coming out in France until April because the Paramount film *Benjamin* has been such a hit.

I will not be sending you a copy of my script for *Stolen Kisses,* which I am shooting at the moment, because it is just a nostalgic, romantic comedy, budgeted at 250,000 dollars and largely improvised!

My next project is a more important one, *Waltz into Darkness,* adapted from a book by William Irish, with Catherine Deneuve and Jean-Paul Belmondo. I bought the rights to the book from Fox and I am hoping to make it for United Artists. I have written a first draft of my adaptation which I'll send you as soon as it has been translated into English, within the month.

I hope Mike Korda will soon have some good news about the Hitchbook for me; I see the reviews have been very good and I hope sales do as nicely.

I hope that the length of this letter is some compensation for its tardiness and I look forward to hearing from you soon.

Please give Mrs Hitchcock my best regards.

Yours very sincerely,
François Truffaut.

## THE SEVENTIES

After the debacle of *Topaz*, Hitchcock's career picked back up with *Frenzy*, based on the Arthur La Bern novel *Goodbye Piccadilly, Farewell Leicester Square*. Anthony Shaffer penned the screenplay. The process was routine and there are no surprises in the well-documented Hitchcock files.

After *Frenzy*, Hitchcock considered several projects: Elmore Leonard's *Unknown Man #89* was one that seemed promising, but not even a treatment exists for this. *Family Plot*, Hitchcock's final film, was based on the Victor Canning novel *The Rainbird Pattern*.[4] For this project, he returned to Ernest Lehman. Here the files explode again.

Lehman kept every draft for this film and for *North by Northwest*. The *Family Plot* files are replete with more than 500 pages of transcripts from script meetings with Hitchcock. These, because of their size, could not be printed here. They are, though, indicative of the working style he had cultivated for fifty years. Hitchcock, alone with the writer, dreaming up schemes—twists in character and narrative, set pieces that have come to define Hitchcock films. For several drafts of *Family Plot*, Hitchcock had tried to include a subway sequence in the film. The pair could never work out a proper excuse though for the sequence—so it was out. Hitchcock loved to include these kind of set pieces, but only if it served the story.

Sadly, the film does not match the dreams of Lehman and Hitchcock. While it has its own charm, *Family Plot* betrays the age and perhaps lack of interest of the director.

His final project, *The Short Night*, is well documented in David Freeman's book that includes his unproduced screenplay. The screenplay reads promisingly enough and it is the only unproduced Hitchcock screenplay published thus far.


## CONCLUSION

Hitchcock said on many occasions he would never "go to the floor without a solid screenplay." With the rarest of exceptions, this rule was followed by Hitchcock. After the screenplay was finalized, the difficult and compromising process of making the film began.

[4]Hitchcock at first rejected the novel.

# chapter three
# PREPARING THE VISUAL

*You have to remember that as well as being a creative person,*
*I am a very technical person. The actual exercise of technique*
*is very important to me, the practical solution of technical*
*problems. I have always needed to do things, never had much*
*taste for philosophizing about what to do.*

—HITCHCOCK TO JOHN RUSSELL TAYLOR

during the scripting process, Hitchcock was simultaneously involved with the preparations for filming, the process by which Hitchcock and the screenwriter's dreams began to live. Sets were designed, storyboards drawn and flat, paperbound characters given the flesh and blood of actors. In some cases, the second unit work—the filming of location and transparency material that will be needed during the actual production—began. For example, the second unit work began on *Vertigo* nearly a year before actual filming began with the actors, but in most cases, the advance crew work doesn't anticipate a production by such a lengthy period.

Hitchcock did much storyboarding himself, but the finer more elaborate work conceived for his later films is largely that of other artists. Still, the artist would certainly have worked with Hitchcock, his sketches, and the screenplay.

Despite his legendary use of storyboards, it was only very rarely that Hitchcock storyboarded an entire film. *Lifeboat* and *The Birds* were extensively storyboarded. The rest of his films would have storyboards done for key sequences: the crop dusting sequence from *North by Northwest*, the shower sequence from *Psycho*, the car scene in *Family Plot*.

Hitchcock was also decidedly hands-off when it came to his fellow craftsmen.

"On a Hitchcock film, it was all in the script. We had meetings, but Hitch generally left us on our own," art director Henry Bumstead recalled. "He gave us a great deal of freedom to do our own work. When you did a Hitchcock film, you knew that your very best was required. Anything less would have been unacceptable to Hitchcock."

"We would discuss the overall plan and conception—and, of course, any special shots that needed advance planning," Leonard South recalled. South was the camera operator for Robert Burks on most of the Hitchcock films and the director of photography on Hitchcock's final film, *Family Plot*. Hitchcock used the English system for his films, which meant the director of photography was in charge of the lighting and framing of the shot and the camera operator was in charge of the physical operation of the camera.

But here again, Hitchcock let his professionals work on their own. "We had our assigned tasks and we knew exactly what Hitchcock wanted," South remembered. "On a Hitchcock film, there was never any question. He always knew exactly what he wanted."

"We liked to plan everything. Hitch didn't like surprises on the set or during the production of a film, so we spent a lot of time in preproduction. It paid off," said Herbert Coleman. He was Hitchcock's associate producer for his cycle of classic Paramount films beginning with *To Catch a Thief*. He began with Hitchcock as an assistant director on *Rear Window*.

"*There* was a film which took a lot of work. The set occupied an entire soundstage at Paramount and we had the difficult challenge of choreographing what Jimmy sees across the courtyard," Coleman remembered.

Coleman was involved in what can be an enjoyable preproduction task, that of looking for locations.

"That was a great thing about a Hitchcock film—we got to go to some great places. I loved Monte Carlo, the South of France. I think *To Catch a Thief* was my favorite film with Hitch because of the location work. Hitch also let me shoot the car chase along the Riviera, so this film has special memories for me," Coleman remembered from his home in Salinas, California. Not far from there is the location he found with his daughter for that important and personal Hitchcock film *Vertigo*.

"Hitch had wanted Mission Carmel, but when I got there, I found it was too beautiful. We wanted something more forgotten, something that looked the way it did a hundred years ago. It was my daughter who recommended that we look at San Juan Bautista, which was perfect for *Vertigo*."

During Coleman's tenure as Hitchcock's associate producer, Hitchcock filmed in a variety of locations: the French Riviera, Morocco, London, Virginia, and the San Francisco Bay Area. Coleman did not work with Hitchcock on *Psycho* and only returned to work on the troubled *Topaz* in 1968.

"There's no doubt that Hitch was a genius. Those were special years for me," Coleman said. (After Hitchcock, Coleman went on to produce and direct a number of films, the most notable with war hero Audie Murphy, a friend of Coleman's.)

Casting is another preproduction task. Hitchcock often knew well in advance who his stars were. For example, the films with James Stewart and Cary Grant began as productions with these actors attached (both men were involved in a limited way with the preparation of the script and were paid a percentage of the film's profits). If Hitchcock didn't know, he began casting immediately.

"Sometimes we would go through pages of possibilities and then we would sit through whatever we could find for the actor in the screening room," Peggy Robertson remembered. Robertson worked with Hitchcock longer than any other associate besides Alma. She began as his script supervisor for *Under Capricorn* when she was Peggy Singer. When she moved with her husband to the States in the late fifties, she rejoined Hitchcock on *Vertigo* and remained with him to the end of his career.

Robertson, who died in early 1998, was a tremendous source of information for this book and my book on *Vertigo*. Her work as script supervisor and later special assistant to Hitchcock has left the closest we will have to a written work history of the Hitchcock years from 1957 to 1980.

"Hitchcock was very organized and very particular. We often would try to keep his name out of the preliminary casting, because once an agent learned he was dealing with Hitchcock, the actor's price would begin to climb," Robertson recalled.

Robertson pointed out that it was over just such a financial problem that a proposed Hitchcock film collapsed.

"Robert Bloch's agent kept asking for an amount that Hitchcock wasn't willing to pay, so that project ended," Robertson said. To be fair to Bloch, he recalled to others that Hitchcock had wanted him to work without pay during the screenplay's development. A look at the records indicates that Hitchcock never asked Bloch (or anyone else for that matter) to work without pay. There were several letters from Bloch's agent about money and several replies from Hitchcock's office about the terms being unacceptable.

What follows are the nonscript preparations for the films: set designs and floor plans, the famous storyboards, memos concerning possible actors for specific roles, and excerpts from some fascinating meetings with production personnel for some of Hitchcock's later films. All of the elements play an important role in making what's happening in the script more concrete.

In most films, sets are built in pieces—one room on one soundstage, the other room on another. It's rare that an entire set is built contiguous. (I can think of only one film for which this was done: *The Magnificent Ambersons*.) So the plans are often of separate rooms, or rooms that are open like a stage play.

Storyboards are cartoonlike drawings of what the filmmaker actually wants on the screen. They have become a necessity for today's films, which are filmed with so much special effects work, therefore requiring a most exact planning. Hitchcock storyboarded from the beginning. His goal was to limit expenses and to fully visualize the film. One of Selznick's first complaints about Hitchcock was his refusal to film a variety of angles in a film. Hitchcock filmed only what he knew he would need—cutting the picture in the camera. This severely limited the possibility for change in the editing room and ultimately Selznick's power as producer.

In a traditionally shot film, the director would first shoot an establishing shot—usually the entire scene from a standard distance. Then they would go in to do close-ups and two shots (two actors talking or standing together) and even later what are called "pickups"—detail shots (hands opening an envelope, the contents of the letter, the fidgeting feet). All of this material is then given to the editor, who uses it to cut together the scene.

Hitchcock, having storyboarded the most important scenes of the film, filmed only the shots needed and provided no "coverage" for second-guessing producers. It is an economical approach, but Hitchcock was not concerned with economy at this stage of his career. His primary concern was having the movie end up a Hitchcock film and not a Selznick film.

The transcripted conferences are a little unusual for a director of Hitchcock's era. The earliest transcript I discovered was a rather innocuous discussion with some production members during the editing of *Under Capricorn*. The ones excerpted here are the more complete transcripts from his last major production phase at Universal Studios.

## *The 39 Steps*

Hitchcock did his own storyboarding for his classic *The 39 Steps*.

Hitchcock's rendering of the film's opening sequence of *The 39 Steps*. Storyboarding can give a sense of the editing and framing.

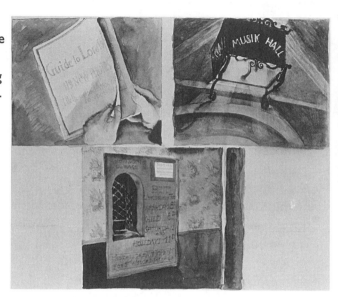

After meeting the mysterious woman at the music hall, Richard Hannay brings her back to his borrowed flat. The finished sequence is as evocative as Hitchcock's original drawing.

After the mysterious Annabella Smith is murdered, Hannay must flee London for his own safety and to find the leader of the spy ring. He eludes the police on a bridge in Scotland.

Hannay continues to run from the police in Scotland. Hitchcock's heroes, like Shakespeare's, are often tossed into the wilderness from their more sophisticated city dwellings.

Hannay alone on the Scottish moor. Compare the framing and lighting in this sketch to the stills from the lost film, *The Mountain Eagle*. The similarities are remarkable.

## Young and Innocent

*Young and Innocent* was one of Hitchcock's more popular British films with audiences on both sides of the Atlantic. Hitchcock had extensive storyboarding done for this very professional-looking (i.e., American-looking) film. These renderings were not drawn by Hitchcock but by a Gaumont production designer working from Hitchcock's sketches and the screenplay; they are set designs as opposed to storyboards, which show action.

The mill set design from *Young and Innocent.* Mills appear in two other Hitchcock films—the earlier silent *The Manxman* and the later American film *Foreign Correspondent.*

Erica Burgoyne's family dining room. The family scenes in *Young and Innocent* bear a striking resemblance to the family scenes in the later *Shadow of a Doubt.*

The interrogation room. Whether in a small town or a city, Hitchcock's halls of justice have high ceilings and tall windows.

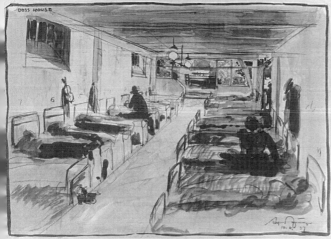

The doss house where Old Tom spends the night. Hitchcock would return to the London doss house for *Frenzy* forty years later.

The car men's shelter. In the States we would call this a roadhouse or a truck stop. Hitchcock more often set his films in the lower-middle-class world than the world of wealth.

The hotel ballroom set for the film's final, magnificent crane shot.

## THE AMERICAN FILMS

The high professional standards of the Hollywood film were an important reason for Hitchcock's move to the States in 1939. He had visited once before and as a boy had memorized maps of New York City. It was, in fact, the opening of an American studio in London that prompted his entry into the film business (the 1920 Famous Players-Lasky studio at Islington).

Professionalism must have been part of the motivation to sign with David O. Selznick. There was no other producer as involved and as committed to high standards working in Hollywood and Hitchcock must have been flattered at his interest. His initial project was to be a film about the R.M.S. *Titanic.* Selznick may have shown some alarm at the proposed cost, as Hitchcock wanted to buy an actual ocean liner and sink it. Instead, the first Selznick and Hitchcock film was to be based on a bestseller: *Rebecca* by Daphne du Maurier. (Selznick was still in production/postproduction with another bestseller, *Gone With the Wind,* at that time.)

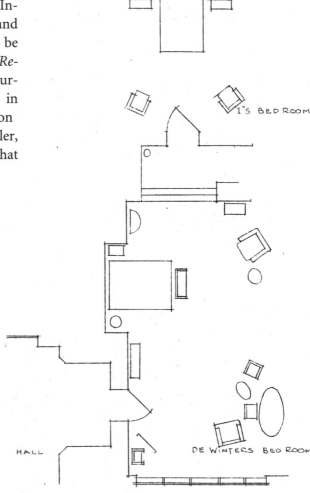

The floor plan for Maxim de Winter's bedroom

## *Rebecca*

Much of the design work for Manderley, the stately mansion which Rebecca haunts, has been reproduced elsewhere. Of interest, though, are the floor plans for the sets. For example, I wasn't aware until examining these plans that Maxim de Winter's bedroom in Manderley adjoined "I" 's. This floor plan is a classic Hollywood set. Notice that there are not four walls—the set was only built for what the camera would see.

A slightly more enclosed floor plan is the upper passage to Rebecca's room. This is quite memorable in the film—it anticipates slightly those beautiful corridor shots in Jean Cocteau's *La Belle et la Bête*.

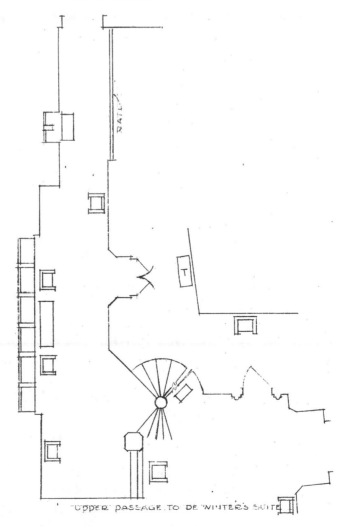

The upper passage
to Rebecca's suite

The morning room design is another nearly complete room. The plan indicates which doors lead where, something poor "I" could have used in this confusing house. The disjointed filming of the house adds to the film's overwhelming feeling of uncertainty. Certainly, like "I," we never feel at home, despite the overall sunniness of the morning room.

The morning room

· MORNING · ROOM ·

:TO · CORRIDOR ·

TO · GREAT · HALL ·

The only full four-wall set is the dining room, which on paper is as austere and intimidating as it is on film.

Another nearly complete set is the Great Hall set, which must only rival the halls in Selznick's *Gone With the Wind*. This design also helps in giving us a handle on the general layout of the house, since the hall appears to occupy the center of Manderley.

Finally, the only comfortable room in the house: the library. Much of the film takes place here and it is the only room where we see Max and "I" enjoy some warmth together. Even this floor plan has a much more cheery aspect than the earlier designs.

All the exteriors of Manderley are quite obviously model shots (as nice as they are) and these sketches give an idea of the scale of the model. Hitchcock had used models throughout his early days. He would continue to use them through *Under Capricorn* (another film where the house is a character).

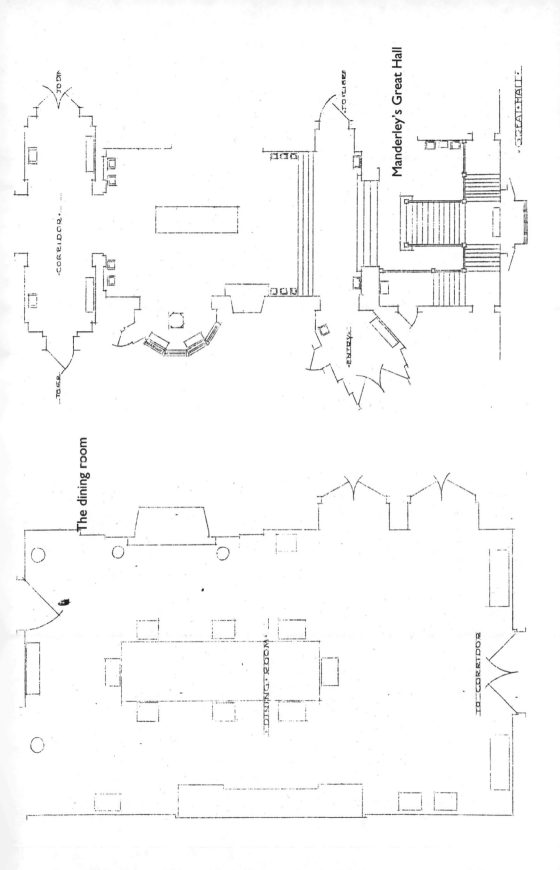

The dining room

Manderley's Great Hall

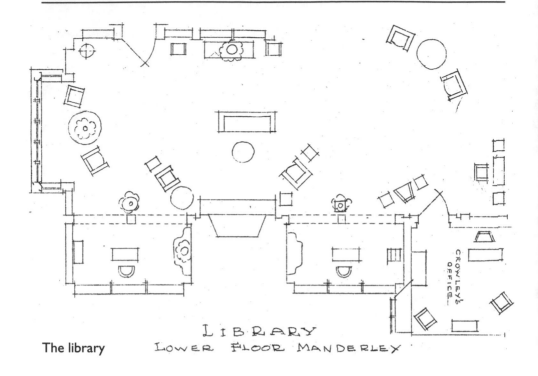

LIBRARY
LOWER FLOOR MANDERLEY

The library

Two views of the ghostly Manderley as seen at the beginning of *Rebecca*

During this design work, Hitchcock and Selznick were struggling to fill the house with the right actors. The following memos show how wide a net the two were casting for just the right "girl" to play "I":

SELZNICK INTERNATIONAL PICTURES, INC.
Culver City, California

Inter-Office Communication

TO    MR. DAVID SELZNICK    cc  Mr. O'Shea    DATE    July 19, 1939
FROM  Alfred Hitchcock          Mr. Schuessler  SUBJECT  GIRL FOR "REBECCA"

MIRIAM PATTY ............................... Too much Dresden china. She should play the part of the cupid that is broken—she's so frail.

MARJORIE REYNOLDS ...................... Absolutely not the type—too much gangster's moll.

BETTY CAMPBELL .......................... Too ordinary—too chocolate-box.

PAULINE MOORE ............................. Was the best of the three readings this morning. Might be worthy of a photographic test.

MARY HOWARD ................................ Reading to come, but most intelligent.

ELLEN DREW .................................... Possibility. But my feeling was that she was a little too self-possessed, however I have to defer an opinion until I hear her read.

SIDNEY FOX ..................................... No quality of gentility at all—too pert.

MARY TAYLOR ................................. Not suitable.

JEAN MUIR ....................................... Tested. Too big and sugary.

HEATHER ANGEL ............................. Good reading and test, but unattractive to look at.

LUCILLE FAIRBANKS ....................... Tested. Not the right quality at all.

JOAN FONTAINE .............................. Tested. Possibility. But has to show fair amount of nervousness in order to get any effect. Further test to see how much we can underplay her without losing anything.

ANNE SHIRLEY ............................... Not available.

ANDREA LEEDS ............................... Waiting for Mr. Whitney to speak to Mr. Goldwyn.

RENE RAY ........................................ Tested. Competent but hard in type and therefore unsuitable.

VIVIEN LEIGH .................................. See Page one.

KATHRYN ALDRICH .......................... Too Russian looking.

AUDREY REYNOLDS .......................... Excellent for Rebecca who doesn't appear.

ANITA LOUISE .................................. Very interesting. Her reading was competent, but she doesn't look anything like a companion.

JO ANN SAYRES ............................... Too sophisticated, but reading to come.

ALICIA RHETT .................................. Homely. A bit too old. But reading to come.

LOUISE CAMPBELL ........................... Possibility. Waiting for test.

FAY HELM ........................................ Her reading was quite good, but I don't think she looks attractive in person at all—slightly homely. However, waiting for test.

GERALDINE FITZGERALD ................. Not available.

JULIE HAYDON ............................... Awaiting test from New York.

JEAN ROUVEROL ............................. Not available—awaiting motherhood.

ANN RUTHERFORD ........................... Not available.

TESTS are being arranged for:

LOUISE CAMPBELL
ELLEN DREW
MARY HOWARD
ANITA LOUISE
JOAN FONTAINE
PAULINE MOORE
FAY HELM
ANDREA LEEDS
FRANCES DEE

SELZNICK INTERNATIONAL PICTURES, INC.
Culver City, California

Inter-Office Communication

TO      MR. DAVID SELZNICK    cc  Mr. O'Shea      DATE      July 21, 1939
FROM    Alfred Hitchcock            Mr. Schuessler  SUBJECT   MORE GIRLS FOR
                                                             "REBECCA"

| | |
|---|---|
| EVELYN KEYES: | Reading. Too much like an actress—no reality. |
| AMANDA DUFF: | Ordinary. |
| ALICIA RHETT: | Still homely. Read with a faint whiff of old lavender—very pale and uninteresting. |
| LYNN ROBERTS: | Unsuitable. No reading. |
| CAROLYN WHITTINGHAM: | Too matronly. No reading. |
| SIDNEY FOX: | Reading not good, for which she apologized. |
| JOYCE COAD: | Unsuitable. No reading. |
| MARION CLAYTON: | Too old. No reading. |
| FRANCES DEE: | Questionable personality and very snooty, but worthy of a test. |
| MARY HOWARD: | Impressionable reading. Waiting for test. |
| SHIRLEY LOGAN: (Para. Test) | Too big. |
| PATRICIA MORISON: (Para. Test) | Totally unsuitable. Looks exactly like Rebecca. |
| JULIE HAYDON: (N.Y. test) | Pale and uninteresting. |
| WELD & FLETCHER (N.Y. test) | Grotesque. |

SELZNICK INTERNATIONAL PICTURES, INC.
Culver City, California

Inter-Office Communication

TO    MR. DAVID SELZNICK            DATE        August 19, 1939

FROM  Alfred Hitchcock              SUBJECT     TESTS FOR "REBECCA"
                                                ANN BAXTER
                                                JOAN FONTAINE
                                                MARGARET SULLAVAN

I showed the tests of Ann Baxter, Joan Fontaine, and Margaret Sullavan to Mrs.
Hitchcock and Miss Harrison.

Mrs. Hitchcock's opinion was that Fontaine was just too coy and simpering to a degree
that it was intolerable. She thought her voice was irritating and was distressed about
the whole thing. Miss Harrison's comments were roughly the same.

The opinion of Ann Baxter is that she is much more moving [except] a fear that she
would not be able to play love scenes due to her age and lack of experience.

Both opinions agree that Sullavan is far ahead of either of them, but should be made
less sure of herself and characterized more as the girl in the book. Miss Harrison says
that Sullavan, if she enacted the part, would help to relieve the monotony which might
arise through the terrific number of scenes the girl has to play.

The opinion seems to be that Ann Baxter would be definitely second choice after
Margaret Sullavan. Another thing mentioned by both in Baxter's favor is that her voice
has a quality that could be taken easily for either English or American in the same
manner as Ronald Colman's.

AH:cs

It was nothing like the hyped search for Scarlett, although there was an
attempt to capitalize on the *Rebecca* search as had been done with *Gone With
the Wind*. It is interesting that Alma and Joan Harrison's third choice should
become Hitchcock's first choice.

# *Lifeboat*

*Lifeboat* was a great technical challenge—something Hitchcock lived for in
a production. I think it kept him interested in the production process once the
plot and characters had been developed. This tight film for 20th Century-Fox
had its share of challenges.

This was the first Hitchcock film to receive extensive storyboarding. Other films had the periodic scene storyboarded (some had no storyboards—I could find no storyboards for *Rebecca,* although I'm sure there must have been some) and keep in mind that storyboarding was not the norm as it is today. Steven Spielberg and George Lucas's extensive use of storyboarding has altered what's expected during preproduction from most directors.

I've selected three moments from the film's storyboards. There are hundreds of pages, far too many to reproduce here, and frankly, for such a static film, of little interest. The first set of boards shows how Hitchcock envisioned the beginning of the film. The necessity of these boards is obvious, as models would have to be built and the studio tank would need to be filled with debris.

Storyboards for the opening sequence of *Lifeboat*

1.

SCREEN AND CREDIT TITLES
OVER FUNNEL WITH WHISTLE
SCREAMING OVER SHOT –

2.

FUNNEL STARTS OVER AND
DOWN TO RIGHT –

3.                          4.

CONTINUATION —                 WHISTLE GOES UNDER,

5.                         (6.)

DISAPPEARS IN TERRIFIC     SMASHED LIFE BOAT
UPHEVAL OF FOAM & STEAM   SUDDENLY SHOOTS UP —
& AIR —

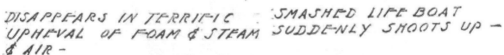

(7)

TOWARDS CAMERA AND —

 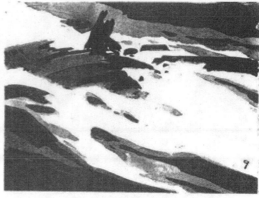

SETTLES BACK SO THAT WE
READ "FRANCES SWEENEY".

LIFE BOAT ROLLS OVER AND SINKS

The next boards were rather unique in their size and drama. They appear to be during an early moment in the film when the last members of the lifeboat are rescued.

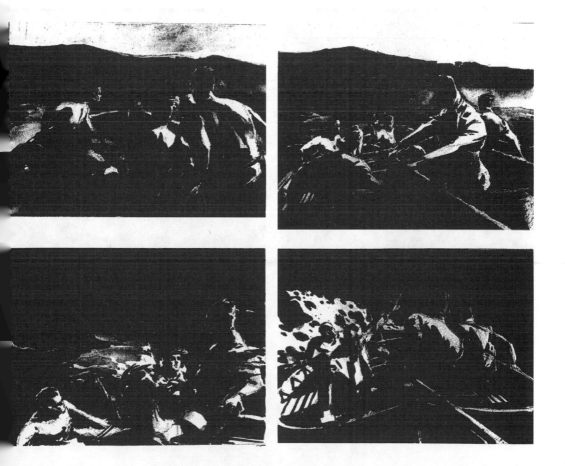

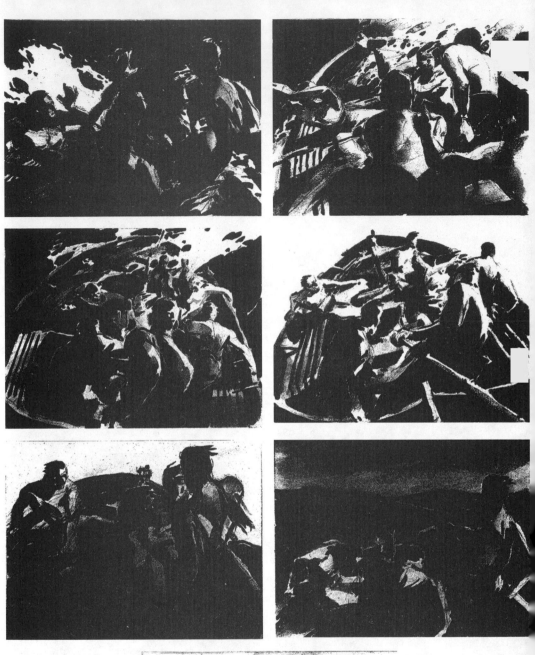

The final sequence is from the most dramatic moment in the film. As those in the lifeboat are approaching death through hunger and dehydration, a ship is finally sighted and signaled. Unfortunately, it is a German ship, which is attacked before the lifeboat is rescued.

In an effort to save their ship, the Germans steam straight for the lifeboat. These boards portray the drama that follows:

Sc #310 - SERSEN MIN. SUPPLY SHIP BEARING DOWN AT FULL SPEED - SHELLS SPLASHING.

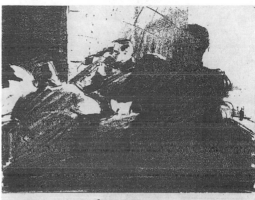

Sc #311 A PROC - SERSEN PLATE - SHIP COMING -

Sc #311 B. PROC - SERSEN PLATE - PROW BOW WAVE

Sc #311 C - LIFEBOAT BUMPED BY SIDE OF SHIP.

Sc #311 D.    CONTINUATION.

Sc #312    PROC OR ON LAKE - C.U. OF PEOPLE

Sc #312 A - FULL SHOT OF BOAT AND SHIP.

Sc #312 B - C.U. OF PITT.   PROC OR ON LAKE.

Sc #312 C - PROC. SERSEN PLAT. PROPELLERS.

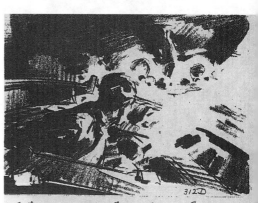

Sc #312 D - PROC - SERSEN PLATE - CONTINUATION

Sc #313 - Proc Sersen Plate - Shell Strikes
     Behind Life Boat.

Sc #314 - Proc-Sersen Plate - Shell Strikes
     Nearer - (Sc #315)

Sc #315 Proc. Deluged with Water.

Sc #315 A Proc - Faces Light up at Terrific Explos'n
     Debris Falls -

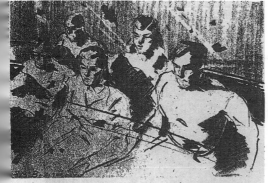

Alternate Angle - of Sc #315 B.

Sc #316 - Sersen Min. Ship Burning.

Sc.#317 - PROC - LIGHT FROM FIRE DIES DOWN.

Sc.#318 - SEKSEN MIN. SHIP SINKS -

## *The Wrong Man*

Hitchcock often dealt with the theme of the innocent man wrongfully accused of a crime. In *The Wrong Man,* he worked with the true story of Christopher Emmanuel (Manny) Balestrero, an innocent who was falsely nabbed by the police. In style, it is his most British film: black-and-white, realistic settings, and natural sound and music. He had contemplated the traditional cameo for the film, but ultimately felt that the director popping up at any time in the narrative would disrupt the documentary effect he was giving the movie. Instead, Hitchcock devised this introduction, which he scripted and storyboarded.

This is Alfred Hitchcock speaking. In the past I have given you many kinds of ~~~~ suspense pictures, but this time I wmed like you to see a ~~~~ different one. ~~~~ This differeuce lies in the fact that this is a true story — every word of it. And yet it contains elements that are stranger than all the fiction that has gone into many of the thriller fictions that I've made before.

## Vertigo

Much of the extraordinary advance work on *Vertigo* was published in my book on that film. Henry Bumstead's elaborate blueprints for the *Vertigo* sets, however, were not discussed. Although much of this film was shot on location, all of the interiors and some of the exteriors were re-created in the studio. For example, although 900 Lombard is a real exterior that is used for several shots, all of the dialogue shot at the house's door was done on a Paramount soundstage.

Here are Bumstead's (blueprint) designs for the bookstore, Gavin Elster's club and tower.

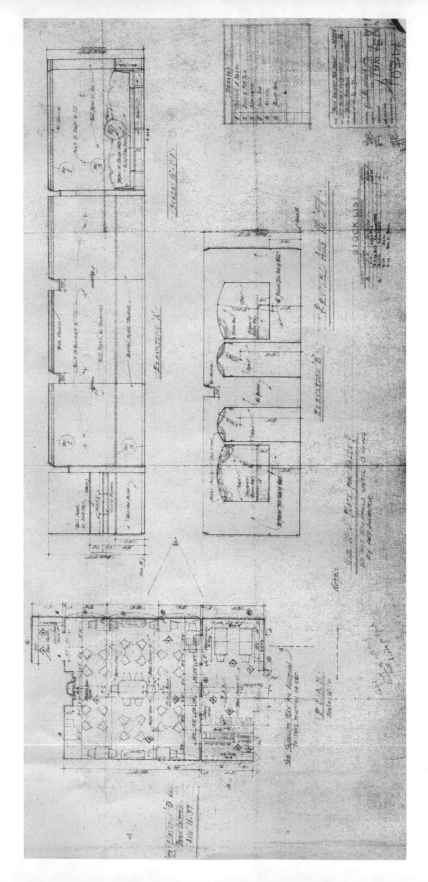

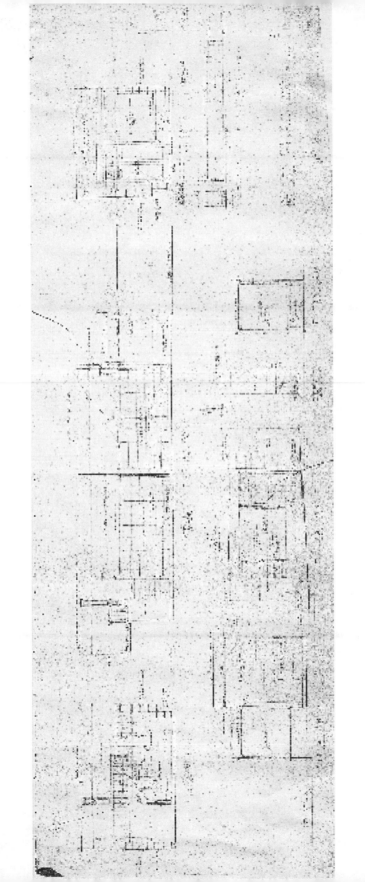

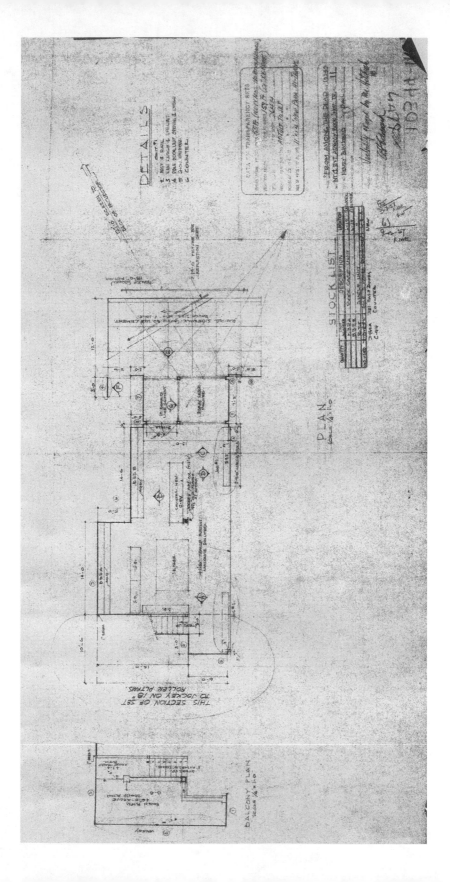

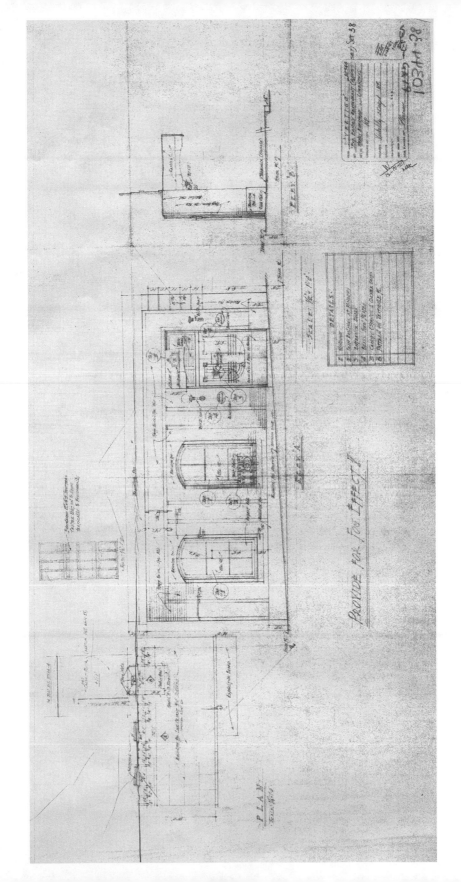

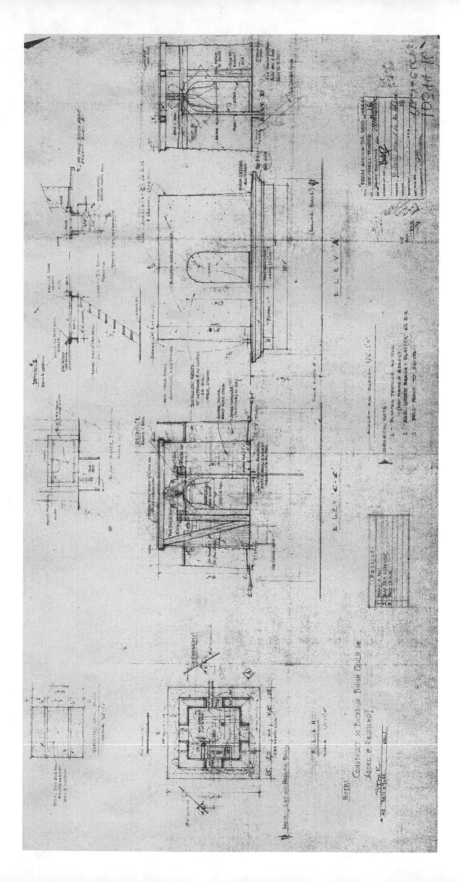

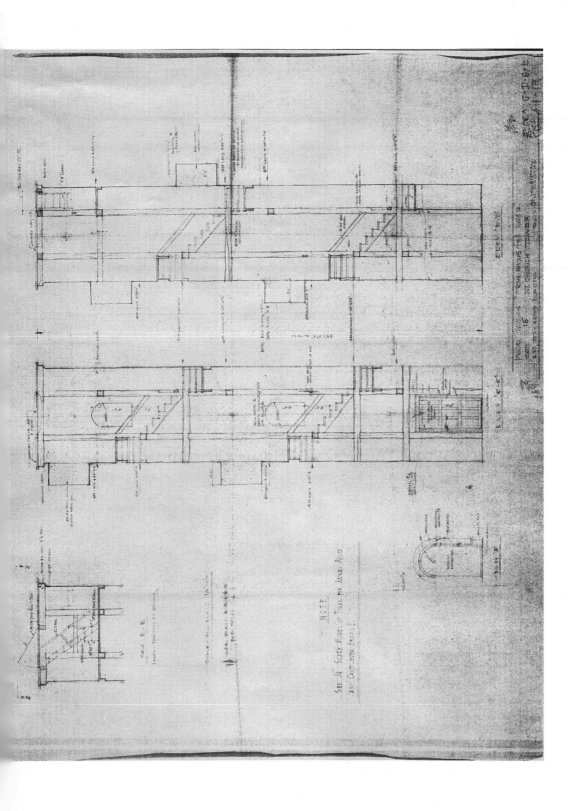

## North by Northwest

After the heavy *The Wrong Man* and *Vertigo, North by Northwest* is a liberating experience. Hitchcock seemed to enjoy this production from the first moments in his study with Lehman to its conclusion at the summer 1959 release.

Like *Lifeboat,* much of this film was storyboarded, including the justifiably famous crop duster sequence. Before getting to these boards, it is useful to see at least one diagram that every filmmaker makes—sometimes in advance (which Hitchcock preferred), sometimes scratched out nervously on the set. The camera plot is a practical map of the set/location, the actors, and where the cameras will be positioned.

This is the camera plot for the Oak Room scene at the beginning of the film:

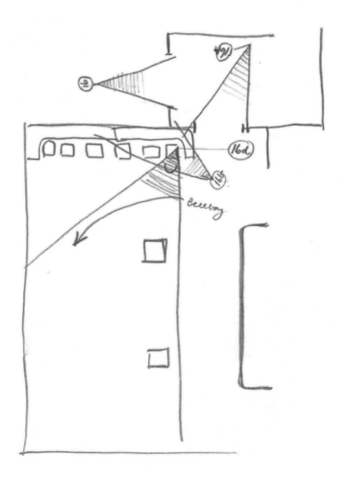

The bar is on the diagram's right, the long row of booths that Roger O. Thornhill sits briefly at are at the top of the diagram. Outside the bar is the foyer where the two henchmen kidnap Thornhill. The numbers refer to shot numbers in the shooting script. The partially shaded in V's are what the camera will shoot. This sketch (and there are at least a dozen that survive from this film) were more than likely drawn by Hitchcock with Robert Burks.

## The Crop Dusting Sequence

Next to the shower scene in *Psycho*, this is Hitchcock's most famous moment. Roger Thornhill has been sent to this desolate site in Illinois to meet the elusive (and, we know, imaginary) George Kaplan. It is a setup by the spies Thornhill is unknowingly trailing. After waiting for some time, he is pursued from the air by a crop duster. The scene is harrowing (and imitated many times since then—as recently as *The X-Files: Fight the Future* movie) and fully realized during this preproduction process on paper.

The following storyboards for *North by Northwest* were drawn by Mintor Huebner, who had worked with Hitchcock on *Strangers on a Train*. Huebner was given free reign by Hitchcock to develop the sequence based on what Lehman and the director developed in the screenplay. The filmed sequence remains remarkably true to these designs. What images are Huebner's? Hitchcock's? Lehman's? The answer, which makes empiricists uneasy, is all three. It is Hitchcock's sequence—but it is his sequence as realized by Lehman and Huebner.

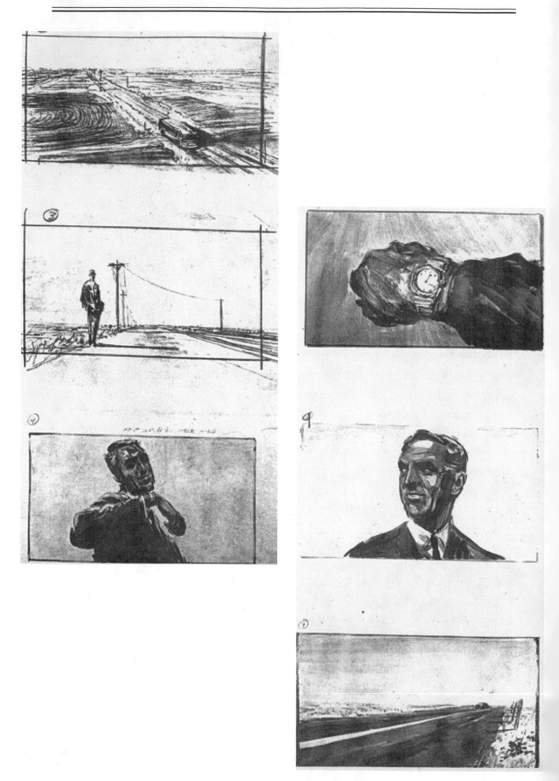

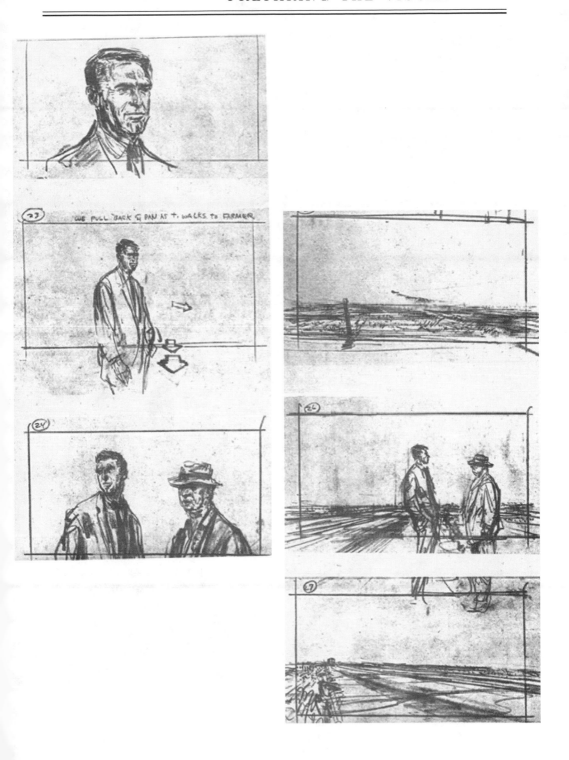

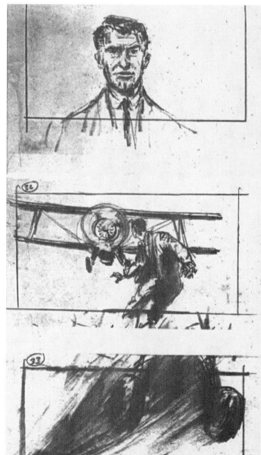

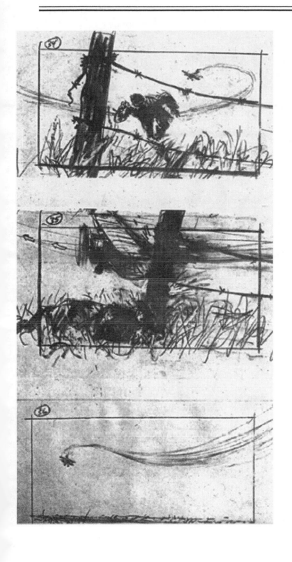

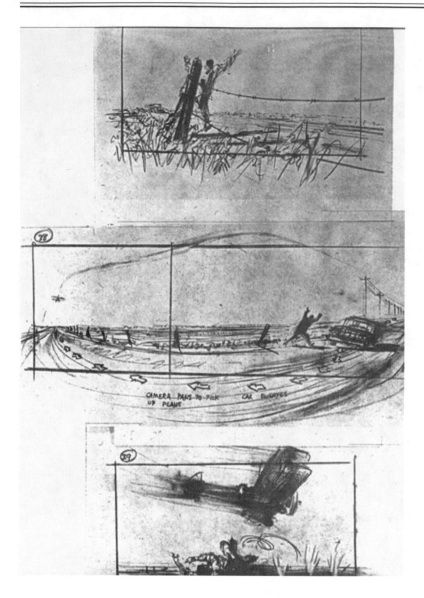

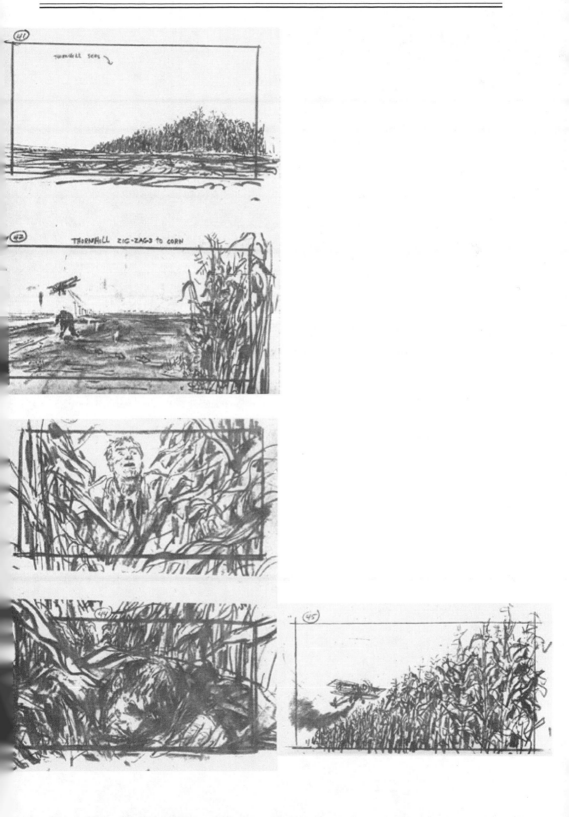

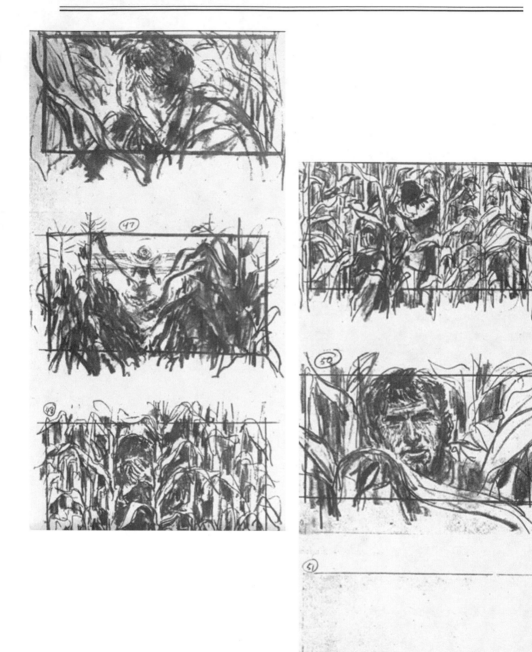

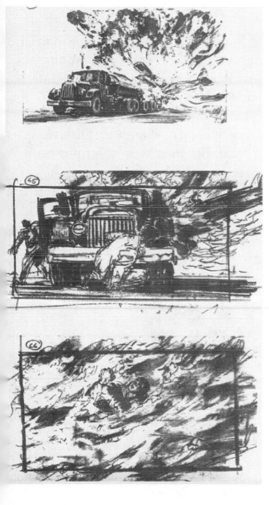

## Mount Rushmore

Hitchcock had initially tried to get the National Park Service to allow him to film on Mount Rushmore, but he was quite naturally refused. Thus, Mount Rushmore and the nearby fictional Mendoza ranch house were built on MGM soundstages at a combined cost of more than $50,000. The striking Frank Lloyd Wright-style house was almost as expensive as the stone monument.

The chase across the presidents' faces was prepared, along with the scene prior to it, in these storyboards. The first set of drawings is how this process would often start: a rough sketch by Hitchcock.

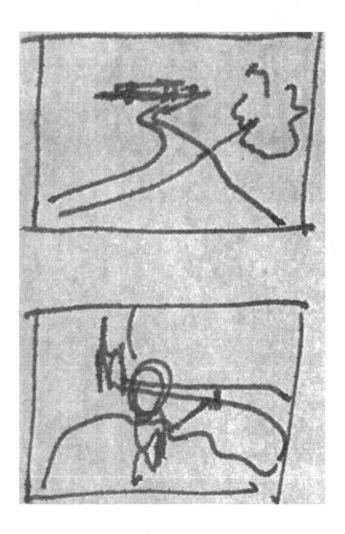

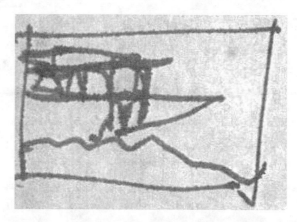

These were then transformed by an artist into more dramatic images.

SC 170

170A

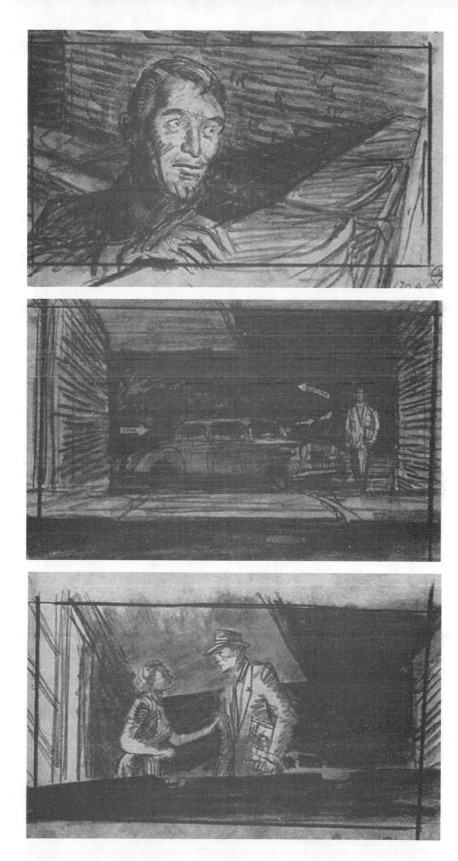

BACK OF MT. RUSHMORE MONUMENT
MATTE PAINTING.                                    Sc 234x 5

√ Slate 5 70

C.U. EVE -THORNHILL                              234/x6
LOOK OFF LEFT
(SET - STG. 25)

③

✓ 5·79

V. P.  FLASH LIGHT IN FOREST·
(SET STG 25                              SC 234×|7

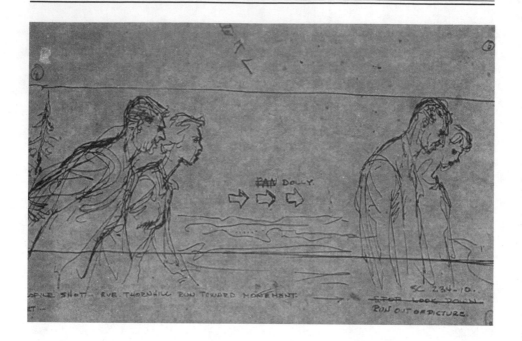

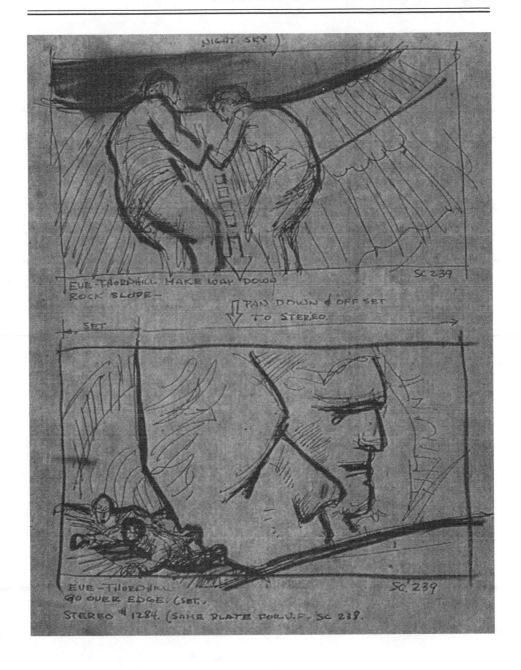

EVE-THORNHILL MAKE WAY DOWN
ROCK SLOPE-                                    SC 239

PAN DOWN & OFF SET
TO STEREO.

SET

EVE -THORNHILL                                 SC. 239
GO OVER EDGE. (SET.
STEREO # 1284. (SAME PLATE FOR V.F. SC 238.

## *Psycho*

Here again, we are on well-traveled ground, thanks to Stephen Rebello. I did uncover these sketches made by Hitchcock in his files for the famous shower sequence. The Saul Bass storyboards were recently published on the Universal Studios' *Psycho: Special Edition* (laser/DVD). Close observers will note there are actually several distinct differences between the Bass conception and the final version. These drawings, while only a frame or two and extremely abstract, give an idea of Hitchcock's input. The debate, well discussed in Rebello's text, over this scene and Bass's input is familiar. These storyboard frames tend to tip the scales in Hitchcock's favor by showing, as in the case of the *Psycho* screenplay, Hitchcock collaborating fully in the visualizing process.

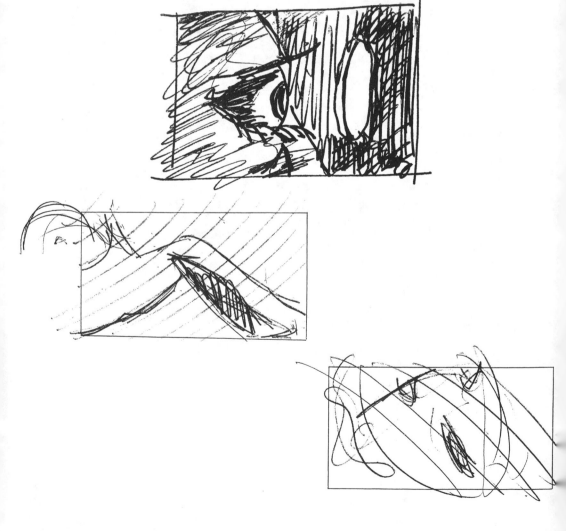

## *The Birds*

Hitchcock's most challenging film from this period was undoubtedly *The Birds*. With so many special effects shots, advance planning was essential. The attacking birds were matted into the film after the principal photography, so each attack needed to be carefully planned so that the action would match the effects work.

A most important aspect of this production was the rounding up of the actual birds to be used for the film. In order to do this, a bird wrangler was hired to catch birds (seagulls, for example, were found at Bay Area garbage dumps) and to make every effort to keep the mortality rate low. Surprisingly few birds perished during the production, although quite a few were hurt during the initial roundups.

Hitchcock wrote a list of shots that would be required during the preproduction period. Much of the material would be needed for background plates during rear projection. Rear projection is often used during close-ups. Hitchcock preferred to shoot close-ups in the studio, where he had better control of the lighting.

Of the extensive storyboards, the following schoolyard sequence is one of the more effective in the film: Melanie Daniels waits outside the schoolhouse while the birds ominously flock behind her on the children's playground equipment. There Melanie and the schoolteacher try to lead the kids to safety, but the birds attack. Those of us who were youngsters at the time of this film's popularity in the sixties are unable to forget this scene.

Hitchcock had signed a cool new blonde to debut in *The Birds*: Tippi Hedren. Alma Hitchcock had spotted the young Hedren in a television commercial (which Hitchcock parodies at the beginning of the film) and Hitchcock, after some friendly negotiation, signed the untested actress to a seven-year exclusive contract.

Pre Production Shots

Sc 51-57,    A high spectacular shot
of car proceeding away from
camera around Tomales
Bay. Road should be
curving.

Alternative.    Same shot on
Coast highway.

Sc 58a    A high shot with car,
showing Bodega Bay in distance

Sc 59    as script.

Sc 63    as script.

sc 64    as script but to be shot
in Bodega. The viewpoint should
be taken starting with first
building on main highway
opposite schoolhouse road
and proceeding thru town
going north.

All plates for Melanies' close ups
should be taken at ~~½~~ three
quarters in order to get correct background

Sc 75    View of Bay &c as seen from Post Office
This is a matt shot showing Tides
with matted Town (Back lot) in foreground.

Sc. 104    A very long spectacular shot.
of the boat with Melanie steering
crossing the bay from the Tides
to the Brenner Home. Left to
Right progression.

Sc 104a   Another angle of the
boat crossing the bay, but
shot so that we can progress
the boat further. ~~~~~~~~

Plates straight back and
three quarters right for Melanies
close ups.

Sc 106   ~~Shooting over the bow of the
boat, a forward moving shot
showing the Brenners house ahead
with action so indicated in
the script~~

~~~~~~~

Scenes 139 etc   Mitch's car racing
around the bay to the
tides as seen by Melanie

Plates for Melanie. Side on
and 3/4 and straight back.

Sc 173   Melanies car ~~~~~~
approaching and arriving
at the Brenner House.

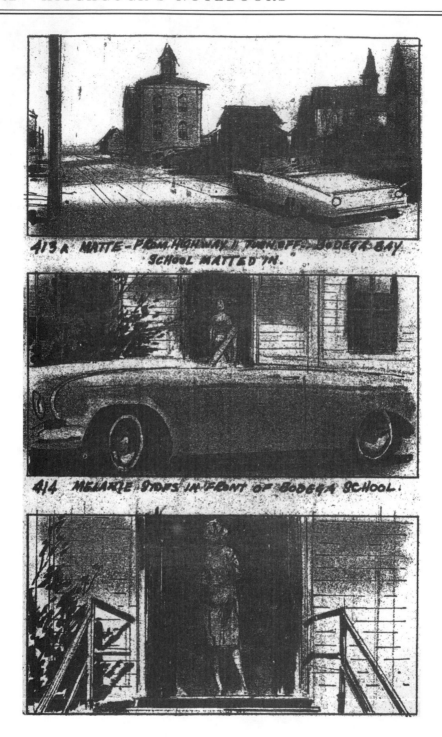

413 A MATTE - FROM HIGHWAY 1 TURN OFF. BODEGA BAY
SCHOOL MATTED IN.

414   MELANIE STOPS IN FRONT OF BODEGA SCHOOL.

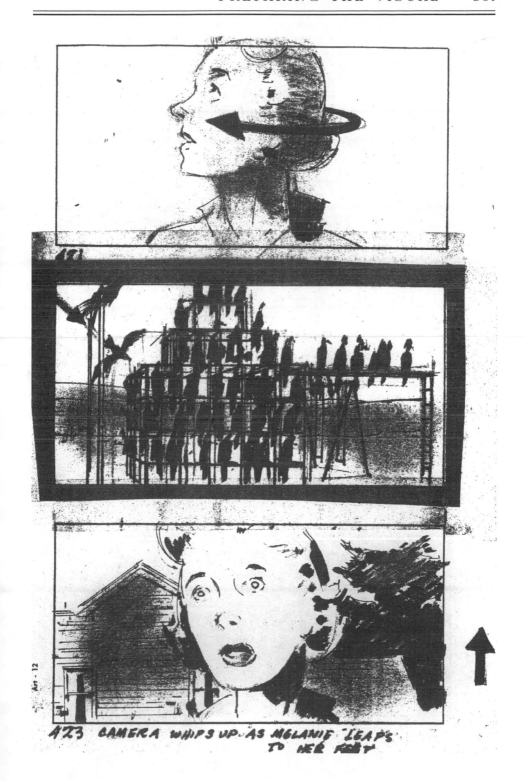

423 CAMERA WHIPS UP AS MELANIE LEAPS
TO HER FEET

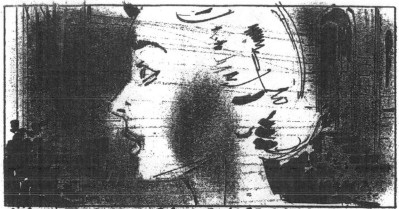

426 - TURNS WITH BACK TOWARD CAMERA
GOES TOWARD SCHOOL - CAMERA FOLLOWING

426 A    MOVING P.O.V.

Ar - 12

CONTINUATION OF 426 - CAMERA STOPS AS SHE
HEADS FOR STEPS AND GOES UP.

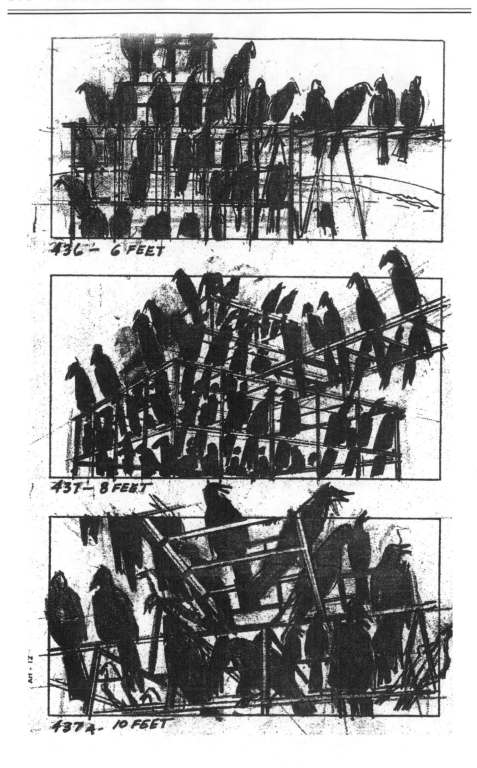

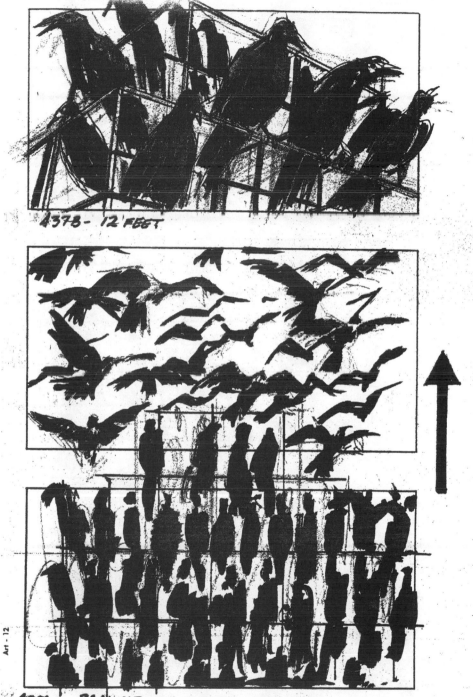

4378 - 12 FEET

137C PAN UP AS CROWS FLY UP AND OVER CAMERAS

389 - MOVING - BIRDS FLY BETWEEN MELANIE AND CHILDREN - LIVE BIRD SWEEPS BY IN F.G.

390

441 BIRD BITES RUNNING GIRL

441A

441B    Prepyze

Art - 12

441C

441G

441.H

441J BOY DUCKS BEHIND POLE - BIRDS GO BY
ON LEFT AS ANOTHER ATTACKS FROM RIGHT.

Art - 12

441 K

441 L

Art - 12

441 M

441N

441P - ANNIE DRAGGING SLOW CHILD

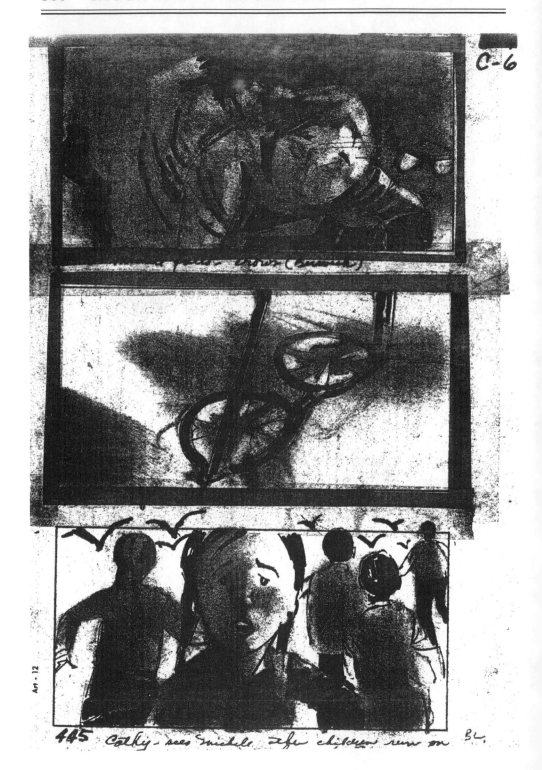

445 Cathy sees Michele. The children run on BL.

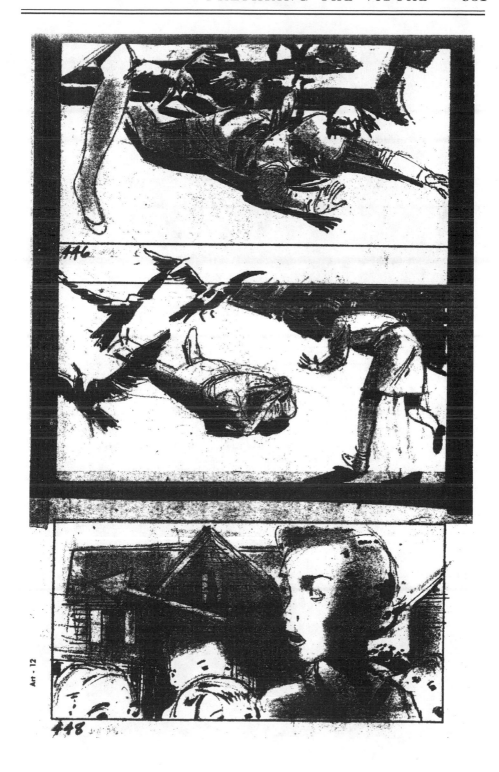

450A- MELANIE DRAGS CHILDREN OUT CAMERA RIGHT

451- THEY HEAD FOR STATION WAGON

452

Hitchcock was determined to shape the perfect actress in Hedren, so unusually long (for Hitchcock) meetings were held with her to discuss the role of Melanie and her development in the film. Transcripts have been kept of these meetings with Hedren and they provide a unique look at how Hitchcock developed character in a film—and how he felt an actor should do the same.

Hedren rarely speaks in the transcripts, other than to clarify a point or to question a motive. The following, then, is almost a monologue by Hitchcock:

Recorded February 24, 1962
Tape #1

I thought, perhaps, that the first thing we ought to do XXXXXXX i just to go over the character as a whole. You know, generally speakingin terms of the background and the general shape of her development.

Now what do we know about her? We know that she is very well appointed, very well dressedXX. She issmart, sophisticated; apparently she <u>looks</u> sophisticatedXX (I'm talking when we first see her in the picture), and then a little bit of her background comes outX so that generally speaking, as I said, we get a picture of a girl who is, at first sight, well off, XXXXXXX XXXXXX XXX well appointed and, as we learn in the scene, obviously a woman with a sense of humor; otherwise, we wouldn't talk about her going in for practical jokes. XXXX

We're going to show, you see, that XXXXXXXXXXXXXX she is, to some extent, a fairly extremeX.I would say that extreme in the sense that when she found out that she was going to have to go all the way up to Bodiga Bay, she didn't say, "Oh, the hell with it" and then throw THE BIRDS away and forget the whole thing. You know, she kind of XXX went throughX with it. Now what's this based on? This is based on, which we'll deal with later when we come down to the individual scenes, that she has been attracted to the young man . . . no question about that.

Now, as she goes along, she finds herself in the company of literate people, but a little more sober in their whole setup, their mental setup, than she has been. She probably is capable of it as well, you know? But Lydia is a serious woman. X After all, Lydia has a husband who was well off. He was probably a director of a San Francisco corporationX and, after his death, left her reasonably comfortably off. I imagine they lived in San Francisco in an apartment and had this farm as a weekend place. There are some people up in Bodiga Bay we have encountered of the same . . . except they sit indoors and drink allday. They're quite different to our people.

And Their Mitch has been, you know, to a good XXXXXXXX school and college . . . but these people, XXXX generally, they're not entirely frivolous people. They're pleasant people and, as I say, literate, educated. I imagine if they hadn't had the money, they would have been kind of bohemians almost, you know. And this is the group to which she finds herself. Well, of course, they're a little . . . they're a type of person which she has met, occasionally, from various groups she's been among in San Francisco whether socially or what have you, you know. So I think there is a kind of, like anyone moving into a different atmosphere, there's a kind of a toning down that starts, you see.

Now she finds herself involved as a kibitzer, as an onlooker to a little situation which she learns from the schoolteacher. She finds, in other words, something she's never probed into before; that people have problems. They have, you know . . . emotions and so forth which she's been aware of through plays and novels and a fair amount of gossip that she's heard. I don't know whether (she may have done) but let's say, for the purposes of our story, she's never really been face to face with it, and when she meets Annie, you know, the teacher;.I think she's inclined to look at her objectively saying, "Well, this is an interesting XXXX character. I never met this sort of person before." And you XXXXXXXXXXXXXX haven't, because in the remoteness of this setting and the mere fact that you're away from the city, they're away from the city, I suppose it generates a kind of X expression from somebody who normally wouldn't do it, if you were in San Francisco. So that the little kind of interchanges that she gets from Annie give her a kind of little thoughtful glance.

Tippi—It seems to me that meeting Annie and talking to her, she realizes that Annie has a purpose in life. Annie has found something that she wants to do.

Oh, she says that, too.

Tippi—Yes. Would this give Melanie a sense of inadequacy? I wouldn't say at this phase. Well, it'll only be a kind of a glance on her face, you know, but I don't think it impinges itself too much. I'm sure she drove away to San Francisco again that night. It'd be off her mind pretty well, you know. Now, of course, now she moves then into another aspect. She now moves to the other side of Annie's story: The mother and the boy, Mitch, you see, and, again as she gets into this atmosphere, and the ten-year-old daughter, they're all kind of fresh to her. I won't say strange, youknow, that'd be making her from outer spaceX or something, but they're kind of fresh to her, and I think her general attitude is one of . . . she looks at them as it were . . . not questioningly, but it's well..well "Rather interesting people, I wonder what the XX mother's really like", you know, and she begins to speculate on what Annie has told her generally about the relationships, you see. And now of course, out of this, comes the beginning of The Birds. Now the gull attacks, you see. Merely . . . it hasn't any particular effect on her, She was hit by one gull, you know, and there's not too much to it. And that passes from her mind.

Having put these people in a certain category, she is a little bit taken aback by Mitch's approach to her, and that's why she resents it. Like when she's leaving the town that night . . . when hesays, "I'd like to meet in San Francisco, and let's have some fun," you know. Had she been among San Francisans, you know, and somebody from Burlingame . . . some guy from Burlingame had made that crack, she'd have just XX turned her back on him and said, SSS "The hell with it." I think she's already been attracted to the young man,and there's a kind of a bit of a disappointment that she finds, because she's beginning to get interested in these sort of people, you see, as a fresh thing that she's come across, and I think that there's a general sobering up here. Actually, this is a scene that progresses her a bit further You know, her disappointment and the way she drives off in, what shall we call it, slightly elevated dugeon, high dugeon, but not too high. And, but of course, Annie, later on, when he rings back and apologizes to her and projects her a little bit back into the group, you know, andthat's when she does go to the party the following day, and so forth, and it's that night that there's a bit attack by the birds.

Well now by degrees, what are we getting? We're getting . . . she's getting abit unnerved by the bird situation, and it's getting mixed up a bit with her attitudes towards the young man. I think it's the attack by the thousands of birds that came in the room which forces her to stay the night, you know, and that things are getting serious, set up another mood for her, and brings out the emergence of the scene between Mitch after he's been burning the birds, you see, and I thinkX that the love scene that takes place there is . . . has been a combination of the thing that she saw in the bird shop. But the externals that are happening . . . the bird attacks and there's something funny here . . . gives her a kind of a funny feeling. It's people beginning to, in extremes, like in an air raid, get very e motional. It's a reaction; it's a XXXXXXXXXXXXXXXX reflex action, really. I think XX this is the thing that sends her into this love scene with him. It projects it earlier than it would have occurred in a. . . . it would've taken much longer if it hadn't been for these circumstances. This is what theX bird attacks are doing. It's projecting everybody, as it were, into emotions that would not normally come in X such a way.

And now, of course, when the mother XXXX returns, you know, horrified at what she's seen at the farm, and she has this scene with Melanie, she finds that her relationship with the young man has gotten onto a kind of steadiness that she herself is kind of inwardly surprised at. But she's kind of hooked, you know, andX to a point where she's in the Lydia net, as it were. She's in the Annie situation that was, and now, I think, somewhere here, her attitude is that, well,not in these words but, "Listen, you old bag, I'm a little bit different to Annie, you know,..can't fool around with me." And I think that Melanie is a girl of spirit as we're going to see later on. She was . . . she showed some of her spirit when she rejected the boy the night before. She has an independence; there's no question about that. And I think her attitude toward Mrs. Brenner is a kind of a"chin out"sort of thing. But she's not stupidly antagonistic or anything like that. I think she has enoughX confidence to say, "Look, Mrs. Brenner, don't worry. I can figure this thing out." That's the nice thing about Melanie . . . when XXXX Lydia worries about her daughter . . . XXXXXXXXXXXXX She's not so small as to not be generous even to this woman. I think she feels that superior to her. I think she then and there discovers when Lydia says "I feel so helpless" , and after all, Annie's indicated this, there's a certain element of feeling sorry for her. Then she goes off with the child, you see. From that point on, she's really involved in the whole town's situation . . . the telephone call to her father . . . and I think she's behaving in a very matter-of-fact, XXXXX business-like way . . . no intention of going back to San Francisco now. I'm in with this, and I'm with Mitch and so forth, and her general a ttitude is definitely a businesslike one and the flippancy is going, is gone almost, now. And then, of course, after that comes the attack of the gull which is purely a physical thing, actually. And then, finally, to the death of AnnieX which moves her considerably. I mean it moves her not necessarily to the point of tears but it's areal soberin thing on her. I think that the death of Annie is a big turning point in Melanie's whole outlook. XXXXXXXXXXXX XXXXXXXXXXXXX Even when Xhe's prepared to think only of Cathy and dash away in the car and get Cathy out of it, it's XXXXX Melanie so, you know, only for them.X It's . . . I know you want to get Cathy out of the way but . . . and I think this is a very important turning point.

And then, of course, you see you get . . . back at the house, you see, I think that Melanie there in the house has more or less taken over from Lydia. I think Lydia's gone. She went kaputX when the thousand finches came throughX. Well, I don't know howXXXXX . . . we'll have to look at it in the script . . . but I think that, you know, Melanie's getting the coffee or . . . I think she's. . . . I think we show a picture there . . . and I think that I'll photo graph it, too. I think that Lydia recognizes this, too. She sees the positive qualities in these circumstances,.tXXX the strength that Melanie has. And I think it's important for us to show that, in this area, because want to build up to that moment when she shuts herself up in the room. That we feelXXXthis isn't a thing done out of the blue, this is a different Melanie than we started with, when she locks herself in the room. I know that she does it in a self-sacrificial way. I think we have, as I was telling you earlier . . . I think we have to show a certain hesitancy and XX an in conclusive moment until she slams the door. But from that point on, of course, Melanie is hors de Combat.

No doubt we have to, in the final car sequence . . . we know we have terror on the faces at the final attack and we have . . . but I think that in the car, until the final attack, Melanie is pretty well knocked out by . . . you know, she's bandaged up and pretty XXXX badly knocked about. She's more or less in the arms of Lydia then, you see. I think at some point we have to have a kind of a little touch of association between her and Mitch. Maybe it's her hand on his shoulder or something, I don't know what. We'll have to work something out that isn't corny, but rounds XX this out a little bit . . . if we should put over the fact that she's not going to be mothered by Lydia the rest of her life. EndX of memorandum.

1.  The Bird Shop Sequence.

This is our first introduction to Melanie. We know how she's dressed, we know XXX her general poise, her authority, her self-possession . . . and she will look the part, I'm sure. Now when the young man comes in, the first thing she notices is his physical attraction. But, on the other hand, she certainly is, I think, amused within herself that it's kind of a ridiculous note that the young man should come in for love birds. I think X her sense of humor starts there when she decides to . . . take. . . . well it's not his gag. He knows who she is, you see. I think, although it's not indicated in the script, he deliberately starts the thing, you know. He does it because he knows that she's a practical joker . . . always has been. And she fallsX for it. Now I think that Melanie is X quite a good actress. We see just for a moment how her expression changes when she realizes that, apparently, he has mistaken her for the bird shop attendant, and she goes along. Now I think thatthis should be played with quite a dead pan. I don't think XXXX we ought to play it with a kind of a secret smirk on her face. The words take care of it; the attitude takes care of it, and the mere fact that she should behave like an assistant in a bird shop. I think it's more amusing to play it straightX than to attempt to give her what I call "little twinkles of the eye". And her embarrassmen or awkwardness comes out when the straight dead pan expression with which she is playing breaks down now and then. It gives us a chance, in other words to show awkward moments when he says, "Are these love birds" and "Well, no, they're XXX canaries . . ." So that if she's playing it cute, and we see an amused expression on her face, it doesn't give us room for the change of expression for awkwardness. It's too extreme. In other words, they go from what I call "the twinkle in the eye" to the embarrassment of X not knowing the right birds. But a dead pan, in other words, "all is well, I'm in control of the situation", you see, is stronger for us when she's not in control of it . . . when he asks difficult questions that she can't answer. And then, of course, we come to the point where he does catch the bird, and then puts Melanie Daniels back into her gilded cage.

Now I think the change here should be a change of tempo. I'm not too certain whether we ought to play it . . . "What, what did you say?" I don't think that's Melanie, not our Melanie. It's a take—we'll put Melanie back into her cage. "What did you say?" "I said Melanie Daniels." "How did you know my name?" Not XXXXXXXXXXXXXXXXXXXXXXXXXXXXXXXXXXX "Hh, hh, how did you know my name?" We don't want any of that. I don't think that's . . . that's kind of what I call corny playing, almost. We don't want that.

The thing that gives you the comedic thing is the change in timing. Now, when he says, for example: he says XXXXXXXXXXXXXXXXXXXXXXXXXX "Back in your gilded cage, Melanie Daniels." "What did you say?—How did you know my name?" "Well, a birdie told me. Good day, Miss Daniels." "Wait a minute,' XXXXXX she says. "Hey, wait a XXXXX minute." She says, "I don't know you." "Ah, but I know you."

"How?" "The man in court." "We've never been in court or anywhere else." She's really annoyed now, you see. Because those who make jokes do not like them played on themselves. But her annoyance is merely a set expression, you see, which is equally comic. It's as comic as . . . well, I call it "corny annoyance" on the face. It's more subtle, you see. He says, "Do you remember one of your practical jokes that resulted in the smashing of a plate glass window?" "I didn't break that window." It's still . . . we've got to keep her in her own line, you see. He says, "No, but your little prank did.X The judge should have put you behind bars." "What are you? Policeman?" He says, "I simply believe in the law, Miss Daniels, and I'm not too keen on practical jokers." "What do you call your love birds if not a practicalX . . ." "Ah, but I do love those birds." "You knew I didn't work here. You deliberately . . ." You know, she's real annoyed, but she's suppressing it. We've still got to keep her in the type that she is, and, as I say, we don't want to make it dull. It'll depend how it's rehearsed; how they play with each other . . . How you and Rod Taylor jump in on each other. But the main thing I want to make clear at this point is that I don't think we should play it with what I call "on the nose," expectant expressions and . . . It's high comedy. It should be played for real high comedy. A high comedy is played like drama. It's the situation that carries you, you see. I mean, when she XXXsays . . . he says,XXXX MITCH—"I recognized you when I came in. I thought you might like to know what it feels like to be on the other end of a gag. What do you think of that, Miss Daniels?" I think you're a louse. Good day." And he says, "Madame, I'm glad you didn't get your love XX birds." "I'll find something else." You see, her annoyance is only X in the tempo of the speech. You see what I mean? Not a XXXXXX corny "I'M GLAD YOU DIDN'T GET YOUR LOVE BIRDS!" This is old hat stuff, you know. I wouldn't want to play it like that. That makes her a cheap little girl, you know. "I'm *glad* you didn't get your love birds," see . . . the spelling it out . . . your tempoX but the little bite that comes into it there.

Now, of course, we get a change. He XXXX says, "See you in court some day." You see, that . . . "Who was that," angry to him. He says, "I have no idea." Now, there's a change on her face, and this is very important, here. After he's gone, of course, again I'm going to give you what obviously will happen. We see a kind of a half smile come on her face, and she goes to the windowX to get the car number. This is the corny way of doing it. I think it's just a little malevolent thought, you see. This is Melanie back at the practical joker again. I'll get him, you know. And it's got to have a double thing. It's got to say she's fallen for the guy. And now we sayXXXXXXXXXXXXX what's she gonna do now, the audience, see her. But she just looks. The look should be a steady one, no secret smile, no sauciness or anything like that. She just looks and then goes back . . . pencil . . . writes the number down.

TIPPY X Now when she goes to the door . . . that's when she's looking at the license plate.

Yes, that's the expression . . . see, she follows him to the door, and the expression must be there when she's looking at that license plate, 'cause that's when she decides to go further with this encounter. That's what it amounts to. She wants to see the XX guy again.

There's been enoughX in this little, tiny conflict here, this little battle, battle of wits, to make her want to see him again. And that's the root, that's the end of this scene. And that look at that number plate mustn't be too calculating. It's only a matter of a pause.

It's the look . . . and watches and then goes back. The amount of time that we spend on that look . . . if it's too short, it's just getting the number. But it's lookingX X we cut to the number, and then she goes back. In other words, she's got the number . . . XY 5472 . . . you see, there's a beat or two. Now, I can cut it either way. I can cut it as she's looking . . . looks at the number, and rushes back to put it down. You see, that's another way of doing it . . . it might work either way. That's a matter of split second timing in the cutting. However long I stay on her face, the front part, you see. See I can make her go and look, look after him then flash to what she sees, XXXXX the guy getting into the car. Then her eyes drop; we cut to the number, you see . . . then she dashes back. You see, and give me a paper and pencil to write the number down. Now that gives you the effect of "He interests me, that's the number of his car. I will make a note of it." You see, done that way. But we have to be very careful that that expression must tell us she's fallen for the guy. Now to what degree, we'll have to see how it works out on the stage. But this is the thing you can think about. So that's the bird shop. Do you have any questions on this at all?

Can't make out replyX from Tippi.

Don't take any notice of that for this reason. She wouldn't have taken down that car number unless she had a purpose. What she does after that is merely mechanical. It's who does the car belong to? . . . following through. It wouldn't come at that part, you see. She's already doneXXX . . . the mere fact that she's taken down the car number, per se, that's the end of it. Her determination to contact him again occurs the moment we flash that car number. The moment she says, "Give me a pencil and paper," we know she wants to see him again. It's there. Well now, what happens after that. XXXX We merely establish that her father is on the newspaper . . . That's exposition. How she gets the number we're using there. We're using how she gets the number to tell the audience more about her.

Do you feel anything else that you would like to ask there?

TIPPY: No. End of sequence

THE APARTMENT

It seems to me the next thought we have to put over from Melanie's standpoint is the problem she has in being stuck with a couple of love birds. You see, the information she received from the newspaper office was that XXX Mr. Mitchell Miller lived at 497 Taylor Street, San Francisco. She goes there with the birds, ostensibly to leave them outside the door . . . after all, let's assume that they're well fed, and they'll only have to wait an hour or two if he's out, or what have you . . . or until he comes out the door. Then she discovers that he doesn't live there for Saturday or Sunday, so we have to have a moment at the end of the sequence out side of his apartment, after his neighbor has told her that Mitch Miller lives in Bodiga Bay . . . Now what's her expression here? This is where we have to be very careful, because someon might say, well why doesn't she take the birds back to the bird shop and give up the X whole idea? And I think it would be an interesting thing . . . I know it isn't in the script . . . but we have to put it over, but she looks at the birds, looks at his door . . . in other words, we should reprise the fact that she wants to see him again. You see, because I think in the script Melanie says, "Well, where did he go?" Man XXXsays, "Bodiga Bay.X He goes up there every weekend." "Bodiga Bay, where's that?" "Up the coast, about sixty miles north of here."

"Sixty!..oh." Man says, "About an hour and a half on the freeway or twohours if you take the coast highway." "Oh . . . I'd hold the birds for him, but I'm going away myself. Someones got to feed them, I suppose." Melanie, now the script says "in utter despair, now." "Yes, yes, someone's got to feed them." Man, "I'm awfully sorry."

INTERFERENCE ON TAPE UNTIL:

That puts her in a mood of exasperation. I don't think that's correct.

Tippy: Then these love birds are her one main source to see him again.

Well, this is the point you see, so that her expression when the man says, "I'm awfully sorry," puts his key into his lock, opens the door and goes in, now she's left alone. . . . in the hallway, holding two lovebirds. She has to look down at the birds, look up . . . 'what shall I do with them?," look at his door. Maybe we'll arrange it so that his name is on the outside or something. Now she looks out again from his door, then maybe we'll put the vestige X of a little, tiny smile on her face. Just a tiny, oh, a nuance, hardly notice anything. Now you're XX dissolved, on the way to Bodiga Bay. You see the difference? This is not correct, you see, because if this is correct, where she says, "Oh, shut up," to the birds, then I would say s he would have taken the birds back to the store. She defeated her . . . her gag has gone wrong. She's arrived to deliver two birds, he isn't there, the man says he's out of town, "Yes, I'm sorry, I would have taken them in myself." "But, Madame, you're stuck with two birds." So maybe her look is not a smile. Maybe it's a look of determination which says, "You're going to get to him somehow," you know. It can be that. Let's for a moment think about this. She took the trouble to get the number of his car, she bought the birds, paid for them, got his address and went to deliver them. Now allthis, then, we know that it's in her spirit of the way that she liked to . . . her way of getting acquainted, because let's think of what might be in the back of her mind. If he gets the birds , he's bound to follow through. Go back to Mrs. Magruder. "I didn't order the birds, Mrs. Magruder." X She would say, "No." He would say, "Well, who did?"knowing all the time it was Miss Daniel. xx Now starts the train of contact. He would have sent a note saying, probably, "Well, you needn't have done it." Then you would have sent a note back, "Very well, send the birds back toXX me," which he wouldn't do. This sort of going on but, by this time, they're sort of together, you see. So this is what her purpose. Now, what she has to decide here is, does she want to renew the acquaintanceship badly enough to go sixty miles? And this is what the expression on her face must say. Now, if it's a smile when she looks at his door, it could be a kind of a tiny, tiny, little look of, shall we say, mischievious determination. It's a humorous determination that we see on her face. You know, sort of very fine shadings of expression here. But they've got to say for us what's in her mind, because you answer it by a car whizzing along the highway . . . a long shot of a car winding itself through a very scenic shot. But we've answered it . . . Now, there's another way of doing it, what I call the cute, movie way, is following this, you know, full of annoyance so that at the end of this sequence you could follow this routine but I don't know whether it's so good . . . It's the usual thing where you say, "Well, that's the end of that." But any audience knows that the hero and the heroine . . . they're going to know that, in this film, they're going to meet again. They know very well that they're not going to part forever at this stage of the movie. Let's face it. Now there is a certain style treatment where the style is to show anger and then answer it by her doing the opposite of what you would expect her to do . . . to go North. But at the end of the sequence her face would say, oh, the hell with it,.oh you shut up, birds. And then, next thing you see, XXXX it's supposed to be a surprise to the audience . . . "Oh look, she's gone after all," they say. Well, I'm not so sure . . . that's what I call a little "cute," you know? I'd much rather keep our character true XXXXX in terms of she looks at his door, looks out, and keep XXXa kind of a thought on her face . . . mischievious thought, not overdone. And the next thing you see, there she is . . . on her way. But, of course, the thought will be telegraphed, and she's on her way, but I don't think, in the space of four seconds of film,we should withhold this from the audience. These are little tricks that. . . . we've done these in movies for years, you know Theydo one in "How to Succeed in Business Without Really Trying" . . . you know, they have the head of the advertising department in his chair there, and we know the young man's on the way up, so they black out and the lights go up again, and there's the young man in a chair . . . well, I know Frank Loesser, he stole that from the XXXXXX movies, butXXXXXXXXXXXXXX unfortunately, that's a very old-fashioned movie. So, we'll have this changed from the script, put into these notes and maybe the next time I talk to Evan HunterX, I'll, you know, tell him that we've talked this over and there might be an alternative. I'm not sure, though, that this ending is right. It may be that we have to justify why she goes sixty X miles. Now what justification can there be, except that she wants to see him again. And we can only do that by whatever expression . . .

TIPPY: But does she realize this yet?

What?

TIPPY: That she wants to see him.

Well, I've just said, she's gone to allthe trouble . . .

TIPPY: I know, but it's um . . . well, I'm going according to the script, that she doesn't quite realize that it's really Mitch she wants to see instead of going through with the practical joke, until she's in the XXXX boat and she thinks she's not going to get any reaction from him.

Oh, but, XXXXX yes. But this is a long range thing. You see, this is Melanie Daniels using her practical jokes knowing there's gonna be a reaction. It must be. What would she go to all this trouble for? It started whenshe got the car number. I'm sure she wants to see him again. You see it's a very different thing, when later on in the story, she XXXX wants the minah bird to speak, you know, to give to her aunt . . . and make it say something dirty. Well, that's the thing, you know . . . that's an ordinary practical joke, but here, you see, you've already had a conflict in the shop . . . there's been an association between the two. They have a kind of a

INTERFERENCE ON TAPE UNTIL:

XXXXXXXXXXXXXXXXX I can't, you see, I can't believe that she would sixty miles to carry out a practical joke on the strength.

MORE INTERFERENCE UNTIL:

Maybe she wouldn't admit it to herself. If somebody said to her, "YOu mean you came all this way to deliver a couple of birds?" "Well, I had nothing better to do, you know, I didn't want any lunch . . . a little ride up there. What's it take me? Three hours. Doesn't matter much . . ." She'd defend it that way. Or she'd find some excuse.

Well, I really think that, especially later on

MORE INTERFERENCE

End

XXXXXXXXXXXXXXX JOURNEY TO BODIGA BAY

All we have here are a series of closeups of her driving. These will be done in the studio. They'll be forward shots of the road ahead and back on her face. Now we have to decide what expression; what she's thinkingX on the drive. Scenery, is it nice scenery? I don't think she ought to lookX coy, saying, "Oh, isn't he going to be surprised when he gets the birds." No, I don't we'd want anything like that. I think we should put over in the expression a little tiny sense of mischief, you know? And that's about all we'll need here. There'll only be about three or four cuts. But to keep it alive, you know, we just don't want to get a dead face without any thoughts going in it at all.


AT BODIGA BAY

In this sequence we have her going to the post office. She is now with other characters so it's a fairly practical, straight-forward request to the postmaster for the address and the building up to wanting to surprise the . . . I think, if anything, she should be quite casual. She should be XXXX purposefully casual toward the clerk, especially when s he says to him, "Isn't there a back road I can ttake?" X And he XXXsays, "No, that's the road, straight through the town, etc. etc." That's where she becomes casual. I want her to surprise him. "I wanted to surprise him. I didn't want to come right down the road where he could see me." It's a surprise, you see. And he talks about the boat, you see. When he says "Have I handled an outboard motor boat?" "Of course," you know, don't be indignant about it. "Of course." "Want me to warm it up for you?" "Thanks." "In about twenty minutes?" ". . . named Daniels, O.K." That's all. Then she wants the little girl's name, you see.

Now, we have a moment here. It's marked in the script scene 78, close shot, Melanie. It says, abruptly she gets a new idea and turns back toward the post office. Now, she's got a note in there for him, hasn't she? Which later on she tears up, doesn't she . . .
INTERFERENCE Where does she tear up the letter?
TIPPY: Well, she tears up the letter now and she gets the card for the little girl . . . the birthday card at the general s tore. But she talks about the letter . . . later on.

Yes, I know she does . . . much later on. Well, there's certainly a moment when, you see, after all we have a change here. She's after Mitch Miller; now she wants to know the little girl's name. Well, we'll have to look at that. It seems to me, when you ask for the little girl's name, you don't really have a reason. See, she reaches in her purse for the envelope, she looks at the envelope and then begins tapping it on the edge of her XXXXXX purse, thinking, reconsidering. Abruptly she gets a new idea and turns back to the post office. Well, we'll have to put that over very clearly there . . . that she looks at the envelope and then goes back.

(out via Hitch instructions on tape)
End of sequence.


Tape #2
SCHOOL TEACHERXSEQUENCE

When she arrives at the school teacher's house, the first things she's conscious of is Annie's examination of her. Annie comes out from gardening and so forth . . . then we should have just a little touch of self-consciousness. But not beyond Melanie's ability to control any situation . . . sort of, it's just a steady exchange of looks, because we've got here, you see, where Melanie says . . . Annie says, "You're leaving after you see Cathy," and Melanie says, "Well, something like that . . . I'm sorry, I don't mean to sound mysterious." Annie says, "Well, it's none of my business." I think there Melanie's attitude is a kind of a steady look . . . I think she's very controllable, because the script says here—"Melanie, by her silence, affirms that it *is* none of Annie's business." I think her self-consciousness is only related to the first meeting between the two. I think it's in the script here . . . Page 26, and you see we describe in scene 86 what she looks like . . . Annie, you see . . . "She's puzzled by Melanie, who, exquisitely dressed and groomed, seems out of place in Bodiga Bay. She studies her openly." This is what I meant when I said that . . . see, Scene 88, there's no reference to that in the script. But if we have Annie studying her openly, you know, just for a moment. Melanie could . . . I think we might give her a touch of the hand going to the front of the fur coat; something very XXXXX tiny, you know. And she might react to that ever so slightly.

Now we're getting down to t he details about Cathy and I think, here, Melanie, when questioned by Annie, "Did you want to see Cathy about something? "Well, not exactly," says Melanie. "You a friend of Mitch's?" "Well, not really." The awkwardness comes out of the fact that . . . No, it seems to me that Melanie has gotten by this awkwardness with Annie, really gets down to her own inner thoughts of the real purpose of her journey . . . not Cathy, but it's to renew acquaintanceship with Mitch. I think if there's any awkwardness here, that's the reason for it . . . not the practical joke any more. Cathy and the thing are theXXXXX surface thing, but when Annie says, "Did you want to see Cathy about something?" . . . That's the birds and the practical joke. She might have answered . . . well she does say here, "Well, not exactly," meaning XXXXXXX ZZZZXXXXXXXXXXXXXXXXXXXXXXXX "I'm playing a practical joke on Mitch who wants to give these birds to his XXXXX sister as a birthday present." But when Annie says, "Are you a friend of Mitch's?" . . . this calls for just a beat. "You a friend of Mitch's?" says Annie. "No, not really" . . . there's a tiny fraction of a beat there which Annie would be quick to pick up, because in the script Evan's written, "there's an awkwardness here" . . . Annie wants to know more, you see.

Now, Annie goes on. She talks about her garden. Now Annie's probing mor "Do you plan on staying long?" Melanie XXX says, "No, just a few hours." "Yo leaving after you see Cathy?X" . . . that's a dirty line, you know. Melanie . . . I think she almostX resents that line, but she mustn't show it. She's too smart . . . she's too poised to show it. Well, something like that. Then she says . . . this is another sign of it, "I'm sorry, I don't mean to sound so mysterious," and Annie says, "It's none of my business." You see . . . "Well, I'm getting on my way. Thank you very much," and walks toward the car. ANNIE, "Did you driv up from San Francisco?" You know, this Annie is really getting her down a bit. "That's where you met Mitch?" "Yes." I think the tone of the "yes" there is important. It should be a flat "yest". "Yes, but it's none of your business She says, "I guess that's where everyone meets him." Melanie looks at her on the word "everyone." Now here's a beat . . . she should get behind the wheel looking at Annie all the time. "Now you sound a bit mysterious, Miss Hayward."

So it's a nice scene . . . I think it should be played . . . I'll photograph it to get the benefit of these looks, but we should observe every nuance . . . because every look and every pause . . . you can see in every beat and give us a meaning, you see. And I'm sure when you get together with Miss Pleschette, you'll be able to work out the timing which is so important.

TIPPY: During this conversation, they're both getting the idea that they're both eyeing each other.

More than that, they're thinking a lot . . . about each other, too. Annie well let's face it, Annie sees a girl in a mink coat asking XX for the Brenner house . . . and she's very, kind of awkward. She's not exactly clear in her answers. She wants to see Cathy, "Is she a friend of Mitch?" "Yes." You know Annie knows what Mitch is. She's had him; she's had something of him. And the mere fact that woman mentions Mitch tells Melanie right away there must be something . . . especially when she says, "Now you sound a bit mysterious." She didn't know . . . "well, I'm an open book XXXX maybe, or maybe a closed one." See the reaction to these are not lost on Melanie and we've got to photograph them However, where she says, "Maybe a closed one," Melanie's eyes run her up and down just for, oh, the tiniest flicker. Then Annie changes the subject, says, "Pretty, what are they?" "Love birds." "Well, good luck, Miss Daniels." See the meaning of the word XX "good luck." I didn't get any luck there. So there's plenty in it Tippy. Plenty in this scene to play . . . a lot to play. A lot of coming and going here with the changes in attitude between each other. First she's mysterious, then the other one's mysterious.
END OF SEQUENCE

THE JOURNEY IN THE BOAT TO BRENNER HOME . . . AND ALSO THE JOURNEY BACK AFTER DEPOSITING THE BIRDS

Now we have the incongruous situation of a girl wearing XX a mink coat sitting in an outboard motor boat, and, while she does meet a fisherman who guides her to the boat, etc., we've already been told that she handled an outboard motor boat, but I don't think we want to repeat the same thought with the fisherman. There's nothing to be gained fromXXXXXXit . . . her feeling awkward . . . and I don't thinkwe should stress it when she gets into the boat. But once she gets into the boat, there'll be a fair amount of wind on her face . . . these'll be done in the studio, anyway . . . but let's think about Melanie's attitude as she gets nearer to the Brenner home. I think we should try to put over one point, and we'll try and find out when that moment shall be. Is the fact that she reacts to the remoteness of their farm . . . but it's pretty . . . when she . . . what we shall show from her viewpoint in that boat approaching the house . . . it's pretty isolated. I think for a moment she'll say, "What am I doing coming out here in a boat? How did I find myself in t his situation coming to such a remote spot as this?" And I think just for a moment we might put over on the face, somewhere or other, "It looks so remote . . . I wonder if the man was right . . . and, maybe I better go back." MaybeXXXXXX we might put in a waverin so that we don't just get a straight face looking which is what we're liable to get approaching this house . . . because the shot that we're going to get will be a closeup of you at the tiller of this boat with the wind blowing . . . and then she'll pull her coat up . . . I think we might even try and get a little more amusement out of it if we did give it a bit of wind. It depends how choppy the water is, but she pulls the coat up around her neck andX we get the shiver and she looks over her shoulder back to the shore . . . and let's try to put over, if we can . . . in pantomime of XXXXXX course, when we come back to the studio . . . of her literally saying, "How the hell did I find myself in this silly situati which it will look. I don't we ought to haveX XXXXX her calmly sitting there, chugging away as though she's on the river, enjoying herself. I think we should put over

. . . you know . . . We can't have any soliliquies or talking to herself, but it would be nice if we could have a line for her to say, "Well, this is the silliest situation I've got myself into." I think we should try and put that over with almost a determination to turn back . . . but then I think, at that moment her eye should catch sight of Mitch coming out of the house wit his mother and Cathy . . . where she sees Cathy and the mother get into the truck and drive off. As they drive off, we'll make her eyes follow the truck, and Mitch is standing there . . . and maybe she just preens herself a little bit . . . "Look, XXXXX/XXXXXXXXXX he's alone . . ." you know, "Might be rather fun, maybe I'll get him alone there or something" althoughX she has no intention of this. I think we should let the moment recur where we keep alive the purpose of the whole thing . . . a girl on the make . . . in the most elaborate circumstances . . . So then he goes off into a barn and now we're dealing mostly with the mechanic of her XXXXXXX depositing the birds which will be . . . when she gets out of the boat, the camera will be on the long dock that sticksout into the water, and we shall follow her in a close shot and we'll constantly cut to the barn where Mitch has gone, you see, and disappeared, so we get a little . . . we want to get her a little furtive here. It's in fun now with the hope that she isn't caught in the act. People always enjoy seeing someone doing something without being discovered, as to whatever form it takes. Even if you have a . . . sometimes in a movie you have a villain creeping in, whatever it is. And the audience, for some reason or other, whether there's a touch of larceny in everyone or something, I don't know. But they always say, "Quick, quick, before you're found out. Get out, get out." So on her face there's a little caution and the look of her hurrying up to the house and dumping the birds in the room on the table and hurrying out. Her movements here are important. It's not exactly tip-toeing although it's in the open air, you see . . . but the body should be stealthy and so forth and back to the boat, and she gets in the boat and pushes the boat away. At that time, he comes out, you see. And now she ducks and her eyes, we'll photograph her eyes coming over the edge of the boat, looking out. And he rushes out, she sees this little figure rush out and look everywhere. Then he goes back in, you see . . . so she'll enjoy this now . . . and she sees him put up the binoculars and then we cut close to him with the binoculars up. Now we see what he sees . . . and this a close view of this face who turns, and sits up and turns her back and starts the boat away. And the XXXXX timing . . . I don't know how it cuts, exactly, but by the time he gets onto the . . . by the time she gets the boat going . . . she's chugging away . . . I think that's when she looks over her shoulder and he really recognizes who it is . . . through the binoculars. Now we go back to her point of view, and from her point of view she sees him, you see . . . and he gets in the car and starts to race around the bay. She crosses it direct and goes back to the Tides. But his car goes right around the bay . . . so it intercuts. And now the trick starts Now she's really satisfied . . . so it's not too strongly played; it's played with a kind of a smug satisfaction . . . you know, a little bit of a XXX smile, the wind'll be blowing her hair and her eyes watch his car . . . cutting back, cutting back, you see. And there, finally, on her face, she sees him waiting on the dock. I don't think she's displeased at all. . . . and there he is waiting on the dock, at that moment . . . when the gull strikes. And then she changes completely. You see, this gull should strike when her mood is cozying itself up for another meeting with him. That's all she's thinking of . . . then boom, this thingX arrives.

TIPPY: Now how does this . . . yeah, whenX the gull hits her . . . how

Well, I was going to change that. Actually, from this point on, it hits her . . . she's sort of hurt. Her hand goes up to her head and she just looks up to see what it was, and from her viewpoint sees this gull flying away, you see. By this time, by the time we go from her closeup, we shall cut to the boat practically coming alongside the dock and he's hurrying down and gets toherX and helps her out, and the fisherman comes in the background. So then we shall probably follow the two of them up..but her behavior at this point is one of just distress and injury. I don't think there's room for us to put anything into her face or anything into her mind except for the meeting and all the fun's gone for the moment, because it was rather a big bang..and her hand's showing blood, you know . . . bleeding and all this XX sort of thing . . . so that we don't deal with anything here except just the plain distressof what has happened to her. Now and then he helps her, then we get them up to th Tides restaurant. You see, we've got a walking shot across the car park there up to the Tides, inside the restaurant, you see. And now we get down to the practicalities of the bandaging you see.
END OF SEQUENCE

## THE FIRST SCENE INSIDE THE TIDES RESTAURANT WITHXXXXXXXXX MITCH AND MELANIE

This is inside the Tides restaurant when Mitch mends her head wound. I think the first . . . where she starts to say, "SoX you're a lawyer," I think her manner is kind of . . . she should kind of cover up the whole visit with a kind of purposefully off-hand manner. Where she says, XXXXXXXXXXX "Oh, so you're a lawyer," you know, just be nonchalant. But it's a calculating nonchalance, you know . . . "So you're a lawyer." "That's right, what're you doing in Bodiga Bay?" "Do you practice here?" "No, San Francisco . . . what're you . . ." "What kind of lawyer?" "Criminal." "That why you've got to see everyone behind bars?" Here is a point when she says, "behind bars," here is a point of going back to the bird shop, and her attitude of a slight disdain for him, of course this is put on . . . until she says, "I was coming up here anyway." Now she's a little on the spot so that her speech becomes a little measured, because she's thinking. Her tempo slows up a bit here. In other words, the other stuff she can rattle off, you know "So you're a lawyer," and so on and so on and so forth. But the moment he says, "Besides, I was coming up anyway," . . . she says, rather. MITCH,XXx "What for?" "To see a friend of mine." Now she's going to slow a little, because she's got to XXX figure XXXXXXXXXX things out . . . says "Oh, careful." "I'm sorry," and then he says, "Who's your friend," and there's another pause . . . she's thinking . . . she says, "Annie, Annie Hayward." Now she's got the name out, now her tempo can change a bit. He says, "Well, small world . . . Annie Hayward." "yes" . . . you know, XX a little defiantly . . . "Yes," that kind of intonation. Mitch says, "How do you know Annie?" "We went to school together." In XX other words, I don't XXX think she's hesitant. She merely XXXXXX thinks a little bit, and so her timing slows up just a touch. And Mitch says, he doesn't believe it, of course, he says, "How long will you be staying?" "Day or two . . . maybe the weekend." Now, of course, there's a little bit about the razor, but that's XXXXX obvious there. Now we go into t he covering of the cup, and now, suddenly, he says, "So you came up to see Annie." "yes . . . yes. So what," you know, "None of your business." That's her attitude. She'd like to put on the facade of asserting herself, until he says, "I don't believe you. I think you came up to see me." Now she looks and XXX

says, "Why would I want to see you, of all people." She's quit . . . this girl, Evan has tended to write her a little awkward and XXXXXXXXX hesitant, but I think she's smart enoughX to be ready with a lie . . . and ready to put on a . . . you know, "Why would I want to see you, of all people?" She puts almost conviction . . . she creates conviction of her own in her voice. And then heX says, "I don't know. It seems to me you've gone to a lot of trouble to find out who I was and where I lived and . . ." you see, this is true. This is what we've been talking about in the first reel, in the early stuff . . . this is true, you see. And she just brushes that off, "No trouble at all, I was to call at my father's paper, I was X coming up here anyway." Then he persists, "You like me, huh." He persists, you see. SHe says, "I loathe you." I think she should be very calm . . . she mustn't say, "I LOATHE you," nothing of that. I should keep it on very high comedyX all the time here. And she shoul read this line, he says "You like me, huh." "I loatheX you. You have no manners . . . you're arrogant and conceited. I wrote you a letter about it in fac but I tore it up." "What'd it say?" "None of your business. Am I still bleeding?" So that she spells out her opinion of him in what she thinks is a fairly controlled and authoritative manner, but not really believing it. If she believed it her face would be flaming, but it isn't that way, you see. After all, she did tear the letter up which said, I mean, that belies any true anger she may have. No, I think that the high comedy is again the essential thing here, and that will emerge from her audacity, her brazenness of the way she lies about her coming to see Annie and her response, you know . . . because she's very inconsistent. If she says "You have manners, you're arrogant and conceited," he obviously doesn't believe a word of it, because she never would have brought the birds up anyway. He's in the XXXXX right here. So, in a way she's on the defensive, but she's doing her very best to carry it off. Now that bottom speech here . . . he says, "All I get for my pains is a hole in the head, right next to the one you already had." And she says, "Look Mr. Brenner" . . . I don't know whether she should be that angry. Of course, he was rude when he XXX said "Right next to the one you already had."
TIPPY: But he's laughing when he says it.

Oh, sure, he's laughing with it. I think she would say . . . I would prefer her to say, "Thank you, Mr. Brenner." You know . . . I think she'd admonish him instead of "Look Mr. Brenner." I don't like that very much. SHe SSsays, "All I get for it is a hole in the head." He says, "Right next to the one you already had." "Thank you, Mr. Brenner." Change that, yes. I think that puts him in his place a bit more than just the angry, you know . . . that's Page 43, last speech.

Now Lydia comes in. X I think that when . . . you see, of course, Lydia will come in as quite a strong person here, when she comes in to this Tides thing. Then I think that, for the first time, here, you know . . . when she's face to face with Lydia, and Mitch says, "Miss Daniels is staying for the week end. In fact, I've already invited her for dinner tonight." which is a lie. Now I really think we can get a little touch of embarrassment here. She says, "No, no" you know. And she's genuine here, now, because she's a little, you know . . . when you get a kind of . . . I won't say that Lydia is going to be a formidable woman, but when another person enters and it's not a . . . it's a person apparently of some consequence, which Lydia will be, I think it would sober MelanieX somewhat. XXXXX Don't you think? I think it should, you s ee . . . and I think all through this I shall be cutting to Melanie. She doesn't have a lot to say, bu she says, "I couldn't possibly come to dinner." And now Mitch and Lydia exchange a discussion about love birds, and they talk in terms of dinner and so forth . . . and, here, I do think that Melanie is a little bit self-conscious . . . just a bit in front of Lydia. What do you think?

TIPPY: I think she would be.

XXX I think she wouldX be, but only in a very, very subdued way. I think what it does, it subdues her expression a little bit in front of Lydia. And she protests, "Where are you staying," and all that. Now she can be . . . "With Annie, of course." And Mitch, "Of course, how stupid of me. A quarter of seven, will that be all right? MELANIE, "Well Annie may have made other plans I'll have to see. Besides, I c an find my own way." "You're sure, now. You won't hire a boat or anything?" I'll probably go to Lydia's face, and that'll give me an opportunity to s how you looking at Lydia, feeling really stupid about the boat. The joke sounds silly. It's flat in front of a third person. It was all right between the two of you, because, as we said, this all starts from the bird shop. But now with Lydia . . . you see I'm not . . . we won't play Lydia stiff-necked or anything like that, but, as I say, a rather responsible, XXXXXXX thoughtful woman, and if she were behaving like Agnes Moorehead, head high and rather hard-faced, I don't think Melanie would give a damn.

TIPPY: No, she could probably stand up to that sort of thing.

Yes . . . but Lydia will, I hope, will look sensitive.

TIPPY: Now, do you want to put any mention of the cut to Lydia in here?

XXXX It's all been done.

END OF FIRST TIDES SEQUENCE


SECOND SEQUENCE WITH XXXXXXX ANNIE HAYWARD - WHEN MELANIE TAKES ROOM

Well, there's not a lot here except that we do have the relationship of these two developing. It comes from the previous scene. She asks for the room for the night. Annie reads a lot into the line on the topX of Page 48 wher Melanie says, "You see I hadn't planned on spending much time here," because Annie uses the line, "Yes, I know. Did something unexpected crop up?" This is Annie XXXXXXX reading more into it, you see. I don't think there's much more we can do with that, do you?"

TIPPY: No.

END OF SEQUENCE


THE FIRST PART OF THE FIRST DINNER AT THE BRENNER HOUSE

Starting on Page 49. Well, it's pretty routine here, because we're dealing mostly with the introduction of Cathy. I think that Melanie likes Cathy.

TIPPY: DoX you think she might be surprised at her feelings toward Cathy because it XXXXX wasn't Cathy that she came up here for anyway?

What . . . there's very little here, you see. CATHY, "Miss Daniels?" "Yes," and flings herself into Melanie's arms . Course I really don't know much about their behavior. Do they really fling themselvesXXX into people's arms?

TIPPY: Yes, children sometimes do. They're very warm . . . oh yes.

They do. Well, that's fine, if you think that's all right. I can't tell which is whichXX . . . well I suppose . . . you s ee, there's nothing about the chicke you know. I not certain whether . . . where he says, "Are you hungry?" and Melanie says, "Famished" . . . why are people always famished? Have you ever used the word famished?

TIPPY: I XX use starved.

I mean, are you that much before dinner? I think it would be better if he said, "Are you hungry?" "Reasonably so" . . . or something like that other than that. Let's leave it for the time being but we'llbring it up later on. Make a note on Page 50 - query famished. Well, there's nothing for Melanie to do while Lydia's on the phone. They're talking about the feed.

Now we have the second part of the dinner. Well, we're coming to our famous piano bit now, aren't we? Well, I think it would be nice if Melanie's attitude was a relaxed one which is expressed through playing the piano. If you're not relaxed, you wouldn't go to a stranger's piano and start to sit down and play something. I would assume that she's been playing already just before Lydia and Mitch went through to the kitchen. But we can see, generally, that Melanie's beginning to feel relaxed with the Brenners as a whole, expressed through the piano playing, the cigarette and the talk with the little girl.

Now, the question is, when . . . XXXXXX you see, Cathy . . . you see, we have to XX watch it very carefully here, because at the opening of the scene Cathy says, "I still don't understand how you knew I wanted love birds," and Melanie says, "Your brother told me." That's fine up to there until Lydia says, "Then you knew Mitch in San Francisco, is that right?" Now we've got to bang the closeup. "Well, no, not XXXXXXXX exactly." Now she's in trouble again. This little thing there . . . she was fine, you know, and Cathy will probably be able to e stablish Melanie's comfort for the moment by delaying Cathy's line. And the moment Cathy speaks, oh, here we go again..so that her reaction, "No, not exactly," . . . then is relieved when Cathy says, "Mitch knows a lot of people in San Francisco, they're mostly hoods," you see. Now, Melanie and Cathy are alone and they t alkX about smoking . . . so we get Cathy and Melanie together There's nothing much for her to do t here, except playing..and the smoking. It's really Cathy's introduction. I think perhaps that during it we might have Melanie conscious of Mitch and his mother in the kitchen. See, according to our script, we only X do it towards theX end when Cathy a sks her to stay for the party and answers toward the kitchen, "I don't think so, Cathy," Melanie says. It'll be the K V voices off in the kitchen that'll make her wonder a bit. In other words, during Cathy's talk on Page 55 about "Don't you like us?" "Of course I do." "don't you . . ." "I don't know yet." "Mitch likes it very much." The moment they do that and she's talking about that surprise party bit and this, you know, I think Melanie can look off toward the kitchen. XXXXXXXXXXXXXXX

Now we get the scene off between Mitch and Lydia which sets up Lydia's attitude. So that will be the end of the dinner sequence. I think it's fairly self-explanatory there. There isn't much we can put . . . there isn't very much XXXX we can add to that.
END OF SEQUENCE

This is the scene where Melanie departs after the first evening with t he Brenners. In this scene, Mitch attacks her. Obviously, his mother in the kitchen previously had, in a way, accused him of bringing home a floozy or an irresponsible type of girl and he himself has already begun to fall for her, don't you think?

TIPPY: Yes, that's explained in that, too . . . with his mother.

His anger, therefore, with his mother is taken out on Melanie as she leaves. That's why he accuses her of all these things. She, on the other han I think rises, she's angry . . . but there's a tremendous amount of control. In fact, I think s he comes through the scene with quite an amount of strength. the ways he answers him with slow deliberation, with a low, controlled accent in her voice, but seething underneath with anger.

INTERFERENCE ON TAPE UNTIL:

And somewhat with an air of finality. She doesn't do very well h ere. I think the whole thing should smack of, "Well, it's been nice knowing you, I'll be on my way . . . thank you for a pleasant dinner . . .

MOREINTERFERENCE UNTIL:

This is the end of the little attraction that started in the bird shop, and, she doesn't realize it, but his attitude springs from the possessiveness of the mother who. . . . this is where it's rooted. Now she's going to find this out when she gets home with Annie later on. And in a sense, we may find out when we come to the scene . . . in a sense, she may be aware of this. We'll look, when we come to that scene, we'll look at it carefully to see whether she can find any mitigating ci rcumstances for Mitch's attitude . . . if we can trace it. It came from the mother. I don't know whether we have that in the script, but we'll deal with that when we come to it.

TIPPY: I don't think so. I don't we have any up until then.

No, I meant with Annie.

TIPPY: Oh, I see.

END OF FIRST EVENING AT THE BRENNERHOUSE

Well, obviously, she returns to Annie's house pretty het up. She's prett mad. I think she does begin to change . . . to lose some of her anger in her interest about Lydia, don't you think? In other words, she is at the end of the scene going to agree to stay over and I can go back to their house. However, when this scene opens, she wouldn't dream of going back to their house. So what causes her change? I can only think, to some extent, the story that Annie tells of the Brenner family interests her somewhat. I think that, where she says, "Would you rather I change the subject?" "I think so." Well, of course, in that early part of the scene, she's obviously not interested at all She despises the little hamlet . . . then Annie tells her story about Mitch Brenner. Melanie says, "I suspected as much." ANNIE, "You needn't XXXXXX worry. It's over and done with a long time ago." I suppose Annie says, "You needn't worry," because she feels that there is something between Melanie and Mitch and Melanie answers it, "Annie, there's nothing between Mitch Brenner and me." I think we should add X "Brenner" there. Annie shrugs. "Maybe there is and maybe there isn't. Maybe there's never anything between Mitch and any girl." "What do you mean?" Now she has some brandy a nd tells the story of Lydia . . . and in the course of listening to Annie's account of her slight conflict over Lydia, Melanie loses some of her XXXXXXX antagonism there toward Mitch in being interested, don't you think? Because obviously we have to change her . . . change her attitude as we go along. You see, on Page 67 Melanie says, "Well, what have you done?" Then she talks about the jealous woman, the "What was it Lydia liked me?" "Then why did she object to you?" "Afriad you' taken it . . ." These are all questions that Melanie puts to Annie. Melanie at the bottom of the page says, "Annie, that adds up to a jealous, possessive woman. What about Mitch, doesn't he have anything to s ay about this?" Now Annie says, "I can understand his position. He went XXXX through alot with Lydia after his father XXX died. He didn't want to risk going through it all again." Now Melanie sees a sympathetic angle here towards Mitch, doesn't she? And Annie tells her why she came back to Bodiga Bay. Now the phone goes, and Mitch comes on the phone. Melanie hesitates when Annie says, "He's waiting," then she rises and goes to the phone. Well, this is a thought of Annie when she XXX listens to the phone call. This is an aspect. Now you have the phone call, you see. He does apologize, and in the whole of that, of course, we see the changes on her face. And in listening to that phone call, of course, we'll have to show and see, not an immediate response, but a kind of hesitancy and then, I think we ought to portray her as a reasonable girl and not a petulant girl . . . you know, she says, "No, won't come" . . . I don't she XXXX ought to have any attitude of "oh, the hell with you." I think that we must assume that he is in a rather apologetic . . . conveying a certain amount of humility, so t hat we can gradually see this change on her face. So therefore, we have to start with a very cool, you know, "Hello? Yes this is Melanie." X I think the voice should start . . . I mean it ought to read something . . . I'll give you a rough idea, something . . . "Hello? This is Melanie. Fine, thank you. No, no trouble at all. I simply followed the road. It's a very bright night . . . what? No, there's no need to apologize. I can understand. Well . . . that's very kind of you. No, I'm not angry. I couldn't. I'm afraid I have to go back to San Francisco . . . No, I wouldn't want to disappoint Cathy, but . . . I see . . . I see, well if you really. All right, yes, I'll be there. Good night, Mitch." You see, there's a transition in the tempo. It starts fast and gradually slows up in accordance with his pleading you see. Now she's doubtful. Now she is, I thinl she's not aware that Annie has beenwatching her. So the way we'll play it, that her final "Good night, Mitch," and then she turns and sees the staring Annie which makes her say, "He wants me to go to Cathy's party tomorrow afternoon. I said I would." You know, as if "I shouldn't have XXXX said it." "I'll be going too, it should be fun, Melanie." Now she's regretting it..seem so pointless. "I'll go to sleep. It's been a busy day." She tries todismiss it . . . only because she's embarrassed, now, in front of Annie. And she changes the subject, holds up the flowered thing. It's Annie, looking at XXXXX her, I think, makes her say, "Do you think I should go?" "It's up to you." "It's really up to Lydia, isn't it?" "Never mind Lydia. Do you want to go?" "Yes. Now, she's almost . . . one moment she's saying, "Well, Annie, she can't put me off, you know, by looking at me." In a way, she's worried by Annie's look and it's almost . . . if she said, "Oh well, I won't go then," you know . . . then she's losing, kind of, face to Annie. But she has to be resolute and answer this steady look of Annie's by . . . you know. And then the gull. And then the very end, the reading, Annie says, "Oh, the poor thing. He probably lost his way in the dark." Now here's the place where we have to get into the voice, the ominous note . . . "But it isn't dark, Annie. There's a full moon." You could read it a different way, "But it *isn't* dark, AnnieX. There's a full moon!" That doesn't carry the same implication of "There's something funny here." So it would read, ANNIE: "Oh, the poor thing, he probably lost his way in the dark." "But it isn't dark, Annie. There's a full moon." (flat, quiet) It's a down, you see. Instead of it being a climactic, end-of-the-sequence note in the voice, she should depress it down. Well, that's all we have for that sequence. I think it's a matter of how it goes along with the other girl, Miss Pleschett Do you have any thoughts at all about it?

TIPPI: No.

It is an important switch after that row outside the house. So there's a lot to convey in t he face here, especially during that phone call. So when it started with a sign of a very cool expression, and then gradually begins to warm up, you see.

END OF SEQUENCE
END OF TAPE #2

Tape #3

THE CHILDREN'S GULL PARTY

Well, we're up on the dunes, now, having a martini. I don't think we want her really drunk. I think as much as we dare go is the use of that kind of speech where one has had a couple of drinks and you begin to articulate more carefully. I think that's about as far as we dare go. I we're going to have to, you know . . . Now and again we're going to hear the sound of the children off down below, so in playing the scene we'll constantly look down there, you see . . . you will, you know. She says, "I have several jobs." "What do you do?" "Well, I do different things on different days." "Like what?" That's the first change of expression there. "Well, on Mondays and Wednesdays I work for travelers aid at the airport." "Helping travelers?" "Yes." I think she looks away from him, I think turns . . . she's embarrassed. Well it grows on her, when she . . . doesn't look away until he says, "Like what?" You're looking at him. "I do different things on different days." "Like what?" "Well, on Mondays and Wednesdays" now you look at the children "I work for travelers aid at the airport." "Helping travelers?" "Yes." And then I think for a moment she recovers and looks round at him. "So what's wrong with thatX Mr. Brenner?" And then she breaks again . . . oh these are very tiny nuances. "Well, on Tuesdays I take a course on General Semantics at Berkeley. That's not a job, of course. I just take it because . . ." It jumps here. "Then on Thursdays and Fridays . . ." Now when the little Korean boy through school, she really feels it kind of stupid. It's so piddling, this thing. Now I think she recovers. "On Fridays, what do you do then?" "Nothing." Now she recover . . . now she's got a joke to make. "I go to bird shops on Fridays." Then she recovers here a bit from this awkwardness. Now she recovers from embarrassmen "You know what I was doing in that shop?" "What?" Now she should work up an enthusiasm for a gag. She always loves a gag, this girl. Now she says, "Well I have an aunt, you see . . . Aunt Tessa. She's seventy years old and very prim and straight-laced . . ." You sort of purse your lips over that. "She's coming home from Europe at the end of the month and I'm going to give her a mynah bird." "What'll it say?" "Well, XXXXXXXXXX you'll think me very bold, sir." "No, tellme." Then she whispers. He laughs, then she does change. "That's silly, isn't it?" "That's just silly and XXXXXXXX childish." I think there again, she builds it up to a big laugh, and then collects herself. This is all part of her . . . in meeting this whole atmosphere . . . this whole . . . the Brenners and she's talked to Annie . . . so her life, her background . . . If she'd been tellin this in the Hungry XX I Nightclub in San Francisco to a group, it would have all gone down very well . . . now it seems kind of out of place here. I think even thoughX she's embarrassed . . . "That's silly, isn't it. Teaching bird to shock my aunt . . . just silly and childish. I think she's not deprecating hersel She's taking a look; an objective look and saying to herself, "You jerk, sound ridiculous." I think she's accusing herself as much as anything else.

There isn't much in the gull attack except that . . . well, we'll work that out mostly on the children.

TIPPI: These were originally bluejays, weren't they?

Yes. We made them gulls because we're near the . . . you know. Somewhere here we had Melanie feel her head. Is that still in here? I think in the end of the scene when she recount about the bird last night at Annie's and the gull ran smack in the front door . . . "Mitch, what's happening?" "I don't know, Melanie. Do you have to back to Annie's?"

"No, I have my things in the car." "Well, you ought to have something to eat before you start back . . . feel a lot better." I think here we need that very sober, you know when he says, "You look (can't make it out) and I am" . . . it's not the attack that shakes her per se. it's the juxtaposition of this attack with the attack of t night before and her own head. In other words, Melanie really represents to the audience the growth of the attack of the bird. You s ee it's reflected in her. In other words, we rely upon, from a story-telling point of view, this is where XXXX we're relying upon Melanie to convey to the audience there's something very strange happening here with these birds.

## THE BIRDS IN THE ROOM

Now I think with the birds in the room it's pretty self-evident that there's a panic INTERFERENCE ON TAPE UNTIL

But in the main, I think Melanie has, as far as I can see, a "screaming, look-out" scene.

### MORE INTERFERENCE

Now here we are, you see . . the attack is over . . . Lydia is gone. I do think at this stage that Melanie should look rather sympathetically and understandingly toward Lydia. It's not in the script. I think this X is another moment when Melanie becomes more integrated into the situation and into the people. So we've got a pretty serious Melanie going for us here . . . and she makes a decision . . . it's very important because . . . we can't . . . it's not covered in the script enoughX, but I have to do that . . . when Melanie says, "I'll take Cathy up to bed"and Mitch says, "Are you staying." MELANIE: "I think I should, don't you?" Lydia observing, making no comment. Well I think it would be nice if Melanie looked, during the sequence, toward Lydia, and realized that Lydia's cracking . . . and it'll be "I think I better stick around," you know, because Melanie looks after Cathy. She may be too presumptious to think that Cathy needs looking after, but I don't think that Melanie staying should come out of the blue. So during the attack, wherever we come upon you, I don't know how we're going to cut it up at the moment . . . but I think that Melanie herself should realize that Lydia's crack and "MaybeX I better stickaround." Now I think, after all, she's fallen for Mitch already, so there's a tie-in here. See, she says, "(can't make it out) with Cathy." Cathy and Melanie go out, leaving alone, Mitch and Lydia.
END OF SEQUENCE

## MONDAY MORNING - THE FIRST LOVE SCENE BETWEEN MELANIE AND MITCH

On Page 93, the opening scene indicates Melanie waking up. We want to change this to Melanie brushing her teeth at a hand basin in the bedroom. The voice is heard off then . . . take place while Melanie is doing her teeth, so she doesn't have an opportunity to find out exactly where Mitch's voice is coming from. She pulls a comb through her hair and makes her way downstairs, after calling out for Mitch. She gets herself some coffee and that's when she looks out of the window in scene 348. She sees Mitch, and her expression after seeing Mitch is one of a little, extra interest . . . Maybe a faint brush of a smile. Then she makes her way out and gathers her fur coat from the hall and goes out to wait for him. After she's waves to him, we do s ee the anticipation on her face which is built up as Mitch comes toward her. And now we see this slight change of expression to one of disappointment when Mitch turns off suddenly and goes into the

house. Of course he comes out again very soon, so her interest XXXXX warms up again when he comes out. Now in the scene that follows I think it should be played quite dead pan, all the humorous comments about birds and the revolution of birds, but gradually, as indicated by the script, it develops into a more serious discussion which automatically leads them into their embrace. I think that's pretty well what we XXXX said in that sequence.
END OF SEQUENCE.

LYDIA'S RETURN FROM THE FAWCETT FARM

This scene concerns itself with Lydia in the bedroom and Melanie attending upon her. In the early stages I think that Melanie is solicitous and rather like a nurse, you know, her general attitude. At the same time, she should have the opportunity when listening to Lydia's story of her husband and so forth, we should be conscious that Melanie has become deeply interested in the type of people she normally, as a socialite, would never hav encountered, so that her listening to Lydia is very important here. It mustn' be just dead pan. It must be . . . she must have some indication of Melanie's being absorbed by this. As I said before, we didn't record it. There is a moment when Lydia expresses her doubt about liking Melanie. I think the key line when Melanie says, "Is that so important, Mrs. Brenner?..You're liking me Up to this point, I think it was on the previous page, 109, when Melanie says, "Would you like to rest now, Mrs. Brenner?" and she starts to move away. Lydia then says, "No, no, don't go yet." That gives Melanie an opportunity to walk slowly XXXX back into the room and then comeX to a sudden stop when she says, "Is that so important, Mrs. Brenner . . . you're liking me?" later on in the scene, Melanie says, "Why don't you try to sleep now, Mrs. Brenner?" I think she drops her rather stiff attitude. I think the stiff attitude is only momentary . . . After she's finished saying, "I think it might also matter to Mitch. I think Melanie, during Lydia's speech, when she says, "I wouldn't want to be left alone. I don't think I could bear being left alone . . . I . . . I . . . forgive me. This business of the birds has me upset. I don't know what I'd do if Mitch weren't here." There I think she regains her compassion for the woman, during that speech. We w ant to watch the listening part there.

And then she warms up more when she offers to go to the school and bring Cathy back. Perhaps we might have a final closeup of Melanie at the door after Lydia has said, "Thank you for the tea." We could even warm her up a little more there.
END OF SEQUENCE.

THE ARRIVAL AT THE SCHOOL AND THE HAPPENINGS THERE

These actions are pretty straight-forward as indicated by the script. It's a matter of how interesting we can Melanie sitting there smoking. There isn't much she can do. We have the voices of the children in the background. The audience's XXXXX interest, naturally, are in the gathering of the birds behind her which Melanie is unaware of until she sees the final bird arrive. That's when she jumps up in alarm and goes into the school to warn Annie. And then the rest is the action of the birds chasing the children and Melanie grabbing the little girl and getting into the automobile.
END OF SEQUENCE

## THE TIDES RESTAURANT SCENE

Now we get a very business-like Melanie. She's on the phone to her father, and she's surrounded more or less with a lot of different types from the town; the restaurant owner, the comic old Mrs. Bundy . . . and here I think we should see Melanie holding her own quite well. I think she's emerging a little with a practical approach toward what should be done, so that she's reasonably aggressive here. I think that when she says her lines . . . and even says to Deke Carter about the television going, "Would you turn that down, please." Not in an unfriendly way but in a very practical way. So her phone call to the father is clear and direct, e specially when she says, "No, I can't come home now, I just XXXXXXXX can't, Daddy. How is it there, I mean, are th birds in the sky? No trouble, huh. No, I don't know when. I simply can't leave now. Tell mother not to worry. Bye, Daddy, good bye." Very practical, she's got business to do. And I think that holds pretty well for her all the way through. Now her conversation with Mitch, we don't hear. We'll probably have to write out . . . I'll write out some special words for that phone call.

### INTERFERENCE

Until she hangs up. And I think it's fairly straightforward. You know, we've got to get a very positive voice, good authority. That'll be most important. On Page 129, bottom of 128 - 129, Melanie says, "I think they were after the children." Let's go back a few sentences. I mean when they talk with Sholes about the flock of gulls catch her. Mrs. Bunday says, "The gulls were after your fish, Mr.Sholes, really. Let's be logical about this." MELANIE; "What were the crows after at the school?" There she underscores it herself. Mrs. Bundy replys, "What do you think they were after, Miss Daniels?" "I think they were after the children." "For what purpose?" "To kill them." very quietly, not melodramatic, "To kill them." Melanie Daniels is a smart girl. She behaves this way. She doesn't dramatize it . . . doesn't let it run away with her. "I don't know why." She mustn't say, (breathless) "I don't know why!" She's still positive, says to the children, "To kill them." Mrs. Bundy, hoping to get on over on her, "Why." MELANIE; "I don't know why." Mrs. Bundy, XX"I thought not, etc. etc." X I think it's very important for Melanie to be well controlled here. I'd like to see her kind of stand out, so th ey have to look at this girl, "Well," you know, they're impress by her. I'll photograph that

### INTERFERENCE ON TAPE

I think on Page 131 where Melanie says, "Maybe they're all protecting the species. Maybe they're tired of being shot at and roasted in ovens and things." Mrs. Bundy, "Are you discussing game birds. Now all birds are not game birds, you know." "I don't know anything about birds except that they're attacking this town." There again, she's got to have bite with this. And I think that goes along just as is. Now we get comments here and there from her until Mitch arrives. Now she doesn't have a lot to say there, after Mitch comes. No, she's pretty well a listener here, until Page 139 . . . until she sees the gulls out of the window
END OF SEQUENCE


## THE ATTACK ON THE TOWN

Now, we get page 141 of the script where Mitch runs out and tells Melanie to stay back in here. She is a witness to the whole of the gas explosion and so forth. Now, we've got to be very careful, Tippi, here, that we don't make our expressions too strong, because we have XXXX a long way to go here. If we explode all our gunpowder here, as it were . . . in other words, if the expression watching the car go up and the gas station blowX up . . . if we wake those express ions too strong, then we've no where to go later. Of course, we do have to go pretty frantic later on. I think what we've got do, maybe after . . . maybe durin I don't khow whether we can do it after, actually . . . XXXX maybe both. But I really think that we ought to get the makeup changed toward the end of the telephone booth and, if not there, by the time they arrive at the school to pick up Cathy and we find the dead Annie there. I think she should look washed out, because we're going to have, in the phone booth, real hysteria.

TIPPI: (Can't understand)

Oh, of course, I've written the whole thing from her point of view, you see. The whole of the attack is from Melanie's viewpoint, so we've got to look at the shape of that from beginning to end and see how we can build it. And I'm not sure that the pale makeup won't be necessary once we get her out of that phone booth. Well, you see, the script is pretty well clear on what Melanie does in her behavior. But we have to bear in mind one thing; she is not only trapped in a phone booth, but she's got to have on her mind, all the time, where's Mitch. Where is he. And you see by the script, I've made her open the doors a couple of times and then be driven back into the booth. So we'll have to XX work that out, because this is where we may, in a subtle way..we might do it in a couple of stages, like the lips down or take that color out of her cheeks . . . maybe in two stages. And then we must . . . I don't know what the hair's going to look like here, but that should begin to go. I think that that pretty well covers the phone booth scene. When they go back into the Tides, of course, that's fairly straightforward there . . . And they run to Annie's house. Now of course, they have to be careful of the crows going by. I notice Evan's put at the top of Page 150B, CLOSEUP MELANIE, realizing that Annie is dead and wonder what Mitch's reaction will be. That's going to be hard to photograph, isn't it. I think that she should more or less freeze here And, by this time, I think we will have changed the makeup so that we'll get the distress in the face with the help of the makeup as well, because I don't think there's too much she can do here except to plead with him . . . "Mitch, don't," when he wants to throw the stone at the birds. "Let's get out of here."

TIPPI: Do you suppose when she's watching him throwing the stone at the birds that she'd be rather calm about it, like "Oh, Mitch, don't.."

No, I think she can explode a bit. I'll tell you why . . . "Oh, Mitch, don't! Get Cathy!" I think it's frantic there, because she was with those birds when they chased the kids down the street. No, I think she's really scared that . . . after all, she's been in that phone booth. She's seen a lot of birds attacking I think she'd be rather frantic, because you've got a contrasting line coming up here . . . on the topX of Page 150C. "Mitch, can't leave her out there" . . . you see. So the big contrast with that line,XXX the XXXXX emotional line, and the other, frantic, "Don't throw the stones at the birds.." there's a difference. It drops there.

Well, they go cautiously back to the car again, and she says, "You drive, Mitch. I don't think they're coming." Now she has to listen t o Cathy's story. I think she's quite dead pan here. I think she's numb with the whole thing . . . because, you know, the death of Annie, after all she does, she says, "Well how will Mitch take it." I think she can XXXXXXXX look at him. I mean, I think we could follow that up as . . . if Mitch comes, then she can look at him and exchange a look between the dead body and Mitch when he comes back . . . and then she says, "Mitch, don't leave her there." I think she says itX not only for humanitarian reasons, but I think she wants . . . you know . . . she was really very much in love with him. I think that thought's in her mind as well so that we'll give it . . . we'll make it a double look. She looks at the body and looks at Mitch and says, "Let's go," and she looks at him; back to the body . . . back at Mitch, "Don't leave her there." I XX think that's the way we can put that over there. END OF SEQUENCE

# *Marnie*

Hitchcock's full monopolization of these conversations were perhaps a portent of disaster with Hedren. He had lost in his bid to have Princess Grace of Monaco (the former Grace Kelly) return to the screen with his next project, *Marnie,* so the project fell to the exhausted Hedren, for whom the production process of *The Birds* had been particularly difficult. During the penultimate attack on Melanie, the actress collapsed in a frenzy when one of the gulls scratched her eyelid. This was understandable after nearly a week of having living and stuffed birds thrown at her.

*Marnie,* fortunately for Hedren, promised to be an even better showcase of her potential talents. The story would feature Hedren as a sexually frigid thief who is caught and blackmailed into marriage by her former employer. It's a fascinating film at every point in the process. Even Hunter wrote the initial drafts of the screenplay and Hitchcock asked the writer to explain to Hedren the psychological complexity of the part:

To Tippi—

Hitch asked me to explain the psychological complex of the character MARNIE. To do this we should first examine MARNIE'S childhood trauma which is the key to her subsequent adult behavior.

At the age of 4 or 5 the Oedipal situation is at its' strongest in all children. This means, in its simplest terms, that MARNIE wants to go to bed with her father and considers her mother a rival for his love. Marnie's father, as we know, is a sailor aboard a ship somewhere in a battle zone. On the night of the incident that will shape Marnie's future life, a sailor whom her mother is entertaining, enters Marnie's bedroom by mistake and approaches the bed. She mistakes him for her father at first and, frightened by the thunder storm outside, succumbs to the sailor's gentleness and kindness. The sequence serves only to reaffirm her own fantasy concerning her real-life father. The fantasy achieves frightening reality when her mother enters the room and mistakes the sailor's friendliness for a sexual advance on the child. In short, Marnie, who wants her father, whose mother is her rival, is presented with a real-life situation in which a father figure displays affection toward her and is immediately attacked by the rival, her mother. The situation ends in the murder of the sailor. Unhappily, this coincides with the death of her father at sea—an event which is never adequately explained to Marnie. In the child's mind, the death of the sailor in her bedroom and the death of her real father at sea become one. The equation to her is clear and simple: "My father made love to me and my mother killed him for it."

How does this relate to Marnie's later behavior? The notion that her crimes are a substitution for sex is not a valid one. She does not rob safes because she desires men. Instead, her crimes are in effect a re-enactment of what happened to her that night in her bedroom. She commits the crimes in an attempt to find a different and more satisfactory solution to the situation. Long ago she stole her father and he was killed for it. Now, symbolically, she steals her father again every time she commits a crime and hopes that the solution will be a different one—he will not die.

Symbolically, the situation <u>seems</u> to change each time she commits a crime, because she then is allowed to enjoy the time-honored symbol for father, The Horse. She is indeed ecstatic whenever she is with Forio. But, a temporary and seemingly satisfying solution to a deep psychological wound is never truly relieving unless someone understands what is causing the emotional disturbance to begin with. Marnie finds no relief. After her scenes with Forio she immediately seeks out her mother each time and, guilt-ridden, gives her part of the money she has stolen. (In a sense, she is returning "father" to the person who rightfully owns him.) The entire pattern is compulsive because she is desperately trying to work out an answer to her childhood experience. She is, if you will, emotionally arrested at the age of 4 or 5. The reason she so fears anything more than casual sexual contact with a man is because any man becomes a representation of her father. If she goes to bed with him, if she accepts his love, something dire and unimaginably horrible will happen. The scene wherein Mark forces himself upon her is graphic proof of this. It comes too close to the childhood trauma, and threatens the entire fabric of her life. She attempts suicide following it.

Hitchcock continued to document his filmmaking process with transcripts with this film. The idea is a blessing to historians and filmmakers, as it gives us a chance to eavesdrop on production conferences that we are seldom privy to. There are three reels of taped conversation between Hitchcock, Hunter, and the film's production designer, Robert Boyle, on the overall production design for the film.

The following excerpts are the most accurate documentary picture of just how Hitchcock worked. Determining the authorship is complex, as these pages will indicate, but they also show that despite the obvious collaboration, Hitchcock was the director. These conversations were held early in the film's scripting (as evidenced by Hunter's presence). Readers will recall that Jay Presson Allen replaced Hunter to do the final drafts of the screenplay.

REEL ONE

| | |
|---|---|
| MR. HITCHCOCK: | The film is going to open with a girl, back view, going into a railroad station at Hartford, Connecticut. At present, I don't know what time of the day we can shoot it because we don't want it full of crowds because it may cover her up. The essential part is that we follow her back view into the station as she goes to the desk or booking office. |
| EVAN HUNTER: | The ticket window. But Hitch, it should be on a Friday evening because she goes directly there from robbing the safe. |
| MR. HITCHCOCK: | Well, we needn't say it's Friday evening as long as we don't people it with too many people, we're going to have put our extras in it anyway however we shoot it there. And she goes to the ticket window and buys a ticket. We still follow her into the station as she looks up and we go up to New York, you see. We go close enough to her to see the color of her hair, and finally she goes on to the platform down toward the train. Or it can be empty waiting for the train to come in. I don't know, we've got to look into that, you see, or you can probably be going east to find out all this information for us. And we end up with a CLOSE SHOT on a rather bulky handbag under her arm. So that would constitute the first scene. We'll have to investigate whether we shoot it all in the station, whether we make a traveling plate of it or what the best way to handle that is, you see. I feel that we ought to cheat like they do in the Italian films and have nobody around if we can. Because otherwise we don't draw enough attention to the girl. The next sequence cuts immediately to an open safe and a crowd around it in an office. This would require an impression of an office, and maybe we can have one of those kind of offices with glass screens around it. So we get an impression of an office beyond, which we can either make as a backing or something because we needn't show too much activity or we can fake a set behind it. And the essence of this scene is that the safe has been robbed and there is a group of people. Mainly that constitutes the scene in which the manager or proprietor or the high official, whoever he may be, is known in the story as a MR. STRUTT, is the selfconscious figure who apparently gave this girl a job, without proper references and we indicate that he was obviously impressed by her other than her ability as a clerk or whatever she was, so he becomes a central guilty figure. So pictorially it's a GROUP SCENE, you see. |

| | |
|---|---|
| MR. HUNTER: | Also, it's an accounting firm, Bob. |
| MR. BOYLE: | Wouldn't Hartford—would it be insurance? Probably would be insurance, wouldn't it? |
| MR. HUNTER: | Well, we want it to be accounting because he comes in later on . . . |
| MR. HITCHCOCK: | He comes in later on in the story. This man is a very important figure, because he comes in, that's why we . . . the scene will be concentrated on this man and we read a complete picture of this man falling for the girl when he shouldn't have done. It's the chief cashier who's a girl—almost accuses him of having an affair with her—which he didn't. As we shall find later. . . . but nevertheless he feels very guilty about the whole thing and he's right on the spot. There're police around and so forth, etc. Now, from that we continue the next scene down a hotel corridor—still back view on the girl and she's now carrying a suitcase which is brand new, wrapped in brown paper and . . . |
| MR. HUNTER: | Excuse me, may I break in here a minute. Do we need to tell Bob what we need in the way of a physical thing in the office since modus operandi's going to figure in this, you know. Her access to the safe. |
| MR. HITCHCOCK: | I don't think so. |
| MR. HUNTER: | We don't? |
| MR. HITCHCOCK: | Not for our opening scene. As long as we show the safe as being robbed, but our dialogue will tell us a lot there. Now in this next scene, following the office scene as I said, we're going down a corridor in a hotel and we can establish this as a hotel by possibly a clear—a floor weight or, I don't know, depends what type of hotel we use. I don't think it should be a big hotel. It should be a small hotel, rather cheesy. But we have to establish within this corridor what it is, you see. |
| MR. HUNTER: | Not too cheesy, you know. Not like the 47th Street ones, off Broadway. |
| BOB BOYLE: | Where are we in this hotel? |
| MR. HUNTER: | New York City. |
| MR. BOYLE: | New York City. |
| MR. HUNTER: | But not a luxury hotel, either. |
| MR. HITCHCOCK: | No. And she finally goes into a room and there we see another suitcase, clothes on the bed, and now she tears the paper in which is the brand new suitcase and there are other boxes on the bed showing purchases, and the scene in this little bedroom constitutes her change of clothes and the cutting out of labels and so forth, you see, and then eventually we go and follow her into a bathroom and she goes 'round behind the door and by this time she's taken off |

probably part of her clothes and we go into the bathroom and we just go to the head and we've never seen her face yet and right on the head down into the basin and we see the dark very dark brown dye flowing out of the hair into the basin. And it just swirls around this dye—and for the first time she lifts her face. The hair is now blond and we see her face, for the first time. Now—we go then to Penn Station or a Greyhound Station. Have we decided? . . . .

MR. HUNTER:    I think the bus terminal would be better. You know, we've had one railroad station . . .

MR. HITCHCOCK:    Whatever it is—it will probably be the bus terminal.

MR. HUNTER:    The Port Authority Bus Terminal on, I think, it's 38th and 8th.

MR. BOYLE:    Not to leave the hotel room so soon. She has no reason . . . she's just trying to pick something that's a nonentity, isn't she? It's neither too poor or too rich. It's some lost hotel.

MR. HITCHCOCK:    Quality of the hotel . . . you're talking about the quality of the hotel?

MR. BOYLE:    Well, yes, I'm going back to the hotel. What kind of a hotel she would pick. Obviously she has money, so she could live anywhere.

MR. HUNTER:    Yes, but she doesn't want to call attention to herself in any way, you see. She's going in there to change her identity really.

MR. HITCHCOCK:    That's all she is. . . . so that she would choose a very quiet hotel. Very quiet, very unobtrusive hotel. So you can debate this again, you know. A girl can get lost in the biggest hotel just as well. You know, so that you see that there are many people up and down the corridors and the elevator and so forth, but. . . .

MR. BOYLE:    Yes, that's true.

MR. HITCHCOCK:    We could debate that, but we don't have to decide that finally now.

MR. BOYLE:    Could be a business hotel.

MR. HITCHCOCK:    Like the New Yorker or the Commodore.

MR. BOYLE:    People come and go all the time.

MR. HITCHCOCK:    As a matter of fact. . . .

MR. BOYLE:    Or the Biltmore across from . . .

MR. HITCHCOCK:    The way to establish that is to establish a facade of a hotel with so many windows, you know.

MR. BOYLE:    Yes.

MR. HITCHCOCK:    So, if you state that fact, you know, a mass of windows . . .

MR. BOYLE:    The Commodore would be very good.

MR. HITCHCOCK:    The Commodore. Anyway . . . we can debate that afterwards. Now . . . the only reason I bring up the question, Evan, as to whether it should be a railroad station or bus

|  |  |
|---|---|
|  | station. Can you leave a suitcase there . . . for good? In the lockups, it's no good. |
| MR. BOYLE: | Well, sure it is. Why not? |
| MR. HITCHCOCK: | Because they empty them every twenty-four hours. |
| MR. BOYLE: | Well, what does she care what they do with it? It'll vanish from sight. She's going to throw the key away, anyway. So they'll take the bag out of the locker and take it someplace else. She's never going to claim it. What does she care? |
| MR. HITCHCOCK: | Right. Well, anyway this bus depot. She deposits the old bag. She arrives with two bags, you see. An old one and a new one. The old bag is deposited and then she goes to the bus with the new bag, you see. And the bus drives off. I think we're going to label it to Maryland, Laurel . . . |
| MR. HUNTER: | Well, no, I play a scene where she buys a ticket to Laurel, Maryland. And he tells her when the bus is leaving and when it's going to arrive and all that. |
| MR. HITCHCOCK: | On arriving at her destination there's a station wagon belonging to a hotel waiting for her at the destination, which we've got at present as . . . |
| MR. HUNTER: | Laurel, Maryland. |
| MR. HITCHCOCK: | Laurel, Maryland, you see. This isn't final, you see. Laurel, Maryland, of course, is a well known race track center and so forth. From here there's a station wagon waiting with the name of a hotel on the side. And she's driven . . . and we may have a couple of ESTABLISHING SHOTS of going through the countryside to establish we're in the country, you see. And then it eventually arrives at what we call the Old Colonial Hotel. This hotel has to have a bit of class about it, you know, it's where retired people can live, there are horse people. It's in . . . it should be a hotel within its own small grounds in this area and it should be related to racing, hunting, you know, that's the atmosphere that we take her into. Because don't forget we've got a strange mysterioso working for us. Because, after all, you've seen a girl who's a petty thief or a small thief changing her hair, clothes and so forth, and now she's arriving in completely contrapuntal surroundings—beautiful countryside and a rather smart or traditional hotel . . . |
| MR. HUNTER: | And she's been here . . . you know . . . she's recognized here . . . she's been here many times before. |
| MR. HITCHCOCK: | Now we come into the lobby. The lobby of this hotel conveys the same quality. And when she goes to the desk a man carries her bag in and the woman clerk recognizes her immediately, addresses her by name and says, 'Your riding clothes came back a week ago' or something or yesterday or whatever we establish . . . 'and they're in your room' or she |

asks, you know. We establish anyway she's left clothes there, which still sets up a mystery. And now she goes from there and we see her change—is that right?

MR. HUNTER: No, I think we should simply show her coming right into where the horse is kept.

MR. HITCHCOCK: That's what I meant.

MR. HUNTER: Oh, I thought you meant showing her change.

MR. HITCHCOCK: No, no, she goes upstairs and from there that indicates she's going upstairs to change and now we go right to the stables where she arrives.

MR. HUNTER: This is another place now. It's not a part of the hotel grounds.

MR. HITCHCOCK: That's why we might have to show the station wagon taking her there. So she might get out of the station wagon at some stables. Now, these stables should be . . . I think they're a type of stable where they train yearlings and other people are allowed to keep horses. This is very important to find out. What kind of stables this would be. She keeps a horse there. But it's vital to our story that she knows about the training of horses, especially race horses. And we have to get that over. You see, what happens now with a regularly trained race horse . . . it goes to stables from one meet to another. That's how it works out now. That, I found out, they don't go back to training stables. In England they do. But they don't necessarily—once a horse has been trained . . . so this should be a training stable.

MR. BOYLE: And also a boarding stable.

MR. HUNTER: It's a boarding stable. She's not training a horse there, she's just boarding it.

MR. BOYLE: Exercise boys and people like that who work with the horses.

MR. HITCHCOCK: And also they might . . . we might choose a place where they have a track . . . a training track.

MR. HUNTER: They would have.

MR. BOYLE: Or training rings, at least.

MR. HITCHCOCK: Well, I know tracks where they have them out here in Northridge. Lot of these people have training tracks. Starting gate, schooling, what they call schooling, and so forth. Now . . . we show her riding, which calls for some beautiful landscapes, and her riding in the distance on this horse. Not any particular way . . . around and so forth . . . and then we go to CLOSEUPS, which will mean plates and things, for her closeups showing her enjoying it and her hair blowing and it's very important that we establish here one big CLOSEUP of the hair blowing and as she's riding . . .

MR. BOYLE: And come back to that.

| | |
|---|---|
| MR. HITCHCOCK: | And it's a motif, you see. It's a light motif that goes through the film. Again, it's going to be presented in such a way that you say, well I don't get this—we want to mystify the audience. The contrast between the thievery and the way she was dressed . . . quite modestly, as a clerk, and soforth, with this proprietory interest in this particular horse riding thing she has. Now, from there we go to visit her mother. Her mother is going to live in Baltimore. In one of those streets where they have all those steps . . . you know, the whitewash steps. This, again, is a tremendous contrast because, you see, we've practically shown we've done all this cinematically. We've told the mystery of this girl in a series of images of pictures and settings and backgrounds. That's why they're all very important because they do make statements all the time. Now we get this cheesy, long Baltimore residential street. It's almost like a . . . you haven't been to Baltimore, have you? Well, it's like the north of England street . . . just the same . . . oh yes, just like the north of England. Rows of houses and chimneys. But the one feature of Baltimore is that people take great pride in their steps because all the houses have one step up from the sidewalk. And they're always done with pumice stone or whitewashed or painted white. You get this vista of all these steps, you see, and she drives down this street, maybe in a taxi. |
| MR. HUNTER: | If we can, Bob, if we can get it near the water someplace . . . |
| MR. HITCHCOCK: | What would be nice if at the end of the street we could see masts of ships because this is very important later on. And they do have them. There are probably streets around there with this terribly sordid atmosphere—the saloon at the corner and the ships down at the bottom. And the taxi stops and she gets out. Then, you know, opens the door—or the door's opened for her. Now she's in her mother's home, which is pretty. . . . it has to be the size of the real house—quite small, narrow passage, the sitting room in the front and the one story up to the bedrooms, staircase up in the hallway. There, of course, we have the scene where she meets her mother and the little woman who looks after her. And we play the whole scene . . . and the girl's familiar with the place and there'll be a kitchen required. |
| MR. HUNTER: | This should be a pretty dowdy place. |
| MR. HITCHCOCK: | Oh, it will be dowdy. Bob, we'll eventually get the photographs of the real interior there. That'll be done. We'll get all that. But the external atmosphere is very important, to show again, the contrast of the riding and she's now in a nice suit, not too showy, but fairly conservative and she's |

blond. And she goes in and now we introduce the mother and now something of her. The fact that she brings gifts to them and that she works for a millionaire and her mother belives her. We characterize her mother as a cautious woman. The mother is grey-haired, but not too unattractive to look at. And so we set her up there. Then we go from there to the outside of . . . again, the railroad station.

MR. HUNTER:     We have her arriving, Hitch, in a new town.

MR. HITCHCOCK:  That's what I mean. This, again, is a motif shot. It must be a bus depot, we can decide this later. Railroad station. What the images must say—here she is again in a new town. CAMERA DOLLIES RIGHT IN to her and almost as she's looking about which way to go—right up to the hair. And it's now red. And from that we go to the inside of a movie house. Evan, I'm just going to record for Bob that if we don't have the ships masts and atmosphere at the end of the street, we can make a matte of it and put it in afterwards.

MR. BOYLE:      I think that's important.

MR. HITCHCOCK:  It's important for later on, yes. So again we have the arrival, as I've just described, and then we LAP DISSOLVE to the interior of a movie house. All we see is the screen.

MR. HUNTER:     Black and white.

MR. HITCHCOCK:  In black and white. Pictures in black and white, but of course, surrounding we're in color and the silhouettes of the people. On the screen we're going to have a little satire on . . . we're going to play a foreign film and we're going to have a couple of Italian lovers, you know, looking down, arm in arm, looking down. Then we CUT to what they see and it's just muddy water flowing in a gutter and they look up at each other and then kiss. And with this scene going on behind us our girl comes up and we now see that she's in usher's uniform. We'll have to have a soft glow light above us, in the gangway behind the seats. She's got a flashlight in her hand and then a couple come and she shows them . . .

MR. HUNTER:     Are we going to use our line?

MR. HITCHCOCK:  No, the line's coming out.

MR. HUNTER:     They're coming out of . . .

MR. HITCHCOCK:  That's later on. That's not now.

MR. HUNTER:     I think we should do it now. Later on is going to be the robbery.

MR. HITCHCOCK:  No, no, she's coming up on her own. We can't have people coming out. See, she comes up and then meets a new couple and shows them down to their seats. Now we're going to go out and do a more or less ESTABLISHING SHOT of the cashier's desk. Right in front of the house with the money tinkling and from that we're going to PAN and she comes out of the door and stands, watching, so we see her intent and then from this point on we're going to establish the manager and how she's popular with everybody, she's so worked herself in, she's popular with the cashier, and so forth and with the ticket-taker and she's well esconced at this movie house. To such an extent that when the manager, and it's about nine or . . .

MR. HUNTER: This is . . . all the people are going in. It's the last show . . . they're getting the last receipts.

MR. HITCHCOCK: And the manager comes down . . . he takes up the takings up to date—there's a few stragglers coming in and . . . in fact, she gives him a hand with it, she's able to come out because the house is nearly full. We establish it's near the end of the evening and she's able to help him carry it up . . . carry the money up and they go up . . . and they go up to the office, his office—that has to be worked out. We've got to work out a whole layout of a movie house and the manager's office, and so forth and where it will be. And she goes in and leaves the money there and walks out. We follow her down and eventually she does a little bit more of her job and the manager comes out again and that's when she says to her girl friend, the other usher, we establish that she says, 'I'm going to the girl's room', and she goes upstairs, instead of going to the toilet. She goes straight to the manager's office, goes over to a filing cabinet, feels in the back, takes out a glove, takes out a key from the glove and bends down and opens the safe. Then you cut—you don't see anymore—and go to the manager who is down in front talking to the cashier or talking to somebody. And he wanders around and we stay with him all the time. He wanders back into the theatre, stands looking at the screen and we show now a couple, same couple—they are looking up into the sky on the screen and there's a big crane with a lot of dirt and they look at it, turn and fall into each other's arms. They embrace and eventually the manager leaves and wanders up the stairs and wanders right outside, almost outside his office . . .

MR. HUNTER: His hand on the knob practically.

MR. HITCHCOCK: . . . and one of the operators is going to be . . . 'Oh George' . . . and the operator comes down and he starts to talk about the condition of the projectors—that, 'That lens must be loose. We've been going in and out of focus, you know, you better do something about it. He says, 'Well, I . . .' and a long conversation between these two, right outside the office, occurs and it goes on and on. See, the timing will be such—it will be worked out timing-wise so that you know that she's only just about had time to do the job. And eventually the phone rings inside the office, so he dismisses the operator and opens the door and goes in and there's nobody there at all. He picks up the phone and he says, 'Well, I haven't had time to count the money yet'. He says, 'I must say it's the best business we've done with a foreign picture for a long time.' And he says, 'I'll call back and when I've counted it I'll let you know what tonight's business was.' He hangs up and turns and goes to the cabinet, takes out the glove, takes out the key, opens the safe and freezes. There's a straight cut to the head and the flying hair galloping on the horizon with the blond hair.

MR. HUNTER: Can I go back on this a minute? Bob. Is Bob going to get us that information we need on the projector?

MR. HITCHCOCK: Oh yes . . . sure.

MR. BOYLE: Oh yes, I can do that. You can have some fun about the projectionist saying these foreign pictures are always out of focus.

MR. HUNTER: We're going to have a man and woman coming out of the theatre and the woman is going to say to the man, 'Well, I don't know what it was all about, but it was lovely.' And he's going to say, 'Lovely' as they go out.

MR. HITCHCOCK: Now, we're on the motif. Just the flying head . . . hair blowing, fame, ecstasy almost, on the horse. And now again we get Philadelphia.

MR. HUNTER: In a long shot.

MR. HITCHCOCK: And the horse goes into a long shot. There's a long dissolve while she's galloping in the land, with this beautiful shot and then we get a long lap dissolve and there she is coming out of the station at Philadelphia. Again, she looks around, camera goes right up to the head, same motif and the hair is changed again. It's a very soft honey-brown. Then from there you see the pencil going down the situations, vacant, in the classified. There's one, assistant cashier. Now we come to Rutlands, which is now going to be the glass works—glass manufacturers. We establish the outside and then we go inside and there she is in the office of the general manager, MR. WARD. This ought to be a very small set of an office so that MARK, the leading man, is sitting on a table behind the door, glancing through trade magazines and she goes in and sits down. The scene is going to play all from this central figure—one of the proprietors, MARK RUTLAND, his name is—from his point of view. As the interview starts he just lays down the magazine because the image he gets is her legs and the way she sits at the chair facing the other man. Of course, as you know, the scene is that she doesn't have sufficient references until our friend, watching her, gives the nod . . . 'Engage her' . . . and she's engaged. She goes out, hardly observing this man behind the door, as the door opens. She may just glance at him, but it doesn't mean anything—she goes out. Now comes the first day in the office. Now we have to establish very clearly the whole set-up which relates to her position. The scene will start—the first day at work will start in the same office of the general manager—who has called the other main cashier—whoever we decide—whatever the technical aspects of it are—introduces her and she's taken off.

MR. BOYLE:      But she's a principle—DAWN.

MR. HITCHCOCK:  Yes, she's one of the principles—her name is DAWN. And she's taken through to this office where you see the set-up and she sets herself . . . here's the work . . . and beyond it is the safe and possibly, it hasn't worked out yet, what the other personnel are . . . and this is some of the information we've got to get from this office and so forth . . . and these offices are adjacent or connected to the factory. But the set-up is our girl is in one division, there's another division, and these could be glass things, and beyond that is a little cubby-hole with a safe in it. And an important factor about this set-up is that there is a drawer, in the inner office, which is locked. This drawer contains petty cash and it also contains, stuck on the inside of the drawer, the combination of the safe, which is a method which we discover they use here. The combination is kept locked in a drawer. So now the scene develops with the arrival of the junior partner, who goes to the safe with his own key, goes to the drawer with his own key and looks in, closes it and goes and opens another thing on the safe which he observes and then the thing that she watches as he goes out is the key chain on his pants.

REEL TWO

MR. HITCHCOCK:  Where are we up to.

MR. HUNTER:     We're up to Terry going out with the key hanging from the chain.

MR. HITCHCOCK:  Did Terry look at her at all? He does, doesn't he?

MR. HUNTER:     Yes, he gives her a big once-over and he also invites Dawn to a poker party that weekend.

MR. HITCHCOCK:  Yes. Our girl now expresses interest in the nature of the company. So Dawn invites her . . . 'why don't you take a look around?' This is where we get our tour of the glass works, and she wanders and we show some of the processes of the manufacturing, especially where they are doing the wine glasses coming on the line and see how that works out. Finally she arrives at the man who engraves those elaborate Steuben things. And another man comes up . . . says, 'Are you interested in our work?' or whatever he makes himself and, of course, it's the leading man, you see . . .

MR. HUNTER:      Who gave the nod to hire her.

MR. HITCHCOCK:      Who gave the nod to hire her. And there's a short scene between them. Does he establish it's a family firm at all there?

MR. HUNTER:      He's going to give a little background of the business in that firm and try to establish some personal contact with her . . . which she fends off . . . keeps it all strictly business.

MR. HUNTER:      The main purport of the scene is that this man was attracted to her right in that office when he gave the nod. This is a further progression of his interest in her. But she's quite unresponsive because she's quite cool and we sense that she's polite but she doesn't want to get involved or anything like that. That we establish.

MR. HUNTER:      She doesn't encourage him in the slightest.

MR. HITCHCOCK:      When she gets back, she . . .

MR. HUNTER:      When she gets back to the office that's when Sam Ward is at the drawer.

MR. HITCHCOCK:      Yes—and now somebody else is at the drawer—the general manager—he's gone to the safe.

MR. HUNTER:      And Dawn tells her that Terry has called back and wondered if she would like to come to the poker party.

MR. HITCHCOCK:      He gave her the once-over and the result of that comes in an invitation to a poker party. And the poker party takes place pretty well as in the book, doesn't it?

MR. HUNTER:      But she's watching this key routine all the time. She's getting this invitation and she accepts it so we get the notion that she's going to the party and wants to gain access to that key.

MR. HITCHCOCK:      And one of the first things she sees at the party is that key chain again. So you can see she's only willing to go to this man's place because there's the key. And, of course, the poker party plays and eventually . . .

MR. HUNTER:      Well, let's tell him . . . do we have to tell him a little about Terry's apartment?

MR. HITCHCOCK:      Yes. Terry's apartment is in Philadelphia. Now, it's got to be fairly comfortable. After all, this man's reasonably well off. He's a partner of the company. The character of it is . . . has there been a woman? His wife left him. . . .

MR. HUNTER:      He's either separated or divorced from his wife . . . one of the two . . . and it's a bachelor apartment now—whether she lived in it at one time or not with him—it's now exclusively his own. He's sort of been playing the field for a year or more with various women around town.

MR. HITCHCOCK:    What we have to find is some block of apartments in Philadelphia. Get some information about some of the interiors.

MR. HUNTER:    It should be a pretty nice apartment though.

MR. HITCHCOCK:    Have it's own kitchen—where they have breakfast—the bacon and eggs and stuff.

MR. HUNTER:    Yes. Remember we discussed this business of an entrance alcove or something separated from where they would be playing poker. So for that later scene we can get him and MARNIE alone in there.

MR. HITCHCOCK:    That will be the lobby, you know, or something like that. Of course, the final scene is that the guy makes a pass at her and she fights him off and so forth. Now, we're back in the office again.

MR. HUNTER:    Right. Where Dawn tells Marnie that Mark has called or . . . they're discussing the poker party and Dawn wants to find out how late she stayed and all that and she lies about it.

MR. HITCHCOCK:    She lies . . . says, 'I left right after you.'

MR. HUNTER:    She had a cup of coffee and left. The phone rings . . .

MR. HITCHCOCK:    She makes some remark about . . . '. . . you didn't rise to it or . . .'

MR. HUNTER:    'Isn't Terry feeling well?'

MR. HITCHCOCK:    'Isn't Terry feeling well?' Yes, that's the remark. The phone rings and it's Mark Rutland. And he wants Marnie to come over with the ledger he needs. He's at his house with a lawyer. They're working over something and he wants Marnie specifically to come over with this ledger that they need . . . and Dawn makes some comment about how the other partner's coming in on it and then takes the key from her own bag and goes to that petty cash draw to get some petty cash to give her for the cab ride. Marnie see that Dawn has a key in her bag. And that's the last we see of that key now for a long, long time or of the safe or the drawer or anything connected with the robbery. From then on nothing about the robbery.

MR. HITCHCOCK:    Now we come to the house of Mark. In this scene, roughly, she arrives. There's another man there, a lawyer working with him over some papers and she's brought something that's pertinent to their discussion.

MR. HUNTER:    Which we need, Bob, we have no . . .

MR. HITCHCOCK:    That we'll get.

MR. HUNTER:    Some clue to the nature . . .

| | |
|---|---|
| MR. HITCHCOCK: | The housekeeper comes in with tea and she observes there are three teacups on the tray. He asks her, Marnie, to pour out the tea and the lawyer says, 'Not for me. I'll have to go.' So he completes his work and goes and then they are left alone. While the lawyer's finishing up she pours her tea and wanders around and then she comes to a cabinet. This is quite important, this cabinet, because it contains pre-Columbian art including a gold necklace and after the man's gone he follows her over and they talk about this cabinet. Apparently his wife collected this soft of stuff and even the necklace . . . she admires this gold . . . this pre-Columbian . . . |
| MR. HUNTER: | His wife is dead. |
| MR. HITCHCOCK: | This gold necklace . . . offers her to try it on, she doesn't want to. The whole object of the scene is that he is trying to indicate to her that his wife has been dead long enough now that he is becoming eligible again. |
| MR. HUNTER: | See, the whole lie is that her husband has recently died. So that he's exploring in this scene whether it's all right for her. It's now all right for him . . . is it all right for her . . . |
| MR. HITCHCOCK: | He has to be very . . . |
| MR. HUNTER: | . . . subtle. |
| MR. HITCHCOCK: | He has to be very subtle and very tentative with it because he barely knows the girl, but yet he's on the make. When she gets embarrassed by it and turns away and goes over, possibly, to the mantelpiece in this room. It should be a very attractive room. A Georgian room. |
| MR. HUNTER: | Yes, and it has stable facilities, Bob, because he later brings the horse there. We decided it should be rather an elegant house, didn't we? |
| MR. HITCHCOCK: | A very elegant house because this sitting room is going to be kept for a reception later on. And it's going to have an upstairs. It should have an entrance hall, a staircase, because on the day of the wedding she's upstairs. |
| MR. HUNTER: | And this is where he used to live with his wife. Definitely. And now he lives there alone with a couple. |
| MR. HITCHCOCK: | Yes, we're going to have a couple. A man and a woman. And she changes something and goes over . . . maybe to the mantelpiece or some other table. You know those small figures of jockeys that race people have to show their colors? We have a couple at home. She admires these, too, and he says, 'Are you interested in racing?' and she says, 'A bit, my father was and so was my uncle . . . they both owned horses.' He says, 'There're my father's colors and there're my uncle's colors.' That leads into the discussion of the interest in horse racing. Which . . . in the book they had the television thing. |

| | |
|---|---|
| MR. HUNTER: | In the meantime we hear distant thunder and the room is getting darker and darker. |
| MR. HITCHCOCK: | So we need a pretty good backing outside that room, don't we? |
| MR. HUNTER: | And there should be a big tree outside in the backyard. Lightning's going to strike that. |
| MR. HITCHCOCK: | And then the storm starts. Now she goes into almost a catatonic state over this thing. At one point—this is why the placing of the cabinet has to be right . . . the French window is blown open and smashes the cabinet of his wife's collections. And shatters it. And finally the girl rushes and she even cowers behind him and makes him turn to hold her. This is the first real contact between the two . . . as a result of this. And we may eventually devise her behaviour as paralleling that when she was a child. Because the thunderstorm was on at the time in the trauma. Out of this discussion of race horses he leads to the question whether she would like to go to the races, one day and so forth. Now . . . do we go straight to the race track. |
| MR. HUNTER: | Straight to the track. |
| MR. HITCHCOCK: | There's no interlude there? |
| MR. HUNTER: | She accepts and leaves. |
| MR. HITCHCOCK: | She accepts and leaves. And now the race track. |
| MR. HUNTER: | The storm passes . . . it calms down. |
| MR. HITCHCOCK: | And we get on the race track. Which we should do with plates. And maybe doubles at a distance. But I can get all the facilities we want there. We may move them away and up into a box to watch a race . . . in the stand there. And the content of this scene is, of course, that there is the first man who says, 'Haven't I seen you before somewhere?' And what is her attitude . . . have we worked out her attitude there? |
| MR. HUNTER: | You see, we're starting a red herring with this thing and the red herring is that she's falling in love with Mark and is not going to do the robbery. The audience thinks. So that when this guy approaches her, her entire attitude is . . . it seems that she doesn't want Mark to find out about this. That she's beginning to like him immensely and is going to reform. So that we slant the scene in that direction. Mark shouldn't find out and she's on the look-out for Mark and when he does come back she covers . . . we're playing it that way. |
| MR. HITCHCOCK: | Following the race track scene he invites her to dinner. At a Philadelphia hotel to meet his mother. He thinks it's less rushing it. He's very tentative about this. |
| MR. HUNTER: | We ought to have a scene in the car as I did in the first draft on the way from the races that night. We need some bridge there from the track . . . to that date. |

| | |
|---|---|
| MR. HITCHCOCK: | So we want to find out a Philadelphia hotel and where he does introduce her to his mother. She begins to realize that this guy's really serious . . . to go to this extent. |
| MR. HUNTER: | And the mother likes her immensely. |
| MR. HITCHCOCK: | At this point we go back to the mother again. Seeing that her own mother . . . |
| MR. HUNTER: | Her own mother. |
| MR. HITCHCOCK: | She's met his mother and there's a scene which is in the book where she discusses marriage, with her mother. So now we feel that the robbery has gotten further away. The man, Mark, is beginning to take over the story, take over the girl, and I don't . . . what's the mother's response to marriage? |
| MR. HUNTER: | She's highly against it. |
| MR. HITCHCOCK: | And now we're back at the office again. |
| MR. HUNTER: | Five o'clock. |
| MR. HITCHCOCK: | Her mother, by the way, notices her hair has changed again. She prefers her as a blond. It's five o'clock at the office. |
| MR. HUNTER: | Marnie is leaving. |
| MR. HITCHCOCK: | Everybody's going home. They go to the girls' room . . . she goes right inside, we show the inside of the girls' room . . . toilets, and she goes right into one and locks the door and stands there. |
| MR. HUNTER: | Lights a cigarette. |
| MR. HITCHCOCK: | You stay with her and you hear the diminishing sounds of the departure, both from the girls' room and the door slamming and the night sounds outside. We stay with her all in the one shot until it's silent. We get the silence there and then she opens the door very carefully, crosses the girls' room, opens the other door and now the lights are going off. She waits a bit and then we see her go forward. Has she got the key in her hand? Unlocks the drawer and looks at the combination, goes to the safe. Then possibly we'll relate this to the night watchman. |
| MR. HUNTER: | And to the glass that's in the factory. Haven't worked this all out yet. |
| MR. HITCHCOCK: | And what she does is that she makes her way out of a back way when she's got the money. We're debating whether she drags against a piece of the glass. I don't know, we haven't worked out the details yet. The details in the factory when she creeps out. But it will relate to the presence of a night watchman. And how she eventually gets away, out of the back door. And down the brick wall side street. We see her go. Now . . . where were we. |
| MR. HUNTER: | Where she gets caught. |
| MR. HITCHCOCK: | We'll detail the robbery—it will cover the factory and this is a question of plates. We're obviously not going to |

photograph in the factory itself. We'll have to do some stills, colored transparencies in there and leave enough open for her to walk through. That's the kind of thing and then go up close to our detailed set.

MR. BOYLE:     Rather than moving plates, you mean?

MR. HITCHCOCK:     No, we don't need to have that. I can remember when I did, back in 1929, I did a chase through the British museum and I had nine transparencies. Just ran the figure through wherever we wanted it . . . for the long shots. Mac Johnson did the same thing in THE PARADINE CASE. We had a woman showing over a house and we just left enough space for the walking figure. And the rest we just plated. So that's the way we would do her. We'll probably go to the Steuben place and in color make a series of long exposures . . . because if there's no one else around you can do it and even in color, if necessary, you can do fifteen minute exposures. And we could almost . . . especially if it's at night with an odd glow, you could do it without any lighting. And do it for what it is there. Because you can have a half an hour exposure if you want to. I remember that's what we did in the British Museum . . . way back in 1929. Half-hour exposures they were. Needle-sharp. They were beautiful pictures. Taken 10 × 8's, blown up and made into transparencies. Big glass transparencies . . . we back lit them. And we used shiftrin in those days, where we matted out part of it. That's what we could do in the glass factory. We could take her any way we want. We could go to that factory with 10 × 8's in color, make the transparencies of them and just matte enough out for where she walks. High shots are the same because you're not going to have a floor to worry about, you see, keep her in the clear. So we'll need to cover that glass factory pretty well . . . for this sequence . . . if we're going to make something of her moving around. And we might even matte out another little corner to show the light of the night watchman. You might relate the two, cross-cut with him if we do it that way. So now . . . we're going to milk the robbery for all we can now. Now we come back again to our motif . . . if she runs down the side street. For example, that side street running, Bob, you know, if we have a high enough camera and a tiny figure we could lay that out on the middle of this roadway here, sometime, and matte round the whole lot and show the factory wall, especially if it's at night. We could back light the figure from one end and continue it on the matte. Maybe we could take the stills and Al Whitlock could paint the mattes, if necessary, because the painting isn't the main cost, is it?

MR. BOYLE:        No, no.

MR. HITCHCOCK:    Where we're going to work pictorially we're going to have to
                  dramatize that robbery, especially when she nearly knocks
                  and smashes a piece of glass. Maybe we might have her go
                  as far as that . . . knocks against one of the pieces and it
                  crashes and you get the night watchman looking to see. So
                  from there we go to the stables again . . . you know, the big
                  head, then again to our long shot . . . but this time, in this
                  long shot, which is very spectacular again, she rides and
                  rides and comes right down into the camera. We'll have to
                  dolly where she pulls her horse up if we can work it. Then
                  we go right up to about a waist shot and she stares and looks
                  and then you cut and there's the man. And we start the
                  scene there and she gets off the horse and the groom comes
                  up to take it. And now, of course, is one of the big scenes of
                  the picture. The dialogue scene of the man, Mark, and the
                  girl. She is now discovered. She's a thief and he says, 'All
                  right, let's go.' Now this long dialogue scene is a scene which
                  is going to be a continuous dialogue scene and never stop . . .
                  a very long one . . . and the first part of it will be when he
                  takes her down from the horse we dolly away from them.
                  Now this may have to be a treadmill, I don't know. It
                  depends on the location and what we choose and so forth.
                  And then as they come forward they're talking and then we
                  cut and we go on their backs. They're still talking, but now
                  we've jumped them right to the door of the inn—which we'll
                  do on the set—we'll match it on the set and go right through
                  the door and we dolly with them up the stairs toward the
                  room. Then we cut again and now she's finished the final
                  packing in the room, the dialogue still goes on, no
                  interruption, and finally she's finished and—there'll be
                  pauses to justify the breaks—but not too long, and we cut
                  straight from there to the two of them in the car. No break
                  in the dialogue at all . . . no dissolves . . . nothing. And now
                  you have your continuation in the car, which covers the
                  whole long scene and he describes the robbery, and over his
                  face you see him describe the big scene back when he gave
                  the alibi for her and he tells her that it couldn't have been
                  you because you had gone to New York to buy your
                  trousseau. She looks and he says, 'You know because I told
                  them we were going to get married.' Now . . . over his face
                  we have to lap dissolve over his face with his voice
                  narrating what you see as a silent scene back in the office.
                  And his words will slightly counter-point and she asks
                  questions and he says, 'Well, Terry, you know, he raised a
                  little question . . .'—but on the screen you see Terry raising

|  | hell. He doesn't tell her the complete truth of what took place in that office. It ends up with the fact that he's going to marry her. The details haven't been worked out . . . but it ends in the car, doesn't it? |
|---|---|
| MR. BOYLE: | And she accepts. |
| MR. HUNTER: | Well, we don't know yet whether she says yes or no, but we go out on her and the next scene is the reception. |
| MR. HITCHCOCK: | And now there is the reception . . . in the home. And we take the camera out of the living room across the hallway, up the stairs and around to the room up top. And in the room she's just changed for travelling. The mother's there and Dawn is there. The mother goes out. His mother. You get then the story from Dawn of what they all thought about it. The office and what she thought and I suppose it all started with the day you went to his house with the ledger. In other words, Dawn expresses for us—'What the hell do they think?'—about this marriage and so forth. Finally they come downstairs and you sense, by they're all very genial, the partners of the firm, and Mr. Ward and so forth, and the only cynical one is Terry, who obviously still thinks she did the job. Then after that they're off . . . to the honeymoon. This reception is not the sort of reception . . . you smell, you sense, that they're very polite to her but there's a tremendous under-current going on which is expressed through the character of Terry, who is the last one to say to her . . . |
| MR. HUNTER: | Good luck. |
| MR. HITCHCOCK: | Yes, good luck . . . you'll need it. Now we get the long shot of the LEONARDO DA VINCI, which we probably can do by borrowing their miniature and getting some ocean stuff at witching hour. And printing their miniature into real ocean of tank stuff, whichever we like. Did you see the end of LIFEBOAT? |
| MR. BOYLE: | Yes. |
| MR. HITCHCOCK: | With a tanker. Well, there we did our whole business of double-printing a tanker into regular water and we even, by changing the perspective, put the tanker in miniature and the full size rowboat coming away from it. So we could devise some shot like that, because you're never going to get a full size shot of that ship at witching hour unless she knew she was sailing out of Genoa harbor or somewhere at dusk and got up to put all her lights on. It's the only way you'll ever get it. Or you'll have to go into that, you see. Now we come inside from the long shot inside the cabin. It's night now. The cabin has to be a bedroom and sitting room . . . a suite. They only have two suites on board . . . we can readjust it to suit our purpose . . . and she's in negligee. He's |

in shirt and pants. And he comes over to embrace her now, now is the moment. And she turns, on him, and walks away and sits in a far corner of the sitting room. He comes to the door and says, 'What's wrong?' and in rather bold language she says, 'It's animal and the whole business is horrible . . .' and the language will be quite outspoken, but it's going to be played with just. . . . he at the door and she talks back from the corner of the settee, which expresses her detachment from him, and the desire to stay away from him. The following day they're leaning over the end-rail . . . not the side of the ship—but they're watching the activities around the pool. There we get the argument from him, 'Why did you marry me?' and she says, 'Because you were going to turn me over to the police.' There're obligations when you're married and he tries to talk her into being sensible about the whole business, but she won't attempt it at all. And then you get the second night in the cabin. He comes to her and she tries to resist—and then she turns her head away and you follow the big head right down onto the bed and you stay on the big head and. . . . you know. . . .

REEL THREE

MR. HITCHCOCK:   We start from the big head. We pan to the open porthole, having established that it's warm enough to have it open, into the moonlit sea. Possibly we'll bring the sound up so that the roar of the sea will increase. You know, there's a roar as the ship goes by. Then you go from that and see the dawn come up by a dissolve. The camera pans back and it's a different lighting and, of course, there you pan back to a different position. You go to two beds, one's empty. He awakens, looks at his clock . . . it's five a. m. and he puts on a robe, slippers and goes out, looks in the sitting room . . . nothing . . . in the corridor And now at dawn you find this man searching the empty ship. There isn't a soul about. Long shots of the promenade deck, going upstairs, the boat deck and this grey atmosphere of this man searching and searching. And finally he runs to the rail—where we previously established—and there, down in the pool, she's floating. Face down. He rushes down and then we see him in long shot fish her out. She's in negligee still, and the body the form is shown through it—we'll probably play it a long way away, until he gets her down and brings her around with artificial respiration—brings her round—some dialogue will be put in there like—'Why didn't you jump over the side?' and she says, 'I hate sharks . . . I'm scared of sharks.' Then we're going to show—these haven't been worked out yet—a series of slides—Kodachrome slides—and they're back home and you get on the screen some impressions of what the honeymoon was like. These will be shots which will establish her attitude, the fact that they were never photographed together, and the only one where they're photographed together they got the hall porter to do and it's blurred and out of focus. And there'll be some scenes she hates—like a scene with sailors in the background. And some of her inner things psychologically will come out during this slide scene. They're not all worked out yet—they're all going to make points. You do see for a moment when she's being nice to an Italian child or something—you see her smiling for once. He says, 'That's a nice one.' She says, 'It stinks.' And she refutes some of the scenes.

MR. HUNTER:   It'll be a half-dozen or so, won't it?

MR. HITCHCOCK:   Yes. In the middle of it dinner is served and now you see a picture. This is important, this room. This is the dining room . . . fairly formal, candle-lit, and of course, she's dressed in the best Bergdorf-Goodman manner.

MR. HUNTER:   A hostess gown.

MR. HITCHCOCK:   And she expresses almost her contempt for the whole thing. She's a prisoner in formality. Doesn't eat the food . . . 'No, thank you.' . . . 'I'm filling up with bread and butter.' You know. And out of this scene comes the problem. Where he's talking her into going to a psychiatrist. And they make a deal that, you know, she . . . he'd always refused to have the horse around, now he makes a deal . . . now she can have the horse. If she agrees to go to a psychiatrist. And now you have her first scene with the psychiatrist. The psychiatrist's office you'll have to find out about. It's pretty uncomplicated, isn't it?

MR. BOYLE:   Just a very simple room. Couch and chair. Desk and some books.

MR. HUNTER:   Pictures on the wall?

MR. BOYLE:   I'd just did one recently. Few pictures.

MR. HUNTER:   I was told recently that psychiatrists nowadays like to . . . instead of . . . the old notion was to have it rather a sterile room . . . you know, wouldn't upset a patient in any way or cause him to speculate about anything other than himself, but that now more and more their own personalities are intruding into the room. Their own hobbies, their own interests, etc., so that the figure is not as remote—which might be something interesting to consider in terms of Roman.

| | |
|---|---|
| MR. HITCHCOCK: | Well, we could look into that. We can probably get some photographs of psychiatrists' offices. There are a couple of men who are most important, but they're over at UCLA—but they might be very formal, those rooms—over at the university. |
| MR. HUNTER: | Our man is not a very formal man. |
| PEGGY ROBERTSON: | They have their own practice, I understand. |
| MR. HITCHCOCK: | Oh, do they? |
| MR. HUNTER: | We can have a warm room. |
| MR. HITCHCOCK: | Peg's got the name of the psychiatrist—local man that we can get the information from. Well, the first psychiatrist scene, of course, is quite a comic one. It'll be played for laughs the way she calls him a dirty old man, and all that sort of thing, . . . she's very outspoken. And after the first psychiatrist scene we return to the horse again. Now she's riding around the paddock. That's why the backing outside that living room may have to indicate this. So she's happy with the horse and he's probably leaning over the rail watching her and so forth. Then there'll be a little scene there and then she's back for the second psychiatrist scene. These psychiatrist scenes are going to show an emergence—that there's more underneath her—gradually. Each one will start comic, but by the time you get to the second one there'll be an undercurrent that there's more in this girl than we realize. Now after the second psychiatrist scene . . . |
| MR. HUNTER: | Is the . . . she calls home. |
| MR. HITCHCOCK: | This is her problem. Now her problem, which hasn't been worked out entirely yet, is she's still got to keep her mother going. So there's a whole element in this area, which we're dealing with, which shows that she's still got to lead a double life even while married to this man, Mark. |
| MRS. ROBERTSON: | She doesn't tell Mark about the mother. |
| MR. HITCHCOCK: | Oh, she can't. Everything will come unstuck, you see. She's still supposed to be secretary to a millionaire, in the eyes of her mother. |
| MR. BOYLE: | Her mother knows that she's marrying . . . |
| MR. HITCHCOCK: | No . . . no . . . |
| MR. BOYLE: | Oh, there were some . . . |
| MR. HITCHCOCK: | No, she discusses about the marriage . . . the mother poo-poos the whole thought of it. She only touches on it. So far as we're concerned story-wise it's that the audience think that she's getting it into her mind that Mark is rather serious about it. Especially as it comes after him going to the trouble of introducing her to his mother. You know, you don't start introducing a girl to your mother unless you've |

got some ideas, and Marnie begins to smell this. And she allows herself to think about it a bit by discussing it with her mother. And her mother poo-poos the whole thing. We, the audience, are allowed to think that the robbery's fading out of her mind, and it's all this man and that the possibility of marriage has taken over. Our shock is that she stays in that toilet one night. See, it's deliberately designed to lead the audience onto one line of thought and suddenly we switch it like that. But coming to the area we're in now you see, we not only have her going to the psychiatrist, but she has a background problem, that's the mother. And, as a result of which, she promises to send money. She phones . . . they don't know where she is. They wait . . . she phones them . . .

MR. HUNTER: She also learns in this call that her mother has been ill.

MR. HITCHCOCK: Now where does this phone call take place?

MR. HUNTER: Well, we haven't decided yet whether she's going to make the call from the house . . .

MR. HITCHCOCK: She might make the call from the house . . . just one call because this one call is going to come on the telephone bill which is going to give him the clue about Baltimore and the number. Well, we haven't followed that line because. . . . there's no place there for him to question her about the bill if he's going to. We didn't follow that . . .

MR. HITCHCOCK: No. Well, we haven't worked that out yet. But there's a possibility she might do it from the house, otherwise it will be from outside from a phone booth. The result of this is that she goes to the poker game again so we're back in Terry's apartment.

MR. HUNTER: It just occurs to me to make the point stronger. She should call Terry and ask him if he's having a poker party.

MR. HITCHCOCK: That's right.

MR. HUNTER: Instead of the call coming fortuitously from him. She should call him and invite herself.

MR. HITCHCOCK: So we get another poker game in which she loses. But there's another scene . . .

MR. HUNTER: With Terry and Marnie . . .

MR. HITCHCOCK: Terry and Marnie, yes.

MR. HUNTER: As she's leaving, where we get under his skin for the first time and see how much he dislikes Mark and what he's capable of . . . we foreshadow what he's capable of at the end of the picture.

MR. HITCHCOCK: See, Terry is . . . does he hint there about the business deal that's going to take place? Not yet?

MR. HUNTER: I don't think so. We're just going to pull that in.

MR. HITCHCOCK: Now you come to your third psychiatrist scene, which is really the explosive scene where she breaks down and cries

|                 | because he's probing too deep. And he gets something out of her. We sense, audience-wise, that she's really a case . . . which begins to make you speculate on the thievery why she's a thief, her mother's background and so forth. |
| MR. HUNTER:     | And the frigidity. |
| MR. HITCHCOCK:  | The frigidity and so forth. This third psychiatrist scene is quite a revelation. I mean, it spurs the audience to know there's much more underneath this. . . . beyond a girl who's frigid and the reasons are beginning to emerge, which of course, build up at the end. This carries over back home when he says they have to go to a special party and there's a meeting, although it may not be necessary to mention to this party—some people are being gathered together and she doesn't want to go because she's in rather a state and says, 'I'm not going to that psychiatrist anymore.' And he senses also that things are going to pop here. Anyway, he talks her into going. And now you get a big explosion—at this dinner party, of course, there are the various people. They're the people who are going to help—he's going to take over—going to sell out, you see. We make this . . . he explains the whole thing—and we do to the audience as well; which is going to double-cross the Terry character. And he explains all this to her and very clear to her because she knows nothing about business so she represents the audience as well. So it will be clearly explained what this party is about. And it has to be explained that the man, Terry, and his father will be at a disadvantage as a result of the whole thing, which is going to build up to your end. His activities at the end. And at the party it becomes quite . . . it becomes quite a suspensing . . . you describe the party . . . |
| MR. HUNTER:     | We're not quite sure yet what's going to happen. How we're going to discover STRUTT, the man from the very first scene of the picture, but he's going to be there and we're going to see him with his wife and either the audience is going to see him first and not Marnie or Marnie's going to see him and try to move away . . . |
| MR. HITCHCOCK:  | We're going to squeeze a tremendous suspense . . . |
| MR. HUNTER:     | We're going to hold off the actual confrontation of the two . . . |
| MR. HITCHCOCK:  | We're never going to show the confrontation . . . |
| MR. HUNTER:     | And then we're going to show Mark in a discussion with Strutt in the background . . . |
| MR. HITCHCOCK:  | And they're looking toward . . . |
| MR. HUNTER:     | And looking toward Marnie while she thinks possibly he's telling Mark about her and then they're going to both start toward Marnie and he's going to introduce Marnie as his |

wife and Mr. Strutt is simply going to acknowledge the introduction and Marnie's going to say, 'I'm awfully tired, Mark, could we go home?' And he says, 'Yes.' and she heads upstairs for her coat.

MR. HITCHCOCK: Wait. As they walk away . . .

MR. HUNTER: As they walk away Strutt just gives a slight turn of his head . . .

MR. HITCHCOCK: It's all being played visually and you sense . . .

MR. HUNTER: We think she got away, you see. We think, oh, he really didn't recognize her and the guy's only. . . . and she goes upstairs to the ladies' room to get her coat and there's Mrs. Strutt and she says, 'You knew my husband, didn't you?', and goes into this business of, 'I saw my husband watching you', and the guy obviously has a reputation as a ladies man and she suspects that Marnie is one of his past flames. And Marnie convinces her that nothing like that ever happened and she comes downstairs and—with her coat—and goes to where Mark, Terry and Strutt are in conversation. We don't hear the conversation—comes up—they leave and go out and we leave Terry and Strutt alone in conversation. Mark and Marnie get in the car and they're driving for a little distance and Mark turns to her and says, 'So, you worked for Mr. Strutt, did you?' Strutt has. . . .

MR. HITCHCOCK: We never do the corny confrontation at all. It all takes place very oblique. But the summation of it is that you don't know, you think . . . my God, I'm glad she's out of that and then the bombshell comes in the car . . .

MR. HUNTER: And then we have a real showdown.

MR. HITCHCOCK: Now comes the big . . .

MR. HUNTER: He explains what the conversation with Strutt was about and gets her to tell him all about the other robberies she's committed. And they're in . . . are we going to do this the same way we did the first one, with the jump cuts and the dialogue. I think that's a good idea, taking them right back from the party, in the car, to the house up to the bedroom, almost a reprise of that earlier scene when he catches her the first time. Now we haven't yet decided . . . you want to do it, I don't . . . we haven't yet decided . . . a time dissolve . . . I want to go right into the next scene but you want to dissolve. However we do it, he calls his friend whom we have planted earlier . . . who is a retired . . .

MR. HITCHCOCK: At the reception . . .

MR. HUNTER: Mark calls his friend who is a retired judge and gets him in the house to get his advice on this thing and he's in the study with Mark and Marnie is in the kitchen and learns that he's there and she goes outside and eavesdrops on what's going on in the study and hears Mark . . .

| | |
|---|---|
| MR. HITCHCOCK: | Asking advice. Asking him what to do . . . |
| MR. HUNTER: | And the judge offers . . . they debate several possibilities and then the judge ends it by saying that he hopes they can work it out some way but if they can't, within the next week or so, he's going to be forced to report it to the authorities because this sort of puts him on the spot. |
| MR. HITCHCOCK: | Now, set-wise. Is this going to take place in the living room or the study? |
| MR. HUNTER: | I think the study, don't you? It sounds more cloistered to me and more private. |
| MR. HITCHCOCK: | We'll have to establish where their study is, but it must have an outside with French windows again, similar to the other French windows in the living room that smashed open. |
| MR. HUNTER: | Oh, I thought that early scene was in the study. |
| MR. HITCHCOCK: | No, it's not big enough to get around that room. |
| MR. HUNTER: | See, I visualized it as sort of a room with a lot of book shelves and perhaps Mark's work desk so that when he's working at home . . . a large room . . . almost a library-study. |
| MR. HITCHCOCK: | But then you wouldn't have the wife's ornaments. |
| MR. HUNTER: | Sure you would. |
| MR. HITCHCOCK: | Oh no, they'd be in the drawing room. Oh sure, glass cases like that. Oh yes, they wouldn't be in his study. Her collection? |
| MR. HUNTER: | Would he have the jockeys in the living room? |
| MR. HITCHCOCK: | Might . . . might. |
| MR. HUNTER: | Well, I don't know. |
| MR. HITCHCOCK: | We'll have to do that later. |
| MRS. ROBERTSON: | Why is the judge saying he'd be forced to disclose . . . Did Mark use a fictitious name or didn't he? Did he say it's my wife and . . . |
| MR. HITCHCOCK: | Oh yes. He tells the truth . . . the whole story. |
| MR. HUNTER: | And you know, I just said a week. We haven't decided yet whether there's going to be a time limit or anything, but . . . |
| MRS. ROBERTSON: | Mark would say a friend of mine . . . |
| MR. HITCHCOCK: | No . . . no, he tells the judge . . . oh, sure. |
| MR. HUNTER: | He levels. He gives it to him absolutely straight. |
| MR. HITCHCOCK: | The judge says, 'Well you know, I can keep this to myself for a time, but after all remember I'm an ex. . . . I may be retired but . . .' You know, he could have been a federal judge, which . . . he'd have to tell. |
| MR. HUNTER: | Otherwise he's an accomplice, isn't he? |
| MR. HITCHCOCK: | Sure. |
| MR. HUNTER: | After the fact . . . because there has been money stolen. |
| MR. HITCHCOCK: | Oh, no question about that . . . she's committed felony. |
| MR. HUNTER: | Many of them. |
| MR. HITCHCOCK: | That'd be a nice name for a girl . . . Felony. |
| MR. HUNTER: | Felony Daniels. |

MR. HITCHCOCK:     Now, of course, you get her . . .

MR. HUNTER:     She flees—she goes upstairs and packs—grabs some jewelry from the drawer.

MR. HITCHCOCK:     Her jewelry is the only thing she's got.

MR. HUNTER:     And we establish the jewelry earlier . . . and runs home to mother. Her idea is simply to hide out for a while and then go. She'll work it out from there. She's taken the jewelry so that she'll have some money when she needs it.

MR. HITCHCOCK:     Now we're back in the Baltimore street and into the house and, of course, . . .

MR. HUNTER:     She comes in . . . no, we've . . . we decided not to use the phone call.

MR. HITCHCOCK:     Oh, did we?

MR. HUNTER:     Yes.

MR. HITCHCOCK:     Why was that?

MR. HUNTER:     Because they would have asked . . . is Marnie there? And she would have said yes, here she is and give her the phone. We were debating an idea of having the phone . . .

MRS. ROBERTSON:     . . . calls her Marnie and Mark calls her Marnie.

MR. HUNTER:     Yes. They all call her Marnie now after the first time she's caught. We were debating whether . . . when she gets there, of course, the mother is dead and Lucy tells her that, but we were debating whether the phone should ring so that we know that Mark and the other guy are tracing her through the phone bill and have traced it to this number and now . . .

MR. HITCHCOCK:     You can do that. You could have the phone ringing while she's outside the house. And Lucy's a long time answering the door and she hangs up and Lucy says, 'Oh, someone just called for you.' That would make Marnie very worried wouldn't it?

MR. HUNTER:     Yeah . . . she'd run like hell.

MR. HITCHCOCK:     Anyway, we establish the mother's death there. And, of course, the mother's been dead for a few hours or more.

MR. HUNTER:     She's already called . . .

MR. HITCHCOCK:     The morticians and people, the doctor's gone and the morticians are on the way and while she's in the room with the mother, Lucy says, 'The morticians are here', and she says, 'Tell them to wait.' They're waiting to take the body away. And that's when she begins to go through the effects of the trunk under the bed. Now, of course, out of this comes the information as to what her mother was and Lucy begins to tell the story. We're going to have a flashback, you see, of what happened, that men tapped on the window, mother took her out of the bed she was in, put her into another room, and a kind of rough sailor comes into the room to the child, and the mother, fearing that he's going to attack the child, pulls him off and kills him and the child is a witness to all this. And the press reports indicate that the mother was defending her child, although we show the sailor had no intention at all. She was acquitted, wasn't she, the mother? Now, the whole of this is we're going to devise a form of flattery, we're not going to do it like they did in Freud by putting an oil diffuse around the edge, that kind of thing which is kind of old hat, we used to do that in 1922. Take a glass, get vaseline, put it around the edge of the glass, slide it into the front, so that it blurs the edges and the center's clear. That's the oldest form of diffusion, vaseline diffusing. We're probably going to do sharp cutting.

MR. HUNTER: But we're going to make it so that present action seems to flow into past action in a continuous line.

MR. HITCHCOCK: By cutting. Marnie will be in the same position, see, as she was as the child and when we cut we're going to cut to washed-out color. We have full color as the present. The washed-out color is the past, but they are intercut. The images will . . . we're going to try and avoid the conventions of the dissolve or the fade or the soft or the blurred.

MR. HUNTER: See, Marnie is going to reinact the story in a sense. Instead of remembering the story, she's going to reinact it so that when she remembers going under the bed, she'll look under the bed and we may even see the girl, Marnie, looking out.

MR. HITCHCOCK: She'll see herself under the bed.

MR. HUNTER: She'll lift the thing and look under the bed and the child, Marnie, will be looking out so it'll be almost a continuous thing, if she backs into a corner of the room we could do a quick cut on the child backing into the corner. Be interesting.

MR. HITCHCOCK: So the layout must cover these both bedrooms. And during this, of course, the husband arrives with the psychiatrist.

MR. BOYLE: Pardon me, you said both bedrooms. Isn't this the same house that they lived in, or not?

MR. HUNTER: Yes. But we need to show the mother's bedroom and also Marnie's bedroom.

MR. HITCHCOCK: This may be upstairs.

MR. BOYLE: I see.

MR. HUNTER: This thing has taken place in Marnie's bedroom.

MR. HITCHCOCK: It's upstairs, you see, the two upstairs bedrooms. And finally the husband does arrive. . . .

MR. HUNTER: It has to be downstairs, Hitch.

MR. HITCHCOCK: Does it? Why?

MR. HUNTER: Because they rap on the window.

MR. HITCHCOCK: That's right, yes.

MR. HUNTER: Unless they have a long ladder. But the signal is when the sailors arrive at the house they rap on the window and Marnie hears this each time.

MRS. ROBERTSON: There's a reprise with the husband . . .

MR. HUNTER: No.

MR. HITCHCOCK: Well, we'll have to look into that.

MR. HUNTER: Yes. As to just where the layout of the house . . .

MR. HITCHCOCK: Well, the climax comes with the morticians taking the body away and Marnie returning and we have another scene inside a car with the return and some of the psychiatric explanations by Roman.

MR. HUNTER: The psychiatrist.

MR. HITCHCOCK: The psychiatrist. And now you feel that it's all . . . you know, we've forgotten one thing . . . what about the judge and all this sort of business and so forth, and finally they're almost going back home. The audience will be . . . by all this flashback lulled into this until she arrives outside their home and the front door opens and there—inside the room—inside the hallway—are the police, Terry and Mr. Strutt. And they stop, they're going out to the car, and they play the scene, their first real love scene, right then and there, floodlit by the open door and the people waiting, and she says, 'The only way I'm ever going to come back to you is after I've been through that door.' And that's when she makes her real simple approach to him. And then you get the final scene inside the hallway about which will be very matter-of-fact. Miss so-and-so, you know Strutt, yes I know Strutt. Terry stands there—'Well, do I have to come along now or shall I pack her bag, no, no, no, I think we can . . .

MR. HUNTER: Oh, we do that?

MR. HITCHCOCK: . . . bail . . . something like that.

MR. HUNTER: I thought we were just going to take her on the walk to the door.

MR. HITCHCOCK: Well, that's awfully corny. It's like a movie. I think we ought to discuss whether she's going to have bail . . . just give a flavor of being arrested and so forth. So that front of that house will have to be built or the doorway alone, enough of it.

MR. BOYLE: Maybe. At least the front. Maybe some more.

MR. HITCHCOCK: Steps, you mean, have it up on a platform because you've got to look right into that hallway. Stairs going up and everything, so you might have to go to the extent of building that whole thing up on a platform.

MR. BOYLE: Well, that you could see when you see what your action is. It might be that it's a separate set and . . . it's good. What is the rush now for—you know—I can see it . . . that's one of the things I suppose she left, and that is of not telling him

| | |
|---|---|
| | about the mother. In other words, she was only telling him as much as she needed to. |
| MR. HUNTER: | If she tells him about the mother then he'll say, 'Well, let's meet mother. You mean to tell me you have a mother living in Maryland? Well, let's go meet her . . . ! And then she'll go meet mother and mother'll eventually say, 'What happened to your job with Mr. Pemberton? My daughter used to work for a millionaire, you know and travel all around the country.' And Mark'll put two and two together and begin figuring out that she never worked for any millionaire that she was a thief. You know, a repeated thief. |
| MR. HITCHCOCK: | Oh yes, she . . . she'd open up a whole can of peas by . . . |
| MR. HUNTER: | And not only that, but her mother all through her life has warned her . . . don't get involved with men and. . . . |
| MR. HITCHCOCK: | All right, you can close it now. Thank you. |

## Kaleidoscope

Despite problems with the developing script, Hitchcock began the meticulous preparation for this project. He wanted this film to be different from other Hitchcock films, for he had been impressed with the recent wave of Italian filmmakers—especially the work of Michelangelo Antonioni—and he wanted desperately to try to capture the spirit of the times, but with that special Hitchcock twist.

For this dark "love" story, Hitchcock wanted to film using natural light, with a portable camera and unknown actors. In short, he wanted to reinvent the Hitchcock film. To do this, he hired photographer Arthur Schatz in New York to conduct a series of film tests using various faster new color films. The footage is remarkable, as it follows the intended screenplay, filming at various locations in New York that he and Benn Levy had worked into the script.

This footage, shot without sound and, to this day, still unknown actors, is an incredible glimpse into what could have been. Surely, this is remarkable stuff that would have altered our perception of Hitchcock's final decade. The impact on cinema would have been substantial. Hitchcock would have re-emerged at this late point in life at the forefront of style.

The project excited Hitchcock, but shocked Universal. *Topaz,* a disaster in any terms, is even more painful when put in the light of what *Kaleidoscope* surely would have been.

The following is the report on the extensive test footage that was shot. Four reels of footage equal approximately forty minutes of footage. Edited into a workable film sequence, this is approximately ten minutes of screen time. Even though the report indicates that the footage was shot by Arthur Schatz, he claims never to have even seen a film camera present (despite the fact that stills that he admits he shot are of the very same scenes and actors).

## 35 MM Film Shot by Arthur Schatz in New York on New 54 Stock                                         July 23, 1968

REEL 1

INT. BEDROOM—CLOSEUP (Take 1)
This is not pushed. The other one where you see more prevailing light in the darkness is the pushed roll.
Shot at 2.5, 150 watt standard Tungsten bulb (in the bed lamp). A little daylight, you can see the reflection. The tones are reddish. Probably due to red bed lamp.

(Take 2)
$^1$/₂ stop additional exposure, f.2, no push. Absolutely no light, just daylight coming in from three windows. Almost total darkness.

INT. ART STUDIO (Take 1)
No push. Normally exposed for daylight ASA 64 with an 85 filter. If it looks slightly actinic it's because of the tremendous overcast sky. The range in stops (where he starts with the first students, talking to them and then walking to the ladder) is almost $^3$/₄ stop difference. We made no correction for it. The film held it. This is evidence this stock can be used outdoors on overcast day.

REEL 2

INT. BEDROOM (Scene 2 Take 1)
Pushed. Almost total darkness. The meter read right off her face rather than the wider shot which she moves in and out of. This sequence has 250 watt Halogen (weighs about $^1$/₂lb!) bounced about 20 feet away. As camera pans around room in this scene, this 250 watt Halogen just fills in the darkness ever so slightly, so you can see a little more detail.

(Before she turns on the lamp) If the Halogen bulb were bounced off an absolutely white source, the color would be a little more true, but we just bounced it off a 20 year old mouldy, yellowish ceiling, which is what it reflects.

Scene 2 Take 3
Same thing, open a fraction of a stop more. Identical exposure, the two absolutely matched up.

Scene 2 Take 4
This goes down a $^1$/₂ stop. This is darker than the other one.

REEL 3

ART CLASS

Straight daylight.
Important: Exposure strictly for silhouette effect. Meter reading done outside. The

reading was made for the outdoors and nothing indoors; look how it holds the shadow in the model, you can see details in the faces. It was shot strictly for silhouette effect. There was enough leaway to give a little detail in the peoples' faces. It is unpushed, straight ASA 64. Could have made greater silhouette by under-exposing another stop.

(Take 2)
Start on closeup model's face.
This is unpushed, ASA 64 with the 85 filter.

Scene 6 Take 1 (INT. BATHROOM)
This is where the pink light, the back 60 watt bulb, throws it a little bit. Two 60 watt bulbs and the one closest to us would have bounced out to us directly. But the pink bulb warmed up the color a little bit.
Tungsten. No push. Evening—but still daylight (about 8 P.M.)

Scene 6 Take 2


REEL 4

ART CLASS
Closeup model's face (sipping coffee)

and
INT. BREAKFAST SCENE
No push.

Scene 8 Take 1
Closeup, woman's face.
Odd stock roll bought in New York. $^{52}/_{54}$ but a different emulsion. Just wanted to see if you had bad emulsion problems how it would match up.
Shot Tungsten 100, no filter, no push. Has one 500 watt Halogen bulb bounced from about 10 feet away. Not directly on her, just bounced.

Scene 8 Take 2
Same thing for this take.


# *Family Plot*

Hitchcock's final film was prepared with just as much care as his earlier films. Donald Spoto reproduced the storyboard from the out-of-control car scene in his book *The Art of Alfred Hitchcock*. Hitchcock drew several sketches and floor plans for the production.

One of the film's finest scenes takes place at the San Francisco Cathedral. The film revolves around a pair of kidnappers who ask for high-priced jewels as ransom. The kidnappers, à la Hitchcock, stage a spectacular kidnapping of the cathedral's bishop in front of the entire congregation. Hitchcock was always amused at how reserved people were in church no matter what occurred and the scene works extremely well.

Hitchcock drew these sketches in advance of shooting the scene:

EXT. BLANCHE TYLER HOME

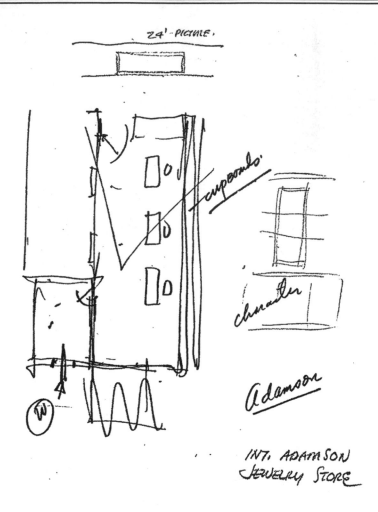

24' - PICTURE.

cupboards

character

adamson

INT. ADAMSON
JEWELRY STORE

## CONCLUSION

Here the dreaming must end and the hard work of actual film construction must begin. The next arena is filled with compromise, according to Hitchcock. Not the compromise with fellow artists, but the inevitable compromising of the perfect film dreams he has built with his writers and production team.

Hitchcock on the set does not reveal the active genius in preproduction. Instead, he must be The Director.

# *chapter four*
# PRODUCTION GALLERY

*The motion picture is not an arena for a display of techniques.
It is, rather, a method of telling a story in which techniques,
beauty, the virtuosity of the camera, everything must be
sacrificed or compromised when it gets in the way
of the story itself.*

—HITCHCOCK

f or a man enamored of publicity and the process of filmmaking, it is surprising that there are not more photos of Hitchcock at work, especially
since Hitchcock did enjoy the staged shot. A somewhat shy fellow in
strange settings, he was not at all shy on the set. And the photos that follow,
some never published before (others quite famous), will serve as a visual counterpoint to the remembered working Hitchcock.

The first is perhaps the most famous early Hitchcock still: The Master directs *The Mountain Eagle*. To his right is Alma Reville, his future wife. The still
is a wonderful performance (the position of the still camera would make filming impossible, so it must be staged), but it does give a sense of the dynamo
young Hitchcock was. Home movies from this time period show a much more
animated young man compared to the Buddhalike presence he cultivated in
the fifties and sixties. Like the still from above, this is one of the few souvenirs
left from this now lost film. It was his second complete feature. (His first
complete feature was *The Pleasure Garden*.)

The winning team (shown opposite). John J. (Jack) Cox and Hitchcock on their very first production together: *The Ring*. In 1943 Jack Cox recalled to Frank Sainsbury (in *The Cine-Technician*, a magazine of the time) their work together, beginning with their rushed meeting after Hitchcock's original cameraman on *The Ring* walked out over a salary dispute:

"The next day they sent for Jack, told him they'd got a lovely Mitchell for him, and he was to work on Hitch's picture. That was all very well until Jack found out what his first day's assignment was to be: they were making *The Ring*, with Carl Brisson, and they'd built a lovely Fun Fair for it out on the lot. Jack's first day's work, with a hand-turn Mitchell he'd never used before, was a sequence of 18 camera dissolves of the various Fun Fair sideshows. Jack sweated blood over that day's work and didn't sleep at all that night. But when they saw the rushes next day, everything was the white-headed boy. He was Hitchcock's cameraman right the way through, until Hitch left [British International Pictures] . . .

"Of all the directors he has worked with, Jack liked Hitch best, for his quick mind, lively ideas, and workmanlike way of setting about the job; they were

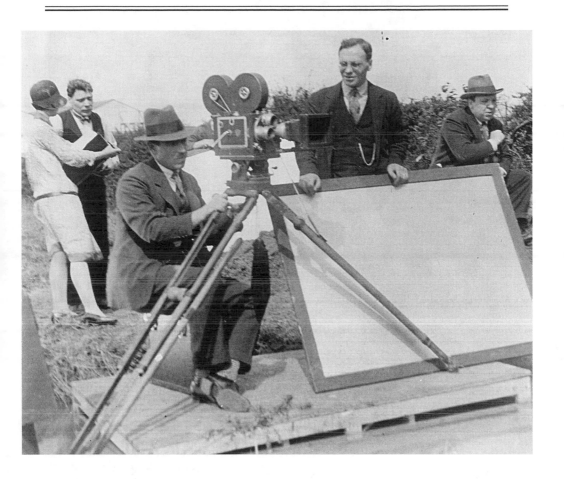

always going into conference together and thinking up new narrative gags and camera treatment . . .

"Hitch, whose charming wife had been his script girl, had a town flat and a country place and they used to entertain very lavishly, with lashings of champagne and so on, says Jack, with a far-off reminiscent look . . ."

*The Ring* is an excellent film—and one Hitchcock loved dearly. He remembered to Truffaut and others the film's first screening and the audience bursting into applause after the first montage. Like its predecessor, *The Lodger,* the film forever established Hitchcock's place in British cinema history.

*Champagne* was not as critically or financially successful as *The Ring* or *The Lodger,* but the film is in no way a failed enterprise. The following is a terrific (if slightly blurry) shot of Hitchcock directing the scene. Despite his reputation to do otherwise, Hitchcock often worked with the actors on the set. Again, that is Jack Cox behind the camera (this time without the hat and a slightly less dour expression).

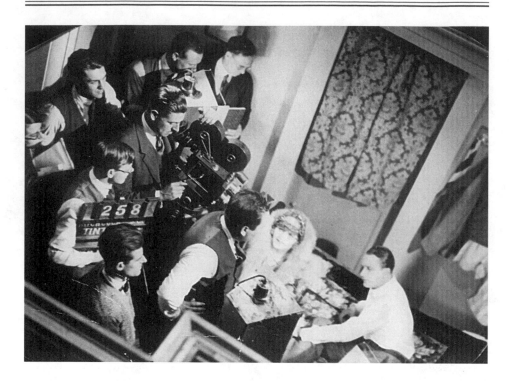

Two cast photos from *The Farmer's Wife*, an often unfairly disparaged film. I liked this one quite a bit (Hitchcock's pastoral films are not only engaging melodramas but they are also some of the most beautifully shot films in his canon) and it's curious that there exist two photos like this for the film. The garden set photo is very interesting. Jack Cox (again looking quite dour, which

is so odd, since he was described as a mostly gregarious man) is by the camera. Hitchcock is squeezed onto this wooden bench with the film's star and character actress. Lounging is the famed character actor—who Hitchcock evidently became good friends with. And then there is the young woman at the typewriter. In the last photo, the director is appropriately positioned next to the film's love interest and the champagne.

*Number 17* is a bizarre, almost experimental "art" film which ultimately fails. This is a terrific still, though, of the director looking up to his daughter, Patricia, during the filming.

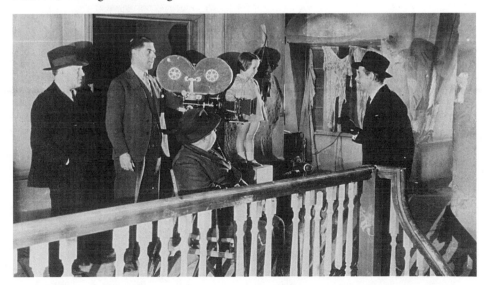

Below is a terrific shot of Hitchcock on the set of *Rich and Strange,* which was filmed at Elstree Studios. At the far right, the camera and crew are preparing to shoot the protagonist as he returns home from work with a malfunctioning umbrella—Hitchcock stands at the end of the street with his hands on his hips, watching the actor go through a rehearsal—the set has been soaked and façades have been built for the row of homes that will be matched to the model that can be seen just above the camera setup. At the far end of the stage is a painted backdrop for the factory our hero is coming from.

The next still is a rare one of one of the full sets for *The 39 Steps.* Hitchcock and the camera are not in the shot—it appears to be the set for Hannay's escape from the Scottish jail—indeed, Hannay is at the very center of the shot in the distance. The camera could be off to the left of Hannay or behind the still photographer. Judging from the action in the shot, my bet is that the camera is to Hannay's left—and the cars and crowd are preparing to move in Hannay's direction past the camera.

Following is a more familiar still from *The 39 Steps.* Hitchcock is just beneath the lens, filming Hannay (Robert Donat) and Pamela (Madeleine Carroll) in the Scottish countryside. Hannay appears to be whistling the signature tune: "Mr. Memory." *The 39 Steps* became an international success, placing Hitchcock on the international map and bringing him to the attention of producer David O. Selznick. Its predecessor, *The Man Who Knew Too Much,* was also a hit, but the studio had no confidence in the film and placed it as the

second bill to a now forgotten "A" film. Despite its second billing in England, the film did record business and garnered good reviews in London and the States. This success and the success of *The 39 Steps* gave Hitchcock an enormous amount of power in the small British film industry pond—certainly, none of his films were ever second-billed again.

A remarkable candid shot on the set of *Secret Agent*. Just what were they talking about?

A less candid moment—from the film's dramatic conclusion. Hitchcock is again in his favored position, right below the camera, watching the action. *Secret Agent*'s ending, as described in Chapter Two, "Building the Screenplay," went through a number of drafts, but it always concluded with the dramatic train wreck. Notice the production assistant holding the flare just off camera for the smoke.

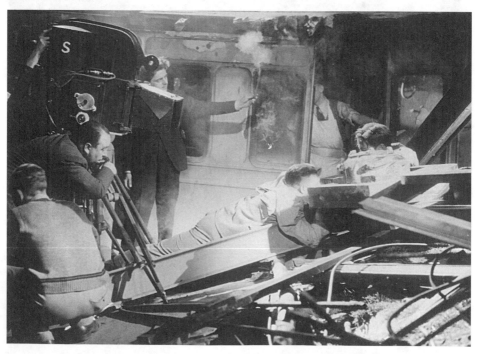

Making do with as little as possible, Hitchcock uses a narrow lens and a tightly packed crowd to give the impression of an extremely large crowd gathered for the Lord Mayor's Parade. At first glance, this looks like a location shoot, but this is the back lot of Lime Phane Studios, where most of *Sabotage* was filmed. Hitchcock is leaning against a makeshift rail, talking to a very animated young extra. *Sabotage* is probably Hitchcock's darkest film after *Vertigo* and featured the American star Sylvia Sidney. Sidney remembered working with Hitchcock:

"I don't remember much. Hitchcock liked things. He was always shooting things—hands, knives, birds. He didn't seem too interested in people. But he wasn't unpleasant and knew what he was doing. We had no idea what was happening, but Hitchcock knew. I remember not thinking much of the murder scene—which just did it. Hitchcock would say, 'Look this way—look that.' He was a funny man. Oscar Homolka [Sydney's costar], he was very old school. Very old-fashioned about his acting. I had a hard time with that."

The young boy at the center of this still is the young Desmond Tester (who, according to Sydney and others, would always blush when Hitchcock would

call him "Desmond Testicles"). He has a very important role in Hitchcock history—he plays the young boy that Hitchcock kills in a bus explosion. The killing angered many patrons and Hitchcock later conceded that it was a mistake.

Another scene on the Elstree back lot—this time a night shoot. Notice that the Bijou on the lot is located across the street from the High Street tube entrance, which is not the case in the film. The effects work in *Sabotage* is quite fluid, only rarely noticeable. Again, Hitchcock is crowding the scene in front of the Bijou to make the street appear busy. Hitchcock is to the left in the still.

The Lord Mayor's Parade with the enormous Westminster backdrop. The scene is very effective in the film. Hitchcock loved to use backdrops and all manner of in-camera special effects to create shots.

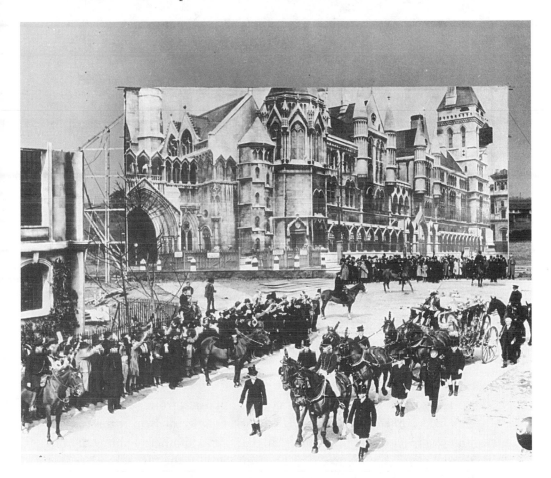

The dynamic Hitchcock positioned in his favored location (next page), this time on the front of the dolly beneath the camera—notice the cigar in Hitchcock's right hand. A cigar smoker for most of his life, the sound of Hitchcock opening and lighting a cigar is one of the more familiar sounds on the historic Truffaut tapes—almost always at the end of a taped luncheon (one should never listen to the tapes on an empty stomach). He preferred the Dunhill Cuban line: the Flor de Allones. (Dunhill no longer manufactures Cuban cigars (they did so until the early nineties) and they no longer even manufacture the domestic line of Flor de Allones.)

The massive (and magnificent) crane shot (opposite) from *Young and Innocent.* This light comedy thriller was Hitchcock's last great British thriller (*Jamaica Inn* was Hitchcock's final film in England) and another big hit with both British and American audiences. The final moments of the film take place in a posh hotel ballroom as the camera (and the film's heroes) track in on the twitching eye of the murderer. The shot begins from a high corner of the ballroom and slowly moves across the room to the bandstand, down to an extreme close-up of the twitching eye. The shot is very complicated. It requires this enormous dolly and crane, which are maneuvered through tables that are being hurried out of the way just out of camera shot and through dancing couples who part out of the lenses' range for the crane, dolly, and camera to the bandstand and ending just inches from the drummer's face. The shot required fourteen men to help move and operate the dolly/crane and two men to operate the camera—one for the camera and one to pull the focus. Hitchcock cannot be seen in the shot. Is he in his usual position, this time at the top of the crane, sitting beneath the camera's lens?

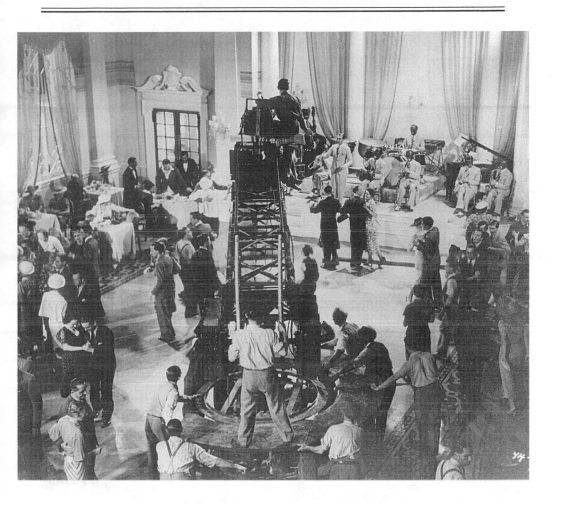

Hitchcock, now in America (next page), gives some direction to Herbert Marshall and Joel McCrea on the set of *Foreign Correspondent*. This is a great film—well designed with some very effective Hitchcock moments. It warrants the four-star status it is often given when shown on TV—which is not frequent enough. The film was an independent production from Walter Wanger with the production designed by William Cameron Menzies. This independent status means that it is often neglected by video companies. It is currently out of print in any laser format and difficult to find on tape. This was Marshall's second Hitchcock film—he also starred in Hitchcock's *Murder!* (based on the play *Enter Sir John*), Hitchcock's second sound film.

On location. Once in the United States, Hitchcock began to get out of the studio. His first film shot on location was *Shadow of a Doubt*. This scene is at the Santa Rosa train station just before Uncle Charlie arrives. In the right corner of the still, Alma and Joan Harrison sit behind one of the light stands.

Hitchcock at work with Thornton Wilder.

Rehearsal. Another myth was that Hitchcock never worked with actors. The truth is he often worked closely with actors and always rehearsed. *Rope* demanded a much more elaborate rehearsal process—both before filming and during filming.

For parts of *Under Capricorn* (see opposite), Hitchcock tried to use the long take technique that he developed in *Rope*; this still shows the crane used with the large Technicolor camera. This strenuous process is described by Jack Cardiff, the film's director of photography:

"We would rehearse one whole day and shoot the next day. Good recorded sound was impossible: the noise was indescribable. The electric crane lumbered through sets like a tank at Sebastopol, whole walls cracked open, furniture was whisked away by panting prop men and then frantically replaced in position as the crane made a return trip. The sound department did exceptionally well just to get a 'guide track' [picking up dialogue above the din so that the correct soundtrack could be matched to it later].

"When we had made a successful ten-minute 'take,' everyone had to leave the studio except the sound people, Hitch, the script girl, and the cast, who would then go through the motions with dialogue without the camera. Amazingly, by sliding the sound tape backward and forward, it all came together . . .

"He never looked through the camera, saying instead, for example, 'Jack, you have the thirty-five lens on and you are cutting just below the knees—right?' And right he always was.

"I watched him once during a ten-minute take. He had his back to the actors, aimlessly looking down at the floor, and at the end, when he had said, 'Cut!' he made only one comment to my camera operator, Paul Beeson: 'How was that for you, Paul?' On Paul's nod, he would signal his acceptance of the whole reel. More puzzling, he hardly ever saw the rushes of the day's work. The editor would keep him closely informed, but Hitch knew exactly what he was getting on the screen. From the moment he had drawn pictures of the camera setups, he had it all firmly in his mind.

"I had been much more involved than usual in the preproduction planning. Usually I tried to dream up ideas for dramatic lighting, but on *Capricorn*, I had for the most part to work out how on earth I could possibly light so many sets at once! I worked more closely with the director than usual.

"Practically all of Hitchcock's dramatic ideas were visual. If a cameraman is supposed to 'paint with light,' Hitchcock painted with a moving camera."

Hitchcock is pictured here on a smaller dolly for the same film. Details: notice the tape measure just below Hitchcock's knees beneath the large Technicolor camera. This is an indispensable tool for the camera operator. Focus is often determined by measurement, rather than just eyeballing it through the lens.

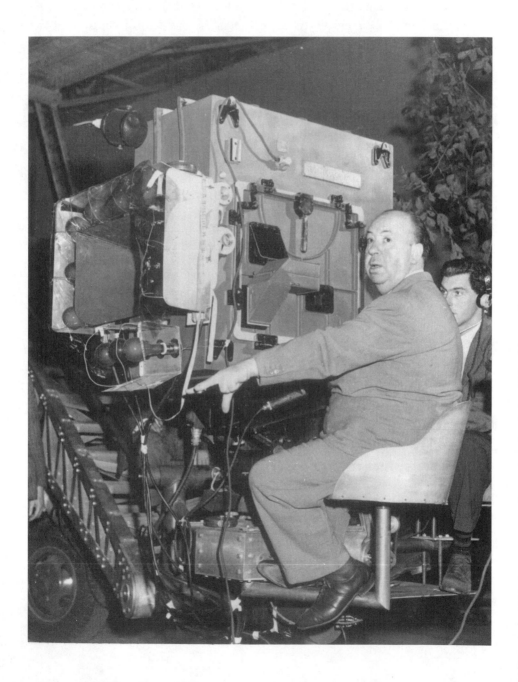

## Strangers on a Train

Father and daughter at work on the *Strangers on a Train* set.

During the climactic merry-go-round sequence, the director shares a private moment with a member of the cast. Who said actors aren't cattle?

Setting up the spectacular ending. The merry-go-round sequence is one of film's most surreal moments. I always find it deeply disturbing. The process of filming the sequence was difficult, time-consuming, and dangerous. In both photos, Robert Burks and Hitchcock plot the camera angles.

*I Confess* was intended as a Transatlantic Pictures film, but the company ended production. Warner Bros. purchased the rights from the company and Hitchcock directed it after *Strangers on a Train*. This is from the flashback set.

## Dial M for Murder

Hitchcock at work. Every cameraman Hitchcock worked with remarked on the sketches he would produce on the set to help position the camera and frame the shot.

The wheels are turning. Samuel Taylor and other writers spoke of Hitchcock's need for quiet reflection. Here he meditates on the set for *Dial M for Murder*.

The side many visitors saw of Hitchcock on the set. His sets were often closed. He liked a controlled, quiet environment for his cast and crew. Voices were seldom raised—unless a private meditation was disturbed. On the *Dial M for Murder* set.

Classic Hitchcock. Hitchcock enjoyed *Dial M for Murder*—it was his first production with Grace Kelly, with whom he would work on two more films. They became very close friends. John Williams was another favorite of Hitchcock's. He had a small role as a barrister in *The Paradine Case*—and went on to do *To Catch a Thief* and one of Hitchcock's television episodes (*Banquo's Chair*). He was reprising his Broadway role for *Dial M for Murder*.

Hitchcock's first Paramount film, *Rear Window,* was an enormous challenge. It was also an enormous hit and solidified his relationship with the studio. He stayed with Paramount through 1961. Hitchcock (opposite, top) with the microphone that allowed him to speak to the actors in the far apartment set. Robert Burks, who worked with Hitchcock on *Strangers on Train,* stands to the right of the camera.

On the Moroccan restaurant set of *The Man Who Knew Too Much.* This is my favorite set in the film. Designed by Henry Bumstead, it looks real to me. I didn't know until recently that it was a set. It's also a very nicely done scene—one of the scenes in the American version that makes this one superior to the early British film. Hitchcock sits next to the standing Robert Burks.

Hitchcock and Burks (to his left) discuss the setup for a shot on location in Marrakech. The Hitchcocks and Jimmy Stewart and his wife both enjoyed their time in northern Africa—so much so that they were tempted to return to the Continent to film *Flamingo Feather*. Hitchcock and Alma did return in the summer of 1956 with his production crew to look at locations, but while on this trip they decided not to film *Flamingo Feather*. *Vertigo* became his next production. San Francisco's climate was a little more friendly than South Africa's.

## The Wrong Man

A revealing still of an unused shot from *The Wrong Man*. Hitchcock decided to cut his cameo for the realistic drama. Instead, he chose to introduce the film in silhouette.

Hitchcock on location and directing the actors. Hitchcock always claimed to be afraid of the police—here he seems to have no problem as The Director. Actually, much of what Hitchcock said concerning police and cars was just publicity fodder. Hitchcock taught his daughter how to drive—and often enjoyed driving through scenic California. And in an irony considering his phobia, he was made an honorary deputy in Santa Rosa during the filming of *Shadow of a Doubt.*

# *chapter five*

# PUTTING IT ALL TOGETHER: POSTPRODUCTION

*That last ten seconds on the screen—*
*we took three months to do it.*

—HITCHCOCK ON *The Birds*

t he final step in film production is called postproduction, when the director must pull all the various production threads together and complete
the film for distribution. It can be a fast process or a slow one.

Hitchcock tended to have a fast turnaround in post. The process at this
point was accelerated by his production techniques—his intense planning before shooting and his filming only what was specifically required (not provid-
ing too many options) allowed editors and composers to work quickly with
the material as the film was being shot. In most cases, Hitchcock was able to
view a first cut within a week or so of the film's completion.

Hitchcock fans will find that Hitchcock's input at this point was a tad
perfunctory. After all, in many ways, his task was complete. As he said often
during production, he had already provided the instructions—it was up to his
team to fulfill the film's needs.

For example, for a man who expressed his love and appreciation for all
kinds of music and who especially understood the importance of music to film,
Hitchcock seemed to have little to say about the music in his own films. After
a diligent search, nothing could be found concerning the music for his "silent"
films, which seems unimaginable, since the music played for *The Lodger* would
seem all-important.

What can be determined about Hitchcock's postproduction methods can
also be said about his creative methods in general: Hitchcock loved to build

teams that worked from one film to the next. His creative staff from 1950 to 1964 was remarkably stable—with the same team shooting, cutting, and scoring the film except on a few occasions. (He worked with Robert Burks, his director of photography, on every film from *Strangers on a Train* through *Marnie*—except *Psycho*—and George Tomasini was his editor on every film in this period. Bernard Herrmann scored every Hitchcock film from *The Trouble with Harry* through *Marnie*.)

The dissolution of this team (the Chicago Bulls of filmdom) was tragic in every sense for Hitchcock. He lost both Burks and Tomasini to early deaths (Burks in a fire and Tomasini to a heart attack) and his famous parting with Bernard Herrmann will be discussed in this chapter.

Sadly, of course, the great unpublished film *Kaleidoscope* never saw production or postproduction. This film, like many of the other unfinished dreams of Hitchcock, awaits another dreamer to complete it.

## *Rebecca*

Hitchcock loved to claim that he never had previews. Even his colleagues will tell you that he never had previews. This was never true. The only period that I could find where Hitchcock did not have public previews was the later Paramount period (but even here, as the *Vertigo* story shows, Hitchcock held informal previews for friends and associates). I suspect that the record is merely incomplete because Hitchcock's primary concern was always the overall effect of the film with the audience. The proof is that he made significant changes over the years directly in response to audience surveys after previews.

Previews, for the uninitiated (in the Los Angeles area, they are a daily occurrence and most people have, at one time or another, been stopped by studio representatives to be invited to an evening screening), are invitation-only screenings of an early cut of the film. After the screening, the audience is expected to fill out questionnaires judging the film's success (or failure). In England, films were often displayed at trade shows, where reactions were measured. Hitchcock's first American film was with the undisputed master of the audience survey: David O. Selznick. Here is the audience survey and the tallied responses from the December 25, 1939, preview of *Rebecca* (just a few weeks after *Gone With the Wind*'s heralded premiere):

## Summary of 266 Preview Questionnaires
## (Compiled January 4, 1940)

#1.   HOW DID YOU LIKE THE PICTURE?

179   Excellent
 74   Very good
  9   Fair
  0   Poor
  4   No Answer

#2.   WAS THE ACTION OF THE PICTURE ENTIRELY CLEAR? IF NOT, WHERE WAS IT CONFUSING?

178   Yes
 52   No Answer
 11   Followed action of book very well.
 16   Confusing (Where not clear listed under sequence heading.)

#3.   WAS THE SOUND ENTIRELY CLEAR AND COULD YOU UNDERSTAND THE DIALOGUE? IF NOT, DO YOU RECALL WHICH PARTS WERE NOT AUDIBLE?

173   Yes
 52   No Answer
 40   Not Clear (Where parts inaudible listed under sequence heading.)

#4.   DID ANY PARTS SEEM TOO LONG? WHICH PARTS?

113   No
 86   No Answer
  7   Yes (but didn't tell where)
 18   Picture too long (one card said cut out 30 or 40 minutes)
  6   First half too long (half of these cards specify " 'I' in house."
 33   Some parts too long (Where too long listed under seq. heading.)

#5.   HAVE YOU ANY OTHER SUGGESTIONS TO MAKE?

 98   No
 92   No Answer
 76   Suggestions listed under sequence headings and miscellaneous.

#6.   CONCERNING FUTURE PICTURES WITH LAURENCE OLIVIER:

181   I will go to see other pictures because Laurence Olivier is in them.
 69   I like Laurence Olivier very much but would not go to see pictures just because he is in them.
  5   I don't much care one way or the other about Laurence Olivier.
  0   I wouldn't go to see a picture with Laurence Olivier.
 11   No Answer
  3   Best he has done.

#7.  CONCERNING FUTURE PICTURES WITH JOAN FONTAINE:

   143  I will go to see other pictures because Joan Fontaine is in them.

   93  I like Joan Fontaine very much but would not go to see pictures just because she is in them.

   10  I don't much care one way or the other about Joan Fontaine.

   0  I wouldn't go to see a picture with Joan Fontaine.

   18  No Answer.

   3  Fontaine too drooped and meek.

   2  Too much of Joan Fontaine.

   1  Would like picture of Fontaine.

#8.  CONCERNING FUTURE PICTURES WITH JUDITH ANDERSON:

   68  I will go to see other pictures because Judith Anderson is in them.

   114  I like Judith Anderson very much but would not go to see pictures just because she is in them.

   44  I don't much care one way or the other about Judith Anderson.

   6  I wouldn't go to see a picture with Judith Anderson.

   36  No Answer.

   1  Judith Anderson perfect.

   2  Would like to have seen Gale Sondergaard in the part.

   6  Said all actors excellent.

   4  Said George Sanders very good.

### COMMENTS ON LENGTH:

18  Picture too long. (One card said cut out 30 or 40 minutes.)

 6  First half too long. (Half of these cards specify " 'I' in house.")

 4  Some scenes in the house boresome and tiresome.

 9  Don't cut.

### COMMENTS ON DIRECTION, PHOTOGRAPHY, ETC.:

1  Don't like English pictures.

1  Mr. Hitchcock's building suspense beautifully timed.

2  Excellent photography.

1  Slightly underlighted.

### SOUND:

4  Not clear because of English accent.

1  English accent in this picture easier to understand than in most.

2  Kissing too loud. Whistle sounds evident.

1  Fontaine speaks at one time with no sound.

Olivier:

   5  Talked too fast at times (3 cards didn't specifically complain of Olivier.)

   11  Olivier difficult to understand.

Fontaine:
   2  Not clear.

## COMMENTS ON STORY IN GENERAL:

1  First part better than last.
12  Followed action, characters and mood of book very well.
1  Too much dialogue.
1  Too much footage without dialogue.
1  Some of the dialogue too direct.
1  More comedy relief.
1  More like it.
1  Seemed amateurish, didn't bring out important points clearly enough.
1  Story held person spellbound.

1  Maxim riled too often by "I".
1  Maxim's bluntness hard to explain till toward end.

4  Cause of Rebecca's death should be brought out sooner. At first believed Rebecca drowned in surf.
1  Never found out if Maxim killed Rebecca or if she died of cancer.

2  Rebecca brought to Olivier's mind too much.
1  Rather weird in spots.
1  Hope it gets by the Hays' office.

## COMMENTS LISTED ACCORDING TO SEQ.:

### "I'S" VOICE OVER MANDERLEY:
1  Inaudible (possible it was due to stir of patrons)
1  Shorten
1  Spoils picture because they knew heroine lived through it all.

### MONTE CARLO SEQ:
7  Rather confusing.
2  Too abrupt.
1  Change of locations not clear.
8  Too long (1 card said too many long drives.)
1  Needs another preface, confusing who Rebecca is.
4  Death of Rebecca should have been told sooner.

2  Mrs. Van Hopper does too much dry talking—could rewrite beginning.
1  Part of Mrs. van Hopper too long and out-spoken.
3  Leave out part where Mrs. Van Hopper asks "I" if she has been doing anything she shouldn't.
1  Leave out a little of Fontaine's confusion.

1  Maxim's dialogue muffled in hotel dining room.

4   Some of first part inaudible.
2   Dialogue rather confusing.
2   Hard to understand Maxim in automobile.

ARRIVAL AT MANDERLEY:
1   Mrs. Danvers seemed young for having been in family so long.
1   Mrs. Danvers part could have been made clearer.
1   Manderley drives too long.
4   Too long when "I" meets servants.

MANDERLEY:
6   First half too long.
1   Olivier's love for Fontaine shouldn't be held until the end.
3   Fontaine too drooped and meek.
3   Showing Mrs. Danvers' eyes so much took away from feeling of the difficult part.
4   Some scenes in the house seem boresome and tiresome.

MORNING ROOM:
1   Too long.

GILES AND BEATRICE LUNCHEON SCENE:
1   Joke Giles tells at opening of scene inappropriate.
2   Giles hard to understand.
1   Maxim's good-bye to sister—dialogue not clear.

COVE:
2   Ben's part in story confusing. (1 said quite a character in book)
1   Who was the skeleton in the small beach cottage?

HONEYMOON MOVIE:
2   Maxim shows too obviously death of Rebecca was at his hand when "I" refers to gossip.
1   Confusing.
3   Too long.
1   Not clear in sound of dialogue.
1   Motion picture camera on a tripod couldn't have made zooming shots which Maxim's camera did.

FAVELL'S VISIT:
1   Leave out facial expressions and character changes of Favell.
1   Didn't know what voices upstairs were about until the end.
2   Why did Favell make this secret visit to Mrs. Danvers?

MRS. DANVERS SHOWS "I" REBECCA'S CLOTHES:
7   Too long.
4   Said Rebecca's room (and didn't mention which scene).

FINDING REBECCA'S BOAT:
4   Too abrupt from evening of ball to morning when they find Rebecca's boat.
1   Seems unlikely freighter would ram the boat. Action not very clear.

DECIDING ON COSTUME FOR BALL:
1   Too long.

CONFESSION SEQUENCE:
1   Maxim turned his back on the audience too much.
1   Could end picture after this sequence.
1   Good Photography.

COL. JULYAN LUNCHEON SCENE:
1   Too long.

CORONER'S COURT:
3   Too long.
1   Time on clock in courtroom is wrong.

EXT. CORONER'S COURT:
1   Too long.

INN SEQ.:
1   Person said: "Have my doubts about part: 'Have you been behaving yourself' "?

DR. BAKER'S:
7   Thought the line "Is cancer catching?" could be eliminated. (One said it causes one
        to lose the beauty of the story.)
2   Cut out: "Was she going to have a kid?"

BURNING OF MANDERLEY:
1   Excellent.
2   Author's version more effective.
6   Mrs. Danvers and candle too long. (2 said too melodramatic)
1   Tone down ending—part of Mrs. Danvers.
4   Too drawn out.
1   End at reunion.

MISCELLANEOUS COMMENTS:
2   Why wasn't Fontaine's hair fixed more attractively.
1   Shouldn't have swearing if children see picture.
1   Why isn't "I's" name revealed in picture.
2   Would like to have seen one picture of Rebecca.

The audience response was extremely positive—future films were sometimes not so warmly received. In fact, the only noticeable concern from the responses had to do with the film's length and understanding Laurence Olivier. The previews for *Topaz,* attended by Hitchcock, garnered some of the worst responses in the studio's history.

The *Rebecca* previews take us out of the postproduction process order, but they are an important part to the process—often this is where mistakes are caught with fresh eyes. Peggy Robertson recalled that it wasn't until a final screening (and it was too late to do anything) that she noticed someone standing in the background of one of the long tracking shots from *Under Capricorn.*

"Hitchcock didn't seem at all disturbed. He said, 'Peggy, we've seen this film countless times and we've just noticed it. All we're concerned with is getting it by the audience once—they'll never notice.' And you know, no one has ever mentioned that mistake," Robertson pointed out.

## *Rope*

When Sidney Bernstein and Alfred Hitchcock first planned the filming of *Rope* as a continuous single take, the idea was heralded as a way to be creative and save money. Unfortunately, the execution of the long ten-minute takes was never simple. A single error meant an entire reel of film would be worthless. For example, Hitchcock discovered after a week's work that the color was wrong outside the apartment windows and all of the footage had to be reshot.

The trouble did not end with the production. *Rope* required only ten edits—the breaks between each reel.[5]

The following is the reel break list for *Rope*. A careful reading reveals that Hitchcock cheated a bit on the last cut—reel nine is only five minutes long and

| | REEL BREAKS | |
|---|---|---|
| R 1 | CU strangulation<br>Blackout on Brandon's back, after panup books. | 1—11 |
| R 2 | Black, pan off Brandon's back.<br>CU Kenneth "What do you mean?" | 12-24 |
| R 3 | Two boys cross to greet Janet.<br>Black on Kenneth's back after "No, that would be too much of a shock". | 24-35 |
| R 4 | Black on Kenneth's back, reveal Mr. Atwarter and Phillip at piano.<br>CU Phillip "That's a lie". | 36-46 |
| R 5 | CU Rupert seated by piano.<br>Black on Brandon's back "Aren't we all missing David." | 46-56 |
| R 6 | Black pan-off Brandon's back. "Two desserts Mr. Kadell".<br>Three shot "There's something upsetting both of you." | 56-66 |
| R 7 | Med. shot Mrs. Wilson "Pardon me, sir".<br>Black on Brandon's back as he calls garage. | 66-78 |
| R 8 | Black pan-off Brandon's back to Phillip "Who are you calling?"<br>CU Brandon's hand in gun pocket. | 78-87 |
| R 9 | CU Rupert is aware of gun.<br>Black out on lid of chest. | 87-92 |
| R 10 | Black pan-up from lid of chest.<br>FIN | 93-95 |

[5]Before the platter systems that all modern theaters use, most theaters were equipped with two projectors, which required a changeover between reels. That's why when you watch older movies you see a dot or mark in the upper-right-hand corner of the film every ten minutes or so. This was a cue to the projectionist to prepare for the change to the other projector. Today, films are edited together onto a horizontal platter that can usually hold the entire film.

reel ten is only two minutes long, while the other eight reels are the typical nine to eleven minutes long. He needed the cut at an earlier point in reel nine—so that's where the reel break is!

The numbers originally handwritten to the right are the film's timing at each point.

## Strangers on a Train

Hitchcock's first film of the fifties was an enormous success, owing in part to the director's inventive cross-cutting at key moments. A classic sequence is the tennis match that is cross-cut with Bruno's retrieval of the lighter, followed by the dramatic denouement on the merry-go-round.

Here are Hitchcock's cutting notes for this sequence. They begin with a roughed-out list. Hitchcock divided the page into two columns—Bruno and Guy—and then began to bounce the film back and forth between them. He included a rough visual sketch for the editor to use as a guide. After this informal presentation is a more formal listing of the order for the cuts.

This final list goes on to the film's final moments and includes the instructions that there should be no "tag" ending. This refers to the semicomic moment on the train when a minister asks for a light and the couple ignores him. This ending was added to the American release, but kept off the British version for good reason (as the current Warner Bros. DVD of *Strangers on a Train*, which includes both cuts, demonstrates).

| BRUNO | GUY. | |
|---|---|---|
| — | Ⓐ Game starts | |
| Bruno leaves | — | |
| — | Ⓑ Play. | 70 |
| Bruno in cab | — | |
| — | Ⓒ Play. | 60 |
| Bruno answers Stew | — | |
| Bruno on train | Ⓓ Play. ENDS 2 all 2nd set G near | 50 |
| | Ⓔ Play G near | 40 |
| LAP  DISSOLVE | | |
| BRUNO ARRIVES | | |
| — | Ⓕ Barbara goes | ? |
| BRUNO + MEN | | |
| — | Ⓖ Barbara returns | ? |
| BRUNO DROPS IT | | |
| | Ⓗ Play. ARCHIVES ISSUE | 30 |
| Bruno gropes | — | |
| | Ⓙ Play. | 20 |
| BRUNO gets it | | |
| | Ⓚ Game ends. | |

375

gets it

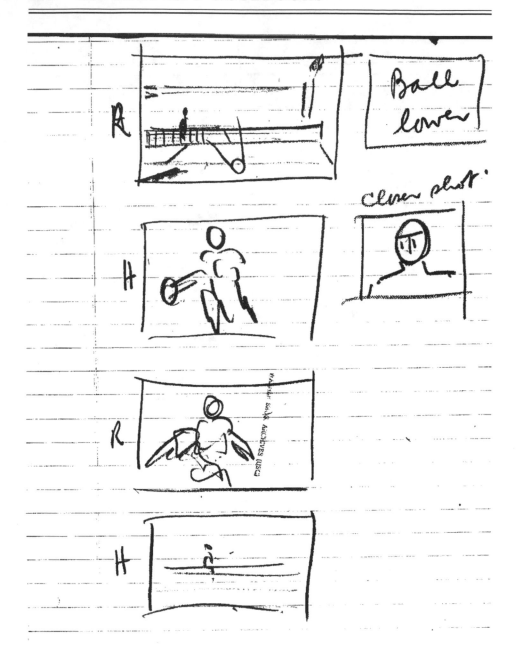

CU ....Guy serves

LS ..(Guy's viewpoint) Reynolds returns ball.

CS ... Buy returns ball.

MS ...(net in fg) Reynolds misses. LINESMAN'S VOICE: "Out"

LS ... Guy crossing to next service court. UMPIRE'S VOICE:  "15-Love")

CU ... Guy serves

LS ... Guy's viewpoint) Reynolds misses

CU ... Guy looking at his ace serve  UMPIRE'S VOICE:  "30-Love"

MS ... Reynolds gets ready to receive serve

MS ... (dbl) Guy serves

MS ... Reynolds returns

CLOSER SHOT: Guy runs across and returns

CLOSER SHOT: Reynolds returns

MS ... Guy lobs

MS ... Reynolds smashes

MS ... Guy misses

CU ... Anne - anxious. UMPIRE'S VOICE:"30-15" and mentions point is/Reynolds Ray

LS.... Guy serving (Forest Hills shot ?)

MS ...(Guy in f.g, Reynolds returns ball out. LINESMAN'S VOICE: "Out"
                                 UMPIRE'S VOICE: "40-15"

MS ... Flash. Guy receives ball from ball boy

CS ... Guy gets ready to serve.

MS ... Reynolds waiting.

MS ... Guy serves

CS ... Ball into net. UMPIRE'S VOICE: "Fault"

MS ... Guy serves again.

MS ... Reynolds lobs

BIG HEAD : Guy smashes.

LS ... Flash - Crowd applauds.     *ump Voice "Game to Mr Haines."*

CS ... Guy moves around back of umpire's chair, looks at clock.

INSERT ;;;Flash of clock.
        BRUNO LEAVES HOUSE.

                                                              2.


    BRUNO LEAVES HOUSE

CS  ANNOUNCER - over shoulder, with play beyond] saying in effect
    that  Guy Haines seems to be rushing his game - very unlike him,
    etc.

MS .. GUY dashing backwards and forwards across base line in middle of
      a volley.

MS .. Reynolds doing the same.

CS .. Guy : similar action.

        BRUNO IN TAXI

BRUNO IN TAXI

Eagle Shot - crowd and play

LS .. Play under awning

MS - pressmen

CS .. Anne and Barbara

CS .. Hennessy and Hammond

CS .. Linesmen and ball boys

CU - Umpire watching

BRUNO ARRIVES AT DEPOT
~~(Possibly~~ dissolve, ~~possibly not - decide later.)~~

LS .. Establishing crowd and play

Cu -- Guy smashes

LS -- Crowd applauding  UMPIRE'S VOICE: ~~Mr. Haines leads~~
③ *Announces*.                        "Mr. Haines leads - one game to
                                       love in the third set."

CS -- Anne and Barbara - dialogue, script scene 393

MS - Barbara passes Hennessy

Play - with umpire in fg.

BRUNO ON TRAIN

Play from under awning

CU   Anne - looks anxiously over shoulder

Barbara gets out of cab

Insert trousers

Milling crowd by name board (piece of Plate)

Barbara passes Hennessy

Barbara joins Anne

④ *Announcer*
Low shot - both Guy and Reynolds playing

MS   Guy playing hard on base-line (dbl)

CS   Reynolds viciously smashing forehand

BIG HEAD - briefest piece of Guy going forward as if missing ball.

FLASH - crowd applauding

CU......Umpire:  "Game and 3rd set to Mr. Reynolds.  Mr. Haines
                  leads two sets to one."

CU.....Anne, distressed.

MS.... Guy, behind umpire's chair, looks at:

Insert..Clock

QUICK DISSOLVE

BRUNO GETS OFF TRAIN AND DROPS LIGHTER

### BRUNO DROPS LIGHTER

CU - ANNOUNCER, saying in effect that set score is two to one, Haines leading, and that game score is ten all, and that if Haines wins this and the next game he wins the set and the match.

LS - General exciting play.

### BRUNO DIALOGUE SCENE WITH MEN

LS - Play - in which Guy wins point. UMPIRE'S VOICE: "Game to Mr. H."

CU - ANNOUNCER, excited, saying in effect "This has been a long set." Haines needs only one more game to win the match. Both men look tired."

LS - General exciting play.

### BRUNO KNOCKS LIGHTER OFF LEDGE

CS - Guy playing

CS - Reynolds returns

CS - Guy wins point. UMPIRE'S VOICE: "Score is 40-30."

CU - ANNOUNCER: "Haines now leads forty to thirty. It is match point. He wins the match if he gets the next point."

- Play - Reynolds wins point. UMPIRE'S VOICE: "Score is deuce."

LS - Crowd

### BRUNO REACHES FOR LOWER LEDGE

LS - Players poised. UMPIRE'S VOICE: "Advantage Mr. Reynolds."

LS - Reynolds serves.

CLOSER SHOT - Guy returns.

"          - Reynolds returns.

"          - Guy scores. UMPIRE'S VOICE: "Score is deuce."

CU - Reynolds serves

CU - Guy returns

CU - Anne

CU - Reynolds scores. UMPIRE'S VOICE: "Advantage Mr. Reynolds."

p.6

### BRUNO'S FINGERS REACHING FOR LIGHTER

MIS.. Play. Haines scores. UMPIRE'S VOICE: "Score is deuce."

BIG HEAD: Reynolds serves.

BIG HEAD: Guy returns

LS       Crowd applauds. UMPIRE'S VOICE: "Advantage Mr. Haines."

### BRUNO'S FINGERS GET LIGHTER
### BRUNO HURRIES AWAY

LS  Play.

CU  Guy smashes - wins point.

Rushes to net

Etc.

REEL  11                    STRANGERS
                                  Cutting notes - 2/1/51

After seedy characters last line and exit, cut to CU Bruno, with Bruno
looking down when we cut to him, and looking up for end of cut.
          CUT TO
what he sees : sun in sky.
          Back to
CU Bruno still looking up.
Repeat same pattern in 2nd series of Bruno looking at sky.

DISSOLVE, not cut from Guy in train to Bruno.

Look for piece of film to precede Bruno's rising to join queue - something
to accentuate it has grown dark.   Perhaps flash of queue, using piece
from angle in which Bruno now joins queue but isn't recognizable - for his
viewpoint shot in this instance.   To intercut with flash CU Bruno looking
out.


Go quicker to Bruno after he joins queue

Trim LS viewpoint boatman and detective that precedes CS their conversation

Trim end of next cut Bruno - don't have him touch his hat.

Trim CS Bruno ahead of boatman talking to girl in booth

Add few frames to Bruno's viewpoint of boatman telling detective he's
spotted the killer

Trim policeman walking toward Bruno

Trim off Bruno narrowing his eyes when he sees Guy.

Trim beginning of Guy walking toward him

Trim 1st shot of Bruno (LS) from Guy's viewpoint

Trim Guy's viewpoint of Bruno, before Bruno turns and runs

Trim beginning of angle in which Bruno gets on machine. Use just flash of
him leaping on

Trim 2 men running after Guy , in angle before Guy gets on merrygoround

Start Guy earlier, with his back closer to camera, in angle in which he
gets on merrygoround

Add few ft. to shot of machinery before it speeds up

Trim CU Bruno wanting to jump from merrygoround - don't have him look down
before viewpoint of whizzing exterior

Lengthen section of fight which comes between Turley scene and scene of
old man saying "I can manage it".  (More cuts.)

After cut of old man going under: trim beginning of next angle, of fight,
so that when we come back to fight here, Guy is almost being flung off.

When Guy is flung behind the horse : cut immediately to CS with Guy
hitting Bruno in the jaw (eliminates whipping with strap, etc.)

Trim mother crying "My little boy!"..

Trim next cut of screaming girls (2nd time they're used)

Everything intercutting with fight should be just flashed - trim all

Start TRACK of woman screaming earlier, as little boy starts to roll
toward edge of merrygoround

Substitute another scream track for above.

Added cut of old man under merrygoround to come in right after girl
on the horse and Bruno smashing Guy in the jaw.

Lose next piece of fight - picking up on CS with horse's hoof coming
down.

Trim two girls on merrygoround

Trim next cut - mother with little blonde boy

Examine other take which shows Guy floating in the air.  Presently
the film doesn't seem to get this over.

Intercut flash of older mother onlooker when Bruno is smashing at
Guy's knuckles - couple of cuts before old man under merrygoround


~~xxxxxxxxxx xxxxx xxxxx xxxx xxxxx xxxxxxxxxxxx xxxxxx xxxxxxx xxxxxxxxx xxxxx~~
REEL 12

Add a beat to beginning of CU Guy after Bruno says (dying scene),
"They got you at last, eh, Guy?"

After Turley says, "...besides he says he hasn't got it," CUT TO
CU Guy, desperate, very anxious, and off scene hear "I think he's
going".  Still in CU, Guy looks down.
       CUT TO
CU Fist.   Hear off scene "He's finished", then fist opens.
       CUT TO
Turley - bends down to get lighter, etc.......

Put back "Very clever fellow" section.


Fade out, Morton Home, before ~~Katharinx~~ Senator's line, starting fade
right at end of Anne's line "..looks funny in his tennis things".
(All right to have action of father rising, etc., without his track,
come in fade.)


No train tag.

## *Dial M for Murder*

A film is screened countless times during the postproduction stage. Different elements are slowly added and adjusted. Special effects and other shots that may not require the actors are often completed during this stage (which accounts for the lengthy gestation period of the modern film, which is so often filled with special effects).

The following memo from the production of *Dial M for Murder* is typical of the kind of work that goes on in a film's final months:

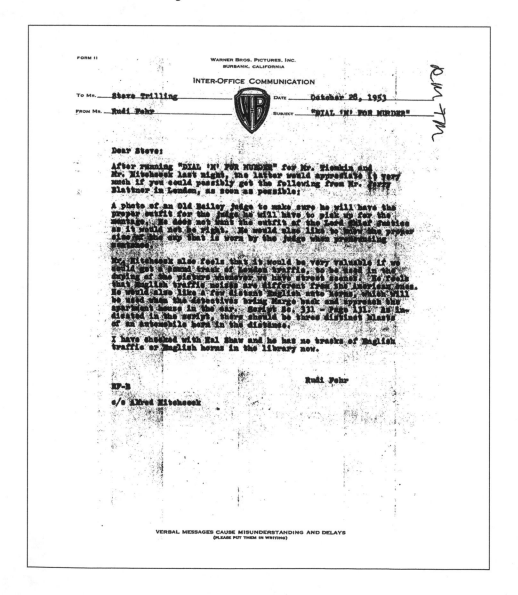

The next memo reveals a number of aspects of Hitchcock's process. First, he is involved with Dimitri Tiomkin, the film's composer, at least to the point of screening the film with him and no doubt discussing with him the overall effect he's after. Hitchcock is also concerned with the film's authenticity, and has requested photos and descriptions of the sentencing process. And finally, he is even concerned with the sound—that distinctly British traffic noises are used as background noise, as opposed to American. Ultimately, it is these fine details that raise fairly standard thriller material to something that can be appreciated on more than one level. At the very least, it's an instructive exercise in the British judicial process.

COPY

WARNER BROS.
ELSTREE STUDIOS
BOREHAM WOOD, HERTZ

4th November 1953

Mr. Steve Trilling,
Warner Bros. Pictures Inc.,
West Coast Studios,
Burbank, California

Dear Steve,

re:   DIAL M FOR MURDER

Further to my letter of the 2nd enclosing authentic "black cap" as worn by Old Bailey Judge, and my cable of the 3rd in which I advised you:

"AIRMAILED TODAY COLOUR PHOTOGRAPH BAILEY JUDGE"

In order to save time I had the photograph despatched direct from the photographers.

We were able to borrow a "Bench Wig" from a Judge and also the clothes as they are worn so you will find therefore, that the photograph should be correct in every detail.

You may be surprised by the wig, which is not the curly full-bottomed wig usually associated with judges. The reason why popular conception has been misled is that photographs cannot be taken of judges inside their courts, and are only taken on ceremonial occasions, when they wear the full-bottomed wig. The little half wig which you will see in the photograph is the one they wear while presiding at a murder trial at the Old Bailey.

Bestest,

Jerry

P.S. Hope to dispatch Dial 'M' sound effects next few days.

C O P Y
  O
    P
      Y

### Procedure on donning the "Black Cap"

After the Jury has given the verdict, the Judge asks the prisoner whether he has anything to say.  Then there is a proclamation for silence, read by the Clerk of the Court.  The Judge's Clerk (who sits beside the Judge) then takes the black cap, which is lying on the desk in front of the Judge, and places it on the Judge's head. The Judge passes sentence, and the Chaplain says "Amen.  And may the Lord have Mercy on your soul."  The prisoner is taken away and the court is cleared.

NOTE

The cap is worn flat on the head with the point marked over the forehead. The Judge's clerk sits on the Judge's left and the Chaplain on the Judge's right.

The work on *Dial M* paid off, as this congratulatory memo suggests:

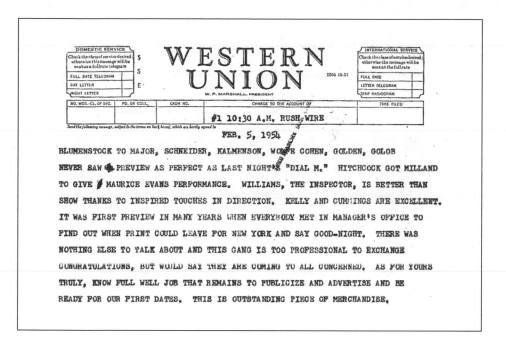

WESTERN UNION

#1 10:30 A.M. RUSH WIRE

FEB. 5, 1954

BLUMENSTOCK TO MAJOR, SCHNEIDER, KALMENSON, WOLFE COHEN, GOLDEN, GOLOB
NEVER SAW A PREVIEW AS PERFECT AS LAST NIGHT'S "DIAL M." HITCHCOCK GOT MILLAND
TO GIVE A MAURICE EVANS PERFORMANCE. WILLIAMS, THE INSPECTOR, IS BETTER THAN
SHOW THANKS TO INSPIRED TOUCHES IN DIRECTION. KELLY AND CUMMINGS ARE EXCELLENT.
IT WAS FIRST PREVIEW IN MANY YEARS WHEN EVERYBODY MET IN MANAGER'S OFFICE TO
FIND OUT WHEN PRINT COULD LEAVE FOR NEW YORK AND SAY GOOD-NIGHT. THERE WAS
NOTHING ELSE TO TALK ABOUT AND THIS GANG IS TOO PROFESSIONAL TO EXCHANGE
CONGRATULATIONS, BUT WOULD SAY THEY ARE COMING TO ALL CONCERNED. AS FOR YOURS
TRULY, KNOW FULL WELL JOB THAT REMAINS TO PUBLICIZE AND ADVERTISE AND BE
READY FOR OUR FIRST DATES. THIS IS OUTSTANDING PIECE OF MERCHANDISE.

## The Man Who Knew Too Much

During his high period, Hitchcock often wrote detailed notes concerning how the sound should be handled. These notes are organized by film reel—which in a standard 35mm print is approximately one thousand feet (or ten minutes) in length.

The best example of the kind of notes Hitchcock provided for the sound element of the film are from the 1955 remake of *The Man Who Knew Too Much* (in the notes, there are references to temporary tracks—these are sound-tracks that are laid down by the editor just to fill in the blanks, so to speak). These notes are instructive and, frankly, uniquely entertaining to read:

## "The Man Who Knew Too Much" Notes

REEL I

In the opening scene on the bus we should have regular interior sounds of the tires on the roadway and the purr of the automobile engine. At the very outset, the ring of the cymbals should carry over into the whine of the tires on the roadway.

In order that the voices of our principals shall not dominate everything else we should occasionally hear some French conversation and maybe some laughter from the French women in the bus. This should be spotted all the way through this bus sequence. Now and again we ought to hear the whine of the tires as they turn corners and we shall need an especially loud sound of tire screech when the brakes are suddenly applied which causes the little boy to lurch and grab the Arab woman's veil. This pretty well covers the amount of sound we shall require in this scene.

To repeat, it is essential that we hear other voices, otherwise just the voices of our principals will make the thing sound stagey, which should be avoided at all costs.

In the scene in the long shot where the bus arrives outside the city walls and goes through the arch, we should hear a general sound of traffic. And especially when the Arab woman on the bus approaches near the camera we should hear the bicycle bell so it will give the impression that the Arab woman is ringing the bell for the camera to get out of the way.

Once we are inside the city walls we should hear general crowd noises and voices and perhaps our first impression of some distant Arab music. Some of the voices that we hear when we do the close up of the bus plowing its way through the crowd should be loud and protesting as though they resented being forced out of the way by the intruding bus.

For the arrival of the bus in the main square in the Place De La Fna we shall, for the first time, hear the mixed sounds of the various drum thumping and the other sounds that come from this market of which we already have tracks.

Again the babble of voices and also bear in mind the sound of horse traffic here when they are conversing at the door of the omnibus.

It may be difficult to do this but if we could hear the laughter coming from Louis Bernard in the distance, it might help us a little bit here dramatically.

A special note: going back to the entrance of the bus through the arch on the inside of the circle, we should have the horn honking for the people to get out of the way which should justify the protesting voices.

REEL II

During the carriage ride from the main square we should hear the music of the various vendors slowly fading from us as we get further and further away. There naturally should be general traffic noises to match what we see on the screen and the regular clippety-clop of the horse's feet of our own carriage.

When we turn from the archway into the street it just calls for normal traffic noise. And then as we get beyond the city walls, the traffic sounds should diminish so that we get the feeling that we are now in a much quieter part of town.

This continues as we enter the grounds of the Mamounia Hotel. Naturally, horses' hooves should sound all through this, especially those across the picture on our way in. There should be French voices heard from the people in the entrance of the Mamounia Hotel and those who are walking around in the forecourt. There should also be faint distant traffic noise heard as though coming from the main street outside.

In the long shot which now has scene missing but will later become the evening shots of the mosques, we should permit ourselves very faint market square music and sounds because these actually do continue until quite late in the evening.

When we first come into the hotel suite of the McKennas we should start by hearing Doris humming the song that the little boy takes up. The humming could actually develop into murmured words of the song here as well.

When we get onto the balcony we should again very faintly hear the Arab music in the distance as though floating over the night air. But when we get inside the room this should diminish so that we get the effect that this can be heard with any clarity only when you are actually on the balcony itself.

While we are on the assassin in the doorway we should hear a couple of doors opening and shutting down the far end of the corridor.

When we cut to Louis Bernard after the assassin has gone we should hear the footsteps of both Jimmy and Doris as they cross the room and approach Louis Bernard, because at present we are long enough on him and so long off them that we must be reminded of their presence. However, during the close up of Louis Bernard and while the footsteps are crossing the room we should still hear faint marketplace music coming over.

It might be a good idea when we are on the balcony to put in some night noises like bullfrogs and crickets and also again a faint airplane sound might be interesting.

In the Arab restaurant we should hear soft distant Arab music coming over. We should also hear French voices and laughter from the other patrons in the restaurant.

<u>REEL III</u>

In this reel the atmosphere in the restaurant as in Reel 2.

In the marketplace, of course, we get the general sounds from the various drumbeats and we should particularly hear both the fast music of the dancers and in the distance the music of the acrobats at the same time. And the Teller of Tales should be an equal blending of this. But each time we move backwards and forwards we should let whatever music we are closest to dominate the scene. Naturally there will be other distant sounds as well, including traffic.

In the walk taken by Jimmy and Doris we naturally will hear a blending of all the sounds.

We must be careful to make sure that the sewing machines are loud enough above the marketplace sounds.

When the chase is first seen our group's attention should be drawn to it by the yells in the distance accompanied by police whistles. Once we get into the souk, our marketplace noises should diminish and be replaced by local sounds, including exclamations from people who are watching the chase. These should thin out when we get into the dye market so that by the time we arrive at the point where the new Arab killer joins we should be practically in silence except for the running footsteps. But the moment we go down to the close shot of the stabbing we should very faintly begin to hear the marketplace sounds coming up again. These, however, should be kept pretty low so that we hear very clearly the loud cry of pain from the stabbed Arab. Then, as he turns the corner in close shot, we can bring up the marketplace sounds to the full again, though not quite as full as we originally had them. They should still be fairly distant as though at the other end of the square.

Special note: do not continue police whistles except at the beginning of the chase.

<u>REEL IV</u>

These marketplace noises should remain as the end of Reel 3, and should die down somewhat during the scene between Jimmy and Louis Bernard. We should hear the arrival of the ambulance, which I think is a bell, and we should hear all the excited murmurings of the Arabs around us.

I would particularly like some loud noise to drown the little boy when he says, "I want to see a French police station" so that we don't hear him at all. It could be an Arab yelling at somebody, or it might be a gear changing on an ambulance, or an ambulance starting up because we see it later starting up in the back of the picture. But whatever it is it should kill the little boy's line as much as possible.

As we have started the sequence here with distant noises as our couple walk along toward the police station, we should bring these sounds up until they reach quite a loud pitch, although not loud enough to drown the dialogue so that when we immediately come to the courtyard of the police station we hear almost a quietness with only the faint marketplace sounds in the distance.

Inside the police station corridor, I think we merely need to hear some distant voices in French and the opening and shutting of doors with a bit of echo on them.

Inside the inspector's office we should hear only the faint traffic sounds and marketplace noise with special reference to the bus which turns during the scene.

Incidentally, we should also establish one or two telephone bell rings and some typewriter noise in the early corridor scene and also spot carefully the telephone bell ring that causes the assistant to come in and say Mr. McKenna is wanted on the telephone. Our office noises should come up again when Jimmy emerges into the corridor to go to the phone, and should remain so when he is on the phone, but not strong enough to interfere with our drama.

Also special note to change the Arab's voice over the telephone and add additional lines so that they can be heard when we see Jimmy's big head with the earpiece come on the screen.

## REEL V

The same general noise regarding police station atmosphere in this reel apply both as to corridor and the police inspector's office.

In the carriage scene that follows we hear naturally the sound of the horse's hooves and the marketplace sounds. I think it would be a good idea to let them increase as our journey goes on so we feel that just as we lost them in the police station, we are approaching them again. Then they will drop out altogether outside the Mamounia Hotel, where we just need the local sounds of French voices and the occasional traffic.

Up in the room where Jimmy tells Doris about the lost child, just an odd distant motor car horn from the cars in the distance and that is all we need here.

Naturally over the long shot of the mosques at night we will hear the long prayer and this will continue over the scene where Jimmy is packing. We should continue this over the whole scene that follows when Jimmy tries to revive Jo and get her to depart for London.

## REEL VI

The exterior of the airport should contain all the necessary atmospheric sounds with the cheering bobbysoxers brought into proper perspective, because the temporary tracks at present are a little loud and out of proportion. We do not necessarily have to hear the voices of the officials quite so loud as at present. They can even be lost as might the rest of the noise. So it should be the cheering kids and takeup noises that dominate the scene.

When we get near the entrance of the arrival and departure room, the kids should subside altogether because they would have lost sight of Jo Conway by this time.

It will be noted at the airport office that there was a shadow moving over the airport circle in the background. This should be accompanied by the sound of a loud plane that has just taken off and passing over the building.

We should have other distant takeoff noises during the whole of this sequence. And perhaps we could hear distant footsteps up and down the office corridor and again some typewriters, telephone bells and the slamming of glass doors. Also include in these background sounds the faint noise of the public address system, arrival and departure flights, etc.

In the Savoy suite we should hear faint traffic noises, maybe a quarter hour of Big Ben in the distance and some tugboat sounds on the Thames nearby. Make sure these tracks are from London because the horn noises are quite different from those in America.

REEL VII

The scenes in the hotel room continue with the same sounds as indicated above.

In the Camden town street we should retain something of the suburban characters of the barking dog and the distant hammering iron.

Now the question of the footsteps. These are very very important. The taxi that drives away after Jimmy gets out should be taken down as quickly as possible because we want no other sounds other than very distant traffic noises because the predominant sound is the footsteps of Jimmy Stewart. They seem to have a strange echo to him because they almost sound like a second pair of footsteps. Until he stops to test it and the echoing footsteps also stop. When he resumes, they resume. And to test it further he stops again, but this time the echoing footsteps continue. Then he slows down and the echoing footsteps slow down. Now as he proceeds, the echo gets louder but his own footsteps remain the same volume. And when he looks around the second time we see the reason for the echoing footsteps. They belong to the other man. Now the two sets of echoing footsteps are heard. The quality of echoing footsteps diminish and they become more normal than Jimmy's and remain normal as the other man passes Jimmy and crosses the street to enter the premises of Ambrose Chappell.

Make sure that the bell that Jimmy presses at the taxidermist's door is rather a weak one and has quite an old-fashioned quality. Don't have it a very up-to-date sharp ring because it would be out of character with the place.

Once Jimmy is in the room there should be just faint sounds of men at work, a cough or two and perhaps a bit of filing noise, an odd tap of a light hammer, etc.

Mr. Tomasini has special notes concerning the re-dubbing of Jimmy's lines after Ambrose Chappell, Jr. has said they have no secrets from their employees.

Note that the correct amount of dialing should be heard when Ambrose Sr. dials.

When Jimmy opens the door to exit let us hear some outside traffic noise and banging iron noise again and barking dog noise just for a brief moment.

Back in the Savoy suite the same sounds apply but it would be wise to avoid Big Ben again. Otherwise we would be committing ourselves to certain times which we should avoid.

Outside Ambrose Chapel again some suburban noise, distant children's cries at play, and the odd traffic that goes by at the end of the street.

## REEL VIII

Interior of Savoy Hotel suite should be the same sounds.

Outside the chapel, the same as previously indicated. And inside the chapel just faint external traffic noises all the way through.

Watch out for balance of Bernard Miles' voice in the room after he has played the record because it at present sounds phony.

After Jimmy and Doris walk across the street toward the chapel we should hear the faint choral music which comes from inside, which increases as they get nearer and nearer to it.

## REEL IX

The choir singing should remain as is and make sure when Jimmy and Doris sing that his voice is pretty much the same volume as the rest of the singing. Or rather should I say the rest of the singing should be brought up to maintain the same level throughout. It is only when Doris sings that it should be brought up to the rest so it direct attention to her.

There should be some advancement to the noise of the people walking out. As when Edna, the organist, walks down there should be continuous talk.

Make sure the sound of the locking door is very clear.

We should also, when the camera moves to the door, hear the shuffling feet running down the stairs.

We should also hear the feet of the thug with the blackjack coming down the stairs.

At present the track of the little boy seems a little too near, especially his banging on the door. This should be much fainter and farther away. As a matter of fact, the present track is bad because the yelling sounds farther than the door knocking. Both should be of equal volume.

The sound of the blackjack on the head is not good. If it is convenient, could an extra be hired who is willing to have a real blackjack hit on the head so that we get the actual sound.

The exterior of the chapel follows the same pattern of sound as indicated previously.

There should be no particular background noise for Woburn's office because it is now late evening. Behind Woburn's scene put in a half hour of Big Ben. Choose the spot where we are on him long enough to play before we overlap into Doris's scene.

Doris, in the phone booth, should have a little distant traffic noise.

## REEL 10

Outside the chapel there will be the usual traffic noises and distant children cries as established previously. When the police car arrives and they begin to go around to examine the place, when we go inside to Jimmy lying on the alter we should hear the distant banging or perhaps the sound of a front door bell ringing indicating the police's attempt to rouse someone.

Back in the street we get our regular noises again until the car drives off.

Inside the chapel we hear the sound of a car driving off when Jimmy is going from one door to the other.

Outside the rear of the embassy, of course, will be the usual traffic sounds, buses going by, etc. These should be carried over faintly as the baldheaded embassy official goes into the kitchen when we should hear no more external sounds at all.

Inside the kitchen our present track will pretty well be satisfactory.

Outside, when they take the boy in, we're back to traffic noises again.

In the kitchen corridor we should hear the passage of four or five people's footsteps crossing the kitchen and then the sound of a door opening and slamming.

We should hear murmured crowd noises and these should build as the bell tolls. We must make sure when we go up to the belfry that we hear it very loud. It must drown all other sounds, street noises and everything else, and only diminish a little bit as Jimmy lowers himself on the roof.

Outside the Albert Hall we want the chatter of people, traffic moving by and the general crowd noises in the lobby. When Doris crosses the lobby her attention is drawn to the arrival of the Prime Minister by a sudden hush on the part of everyone because their attention is drawn to this little element of a ceremony. Also we should hear the faint tuning up coming from inside the Albert Hall.

We will hear applause coming as Doris enters as roughly indicated as at present. There should be especially three distinct sets of applause: one for the concert master which may be heard off; second for the soloist; and third for the conductor.

I imagine we have the track but when the hush falls on the hall when the choir is given the signal to rise, we should hear a concerted sound of the rustle of dresses and the noise of the standing up.

## REEL 11

In this reel of course the main sound will remain exactly as the existing music track from beginning to end. It will be noted that we have taken dramatic license to preserve the same volume of sound whether we are in the hall, the lobby or the corridor and this should remain so in order not to disturb the music unity of the cantata. The hubbub of the crowd should start a bit as Doris has screamed. In other words, she screams and altho there is an immediate response it should grow until the assassin falls, then it should treble in intensity because of the new element that has come into the disturbance.

We should not hear any clear words in her explanations or any from Jimmy Stewart up in the box. We should still get the effect of pantomime but the sound is too loud and the hubbub is too great to hear any actual words they are saying.

On reflection, it might be a little helpful if we would let Doris's voice of explanation to the manager at the end leak through here and there.

## REEL 12

In this reel, in the lobby there is a general hubbub, the running feet of the police, the shouts, "what?" "who?", other people wanting to know what is happening, etc. Be careful here that the voices used must be English voices.

The hubbub should subside a little upon the Prime Minister coming down the stairs and the moment he is gone, the hubbub should be resumed so that we dramatize his little scene with Doris at the bottom of the stairs.

Once we are up in the Green Room, we should hear faint bus traffic going by and a few horns, etc.

As soon as we are in the embassy I think we should have no atmospheric sounds at all because here we are going to rely upon the background music to dramatize this whole scene at the embassy between the Draytons and the ambassador.

When we come back to the Green Room again we resume with our faint traffic noises, etc.

When Jimmy and Doris are on the way in the taxi we get regular taxi interior noise and other passing traffic. This again is reduced to a silence when we get into the lobby of the embassy. And the only sound here should be the hubbub of polite voices coming from the ballroom. Please make sure these are polite voices and not a raucous crowd at the Coliseum.

Incidentally, just to revert to the Green Room, whenever the door opens and closes in the Green Room, either on the part of the detectives or the solitary detective who comes in later, we should let the hubbub of the lobby come into the room.

## REEL 13

In this reel, once we arrive in the ballroom we enlarge the polite hubbub that we heard in the hallway previously. We should reduce this to almost silence as Jimmy and Doris enter so that it matches the curiosity of the guests on seeing two people in ordinary day clothes coming into the room. There should then be a polite silence during the introductions to the Prime Minister and the moment he says, "Jo Conway has consented to sing for us" there should be murmurs of approval and perhaps one or two little light handclaps from the back of the room. Then there should be a shuffling of chairs and a general settling down sound as Doris sits at the piano. During the silence here it might be good to hear odd taxi horn from the street outside so as to remind our audience that we are still in a big city.

When Doris starts to sing we must make sure that she is deliberately projecting her voice and this is most essential when we come to the voice laid over the exit door of the ballroom. And then when we come into the hallway for our first pan shot we should still feel conscious that she is singing loud deliberately.

As we go up the stairs, naturally the voice perspective increases until we actually come into the room. Once we are in the room the voice should be very faint so that we feel it is more easily recognizable to the little boy than it is to Mrs. Drayton.

Once we are back in the ballroom naturally the volume returns ILLEGIBLE reach the point where Jimmy gets into the hallway and our volume should match up previous volume for ILLEGIBLE full.

It should drop a little XXXXXXXXX.

As Jimmy mounts XXXXXX.

Up in the room the voice of Doris should drop as previous and when the little boy starts to whistle he should be quite shrill.

Once we are back in the ballroom the whistle at first should not be heard because Doris's voice is much louder and drowns any sound of it. It is only when there is. a break or a pause in her song that this whistle comes through as roughly indicated as at present.

This should be heard by Jimmy as well but it should be so faint that it might, to the rest of the people in the room, sound like a passing boy in the street whistling.

The whistling should only be heard spasmodically as Jimmy moves down the room until he gets outside the door. But this time the whistling should stop because obviously the little boy has broken down upstairs.

About this time the first song is ending to a round of polite but not too enthusiastic applause. We then hear the chords played on the piano and Doris starts her second song.

We now go to the back stairs where Drayton is about to go up to the boy. Here we make the song quite unobtrusive so as not to draw Drayton's attention to it too much.

Back in the hall as Jimmy mounts the stairs, we return to our previously established volume.

Up in the room we are back now to the voice being very faint. As Mrs. Drayton starts to rise from the couch the first faint sounds of footsteps on the back stairs are heard. These should increase in volume as she crosses to the window and returns to the boy. At one point the footsteps should be cut off by the sound of a door closing. So we are now in mid-air. We don't know whether they are coming along or not. As she looks at the door handle we hear the soft tread of the footsteps come in again as though they change from back stairs to carpet. Then the door handle turns and the door flies open as Mrs. Drayton screams. The voice of Doris below naturally comes up a step or two.

From this point on, after Drayton's entry, the background remains Doris's voice and, during the descent of the stairs, increases in volume just as it originally decreased as we went up the stairs. It breaks off when the shot goes off and from this point on we hear the hubbub roughly as it is at present in the picture.

This hubbub drops to the silence of the Savoy Hotel room until the door opens and the McKenna family return. After Jimmy Stewart's line about going to pick up Hank, Mr. Herrmann will take over.

Special note: when we get back to the apartment, a couple of ladylike snores might be permitted here.


Notice that Hitchcock, throughout their career together, gave Bernard Herrmann a very free hand in how he developed the music for his films.

Unfortunately, this free hand ultimately led to the disastrous falling out over *Torn Curtain.*

# The Birds

*The Birds* was an enormously complicated film at every step of the process. Regardless of where one might stand on just where *The Birds* critically fits in the Hitchcock canon, all must concede the film is a technical achievement.

The film's strength lies not only in its well-planned and believable special effects, but also in its careful editing. In particular, there are two outstanding sequences. The first scene is known as the Crow Sequence (for which the storyboards are included earlier). Hitchcock wrote out these notes on how the scene should be assembled in the editing room:

CROW SEQUENCE (1)

1. Melanie's car turns and goes up School Road.

2. Closer shot car coming to a stop outside school. Melanie alights and goes up steps to school interior.

3. Medium shot. Melanie emerges and strolls up street toward Annie's House.

4. Melanie turns back and seats herself on seat in front of play yard.

5. A side profile of Melanie as she sits. Size of shot has seat on bottom of screen we are shooting toward 3/4 school.

6. 3/4 angle on play yard behind Melanie. A crow alights on the Jungle Jim.

7. A nearer cut of Melanie same angle as previous.

CROW SEQUENCE (2)
continued

9. Nearer shot of Melanie smoking. Same angle. Just above waist – bust shot.

10. Play yard again 5 more crows arrive.

11. Head and shoulders of Melanie. Hold for 20 or 30 feet. She looks up.

12. A crow is coming down toward her

13. Same as 11 but head turning right to left & looking up.

14. Crow moving down and left to right sky or Annie's roof background.

15. Same as 11 but body turning to follow crow.

16. Crow descending to yard and revealing 200 crows all over Jungle Jims and

**CROW SEQUENCE cont. (3)**

18 The Play yard full of crows.

19 Big head of horrified Melanie

20 The Play Yard

21 Big profile of Melanie. She turns with back to camera and goes toward school looking across at crows as she goes away. The camera follows her so that her image becomes smaller as she goes up steps into the school.

22 A side on dolly shot of the crows to cut into the first part of 21.

23 After this, follow existing script for school interiors.

23-24 A full shot - straight on of all the crows. say 6 feet long.

24-25 A nearer shot and another angle of 24   8 feet long.

25-26 Closer still and a "   "   "   "

---

**(4)**

27-28 A full screen of crows - about 50 or more. - the shoot off - the feet pattering. Suddenly the crows rise - the camera pans up with them.

28-29 The full shot showing the children running toward the camera - Annie herding them at the rear. The crows - about 200-many over the schoolhouse roof and descending toward and reaching the running children. Shot as a plate with 6 or 7 children in front on a treadmill with the mechanical birds coming into top of screen as though continuing on from the plate. The birds swing around and among the foreground children.   15 feet

29-30 A side view of running children with Melanie in front urging them forward. Birds fly between them 2 or 3 others wheel around 1 here

---

**CROW SEQUENCE (5)** continued

30-31 3 or 4 children running Birds overhead - one or two children spread out as others come in from sides, and take their places. Birds swerve in and out-   3 feet

31-32 A nearer side or view without Melanie Birds wheeling in and out others overhead   3 feet.

34-35 A 3/4 Back of 2 children running both or birds over head and others wheeling. Screen almost full of Birds   2 feet

36-37 C.U. Feet running.

36 37A (see end sheet No 8)

38-39 One screaming child as Bird swoops from top down to lower right   1 foot.

41-42 Head & Shoulders of Boy who ducks behind pole - Bird goes by as another attacks him from right hand side.   2 feet.

---

**(5A)**

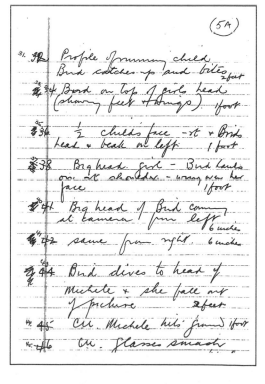

31 32 Profile of running child Bird catches up and bites   2 feet

33 34 Bird on top of girls head (showing feet + wings)   1 foot

35 36 1/2 child's face - it + Birds head + beak on left   1 foot

37 38 Big head girl - Bird lands on off shoulder - wings over her face   1 foot

39 41 Big head of Bird coming at camera from left   6 inches

41 42 same from right   6 inches

43 44 Bird dives to head of Michele + she falls out of picture   2 feet

44 45 CU. Michele hits ground   1 foot

45 46 CU. glasses smash

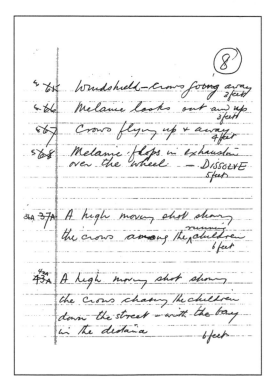

CROW SEQUENCE (6)
continued

47  Flash Kathy sees & turns back. Birds swirling around. 2 feet

48  6 Birds descend on fallen Michele – legs running by. 1 foot

49  Kathy rushes in she disperses birds & bends to pick up Michele. 3 feet

50  Side on. Melanie stops, looks back & sees Kathy and Michele – heads of other children rush by in foreground. Birds swirling. Melanie dashes out left. 2 feet

51  Side on. Melanie reaches Kathy & Michele – Michele now on feet – Birds swirling. Melanie looks about – sees 3 feet

52  Station wagon across the street. Birds swirling about. Children running by. 2 feet

53  Melanie drags Kathy & Michele to wagon – shot shows Bay in distance and children running on to bottom of street


CROW SEQUENCE (7)

54  Shooting inside wagon across front seat. The three scramble in Kathy first then Michele and Melanie last – door slams on crows swooping around. Kathy & Michele screaming with fright. 8 feet

55  Thro' the windshield we see crows attacking. Bay & running children in distance. 3 feet

56  Faces of the three – Birds fluttering on Rear window. 3 feet

57  Melanie – wheel in f.g. she starts to slam hand on horn ring. 3 feet

58  Crows attacking side window. 2 feet

59  Hand on horn ring. 2 feet

60  Kathy & Michele's faces huddled together. 2 feet

61  Melanie's big head. she looks down. 2 feet

62  C.U. Knob of wiper – her hand comes in & pulls it out


(8)

65  Windshield – crows going away. 2 feet

66  Melanie looks out and up. 3 feet

67  Crows flying up & away. 4 feet

68  Melanie flops in exhaustion over the wheel – DISSOLVE 5 feet


37A (36A)  A high moving shot showing the crows among the running children. 6 feet


43A (43a)  A high moving shot showing the crows chasing the children down the street – with the bay in the distance. 6 feet

Two other harrowing scenes are the attack on the birthday party during a game of blindman's bluff and the attack on the town while Mitch Brenner (Rod Taylor) and Melanie Daniels (Tippi Hedren) are at the Tides Café. Here are Hitchcock's original handwritten notes for the editing of these sequences (the interlinear clarifications are from one of Hitchcock's assistants):

Shots.

1  Gull swooping  Bird Poo
2  Hits Blindman — "Don't touch."
3  Gull swings back.
4  Reaction Annie — head swing.
5     "    Mitch + Melanie — slant fwd.
6  2 Gulls downward sweep.
   (Annie ducks yelling + Kids.
   look up + scatter.
7  Lydia reacts.
7a  Blindman groping  7b Gull coming
                      7c Lydia grabs her. away
8  Gulls dives between mothers who
   Kids in f.g. running by.
9  Gulls in sky coming down
10  Mitch comes back with broom
    starts to swing at gull
    in f.g.
11  Kid running to bank
12  Gull following.
13  Kid flings body onto bank
14  C.U. Gull smashes in Kid.
15  all Run to hurt child.
16  They reach child, some
    look up.
17  Gulls going away.

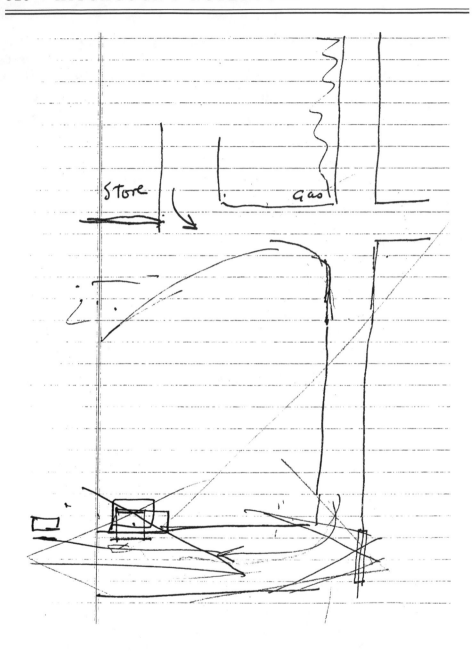

Tides attack    (1)

(473b) (1.) Viewed from the side window of Tides
~~Sky full of gulls~~ – 3 or 4
diving down toward highway
over roof of Tides office. ~~Two~~ Two
more swoop ~~off~~ into foreground
of Tides side window and out to
left.

(473c)    AS 15.

(473D) (2) The first gull reaches the
gas station ~~but~~ misses the
attendant who is in the
act of filling a car – the
owner is seen retreating into
the men's room.

? NO.    Flash Group at Tides window

(3) A nearer view of the gas station
a second gull hits the man
on the back – he falls – hits his
head on the pump & the
collapses over the gasoline
hosepipe, pulling it out & ~~&~~
causing it to spill. The third
and fourth gulls swoop by.
The gas begins to flow away.

(476) (4) After first part of scene 476 we
come to windows and over Melanie's
shoulder we see the men arrive
to rescue attacked gas station
attendant. Three or Four gulls
are still ~~and~~ attacking and they

Tides attack                    ②

flutter away as the men appear
to beat them off. This angle is
~~shot~~ shot from same distance
as N⁰ 2 (Sc 473d) Suddenly
Melanie in the foreground turns
in full profile and looks down

⑤    On the sloping pavement trem-
     ~~bar~~ a stream of gasoline
     is [?] flowing toward the right,
     into the compass.

(477)²    AS 15.

(479) ⑥   The camera follows the flow
          of gas back to the station. (The
          camera is [?]

(479a)    A. [?]

(480) ⑦   the gas reaching the [?]
          [?]. It has
(481)     flowed under the car.
          AS 15
(482)     AS 15.
(482a)    AS 15 (added to script)
(483) ⑧   The big blow up of the parked
          car. The man is enveloped in
          flame.
(484)     AS 15
(485)     ~~[?]~~ as revised in script.

Tides attack ③

486 | A very high shot shows the beginning of the people of the town rushing around the car park and the streets across the highway, endeavoring to put out the two fires. We see automobiles coming to a stop on Highway one, and the oil smoke beginning to rise from the burning gas station and the parked cars. Some men have managed to start a fire hose and have trained it on to the burning cars. Suddenly the foreground begins to fill with close wheeling gulls. The whole picture becomes obliterated by the foreground birds who seem to swoop down on the town.

487 | A raking shot outside the Tides Restaurant showing the phone booth and Motel office in the b.g. People are rushing out from the restaurant and look up in alarm at the sky. Gulls begin to descend into the scene driving the people back into the restaurant. Melanie is seen in the distance calling for

The process of placing the birds on the screen with the actors is called "matte work." There are several ways two images can be matted together. During preproduction, Hitchcock's production team researched which matte process would be the best to use for *The Birds*. He chose the second process described below (which accounts for Ub Iwerks's credit on the film).

## Travelling Matte Systems in General Use

1. <u>COBALT BLUE</u>—color separation process using a special cobalt blue paint on muslin or blue dye on a transparent screen.

   The painted muslin is lit from the front using any convenient light—arcs or incandescent.

   The transparent screen is lit from behind using banks of photo floods.

   In this process the matte is made from the blue register of regular color neg.

   <u>Advantages</u>—The chief advantage of this method is the availability of equipment—lights, cameras, and any one of the various sizes of film in current use—35mm, VistaVision, 65mm, etc. It is even possible to shoot outdoors using sunlight.

   <u>Disadvantages</u>—
   - (a) Color, particularly in the blue range is practically impossible unless the blue is very light. Certain greens and magenta are difficult to obtain.
   - (b) The matte (made from the blue separation) is, in effect, a dupe and has a tendency to be less accurate than mattes made directly in the camera, i.e. Sodium Vapour. This often results in the familiar blue line around the figures. Printing care can reduce this hazard (enlargement or reduction of the foreground strip). This system is now being used by
     - (a) M.G.M. (information received from Robert Hoag, head of optical dept.),
     - (b) U.I. (discussed use with George Golitzen, head of Production),
     - (c) Columbia Pictures—Larry Butler (special effects),
     - (d) Fox—William Abbot
     - (e) Paramount—Farciot Edouart.

     NOTE: This system is the one in general use and seems most adaptable to the varying film sizes and available camera and lighting equipment.

2. <u>SODIUM VAPOUR</u>

   This is also a color separation process but uses the very thin sodium band in the approx. center of the spectrum. It seems least affected by the other colors and allows a complete range of foreground colors. The screen is muslin painted yellow and lit by sodium vapour lamps.

   Two strips of 35mm film are used—one is a regular color neg. and the other is sensitive to the sodium light for the purposes of the matte strip.

   The camera now in use is the Technicolor camera with a beam splitting lens or prism.

   <u>Advantages</u>—Since the sodium band is not affected
   - (a) by yellow pigment color a complete range of color is available in foreground subjects. (In the cobalt color separation method any strong blue would make its own matte.)
   - (b) The matte is made at the same time as the foreground subject to be matted and the result is a more accurate matte than those 'duped' in the other processes.
   - (c) Extremely fine detail without the usual line or halo is possible—for example, smoke, lace or net, hair, string, etc. Fast moving objects which tend to blur i.e. birds, running figures, etc. are reproduced with the blur.

NOTE: If needed, the background can be printed in or out of focus to blend with foreground subject. (This is possible in the other processes also.)

Disadvantages—The chief disadvantage is the lack of special equipment.

(a) At present, Walt Disney Studios have the only (24) Sodium Vapour lamps available. These lamps will light a screen 30' × 50'.

NOTE: If a larger area than this is required it is possible to put a small screen in the foreground with a hole in the center to shoot thru to the larger screen. This would not allow action to cross the entire frame but could be useful in some shots.

If more lamps are required they must be purchased in England (according to Ub Iwerks the American lamps have not proven satisfactory.)

(b) The film is limited in size to 35mm for use in the Technicolor camera.

NOTE: The background, however, may be shot in VistaVision or Panavision where a sharper (less grain) image is required and reduced to 35mm in the printing.

(c) Technicolor camera must be rented.

(d) Use of special 'beam splitter' prism for the Technicolor camera. There is only one available at this time (Walt Disney Studios) although both W. Disney and Universal-Int. are contemplating additional lenses in the near future.

NOTE: The printer is owned by W. Disney and can be adapted to VistaVision or Panavision backgrounds. It is an instrument of great accuracy and latitude—allowing variations in size of background as well as placement of foreground, in relation to background.

NOTE: Although this system is not in general use (due to the above reasons) it appears to be the most accurate and to allow the best color reproduction—(Most of the persons talked to admit to its superior quality.)

3. ULTRA VIOLET AND INFRA RED

Since these systems involve the invisible bands at both ends of the spectrum they have similar problems. While they are essentially the same process as Sodium Vapour—existing lenses are incapable of a sharp focus in these invisible bands. Usually a dupe must be made for the matte so that the line or halo problem is similar to that in Cobalt Blue.

Warner Bros. and Fox have used these processes but seem to be favoring the Cobalt Blue at this time.

Color difference in Mercury vapour light similar to problem in Blue.

Since each method has limitations it would appear that, if production permits, the ideal solution would be to consider the needs of each individual shot in the picture in terms of the best possible method.

For example:

1) Very long shot (small figure) with action across screen requiring 60' or more in width—Cobalt Blue should be used.

2) C.U. with background not in sharp focus—background projection.

3) Med. Shot. birds flying in foreground. Sodium Vapour.

4) L.S. on exterior—Blue backing.

The work in *The Birds* is outstanding (and certainly far superior to the rear screen work generally dismissed in his next film, *Marnie*).

Another progressive aspect to *The Birds* was the soundtrack. Bernard Herrmann provided some overall ideas concerning the sound effects for the film, but Hitchcock insisted on no musical score. Instead, he had Remi Gassmann and Oskar Sala design a provocative electronic soundtrack (which was recorded in Germany). His notes, below, are as fascinating as (but more experimental than) his notes for *The Man Who Knew Too Much*.

## Background Sounds for "The Birds"

There will be two kinds of sounds in the background of this picture. One will be natural sounds and the other will be electronic sounds.

In the following lists of sequences, following the number of the sequence we will indicate in parenthesis which is natural and which is electronic.

As far as can be indicated at present, it is our intention to do the natural sounds in the studio here and leave the electronic sounds to be shot in Germany.

REEL 1

1. (ELECTRONIC) Title backgrounds as will be seen behind the titles, we have silhouetted flying birds. These will vary in size, start in very close. In fact, so close that they almost take on abstract forms. For the electronic sounds we could try just wing noises only with a variation of volume and a variation in the expression of it in terms of rhythm. We could also consider whether we have any bird sounds such as crow or gull sounds or their electronic equivalents, or a combination of both wing and bird cry sounds.

Whatever sounds we have in behind the titles the question of volume should be carefully gone into in view of the fact that we are not using any music at all. So therefore in a sense the volume is a very important factor here.

2. (NATURAL) This sequence calls for San Francisco street sounds including that of the cable car and general passerby sounds. When Melanie looks up to the sky, we should put in some faint cries of gulls in order to create the unusual nature of their numbers. It should be debated whether this faint distant sound should perhaps not be a natural one but a stylized one electronically made.

3. (NATURAL) The bird shop, the existing background sounds of birds singing, twittering should remain. In the opening shot as Melanie comes through the door, we should hear the traffic noises coming from outside including perhaps another cable car sound. As the camera pans her around the top of the stairs, removing the front door from our view, we should fade away the traffic noise. When we cut back to the arrival of Mr. Brenner, we should bring up the traffic noises again and, in order to avoid a jar, we should just softly bring it up before we cut to the entrance.

Again the traffic noise should subside as we pan him up the stairs and the front door disappears from view.

Traffic noises should resume when Melanie is panned down the stairs to the front door. As she looks out, we see Mr. Brenner's car going away so we should now put in full traffic noises.

## REEL 2

When Melanie turns and goes back to mark down the number of the car, traffic noises should be taken down. And in the final scene while she is on the phone, we should just have a token sound of traffic so that her dialogue is not interfered with. NOTE: Hold down Mrs. McGruder's scream when the bird goes loose.

4. (NATURAL) Apartment hallway, downstairs as Melanie's feet and the cage she is carrying come through from the street. We should have just casual traffic sounds; in other words an automobile or two passing by. This sound should be cut off suddenly as the elevator doors close.

5. (NATURAL) Inside the elevator we just hear the hum of its rising from one floor to another. There are no external noises.

6. (NATURAL) Upper landing. We hear the elevator doors opening and the emergence of the two characters as they walk down the corridor. It seems the only sounds we have in this scene should be faint automobile horns to remind us that we are still in the city. Perhaps an occasional cheep should be heard from the lovebirds.

7. (NATURAL) The journey to Bodega Bay. Sounds here are fairly self-evident. We need the sounds of the automobile from the driver's point of view, accompanied by the screaming of tires on the curves and then the distant, faint sounds of the automobile when seen in the long shots. Traffic sounds should increase when we see the car tear into the center of town. This continues until Melanie enters the general store.

8. (NATURAL) Inside the store we just hear an odd automobile or two pass by. When the couple emerge onto the front porch of the store, our traffic sounds should come up but they still do not have to be too busy. Again, just an odd one or two passing and perhaps distant voices of people. When we go back into the store, the traffic sounds should be a little louder because the door has been left open and this will continue until Melanie departs.

9. In the second section of the store scene we should hear someone, unseen, moving boxes around so that we can account for the normal voice off.

10. (NATURAL) At Annie's. The car going up the road is self-evident sound. During the scene between the two women, we could perhaps hear the o.s. voices of children playing.

## REEL 3

11. (NATURAL) sound, the envelope, outside the general store. Here again we need

occasional travel sounds and perhaps as we get down to the dock we could begin to hear some gulls occasionally making sounds. The rest of the sounds should remain as they are at present in the picture, that is the quantity of the footsteps on the pier and down to the starting of the outboard motor.

12. (NATURAL) The journey to and from the Brenners' house. The early part of the journey across the bay should obviously have only the outboard motor boat sounds varying with the nearness or distance of the image. When Melanie arrives at the Brenner house and switches off her motor, we should only then hear the sound of the Brenners' truck departing. After this, she paddles to the dock which calls only for water sounds and perhaps an odd gull or two. The rest of the sound when she goes along the dock into movements should not have any sound. Melanie starts the outboard motor again. Here the sound of her own outboard motor drowns out any other sound, such as the car racing around the bay, so we would not need any sound of this.

13. When we see the first cut of the dock we should hear o.s., the motor being cut off so that she is drifting in when the gull swoops down to attack her. After the gull has hit Melanie, the rest of the sounds remain as in the picture except that we do not need any more outboard motor sounds. Just the lapping of water and the existing sounds as they are at the moment which will take us right up to the entrance into the Tides Restaurant. There might perhaps be an occasional automobile, but at present the footage is so short that this might not be necessary.

14. (NATURAL) Inside the Tides. It will be sufficient if we have a general murmur of customers and perhaps a few orders being given to the kitchen through the half-open door. We might get a little traffic sound as the door opens and Mrs. Brenner enters.

REEL 4

We should also consider bringing up perhaps some o.s. laughter from the customers here where there is a conversation between Melanie and Mitch and Mrs. Brenner. Through all this should be the sounds of glass and china being collected or moved around.

15. (NATURAL) Second Annie scene. There are no particular sounds to add here except those which are on the film at the moment perhaps and the migrating birds shot should be played natural as well. The sound of the migrating birds should come ahead of the shot so as to draw the two women's attention to it.

16. (NATURAL) Melanie's arrival at the Brenners. It would be nice to suggest that we are on the far reaches of the bay and the only way that seems possible is to have some faint gull noises and these should continue right through the scene until the family and Melanie enter the house.

17. Inside Brenner home before and after dinner. Here the sounds remain practically as they are in the picture. NOTE: The MUSIC DEPARTMENT should pay special attention to the ironing out of the piano sounds so they come in proper sequence.

REEL 5

18. The departure of Melanie. Although we don't show them, immediately at the end of this sequence, Mitch is going to look up to the phone or power lines and see that it is completely covered with blackbirds. There is a possibility that we could have a kind of murmuring sound that could have a kind of restive quality so therefore this should be established at the beginning of the sequence and brought up a little louder at the time we see them, and remain louder until Mitch turns and re-enters the house. Over this, of course, come the NATURAL automobile sounds, the starting and departure of the car.

19. (NATURAL) Inside Annie's at night. There are no sounds necessary beyond the existing ones in the picture. This includes the thud of the gull against the front door.

REEL 6

20. (NATURAL and ELECTRONIC) The children's party. The first part of this sequence should have just the natural sounds of the children's game. This should continue all through the scene on the top of the dunes, Melanie and Mitch, with its natural perspective and then the electronic sounds should start with the attack by the gulls. It will be very necessary to watch that the screams of the children and the screams of the gulls do not sound the same. There will be obviously the need for careful examination of this. The end of the sequence the screams of the gulls should fade away in the distance at the same time that the children's cries finish off, so that we end with a silent background broken only by the dialogue of the characters.

21. (ELECTRONIC) The second bird sequence. The overall sounds in this sequence should have a quality of shrill anger as though the birds in their own particular way were invading the room and almost screaming at the occupants. The quality of this sound should assail the ears of the audience to perhaps an almost unbearable degree. It should not necessarily have volume, but the quality of the shrill notes should be something like the effect of the screech that you get if you scrape two pieces of metal together. There should be some build-up but nevertheless, in view of the sudden rush and such a quantity coming in together that the sound should start with a fairly comprehensive amount at the beginning of the scene. Naturally accompanying this but in a much lesser degree, we have the sound of the little wings beating. Perhaps there should be some sprinkling of thuds where birds hit the walls and other objects in the room. In addition to all this, there are the sounds, of course the NATURAL sounds, of the flicking of the napkin by Mitch, the tipping of the table and the thrusting of it to the fireplace, etc., etc.

22. (NATURAL) sound—The sheriff sequence. There is nothing required for this sequence except the natural sounds that we already have in the picture. At the end we should hear Melanie open the door to go out to her car.

REEL 7

23. (NATURAL) The morning after the birds. The voices here should be brought into line in relation to the location of the various people as heard by Melanie from her room.

24. (NATURAL) sound. Fawcett's farm. Upon Mrs. Brenner's arrival we should hear a few natural farm sounds, but definitely no chicken sounds. After Mrs. Brenner has entered the house, we should be in silence so that we can hear the choking sounds of Mrs. Brenner when she dashes out and just the simple sounds of the roaring truck as she dashes back to her home.

25. (NATURAL) sounds. Mrs. Brenner and Melanie in the bedroom. There are no particular sounds required here except those that we already have in the picture.

## REEL 8

26. (NATURAL and ELECTRONIC) The school and crow sequence. At the start we get Melanie's car approaching and coming to a stop outside the school. In the background we hear the children singing. Melanie goes in and the singing naturally becomes louder until Melanie is in the schoolroom proper. She exits and the sound of the children singing diminishes again, and stays at same volume while she is seated on the bench. We should not hear any sounds of the crows arriving because we assume that the children's voices would cover this. Finally when Melanie returns to the school, we continue the NATURAL sounds in the proper perspective inside the schoolroom. Then after the children have started to exit, we go back to the crows. We should have a silence with an odd flapping or two of the wings because we assume the children will tiptoe out. Suddenly we hear the running feet of the children. Immediately there is a tremendous fluttering of wings as the crows rise. In the long shot we see the crows coming over the top of the schoolhouse and for the first time we hear the distant massing electronic sounds of growing anger as they descend upon the children. The sound increases now for the rest of the running sequence. We hear running feet, the odd screams of the children which should not be reduced by the croaking of the crows but should be continuous, but possibly not excessive so we do not get a monotonous humdrum all the time. All this continues until the distant screams of the children are heard going down the street, while Melanie picks up Michele and hurries her across to the station wagon. Once they are inside the wagon and the window is wound up, we hear the banging and flattening of wings and the groans all around the station wagon but with a reduced volume. Finally, the croaking dies away as do the screams of the children and Melanie drops her head on the wheel in complete silence. NOTE 2: MUSIC DEPARTMENT: Practice children singing song, at certain point possibly double the tempo.

## REEL 9

27. (NATURAL) Inside Tides Restaurant. This should be the sound of the inside of a restaurant. The general murmur and laughter of customers but as the scene proceeds and the voices of our immediate participants become raised, the background sounds should become subdued for a moment as though all the customers were listening. Then the sounds of these customers should fluctuate accordingly. In addition, when the kitchen door opens, we should hear the growing sounds of voices and china, etc., coming from the kitchen. It is very essential to make sure that this background sound indicates a preoccupation by the rest of the

customers, otherwise we will get the feeling that our argumentative voices in the front would have created a continual listening silence from the rest of the customers.

## REEL 10

28. (ELECTRONIC) The attack on the Tides. At the beginning of this sequence when we are inside the Tides and people are rushing out and in, we should hear some individual screams of gulls to justify the fact that an attack has begun. This should continue right through the fire scene until we get to our very high shot.

Before the mass of gulls appear in this high shot we should begin to hear them o.s., faint but the volume growing. It should start to mount as we see the gulls appear in the f.g. of our high shot and then increase as their numbers increase. The volume should increase until our screen is covered with descending gulls. This naturally should be all electronic. When we are below on the ground, we should increase our volume much more and then once Melanie is in the phone booth we should drop it only a little, just enough so that we do not lose impact of the screams of the birds but merely make the audience conscious that Melanie is enclosed. This volume should continue until she emerges and the volume should rise again until Mitch and Melanie get into the Tides Restaurant. Then it should drop considerably so that we get a sense of being cut off from the outside.

29. (ELECTRONIC) Inside the Tides after the attack. As we have said above, we need to drop the sound considerably to get the comparative silence from the outside in order to dramatize the stony-faced women in the restaurant. During this sequence the attack sounds should decrease so that we can justify Mr. Carter's coming in to say "they're going" so that when they run to the window and see the departing birds, we match the faint sounds of their screaming departure.

## REEL 11

30. (ELECTRONIC) The death of Annie. In this sequence we should have only the faintest brooding and NATURAL sounds of the crows that have paused between their attacks. This sound should be quite subdued so that it does not detract from the silence of death which should surround the cottage of Annie. We might even consider, although we shouldn't be definite about it, an odd croak or two from the murderers on the porch roof as though they are satisfied with their handiwork. Naturally at the end we will hear the sound of the car starting and driving off but even this should have a careful note of only a moderate engine acceleration so as not to spoil Cathy's outburst.

31. (NATURAL) The boarding-up sequence. In this sequence both inside and outside the house we should have complete silence except for the radio announcement and even the birds that are moving to Santa Rosa should pass by in silence so that for this sequence we need nothing but the hammering sounds and the natural sounds in the room except for the radio.

REEL 12

32.  (ELECTRONIC) Outside attic. This is the sequence which already has a sample of the electronic sound on it.

Generally speaking, the effects obtained electronically here would be fairly satisfactory except that there are matters of synchronization that should be corrected, such as the excessive sound of pecking at the door when Mitch goes into the bathroom. It is so loud now that he would obviously hear it before he went in and there are, generally, things like this that have to be adjusted. Another example is that we should definitely hear them fading away to justify Mitch's remark.

Missing from the present scenes are, of course, the natural sounds of the people moving around when these are replayed they should still be so subdued that we only hear a trace of them.

REEL 13

33.  (ELECTRONIC) Before the attack. This sequence should start in silence until the sound of a wing flutter is heard, which attracts Melanie's attention. Now this wing sound should be very simple and unmenacing. In fact, it should never be so strong as to warrant Melanie's waking up Mitch. Now she moves over toward the lovebirds and while she is there, a third flutter comes from the direction of the stairs. This draws her attention away from the lovebirds and motivates her ascent. The fourth flutter should come just before she mounts the stairs and this should be a shade louder to indicate its source when she reaches the top and should be heard again but not quite so strong because it would indicate to her by the turn of her head that it is not necessary to go down and bring Mitch up the stairs. To repeat, there are two wing sounds at the beginning before we see the lovebirds. However, we should make absolutely sure that it seems always like a sound of one bird only flapping its little wings.

34.  (ELECTRONIC) The attack sequence. It is very essential in this final attack by the birds in the attic that we give the sound a quality that gives this volume but is not of such a serious quality as to cause the people downstairs to be awakened by it. In addition, the thud of the birds against the girl's body should also have an impact but I repeat a soft one. Melanie's actions have already been made and they are also of such an inarticulate nature as to be lost almost among the sound of the flapping wings. It is also the question of the flashlight hitting the birds. This has to be taken into account. The o.s. dialogue when the people below are awakened should start as soon as Melanie slams the door and this off screen dialogue consists of the sound of Lydia's voice but, more prominent, Mitch's voice including the sound of his footsteps running up the stairs. Naturally, there should be banging on the door and finally the opening and closing of it and removal of Melanie. Once Mitch has started to open the door, we can afford to bring our volume up climactically.

REEL 14

35.  (ELECTRONIC and NATURAL) Final sequence. As Melanie is brought down the

stairs and the sound of the fluttering birds has been cut off by the closing of the attic door, we should begin to fade these sounds away as we get into the ground floor level. From this point on, we operate in silence and natural sounds until Mitch opens the door to the yard and for the first time sees that not only is the house and yard but also the whole area is covered by birds.

If it is at all feasible, what we would like to have electronically, is the equivalent of a brooding silence. Naturally, to achieve some effect like this will necessitate some experimentation. Maybe the whole time there is a murmur of the lowest keyed bird sounds. Whatever it is, however, should give us a feeling of a waiting mass, that if they were unduly disturbed, an attack would start again. The question as to whether individual crow sounds should be interpolated especially at the sight of Mitch should be debated.

At the end, the most important NATURAL sound is that of the automobile engine which should start cautiously and then feel its way through the birds and it picks up speed once it leaves the area of the farm. Now we should hear that part of the departing car getting fainter and fainter even after it has turned the bend. Once the sound of the car has died away, and we are left alone with the birds, all we should hear is this brooding, massing murmur which should continue until the picture fades out. When at last at the end of the fade, we should come into silence for the very end of the picture when the company trademark appears.

I love the instructions for the last reel, which request a "brooding silence." That sounds so Hitchcockian and it is indeed the effect one experiences during the final moments of *The Birds*.

## *Marnie*

I think it's obvious by this point that I enjoy this particular Hitchcock film from the sixties more than any other. Hitchcock, however, did not share my opinion. After his disillusionment with Tippi Hedren, he was barely involved in the postproduction process. He admitted that he allowed sloppy rear screen work for the hunt scene and an incredibly obvious backdrop of a docked ship at the end of Marnie's home street.

The film has a special charm of its own, but I would be the first to admit that it may be an acquired taste. *Marnie* was a complicated movie for the production code: a thief is caught and blackmailed into marriage, then raped during her honeymoon, discovers that her neurosis was caused by an attempted rape when she was a child and her accidental killing of her prostitute mother's client. With all of this, the studio was nervous over some dialogue at the very end of the film. Marnie's mother finally confesses her daughter's role in the death of her "John" and, in doing so, also elaborates on just how Marnie was conceived.

Literally in the eleventh hour, Hitchcock agreed to trim a few of the lines from the film. Many prints had already been shipped to the "exchanges" (the places from which the film would be distributed to local theaters), so the change would require the exchange to cut the release prints or the studio would ship out new reels to be cut in. Or they would just let two versions float around.

They chose the final option, as I've seen both versions in privately owned prints. The edited version is often shown on commercial television, but the unedited wide-screen version gets shown on the Turner Classic Movies cable channel.

---

UNIVERSAL CITY
STUDIOS          INTER-OFFICE COMMUNICATION                    Misc. 1
UNIVERSAL CITY
CALIFORNIA

Date June 10, 1964

Copies:

To ____ MR. EDD HENRY ____                    ☐ _____

From ____ PEGGY ROBERTSON ____                ☐ _____

Subject ____ "MARNIE" #9403 - ____            ☐ _____

BASKETBALL SWEATER DIALOGUE

BERNICE'S dialogue in the picture now reads as follows:

"You know how I got you, Marnie?
There was this boy, Billy, and I
wanted Billy's basketball sweater.
I was fifteen. And Billy said
if I'd let him, I could have the
sweater. So I let him. And then,
later on, when you got started, he
run away. I still got that old
sweater. And I got you, Marnie.
Then after the accident, when I
was in the hospital, they tried
to make me let you be adopted.
I wouldn't. I wanted you."

Mr. Hitchcock's suggested cuts are the elimination of the
underlined portions above. Therefore, if these cuts are
made, the dialogue would read as follows:

"You know how I got you, Marnie?
There was this boy, Billy. And
then, later on, when you got
started, he run away. When I
was in the hospital, they tried
to make me let you be adopted.
I wouldn't. I wanted you."

I've just talked to Paul Rutan at Technicolor, who told me that
there are 350 prints now out at the various Exchanges. Of these
350 prints, 55 prints have been sent abroad.

I talked to George Tomasini; and if you wish, he will come in
tomorrow during the noon hour and make these cuts in the studio
copy which is in our cutting rooms. You can then look at the
recut sequence, and George can replace it at once. Please advise
me if you would like this done so that I can advise George.

PR/pp

## *Torn Curtain*

Hitchcock's fiftieth film began with such promise. An all-star cast (including Julie Andrews and Paul Newman), a strong script (story by the Hitchcocks, screenplay by Brian Moore), and a strong production team (despite the losses of Robert Burks and George Tomasini). And, of course, a return of Bernard Herrmann, his friend and best composer.

Nonetheless, the production soured. Hitchcock and Newman did not get along—Hitchcock took enormous exception to Newman's detailed notes on the script and to the lengthy time the actor required to get into character. Then the mood turned worse in postproduction. The failure of *Marnie* (critically and at the box office) placed an enormous personal and professional pressure on Hitchcock. Universal wanted a marketable soundtrack for the film and, according to Hitchcock, he had personally vouched for Herrmann to a reluctant studio. Herrmann allegedly promised a more youth-oriented score—something modern and jazzy.

Hitchcock arrived for the film's scoring to hear a score that was undoubtedly brilliant, but unmistakably Herrmann—dark, heavy, bombastic—in short, the complete opposite of what Universal and Hitchcock had hoped for. There was a scene. Hitchcock scrapped the recording session and fired Herrmann. The two never enjoyed each other's company again.

But the collaboration seemed promising enough when it began. This telegram from Hitchcock to Herrmann on November 4, 1965, not only outlines his concerns about the music for *Torn Curtain*, but reveals his frustration with the current nature of film music:

```
ADJO41 INTL (UNIV INTL PICT)
    TDL WUX UNIVERSALCITY CALIF 394 NOV 4
LT BERNARD HERRMANN
    11 CUMBERLAND TERRACE REGENTS PARK LONDNW1 (ENGLAND VIA RCA) DEAR
BENNY TO FOLLOW UP PEGGYS CONVERSATION WITH YOU LET ME SAY AT FIRST I AM
VERY ANXIOUS FOR YOU TO DO THE MUSIC ON TORN CURTAIN STOP I WAS EXTREMELY
DISAPPOINTED WHEN I HEARD THE SCORE OF JOY IN THE MORNING NOT ONLY DID I
FIND IT CONFORMING TO THE OLD PATTERN BUT EXTREMELY REMINISCENT OF THE
MARNIE MUSIC IN FACT THE THEME WAS ALMOST THE SAME STOP UNFORTUNATELY FOR
WE ARTISTS WE DO NOT HAVE THE FREEDOM THAT WE WOULD LIKE TO HAVE BECAUSE
WE ARE CATERING TO AN AUDIENCE AND THAT IS WHY YOU GET YOUR MONEY AND I
GET MINE STOP THIS AUDIENCE IS VERY DIFFERENT FROM THE ONE TO WHICH WE USED
TO CATER IT IS YOUNG VIGOROUS AND DEMANDING STOP IT IS THIS FACT THAT HAS
BEEN RECOGNIZED BY ALMOST ALL OF THE EUROPEAN FILM MAKERS WHERE THEY HAVE
```

SOUGHT TO INTRODUCE A BEAT AND A RHYTHM THAT IS MORE IN TUNE WITH THE REQUIREMENTS OF THE AFORESAID AUDIENCE STOP THIS IS WHY I AM ASKING YOU TO APPROACH THIS PROBLEM WITH A RECEPTIVE AND IF POSSIBLE ENTHUSIASTIC MIND STOP IF YOU CANNOT DO THIS THEN I AM THE LOSER STOP I HAVE MADE UP MY MIND THAT THIS APPROACH TO THE MUSIC IS EXTREMELY ESSENTIAL I ALSO HAVE VERY DEFINITE IDEAS AS TO WHERE THE MUSIC SHOULD GO IN THE PICTURE AND THERE IS NOT TOO MUCH STOP SO OFTEN HAVE I BEEN ASKED FOR EXAMPLE BY TIOMKIN TO COME AND LISTEN TO A SCORE AND WHEN I EXPRESS MY DISAPPROVAL HIS HANDS WERE THRON UP AND WITH THE CRY OF QUOTE BUT YOU CANT CHANGE ANYTHING NOW IT HAS ALL BEEN ORCHESTRATED UNQUOTE IT IS THIS KIND OF FRUSTRATION THAT I AM RATHER TIRED OF BY THAT I MEAN GETTING MUSIC SCORED ON A TAKE IT OR LEAVE IT BASIS STOP ANOTHER PROBLEM THIS MUSIC HAS GOT TO BE SKETCHED IN AN ADVANCE BECAUSE WE HAVE AN URGENT PROBLEM OF MEETING A TAX DATE STOP WE WILL NOT FINISH SHOOTING UNTIL THE MIDDLE OF JANUARY AT THE EARLIEST AND TECHNICOLOR REQUIRES THE COMPLETE PICTURE BY FEBRUARY FIRST SINCERELY

                                                                        HITCH

Herrmann did not hesitate in responding. And you can see from the tone how Hitchcock would feel betrayed three months later when he heard Herrmann's score. But the tone also betrays a slightly patronizing attitude, which may have antagonized Hitchcock:

TWUE262 SSA224 L NHA125 (0 CDU595 CTC154
LHC420 TLH045) 213 48 PD INTL FR
CD LONDONLH VIA ITT 5 1700
ALFRED HITCHCOCK
UNIVERSAL STUDIOS UNIVERSALCITY UNIVERSALSTUDIOS (WUX LOSA)
DELIGHTED COMPOSE VIGOROUS BEAT SCORE FOR TORN CURTAIN ALWAYS PLEASED
HAVE YOUR VIEWS REGARDING MUSIC FOR YOUR FILM PLEASE SEND SCRIPT
INDICATING WHERE YOU DESIRE MUSIC CAN THEN BEGIN COMPOSING HERE WILL BE
READY RECORD WEEK AFTER FINAL SHOOTING DATE GOOD LUCK
BERNARD.
151P PST NOV 5 65

These are the notes Hitchcock eventually sent Herrmann for the music score. Notice that despite saying publicly otherwise, Hitchcock did intend music for the scene where Gromek is killed (scene 111). (This music has been recorded on several occasions, and the entire Herrmann score has recently been recorded by Joel McNeely for Varese Sarabande.)

## Music Notes—"Torn Curtain"

Music Starts:  On opening of "TORN CURTAIN"

I feel that the Main Title should be an exciting, arresting and rhythmic piece of music whose function would be to immediately rivet the audience's attention. Irrespective of the abstract designing of the titles and their background, the music could be, and should be, written before this is achieved.

I would estimate that the timing should be the normal one that we've always had—between 1:15–1:30 secs.

Music Ends:  Scene 10  — Passengers in dining room.

Music Starts:  Scene 11  — Knock on cabin door.

Music Ends:  Scene 17  — Armstrong closing cabin door.

Music Starts:  Scene 19  — Manfred's: 'The lounge. Good'.

Music Ends:  Scene 26  — Sarah in Armstrong's room: 'Darling, we've got connecting rooms'.

Music Starts:  Scene 26A  — Armstrong rushing from shower: 'No, wait!'

Music Ends:  Scene 28  — Manfred to Sarah in lounge: 'Ah, Miss Sherman'.

Music Starts:  Scene 29  — Sarah to Manfred in lounge: 'Good'.

Music Ends:  Scene 31  — Manfred to Sarah in street: 'How long have you actually worked with Professor Armstrong?'.

Music Starts:  Scene 31  — Sarah to Manfred in street: 'Don't you approve of marriage?'. Manfred: 'Of course I do'.

Music Ends:  Scene 32  — Freddy to Sarah: 'Why didn't the Professor come 'imself?'

Music Starts:  Scene 32A  — Sarah: 'Thank you', as she and Manfred exit bookstore.

Music Ends:  Scene 34  — On Armstrong's: 'Thank you', as he takes book from Sarah.

Music Starts:  Scene 34  — Travel Clerk to Armstrong: 'Your tickets, sir'.

Music Ends:  Scene 51  — Tour Official to Clerk: '. . . suitcases gone astray'.

Music Starts:  Scene 51  — Travel Clerk to Sarah: 'Yes, Miss, behind the Iron Curtain'.

Music Out:  Scene 56  — Armstrong sees Sarah for the first time in plane.

Music Starts:  Scene 58B  — Armstrong to Sarah: 'You understand?' and he walks back to plane seat.

Music Ends:  Scene 69  — Ballerina stepping out of plane door, posing for Photographers.

Music Starts:    Scene 83D — All exiting from Terminal as Vice Minister says: 'Come this way'.

Music Ends:      (just a bridge)

Music Starts:    Scene 86    — Ext. Hotel Berlin

Music Ends:      Scene 89    — Armstrong enters Sarah's room: 'Sarah, well. . . .''

Music Starts:    Scene 89    — Armstrong and Manfred exit Sarah's bedroom as Armstrong says: 'You can rest a while'.

Music Ends:      Scene 90    — As we enter a Hotel Room with tapes playing.

Music Starts:    Scene 92    — Sarah in bed—a knock on her door.

Music Ends:      Scene 92    — Sarah says: 'Come in'.

Music Starts:    Scene 92A — Insert—The Note

Music Ends:      Scene 98    — Interior Museum.

Music Starts:    Scene 99    — Armstrong exits Museum, running.

Music Ends:      Scene 104  — Farmer's first speech on Tractor.

Music Starts:    Scene 105  — As Farmer says: 'It's mean soil up there'.

Music Ends:      Scene 111  — Armstrong asks Peasant Woman: 'Is there a back door here?'.

Music Starts:    Scene 111  — As soup smashes against telephone on wall.

Music Ends:      Scene 111  — As gas jets are turned on by P.W.

Music Starts:    Scene 111  — As second gas jet is turned *off* by Peasant Woman.

Music Ends:      Scene 116  — Armstrong entering Gerhard's office.

Hitchcock's increasing irritation with Universal's interference is readily apparent in a series of memos in March and June 1966.

INTER-OFFICE COMMUNICATION                    Misc. 1

Date **March 18, 1966**

Copies:

To    PAUL DONNELLY                        ☐ EDD HENRY

From  ALFRED HITCHCOCK                     ☐ JOE DUBIN

Subject  "TORN CURTAIN" - CREDITS          ☐


I have received a note from Joseph S. Dubin to the effect
that the name of a set decorator, John McCarthy, should
be included in our credits.

I never saw John McCarthy during the whole of our
production. Who is he? I know you'll answer that he
is the head of a department, but who is he as a contri-
butor to our picture? If Mr. McCarthy thinks he should
be included in our credits, then I think that Governor
Brown also should be included, because he came on the
set, and I shook hands with him, and that is more than
I did with Mr. McCarthy.

                    Emphatically yours,


---

INTER-OFFICE COMMUNICATION                    Misc. 1

Date March 18, 196

Copies:

To    EDD HENRY                            ☐

From  ALFRED HITCHCOCK                     ☐

Subject                                    ☐


Dear Mr. Henry,

        In the list of comments on the credits I received
from Mr. Dubin there was a mention concerning a 'custom'
of putting the name of 'Edward Muhl, in charge of
production'. What is the point of this insignia?
Am I to believe that 1,000, or if we are successful, 1,050
people are looking at the screen and on seeing the words
'Edward Muhl, in charge of production' an agreeable
murmur goes over the audience? If so, then I have no
further comment.

        However, I am reminded of an Apocryphal story that
is told concerning a dispute among a family of three
about which picture they should go out to see that
evening:-

                "The father said, "I'd like to
                see the Laurel and Hardy comedy".

                "Oh no", said the mother, "I want
                to see that Greer Garson picture".

                The daughter intervenes rather
                emphatically, "I don't want to see
                either of those pictures, what I
                want to see is that Edward Muhl
                picture around the corner".

                        Yours informatively,

Finally, this memo about interruptions during the screening with his friend
Lew Wasserman, the head of MCA.

---

UNIVERSAL CITY
STUDIOS
UNIVERSAL CITY
CALIFORNIA

**INTER-OFFICE COMMUNICATION**          Misc. 1

Date __June 1, 1966__

Copies:

To __PEGGY__                                      ☐ _____

From __MR. HITCHCOCK__                            ☐ _____

Subject __TODAY'S SCREENING OF "TORN CURTAIN"__   ☐ _____

Please call Edd Henry and ask him to make sure that during
this morning's running no phone calls should come into the
projection room.  Would you also ask him to check with the
secretaries of Wasserman and Rachmil to make sure this is
done.  The last time we ran I made the same request to the
switchboard and asked them not to put any calls through,
nevertheless while Bud and I sat there in the back calls
would come through and flashed on the phone, but we
ignored them.  So you see, in spite of requests to the
switchboardthey still insist on putting calls through.
Tell Edd Henry all this, in addition explain to him the
reason for my caution is that when at Paramount and
running a picture for the first time, Don Hartman used
to have continuous long phone conversations while watching
the picture at the same time.  This so angered me that
I once took the opportunity of calling Hartman's secretary,
without his knowledge, telling her not to put through
any calls on any account.
Tell Bud that when the final trademark appears, before
the roll-up titles, bring theatre lights on, during do not
keep them down while the names roll by, because, at present, they
an addition.

9:10  Mr. Hitchcock just talked with Mr. Wasserman and all
      the memo has been done up to paragraph which starts...
      "Tell Bud that when...."

      Also, Peggy, tell Bud that if he sees any lights
      flashing on the phone not to answer them as I
      have arranged with Mr. Wasserman that no calls
      should come through.

## *Topaz*

This film—I think it's Hitchcock's most problematic—provides the best insight into the postproduction process. For reasons that are not clear, Hitchcock had the following phone conversations recorded and transcribed. Hitchcock and Herbert Coleman, his associate producer, are at Hitchcock's favorite hotel: the Villa D'Este in Gernobbio, Italy (it was a reunion film for the two—they worked together exclusively during Hitchcock's Paramount years, parting on *Psycho*). *Topaz* is now near the end of postproduction and the two are talking with Peggy Robertson, Hitchcock's assistant, on September 17, 1969, and then the three are joined by the film's editor, Bill Ziegler, on September 18.

The conversation revolves around the ending to *Topaz*. Hitchcock shot three different endings for the film (all of which are preserved on the current *Topaz* video edition) and they are discussing what they hope will be the finished one. This transcript allows the reader to eavesdrop on the kind of discussion that is typical between a director and editor at this stage of the film production process.

Conversation at Villa D'Este, Cernobbio, Italy
(9 hours ahead of L.A. time)

September 17, 1969

MR. HITCHCOCK: You don't have the film yet, do you?

PEGGY: It's not coming in until 9 o'clock our time this evening.

MR. HITCHCOCK: Then I'll talk to you at this time tomorrow.

PEGGY: Bill Ziegler is out sick. His vaccination took very badly.

MR. HITCHCOCK: Why was he vaccinated?

PEGGY: To go abroad.

MR. HITCHCOCK: Oh, I see.

PEGGY: And it's taken very badly and he's been running a temperature. I talked to him yesterday—it was around 104. We don't know how it will be today. But I talked to Bill Hornbeck and we assume if he isn't better tomorrow that we'll have to get someone else in. Or do you want to wait?

MR. HITCHCOCK: No, I tell you what you'd better do. When I call you tomorrow night, you'd better have the phone hooked up to a technical . . .

PEGGY:            We've got it on now. We are on a tape recorder now.

MR. HITCHCOCK:    Yes, well there's nothing to say now. I've seen the film this morning and I think it would be better if you and Hornbeck see the film. Then I'll dictate tomorrow night.

PEGGY:            All right, fine. Well shall we.

MR. HITCHCOCK:    Call me whatever time you're ready. I'll be here tomorrow evening around this time.

PEGGY:            As soon as we've seen the film, we'll call you.

MR. HITCHCOCK:    Yes, you call me. Hold a minute, Herbie wants you.

PEGGY:            Yes, I want Herbie.

HERBIE:           Hi, Peggy.

PEGGY:            Hi, Herbie.

HERBIE:           Just want to tell you, this is much too good for me.

PEGGY:            I should think so too. What are the rooms like?

HERBIE:           You've been here, haven't you?

PEGGY:            No.

HERBIE:           Well I'm in Hitch's bedroom now, and it is absolutely beautiful. Alma is looking over the Lake and it just looks gorgeous.

PEGGY:            How long are you going to stay, a couple of months?

HERBIE:           I just resigned from the studio.

HERBIE:           Let me tell you the arrangements for the film so you'll know.

PEGGY:            Thank you, we'd like to know.

HERBIE:           Now I had a hell of a time at Technicolor yesterday trying to get to Technicolor and back in time to get the film sunk and have transfers made so Hitch could see the film. We were going to put in the wild track but we didn't have time. What they thought they were doing is sunk it up, and for Hitch to see it here, double track sunk up, but it was all out of sync and everything, but as far as the picture's concerned, it's fine. The print we saw was a little dark but the print they sent to you was one—one point lighter. I explained that to Hitch and he agreed. Now it was shipped last night, yesterday, to Technicolor from here, so Bill should get in touch with Giff so he can grab it the minute it comes in.

PEGGY:            Now, Herbie. We know this. We know that it is coming in on the Pan American between six and seven tonight, our time, and Giff has just given Jeff the Waybill number. What we don't know is, where is the sound—is that in the same shipment?

| | |
|---|---|
| HERBIE: | The sound was supposed to be sent direct to Bill Hornbeck. |
| PEGGY: | The sound sent directly to Bill Hornbeck. |
| HERBIE: | Yes, because London always sends everything direct to Bill Hornbeck, they say, after instructions. I told them to send the transfer track—the 35mm track, you know, transfer—so they should have that first. That transfer includes all of the original sound shot during the shooting as well as a lot of wild tracks made in a building nearby, later. |
| PEGGY: | Right. |
| HERBIE: | Have you got a pencil. |
| PEGGY: | Yes, it's been recorded. You're being recorded. |
| HERBIE: | Now in addition to the wild track, that is the addition to the sound that you're getting, it was being shipped last night to Bill Hornbeck, so get in touch with him. A day later, or tonight, our time, they are shipping the ¼″ tape. Now you will hear many many readings about the dialogue that Hitch had them record wild, but the ones he wants to use, and he hasn't heard the last two yet, but I know it's what he wants used. Hitch had the last line of dialogue changed for Frederick Stafford to say: "ANYWAY, THAT'S THE END OF TOPAZ". That's what he wants to use. |
| PEGGY: | "ANYWAY, THAT'S THE END OF TOPAZ". |
| HERBIE: | Yes. You'll find that on the last two tracks, on that track you're getting. Now I can tell you what Hitch wanted, the selection he made, I'm not sure about these slate numbers but, on the first Take of the two people coming in and Dany progressing on up the steps and Stafford stopping, he wants the second Take. |
| PEGGY: | The second Take. |
| HERBIE: | Yes, I think it's P-1, but I can't tell you what the print number is. No I'm wrong, Peggy, I put it down on a piece of paper in the projection room. He wants the first Take of his entrance, where he stops and looks off and sees Piccoli. |
| PEGGY: | First Take of Andre's entrance. |
| HERBIE: | Yes, I think it's P-1 Take 1, but I'm not sure. |
| PEGGY: | All right. It will be the first one anyway, where he stops and looks off screen. |
| HERBIE: | Yes. Now when you open up on him standing there looking, and he smiles off, looking at Piccoli and then goes up the steps where he rejoins Dany Robin waiting, he wants the second Take of that. I think that slate was P-3. I don't know the Take number, but it was |

definitely the second Take of that. Now we made 3 Takes of Granville, two of them were shot *silent* and one was shot sound, you want the third Take of that.

PEGGY: With sound.

HERBIE: Where he says "Bon Voyage".

PEGGY: So that you can hear him.

HERBIE: Well know he wants just to pick up—there's an airplane that passes behind the shot of Dany and Frederick boarding the plane, and he wants the sound of that plane to be picked up and built up to where you don't actually hear the words. When you talk to Hitch after you see it, I kind of think he will probably change his mind if you probably very faintly hear it. Anyhow, that's a definite question to ask him after you've seen the film.

PEGGY: Yes, right.

HERBIE: And the ¼" tape you can tell Bill was shipped off tonight.

PEGGY: Tonight?

HERBIE: That is, it was mailed to Bill Hornbeck.

PEGGY: Now wait a minute, this is Wednesday. It was sent off Wednesday—Wednesday night.

HERBIE: Yes, the ¼" tape. The transfer went off last night. Okay.

PEGGY: Okay.

HERBIE: I asked them to send a cable about Lennie and Kunkel leaving today, and I'm assuming they did that. You can check with Marshall Green.

PEGGY: All right.

HERBIE: They sent it off this afternoon, I think it was 2:30.

PEGGY: Oh, I see, right, okay.

HERBIE: The cable was supposed to be sent telling the arrival time, whether they would need to be met, and on what flight they were on.

PEGGY: It was sent to Marshall.

HERBIE: That's right. Now all of the equipment will be shipped back on Friday with the exception of those big stands that you sent over here, you know, that held the signs?

PEGGY: Yes.

HERBIE: I saw no reason to pack that tremendous box back you know because it was just two wooden sign holders. Now also I've told them to leave Dany Robin's fur hat, and the hat and gloves we bought for Piccoli, in Ascarelli's office in London, until someone decides whether they want to ship back because you have to pay duty on top of everything that's paid up to now. So you can ask Vince Dee if he wants the hat and gloves of Piccoli and the fur hat that he had made at Balmain's for Robin which cost us $150—does he want those shipped back and pay the duty on them. Then we can let them know in a little while what to do. Okay.

PEGGY:     Okay. Now are you going to be there tomorrow?

HERBIE:    Yes. When you talk to Hitch tomorrow night, I'll be here.

PEGGY:     Fine.

HERBIE:    Okay, Peggy.

PEGGY:     Will talk to you tomorrow.


Conversation at the Villa D'Este, Cernobbio
(9 hours ahead of L.A. time)

Thursday, September 18, 1969

HERBIE:    Did you see the film?

PEGGY:     Yes. Speak a bit louder, Herbie.

HERBIE:    Did you see the film?

PEGGY:     Yes, we saw it and Bill's here listening in too, and you're being recorded.

HERBIE:    Did our tracks come in as well? Have you listened to them? Did you make heads or tails out of what I told you of the last two takes on the track?

PEGGY:     With 'anyway'.

HERBIE:    Yes. Where he said 'anyway'.

PEGGY:     That's right, and the last ones of her, she said 'they' instead of 'them'.

HERBIE:    That's correct.

PEGGY:     Yes, we have those.

HERBIE:    And now the film was all right?

PEGGY:     The film's fine.

HERBIE:    No problem?

BILL Z:    No, Herbie, none at all. It came in fine we sunk it right up and everything's fine. Where is Hitch? We need to talk to him now to cut it.

| | |
|---|---|
| HERBIE: | You do! |
| BILL Z: | We've been trying to get hold of Hitch since this morning. |
| HERBIE: | He's sitting right here, why didn't you call? |
| BILL: | I'd say, where's 'here'? |
| HERBIE: | We're in the Villa D'Este. |
| BILL: | For heaven's sake, we've been trying to get a line through since early this morning. We've been sitting here, sweating. |
| HERBIE: | We put the call in about 45 minutes ago, I should imagine. Bill, were you able to take the track and move the words around so they would fit the mouth alright? |
| BILL: | Yes, we can print that, Herbie, there's no problem on tracks, I simply want to know the cutting procedure. |
| HERBIE: | Well here, I'll give you Hitch and he can tell you exactly how he would like to have it. |
| PEGGY: | Herbie, Herbie. |
| MR. H: | How are you, William? |
| BILL: | I'm fine, Hitch, and you? You sound fine. |
| MR. H: | First of all, you have enough film of Aeroport de Paris, haven't you. |
| BILL: | Right. |
| MR. H: | Well now you go from that to the longer shot where the both of them go in, and Andre turns and looks. Now you have enough on the front of the zoom to the other man so as you read the word 'Moscow'. There's not too much. |
| BILL: | That's the only critical spot, Hitch. |
| MR. H: | I know, but leave enough to read the word 'Moscow'. Now once you've gone in and he raises his hat and turns to go, let Granville turn and continue up. In other words, don't cut him while he is still looking at Devereaux. The cut should be back to Devereaux right in the middle of his laugh—'the nerve of that fellow' you know. Now he goes up and the wife says her words and then he replies and then he says: "Anyway, that's the end of TOPAZ". |
| BILL: | Yes, I understand that. |
| MR. H: | Now, the point is this. We only want to faintly hear the words from Granville: 'Bon Voyage'. The track of the airport should be carefully put together, you know, for there's no intention to actually hear the words. We've zoomed in and he's not supposed to be that near, you know. You understand this. |

| | |
|---|---|
| BILL: | Yes, we'll handle that properly, Hitch. |
| MR. H: | When he says, 'That's the end of TOPAZ, anyway', try and get it so he turns away on the end, and then . . . |
| BILL: | Direct cut. |
| MR. H: | And then we cut to—are you going to dissolve to the . . . |
| BILL: | (interrupting) no at this point our direct cut, it's a nice snapper. |
| MR. H: | It is? |
| BILL: | We dissolved through the airport but after this sequence I should say we should direct cut to "MISSILE CRISIS OVER". |
| MR. H: | Right, okay. Now one other point. Have you talked to Maurice Jarre about music? |
| BILL Z: | Peggy has. |
| PEGGY: | I talked to him yesterday, Hitch. He's using the TOPAZ theme. |
| MR. H: | Yes. Now here's my point. If you will recall, Maurice Jarre was very concerned at one point about the conflict of music and traffic. |
| PEGGY: | Yes. In Copenhagen. |
| MR. H: | I think it is very important in this sequence to hear airport noises, and all that kind of thing, and I will recommend to Jarre that we don't start the music until the newspaper cut. |
| PEGGY: | Right. |
| MR. H: | What were you going to say, Bill? |
| BILL: | I was just going to say okay, yes. |
| MR. H: | Otherwise if you try and leave TOPAZ the moment you see Aeroport de Paris, you're going to have a conflict between music, airplane noises, and dialogue. |
| BILL: | Right. You also anticipate your end, which you should not. I think having the music just come in on "MISSILE CRISIS OVER" is more of a snapper. |
| MR. H: | Yes, I agree, you're right. So I wouldn't attempt to bring the music in, and Peg, you must tell Maurice Jarre that I think, in view of our previous experience with this sort of thing, we should not bring the music in until we see the end. |
| PEGGY: | Right now, Hitch, in view of this for both endings we would have the same music, wouldn't we? |
| MR. H: | Well, if you do the man who has shot himself and you go to the newspaper, the same music will do. |

PEGGY:    That's what I mean.

MR. H:    Yes. Then we put the Juanita Theme as the play-out music.

PEGGY:    In both cases. Now, this is going to be the TOPAZ Theme but upbeat?

MR. H:    Right.

BILL:    This ending that we have now is so very good that I hope to heavens we can avoid the suicide bit. Do you agree?

MR. H:    The only reason the suicide came up, I'm afraid through the French Office here, oh my god what will the French government say by letting him get away with it.

BILL:    I understand.

MR. H:    So that ending with the shot on the secret house is an emergency.

BILL:    I understand it's intent, Hitch, but after seeing the daily, it is frankly, in my estimation, very, very good. It increases this snap around the end tremendously. I believe the acting on the part of Nicole and Andre are very sincere. You believe exactly what they said that he is too clever.

MR. H:    That's right.

BILL:    And I would hate very much to see but this ending, be our aversion.

MR. H:    Bill, actually, you see, this is really the correct ending. In every case, whether it by Philby, Burgess and MacLean, they've all gotten away with it and they've all gone back to Russia. That's why I'm correct. The only piece of license we are taking here is by labelling the plane to Moscow. He would have taken the plane to Geneva then to Prague and then to Moscow. But it's too late at the end of the film to explain that. So that is actually the license we have taken.

BILL:    Yes, but my point was, Hitch, in the event that there is an objection on the part of the French, shall we just swallow things and just have two versions rather than the bad version for all releases?

MR. H:    Oh I wouldn't attempt to have the other version for any of our other releases. I am only talking about the suicide for the French version only.

PEGGY:    When we send it over to you Hitch, scored and dubbed, you want two versions scored and dubbed for France.

MR. H:    No, I don't. I want you to take that second version—the suicide version—roll it up and put it away and don't tell anyone.

PEGGY:    We just score and dub it.

BILL:    (interrupting) yes, just quietly it will be ready . . .

MR. H:          . . . in case of emergency.

BILL:           Hitch, one question. Would you consider, in view of the fact that when Andre looks off, we must run a short beat to show Moscow and Aeroflot. Would it be better, perhaps, to have the doors close, we go to Moscow Aeroflot and see him start up the gangway. Now to Washington, and the two come on, he looks, and looks directly to the zoom, back to Andre, who laughs and goes on up.

MR. H:          No, you must Aeroport de Paris, and you must show what appears to be the normal ending: Devereaux's got his job back. Then you go to the look. Don't reverse it.

BILL:           Then as he looks, I must hold just a peek long enough to show Moscow Aeroflot.

MR. H:          Right. That's all right, I don't mind that.

BILL:           But I must sell that momentarily, Hitch.

MR. H:          Okay.

HERBIE:         Bill, cut the film the way you two have discussed it and make a temp dub and ship it to Ascarelli in Paris to arrive there Monday afternoon late.

PEGGY:          But we won't have the score, Herbie. It won't be scored.

HERBIE:         How long will it take to get it scored?

PEGGY:          The music was planned to be scored next Wednesday or Thursday morning.

HERBIE:         Well that's too late for Hitch to see it.

BILL:           Also, Herbie, you see I have to have negative cut and a print made, I have to keep the work print. Have the negative cut and the print made.

HERBIE:         What if I send you the other print that we've got here, can you work with that?

BILL:           No I say Herbie to have a fresh print, I can send him the work print for approval.

HERBIE:         That's the most important thing because otherwise if you go ahead and assume that the work that you've done is all right, and it is changed, then it is going to be too late for these people.

BILL:           All right, Herbie, we'll get right on it and get it done as soon as possible. We'll have to send it without the score.

HERBIE:         Hitch will be there on the night of the 22nd, 23rd, 24th 25th and 26th that I know of.

| | |
|---|---|
| BILL: | You see, the thing was, Herbie, the last I spoke to Hitch I said, I think, I want you to approve before we cut negative. He said no, it is very obvious, it will be specific and he has just given us specific instructions and to go ahead, and that will be it. |
| HERBIE: | Yes, but I think he still has to see it, Bill. Now I've got another print of the material here which I'm going to send (ship) to you tomorrow, and you'll have that—tomorrow's Friday—it will arrive on Saturday and you will have it in your hands Monday morning. |
| BILL: | Right. But he wants this cut and dubbed and back in Paris by Monday. |
| HERBIE: | Well, by Tuesday afternoon. |
| PEGGY: | With a score? |
| BILL: | It's impossible. |
| HERBIE: | If you have no score obviously—if you're not going to score until next Wednesday or Thursday—I think the important thing is before you score anything Hitch sees it too. |
| PEGGY: | Then there's no point in dubbing is there? |
| HERBIE: | It's awfully important for the level of the over Piccoli. |
| BILL: | Well you see this will take time. My end of it will not consume much time, Herbie, but to get sound effects cut and to get this re-recorded and dubbed and then get it in shape and so forth, I don't believe we can have it there Monday/Tuesday. |
| HERBIE: | Will it be ready Tuesday? |
| BILL: | We'll sure as hell try but we'll just have to play it by ear. |
| HERBIE: | If you wait til Wednesday, Bill and Peggy says even Thursday on the score, then it can't possibly get to Paris while Hitch is there. I think Hitch should be in Paris with that film so they can tack it off of the print they've got here and look at it. |
| BILL: | Well, Herbie, you see here again if that's what you want to tack it on and look at it I am going to have to send a separate picture and track. You can't cut that into a composite. And if you want a composite to tack it on there, we're going to have to cut negative. |
| HERBIE: | No, you can't do that. You can't cut negative on it. |
| BILL: | Then we're going to have to send separate picture and track only. |
| HERBIE: | Okay, okay. Bill will you do that as soon as possible without waiting for the score because Hitch has a very definite point where he is going to score. |

| | |
|---|---|
| BILL: | Right, well he just explained this to us. He explained to us exactly where the score starts which is on the cut to the end title. |
| HERBIE: | That's right. So we don't have to worry about the score. The important is to get the picture and track sent to us with the temp dub of the airplane noise to get the level of the sound covering Piccoli's 'Bon Voyage' to Andre. |
| BILL: | Well, Herbie, I don't know. We'll do everything we can. With these schedules here, to get into dub, to get the loop lines cut—Wally Reynolds is on vacation—to get these loop lines cut in, and to dub it and get a print back, & ship it I don't know, I can't give you an answer right now. |
| HERBIE: | Bill, do the best you can, and try to get it to Hitch before he goes to London. |
| BILL: | Absolutely, we'll do our best Herbie. |
| HERBIE: | Okay. Just a minute. |
| MR. H: | When dubbing of the airplane sound comes on, you know, we still have the exit of Granville through the doors. It's silent. Right. Make a note that when they dub and the words Aeroport de Paris come on—hit it, his plane taking off now. As we're not going to have any music, let's have the music of airplanes. |
| BILL: | Ext. Airport—hit it. |
| MR. H: | And with the plane going off. Keep that plane noise going all the time. |
| BILL: | Right. We see the same plane in the background too taking through. |
| MR. H: | We see that as well. In other words, make sure the moment we see the words Aeroport de Paris we get a big contrast of a jet taking off right over the words Aeroport de Paris in contrast to the silent exit of Granville. Okay. Keep the airplane noises going. |
| BILL: | Right, Hitch, I've got it. Question: You have not mentioned anything in choice on takes. |
| MR. H: | Hold a second. |
| PEGGY: | Yes, he has on those. He wants the first take of the entrance where they stop and look off and see Piccoli. |
| HERBIE: | Bill, I spoke to Peggy last night, and its Take 1 on P-1 which is his entrance, and Take 2 on the dialogue scene. Take 3 on Granville. |
| BILL: | Is that right, Peg? |
| PEGGY: | That's right. |
| BILL: | You also said, Herbie, that Hitch might change his mind today, that's why I'm checking with him. |

HERBIE:          No, that's what it is. And he just faintly wants to hear the 'Bon
                 Voyage' to Andre.

BILL:            I understand.

The suicide version, which both William Ziegler and Hitchcock spoke of derisively, was an effort to placate the French censors who were unhappy that the spy escaped without punishment. This was, unfortunately and against Hitchcock's wishes, how the film was ended.

During the conversation with the editor, several terms were tossed around that may have been confusing. When a film is in postproduction, an editor works with what's called a "work" print. This is a simple, often unattractive print that he can cut, recut, and recut again without damaging the negative. The negatives, sometimes called the "o-negs" (for original negatives), are never touched until the cutting is sure. You only get to cut the original camera negatives once—to have to recut an o-neg means permanent damage in some form to the film (a work print, therefore, allows the editor limitless variations without disturbing the camera negatives).

This is why Ziegler is continually questioning Hitchcock and Coleman and how "sure" they are about this ending because once he cuts the negative, that's really it. Ironically, this was not the ending that the film was released with—and if you watch *Topaz* closely, you can see some degradation to the print when they cut away to a very awkward shot of the spy's hideaway.

Just to go a little further, the print that you watch at your local cinema is printed from a special print called the "internegative." The internegative is made directly from the interpositive—which is made directly from the o-neg. And it is from this internegative that all other prints will be generated—the o-neg is carefully sealed and preserved and taken out only whenever the interpositive has become too worn to be used to strike new prints.

The original negatives are used to make only half a dozen or so prints. These prints are usually used at the premiere movie houses in the major cities.

The o-negs are considered gold—if something happens to these negatives, the studio essentially loses the film. When preservationists talk about losing films, the first line of battle is to find and preserve the film's camera negatives. If these don't exist, you hope that a decent print still exists. But the purity of the film will be forever lost if the negatives are lost or damaged.

When Robert A. Harris and James C. Katz restore a film, they are working very carefully with the camera negatives. Their work, which is desperately needed (each hour the camera negative is stored improperly, the more potential damage occurs), is therefore filled with its own suspense. If they screw up here, the mistake is permanent. The positive side is that if their work is done properly, the film regains the life it once lost.

One final story on those precious o-negs. During the conversation above, the filmmakers discussed Technicolor several times. Technicolor is the company that prints most of the films made today. They are continually looking for ways to save and restore color films. The situation became imperative when after the Northridge, California, earthquake the Technicolor storage facility was flooded by fire sprinklers going off—basically drowning the original negatives to half a dozen different productions at the time. The negatives had to remain underwater (where they were technically safe) until Technicolor could come up with a way to remove the negatives without damaging them. A way was found—but had they not prevailed, several million dollars' worth of film would have been permanently destroyed.

# chapter six
# KALEIDOSCOPE
# AND OTHER
# DREAMS
# DEFERRED

*[Is there anything you regret not having done?] Being a criminal lawyer, maybe. And some movie ideas that I haven't yet been able to incorporate into a workable screenplay. And Mary Rose, which I really wanted to do, but they didn't want to let me. Do you know, it's written specifically into my present contract that I cannot do Mary Rose?*

—HITCHCOCK TO JOHN RUSSELL TAYLOR

S ecrets. Hitchcock didn't like to keep secrets. Secrets brought on suspense, and despite being the Master of Suspense, he took every effort to eliminate that torturous emotion from his life.

*Torn Curtain.* The film cost Hitch more than what was on the books. His own anxiety over a project personally developed, then strangely, at the beginning of production a complete lack of faith in the material. There were many times he would go so far, then realize there was some deep, structural flaw in the material and he would quickly and, in a way that always saved face, abandon it. *Torn Curtain,* Hitch realized too late, was one of those projects.

He felt betrayed by Herrmann. He had made it clear that he wanted a new sound, anything to help save this disaster of a movie. He wanted a profitable tune. Yet when Hitch went to the first recording session, it was the same old Bennie. Herrmann didn't seem to understand that the world was turning and that they had better run to catch up or they'd be dinosaurs.

But Hitchcock knew he had lost a good friend and a once-trusted creative companion. He preferred to entrust a picture with a group of talented people who he knew would not betray the "Hitchcock" image. But the image had to adjust. Other directors were beginning to out-Hitch the Master and he could tell that audiences were no longer reacting to his slightly Victorian melodramas.

There were other losses that affected Hitchcock deeply. His two other most trusted members of the creative team were gone: Robert Burks, his cinematographer, and George Tomasini, his editor, both died early, startling deaths. Burks had tragically burned to death after nodding off while smoking a cigarette in bed. And Tomasini, the giant, gentle, charming man who was married to silent film star Mary Brian and who was Hitchcock's editor for more than a decade, had hiked off hunting with some friends and dropped dead of a heart attack.

All of this built enormous pressure on the normally placid director. The sudden indifference of his own studio was no comfort. Colder comfort too that its chairman was Lew Wasserman, a longtime friend and career guru. The times called for slightly desperate measures. Wasserman was putting heavy pressure on Hitchcock to do another "big" picture—a bestselling novel with big stars. But there were no stars. The men and women he had worked with were either too old or not working. He thought of Paul Newman and those long moments on the set while he tried to work out why his character would walk through a room. It wasn't just that this annoyed Hitchcock; the very questioning of character development was taken as an implicit distrust of his ability.

It was time for a bold move. Something to shake things up.

Hitchcock had an idea for a film, a variation on *Psycho* thematically and technically. His contract with Universal allowed him a certain degree of freedom, so he used that to begin a project he called *Frenzy*. His old friend Benn Levy worked with him through the first draft, but it was Hitch who wrote the lengthy treatment and the draft during the summer of 1967.

Levy was a curious choice. The two had not worked together since Hitchcock produced Levy's film in 1932, *Lord Camber's Ladies*, where, according to the biographer John Russell Taylor, they parted on less than gracious terms.

Whatever the circumstances, Levy flew in from London in early 1966 and the two immediately went to work on a treatment, then a screenplay. During the process, the pair went on a location tour of New York City, the mothballed fleet on the Hudson River, and a nearby waterfall.

The details of the film's plot were briefly outlined in the screenplay chapter: *Kaleidoscope* is an Americanized version of the story of Neville Heath, a murderer from London, the so-called "baby-faced killer." The screenplay includes three classic Hitchcock set pieces. The first scene, the murder at the waterfall, was reproduced in the screenplay chapter. The second brutal killing takes place on one of the mothballed ships. The third is the finale at an oil refinery with the large oil tanks painted in primary colors.

The script that Levy developed was not fully fleshed out.

Hitchcock's screenplay (parts of which were reproduced earlier) is the best of all the versions of this disturbing story. Howard Fast and Hugh Wheeler's versions make fundamental changes in location and character that dilute the effect of the story. The Hitchcock script has its own weaknesses in the third act, but typical of Hitchcock, the story is as close to the bone as possible, which, in my opinion, serves the story well.

The studios did not care for Hitchcock's draft. Hitchcock did not care for Howard Fast's draft. Then the studio ultimately rejected Hugh Wheeler's version.

Donald Spoto, without reference and in his only mention of the project in his biography of Hitchcock, describes a humiliating MCA executive meeting where Hitchcock's carefully prepared presentation (including slide and film work) was rejected by Wasserman. Peggy Robertson confirmed that such a meeting took place, although the intervening years had softened her opinion of the impact. Her recollection of this project was keen, though. She recalled that it was important to Hitchcock and that its failure had nothing to do with the popular notion that he felt it was too close to *Psycho*. This project, according to Robertson, was one that Hitchcock wanted to complete.

She also indicated that much of *Kaleidoscope*'s flavor was translated into the 1970 *Frenzy*. There are some similarities between the two films. The killer is charming (certainly more charming than the film's hero); the brutality of the first on-screen murder is remarkable in the Hitchcock canon (just as brutal as *Kaleidoscope*'s second murder in the mothballed shipyard); and the offscreen murder of Babs is handled in much the same way the first murder is handled in *Kaleidoscope* (the camera pulls way back so that the murder takes place out of our presence). The differences between the two, though, are fundamental and it shouldn't be assumed that other than the casual similarities just listed there is any connection between the two *Frenzy*s other than the name. The first *Frenzy* is primarily about the handsome psychopath and then his female pursuer. The second one is primarily about the unattractive innocent man who is framed by his charming psychopathic friend.

Hitchcock went further in the development of this project than any other unrealized production (including his famous final project, *The Short Night*). In addition to all of the script work, he commissioned secret film tests to be shot in New York City. The tests were primarily intended to compare different film stocks in low-light settings. Hitchcock gave specific instructions as to content—

the test scenes amounted to full mock-ups of actual scenes from the screenplay, using unknown actors and models. The result is nearly an hour of silent footage (the clapper reads *Kaleidoscope*).

The first scene is of the young model getting up from bed in her New York apartment. She's nude as she rises in the scene—lit only by natural light—and walks to the bathroom. The camera remains fixed as it does a full 360-degree pan of the apartment—starting with her rise from the bed and following around to her entry into the bathroom.

The second scene is at the artist's studio, where the young killer meets the nude model. There are several dollies and elaborate pans of the artists (including the young man intended as the killer) at work. There is definitely an Antonioni-influenced look to the footage. All of the actors are hippies—a deliberate choice of Hitchcock's. In the film's research files are dozens of clippings on hippies and their lifestyle.

Contrasting the research work on the hippies, Hitchcock included two books on Heath and several muscle magazines (thinly veiled gay pornography at the time). Hitchcock told one of the still photographers that he even intended to show the young man masturbating in bed (and having his mother catch him).

That young photographer was Arthur Schatz. Schatz did only color still work and wasn't present during the filming sequences. He does recall meeting with Hitchcock and Benn Levy at the St. Regis.

"I did a lot of work for *Life* in those days and a friend in the London office called me one day and asked if I'd like to do some work for Hitchcock—as if I'm going to say no.

"So I go to meet Hitchcock at the St. Regis. And, of course, it's a beautiful suite and he's extremely nice. And then he does something I'll never forget. He asks if I'd like a drink—I say sure. I think I asked for Scotch and water—I think I was drinking Scotch at the time. So he calls down to room service and requests the drink—and they ask him what kind of Scotch—and he just says, 'Why the very best, of course.' That was Hitchcock for me.

"Basically, he wanted a lot of shots of various New York City locations with actors. He gave me total freedom as to how to do it. I remember riding around the city with him—Hitchcock in the front passenger seat (I was sitting in the back)—and as we reached the locations, he would tell me the story of what was happening in the film. He really was a great man to work with.

"So I did the work—I was fast. I never liked to waste time. In fact, I remember he wanted the material right away—so we used the latest techniques in getting photostats to him.

"I eventually remember taking the slides out to him in Los Angeles. I remember watching them with him and someone else in his basement screening room. He loved the work. He was very complimentary and seemed very excited about the project."

Schatz never heard from Hitchcock again, although he seemed to recall learning that the project died:

"If I remember right, I seem to remember hearing from his assistant that the studio wanted him to do some big-budget thriller instead. I was disappointed. *Frenzy* sounded like a good film."

Another photographer on the project was Steve Kapovich. He did only black-and-white still work at the mothballed fleet on the Hudson River. Kapovich remembered doing the single day's work. He never met Hitchcock (although he knew who he was shooting material for). He had nothing substantial to offer other than that he was given specific instructions about what to shoot but not how. He merely reiterated what all of the professionals have said throughout the book: Hitchcock gave specific instructions, but gave you complete freedom on how you accomplished it.

The film crew and the actors remain unknown. After diligent searches around the country, not one of the people involved in the actual filming could be found. The filming was completed July 14 through July 17, 1967, in Manhattan—and that's all that's known. The actors are unrecognizable from the footage and, I suspect, short of broadcasting the footage on national television, they may remain unknown (if the cameramen could be found—or the person(s) who organized the shoot could be found, they would surely have releases for each of the participants). Unfortunately, Schatz no longer recalls where those records might be kept (or even if they were kept—Schatz likes to describe himself at the time as a "dumb schmuck photographer").

The footage is all that remains—and that may have remained lost had it not been for Richard Franklin (director of *Psycho II*), who helped the family clean out the Hitchcock home after Alma's death in 1982. The material, labeled *Kaleidoscope,* was turned over with all of Hitchcock's other papers to the Margaret Herrick Library at the Academy.

Once filed there, it essentially became invisible to most researchers. The film is not catalogued with the paper archives—it is only catalogued in the film archive under the name *Kaleidoscope,* which would mean little to the casual researcher.

Ironically, it was in just such a casual conversation with the Academy archivist Michael Friend that I learned of the footage and was able to make the connection to boxes full of files stored on the floor above. The connection (it can hardly be called a discovery) illuminated the few lines in Spoto's biography and the other more substantial references in Truffaut's revised *Hitchcock* and in his posthumously published letters. The unproduced *Frenzy* was not a mere footnote on the road to the produced *Frenzy*. This project was an intended turning point in Hitchcock's career—a turn that the studio denied him.

It also puts several events in perspective. The first is the debacle over *Topaz.* This was a project that was never fully under Hitchcock's control, plagued as it was with one technical problem after another. The film has its isolated moments and it is a testament to Hitchcock's abilities that he was able to spin some gold out of this confusing pile of plot. After *Topaz,* Hitchcock would take a long break before shooting *Frenzy.*

Consider as well Hitchcock's attitude toward Universal at the time. After *Topaz,* Hitchcock purchased a controlling stake in the company through a stock trade—he traded *Psycho* and the syndication rights to his television series to MCA for enough stock to make him the third- or fourth-largest stockholder. It was a wise move for both parties.

Hitchcock regained the control he lost during the sixties at Universal—his first project with this power was in many ways a thumbed nose at management. *Frenzy* was not very appealing to the company (to be fair, it would be difficult to imagine any film studio that would find it an appealing project). To lessen Universal's control, he filmed the entire production in London with the required British crew.

In Hitchcock's final work, *Family Plot,* Bruce Dern was chatting with Hitchcock as they filmed on location in San Francisco. The shot involved a clean garage door that Dern joked should have graffiti in order to look realistic. And what should the graffiti say? Very dryly, Hitchcock replied: "Fuck MCA."

On the surface, MCA went out of its way to make Hitchcock comfortable in his final years. The relationship could not have been easy as the director aged and his health began to deteriorate. But like it or not, there were hard feelings and these appear to chart back to the rejected 1967 *Frenzy.*

The loss of the project had a wider, more pronounced effect on Hitchcock's work. Had the 1967 *Frenzy* been produced, its brutality and cinema verité style would have been ahead of the films from this period that did break down the studio's stylized violence: *Bonnie and Clyde,* even *Easy Rider.* Here was one of cinema's greatest directors (perhaps the greatest) proposing a groundbreaking film that would have eschewed the American studio style for the kind of filmmaking Hitchcock was seeing in France and Italy.

More importantly, the 1967 *Frenzy* would have returned Hitchcock to the kind of dark realism that characterized his British films. That may be the only explanation for Hitchcock bringing in Benn Levy, the only surviving writer from that early period who would work with him. Hitchcock queried a number of British and American writers—including Paddy Chayefsky and Sidney Gilliat—but they refused him either because they didn't like the project or because of other commitments. The 1970 *Frenzy* production was described by many participants as having a homecoming feel to it. He chose locations that resonated personally, like Covent Garden.

In addition to the 1967 *Frenzy*, Hitchcock returned to that beloved project from his youth, *Mary Rose*. It was during this period that the project came as close as it ever would to being made—which is not very close.

*Mary Rose* is a play by J. M. Barrie that Hitchcock maintained the rights to until 1987 (well after his death) and was the unrealized project that Hitchcock mentioned the most often in interviews. He liked to claim that it was the one project that Universal stipulated in his contract that he could *not* do—but this could not be verified and appears not to be true. It was, in fact, during his Universal period that he had the only screenplay commissioned for *Mary Rose*.

The screenplay, which follows the original play very closely, was written by Jay Presson Allen, who had written the final version of *Marnie*. Allen got along very well with Hitchcock and the screenplay for *Mary Rose* is quite good. The story is of a young couple on their honeymoon on the Irish coast. During their stay, they take a boat out to a small island that looks romantic but the locals claim is haunted. While there, the young girl (Mary Rose) begins to hear voices and wanders away as the husband and the boatmen prepare to leave. They search the entire island (which is quite small), but she cannot be found.

Years go by and the war intervenes, but one day Mary Rose returns—just as she was the day she vanished. Its structure is more short story than fully a three-act screenplay, but Hitchcock had been attracted to the story ever since he saw a production of the play in his youth. (He even referenced that production during the making of *Vertigo*. The play's original recorded music and sound effects were sought out and sent from England as inspiration for Herrmann.) The screenplay was as far as *Mary Rose* ever went. Like the character, the script disappeared into the files, waiting for its youthful return.

Hitchcock tossed about quite a few projects during this time. He considered another John Buchan novel, *The Three Hostages,* but this never went beyond the daydreaming stage. (The Buchan estate wanted too much for the property.) Hitchcock purchased the rights to Elmore Leonard's *Unknown Man #89* and passed on the novel to Ernest Lehman to develop, but nothing came of it. He also considered screen versions of Robert Louis Stevenson's *The Strange Case of Dr. Jekyll and Mr. Hyde* and H. G. Wells's *The Food of the Gods*—but neither went beyond rereadings of the novels.

Another, even stranger project was called *The Attorney*. In this story, a wealthy woman is being blackmailed by her gay husband—he had her photographed in a compromising position after slipping her a mickey. The project never went beyond the rumination stage.

Prior to his Universal period, Hitchcock's biggest unrealized project was *No Bail for the Judge,* which was to have starred Audrey Hepburn.

The story went through numerous drafts by Samuel Taylor—all of which are quite good. (Taylor contributed his own story idea to Hitchcock during the sixties—a fascinating modern Greek tragedy called *In Another Country.* Hitchcock wasn't interested.) But Hepburn pulled out of the project and Hitchcock, described by everyone involved as furious, went on to do *Psycho.*

The fifties had very few unrealized dramas for Hitchcock. *No Bail for the Judge* and *Flamingo Feather* (a project Hitchcock dropped for *Vertigo*) are the only two that had any serious possibility of being made.

Hitchcock did consider during this time an odd play called *The Queen of the Rebels* by Italian playwright Ugo Bettie. One letter suggests that Hitchcock even considered mounting a stage production of the play with Joan Fontaine in the lead. None of this ever happened. The brief synopsis filed with the two English translations of the play give a sense of what may have attracted Hitchcock to the project:

It's set in an imaginary Balkan revolution. A coarse and selfish adventuress spots the disguised queen, who's on the run among a busload of refugees. So to spite her lover, who's a sentry, she gives the terrified woman a chance to run for it; and is then caught in the trap of being suspected herself of being the hunted queen—a role that she assumes, first out of bravado and then as the character grows magnificently before our eyes—out of the realization that she, a common prostitute, actually has the power to be a queen and to go to the scaffold if need be with all a queen's nobility.

His Transatlantic period had several unrealized projects. *I Confess* walked a tightrope for several years before it was realized, but *Dark Duty* from the novel by Margaret Wilson did not have the same fate. Hitchcock wanted to make a prison drama and, in particular, was attracted to the anticapital punishment stance that the book took. The project was intended to follow *Under Capricorn,* but *Dark Duty* didn't survive the failing of Hitchcock's company. (Curiously, Hitchcock took another look at the project in 1963 as a possibility.)

Another Transatlantic project that never made it was the story of Jack Sheppard, the notorious criminal who managed to escape from Newgate Prison in the 1700s on several occasions. Hitchcock seemed to like this project and, even though it ultimately didn't go very far in development, he developed an opening for the film. A crying baby, who is being christened, is unconsoled until his mother's breast is unveiled—a large smile, then he goes to suckle. Hitchcock would then shoot a closeup of the baby's head, which we then see is now a young man's head, as we pull away from the couple, who are amorously engaged.

As late as 1954, Hitchcock still maintained the rights to the material.

*Bramble Bush* was another project from this period that was being developed under Hitchcock's Warner Bros. production deal. Warner Bros. purchased the rights to David Duncan's novel in 1952. Hitchcock began working on the project with screenwriter George Tabori the same year. The novel is about the adventures of a soldier of fortune who is trying to get home to San Francisco from Mexico. His American passport is no longer valid, so he becomes Philip Tremaine (the novel was eventually made as Anontioni's *The Passenger* with Jack Nicholson).

In light of the Antonioni film (and Hitchcock's own interest in the Italian director), it is interesting to see the difference in the development of the project. Tabori eventually left the film. (In a letter to Alma and Hitch, which suggests that they were both at work on the film, Tabori claimed that he could no longer tolerate the studio system.)

Before he left, though, they began to shape the film. The following is a shopping list of changes that they felt needed to be made in translating the novel to the screen:

a. Controversial political and economic aspects of the story must be eliminated
b. Movement of the hero from Mexico to San Francisco must be properly motivated
c. The hero's reason for continually returning to the scene of his greatest danger must appear not only logical but necessary and inevitable
d. The final scene should see the hero cleared in the eyes of the world and should involve other major characters than himself.

Tabori's brief outline of how the film would be shaped:

a. Hero is anxious to enter U.S., where he is wanted for a minor crime.
b. Meets villain who resembles him, gets hold of villain's papers, enters country
c. Finds that villain whose identity he has assumed is wanted for murder; finds he is subject for frame-up and is supposed to take rap for villain
d. Meets villain's sister (and rest of family); strong relationship of mistrust and attraction to sister
e. Hero arrested, escapes, hides, pursued both by police and villain
f. Hero tries to clear himself, can only do so by exposing villain
g. Resolution, positively, of relationship with sister; climactic final encounter with villain.

Not at all that different in structure from the film realized by Antonioni.

Perhaps the most outrageous plan dates from immediately after World War II when Hitchcock and Bernstein had only just formed Transatlantic Pictures. Hitchcock announced the project in a telegram to Sidney Bernstein:

493 BEVERLY HILLS CALIF 405 1/52 10
NLT SIDNEY BERNSTEIN CX 545
ARLINGTON HOUSE PICCADILLY LONDON
WOULD LIKE TO GET YOUR REACTION ON THE FOLLOWING IDEA FOR OUR ENGLISH
PRODUCTION THIS IDEA WOULD ILLUSTRATE ITSELF CLEARER TO YOU IF I INDICATED
THE BILLING WHICH WOULD BE QUOTE SYDNEY BERNSTEIN PRESENTS CARY GRANT AS
ALFRED HITCHCOCKS HAMLET A MODERN THRILLER BY WILLIAM
SHAKESPEARE UNQUOTE STOP AS YOU WILL SEE THE IDEA IS TO TAKE THE SHAKESPEARE
TEXT AND TRANSCRIBE IT INTO MODERN ENGLISH THE PLAY WOULD HAVE AN ENGLISH
SETTING AND WOULD BE PRESENTED AS A PSYCHOLOGICAL MELODRAMA I WAS OVER
TO SEE CARY GRANT YESTERDAY AT WARNERS STUDIO AND HE EXPRESSED GREAT
ENTHUSIASM FOR THE IDEA I TOLD DAN OSHEA ABOUT IT AND HIS REACTION WAS THAT
IT WOULD BE A TERRIFIC PIECE OF SHOWMANSHIP THE MOST ESSENTIAL THING WOULD
BE TO MAKE CERTAIN THE PUBLIC REALIZED THAT THEY WOULD BE SEEING A MODERN
STORY THE PROCESSES REQUIRED TO GET A SCRIPT OF THIS WOULD BE AS FOLLOWS
FIRST OF ALL TO GET A PROFESSOR OF ENGLISH TO TAKE THE ORIGINAL PLAY AND DO A
MODERN LANGUAGE VERSION OF IT THEN TO TURN THIS INTO A FILM TREATMENT AND
TO REINTERPRET THE SITUATIONS INTO MODERN IDIOM AFTER THIS PROCESS HAS BEEN
COMPLETED THE THE NEXT STEP WOULD BE TO TAKE THIS TREATMENT WITH ITS
STRAIGHTFORWARD ENGLISH DIALOGUE AND HAVE IT GONE OVER BY A TOP
PLAYWRIGHT FOR THE FINAL VERSION NATURALLY I AM CONCERNED ABOUT
MAINTAINING SECRECY ON THIS BECAUSE THE IDEA IS IN PUBLIC DOMAIN AND COULD
EASILY BE STOLEN IF IT LEAKED OUT BECAUSE IT IS A VERY HARD THING TO REGISTER
FOR PRIORITY DO YOU THINK A SIMULTANEOUS ANNOUNCEMENT BOTH HERE AND IN
LONDON WOULD BE THE BEST MEANS OF SAFE GUARDING THE PROPERTY ASSUMING
YOU LIKE THE IDEA DO YOU THINK IT POSSIBLE FOR YOU TO FIND SOMEBODY TO DO
THE FIRST DIALOGUE TRANSCRIPTION IN DIALOGUE FORM PREFERABLY A PROFESSOR
OF ENGLISH BUT DEFINITELY NO ONE IN SHOW BUSINESS AFTER THIS IS COMPLETED
THEN I WOULD LIKE TO HAVE SOME STOOGE WRITER CUT HERE SUCH AS JOCK ORTON
WHO WOULD BE INEXPENSIVE BUT WHO WOULD CARRY OUT MY IDEA FOR THE
PICTORIAL AND INCIDENTAL TREATMENT OF THE ACTION I THINK HE COULD BE GOTTEN
FOR AROUND FIVE HUNDRED DOLLARS A WEEK WITH A SIX MONTHS GUARANTEE THE
FINAL PHASE WE COULD DISCUSS TOGETHER WHEN YOU GET OUT.
HERE PLEASE TELEPHONE ME IF YOU NEED ANY CLARIFICATION LOVE HITCH =
ALFRED HITCHCOCK.

554    HITCHCOCK'S NOTEBOOKS

That's as far as the project went. As difficult as it is to imagine Cary Grant as the Danish prince, it was actually a scholar—who was publishing his own modern English *Hamlet* and who immediately sued Hitchcock—that helped kill the project. Hitchcock's lawyers said the scholar had no case, but his fascination with the project cooled.

# *chapter seven*
# FADE OUT

*I warn you, I mean to go on forever!*
—HITCHCOCK TO TAYLOR

itchcock's marketing methods became legendary after *Psycho*, which was the most dramatic marketing trick in the canon. By not allowing late seating, he generated extra interest and long lines as ticket buyers waited for the next showing.

But the *Psycho* stunt aside, it is thought that Hitchcock became a remarkable pitchman for his films after the introduction of his TV series in 1955. There is, of course, the famous Hitchcock-led tour of the *Psycho* set for that film, and Hitchcock made appearances in his trailers for nearly all the movies made at Universal (with the exception of *Topaz*). The only other director who made such prominent appearances in his trailers was Cecil B. De Mille—and the two, to this day, are easily the most recognized film directors (discounting a director who may also be a star, like Charlie Chaplin).

Hitchcock as the on-screen salesman actually debuted years earlier in a trailer for *Spellbound*. I could find no record that this trailer exists anywhere, but the script certainly hints at the style and humor of his later trailers. The commentary of putting dreams on the movie screen is a fitting conclusion to *Hitchcock's Notebooks*.

```
                        VANGUARD FILMS, INC.
                      CULVER CITY, CALIFORNIA

                      Inter-Office Communication

    TO      MR. HITCHCOCK                  DATE August 24, 1945
    FROM    PAUL MacNAMARA

    SUBJECT  SPELLBOUND TRAILER


        The trailer on "Spellbound," seems to me, could be much more
        ingenious.

        I have talked to Selznick regarding the idea of making a new
        one and making it about you.

        He agrees and thinks it would be a good idea.

        Roughly, my idea was that you would discuss on the screen in
        lecture fashion the fact that everyone is a potential murder-
        er, etc., etc.

        There might be direct questions that you would ask the aud-
        ience -- "do you know that the person next to you might be a
        potential murderer" -- "do you know that in your own mind you,
        too, might be a murderer," etc., etc.

        Other emotions might be touched on in which audience partici-
        pation would be included (including some laughs), "some of you
        are holding hands," etc., etc.

        However, no clips of the picture would be used except in which
        your voice would be the sound and your explanation as to why
        it was handled that way would be that every bit of the picture
        "Spellbound" was so important to the plot that it was decided
        not to show to audiences anywhere any part of the picture in a
        piece-meal state.  (The use of the clips in this fashion, how-
        ever, would show the stars).

        Perhaps the thing should be presented as a short rather than
        as a trailer.

        Undoubtedly, Dr. Romm might be able to provide us with some
        questions that would be helpful in the preparation of a
        script.

        In any case, I think that there is a basically good idea here
        and with the proper development we might be able to work out a
        sensational advance salesman for the picture "Spellbound."

        What do you think?

                                                PM

    PM:eh
```

SUGGESTED TRAILER MATERIAL FOR "SPELLBOUND"

Mel Dinelli
Sept. 3, 1945

FADE IN

INT. PROJECTION ROOM SEMI-LONG SHOT (FROM REAR OF ROOM)

A man is sitting in the middle of the projection room, his back to the camera. The room is lighted, and there is nothing on the square patch of screen in the background. The man sits quietly looking up at the empty screen; after a moment, he begins to speak, without turning.

**Man**

**There are stranger things in heaven and earth, Horatio, than are dreamed of in our philosophy. . . . Shakespeare said that. . . .**
*(pause; then the man turns casually, looking fully into the camera and into the audience's face as he places one arm leisurely over the back of the seat)*

THE CAMERA MOVES IN TO

CLOSE SHOT    THE MAN

THE SELZNICK STUDIO
CULVER CITY                    CALIFORNIA

September 4, 1945

Mr. Alfred Hitchcock
c/o The St. Regis Hotel
Fifth Avenue
New York City, N. Y.

Dear Hitch:

Here is the suggested trailer material for
SPELLBOUND, starring Alfred Hitchcock.
There is not the humorous device in it
that I would like to get, but we are still
working on that phase.

Also, for a conclusion, I would like to
get some challenging question that we
could leave with the audience for them to
take home and stew about. We plan to see
Dr. Romm this afternoon to see if she could
suggest any such device.

Sincerely,

Paul MacNamara

PM:eh

Man

I'm Alfred Hitchcock . . . and I've just finished directing a picture which deals with some of
those strange things Mr. Shakespeare spoke of . . . it's called "Spellbound", and it stars Miss
Ingrid Bergman and Mr. Gregory Peck. . . .
(as he speaks, he turns and looks up at the screen before him, as he does so,
the lights go down.

THE CAMERA PULLS BACK TO

MEDIUM SHOT    THE PROJECTION ROOM SCREEN

On the screen we begin to see the scenes in which Constance comes to J.B.'s room for the first
time after his arrival at Green Manors; although the character's mouths move as they speak the
dialogue, we do not hear it. (The above scenes are SHOTS 71, 72, 73, 74, 75, 76, 77, 78, 79,
80, 81.

Mr. Hitchcock

Usually in a trailer, we're able to let you hear scenes from the pictures . . . but we can't in
this one . . . this story, "Spellbound", is too carefully knit . . . if we were to allow you to hear
actual dialogue, it would destroy the suspense of the story when you view it as a whole. . . .

MEDIUM LONG SHOT (ANOTHER ANGLE)

Mr. Hitchcock is in the foreground, the projection room screen in the background.

**Mr. Hitchcock**

**But I can tell you this much . . . it's a love story . . . and it's a story about murder . . . about quiet murders . . . not of the dark alley variety . . . but murders over a breakfast table. . . .**

On the screen back of Mr. Hitchcock we go into the scenes which show Constance and J. B. on their way to Gabriel Valley. (These scenes are not in the script which I have.) These are the scenes in the dining car in which Constance talks to J. B. as she cuts food on her plate. He listens but his attention is focused on her knife. It ends with the close up of J. B. as the train whistle comes in with startling effect. Although we do not hear dialogue, we hear all sound effects.

**Mr. Hitchcock**

**"Spellbound" is a story about murders over a glass of milk. . . .**

We view the scenes in which Brulov gives J. B. the glass of milk while the former holds a razor in his hand. The scene winds up with the closeup of the milk in the glass, coming toward the camera, filling the screen and turning it white. These are shots 252, 253, 254, 255, 256.

CLOSE SHOT    MR. HITCHCOCK

He is looking directly into the audience, and there is the illusion of his speaking directly to definite members of it.

**Mr. Hitchcock**

**"Spellbound" is also a story about minds . . . about what happens to them when they are disturbed by real, or imaginary things . . . did it ever occur to you that the person seated next to you at this moment . . . the one you came into the theater with . . . might be a potential murderer? That he might actually have contemplated murdering** *you***? . . . How do you know he hasn't . . . what do you** *really* **know about him? What do you know about his dreams . . . what actually goes on in his mind . . . has he ever opened the locked doors of his mind and revealed the things that are hidden there?**

As Mr. Hitchcock speaks, we see on the screen back of him the scene in which the series of doors open. Shot 82 from the script. Mr. Hitchcock continues to speak.

**Mr. Hitchcock**

**Maybe you know about one of those doors, or maybe two . . . but there are others . . . there's a whole succession of doors in the human mind . . . and very few people expose themselves beyond the first or second. . . . "Spellbound" deals with methods by which the individual is forced to open those closed doors . . .** *all* **of them. . . .**

The projection room screen is blank again, and Mr. Hitchcock turns to look at it a moment, without speaking.

**Mr. Hitchcock**

**That screen up there is like a mind . . . we here in Hollywood can make anything happen there. . . .**

Here we go into the scenes in which Constance and J. B. come down the slope on skis. It is the shot which ends with them coming close to the precipice. These are shots 327, 328, 329, 330, 331, 332, 333, 334, 335, 336, 337, and part of 338—we do not show the marble balustrade or the small boy who falls into the spiked railings.

**Mr. Hitchcock**

**We can also show you what a man dreams. . . .**

Here we go into the more spectacular shots from the dream sequence of the picture. These are the impressionistic shots, such as 289, 292, 294.

**Mr. Hitchcock**

**Yes, we here in Hollywood can make anything happen on the screen . . . but our powers are dwarfed compared to what** *you* **. . .**

*(he turns to look into the audience)*

**. . . can make happen in your mind . . . for instance, how many times have you actually murdered someone . . . I mean in your mind. . . .**

On the screen back of Mr. Hitchcock we go into the shot in which Dr. Murchinson's hand is in the foreground holding the revolver which he aims at Constance as she rises slowly from her chair and she walks across the room. We hear no dialogue, no sound effects, no music—it is very quiet. Just when we get to the point where Constance is about to go out the door, there is the startling effect (with sound) of the film breaking—it flaps around the reel noisily. This is shot 371 from the script.

**Mr. Hitchcock**

**Too bad . . . the film broke . . . it's just as well . . . we couldn't allow you to see what happened next . . . it might spoil your enjoyment of "Spellbound". . . .**

*(pause)*

**In case I've forgotten to mention it, the title of this picture is "Spellbound" . . . it's a Selznick International Production, and it stars Miss Ingrid Bergman and Mr. Gregory Peck. . . .**

THE CAMERA MOVES IN

VERY CLOSE SHOT   MR. HITCHCOCK

He looks directly into the audience.

FADE OUT

This is how I prefer to remember Hitchcock—alone in a darkening theater, waiting to fill the empty screen with his dreams.

Lions

# sources and bibliography

The principal sources for *Hitchcock's Notebooks* were Hitchcock's production files held at the Margaret Herrick Library of the Academy of Motion Picture Arts and Sciences. Author interviews with members of Hitchcock's creative team were another important source. The interviews were conducted in 1996–98 (with the exception of the comments from Charles Bennett, which were from interviews conducted in 1991–92).

For information on Hitchcock's life, the author's own research in Hitchcock's personal and production files as well as the two biographies listed below were the principal sources of dates and information.

## BIBLIOGRAPHY

Auiler, Dan. *Vertigo: The Making of a Hitchcock Classic.* New York: St. Martin's Press, 1998.

Boorman, John and Walter Donahue, *Projections 4, 4½, 7 & 8.* London: Faber and Faber, 1993–1998.

Bogdonavich, Peter. *The Cinema of Alfred Hitchcock.* New York: Museum of Modern Art Film Library/Doubleday, 1963.

———. *Who the Devil Made It.* New York: Alfred A. Knopf, Inc., 1997.

Cardiff, Jack. *Magic Hour.* London: Faber, 1996.

Cronyn, Hume, *A Terrible Liar,* New York: William Morrow and Company, 1991.

Gottlieb, Sidney, ed. *Hitchcock on Hitchcock.* Los Angeles: University of California Press, 1995.

Hunter, Evan. *Me and Hitch.* London: Faber, 1997.

Kuhns, J. Lary, "Early Hitchcock" (unpublished), 1996.

Leff, Leonard. *Hitchcock and Selznick.* New York: Weidenfeld & Nicholson, 1987.

Low, Rachel, and Roger Manvell. *The History of the British Film, 1896–1950.* London: George Allen & Unwin, 1948.

"The MacGuffin," (Australian Hitchcock journal)

McGilligan, Pat. *Backstory.* Los Angeles: University of California Press, 1986.

———. *Backstory 3.* Los Angeles: University of California Press, 1997.

Perry, George. *The Films of Alfred Hitchcock.* New York: E. P. Dutton, 1965.

Rebello, Stephen. *Alfred Hitchcock and the Making of Psycho.* New York: Dembner, 1990.

Rozsa, Miklos. *Double Life: The Autobiography of Miklos Rozsa.* London: The Baton Press, 1982.

Ryall, Tom. *Alfred Hitchcock and the British Cinema.* London: Athlone Press, 1996.

———. *BFI Film Classics: Blackmail.* London: British Film Institute, 1993.

Sloan, Jane E. *Alfred Hitchcock: The Definitive Filmography.* Los Angeles: University of California Press, 1993.

Smith, Steven C. *A Heart of Fire's Center: The Life and Music of Bernard Herrmann.* Los Angeles: University of California Press, 1991.

Spoto, Donald. *The Art of Alfred Hitchcock* (Second Edition). New York: Doubleday, 1992.

————. *The Dark Side of Genius: The Life of Alfred Hitchcock.* Boston: Little, Brown, 1983.

Taylor, John Russell. *Hitch: The Life and Times of Alfred Hitchcock.* New York: Da Capo Press, 1996.

Thompson, David. *A Biographical Dictionary of Film.* New York: William Morrow, 1981.

Truffaut, François. *Hitchcock.* New York: Simon & Schuster, 1967.

————. *Letters.* London: Faber and Faber, 1989.

Tweedssmuir, Susan. *John Buchan by his Wife and Friends.* London: Hodder and Stoughton, 1947.

## INTERNET

Alfred Hitchcock Scholars/"The MacGuffin" website
www.labyrinth.net.au/~muffin/

# index

Page references to illustrations, photographs, and original memoranda appear in italics.

# About the Author

Dan Auiler is the author of *Vertigo: The Making of a Hitchcock Classic.* He lives in Los Angeles with his wife and daughter.